ACCLAIM FOR TAD SZULC'S *POPE JOHN PAUL II: THE BIOGRAPHY*

"As close an account as we are likely to have of the way a particular culture and era gave birth to this very Polish Pope. . . ."

—Margaret O'Brien Steinfels,
The New York Times Book Review

"The most useful biography that has yet appeared in English on the Pontiff's background."

—Colm Tóibín, *The New Yorker*

"Brimming with revelations. . . . An extraordinarily candid portrait of the Polish pontiff and a timely look at the Church's internal crisis. . . ."

—*Publishers Weekly*

"Important and illuminating. . . . The book's chief claim has been in revealing heretofore unknown or underreported aspects of the Pope's remarkable ascent and behind-the-scenes diplomacy. . . . Still most readers, and especially Catholics, may find Szulc's book more rewarding for showing how the Pope's Polish roots and mystical beliefs help explain his positions on such divisive issues as birth control, women in the priesthood, and priestly celibacy. . . . The author enjoyed extraordinary access to his countryman. . . ."

—Thomas Kunkel, *Lexington* (KY) *Herald-Leader*

MORE PRAISE FOR TAD SZULC'S *POPE JOHN PAUL II: THE BIOGRAPHY*

"Adds fresh details to the portrait of John Paul II. . . . One feels through Szulc's guidance as though one has met Wojtyla in the flesh."

—Michael Novak, *Washington Post Book World*

"Szulc's long experience covering international affairs for the *Times* stands him in good stead when he writes of the Pope's involvement in world affairs, especially in Eastern Europe. Not surprisingly, the sections of the book dealing with John Paul II the Pole and John Paul II the statesman are the book's strongest. . . ."

—Michael D. Schaffer, *Tampa Tribune-Times*

"[A] thorough and intriguing biography. . . ."

—Philip Seib, *Dallas Morning News*

"Tad Szulc enjoyed unprecedented advantages. The Vatican gave him wide and exclusive access. . . . Szulc can take credit for providing a wealth of invaluable detail. . . ."

—Richard Griffin, *Boston Book Review*

"[A] well-written book that deserves, and no doubt will get, a wide readership. . . . An accurate portrait of the direction taken by the largest religious organization in the world under the leadership of John Paul—and where it might go after he's gone."

—Ernst-Ulrich Franzen, *Milwaukee Journal-Sentinel*

"What is closest to Szulc's heart—John Paul's outreach to the Jewish people and the State of Israel—is a story he tells well. What Szulc knows from personal experience—the life of a small Polish city during the interwar years—he describes with sympathy and insight. What he can grasp as a man conversant with Polish literature—the special character of Wojtyla's poetry and plays—he writes about sensibly."

—George Weigel, *Seattle Weekly*

"Informative and illuminating. . . . A coherent, balanced, and plausible story of the Pope's 'central role in helping to bring about the demise of communism.'"

—*America*

Books by Tad Szulc

Twilight of Tyrants
The Cuban Invasion *(with Karl E. Meyer)*
The Winds of Revolution
Dominican Diary
Latin America
The Bombs of Palomares
Portrait of Spain
Czechoslovakia Since World War II
Innocents at Home
The United States and the Caribbean *(editor)*
Compulsive Spy
The Energy Crisis
The Illusion of Peace
Diplomatic Immunity *(a novel)*
Fidel: A Critical Portrait
Then and Now: How the World Has Changed
Since World War II
The Secret Alliance
Pope John Paul II*

*Published by POCKET BOOKS

POPE JOHN PAUL II

THE BIOGRAPHY

TAD SZULC

POCKET BOOKS
New York London Toronto Sydney

This book is in memory of
IRENA MONICA BARUCH WILEY

POCKET BOOKS, a division of Simon & Schuster, Inc.
1230 Avenue of the Americas, New York, New York 10020

ISBN 10: 1-4165-8886-8

ISBN 13: 978-1-4165-8886-3

First Pocket Books printing April 1996

10 9 8 7 6 5 4 3 2 1

Cover photograph by Grzegorz Galazka/ "Inside Vatican"

Printed in the U.S.A.

For information regarding special discounts for bulk purchases, please contact Simon & Schuster Special Sales at 1-800-456-6798 or business@simonandschuster.com

PREFACE

When Pope John Paul II and I first discussed my plans to write his biography, the Holy Father remarked that "a biography must be more than dates, facts, and quotations . . ." It must convey, he said in Polish, "the person's heart, soul, thoughts. . . ."

In the nearly two years that have elapsed since the 1993 conversation, I had the privilege of watching John Paul II and listening to him in the privacy of his dining room in his apartments at the Apostolic Palace, in his conference room where we joked in Polish, in the public halls of the Vatican, aboard airplanes as I accompanied him on trips to Mexico, Jamaica, the United States, the Baltic countries, and the former Yugoslavia, in great cathedrals of the world and modest suburban parish churches.

I took the pope's advice to study in depth Polish history and literature—his own intellectual and emotional mainstay—and looked up old friends and acquaintances he suggested I should see in Poland and elsewhere. Then I took it upon myself to work through, with much enjoyment, his immense literary output: poems, dramatic plays, essays, books on morals and ethics, articles, letters, travelogues, homilies, and sermons.

I hope that I was able to capture the essence of the persona of Karol Wojtyła of Kraków and John Paul II of the Holy See, and to live up to his counsel.

PREFACE

This is not, of course, an authorized biography, and it is entirely my fault if I have not met his standards. But the Holy Father has afforded me extraordinary access and has shown me great kindness—which has made this book possible in the first place. For this, I thank him. And I know that he will appreciate that I have striven to produce as objective a biography as I could.

T.S.
Vatican City, Kraków, Warsaw, Washington, D.C.
April 1995

PART ONE

CHAPTER 1

Karol Józef Wojtyła was born together with the Polish Miracle.

On Tuesday, May 18, 1920, the day of Wojtyła's birth in the small southern Polish town of Wadowice, Marshal Józef Piłsudski was being triumphantly received in Warsaw, the capital of the newly independent Poland, as the conquering hero of the war with the Soviet Union. Only ten days earlier, Piłsudski's young army had seized Kiev, the principal city of the Soviet Ukraine—Poland's first major military victory in over two centuries.

Three months later, on August 15, the Feast of the Assumption of Our Lady, Polish forces commanded by the marshal repulsed at the gates of Warsaw a powerful Soviet counterattack. It became immediately known as the "Miracle on the Vistula," the river bisecting the capital.

The Soviet defeat at Warsaw doomed the advance that, if unchecked, might have continued toward war-shattered Germany and Western Europe, implanting communist rule there. Lenin and Stalin had elaborated a plan to achieve this goal and the Soviets had already occupied Lithuania and Byelorussia in their westward offensive.

The 1920 Miracle on the Vistula was reminiscent of the battle of Vienna in 1683, when Polish King Jan Sobieski destroyed the Turkish armies of the Grand Vizier, Kara

Mustafa, thereby preventing the Ottoman sweep across the face of Europe.

Indeed, Karol Wojtyła and the resurrected Poland, partitioned for 123 years among her three predatory neighbors—Russia, Prussia, and Austria—came to life virtually at the same time.

Poland's rebirth was the direct consequence of World War I and the rout by the western Allies of the German empire (which grew out of former Prussia) and the Austro-Hungarian empire in 1918, and the previous year's collapse of the Russian empire, smashed militarily by the Germans and swallowed by the Bolshevik Revolution that soon followed. Her reconquest of national sovereignty was part of the most radical redrawing of the map of Europe in centuries.

And the Poles had powerful backers and advocates throughout the world as they strove to regain independence. The first to speak out publicly in their favor was Pope Benedict XV, whose sympathies throughout the war were quietly on the Allied side (which included Italy) and who had a special place in his heart for Poland's fierce devotion to the Roman Catholic faith for nearly one thousand years. In messages in January and August 1917, the pope urged the restoration of an independent Polish kingdom. Poland and the papacy always had a unique relationship—and would go on nurturing it over the coming decades.

The next endorsement, rather self-servingly, came from Russian revolutionaries in Petrograd whose provisional government proclaimed in March 1917 that the creation of an independent Poland would be a "hope-inspiring step toward lasting peace in future Europe."

But the most important move in support of the Polish cause was the peace program presented by President Woodrow Wilson in a message to the Congress of the United States on January 8, 1918. Known as Wilson's Fourteen Points, the program demanded in Point Thirteen that "an independent Polish state should be erected." And on June 3 Poland was recognized by all the Allies as "an allied belligerent nation." There already existed a six-division Polish army in France and Józef Piłsudski commanded a fifty-thousand-man legion in the Austrian-occupied Polish territories.

The Armistice between the Allies and Germany and Austro-Hungary was signed on November 11, 1918, and three days later Piłsudski became provisional chief of state and commander-in-chief of the armed forces. Poland was once more a sovereign nation and, on July 28, 1919, the Versailles Peace Treaty formally recognized "the complete independence of Poland."

But within a year the renascent nation was enmeshed in a war to survive. As Karol Wojtyła was born in Wadowice in the foothills of the Carpathian Mountains, it had triumphed in its first baptism of fire.

In an extraordinary fashion, this convergence of events—Poland's resurrection, a Christ-like phenomenon in the eyes of millions of Poles, Polish victories under the sign of the Virgin Mary, and his own birth and tragic infancy—symbolizes and defines Karol Wojtyła's entire political and religious life. It encompasses his central role in the demise of communism and of Soviet sway in his native land and the rest of Eastern Europe seventy years later. And it is the source of the very special and very controversial character of his priesthood and then pontificate as the head of the Roman Catholic Apostolic Church since October 16, 1978.

To understand John Paul II, the first non-Italian pope elected in 456 years, one must strive to understand Karol Józef Wojtyła, the man. And to do so, it is crucial to grasp and comprehend the fact of his Polishness. This is the essential trait of his personality, an often disorienting blend of conservatism and modernity.

He is the pontiff of the Universal Church of nearly one billion Roman Catholics and a key player on the world diplomatic scene, but he remains a Polish patriot, a Polish philosopher, a Polish poet, and a Polish politician. During his first papal visit to Poland in June 1979, the embroidered insignia on his chasuble—the orphrey—was the Polish royal crowned white eagle with gold letters on blue proclaiming *Polonia Semper Fidelis* (Poland Always Faithful). At Christmas, he sings Polish carols with Polish friends visiting Rome in an informal family atmosphere. He keeps in touch with the Church and political situation in Poland on a daily basis. In his youth, Wojtyła was an actor in dramas celebrating the cult of Polishness, an experience he fondly remembers to this day.

The pope's philosophical and theological thoughts, his reaction to international occurrences, and his interpretation of history must therefore be examined in the light of his personal background along with his familiarity with world problems and politics, acquired in travel on five continents, his towering intellect and erudition, and his massive literary output.

The son of a deeply patriotic and religious retired career army officer and baptized by a military chaplain, Karol Wojtyła is above all the product of the historical Polish renewal whose foundations are rooted in a sense of national identity. The Roman Catholic Church had helped to preserve it over the centuries through the protection of language and culture—the mystical and messianic spirituality.

But as the prolific poet and playwright that he once was, Wojtyła may be even better understood in his human dimension than as philosopher or theologian. His writings reflect his experiences.

From peasant highlander origins in southern Poland, he is at home with the people who till the land and still live miserably in dark huts. Only a generation away from farm life, Wojtyła has deep roots in peasantry. The first known person with the name of Wojtyła was a farmhand named Maciej Wojtyła born in the village of Czaniec in 1765. It is more probable, however, that John Paul II's direct ancestry starts with Bartłomiej Wojtyła, born in 1788, also in Czaniec, who would be his great-great-grandfather. His grandfather Maciej, who was registered in the parish as a farmer and tailor (Latin still being the bureaucratic language in the villages, Maciej was listed as *agricola* and *sartor ex Czaniec*), subsequently moved to a nearby village. Remaining in Czaniec, however, was Franciszek Wojtyła, Maciej's nephew, who led the singing in the village church, a wooden structure built in 1660. The singer died in 1968, at the age of ninety, and Cardinal Wojtyła drove to Czaniec to preside over his uncle's funeral. But the province was full of Wojtyłas: registries list Wojtyła tailors, shoemakers, farmers, harness makers, merchants, "vagabonds," and "beggars." It is not clear if any of them were related to the pontiff.

And like no other pope, Karol Wojtyła had to work for years as a poverty-stricken manual laborer—under the wartime German occupation of his country. This had the merit of exposing him directly to hardships and experiences in human relationships few other priests had known. It taught him how to suffer in silence and dignity, and instilled in him a habit of absolute discipline, which, as pope, he seeks to impose on an increasingly rebellious Church. Wojtyła has always identified with peasants and workers: it is not uncommon for him to appeal publicly for justice for the "working class," an unusual phrase on the lips of the pope—but one, he says, that dates back to Jesus Christ.

He is also identified with the messianic concept of Polish Catholicism, the national idea and religion being inseparable. As a child (and later as priest and cardinal), Wojtyła was irresistibly attracted to Kalwaria Zebrzydowska, a Bernardine Fathers monastery, thirty miles from his hometown of Wadowice, where tens of thousands of rural inhabitants gathered at Easter to witness the reenactment of the death and resurrection of Christ, and at the Feast of the Assumption of Our Lady in August, the Virgin's taking up into heaven. Kalwaria Zebrzydowska has a Way of the Cross, and crowds of believers moved behind the actor playing Christ from station to station, praying and chanting. It was a monumental display of popular piety, and, as a child, Wojtyła was a part of the Passion Play observance. Later, as a seminarian, he had hoped to become a Discalced Carmelite monk, a most mystical calling, and his first doctoral thesis was on St. John of the Cross, the sixteenth-century Spanish mystic.

In childhood, too, Wojtyła absorbed the tradition of patriotism and religion. Catholic since her emergence as a nation-state over a thousand years ago, Poland has been hailed by her messianic bards as "Christ of All Nations," suffering in her flesh for the redemption of other people on earth. This is why, of course, her regained independence was a "resurrection." The most famous Polish epic proclaims, *Vivat Polonus Unus Defensor Mariae!*—Long Live Poland, the Only Defender of Mary! The "Black Virgin" of Czestochowa was crowned "Queen of Poland" in the seventeenth century, when the nation truly needed divine intercession to survive. The mural on the wall of the sitting room of the Warsaw residence of Cardinal Józef Glemp, the Primate of Poland, depicts Marshal Piłsudski, a wounded Polish soldier at the Miracle of Vistula battlefield, and a dying Polish army chaplain blessing the troops.

On still another level, Wojtyła is the product of great personal tragedy and great personal suffering and loneliness, having lost his entire family before he reached the age of twenty-two: his parents' second-born baby, a girl who died in infancy, his mother when he was eight, his older brother when he was eleven, and his beloved father three months before his twenty-first birthday.

His family tragedies inevitably shaped Wojtyła's character as a man and priest. He speaks of them often in private, especially of his poignant loneliness when his father died. And his proclivity for mysticism and romanticism has given him a sense, if not premonition, of martyrdom. He has been at least four times at the door of death.

The figure Karol Wojtyła always venerated the most is Stanisław, the Polish bishop murdered at a church altar in Kraków, then the royal capital, on the orders of a tyrannical king over nine centuries ago. He is now a saint, canonized by the Roman Catholic Church, and a patron saint of Poland. Preparing to leave for Rome to attend the history-making Vatican Council II in 1962, Wojtyła, then a young bishop, told the faithful at Mass in Kraków that "I am leaving the tomb of St. Stanisław for the tomb of St. Peter . . . their greatness is comparable, they complement each other. . . ." He used virtually the same words as cardinal when he left Kraków for the 1978 conclave that would elect him pope.

Today, John Paul II alludes to St. Stanisław when he talks privately about the assassination attempt that almost cost him his life in St. Peter's Square in May 1981. In public comments, he constantly emphasizes that the martyred bishop "always was the patron of moral order in our motherland" and remains "a moral force in our time." Wojtyła, himself Bishop of Kraków for long years, identifies totally with his predecessor, a fervent Polish patriot, at the dawn of the present millennium.

Wojtyła is mystically contemplative, but he is a creature of enormous toughness and stamina, which helped him survive the wounds from the assassin's bullets, major abdominal surgery, serious infections, and numerous accidents over the years, without ever allowing himself to be diverted from the pursuit of his myriad objectives.

Friends who have known Wojtyła over decades insist that prayer and meditation are the principal source of his mental and physical strength and his astonishing capability of restoring his energy—and even his appearance—notwithstanding his punishing schedule at the Vatican and exhausting globegirding jet travel. By any normal standards, this is much too much for a man in his mid-seventies, but until recently no one would dare to suggest that he curtail his activities even by a minute a day. John Paul II is a man with a mission, imposing an overwhelming impression that he fears time is running out for him, with so much more still left to accomplish for humanity and his Church. Yet, by mid-1994, his health failing, he had to start cutting back on his schedule. His final drama had begun.

Wojtyła is said to pray as many as seven hours a day: at his private chapel at dawn, sometimes prostrate before the altar, then with invited guests before breakfast, often in his study next to his bedroom, at Masses and services in Rome or on the road, aboard the plane, and on the back seat of his black Mercedes limousine. The pope has a power of concentration that wholly insulates him from his temporal surroundings as he slides into prayer or meditation, even facing huge crowds at an outdoor Mass. The expression on his broad face is otherworldly, he shuts his eyes so tight that he seems to be in pain, and, occasionally, his lips move lightly in silent prayer. Then, the moment passes, and Wojtyła is alert again, the happy smile is back on his face, and his eyes scan the clergy and the rows of faithful in front of him.

Addressing university students at a Kraków church in 1972, as cardinal, Wojtyła preached that prayer "is a conversation," but it also means "contact with God," and then went on to explain in his methodical way: "Human prayer has different dimensions, very deep ones. And not only different external dimensions: when, for example, a Moslem prays with his great courage, calling out to his Allah everywhere at prescribed times; when a Buddhist prays, entering complete concentration as if removing himself in that concentration; when a Christian prays, receiving from Christ the word 'Father.' . . . So when I pray, when we pray, then all these roads are as one road, completing one another."

As pope, Wojtyła confided, "When I was young, I thought that prayer could be—should be—only in thankfulness and adoration. A prayer of supplication seemed to be something unworthy. Afterwards I changed my opinion completely. Today I ask very much." When John Paul II comes to pray every morning at his private chapel in the papal apartments, a list of special prayer "intentions," prepared by nuns attached to the household, await him on the prie-dieu. A visitor, hesitatingly inquiring after a private lunch whether the pope would pray for his non-Catholic son-in-law awaiting a heart transplant, was told with great warmth: "Naturally, I shall pray for him. What is his name?"

At the same time, this spiritual pope is an activist and workaholic, busy from before dawn until close to midnight. His bedroom window is the last to turn dark along the facade of the Apostolic Palace that adjoins St. Peter's Basilica. And Wojtyła is a lifetime athlete who gave up skiing, his favorite sport, only after fracturing his hip in a bathroom accident when he was just shy of his seventy-fourth birthday. What turned out to be his farewell skiing trip was an overnight excursion to the Italian mountains north of Rome early in February 1994. The Vatican kept secret the fact that the pope did ski on that occasion because doctors advised against it following a fall in November 1993, when he broke his shoulder. However, he was allowed to hike in the mountains, another of his preferred outdoor activities—but not too much—and he is encouraged by his doctors to swim in the pool at the summer residence at Castel Gandolfo.

His determination to achieve his goals is as steely as his single-mindedness in defending his profoundly conservative theological, ethical, and moral beliefs, so unexpected in an otherwise worldly and modern man. For John Paul II is exceedingly open-minded to new ideas and concepts, from philosophy to science and psychiatry. It was this pope who in 1992 formally pronounced Galilei Galileo innocent of the charges brought against him by the Inquisition three and a half centuries earlier for insisting (heretically, a Church court said in 1633) that the sun *is* the central body of our solar system. As it happened, this notion was first developed by Copernicus, a Polish astronomer known in Kraków as Mikołaj Kopernik. And Wojtyła is captivated by astrophysics and theories on the creation of the universe (he is said to accept the theory of the Big Bang so long as it is recognized that it was God's work). Genetics and its impact on Christian ethics fascinates him, although, in the opinion of scientists at the Vatican, genetics may be as much a controversy for John Paul II's Church as Galileo was for the seventeenth-century papacy.

In preparation for the Third Millennium, John Paul II has directed the College of Cardinals to rethink the correctness of the actions of the Church in past centuries, including its stand in religious wars and on the Inquisition, in an undertaking that might, in effect, lead to a fresh version of Roman Catholic history.

The Sistine Chapel (where John Paul II was elected by the College of Cardinals as were most popes since the sixteenth century) was restored on his watch, a monumental fourteen-year project. Michelangelo's *Last Judgment,* perhaps the world's greatest artwork, can now be admired in the pure beauty of the colors with which he painted it on the wall of the chapel behind the altar, after completing the famous ceiling frescoes.

John Paul II personally celebrated High Mass at the Sistine Chapel immediately after Easter of 1994, with all the cardinals present in Rome in attendance, to mark the end of the lengthy restoration enterprise.

Karol Wojtyła is a champion of religious freedom and tolerance—he was among the drafters of the "Declaration on Religious Liberty" issued by Vatican Council II in 1965—and of freedoms, human rights, human dignity, and social justice in every considerable dimension. He has tendered the hand of friendship of his Church to Jews in a manner no other pope had ever done.

But John Paul II tolerates no challenge to what he regards as the Church's unquestionable moral teachings, notably on the sanctity of life, even before conception (therefore no birth-control pill for Catholics as far as he is concerned). And he brooks no dissent from the views he upholds on grave matters. Thus respected theologians who differ from the pope in the interpretation of the Church's truth have been banned by the Vatican from teaching at Catholic institutions.

On the issues of abortion and artificial contraception, euthanasia, priestly celibacy, the exclusion of women from priesthood, divorce, and homosexuality, John Paul II explodes in loud, ominous anger—like a prophet from the Scripture—and more and more frequently so as he grows older and sees the world around him turning unacceptably permissive in moral terms.

He has openly fought the United Nations (and the U.S. government) over population-control programs, for the first time in modern history pitting the Vatican directly against most of the international community. The Church being authoritarian by definition, and compromise of principle not being a Polish character trait, the pope has publicly and vehemently denounced a proposed U.N. text for a declaration by the 1994 International Conference on Population and Development that, in effect, appeared to legitimize abortion on demand and accept artificial contraception methods.

"We protest!" he cried from his window overlooking St. Peter's Square at Angelus noon hour on a Sunday in April 1994, having earlier written personal letters to each head of state in the world, conferred with President Bill Clinton by telephone, and met with the 151 ambassadors accredited to the Holy See to express his overwhelming concern about the "future of the family institution" if the U.N. conference approved the text in favor of birth control.

When Clinton called on him at the Vatican two months later during a European tour, John Paul II told the president how profoundly he opposed the U.N. document. It was the first time that a pope and a U.S. president acknowledged publicly their disagreement on a crucial subject—although they like and respect each other—but for John Paul II this question is one of fundamental principle. He believes he has to give battle with all his resources to prevent what in his view would amount to the enshrinement of the concept of abortion in international law.

And as a pope, Karol Wojtyła is entirely consistent with positions he assumed as bishop and cardinal. In 1968, he helped Pope Paul VI draft *Humanae vitae,* the encyclical reaffirming the Church's ban on artificial contraception. In a February 1974 sermon in Kraków he thundered that "the greatest tragedy of our society . . . is the death of people not yet born: the conceived and unborn."

John Paul II hit the ground running when, two days after leaving a Rome hospital following his 1994 hip fracture, he issued an Apostolic Letter ruling out Church discussion about ordaining women as priests: "I declare that the Church has no authority whatsoever to confer priestly ordination on women and that this judgement is to be definitively held by all the Church's faithful."

In the sixteenth year of his pontificate, John Paul II has thus chosen to launch an unparalleled "Spring Offensive" along all the fronts, as a close associate put it. No Italian pope in centuries has been so outspoken and emotional on matters of doctrine, but now the whole future of the Roman Catholic Church, humanity's oldest continuing institution, may be at stake—and Karol Wojtyła knows it.

In the second half of the twentieth century, the Church has suffered a vast loss of the faithful in North America, Western Europe, Latin America, and the Caribbean, in part because so many Catholic men and women refuse to observe the teachings on contraception or are antagonized by other aspects of Vatican Catholicism they regard as too conservative and out of touch with the world's reality. Some simply stay away from the Church, others join Protestant denominations, notably Pentecostal (that the Vatican calls "ecstatic sects"), where they think they will find more freedom and religious participation. This occurs especially in Central and South America and Mexico, and even in Africa, where John Paul II has made a great personal effort to expand the presence of the Roman Catholic Church. And Islam was, late in the twentieth century, the world's fastest growing religion, chiefly in Africa and the Middle East; there are virtually no Christians in the Holy Land because of emigration and conversions.

Worldwide, there are fewer and fewer priests and nuns, and fewer and fewer vocations. In a May 1994 message, the pope remarked that "it is surprising to note that the greatest shortage of priests is found precisely in Latin America, the continent with the highest percentage of Catholics in proportion to its total population, and, as statistics show, with the greatest number of Catholics in the world."

What John Paul II faces, then, at the threshold of the Church's Third Millennium, is a revolt in the ranks that he hopes to overcome through his "New Evangelization" apostolate without abandoning his principles or any of his doctrine positions. If the revolt keeps spreading, however, he may leave behind at the end of his pontificate a much reduced but hard-core, highly militant, and fully obedient Church. A fighter, Wojtyła may prefer to take losses than to compromise. Sadly for him, these alternatives loom ahead at a time when the world, as a whole, is again in search of religious faith.

There is, of course, a pattern of pontifical confrontation over the millennia. Gregory the Great, who reigned late in the sixth century and was one of the greatest popes—and papal autocrats—wrote once, "I am ready to die rather than allow the Church of the Apostle St. Peter to degenerate in my days." He went on: "You know my character. I am long-suffering, but when I have once made up my mind to submit no longer, I face every danger with joy." The gout-stricken Gregory, according to his leading biographer, was "certainly one of the most notable figures in ecclesiastical history," who "has exercised in many respects a momentous influence on the doctrine, the organization, and the discipline of the Catholic Church."

So in listening today to John Paul II, these stern, defiant words of Gregory—his role model as pontiff, moralist, philosopher, and mystic of martyrdom—inevitably come to mind. Indeed, his choice of words made him sound exactly like Gregory when, fourteen centuries later, he announced in a homily at a suburban Rome church that "I am not severe—I am sweet by nature—but I defend the rigidity principle. . . . God is stronger than human weakness and deviations. God will always have the last word. . . ."

And in these battles, Karol Wojtyła is determined to save humanity as well as his Church from the "culture of death," which he sees in the "contraceptive imperialism" of the West, in the breakup of families, and in the "savage capitalism" that, he claims, has replaced communism as a lethal peril and an evil.

The pope believes that humanity is foundering in immorality as the millennium approaches, and he is profoundly disturbed that all these dangers now rise as well in postcommunist Poland—his beloved Poland, where he daily crossed swords (and pens and words) with the communist regime before his 1978 pontifical election. Indeed, it often appears that he tends to judge the world through the prism of his Polish experiences and traditions. As one of his old friends has remarked, "You can take the Pope out of Poland, but you cannot take Poland out of the Pope."

The Polish pope is a man of touching kindness and deep personal warmth, a quality that evidently he communicates to the hundreds of millions of people who have seen him in person, as he crisscrosses the globe by jet airplane (and hops, skips, and jumps by helicopter from ceremony to ceremony), or on satellite or local television. His smiling face is probably the best known in the world, John Paul II having elevated his mastery of modern communications technology in the service of his gospel to the state of art.

But he really thrives on direct contact with people—individuals or huge crowds—which invigorates him even at moments of utter physical fatigue. In public, he likes to joke, often in a slightly self-deprecatory fashion, in whatever language he happens to be using at the time, and he enjoys the crowd's laughing, applauding responses. It may be the actor in him.

But notwithstanding his extrovert public persona, Wojtyła is a very private man who keeps even those closest to him at arm's length, sometimes imperceptibly. He possesses a very private sense of humor, which he displays at intimate moments, complete with a mischievous glint in his gray-blue eyes and, sometimes, a remark that quite pointedly goes to the heart of the matter—not always in a way complimentary to the person under consideration.

At a lunch or dinner in the plain dining room in the Papal Apartments at the Apostolic Palace—on the third floor—with only a single guest and his two private secretaries, the pope is an amiable host, conducting the conversation in a fashion so relaxed that the visitor quickly forgets that he is in the presence of His Holiness. There are no formalities about second helpings or accepting a second (or third) glass of wine—Wojtyła likes to add a touch of water to his wine—and the meal, an interesting mix of Italian and Polish cuisine prepared by Polish nuns and served by the pope's Italian valet, is abundant; the host himself eats heartily between smiles and makes comments on a variety of themes. It is difficult not to like him.

CHAPTER 2

Karol Wojtyła's Polishness flows from his origins and surroundings. He became imbued from the earliest childhood at home, church, and school with Polish causes, the Polish dimension of religion, and Polish history. It is a long and rich history that Wojtyła learned about his ancient land, triumphant as well as despairing, full of glory and tragedy, victories and defeats, uprisings and betrayals, hopes and deceptions, incredible patriotic courage and destructive nationalism and morbid prejudice.

The stage of the Polish drama was always filled to capacity with heroes and romantic noblemen, patriots and traitors, inspired religious preachers and holy fools, saints and martyrs, geniuses of music and literature, messianic poets, mystics and eccentrics—all elbowing their way to the forefront with charming effrontery. It is a history spanning a full thousand years of combat with Baltic and Slavic pagans, Teutons, Tatars, Turks, Russians, Ukrainians, Cossacks, and Swedes—sometimes in conquest, sometimes in national defense—and, much too often, among the Poles themselves.

Small wonder, then, that the Polish theater faithfully reflected all these high (and low) points of Polish life and history, most notably patriotism and religious faith along with romanticism and mysticism. And small wonder that under all these childhood influences Karol Wojtyła, as a teenager, would turn to drama with its inebriating and electrifying Polishness as his first vocation or, at least, as one of the conduits to his ultimate destiny. His intense exposure to patriotism and religiosity—he was a receptive vessel to both—led him naturally to amateur theater where he could express and act out the sentiments already burning in his soul. Composing poetry came next. In the theater, most of his chosen roles were mystical, religious, and patriotic. Wojtyła was a natural actor, a gift that would serve him well all his life.

Poland became Roman Catholic the moment it was born as a nation-state over a thousand years ago. In A.D. 966, Duke Mieszko I of the Piast dynasty of the Polish pagan tribes, who inhabited the plains between the Vistula and Oder rivers in Central Europe, married Princess Dobrava of the Premyslide dynasty in neighboring Bohemia. Mieszko and his forces had been defeated in battles for the control of the mouth of the Oder by the Teutonic warriors of Otto I, who had succeeded Charlemagne as Holy Roman Emperor of the German nation. He therefore concluded that he could save his domain only through an alliance with the Bohemians and the creation of a strong new nation to challenge the Teutons.

The alliance was formed by Mieszko's marriage to Dobrava, a Christian princess, and his acceptance of Christianity on behalf of his Polian Slavs was part of the accord with Bohemia. In this sense, the birth of Poland as a political entity and the advent of Christianity among the Poles came at the same time in what was known as the "Double Foundation" of church and state. Nationhood and Christianity have been inseparable in Poland ever since in a unique fashion in history—not just as institutions, but as societal phenomena—and sometimes obsessively so, especially in time of national peril.

Actually, Christianity came quite late to Poland, in the tenth century of the Christian era. Because the Slavic tribes in the Oder and Vistula valleys lived in their forests and plains north of the mountain barrier of the Carpathians, Roman legions never reached their territory—and neither did the Greco-Roman culture nor the Christian missionaries. Moving in the wake of Roman conquests (or on their own in more familiar Western Europe), the missionaries made their way with the Gospel to Germany, France, Spain, and even England and Ireland in the west, to the Danubian lands below the Carpathians in the south—such as Bohemia and Hungary—and to Greece, the Balkans, and further east into Muscovy. St. Cyril and St. Methodius, the Greek missionary brothers who were called "Apostles to the Slavs" and fathers of the Slavonic liturgical and literary culture, brought Christianity to Moravia, adjoining Bohemia, in the ninth century, but never set foot among the Piast tribes.

But once Mieszko and Dobrava introduced Christianity there, it took root quickly and easily; for one thing, there was no strong pagan religious heritage among the Slavs to compete with the new faith. The first Polish Roman Catholic diocese was established in A.D. 1000 in the western town of Gniezno, the burial site of the first Polish religious martyr who achieved this distinction barely forty years after the new Christian nation came into being. He was St. Wojciech (St. Adalbert to the West), an archbishop and missionary who was killed among Baltic Borussians whom he sought to convert, and Poland's first patron saint. Martyrdom was an essential part of Polish history from the very outset, a fact Karol Wojtyła was discovering through his lessons in Wadowice grammar school.

The need to choose between the East and the West, in the most fundamental sense of belonging and allegiance, was another essential aspect of Polish history. The first choice was made by the Poles immediately after they acquired their national identity—and, as it happened over the next thousand years, it was for the West. And in this instance, the choice was a religious one, likewise creating a historical precedent.

It stemmed from the deepening division of Christianity between the Latin and Greek churches that followed the breakup of the Roman Empire between the western empire in Rome and the Byzantine empire in the east. The split came after the death in A.D. 337 of Constantine the Great, the first Roman emperor to convert to Christianity, who had decided to move the imperial capital from Rome to

Constantinople, the magnificent city he built in Byzantium on the Bosporus and dedicated to the Virgin Mary. With the empire divided between Constantine's successors, Rome and Constantinople turned into opposite centers of power and civilization as well as of religious influences.

Rome-based Latin Christianity soon found a powerful rival in the growing Greek Christian Church, increasingly known as the Greek Orthodox Church (Byzantium was part of the Hellenic cultural sphere), with their differences emerging both in doctrine and liturgy—and with the Latin losing more and more ground in the East.

Rome no longer had even an emperor of her own after the fourth century, and Pope Gregory the Great, the foremost personage in Europe, had to deal with the Christian emperor in Byzantium on all matters affecting papal possessions in Italy and further west. On religious matters, Gregory communicated with the patriarch in Constantinople, who still recognized the authority of the Roman pope, but ecclesiastic contacts between the two Christian capitals finally broke down. The Nicaea Council in A.D. 787 was the last time a universal gathering of the Christian churches was held. The great schism came in A.D. 1054, when the Latin and Greek churches formally separated.

The Greek Orthodox conquest in the Balkans and the Russian lands resulted more likely—and paradoxically—from its greater and more rigorous theological ritualism on the one hand and from its considerable cultural liberalism on the other. It allowed, for example, the use of vernacular Slav languages instead of Latin or Greek in Christian service—it would take the Roman Catholic Church a millennium and a half to catch up with the idea of permitting Mass in the vernacular—and encouraged the emergence of the Cyrillic alphabet, based on the Greek alphabet, in lieu of Latin. Moreover, the Greek Orthodox Church did not demand priestly celibacy and approved of priests' marriages, as it does to this day. The modern contrast, of course, is that John Paul II is categorically and inflexibly opposed to both practices.

Byzantium, at the same time, was richer and more powerful (and geographically nearer) than Rome as far as the rulers and the people of the Balkans and beyond were concerned. Civilization was flowering in Constantinople while Rome was in the throes of massive cultural decay even when Gregory the Great still reigned as pontiff. Byzantine power forced King Boris I of Bulgaria to accept Christian orthodoxy in A.D. 865. In A.D. 989, the Slavs of Kiev, Poland's next-door eastern neighbors, opted for the Greek Orthodox religion, to be followed soon by the Grand Duchy of Muscovy.

But Poland, born only twenty-three years earlier from Duke Mieszko's marriage alliance with the Christian lands of Bohemia, decided to espouse Rome's Latin Christianity even though the first Greek Orthodox missionaries were beginning to appear along the Vistula. It was a political and strategic decision, as well as a religious one, because it meant alignment with the West instead of the East, and this early move defined Poland's entire future history. Alliances with the papacy in Rome throughout the Middle Ages were the next logical step. It is impossible to say whether the Poles acted from instinct or calculation—or both. From that moment on Poland has been the great western bulwark in that part of Europe, from Tatar and Turkish invasions of bygone centuries to the Miracle on the Vistula in 1920, and the collapse of communism toward the end of the twentieth century.

The schism in 1054 between the opposing Christian churches had drawn with utter finality the basic East-West line across Europe, a line that would resurge time and time again. It reappeared most recently after World War II with the imposition of communism by the Soviet Union in Eastern Europe, though Poland had again succeeded in maintaining allegiance to the West—through cultural and religious resistance—notwithstanding its ruling Marxist-Leninist regime.

And this had become possible in large measure because the original turn toward the West through the Latin Christianity option led to the rise of Latin and Western culture and civilization in Poland. Kraków University, founded in 1364, is the second oldest in Eastern Europe (Prague's Charles University is the oldest), and Copernicus studied there late in the fifteenth century. Latin was the language used even in conversation at that time, remaining the official one in many academic and bureaucratic instances well into the twentieth century. Ideas and knowledge circulated freely among the Poles, French, Germans, and Italians from the Middle Ages, building a body of tradition that defied and survived invasions, wars, partitions, alien yokes and occupations, and all-out campaigns to eradicate and uproot Polishness.

Karol Wojtyła had inherited his Polishness at birth, and he has been building on it as student, worker, seminarian, priest and pope, artist and thinker, patriot, and now world statesman. He has faced all the risks and dangers arising from his mission, and, as he keeps reiterating in public and in private, martyrdom is part and parcel of this responsibility. And it is the memory of the martyred St. Stanisław that is ever present in Wojtyła's mind. He constantly alludes to him, more than to any other figure in Church history—aside from Christ, the Virgin Mary, and the Apostles.

John Paul II is convinced, in a most mystical fashion, that he, too, has been chosen for suffering and martyrdom. He believes that the Virgin Mary, whom he deeply venerates and whose month of piety and devotion is May (as is St. Stanisław's anniversary), has saved his life on many occasions as well as having taught him how to suffer. In private conversations, he also speaks of "Providence looking after me."

Having broken his hip and consequently forced to spend almost the entire month of May 1994 at the Agostino Gemelli Polyclinic in Rome, where he was taken for the first time after being shot on May 13, 1981, the pope has made it clear that he relates his dramatic mishaps to the Virgin Mary and to martyrdom. In the first message he delivered from his apartments' window after returning from the hospital—the Sunday noon Angelus prayer—he said that "through Mary I would like to express my gratitude today for this gift of suffering again linked with this Marian month of May."

John Paul II went on: "I am grateful for this gift. I have understood that it is a necessary gift." Then he made another linkage between his suffering and his battle over artificial contraception and abortion issues advocated by the United Nations during 1994, which happened to be the Church's—and the U.N.'s—International Year of the Family. In most extraordinary language, he said:

> I understand that I have to lead Christ's Church into this third millennium by prayer, by various programs, but I saw that this is not enough: she must be led by suffering, by the attack 13 years ago and by this new sacrifice. Why now, why in this Year of the Family? Precisely because the family is threatened, the family is under attack. The Pope has to be attacked, the Pope has to suffer, so that every family may see that here is, I would say, a higher Gospel: the Gospel of suffering by which the future is prepared. . . . Again I have to meet the powerful of the world and I must speak. With what arguments? I am left with the subject of suffering. And I want to tell them: understand it, think it over! . . . I meditated on all this and thought it over again during my hospital stay. . . .

This was a week before his Vatican meeting with President Clinton, a "powerful of the world," at which their disagreement over the U.N. document consumed the bulk of the time.

John Paul II also touched on the subject in a message to Italian bishops, written at the hospital on May 13, the Feast of Our Lady of Fátima, which coincides with the date of the assassination attempt. The Feast of the Visitation of Blessed Mary the Virgin falls on May 31. The Fátima Virgin, one of the most venerated by Catholics, has her shrine in Portugal, and the pope went there exactly one year after the shooting incident to thank her for saving him—and was attacked (harmlessly) by a demented priest with a bayonet. In a rare public discussion of the 1981 attempt, John Paul II said in his message to the bishops:

> Allow me to think back to what happened 13 years ago in St. Peter's Square. We all remember that moment during the afternoon when some pistol shots were fired at the Pope, with the intention of killing him. The bullet that passed through his abdomen is now in the

> shrine of Fatima; his sash, pierced by this bullet, is in the shrine of Jasna Góra [in Poland]. . . . It was a motherly hand that guided the bullet's path, and the agonizing Pope, rushed to the Gemelli Polyclinic, halted at the threshold of death.

(A month later, the pope told a special consistory of the College of Cardinals that Our Lady of Fátima twice marked his life: when she saved him from the assassin in 1981 and when, with her help, communism collapsed in the countries of the Soviet bloc at the end of the 1980s. "I believe," he said, "that this is an experience that is rather meaningful to all.")

And the strain of Polish mysticism rose again as the pope recalled his visit to Lithuania in 1993, a very emotional experience for him:

> When I was able to contemplate the face of the Mother of God in the shrine of the Dawn Gate in Vilnius, I addressed her with the words of the great Polish poet, Adam Mickiewicz: "O most holy Virgin, who shines forth from the Dawn Gate and defend your resplendent shrine at Częstochowa [in Poland]; just as you saved me . . . from death!" . . . It was an echo, as it were, of those shots in St. Peter's Square that were meant to take the Pope's life. Instead, the fatal bullet was stopped, and *the Pope lives—he lives to serve!*

John Paul II believes that suffering is a foreordained part of his destiny, both as a Christian and now a pontiff, and it has pursued him all his life, from the early death of his closest relatives to illness, accidents, and assassination attempts. But suffering surrounds him, too, affecting his most intimate friends.

Stefan Swieżawski, a historian of philosophy, one of Wojtyła's oldest friends and his former university professor, recalls that at a private dinner at the Vatican in March 1979, the pope, barely five months after his election, opened his heart to him.

"He recognized," Swieżawski says, "that through a strange disposition by God, the most important events in his priestly life are, in some secret way, connected with great suffering of his closest friends. He recalled that his elevation to cardinal was intimately tied to the tragedy of Father Marian Jaworski, who, just then, lost his hand in a terrible railway accident—and that his election at the conclave coincided with such grave illness of Bishop Andrzej Deskur. It looks as if there is a real interdependence of the sacrifice and suffering of friends with events of such magnitude."

Marian Jaworski is now Archbishop of Lwów in Ukraine and remains very close to Wojtyła as friend and theologian. Deskur, a friend since Kraków seminary days, suffered a paralyzing stroke three days before the pope's election. Then president of the Pontifical Council on Social Communication, Deskur was Wojtyła's best personal friend in Rome. Wojtyła went to see him on the way to the conclave, and on his first full day as pontiff, October 17, he visited Deskur at the hospital during the afternoon, driving there in an open automobile. John Paul II subsequently elevated Deskur to archbishop and cardinal, and to this day he invites his old friend to lunch at his private apartments every Sunday when he is in Rome. Deskur, paralyzed from the waist down, lives in a wheelchair, but his mind is crystal clear.

Another great nineteenth-century Polish poet and playwright, Cyprian Kamil Norwid, deeply admired by John Paul II, wrote prophetically about him when he referred to Pope Pius IX: "He is a great nineteenth century man. He knows how to suffer." And John Paul II, discussing Norwid in a private conversation, remarked that "yes, Norwid was very, very important to me, and I still read him."

And it is because of Karol Wojtyła's sense of suffering and martyrdom that the story of St. Stanisław looms so important, both in terms of his own destiny and his vision of the history of Poland.

Stanisław's drama symbolizes the endless church-state tensions and conflicts among Poland's Catholics over one thousand years. Virtually nothing is known, however, about the martyr's actual life, other than he was born in 1030 in the village of Szczepanów near Tarnów in southern Poland (not too far from Wojtyła's birthplace in Wadowice and the parish of Oświęcim—Auschwitz—where millions would be martyred in the Nazi concentration camp) and became Bishop of Kraków on May 8, 1072. There is no record of his family name.

During commemoration in Szczepanów in 1972 of the nine-hundredth anniversary of Stanisław's appointment as bishop, Wojtyła—then a cardinal—stressed in his sermon that the seven years of his tenure, until his assassination on the orders of King Bolesław II ("The Brave"), "left its imprint forever on the destinies of the Church, in the destinies of the motherland." The bishop opposed the king over the long war against the Kiev principality and over his cruelties and immoral lifestyle.

As in his every public mention of Stanisław's martyrdom, Wojtyła's words on that occasion, too, were interpreted as an allusion to Poland's oppression by brutal communist rulers who presumably would not hesitate to murder the bishop defending the rights of the people. The bishop in this case would, of course, be Karol Wojtyła. After the murder on April 11, 1079, the king was chased out of Kraków by an aroused populace and fled to a Benedictine monastery in Bohemia, where he repented and died the same year. Stanisław was canonized in 1253.

This whole saga was an allegory Polish communist authorities did not need. A bloody clash between rioting shipyard workers in Gdańsk on the Baltic coast and the security forces had occurred in December 1970, and Wojtyła's years as cardinal in Kraków were punctuated by sharp disputes with the government over the martyr's memory. Wojtyła missed no opportunity to invoke St. Stanisław in sermons, homilies, speeches, and articles. In the Easter sermon in 1978, the year he would become pope, Wojtyła listed St. Stanisław and the Apostles Peter and Paul in the same breath (the bishop being the first mentioned).

A rock jutting out over the Vistula—known as Skałka in Polish—was the site where the bishop was murdered with a sword blow to the head on charges of pro-German "treason" issued by the king. It had long been a national Catholic shrine, and Wojtyła kept demanding that St. Stanisław's image be carried in procession every year from Skałka to the Wawel Castle's royal cathedral upriver, a recurring quarrel with the regime. In one of his sermons, he reminded the faithful that Polish kings had always led the procession, and that the bishop's death and the king's repentance "have been the spiritual foundations of the destinies of our nation. . . . Polish culture is Christian from its deepest roots. It cannot be torn away from Christianity without destroying it. . . . As Christians, we have the constitutional right to active participation in the benefits of culture; we have the right to mold it according to our convictions."

It must be noted that Wojtyła's devotion to St. Stanisław had long predated his confrontations with the communists, reaching back to his youth and his discovery of Polish messianic poets. That the cult of the martyred bishop was used by him politically against the regime was much more than clever manipulation: it was part of Wojtyła's spiritual as well as pragmatic personality.

Young Wojtyła's favorites among Poland's nineteenth-century writers—an impressive group of immensely talented, patriotic, romantic, religious, and messianic poets and playwrights—included Juliusz Słowacki, who had the gift of prophecy as well. This would become evident to Wojtyła and other Poles much later—in a messianic sort of way. Słowacki, who died at the age of forty in 1849, was the author of the famous play about King Bolesław the Brave and St. Stanisław, appropriately titled *King-Spirit* (as in Holy Spirit), and Wojtyła became intimately familiar with it at readings at the high school amateur theater in Wadowice.

Słowacki and the play entered Wojtyła's life in full during the wartime German occupation, when he combined his manual work at a rock quarry and a chemical plant in Kraków with secret theological studies and secret participation in an underground theater group presenting recitations of great Polish patriotic plays at private apartments before tiny, hand-picked audiences. It was known as the Rhapsodic Theater and it was part of the Unia clandestine organization fighting against the Nazis, the protection of Jews being one of its priorities in Kraków. Wojtyła, as did all Unia members, had to swear a solemn oath upon joining it.

The Polish underground believed that secret efforts to keep Polish culture alive against the proclaimed German *Kulturkampf* were as important as waging guerrilla warfare.

The Poles had learned that during the country's partitions during the nineteenth century, when both the Germans and the Russians strove to destroy the national culture and language, and they would apply the same methods under communist rule following World War II—with Karol Wojtyła's militant engagement.

On November 1, 1941, Wojtyła appeared in a performance of Słowacki's *King-Spirit,* marking the inauguration of the Rhapsodic Theater, at a midtown Kraków apartment where it had to be held early enough in the evening to end before the curfew. Because under the circumstances it was impossible to perform with scenery and costumes, the black-clad actors had to confine themselves to reciting their roles. The only concession to theatricality were candles burning atop the piano on which a member of the group played sad passages from compositions by Frédéric Chopin, another Polish patriotic and mystical genius. The combination of the actors' somber voices, the soul-wrenching music, and the flickering candlelight was eerie and deeply moving.

Wojtyła, then twenty-one, but already very mature and regarded as the leading actor in the Rhapsodic Theater, chose to play the part of King Bolesław, the murderer, rather than that of Bishop Stanisław, the martyr, giving it an unusual and surprising interpretation. Speaking in his beautiful baritone voice (still beautiful a half century later), Wojtyła presented the king not as the assassin, but as the repentant fugitive. He conveyed the lament of the king, once filled with ideals and concern for the fate of his nation, who now bemoaned his fall and warned against the "emptiness of the soul."

In the next performance of *King-Spirit*—there were four of them altogether during the war—Wojtyła sharpened even more his rendition of the wretched king, showing him through bitter reflections as a poor, unhappy man, tragically confessing his sins. Some of his colleagues were critical of the interpretation, but Wojtyła would not change his approach. He believed that his portrayal of the king conveyed the moral dilemma of his life. John Paul II clearly remembered fifty-three years later his Kraków *King-Spirit* performances, correcting a lunch guest who had referred to it as "playing the role." No, he said firmly, "I was *reciting. . . .*"

Asked to define the saint's significance, the pope nodded, saying, "Yes, he was a man of great importance to me."

Karol Wojtyła's fascination with St. Stanisław never ceased. In fact, it grew when he was ordained as priest shortly after the war. Joining the faculty of the Catholic University in Lublin (KUL) in 1954 as professor of Christian philosophy—KUL was the only Catholic university allowed to function in the communist countries of Eastern Europe—the Reverend Doctor Wojtyła gathered around him the university's best historians to discuss the circumstances of the saint's death in 1079. Former colleagues remember long evening debate sessions on the subject at the apartment of one of the historians, with Wojtyła raising questions about different existing versions. It remains unclear, for example, whether the bishop had excommunicated the king, as some accounts have it.

When he was named Cardinal Archbishop of Kraków in 1967 (which made him one of the youngest cardinals of the Church), he named a commission of forensic experts to undertake a scientific investigation concerning the precise manner of St. Stanisław's demise. The inquiry concentrated on the skull because the bishop was believed to have been killed when the sword struck his head.

The skull had to be removed for the study from the reliquary in the chapel of the royal cathedral at Wawel Castle, where it reposes not far from the tomb in the center of the church containing the saint's body. The body and the skull were separated for burial purposes sometime in the Middle Ages. Finding a fissure in the back of the skull, the forensic experts confirmed that the bishop was indeed "executed," inasmuch as the evidence at hand suggested the violent use of a sharp metal instrument. In this fashion, modern science vindicated a patriotic-religious legend, reflecting Karol Wojtyła's penchant for pragmatism and new technology in the service of the faith. After all, he regarded himself as the martyred saint's successor as Bishop of Kraków—and he owed him historical truth.

Wojtyła made his last pilgrimage as cardinal to St. Stanisław's birthplace of Szczepanów on May 7, 1978, and the next day inaugurated what was to be a yearlong synod of bishops of the Kraków archdiocese (the first in forty years) to implement the decisions of Vatican Council II. Consecrated to the memory of St. Stanisław, the synod was to extend to May 8, 1979, the nine-hundredth anniversary of his appointment as bishop—but by then Karol Wojtyła already was John Paul II. Still, he wanted to pay homage to the saint, and when the Polish government begrudgingly agreed to let the Polish pope visit his homeland during 1979, Wojtyła demanded that his trip start on that anniversary date. This, however, was too much for the communist regime to swallow, and John Paul II had to postpone the voyage by a month.

In his first homily as pope, on October 22, 1978, he made a point of mentioning the approaching St. Stanisław anniversary, just shy of a week after his election, but Polish authorities censored this passage—the only passages so censored—in the taped version broadcast in Poland. John Paul II got even, however, when the entire speech was broadcast in Polish over Vatican Radio, then widely heard in Poland. Shortly after his election, he made a pilgrimage to Assisi, made famous by St. Francis, insisting on visiting the church there where Pope Innocent IV had canonized Stanisław.

John Paul II is extremely sensitive to martyrdom in the name of religion, patriotism, compassion, and human freedom. In 1982, he canonized the Polish Father Maksymilian Maria Kolbe, a Franciscan superior with one lung, who died in 1941 at the Oświęcim concentration camp from a lethal phenol injection after offering himself in the place of a fellow prisoner condemned to execution by the Nazis. "He gave his life for a brother," the pope said of Maksymilian Kolbe, the second saint he canonized since assuming the throne of St. Peter.

He regards as martyrs the thousands of Polish soldiers who died in May 1944 in the battle for the hilltop Benedictine monastery of Monte Cassino, a powerful obstacle in the way of the Allied armies fighting their way up the Italian peninsula toward Rome. Polish regiments were in the vanguard of the assault, an unbelievably bloody one, and in a special message on the fiftieth anniversary of the Monte Cassino battle, John Paul II said: "The Church commemorates her martyrs in martyrologies. We cannot allow that in Poland today, the martyrology of the Polish nation should not be recomposed." And more martyrology was added on August 9, 1991, when Franciscan missionaries Zbigniew Strzałkowski and Michał Tomaszek were executed by Shining Path guerrillas in Pariacoto, Peru, for "distributing imperialist products to the people." They were distributing food.

In the spring of 1994, the pope directed his fire at the criminals of the Mafia, something no pontiff had ever done publicly before, and his furious speech on the subject may have added new names to the Church's roster of martyrs. Shortly thereafter, Father Giuseppe Puglisi, also an outspoken critic of the Mafia, was killed near his church in Palermo, Sicily, and Father Giuseppe Diana was murdered in Naples.

CHAPTER 3

The thousand years of Polish history that with its martyrs and heroes had served to mold the personality of Karol Wojtyła were a chain of astounding ups and downs, without parallel in Europe. Within less than four centuries after Duke Mieszko had founded Poland as a recognizable nation-state, it expanded into a veritable empire and a feared European power, stretching from the Baltic to the Black Sea and from the borders of Muscovy to the Germanic lands on the Oder.

Curiously, King Bolesław, who had ordered Bishop Stanisław's murder, had been allied with Pope Gregory VII, supporting his plans for a liberalizing reform of the Church, against the Holy Roman Empire, whose Germanic rulers Otto II and Henry IV desired an equal status with the Holy See in running Europe. That was the beginning of an alliance between Poland and the papacy in Rome that survives to this day, despite lapses on the part of the Vatican during nineteenth-century Polish partitions and even during World War II. It certainly functioned throughout the postwar communist period in terms of Holy See dealings with the Polish Church as a quasi-sovereign entity, especially with the advent of the Polish pope.

Another historical first for Poland came in the 1240s, when her king, Henryk the Pious, in command of Polish and German armies (Poles and Germans cooperated occasionally, if begrudgingly, during the late Middle Ages), blocked the advance of mounted Central Asian Tatars—the "Golden Horde"—in the course of a particularly ferocious battle at Legnica, in Silesia, at the gates of Western Europe. King Henryk was killed on the battlefield, but the Mongol invaders were thrown back.

During the Tatar sweep westward, the Tatars took Kraków, the royal capital, giving rise to one of the most dramatic and colorful Polish legends. A Tatar arrow had pierced the throat of the watchman who stood atop the tower of St. Mary's Church there to warn the populace with the melodic sound of his trumpet when he spotted an approaching enemy. But the arrow, lodged in the throat, stopped the melody in mid-note. To the present time, this is replayed on tape every daytime hour, with the trumpeter's musical lament breaking off in the middle. It was, evidently, Polish destiny over the ages, up to the last decade of the twentieth century, to save Western Europe from invasions from the East.

The Tatar invasion and incursions by the Holy Roman Empire had weakened Poland considerably for a hundred years after the battle of Legnica. The fourteenth century, however, brought Poles unprecedented prosperity and development under King Kazimierz the Great, who during his long reign encouraged trade and protected peasants from exploitation by land-owning nobility, founded Kraków University, built over forty fortresses to defend his frontiers, codified the law, and implemented a currency reform. He was Poland's first truly modern ruler in the environment of Europe at that time.

King Kazimierz also opened Poland's door to Jews fleeing persecution in German lands (German anti-Semitism having preceded Adolf Hitler by six centuries), placing them under the protection of the crown as *servi camerae* (servants of the treasury). Some fifty thousand Jews came to Poland, making the start of the Jewish presence there that reached three million—over 10 percent of the population—by the time the Nazis invaded the country in 1939.

The king was said to have had a Jewish lover—the beautiful Esterka—and whether or not this had influenced his attitudes, Poland became known during the sixteenth century as *Paradisus Judaeorum* (Jewish Paradise). Kraków's prewar Jewish district was called Kazimierz (probably after the king), as is what is left of it today.

Karol Wojtyła's uncompromising pro-Jewish stand represents, by his own admission, the continuation of the position adopted by King Kazimierz, whom he admires as one of Poland's outstanding monarchs. It is part of his Polishness as a history scholar, along with his childhood and adolescent experiences with Jewish friends and schoolmates. In April 1994 he received a delegation of around a hundred Jewish Holocaust survivors at the Vatican on the fiftieth anniversary of the Warsaw Ghetto uprising, an unprecedented event. John Paul II made a point of chatting briefly with each of them, asking where he or she was born. Whenever a survivor mentioned Kraków, the pope inquired earnestly in Polish, "And did you live in Kazimierz? Have you been back there?"

On the issue of Polish anti-Semitism, which still exists and was quite virulent before the war, it is useful to think of King Kazimierz and John Paul II. And, once more, Gregory the Great emerges as the forerunner of John Paul II's ideas in his role as an uncompromising defender of Jews from the fanaticism and oppression of his time. Gregory's biographer cites his grave warning in a proclamation from Rome that "we will not have the Hebrews oppressed and afflicted unreasonably."

It is also worth knowing in this connection (as well as in others) about Cyprian Norwid, the poet and playwright who may have exercised the greatest single artistic, intellectual, and religious as well as romantic influence on young Karol Wojtyła. Unlike his fellow Polish bards of the time, Norwid was also a profound philosopher, another attraction for Wojtyła.

With an intense interest in public affairs, Norwid was among the Polish intellectuals who rose against the anti-Semitism of the Russian occupation authorities, and minced no words about it. After Cossack troops on horseback brutally dispersed a Polish anti-Russian demonstration in Warsaw in the 1860s, singling out Jewish participants for extra beatings, Norwid wrote a poem titled

"Polish Jews," in which he argued that Poland had the "priceless heritage" of two different but great cultures—Polish and Jewish—so close to each other. He presented Jews as bearers not only of ancient thought, but also of an ancient battle tradition. Norwid's biographer described this poem as "an act of justice" toward an often maligned segment of the population.

John Paul II would use almost identical words a century and a half later when he became the first pope ever to visit the synagogue in Rome. And Wojtyła, Norwid, and the Jews were linked in still another youthful dimension. As an actor in the underground Rhapsodic Theater, he recited roles from Norwid's dramas *Portrait of an Artist* and *Promethidion,* a hymn to Polish freedom. One of the players who appeared with Wojtyła in prewar amateur performances was a beautiful Jewish girl named Ida Elbinger. She had been invited to join the secret theater when it was first being planned by Wojtyła and his friends, but she was shot dead by the Nazis on a Kraków street, a tragedy the pope still remembers.

Even before the war, Wojtyła was protective of Jews. Zofia Żarnecka, a university colleague, recalls: "I remember that Karol Wojtyła very often accompanied Anka Weber and played a special role toward her. Specifically . . . he protected her, a Jewess, from aggression by Polish bigots. His attitude toward young Polish bigots—who called themselves 'All-Poland Youth'—was negative, and he did not hide it. . . . He was distinguished by his courageous protection of a Jewish colleague."

Wojtyła was only sixteen, and still in high school, when Cardinal August Hlond, the Primate of Poland, wrote in a pastoral letter in 1936 that "there will be the Jewish problem as long as the Jews remain" and that "it is a fact that the Jews are fighting against the Catholic Church, persisting in free thinking, and are the vanguard of godlessness, Bolshevism and subversion. . . . It is a fact that the Jews deceive, levy interest, and are pimps. It is a fact that the religious and ethical influence of the Jewish young people on Polish people is a negative one."

It is doubtful that Wojtyła was aware of the pastoral letter, and Hlond today is a forgotten figure, despised by the few who remember him for fleeing Poland following the Nazi invasion (Kraków's archbishop, Prince Adam Stefan Sapieha, not only stayed behind, but directed a clandestine seminary where Wojtyła was a pupil and was a member of the Polish underground). Over forty Jews were killed in a bloody pogrom in the Polish town of Kielce, the worst pogrom in postwar Poland, in July 1945—five months before Wojtyła was ordained as priest. Later he deplored those events.

Poland's Age of Greatness, following King Kazimierz's rule, opened dramatically with an extraordinary marriage and a formidable alliance. When Kazimierz, the last king of the Piast dynasty, died in 1370 with no male issue, the country was faced with a complex problem of succession.

Marriages among the royal houses of Europe already being common in the fourteenth century, the first solution proposed by Poland was a union with neighboring Hungary. By previous arrangement, Kazimierz was succeeded on the Polish throne by his brother-in-law, Louis the Great, the King of Hungary, of French-Italian Anjou descent, but *his* death in 1382 reopened the whole question. Because earlier commitments provided for one of Louis's three daughters to inherit Poland from him, Polish nobility, after two years of interregnum, chose Jadwiga, the youngest daughter, and brought her to Kraków to crown her as "King of Poland."

It made no difference that Jadwiga was only ten years old at the time and that she was already engaged to William of Habsburg: it seemed to suit all those concerned (although it is not clear whether the princess herself was consulted). After making Jadwiga "king," the Polish nobles began looking for a husband for her, presumably realizing that at her age she was most unlikely to lead armies to victory in the endless fighting with the Germanic Teutons and the Grand Duchy of Muscovy, both bent on expansion in Central Europe. Besides, Poland needed a powerful ally.

The logical strategic alliance candidate was the pagan Grand Duchy of Lithuania to the northeast, which ruled over all the Ruthenian lands, the vast stretch of territory known today as Belarus and Ukraine, reaching as far south as the Black Sea. The logical matrimonial candidate was Lithuania's Grand Duke Yagailo, who was negotiating marriage with the daughter of the Grand Duke of Muscovy. In the event, the Polish nobility's diplomacy prevailed, and Yagailo agreed to marry Jadwiga, convert Lithuania to Roman Catholicism, and enter into confederation with Poland. They were wed in Kraków on February 18, 1386, when she was twelve (he must have been in his late twenties), the duke having first been baptized, changing his name to Władysław Jagiełło under which he would reign as Catholic king of the vast Polish-Lithuanian Commonwealth. Jadwiga died at the age of twenty-five.

John Paul II has every reason to believe that Polish history is truly mystical. From his earliest days as priest in Kraków—and then as bishop and cardinal—he has held Jadwiga in extraordinary esteem as a queen and as a Christian. In hundreds of sermons and homilies over decades, he linked her with St. Stanisław as a great figure in the history of Poland and of the Church. He had celebrated Masses over her tomb, praying for her to be canonized as a saint by the Church (the decision is ultimately in the hands of the pope). By all historical accounts, Jadwiga was a beloved queen, but there were no specific saintly deeds, like miracles, to be cited. Perhaps Wojtyła venerates her because she was so young when she died, in a sense a martyr in the cause of converting Lithuanian pagans.

Jadwiga is considered to be beatified, the step before canonization, because her cult has existed in the Church for over six centuries. It is known as beatification *Viam Cultis*, and she is called *Blessed* Jadwiga. She is buried in a sarcophagus near the tomb of St. Stanisław at the Wawel royal cathedral in Kraków and next to a black iron cross. Wojtyła prayed at Jadwiga's cross before departing for Rome on October 3, 1978, for the conclave from which he would emerge thirteen days later as John Paul II.

Earlier, Karol Wojtyła celebrated Mass every year on the anniversary of her coronation in 1384.

This anniversary is on *October 16*. And it was on *October 16*, 1978, that he was elected Pope of the Roman Catholic Church. Her name was on his lips the moment he became John Paul II.

In the sixteenth year of his pontificate, in 1994, John Paul II launched formal proceedings for Jadwiga's canonization.

Unquestionably, the marriage was the political and missionary coup of the century in Europe. The new Polish-Lithuanian Commonwealth turned into one of the continent's great powers: it was on par with the German, Ottoman, and Muscovite empires. And it kept growing, incorporating the German states of Prussia and Livonia in the north as well as Moldavia and Crimea in the south. In 1410, the commonwealth forces defeated the Teutonic Knights at the Battle of Grünwald, one of those historically defining military confrontations. Lithuania's conversion extended Catholicism to the north of Europe, keeping it out of the hands of the Greek Orthodox and Russian churches. And Jagiełо and Jadwiga launched the Jagiellonian dynasty, destined to be Poland's greatest and to last nearly two centuries.

Meanwhile, Poland appeared for the first time as the possible homeland of a Roman pope. In 1417, when the Church was thrown into utter disarray by the claims of three rivals to the papacy and a successor had to be found for Pope John XXIII (he was the antipope, and the original one to bear this name and numeration), who fled, Archbishop Mikołaj Trąba from Gniezno in Poland emerged as a skilled mediator.

In those days, nations (and not individual cardinals) elected popes, and Trąba was sent to the General Council in Constance as the representative of King Władysław Jagiełо. It appears that Trąba himself was perceived by other delegations as a promising papal candidate, and he received what was described as a "significant number" of votes. In the interest of unity, however, the Polish afchbishop gave his vote to Cardinal Oddone Colonna, who was elected and took the name of Martin V. (Martin V turned out to be one of the first popes to defend Jews. He issued a bull in defense of Spanish Jews—it was the time of the Inquisition—and forbade priests to deliver sermons attacking Jews.)

In 1565, when the Church was battling Lutheran and Calvinist Reformation, another Pole surged as a candidate to succeed Pope Pius IV. This was Cardinal Stanisław

Hozjusz of Warmia, a widely respected theologian who was in the forefront of the Counter-Reformation struggles and served as president of the last session of the Council of Trent. The council was the center of strategy in the war against Reformation, and Cardinal Hozjusz firmly opposed any concessions to the Protestants on the ground that it would weaken the Roman Catholic Church even further. But Hozjusz declined to be a candidate, despite pressures from fellow cardinals, returning to the Polish-Lithuanian Commonwealth to fight Reformation at home. The new pope was the Italian Antonio Ghislieri, who reigned as Pius V.

Over four hundred years would elapse before the next Polish papal possibility, but Hozjusz may have been one of Karol Wojtyła's role models. Indeed, Cardinal Wojtyła celebrated a Mass in a Rome church in November 1974 during a bishops' synod at which he played a major part, praying for the beatification of Cardinal Hozjusz. Unlike St. Stanisław, Hozjusz is virtually unknown among Poles, but Wojtyła, even more strikingly, spoke of him as a great link between Poland and the Holy See in his homily at Mass at St. Stanisław's Church in Rome (the Polish church) in memory of Pope John Paul I. This was on October 10, 1978—six days before Wojtyła was chosen to succeed John Paul I, who died after thirty-three days on the throne of St. Peter.

Poland's "Golden Age" began to tarnish early in the seventeenth century, gradually at first, as a result of ceaseless foreign wars and simultaneous conflicts among Polish nobility power groups. The internal squabbles encouraged foreign intervention in a pattern that ultimately led to the national collapse although there were moments of great glory, too.

First, King Zygmunt III found himself at war with both the Russians and the Swedes although King Charles IX of Sweden was his uncle. And even before that period, all the sides used religion as a bargaining chip, the Russians offering to convert to Catholicism if they could rule over Poland—Ivan the Terrible proposed it in 1581 to Pope Gregory XIII, who, rather incredibly, took it seriously—

and King Zygmunt playing with the notion of letting his son become the Orthodox Czar of Russia. Pope Clement VII, a former pontifical legate (envoy) to Poland, presided in 1595 over the union between Catholics in Poland and the Orthodox Ruthenian Church in the territories now known as Ukraine. Again, the papacy and the Poles worked hand in hand.

And religion went on dominating Poland's fate. When a massive revolt by Ruthenian Cossacks threatened the country and King Władysław IV died unexpectedly, the Polish nobility decided to elect his brother, Jan Kazimierz; kings at that time were elected by the nobles, not part of a line of succession. Jan Kazimierz was a Jesuit cardinal, which did not dissuade him from accepting the throne. He also married his brother's widow, Queen Louise Marie de Gonzague, the first French queen of Poland. In fact, the new king turned out to be a superb monarch, ending the Cossack rebellion and then defeating the great Swedish invasion.

This latest invasion occurred in 1655, an era the Poles called the "Deluge" because they seemed to be drowning in assaults from all directions. Warsaw, the new capital, was quickly captured by the Swedes, but Poles believe that it was the Virgin Mary that saved Poland at the battle of Częstochowa that Christmas. Częstochowa, an ancient town between Warsaw and Kraków, is famous for its Pauline monastery atop a hill called Jasna Góra (Luminous Mountain), which is the site of the shrine of the "Black Madonna." There, a small band of monks and knights fought off the Swedes, who retreated across Poland. It was one of those Polish religious-military miracles. The Virgin of Jasna Góra is known as the Black Madonna because her face has become blackened over the centuries. The image is a Byzantine icon, supposedly painted by St. Luke the Evangelist on the wooden plank that was the Holy Family's table at Nazareth. She holds the infant in her arm, her face slashed by a saber cut inflicted by a Hussite soldier during an invasion in 1430; the slash mark is venerated as well. It is not known how or when the Black Madonna found her way to Jasna Góra.

The defense of Częstochowa inspired Catholic Poles, suffering under the harsh rule of Protestant Swedes, to fight even harder. King Jan Kazimierz proclaimed the Black Madonna the Queen of the Crown of Poland, the honor she retains today. To John Paul II, Our Lady of Częstochowa is the most venerated virgin in the world as the defender of Poland and symbol of Catholic faith, the two together summing up the best Polish patriotic and religious sentiments. He paid her homage as soon as he came home on his first papal visit.

But the Deluge kept rising. The Swedes occupied Warsaw once more, and the Polish-Lithuanian Commonwealth lost the northern possessions of Livonia and Prussia. Moreover, Poland was devastated by the long years of warfare on her territory. Then, Ottoman Turks embarked on their century-long effort to break into Western Europe. To make matters worse, civil wars erupted among nobility factions and King Jan Kazimierz abdicated in disgust in 1668.

The next elected king was the great military chief and Marshal of Poland, Jan Sobieski, who held off an invading Turkish army at Chocim in 1673. Polish historians believe that Sobieski's victory in that battle again saved Christendom from Asiatic sway.

Sobieski performed an even better miracle on behalf of Poland and Christendom at the battle of Vienna against the Turks on September 12, 1683. He had special ties with the West, being married to the French Princess Marie Casimir d'Arquien de la Grange, bringing Poland into the French system of alliances. As soon as the Turks marched again through the Balkans and Hungary toward the West and besieged Vienna, Sobieski rushed to the rescue with forty thousand men. Following mediation by the papal nuncio in Warsaw, the Austrian empire accepted him as commander-in-chief of the allied armies. Victory came with a charge by Polish cavalry under the king's personal command. It was one of the most significant battles in European history—it halted the Islamic tide before it could engulf Western Europe.

Victory, however, did not mean peace, and one more time the Poles did the bidding of the Holy See. Though the Turks had been smashed at Vienna, they still posed a danger to the West. The following year Sobieski agreed to join the Holy League, organized by Pope Innocent XI, to fight them together with Austria and the Republic of Venice. Inconclusive combat resulted, further weakening Poland, and the country entered the ominous eighteenth century divided internally and no longer fit to stave off disaster.

Soon, she became a pawn in a lethal game between Russia's Peter the Great and Prussia's Frederick the Great, with Austria and Sweden also vying for control over what had once been the powerful commonwealth. Under a Saxon king, August II, who was imposed upon Poland by the Russians and the Prussians, the commonwealth agreed to limit its military forces to an absurd twenty-four thousand men and to let the Russians station their own troops on Polish territory—a foretaste of the future.

For two thirds of the eighteenth century, Poland lived through the "most demoralizing" years in her history, in the words of a Polish historian. He explained: "The Commonwealth ceased to have a foreign policy of its own and had no unified internal administration. The executive power hardly existed, education was neglected, superstition and religious fanaticism were widely spread, and dissipation and drunkenness thrived."

After the death of Peter the Great, pressures on Poland kept rising. Catherine II, who had succeeded to the Russian throne following the murder of her husband, Peter III, signed in 1746 an alliance treaty with Prussia's Frederick the Great, giving her a free hand in Polish affairs. Immediately, she placed on the Polish throne her former lover and the ambassador to St. Petersburg, Stanisław-August Poniatowski, who was crowned as King Stanisław II. He would be Poland's last king.

His ascent was the beginning of the end. Eight years later, on August 5, 1772, Russian, Prussian, and Austrian envoys solemnly signed in St. Petersburg an agreement to partition Poland among themselves. It was the First Partition, leaving a truncated state, which included Warsaw, Kraków, and the port of Gdańsk on the Baltic, but deprived Poland of her traditional provinces in the east, west, and south. Though Kraków remained Polish at the time, the rest of the surrounding province of Galicja was annexed by Austria.

Galicja was the home for multiple branches of the Wojtyła family, spread through the villages of the Carpathian foothills. However, there is nothing to suggest that the good farmers of Galicja knew very much about the partition.

For the next twenty years, however, the crippled Polish state made astonishing advances. It created and expanded new industries, doubled its income, and favored education and the arts. Poland had the only Education Ministry in Europe, and some of the most beautiful architecture flowered under Stanisław-August Poniatowski. In 1791, the Poles promulgated the most progressive written constitution on the continent, leading Edmund Burke to write that "Humanity must rejoice and glory when it considers the change in Poland."

But the joy did not last long. The following year, Catherine II ordered her troops into the eastern section of what was left of Poland, including Warsaw, and signed a new accord with Prussia, which occupied Gdańsk and the balance of western Poland. That was the Second Partition.

An uprising against Russia and Prussia in 1794, launched in Kraków and led by General Tadeusz Kościuszko (who became a hero of the American Revolution after losing his own country), was quelled in savage combat within a year. As a result, the Third Partition was proclaimed by Poland's three neighbors in 1795. The Polish kingdom was formally abolished and all its lands divided among Russia, Prussia, and Austria.

It was *Finis Poloniae*—or so it appeared.

For the next 123 years, Poles strove to preserve their national identity, culture, language, and religion, rising in arms when all hope seemed lost. And that was the time when Polishness in its richest artistic and spiritual expression asserted itself as it never has before or since.

An illusion of national rebirth, lasting barely eight years, was the gift from Napoleon Bonaparte, who created the Duchy of Warsaw in 1807, to reward the Poles who had fought in his armies in defeating the Austrians, Prussians, and Russians in his imperial wars. But his own defeat resulted in the liquidation of the duchy. The 1815 Congress of Vienna confirmed the partition of Poland, though it set up the so-called Congress Kingdom in the Russian part of the occupied country as a Russian protectorate with limited freedoms.

The Congress Kingdom was liquidated, in turn, after the Russians put down the patriotic uprising of 1831–1832 with extraordinary brutality. But turning to the Holy See for support, the Poles were bitterly disappointed in their Church. In response to pleas by Polish bishops, artists, and intellectuals, Pope Gregory XVI condemned the uprising in his *Cum primum* encyclical on June 9, 1832. An angry old monk who had just been elected to the papacy, he described the Polish revolutionaries as "certain intriguers and spreaders of lies, who under the pretense of religion in this unhappy age, are raising their heads against the power of princes."

Rebellions erupted again in Poland in 1848, as they did over much of Europe during that "Springtime of Nations," but, again, the Holy See refused to budge. Adam Mickiewicz, the greatest messianic poet, rushed from his home in exile in Paris to Rome to enlist an intervention by Pope Pius IX, but despite two audiences he failed to elicit a positive response.

While the frustrated Mickiewicz busied himself in Rome organizing a Polish Legion to march from Italy to liberate the homeland (as General Jarosław Dąbrowski, a Napoleonic commander, did with his legion in 1797), another famous Polish poet approached Poland's destiny and the Church's in a most inspired fashion. Juliusz Słowacki, the author of *King-Spirit,* the play about the martyrdom of the Kraków bishop, had concluded that Pius IX was cowardly in his behavior toward the Springtime of Nations, and he turned to poetry to express it. The pope had not only declined to help Poland, but he had fled Rome himself to seek the protection of the King of Naples. Słowacki wrote:

> Amid discord God strikes
> At a bell immense,
> For the Slavic Pope,
> Open is the Throne.
> This one will not flee the sword,
> Like that Italian.
> Like God, He will bravely face the sword,

For Him, world is dust . . .
So behold, here comes the Slavic Pope,
A brother of the people.

Słowacki died a year later, in 1849, at the age of forty. Exactly 130 years would elapse before his prophecy in the 1848 poem came true and the throne opened for the Slavic pope—and Poland's fortunes soared. Meanwhile, another Polish uprising, in 1863, also failed.

But Słowacki, Mickiewicz, Zygmunt Krasiński, Cyprian Norwid, Stanisław Wyspiański, and other Poles of genius went far beyond the struggle for the Polish cause. Living mostly in exile abroad, they created an amazing body of literature—poetry, drama, and prose—that a century and a half later still constitutes the nation's greatest wealth.

And Frédéric Chopin's music, too, was inspired by his longing for the homeland. The great Polonaise was born from the echoes of the bloody Polish uprisings. The Mazurkas express his tenderness for the Polish countryside. The marching song of General Dąbrowski's legion in 1797, also a Mazurka melody, became the Polish national anthem in 1920, the year of Wojtyła's birth: "Poland has not vanished so long as we live. . . ."

It is this treasure of Polishness that has kept the nation cohesive over the last two centuries: the partitions of the nineteenth century, the two world wars, the Nazi occupation, and the communist rule. And it is this treasure of national and religious culture that formed Karol Wojtyła, the Slavic pope.

PART TWO

CHAPTER 4

Predestination is a theological doctrine proclaiming "God's unchangeable decision for eternity of all that is to be" and "God's destination of men to everlasting happiness or misery." St. Augustine, one of the great Fathers of the Church (and its greatest philosopher), accepted the Aristotelian conception of God as "first mover, itself unmoved." His conclusion was that "God's grace is effectual and irresistible" and that "as what God has done He is eternally willed to do, grace involves predestination."

Its meaning has varied profoundly over the centuries and among theologians, but predestination is invoked to raise the question whether, to put it bluntly, Karol Wojtyła was predestined in this particular sense to become pontiff of the Roman Catholic Church. The same question would naturally apply to all the popes of the Church—as it would be to all human destinies in terms of foreordained lives—but the case of Wojtyła is so special and extraordinary that it justifies a modicum of speculation.

From earliest childhood, Wojtyła had displayed an extremely rare but wholesome devotion to God and religion that may suggest in retrospect that he is a "chosen one," if, indeed, God works in this way. Family tragedies were an added component in strengthening his faith. Polish traditions of mysticism and messianism, surrounding him as a youth, inevitably played a crucial role in turning him toward the priesthood. In fact, Wojtyła was directly involved with the Church and its organizations and activities from his youngest years, not as convenient pietism in a religion-oriented society, but as a perfectly natural and logical endeavor for him. A succession of dramatic events and astounding coincidences, bordering on the mystical, occurred during the period preceding the start of his secret theological studies.

As priest, Karol Wojtyła threw himself joyfully into the practice of his calling, deeper and deeper theological and philosophical studies and reflection, and an enormous workload. His spiritual and intellectual qualities and his warm and attractive personality were noticed higher up in the Church where he was able to command vital support along with the friendship of his secular and clerical contemporaries.

Wojtyła always had powerful protectors and advocates—from Kraków's Archbishop (and later Cardinal) Adam Stefan Sapieha, even before he entered the underground seminary, to Pope Paul VI, who held him in the highest esteem, powerfully aiding his ecclesiastic career. His rise in the Church was meteoric.

But, consciously or not, did Karol Wojtyła prepare himself for the supreme honor?

Pelagius, a British theologian of the fourth and fifth century and a contemporary of St. Augustine (then Bishop of Hippo in North Africa), held that free will of man and his conduct, character, and destiny are in his own hands. He added that grace, by strengthening man's moral powers, helps him to fulfill his purpose. In other words, Pelagius posited that by his own actions man prepares himself for his destiny.

Pelagius's views clashed directly with St. Augustine's (the two actually corresponded on the subject) in what was one of the Church's great theological controversies. John Paul II, a pupil of the Dominicans, who followed the teachings of Aristotle, St. Augustine, and St. Thomas Aquinas, is faithful to the Augustinian doctrine that God is "first mover," and he rejects Pelagius. St. Thomas, the thirteenth-century Italian Dominican monk and scholastic philosopher who bears the title of *Doctor Angelicus,* is, along with St. Augustine, the greatest influence on the thought and language of the Western Church. The pope may consider that he was guided in his progress by "God's destination" to "everlasting happiness" in the precise meaning of attaining the Throne of St. Peter—"happiness" in this context being the Church's and humanity's.

As a Thomist scholar, the pope is familiar with St. Thomas's theory of "Divine Concurrence." It establishes the relationship between God's help to man in performing an act and man's performing such an act freely; put another way, it is the result of God's grace and man's freedom to act. This could have conceivably led the pope to the acceptance of such predestination, impelling him to do everything in his power to be worthy of it, as a synergism of theological doctrines. Interestingly, John Paul II wrote in his first encyclical, *Redemptor hominis,* issued March 4, 1979, that through Incarnation "this is man in all the fullness of the mystery in which he has become a sharer in Jesus Christ, the mystery in which each one of the four thousand million human beings living on our planet has become a sharer from the moment he is conceived beneath the heart of his mother. . . . [This] is his 'destiny,' that is to say his *election.* . . . Each man in all the unrepeatable reality of what he is and what he does, of his intellect and will, of his conscience and his heart. . . ." And Gregory the Great, in his biographer's words, understood by predestination "the selection by God of a certain number of the human race, on whom He bestows His grace that they are enabled to acquire merits and attain final salvation. . . . God elects those who He foresees will persevere in faith and good work. . . ."

Be it as it may, the entire trajectory of Karol Wojtyła's life adds up to a formidable project to improve himself in preparation for a predestined future or, simply, for God's greater glory.

No bishop or cardinal in recorded memory has toiled harder as pastor, scholar, intellectual, and de facto political leader (in and out of the Church) than Wojtyła in the prepontifical period. It took thirty-two years for him to traverse the distance from the Kraków priesthood to the Holy See, achieving it at the fairly young age of fifty-eight, with every year bringing fresh accomplishments. In education and erudition as well as in theological, philosophical, and literary output in the formative period, he could be compared only to Gregory the Great, who became pope at age fifty in A.D. 590. He would resemble Gregory, too, in "inexorable severity."

Wojtyła began composing remarkably good poetry in his late teens, appeared at sixteen in the first amateur theatrical play in Wadowice (a Polish messianic drama that he also co-directed), and wrote two biblical dramas at twenty. He spoke fluent Latin and read Greek and German when he graduated from high school. He was awarded his first doctorate (in mystical theology) at twenty-two and his second (in philosophy, accentuating his beloved phenomenology) at thirty-two. His first "political" newspaper article (on French worker-priests) was published when he was twenty-nine.

He served as a Kraków university chaplain and taught ethics at three Polish theological seminaries and at Lublin Catholic University, making friends and impressing people in all walks of life wherever he went. He made lifetime friends among workers at the Kraków quarry and chemical plant where he was a wartime laborer (and simultaneously a secret seminarian), remembering them fondly by name when he was cardinal. As student, worker, priest, or actor, Wojtyła was always the most popular person in his milieu.

A bishop at thirty-eight, he began to be known in Kraków, in Poland, in Rome, and throughout the Church worldwide. A fine, instinctive politician in the best sense of the word, Wojtyła started to build a potential constituency (consciously or not) through more and more key friendships in the Church. He shone at Vatican Council II, delivering six intellectually puissant speeches in impeccable Latin. An increasingly frequent visitor in Rome with growing involvement in the activities of the Curia, he was soon noticed by Pope Paul VI, being named cardinal at forty-seven.

Speaking a half-dozen foreign languages (Italian, Spanish, German, and French being his best), Wojtyła traveled all over Western Europe and attended international Church meetings in the United States, Canada, and Australia, accepting invitations whenever Polish communist authorities were willing to grant him a passport. Everywhere, he befriended cardinals and bishops. At the same time, he regularly invited foreign cardinals and bishops, many of them from the Third World (which would become very important at the right time) to visit him in Kraków where they could observe his tireless pastoral labors.

Before long, Wojtyła was the most important figure in the Polish episcopate, after the aging, old-fashioned Cardinal Stefan Wyszyński of Warsaw, the Primate of Poland. There seemed to be no subject that did not captivate his attention: he organized symposia and conferences of theologians, philosophers, scientists, physicians, lawyers, writers, and journalists to learn their subjects and their concerns as they affected Polish society. As pope, he transplanted this system to the Vatican (and the Castel Gandolfo residence during the summer). He knew then and he knows now how to listen.

Was it therefore logical—or predestined—that with this magnificent preparation Karol Wojtyła would crown his life as pope?

Karol Wojtyła's origins go deep into the soil of peasant Poland. They can be traced at least to the middle of the eighteenth century in the southwestern province of Galicja. Both his parents came from peasant stock, from proud, independent-minded farmers and highlanders of Galicja who speak Polish in melodious tones and ancient words, and nurture their special lore of distinctive native dress, music, and customs. On Karol's father's side, the Wojtyła line begins, as far as it is known, with Bartłomiej Wojtyła, born in the village of Czaniec in 1788, and his wife, Anna Hudecka Wojtyła, born in 1792 in nearby Bulowice. Bartłomiej was a small farmer (he was listed in the parish registry in Latin, as was the custom, as *hortulanus*). Anna was a daughter of Bulowice small farmers, the Hudeckis, but all memory of them has vanished.

The village of Czaniec, in the foothills of the Beskidy Mountains in the Carpathian chain, must have been settled early in the seventeenth century, being once known as Grzanica. Its church, named after St. Bartłomiej (a recurrent Wojtyła clan Christian name), was built in 1660, and its land consisted of forest and stone-strewn fields. Czaniec farming families' added occupation was sewing rough peasant clothing, presumably to increase their tiny incomes. Bulowice, Anna Hudecka's village, was even older, its church having been erected in 1540, supposedly by St. Wojciech, one of Poland's patron saints. Both villages belonged to the parish of Kęt, a small town where St. Jan Kanty, a famous Polish theologian and Kraków Academy professor, was born in the sixteenth century. Sainthood and theology seemed always to hover in John Paul II's background and most remote origins.

Bartłomiej and Anna Wojtyła had four children, two boys and two girls. The boys, Franciszek and Stanisław, must have been outstanding citizens because both were elected as *iudex communitatis*—Latin for community councilman—and Franciszek became county judge. By 1868, they were buying more land for their families. The Wojtyłas were now comfortable, if not prosperous, by the standards of the time in rural Galicja.

Franciszek married a farm girl named Franciszka Gałuszka and they, too, had four children. Their second-born, Maciej, moved to the village of Lipnik, a half-dozen miles away, to work as a tailor as well as farmer, marrying Anna Przeczek, the daughter of the local baker, in 1878. These were the pope's paternal grandparents, but he never knew them. His grandmother died more than a decade before his birth, and Grandfather Maciej died when the boy was three years old.

Maciej had remarried—this time the daughter of a tailor—and they had a daughter, Stefania Adelajda, who died in Kraków in 1962, when Wojtyła was already bishop. She was his half aunt. When he was elected pontiff, his first cousin on his maternal side, Felicja Wiadrowska, was the only living member of his immediate family. He reminded her of it in a very warm letter he penned on the eleventh day of his pontificate, in which he said, "Lord God has ordained me to remain in Rome. It is an unusual act of Divine Providence." He added in this rare intimate letter that "I think much these days about my parents and Mundek" (his late brother) as well as about Felicja's family.

Karol Wojtyła, the pope's father, was born in Lipnik on

July 18, 1879, the year after his parents' wedding. Very little is known about his childhood except that his formal education ended after three years in high school. Karol Senior (as he would be called later) began his apprenticeship as a tailor, following in his father's footsteps, but he was drafted into the Austrian army at the age of twenty-one in 1900—Polish Galicja was then part of the Austro-Hungarian empire—and embarked on what turned out to be a lifelong low-level military career.

Posted to the Count Daun 56th Infantry Regiment, conveniently stationed in Wadowice, some fifteen miles from his native Lipnik, he was promoted within a year to private first class. Karol Senior spent the next three years in Lwów, a city in the east, as guard at the Infantry Cadets' Academy there. He was back in Wadowice in 1904 as sergeant and platoon commander, but the facts of his life over the ensuing period remain murky.

He married convent-educated Emilia Kaczorowska, the fifth of thirteen children of a Kraków upholsterer, in 1906; she was five years younger than Karol (in Polish, endings of last names change, usually to an "a," in the feminine gender). Her father, Feliks Kaczorowski, and the rest of the family were from the small town of Biała in the same Galicja region, moving to Kraków in 1885, the year after Emilia was born. Her mother was Maria Scholz, the daughter of a Biała shoemaker. It is unclear where and when Karol Senior and Emilia first met and why they lived in Kraków for the next thirteen years, although he was apparently still attached to the Wadowice infantry regiment and was promoted during that time to warrant officer. As a quarter-master's noncommissioned officer specializing in accounting, he may have been detailed to a Kraków headquarters unit. He fought in World War I, Wadowice having come under Russian artillery fire, and was awarded by Austria the Iron Cross of Merit with Cluster as "an extraordinarily useful and brave noncommissioned officer."

As a young bridegroom, Karol Senior cut a fine military figure. In their wedding photograph, with Emilia's white-gloved hand on his forearm, he looked trim in his black uniform with a sergeant's three silver stars on each side of his high collar. Rather short, he had a narrow handsome face with an elegant black mustache and a full head of black hair (he became bald some years later). Karol Senior was always a serious man. His army file describes him as "extraordinarily well developed, with a righteous character, serious, well-mannered, modest, concerned about honor, with a strongly developed sense of responsibility, very gentle, and tireless [at work]." His efficiency report praises him for his spoken and written command of the German and Polish languages, his ease with the formulation of "concepts," and for being "a fast typist." His social demeanor is described by the commanding officer as "very pleasant, decent, with good manners."

Following Austria's defeat in the war and the birth of independent Poland, Karol Senior joined the new Polish army, as did many other Polish officers and soldiers who had had to serve with the Austrians, and he was assigned with the rank of first lieutenant to the 12th Infantry Regiment in Wadowice, the Wadowice Lands Regiment, and its Supply Command. He was now a full-fledged officer, a boon in prestige-conscious Galicja.

The promotion was probably the reason the Wojtyłas moved from Kraków to Wadowice in 1919. Emilia's parents died before the war—the pope did not know his maternal grandparents, either—but one of her brothers, Robert, built a modest house in the Dębniki district of Kraków, right on the banks of the Vistula, after spending several years as a Russian prisoner of war. The house would be quite important in the lives of the Wojtyła men during the next war.

Karol Senior and Emilia's first child, Edmund, was born in 1906, in Kraków, where the sergeant served at the Austrian Supply Command headquarters. Their second child, christened Olga, died as a tiny infant, also in Kraków, on an unrecorded date.

Their third child, Karol Józef Wojtyła, was born on May 18, 1920, a year after his parents settled in Wadowice.

John Paul II's birth converged with Poland's resurrection, but it also had a curious time link with the papacy.

Giovanni Battista Montini, who would become Pope Paul VI in 1963, was ordained as a priest on May 29, 1920, eleven days after Karol Wojtyła came into the world.

Montini's first Vatican appointment was as a member of the nunciature in Warsaw, where he arrived on June 10, 1923. As seminarian, he had his first sense of mystical Poland as he read poet Adam Mickiewicz's *Book of the Polish Nation*. His first trip in Poland took him by train to the southern town of Oświęcim (Auschwitz), a short distance from Wojtyła's Wadowice and a half generation from the Holocaust. He went there for the twenty-fifth anniversary celebration of the establishment of Salesian Fathers in Poland, who operated a school in Oświęcim.

Montini remained in Poland only until October of that same year. Yet Poland was always close to his heart. In Warsaw, he had acquired an alarm clock that he kept by his bed for the rest of his life. Later as Paul VI, he had fervently hoped to visit Poland in 1966 on the one-thousandth anniversary of her Christianity, but the communist authorities ruled it out.

There was an even earlier contemporary connection between Poland and the papacy, just before Wojtyła's birth. That was the stay in Poland in 1919–1920, at the time of the national resurrection and the Miracle on the Vistula, of Monsignor Achille Ratti, who within two years was elected Pope Pius XI. Ratti was in Poland as apostolic delegate.

John Paul II was born in a Wadowice house owned by a Jewish family, directly across a narrow street from the town's principal Roman Catholic church, dedicated to St. Mary of Perpetual Succor.

Wadowice was a most unusual town in a variety of ways when Karol Wojtyła was growing up. It was founded in 1327 as a peasant village, maturing gradually into a regional trade and agricultural junction, thirty miles southwest of glorious Kraków, but always basically a backwater in the foothills of the Beskidy Mountains. In 1920, Wadowice's population stood only at roughly seven thousand inhabitants (in the ensuing seventy-five years, it would barely double in number).

Surprisingly, however, the town was an important cultural and educational center. It had electricity from 1907, quite an achievement in rural Galicja. And it was pleasant and rather prosperous, nesting comfortably between the

Skawa River, an effluent of the Vistula, and the Leskowiec hills to the south. The town square and the paved main streets featured neat one- and two-story solid buildings. There were birch trees and a fountain on Market Square. The Skawa was clean and ideal for swimming and diving (boys daringly leaped from the railroad bridge), and the Leskowiec, rising toward the Beskidy peaks in the distance, were excellent training ground for mountain treks and skiing, as well as for warm-weather picnics. The Leskowiec were Karol's preferred hills for long, solitary strolls; it was there that he learned to ski.

Wadowice had no industry apart from a small paper mill, a wire mill, and two establishments specializing in Church communion wafers. But there were many shops and at least two restaurants, including one owned by the mayor and famous for its tripe, a national dish. The town was also a regional administrative center, with a hospital, government offices, and a contingent of public officials whose salaries bolstered the local economy. The infantry regiment gave Wadowice both revenue and prestige.

The Wadowice wafer producers did very well because the town was in the heart of highly religious Galicja—the Kalwaria Zebrzydowska sanctuary was only ten miles away—and Wadowice itself had several churches, a monastery of Discalced Carmelites and a Pallottine Fathers monastery (both had their own schools), convents of Albertine and Nazarethan Sisters, and a parish Catholic House, which often served as one of the town's two theaters for amateur performances.

Strongly Catholic as it was, Wadowice nevertheless had an uncommonly large Jewish population, even by Galicja standards, where Jews had lived for centuries. It was estimated at between 20 and 30 percent, and the Jewish community had a synagogue and a cemetery. And, unlike in much of Poland in the prewar days, virulent anti-Semitism was virtually nonexistent in Wadowice. Until the late 1930s Jews worked as lawyers, doctors, dentists, and merchants, living without friction alongside Catholics, participating in the town's quiet affluence based chiefly on commerce and services. On Tuesday market days, peasants came from the countryside, selling livestock and produce mainly to Jewish merchants.

The best example of harmonious Wadowice relationships was that the Wojtyłas were renting the second-floor apartment in the house on Rynek Street, No. 2, just off the town square, belonging to a wealthy Jewish merchant named Chaim Bałamuth. The Bałamuth family occupied the ground floor of the building where their crystal and glass store was located; Bałamuth also sold motorcycles. The name of the street was later changed to Kościelna—Church Street. The address is now Ulica Kościelna, No. 7. The apartment adjoining the Wojtyłas in the Bałamuth house was occupied by the Beer family, also Jewish. Black-eyed "Ginka"—Regina—Beer, two years older than Karol, was one of the most beautiful girls in town and the best student at the Wadowice girls' high school. They were fast friends, both captivated by the theater. Wojtyła's first appearance on the Wadowice amateur stage was at fifteen, as Ginka's leading man.

Wadowice had fine schools. The girls' high school was highly rated in the region. The boys' high school was one of the best in Galicja. Keen on classics, it taught eight years of Latin and five of ancient Greek.

The school produced an astounding crop of graduates, ranging from John Paul II to fellow Wadowice native Jerzy Majka, who was the editor-in-chief of the Polish Communist Party's daily official newspaper, *Trybuna Ludu,* until the collapse of the regime in 1989 (Majka is ten years younger than the pope). Others were the Reverend Jan Piwowarczyk, the first editor-in-chief of the Kraków opposition Catholic weekly, *Tygodnik Powszechny* (to which Wojtyła contributed scores of articles and poems under his own name and under pseudonyms until the pontificate); Emil Zegadłowicz, one of the most controversial Polish poets, novelists, and playwrights of the first half of the century; war heroes (army generals and privates), an archbishop, several ambassadors, and outstanding artists, teachers, and lawyers. Pupils came from wealthy families, officialdom, and peasant homes in the countryside, but the Wadowice high school was a great social equalizer. Backgrounds meant nothing; a boy's personality, for better or for worse, meant everything.

Over two hundred Wadowice high school graduates died in the two world wars, including scores of Catholics and Jews who were killed in Oświęcim concentration camp, just west of Wadowice, during World War II. Among them were the abbot of the Wadowice Discalced Carmelites monastery and a dozen priests. Karol Wojtyła, already in Kraków, escaped the manhunt in his hometown, which the Nazis had incorporated into Germany (Kraków was part of the so-called General Governorship). Jews were herded into the ghetto the Germans had established in the town and shipped to the death camps.

For such a small town, the cultural level was impressive. Professionals, teachers, and priests—the intelligentsia elite of Wadowice—hungered for literature and theater. There were three public libraries. Spectators filled the two amateur theater auditoriums for performances of classics and modern plays. They came to watch the summer theater, mostly musicals, in the sprawling town park on the outskirts. Wadowice citizens often traveled to Kraków for professional theater—and meals and sophisticated conversation at the big city's elegant hotels and restaurants—and they avidly read reviews of the latest plays and books in Kraków and Warsaw newspapers, especially the capital's *Wiadomości Literackie* (Literary News). In 1922, when Karol was a two-year-old toddler, a Wadowice intellectual group formed a literary group called Czartak, which became quite famous throughout Poland for its provocative manifestos proclaiming Galicja's regional mysticism (mere Polish mysticism was obviously not enough for them).

The Wojtyłas led a quiet, pious life, removed from the cultural ferment, when Karol was an infant. First Lieutenant Wojtyła, always in his army officer's uniform, went on performing his quartermaster's duties at the infantry regiment headquarters. By now he was bald, he wore glasses, and his mustache was modestly trimmed. Emilia Wojtyła, her health steadily deteriorating, looked after the household and after baby Karol. Occasionally, she sewed to augment the family income. Edmund, who was fourteen when his brother was born, attended Marcin Wadowita High School.

Both he and Karol, to judge from early photographs, resembled their mother, with her broad facial planes, rather than their father. And, like their mother, the boys were strongly built, promising to be stout.

At first, Karol was called "Loluś," a baby diminutive, by Emilia. Then he acquired the less babyish but permanent diminutive "Lolek," by which he would introduce himself even at the university, and by which his few very close friends call him in private to this day, even at the Vatican. His mother was inordinately proud of him, even when he was an infant. Franciszek Zadora, then a neighbor of the Wojtyłas, remembers Emilia telling his mother, "You will see: my Loluś will be a great man."

The Wojtyłas' household was very religious, but not oppressively. At the entrance to their apartment from the outside curving iron staircase, a front contained holy water for crossing oneself on the way in and out. There were holy images on the walls and a small altar in the parlor where morning prayers were recited. In the evening and on holidays, the Bible was read aloud by the father or the mother, which was rare in those days among Galicja Catholics, more given to liturgical emotion. Prayers were said regularly as was the recitation of the rosary. Feasts and fasts were observed.

It was his mother who first taught Lolek how to cross himself, and the pope remembers his father as "a very religious man." He said that when he served as an altar boy at the age of ten—his mother had already died—the Lieutenant remonstrated with him for not praying "adequately" to the Holy Spirit. "He taught me a special prayer," John Paul II recalled, "and it was an important spiritual lesson." Over a half century later, he said, this prayer resulted in his encyclical on the Holy Spirit.

But the mood in the three-room apartment was not piously heavy. Religion came naturally to the Wojtyłas, always hospitable to their friends and their sons' friends, but never imposing their religiosity on others. Karol would follow that example.

The Lieutenant, as he was called by all in Wadowice, meticulously read the newspapers and discussed current events at work, at home, and with friends. He was the most respected citizen, friendly to young and old. Karol Poliwka, now a physician in Warsaw, recalls that the Lieutenant taught him how to swim in the Skawa River when he was eleven. Lolek was already a swimmer. Though the Lieutenant was not much of a talker, he occasionally enjoyed holding forth about Polish history and the Great War.

It was a satisfying life for the family, except for Emilia's dangerously weak health. She visited her three sisters in Kraków, but less and less frequently as time went by. The nature of her illness is not recorded, but she became partially paralyzed a few years before her death.

Karol Józef Wojtyła was christened on June 20, 1920, by the Reverend Franciszek Żak, a military chaplain, at the chapel of the Wadowice church, across the street from his house. One of his mother's brothers-in-law, Józef Kuczmierczyk, was the godfather and her sister Maria Wiadrowska was the godmother. The parish register states in Latin that *baptisatus est Carolus Josephus.*

Many of his father's friends and colleagues missed the ceremony because they had been called to the colors to defend Poland from the Soviet invasion then rolling westward across the country. The Lieutenant himself was too old to go into combat. But new responsibilities would soon face him at home.

CHAPTER 5

Tragedy first struck Karol Wojtyła on April 13, 1929, when his mother died at the age of forty-five. The cause of death was listed as myocarditis nephritis, inflammation of the heart muscle and kidney. Karol was five weeks shy of his ninth birthday, attending the third year of grammar school. His brother, Edmund, was a year away from medical school graduation in Kraków. After the funeral, the Lieutenant took his sons to pray at Kalwaria Zebrzydowska sanctuary. He had retired from the army the year before, and now he and Karol would have to live on his meager pension.

Karol had started grammar school when he was six, earning top grades from his first day in class: in the Polish language, religion ("very good"), arithmetic, drawing, singing ("very good"), sports and exercise, application and behavior. The school was located on the second floor and in the attic of the Wadowice district court building, to the right of the church on Market Square and just a few steps from the Wojtyła home. The space was limited, classrooms overcrowded, and the only place the boys had to play during recess was the street in front of the church.

A mother's death must be traumatic to a child, especially an eight-year-old, but Karol demonstrated extraordinary self-control—at least in public—quickly adapting to the new conditions of living with his father alone in the house on Kościelna Street. Deep inside, the suffering was searing. But only ten years later, at nineteen, when he was a student at Kraków University, did Karol Wojtyła allow himself to express it in words, in one of his first poems, written in the spring of 1939:

THE WHITE GRAVE

Over Your white grave
White flowers of life bloom—
Oh, how many years have gone by
Without You—how many years? . . .
Over Your white grave
O Mother, my extinct beloved,
For a son's full love,
A prayer:
Eternal Rest—

The presence of death would never leave the consciousness of Karol Wojtyła. Many years later, he told a friend whose mother had just died, "Well, you are lucky to have had a mother for so many years." His cult of Mary flowered from his mother's death: the natural identification.

In Wadowice, left to themselves, the father and the son, loving each other deeply, lived together superbly. They put their beds in the same room. The Lieutenant took care of the house, cooking breakfast and a light dinner while he and Karol ate the midday meal, the principal one of the day, at the small restaurant of Alojzy Banaś, a few doors down Kościelna Street, where Russian pierogi were the specialty.

It was there that Karol had his first brush with death. Banaś's son was a schoolmate of Karol and they often played together. One afternoon after the meal, when they were alone in the restaurant, the Banaś boy came upon a rifle someone had left behind in the room. He aimed it playfully at Karol and, unaware that the weapon was loaded, he squeezed the trigger. The bullet missed Karol by centimeters. He was ten or eleven at the time.

Daily life was well regulated: school in the morning, the midday meal at the Banaś restaurant, two hours of recreation (soccer and foot racing, or Ping-Pong on rainy days at the Catholic House next to the church), homework, dinner, and a walk with his father. They both enjoyed walking and spent much of the weekend (after church) strolling in and around Wadowice. Karol had no vacation trips, except for visits with the Lieutenant to Kalwaria Zebrzydowska sanctuary.

At home and during their walks, the Lieutenant often spoke German to Karol to teach him the language, although with limited success. In Kraków, Karol had to learn German more systematically, in part because he lived under German occupation, but also because as a seminarian he wanted to read Immanuel Kant in the original; Kant was one of the first philosophers to interest Wojtyła. Then he used a German-Spanish dictionary—evidently he could not find a Polish-Spanish one—to learn Spanish to be able to read the works of St. John of the Cross in *his* native language.

The Wojtyłas were so strapped financially that the Lieutenant, remembering his tailor apprenticeship, took needle in hand not only to mend their clothes and socks when necessary, but also to refashion his old army uniforms into suits for Karol. Zbigniew Siłkowski, one of Karol's closest childhood friends, says that the Lieutenant also would remake into suits *his* father's railway man uniforms. "Karol and I were growing so fast," he recalls, "that what fitted us today, would be too short and too tight in six months."

But the Lieutenant could be playful, too. Another of the pope's old friends remembers finding father and son playing soccer in the parlor on a rainy day, Karol as goalkeeper guarding the door and the Lieutenant firing the ball at him. After Emilia's death, they had no other use for the parlor; the rugs were rolled up and the furniture covered with cloth.

In the Wadowice boys' high school, where Wojtyła enrolled at the end of January 1931 at the age of ten (Polish high schools have eight grades), soccer was the most popular sport. Karol, like other boys, had been playing in improvised games even before high school, but now he could participate in a more organized fashion. He chose to be goalkeeper.

Most of the high school games were between the Catholic and Jewish teams, but Wojtyła often played for the Jews when they needed a goalie. From childhood, Karol had Jewish playmates and schoolmates with whom he enjoyed easy camaraderie. There was Ginka Beer, his beautiful neighbor on Kościelna Street, Jerzy ("Jurek") Kluger, the son of a leading town lawyer (and to this day one of his few close friends), fat Poldek Goldberger, the regular Jewish goalkeeper and precocious music composer whose father was a dentist, Zygmunt Selinger, and Leopold Zweig (all are dead now except for Kluger). It was therefore natural for Wojtyła to play for the Jewish side when asked ("You know," a teammate says, "he was a great guy, but, confidentially, he was a lousy goalkeeper").

Wadowice may have been fairly free of open anti-Semitism as Karol was growing up—even though acts of violence against Jews did explode in the immediate prewar years when extreme rightist groups became dominant in Polish politics—but there, too, the "Jewish Question" was ever present. It was part of the historical Polish obsession with Jews, which existed when three million of them lived in Poland prior to the Holocaust, and went on plaguing the country afterward, when there was a total of barely ten thousand including survivors, their children, and grandchildren.

It has haunted John Paul II's papacy almost from the moment of his election—including the bitter disputes over the Carmelite nuns' shrine at the site of the former Nazi concentration camp in Oświęcim—more than any other non-Church problem, magnifying the whole issue of residual Polish anti-Semitism to an extraordinary degree.

In this context, it was relevant that Wadowice high school boys formed separate Catholic and Jewish soccer teams, and that Karol Wojtyła was always ready to play for the Jews. In most places, this would have been insignificant, but in Poland it carried real meaning, defining Wojtyła's personality and attitudes for the future. The Jewish experience in Wadowice, with his youthful friendships, was among the influences leading him to his role as champion of religious tolerance as Vatican Council bishop and as pope.

And John Paul II is the first to stress that the Wadowice

years were the source of his awareness. He remembers Wadowice parish priest Father Leonard Prochownik preaching in church that "anti-Semitism is anti-Christian" and Polish literature teacher Kazimierz Foryś quoting in class from poet Adam Mickiewicz's 1848 *Manifesto for a Future Slav State Constitution* that "all citizens are equal—Israelites, too."

On May 9, 1989, having ordered the placement of a commemorative tablet at the site of the Wadowice synagogue destroyed by the Nazis, the pope wrote Jerzy Kluger that it would also honor the memory of Jews from nearby who were exterminated. He wrote:

> Many of those who perished, your co-religionists and our fellow countrymen, were our colleagues in our Elementary School and, later, in the High School where we were graduated together, fifty years ago. All were citizens of Wadowice, the town to which both you and I are bound together by our memories of childhood and youth. I remember very clearly the Wadowice Synagogue, which was near our High School. I have in front of my eyes the numerous worshippers who during their Holidays passed on their way to pray there.

Addressing the Warsaw Jewish community on June 9, 1991, during his fourth papal pilgrimage to Poland, the pope said: "Man lives on the basis of his own experiences. I belong to the generation for which relationships with Jews was a daily occurrence." Reminiscing in February 1994 about his Wadowice childhood, John Paul II remarked that "there were so many Jews there" that "the house where we lived was owned by a Jewish family," and that "it is from there that I have this attitude of community, of communal feeling about the Jews. . . . It all comes from there."

The pope said later that his sentiments toward the Jews "go back to my youngest years, when, in the parish church of my native Wadowice, I listened to this psalm [the 147th Psalm] sung during evening Mass":

> O Jerusalem, glorify the Lord;
> Praise Your God, O Zion!
> For He made the bars of Your gate strong.
> And blessed Your children within You. . . .

John Paul II went on to say that "I still have in my ears these words and this melody, which I have remembered all my life. And then came the terrible experience of World War II and the [Nazi] occupation, the Holocaust, which was the extermination of Jews only for the reason that they were Jews. It was a terrible upheaval that has remained in the memory of all the people who were close to these events." Karol Wojtyła, of course, had lived very close to "these events."

Luigi Accattoli, a leading Italian journalistic expert on the Vatican, wrote that "there is something in Wojtyła that didn't exist in his predecessors, something we feel when he speaks of the Holocaust." And on the last day of 1993, John Paul II became the first pope to authorize the establishment of diplomatic relations between the Vatican and the State of Israel, forty-five years after its birth, emphasizing that the long-persecuted Jews had a right to their own nation.

But much as Karol Wojtyła was friendly toward the Jews, many Jewish families in Wadowice began to feel uncomfortable in the late 1930s, when squads of young thugs began smashing windows of Jewish-owned shops and urging boycots of Jewish businesses. Among them was the Beer family, the Wojtyłas' neighbors, who resolved in 1937 that their daughter Ginka should emigrate to Palestine, with the parents to follow.

A half century later, Regina Reisenfeld, the former Ginka Beer, told journalists the story at her home in Israel:

> I knew I was very popular with Polish boys and girls, but there was anti-Semitism, too. There was only one family who never showed any racial hostility toward us, and that was Lolek and his dad. . . . Then we decided to leave Poland for Palestine because we felt disaster faced the Jews. . . . I went to say goodbye to Lolek and his father. Mr. Wojtyła was upset about our departure, and when he asked me why, I told him. Again and again he said to me, "Not all Poles are anti-

> Semitic. You know I am not!" I spoke to him frankly and said that very few Poles were like him. He was very upset. But Lolek was even more upset than his father. He did not say a word, but his face went very red. I said farewell to him as kindly as I could, but he was so moved that he could not find a single word in reply. So I just shook the father's hand and left.

Ginka saw Karol again fifty years after she left Wadowice. She was in a group of former and present Wadowice residents attending Wednesday General Audience on St. Peter's Square, and the pope recognized her when some of her friends shouted her name. Ginka asked him if he really remembered her, and, as she recounts it, John Paul II replied, "Of course I do. You are Regina. We lived in the same house. How is your sister, Helen?" He inquired about others in her family, and when she told him that her mother had died in Oświęcim and her father was killed in the Soviet Union, "he just looked at me, and there was deep compassion in his eyes. . . . He took both my hands and for almost two minutes he blessed me and prayed before me, just holding my hands in his hands. There were thousands of people in the Square, but for just a few seconds there were just the two of us."

Karol was ten years old—shortly after his mother's death—when his father took him to Kraków to see his brother, Edmund, graduate on May 28, 1930, from the School of Medicine of ancient Jagiellonian University. Edmund, whom they called "Mundek," was then twenty-four, and he was charming and immensely popular. The graduation was held in the majestic hall of the university's Collegium Maius, and John Paul II recalled the occasion when he received his *honoris causa* doctorate from the Jagiellonian in the same hall in 1983, during his second pontifical voyage to Poland (the war had cut short his studies there after one academic year and he had not been able to graduate normally from the Kraków university, receiving his doctoral degree there only after postwar studies in Rome).

"The first time I entered the walls of *Collegium Maius* it

was as a ten-year-old boy, still a student in elementary school, to participate in the doctoral promotion of my older brother, a graduate of the Medical School of Jagiellonian University," he said. "Until today, I have before my eyes this solemnity in the University *aula.*"

The year of Edmund's graduation, Karol's father took him on a pilgrimage to Częstochowa to pray before the image of the Black Madonna, the Queen of Poland. He was deeply moved by the experience, returning to the shrine on Luminous Mountain in the summer of 1932, with a school group. Karol had already served two years as an altar boy in the Wadowice church and, as his contemporaries recall it, his religiosity was becoming more and more accentuated.

Meanwhile, tragedy again struck the Wojtyłas. On December 4, 1932, Edmund died of scarlet fever he contracted from a patient at the municipal hospital at Bielsko, a town less than an hour away from Wadowice, where he had worked as an intern since his graduation two years earlier. Karol occasionally visited him there. But a scarlet fever epidemic was now sweeping the region, and twenty-six-year-old Dr. Wojtyła was on duty around the clock. His fellow physicians remember Edmund as a totally dedicated doctor, with a keen sense of humor and a penchant toward playfulness. He often entertained the patients at the hospital by putting on "one-man theater" shows in the wards and otherwise keeping them amused—to the extent it was possible during a major epidemic.

The Wojtyła brothers shared their passion for the theater (Karol also excelled at aping some of his high school teachers) and despite the difference in their ages they were remarkably close to each other and to their father. They resembled each other physically, both with broad, open highlander faces. Both were very well liked in school and among friends and companions. For Karol, the doctor's death was a terrible blow. He was twelve, just completing his second year of high school.

Speaking at Jagiellonian University in 1983, John Paul II mentioned losing his brother, pain still in his voice. "These are events that became deeply engraved in my memory," he said. "My brother's death perhaps even deeper than my mother's death—equally because of the special circumstances, one may say tragic ones, and in view of my greater maturity at the time."

After the funeral, the surviving Wojtyłas published an announcement in a Kraków newspaper to express their gratitude to all the doctors and nurses at the Bielsko hospital for the help and care given Dr. Edmund during his illness "at the risk of their health and lives." They signed it: "Father and Brother."

But Wojtyła's natural optimism and energy prevailed, and he plunged even deeper into schoolwork, sports and exercise, and his ever-growing religiosity. He was at the head of his class at the high school and he was searching for God more and more ardently. Yet Karol was an eager athlete, a very sociable youth with whom it was great fun to spend time. Wadowice girls sighed after him when he became a teenager, but to no avail: the handsome Wojtyła was a dependable friend who did not date. Father Kazimierz Figlewicz, a priest then serving at the Wadowice church as vicar and catechist (religion teacher) at the high school, recalls Karol:

> Those who have met the Holy Father in his mature age, will remember him as a man of reasonable height, slim, with a thin, elongated face—and it will not occur to them that ten-year-old Karol Wojtyła looked quite differently. He was a rather tall boy, but rather on the fat side. A very lively boy, very talented, very quick and very good. He had an optimistic nature though, after a more careful look, one could discern the shadow of early orphanage. . . . He stood out as being very loyal toward his companions, and had no conflicts with the teachers. He studied well. . . . What brought us closer was the altar. Karol Wojtyła was a fervent ministrant. I think that what also brought us closer was the confessional. And conversations and mutual visits. . . .

It was on the occasion of Father Figlewicz's departure for a new assignment in Kraków two years later that Wojtyła first broke into print—at the age of thirteen. As president of the Altar Boys' Circle, he composed a full-page account of the priest's farewell ceremony for the *Little Bell* supplement of the Kraków church newspaper, *Sunday Bell.* After quoting the entire speech by a fellow altar boy ("We bid you farewell with aching hearts"), Karol reported that "From time to time, the speaker had to stop because his own weeping would not let him go on. . . . And [other] boys wept, too, because it pained them to be separated from their beloved patron. Later, they brightened up a bit at the sight of ice cream and chocolate, but sadness and grief certainly remained in their hearts." He was identified "Loluś Wojtyła" in the caption under the photograph of the ceremony. Reminiscing as archbishop in 1964, Wojtyła described Father Figlewicz as "the guide of my young and rather complicated soul."

Karol was fortunate with his teachers, an unusually high-powered faculty intellectually for a town of Wadowice's limited importance—by the time he reached high school Wadowice had only six private automobiles—but fine education was an ancient local tradition. John Paul II remembers the Wadowice teachers well sixty years later, and he makes a point of reminding former schoolmates, when they visit him at the Vatican or in Castel Gandolfo, of the professors' importance in the molding of their characters.

The teacher Wojtyła probably found the most interesting was Father Edward Zacher, a young priest who held a doctorate in science as well as theology and served as the high school's prefect, that is, religious director. He was a physicist, astrophysicist, and engineer. Zacher also skied with Karol and other students. Zbigniew Siłkowski, Karol's classmate since the fourth high school year, wrote that while teaching a course in religion, Father Zacher often "got away from the subject to lead us to the mysteries of the solar system and further on toward the galaxies or to the nucleus of the atom and the secrets of the microcosmos." Siłkowski remarked that "he taught us to think, applying in this endeavor the learning obtained by us in the study of other subjects, but always with the objective of demonstrating that knowledge based on truth never discards God, but, to the contrary, teaches humility toward the Creator."

This is, of course, the view taken by John Paul II in encouraging scientific research—which he does to a surprising degree. And it is interesting to wonder whether Father Zacher's influence loomed behind the pope's decision to clear the name and reputation of Galileo through the work of the special commission he had appointed.

Professor Foryś presumably deserves massive credit for the love and fascination Karol has for the Polish language—Polish philology was his first passion, before theater and before the priesthood—and Poland's great romantic and messianic bards. This remains one of the basic interests in the pope's life. His spectacular command of the classics—Latin and Greek—were a gift from Professor Zygmunt Damasiewicz and Jan Królikiewicz, the high school principal and a classicist of note. By the time he graduated, Wojtyła was absolutely fluent in Latin and Greek. A classmate remembers that he once dazzled even Damasiewicz when he volunteered to explain the differences in the conjugation of regular verbs between formal Greek and the Ionic dialect (Królikiewicz was giving him additional private Greek lessons at the time). The Wadowice high school was therefore the secret behind Wojtyła's ability to stun Vatican Council II with his flawless Latin a quarter of a century later. Hebrew not having been taught at the high school, Karol discovered it only in the seminary and does not dominate it fully.

John Paul II never forgets Wadowice and his schoolmates. In November 1988 he played host at the Vatican to twenty former students from the boys' high school and three from the girls' whom he invited to celebrate the fiftieth anniversary of their joint graduation (the actual anniversary date was in May, but the pope was busy). All the Wadowice schoolmates, including those living in Kraków and elsewhere, received personal lunch invitations when Wojtyła came to Wadowice in June 1991 on his fourth papal visit to Poland. But the most emotional homecoming was the brief stop he made in the town in June 1979, his first time back in the country as pontiff.

One of the lunch guests in 1991 was Halina Kwiatkowska, who frequently played opposite Karol in amateur theater first in Wadowice and then in Kraków, and whose father,

Jan Królikiewicz, was the principal of the boys' high school. Karol danced with her at the Wadowice senior prom in 1938, the first time he is known to have danced with anybody. Kwiatkowska lives in Kraków with her writer husband, Tadeusz Kwiatkowski, and their daughter, Monika Katarzyna, who was the first child christened by Wojtyła, ten days after he was ordained as a priest in November 1946, and four days before he left for Rome to pursue graduate studies.

Wojtyła goes to startling lengths to please old schoolmates, albeit discreetly. When Poldek Goldberger, the Wadowice Jewish goalkeeper and subsequently a dentist in Israel, happened to be visiting Rome, the pope not only had him invited to a choice spot at the weekly General Audience, but arranged for what can only be described as a secret Polish musicale in Castel Gandolfo. A piano was trucked to the little castle on Lake Albano, an hour or so from Rome, and Wojtyła and Goldberger spent an evening of music and song. Goldberger, the Wadowice boy composer, played the piano, and the pope sang old Polish popular songs in his splendid baritone. John Paul II's predecessors were never that lighthearted and informal. It is said that when they were youths in Wadowice, Karol wrote the lyrics to a song composed by Goldberger, an innocuous romantic ballad titled "The Love Letter." The lyrics vanished a long time ago, and it is *not* listed among John Paul II's literary works. Poldek Goldberger has died since.

Clearly, the pope misses the contact with his childhood friends and Wadowice. Jerzy Kluger, the son of the Jewish lawyer, known to Wojtyła and other friends as "Jurek" (a Polish diminutive), now a consulting engineer in Rome, and his English-born wife, Renée, are frequent lunch and dinner guests at the Vatican or Castel Gandolfo, usually summoned by telephone at the last moment. To chat informally in Polish about the past and mutual friends, and away from papal protocol, may be the most important form of mental relaxation for the overworked Wojtyła. The only other persons present at these meals are Monsignor Stanislaw Dziwisz, the pope's Polish private secretary, who is his closest associate, and the Vietnamese private secretary (who speaks no Polish), Vincent Tran Ngoc Thu.

In this unique setting of privacy, Lolek and Jurek address each other by their first-name diminutives. At Castel Gandolfo, Kluger, a onetime tennis champion, and the pope occasionally play Ping-Pong. The Klugers' granddaughter was baptized by the pope (Mrs. Kluger and her daughter are Roman Catholics) and they were the first to be received by him in private audience after his 1978 election. They dined with John Paul II, as family, on Christmas Eve 1993. By unspoken mutual consent, they never discuss Church affairs or politics of any kind.

In Wadowice, Jurek Kluger was among the few classmates who developed the habit of turning up at the Wojtyłas' in the afternoon to do homework with Karol, the school's best student, and to hang around until dinnertime to chat with him and his father. The Lieutenant enjoyed talking with young people. He would read Cyprian Norwid's essays on Chopin to Karol and Jurek, tell them war stories, and quiz them on Polish history dates. Many years later, John Paul II told a French writer that "during all my childhood, I listened to veterans of World War I, talking about endless horrors of battle."

The Klugers lived in a large townhouse at the other end of Market Square, a three-minute walk from the Wojtyłas', and Jurek enjoyed these regular visits very much. He recalls that after a few minutes of initial badinage, Karol would say, "Now, it's time to study," and they would work at the kitchen table. But Karol visited Jurek, too. He came to listen from behind the closed parlor door to rehearsals of the classical quartet conducted by Jurek's lawyer father, a violinist. It was Wojtyła's first exposure to serious music, which enthralled him (Jurek was tone-deaf), and in time he was allowed to listen in the parlor. They also heard soccer games broadcast on the radio.

Antoni Bohdanowicz, another schoolmate who did his homework with Wojtyła, writes in his memoirs that "after we finished each subject, Lolek would leave the kitchen and return a moment later. Once the door was not closed well, and I could see Lolek kneeling at prayer."

Karol's religiosity deepened as he matured, his father's influence unquestionably playing a central role in this evolution. At his First Communion, Karol received a scapular from the Carmelite Fathers in Wadowice; he wears it to this day. From his first day in high school, at the age of ten and a year after his mother's death, Wojtyła would run every morning from the Kościelna Street house to the church across the street to pray for a few moments, then would race down Market Square to Mickiewicz Street where the high school stood. It took him less than five minutes, and he was always on time.

In December 1935, when he was fifteen, Karol was accepted as a member of the Wadowice high school branch of Marian Sodality, a nationwide brotherhood of Roman Catholic youth, a highly spiritual organization. Six months later, he was elected president of the sodality branch and reelected the following year. The brotherhood was devoted to the cult of Mary—hence Marian Sodality—and Karol's attraction to it may have flowed from the memory of his mother. In time, his veneration of Mary became absolute. He also continued serving at Mass, going to confession, receiving Holy Communion daily, and displaying signs of ever-rising religiosity.

Still, his classmates never perceived him as overly religious. One classmate remembers, "He never beat his breast or crossed himself in public for all to see." Faith, then as now, was very private with Karol Wojtyła. And his chairmanship of the Abstinence Circle (the oath was not to drink alcohol for a year) did not denote him as a sissy in a society where even adolescents were hard drinkers and heavy smokers. Though tough discipline prevailed in the school—the students had to wear dark blue uniforms with red stripes on the trousers and regulation caps with visors—young people were generally free to do what they pleased on their own time. And they did. Karol Wojtyła was both liked and respected by his peers. In fact, he was widely admired for his admixture of seriousness and religiosity with friendliness, a fine sense of humor, and involvement in activities ranging from sports and military basic training in the Academic Legion to amateur theater and intensive school homework. He was invariably the best pupil, but he was never accused of being a bookworm.

Dr. Jan Kuś, a classmate, remembers that when they

reached the seventh year of high school—the penultimate year—Karol's friends began asking him, in earnest, whether he planned to become a priest. No, he replied, *Non sum dignus* (I am not worthy). And he meant it at the time. As pope, Wojtyła confided to a French religion historian that in high school and at the start of his university studies, he "rather decisively rejected" the idea of priesthood, convinced that he should be an active "lay Christian," involving himself in helping to solve social problems through the Church. The concept of the Church's responsibility in social justice matters would become one of the foundations of his pontificate; he refined it as bishop and cardinal.

Former companions recollect that Karol was so respected that "nobody would ever use words like 'shit' or 'asshole' in his presence," though it was part of normal adolescent parlance. But he always opened his arms, with a broad smile illuminating his face, to greet fellow students and friends—he still does it today as pope.

Karol Wojtyła always found mentors at critical turning points in his life. The first was Mieczysław Kotlarczyk, a scholarly drama addict with a fierce temperament who introduced him to the beauty of the theater. It would be one of Wojtyła's deepest friendships, and ended only with Kotlarczyk's death in 1978.

Born in Wadowice in 1906—he was fourteen years older than Karol—Kotlarczyk taught at the Carmelite Fathers' high school in his hometown and was the author of the "Living Word" dramatic theory, which placed supreme emphasis on the proper, precise, and clear use of speech and language on the stage. Perfect diction was his passion. John Paul II today is a leading practitioner of this art, the successor of Maestro Kotlarczyk.

They met, probably in 1935, when Wojtyła began to appear in amateur high school productions. In 1931 Kotlarczyk had founded his own amateur theater in Wadowice. But he became quickly involved with the students' theater, leaving his mark on it. Wojtyła wrote many years later that he encountered Kotlarczyk "as the pioneer of the original theater, in the most noble sense of the word, and as the voice of the deepest Polish and Christian traditions, transmitted to us through literature, and above all through the great romantic and neo-romantic literature."

The strands that would be woven into Karol Wojtyła's personality, soul, and intellect—religious faith, patriotism, literary romanticism and messianism, philosophical caution, and overwhelming personal presence on theatrical and world stages—thus began to come together during his teens in Wadowice. His father, his schoolteachers, and the theater mentor he had found were his guides.

For the balance of his high school years, increasingly influenced by Kotlarczyk, Wojtyła plunged into the performance of the dramas spawned by these Polish literary traditions. He was the most active and the most effective single individual in the joint boys' and girls' high school theater group, the Wadowice Theater Circle, as actor, director, producer, and organizer. But he suffered one defeat. His friend Halina Królikiewicz (later Kwiatkowska) won the first prize, and he the second, in a theater recitation contest sponsored by Poland's most famous reciting actress, Kazimiera Rychter. Still, this experience served to underline his approach to all challenges.

Wojtyła had chosen the most difficult imaginable role in the Polish drama: *Promethidion,* by Cyprian Norwid, a philosophical dialogue-poem. Reciting the words of the hero who spoke for "The Good," Karol, incongruously dressed in his dark blue school uniform, opened with the quotation from Paul's Letter to the Corinthians: "For you can all prophesy one by one, so that all may learn and all be encouraged!" But the prize went to Halina for a fable recitation, and fifty years later the pope told her at the Vatican, "Yes, I remember that you beat me that time. . . ."

Wojtyła, however, was vindicated by his spectacular appearance that same year in a performance of *Balladyna,* by Juliusz Słowacki, another intense Polish allegoric drama, in which he played both male lead roles. He acted opposite Halina, whose father, the high school principal, had suspended one of the thespian heroes for threatening to shoot a teacher if he gave him a failing grade. Karol was the other lead hero.

As Halina Kwiatkowska remembers it, the news of the

suspension forty-eight hours before the performance threw the actors into total disarray. "But," she said, "Lolek suggested quietly, blushing with embarrassment, that he could play both roles because the noble Kirkor dies rather early, and he would have time to change costumes to play the ignoble Kostryn." Asked when he expected to learn the second role, Karol replied, "Oh, I know it already. . . . I learned it during rehearsals." Halina's conclusion was the classic understatement: "He had a phenomenal memory!"

Dr. Karol Poliwka, the Wadowice classmate, went even further: "Wojtyła has a computer memory." After meeting his two daughters during a General Audience in Rome, the pope instantly recognized Poliwka two years later at a reception at the Archbishop's Palace in Kraków during the second pontifical visit to Poland. They had not seen each other in nearly forty-five years, but John Paul II said, "Listen, Karol, your two daughters have already visited me in Rome, and you haven't. . . ." Poliwka subsequently flew to Rome for the 1988 high school reunion, and he remembers that the pope "saw us frequently . . . we had breakfast, lunch and dinner with him, and there were conversations and a concert. . . . And he wouldn't let us kiss his ring. . . . But I felt that he was a man of loneliness."

Exposure to Cyprian Norwid's works placed Wojtyła in a fascinating intellectual and spiritual quandary, though he has never discussed it publicly. It was a very Polish dilemma, but extremely relevant for Karol, who was beginning his acquaintance with philosophy and theology. As so many Poles did, he admired the burning flame of Adam Mickiewicz's romanticism and messianism. But even as a young thinker, Wojtyła experienced an intellectual attraction to the cold reasoning of Norwid, who was outspokenly critical of Mickiewicz's "mystical radicalism." Norwid preferred "reality" and the "experience of life," an approach akin to phenomenology that Wojtyła ultimately espoused as his own philosophy. In private conversation nowadays, John Paul II appears to continue to adhere to Norwid, whose favorite definition was "personal scientific experience." The pope's attitude toward the problems of the contemporary world may have its roots in Norwid's citation from St. Paul in *Promethidion:* "So that all may learn and be encouraged." He has assumed the mantle of the Church's unquestionable teacher in morals and ethics.

Wojtyła's horizons were not entirely confined to Wadowice during his high school years. Members of the Theater Circle were often taken by their teachers to Kraków, never missing a performance at Juliusz Słowacki Theater there. And the circle put on performances of its own in many of the small towns surrounding Wadowice. All in all, Wojtyła was gaining a fine education and exposure to universal culture and ideas.

His leadership qualities were also being recognized. Not only was Karol a top student and the elected president of student organizations, but he was in constant demand as the spokesman for the high school on national occasions. He led the uniformed high school contingent in national holiday street parades, right behind the infantry regiment. On an anniversary of the 1791 Constitution, for example, seventeen-year-old Wojtyła was put in charge of a special performance of Słowacki's patriotic *Kordian,* directing it and playing the lead role. And when Archbishop Sapieha came down from Kraków to visit the Wadowice boys' high school on May 6, 1938, Karol greeted him on behalf of the student body.

This was another turning point in Wojtyła's life, though he could not have guessed it. The archbishop, sitting in a red leather armchair, was so impressed by the welcoming speech that he asked the Wadowice parish priest, Father Zacher, what plans Wojtyła had after graduating later that month. Was he thinking of entering the seminary? Zacher replied, "I'm not sure, but it will probably be the university." Karol then said, "If Your Excellency will allow me, I would like to answer myself: I plan to take Polish philology at Jagiellonian University." The severe archbishop sighed, saying, "Too bad, too bad!" The topic came up again at the faculty dinner, and Father Zacher told Sapieha that "this young man has the theatre in his head." The archbishop said once more, "Too bad, too bad. . . . We could use him. . . ."

But Sapieha did not forget Karol Wojtyła. The archbishop, seventy-one years old at the time he met the eighteen-year-old Wojtyła, was one of the most remarkable figures in the Polish Church. He was a formidable protector for a young cleric or priest. Scion of one of the most famous aristocratic families, he held the title of prince. Later, ordained as a priest, he became a doctor of both canon and civil law at the Rome Academy of Ecclesiastic Nobility. He served for nine years as Secret Chamberlain of Pope Pius X, learning everything about the inner workings of the Vatican.

Back in Poland as bishop after World War I, Sapieha displayed his independence when he prevented Apostolic Visitor Achille Ratti from attending a conference of the Polish episcopate he had organized. He insisted that the Polish bishops wished to meet alone. Ratti, of course, soon became Pope Pius XI, and his revenge was to deprive Sapieha of a cardinal's hat. But the tough Sapieha outlived Pius XI—he lived to be eighty-five—and Pius XII in time elevated him to the purple. Between the wars, Sapieha, a tall, ascetic man with a beaklike nose, fought fellow bishops as well as Marshal Piłsudski, the Polish dictator, after his coup d'état in 1926, on matters of principle. In the end, he always had his way. That went for Karol Wojtyła, too, as it would turn out.

On May 14, 1938, Wojtyła passed the exams for his high school diploma. He received the highest grades ("Very Good") in Polish, Latin, Greek, German, history, problems of contemporary Poland, philosophy, and physical education. On May 27, he formally graduated along with forty-one other students. Naturally, he was the class valedictorian. To earn the top grade in Latin, Karol had to provide a forty-minute answer to a first question, a fifteen-minute answer to a second question, and a seven-minute answer to a third question—all in fluent, extemporaneous Latin. The concept behind this exam system was to assure that students spoke Latin as well as they spoke Polish—or almost.

From June 20 to August 17, Wojtyła served, as all high school graduates were required to do, with a youth paramilitary army labor battalion. His outfit was assigned to road building in the mountains south of Wadowice. Karol, wearing an army uniform, seemed to enjoy this first experience with hard physical work. He also peeled potatoes and served at Mass. And, as usual, he quickly made friends. Jerzy Bober, a writer and journalist, remembered meeting Wojtyła for the first time when he reached his tent in the labor battalion camp. "My name is Wojtyła," the young man told him. "I am from Wadowice. Call me Lolek." They became friends for life.

During the summer, the Wojtyłas—father and son—moved to Kraków so that Karol could enter the university in the autumn. He appeared to be superbly prepared in every way for the new challenge, academically and intellectually. Physically, he was in excellent shape. The month of road building under the hot sun hardened his muscles and tanned his skin. Photographs from the period show a confident young man, staring ahead with optimism though slightly stooped since early adolescence. His hair is long and luxuriant down over his neck. The collar of his shirt is folded over the collar of the jacket in the bohemian fashion of the time. Juliusz Słowacki, the poet adored by Karol, always dressed in that studied casual way. It was known in Poland as the "poetic look" or the "Słowacki look."

Nothing in the written or oral recollections of John Paul II's Wadowice period suggests an awareness that Poland and the world were on the verge of a global war during his final high school years and at the time of his graduation. Whether Wadowice was too remote from the centers of the gathering storm or whether its citizens, like much of Poland, simply did not believe that a war was approaching, the impression is that the people there ignored all the signs and portents.

If the Nazis in neighboring Germany posed a danger to Poland, the Roman Catholic Church in neither country seemed to realize it. Although Pius XI had issued his *Mit brennender Sorge* (With Burning Concern) encyclical on Palm Sunday in 1937 denouncing Adolf Hitler's racial doctrines, it had no repercussions anywhere. The text had to be smuggled into Germany, but no priests are known to have read it to the faithful in church. Nor is there a record of its being mentioned in the Wadowice church where Karol Wojtyła worshipped. If Pius XI had reasons to fear a Nazi-triggered war, he gave no public indication of it even as late as spring of 1938.

In Wadowice, nothing disturbed its peaceful existence when word came that on March 12, German troops had occupied Austria, carrying out the *Anschluss* liquidation of that small country. Lieutenant Wojtyła and many of his contemporaries had once served in the Austrian army and fought in the war when Wadowice and Galicja were under Austro-Hungarian imperial occupation. Men's memories are short.

CHAPTER 6

The Wojtyłas, father and eighteen-year-old son, set up housekeeping in Kraków in August 1938 in the tiny basement of a gray two-story house at No. 10 Tyniecka Street, which runs along the western embankment of the Vistula River. The house belonged to Lolek Wojtyła's maternal uncle, Robert Kaczorowski, a master leather maker, who built it after World War I, using old brick and discarded window frames and doors to save money. But it was a solid and respectable-looking structure with a gabled tile roof, two chimneys, and two stovepipes. Two windows each on the ground and first floors looked out on a pleasant, sizable garden with flower beds and tall trees fronting on the street.

Kaczorowski, a bachelor and fifty-one years old at the time, and his spinster sisters, Rudolfina and Anna, occupied the ground floor and the first floor, which was reached by a staircase on the right-hand side of the house. The entrance to the basement was under the staircase, and the Wojtyłas' apartment consisted of two small rooms, a narrow kitchen, and a bathroom. The three Kaczorowskis were the Wojtyłas' only close relatives in Kraków, and they must have charged no more than nominal rent, because the Lieutenant's only income was his meager military pension and Karol held no job during the first year in the city. But the two families evidently led wholly separate lives. Wojtyła does not mention the Kaczorowskis in any of his subsequent reminiscences, oral or written, nor do any of his contemporaries who had frequently visited the house, although the uncle lived until 1962, when Karol already was a bishop.

The house is in an excellent location, and its appearance has not changed. It stands directly across Tyniecka Street from the Vistula, just before the wide river makes its dramatic turn in the form of a bent elbow as it flows north. Behind Tyniecka Street spreads the Dębniki district, a quiet suburb rich in green spaces and woods, even though the city of Kraków proper lies immediately across the Vistula, over Dębnicki Bridge. Looking to his right from the embankment, Karol Wojtyła could see on the other side of the river, just past the elbow, the massive shape of the thirteenth-century Royal Castle atop Wawel Hill and its fourteenth-century cathedral. Beyond the Wawel rises the tower of the Baroque Church of St. Peter and Paul, guarded by stone figures of twelve Apostles. In the distance, to his left, he could discern the spire on the tower of the thirteenth-century Church of St. Mary (where the watchman's throat was pierced by the Tatar invader's arrow) on Market Square in the Old Town.

Kraków has sixty Catholic churches, and in time Wojtyła became familiar with all of them. The Dębniki parish church of St. Stanisław Kostka of the Salesian Fathers on Konfederacka Street, where Karol attended daily the 6:00 A.M. Mass, had been consecrated shortly before the Wojtyłas' arrival. It was about a three-minute walk from their house.

Strolling west along the Tyniecka Street embankment, which he often did with his father or his friends, Wojtyła went past the crenelated-tower monastery of the Albertan Brothers, who, in addition to their charitable works, produced Tormentilla, a salve famous for supposedly preventing loss of hair. Further up, the Salesians had their Theological Institute in a beautiful old building. The abbey of the Benedictine Fathers in Tyniec (hence Tyniecka Street), built in A.D. 1044, is beyond the Theological Institute. And the Vistula was a busy waterway, with big barges bringing coal from Silesian mines in the southwest down to the port of Gdynia on the Baltic, and vessels carrying goods in both directions. In these prepollution days, men and boys fished for pike and perch from the Tyniecka embankment. For a few coins, one could cross the river in a small boat to avoid the bother of walking up to the bridge.

A few blocks south of Tyniecka Street, the Wojtyłas could shop in the stores of the small Dębniki market square and adjoining streets. The neighborhood had the church on Konfederacka and rows of three- or four-story apartment buildings on the side streets. It was a peaceful corner of a peaceful city, Dębniki being a mix of working class, middle-class, and even quite affluent populations.

Kraków was a self-assured cultural and intellectual center, its traditions dating back even earlier than the thirteenth century. The city, built strategically astride the Vistula, was founded by Prince Krakus in A.D. 700, and remained a separate principality until the twelfth century. Then it became the royal capital of the Polish-Lithuanian Commonwealth. Though the capital was moved to Warsaw in 1610, kings continued to be crowned and buried at the Wawel Cathedral until Poland vanished altogether in the partitions of the late eighteenth century. It was always regarded as the royal city. It has the country's oldest university; it probably accounted for the greatest concentration of scholars and theologians (and priests) when Karol Wojtyła came to town. It had the best Polish daily newspaper, the *IKC* (the Polish initials standing for *Illustrated Daily Courier*).

With a population of a quarter million—Poland's population being then under thirty million—Kraków represented a blend of the medieval and the contemporary. It was a trading and academic center, the home of light industry and of ancient churches and museums. It had wealth and aristocracy and quasi-millennial traditions, but it was also a curiously democratic and romantic society.

At Jagiellonian University, most of the professors were what was then known as "progressive," as was much of the student body. Outside, many of the merchant class and workers and low-level officials were identified with the Polish Socialist Party (PPS), a mostly moderate social democratic movement to which Marshal Piłsudski had once belonged, and some were even affiliated with the illegal communist party. Later, extreme right-wing groups penetrated the university, but for others there was no conflict between Catholicism and socialist affiliations. The large Jewish population of Kraków, roughly 20 percent, was very much part of the city's life, from academia to shopkeepers in the Kazimierz district, near the synagogues (in midtown, for example, Corpus Christi Street intersected with Rabbi Meisels Street). It was a lively, pulsating, and endlessly interesting city.

In this Kraków milieu, therefore, it was perfectly normal for Karol Wojtyła, coming from the Wadowice backwater, grandson of peasants and son of a minor retired army officer, to be accepted as an equal among Jagiellonian University students. Along with his late brother, he represented the first generation of Wojtyłas to acquire a university education, and this was part of the slow process of Polish social change.

It made no difference that Karol was abysmally poor, attending class in rough-cloth trousers and a wrinkled black jacket (apparently the only one he owned). His shoes were maintained in an acceptable state of repair by his father. But he always wore a clean shirt. Karol was entirely uninterested in clothes—even when he became bishop and cardinal. He was always tieless simply because he disliked neckties, preferring the poetic Juliusz Słowacki look.

Poverty notwithstanding, Kraków was not hard on Karol, who enjoyed it thoroughly. He was able to enroll at the Jagiellonian presumably because of his excellent high school grades and *matura* (graduating diploma) exams, but it is unclear whether he had been granted a scholarship or exempted from tuition altogether. His father could not have afforded it, the army pension providing basically for food and the most urgent necessities. Karol usually dined at home with the Lieutenant, who did the cooking, but during the day he ate at the university mess hall or at the homes of his new friends.

To reach the university, all Wojtyła had to do was to cross Dębnicki Bridge, no more than five minutes on foot from the Tyniecka Street house, and walk less than a half mile down broad Zwierzyniecka Street to Planty Park. Planty surrounds the oblong Old Town like a belt, and Karol would turn left and stroll along the boulevard, full of trees, lawns, and flowers, for another half mile to arrive at the university. He would leave the Archbishop's Palace on Franciszkańska Street, where Archbishop Sapieha resided, on his right.

The Jagiellonian's main buildings are clustered inside the Planty-bound Old Town, with additional academic structures radiating throughout the area of lovely narrow streets. From the university, it is a few minutes' walk to the Old Town Market Square to visit St. Mary's Church and see the thirteenth-century Sukiennice (Cloth Hall) market building and the statue of Adam Mickiewicz, the bard, in the center of the square. Kraków avenues and streets were named after Mickiewicz, Słowacki, and all the other poets and writers who were heroes to Karol Wojtyła as he started this new chapter in his life.

Wojtyła entered the Philosophy Faculty because it comprised the department of Polish philology, a subject he was determined to study, given his abiding interest in literature, poetry, and drama.

Despite his steadily developing religiosity, there is nothing to indicate that at this juncture Karol was giving serious thought to the priesthood. He joined the Jagiellonian University branch of Marian Sodality and its eucharistic section, as he belonged to the sodality in Wadowice, and he went to Mass and Communion, but the only priest with whom he had occasional contact was Father Figlewicz, whom he knew at school back home and who was now attached to the Wawel Cathedral. He never talked about taking Orders.

Philosophy was one of Jagiellonian's five faculties—the others being theology, law, medicine (from which his brother had graduated), and agriculture combined with forestry—but it was the largest one. With seventy-two professors, philosophy had departments of philology in various languages, mathematics, physics, chemistry, astronomy, geography, zoology, psychology, education, and philosophy proper.

The Philology Department, housed in a classical building at No. 20 Gołębia Street, a few blocks from the main university complex, had some of Poland's leading specialists in this field among its professors—famous names in academia and literature. It also had an overwhelming majority of women among its students, including Karol's Wadowice friend and fellow thespian, Halina Królikiewicz (later Kwiatkowska). A woman student wrote later that "he did not avoid feminine company as a colleague, but he did not seek it."

Signing up for classes for the 1938–1939 academic year, Wojtyła took on an extraordinarily heavy and very unusual load. It offers interesting clues to his personality and interests.

This is the chronological list of subjects as requested by him: Principles of Polish Etymology; Elements of Polish Phonetics; Theater and Drama in Poland Since the Mid-Eighteenth Century, Including "Spring of Peoples" Literature; Analysis of the Theory of Drama; Novels, Memoirs, and Letters of Stanisław Brzozowski; Literature of the Polish Middle Ages; Exercises in Old Polish Literature; Dramatic Interpretation of Stanisław Wyspiański (a famous playwright and painter); Russian Language Beginner's Course; Interpretation of Contemporary Lyricism; Polish History and Geography; Humor, Comicality, and Irony and Their Role in Literary Work; Exercises in the History of Polish Literature; Grammar of Old Church Slavonic (the language in which St. Cyril and St. Methodius preached in the ninth century, bringing Byzantine-rite Christianity to the Balkans and Russia); Introduction to Russian Literature; and Character of Literary Antiquities.

Attending a class of Professor Stanisław Pigon, the favorite literature teacher at the Jagiellonian, Wojtyła volunteered to prepare a paper on a "subject that would not be easy" and would require "a good command of the French language," in the words of the professor. The following week, Karol submitted a lengthy study on "Madame de Staël as a Theoretician of Romanticism," apparently his first written literary effort at the university. He had been taking private French lessons at a friend's home for several months.

Wojtyła also attended outside lectures with regularity, on themes that seemed to point in still other directions in his evolution. Early in the academic year, he heard a lecture about the Legend of St. Alexis and attended one about German schools of Christian ethics, including that of Max Scheler, a subject that would stay with him for the rest of his life.

As usual, Wojtyła made friends very quickly in Kraków. At the faculty, he already knew Halina Królikiewicz and Jerzy Bober, with whom he had served in the labor battalion during the summer. His best new friends were Juliusz Kydryński, a year younger than Karol and son of a professor of Polish philology; Wojciech Żukrowski, who dropped the idea of law to study and create fine literature; and future writers Tadeusz Kwiatkowski (who would marry Halina) and Tadeusz Hołuj.

Kydryński was Wojtyła's closest friend at the time and his conduit to Kraków's intellectuals and artists. Equally obsessed with literature and the theater, Kydryński had appeared as an extra at the Słowacki Theater the previous year, and now had found a kindred soul in Karol.

Kydryński (who died in 1994) remembered Wojtyła as "a strongly built, but not tall boy, with a cordial, disarming smile. . . . He had a broad, round, rather than oval, face, thick dark-blond hair, cut straight in the back (in a home rather than barbershop fashion), and gray-blue eyes, which, often thoughtful and serious, reflected nonetheless a deep joy about life." Then he added: "With all his sense of humor and his unquestioned social charm—which forced all those who came into contact to like him and, after a closer acquaintanceship, to esteem him—and despite his immense sense of companionship and his readiness to join our student lives, Karol was much more serious than us, a bit closed within himself as if he were always meditating about problems that surpassed us. . . . One could feel it."

Wojtyła often visited Kydryński, who lived with his widowed mother, sister, and brother in an apartment on Felicjanek Street in midtown Kraków, fifteen minutes across the Vistula from his own home, and soon was treated like a member of the family. He called Kydryński's mother "Mama," and she made him his favorite dish, scrambled eggs.

It was through Kydryński that Karol met Leon and Irena Szkocki, whose villa on Księcia Józefa (Prince Józef) Street in the Salwator district, almost directly across the Vistula River from the Tyniecka Street house, was a significant center of Kraków cultural activity. Szkocki worked for an insurance company, his wife was a schoolteacher (in the same school as Kydryński's mother), and their villa, called Pod Lipkami (Under the Birches), was the meeting place for writers, poets, artists, and musicians. Writers and poets came there to read aloud and discuss their new works, musicians to play at musical evenings.

The Szkockis took instantly to Karol, also treating him like a family member. Like many other regular guests, he affectionately addressed Irena Szkocka as "Babcia"—grandmother. Their daughter, Zofia, was a pianist who entertained guests with renditions of Bach and Chopin; her husband, Włodzimierz Poźniak, held a degree in musicology. And among the Szkockis' friends, Karol met Jadwiga Lewaj, a teacher of French and literature who lived at the villa. Before long, she was giving him private French lessons. For Karol, the Szkockis became very special friends.

Wojtyła was also most enthusiastic about the thin, intense Juliusz Kydryński. In a letter to Mieczysław Kotlarczyk, his Living Word mentor in Wadowice, he wrote that in Kydryński he found "a colleague who is a spiritual organization man [sic], similar to us. . . . He could be a new brother." He described him as "a wild *homo theatralis,* a sister soul," adding that "we hold symposia at which we read poetry, drama. He knows by heart the entire *Bogumił* by Norwid and many passages from *Wyzwolenie* [Liberation]. . . . We have become very close." He told Kotlarczyk that he and Kydryński had read together "almost all the Słowacki mysticism, then a lot from Mickiewicz, and now again Wyspiański. Besides, the Old Testament from the Scriptures. Yesterday was the day of St. John the Evangelist, and we read together the marvelous passages when Jesus bids farewell to his disciples at the Last Supper. . . ." Deeper and deeper, Wojtyła was reaching into Polish literature as well as the Bible in his search for God and for mysticism.

* * *

His new friendships led Wojtyła to so many extracurricular activities that, considering his heavy academic load, it is hard to imagine when he slept and ate. He joined Studio 39, the drama school of the Kraków Theater Brotherhood; the Living Word cycle of lectures; the Literary Section of the Circle of Polish Philology; the Lovers of Polish Language Association; and the Fraternal Assistance Society of Jagiellonian University Students. The latter was in charge of student housing, but by the time Karol became a member, it had already been taken over by right-wing extremists. For reasons that remain murky, he was elected its president in 1939. He disliked the rightists, and some months earlier he was among the members of the Circle of Polish Philology who actively opposed right-wing attempts to impose *numerus nullus* restrictions on the university's Jewish students, a "zero number" provision expelling them altogether.

Unquestionably, Karol Wojtyła was highly regarded by his friends and colleagues as a quiet, pleasant young man, despite his penchant for being a loner—when not involved in group activities—and his religious commitments. He would never join them, for example, at Kraków's lively bars or cafés. As in high school in Wadowice, Karol and his eccentricities were accepted and respected. It was always that almost imperceptible arm's-length attitude that gained him respect. A woman fellow student wrote that "when he listened in class, Karol Wojtyła had the habit of staring at the professor with enormous concentration—as if he wished to absorb everything." This, of course, remains the habit of John Paul II.

Occasionally, Karol's friends made gentle fun of his religious devotion. Danuta Michałowska, a university classmate and actress, wrote that "as a joke, one day they pinned a card to his desk that said, 'Karol Wojtyła—Apprentice Saint'!" He did not seem to mind.

Wojtyła and his companions were so deeply involved in so many endeavors—including an interest in politics—that in looking back at that period in their lives it is difficult to comprehend how they appeared to ignore the great world events gathering around them. Between September 27 and October 2, 1938, Karol and others received basic military training as members of the University Academic Legion, but it seemed to have little to do with any real threat. The following month, as a university student, he was exempted from regular military service.

That legion exercise happened to come immediately after the signing of the Munich Pact between Hitler and Mussolini and the prime ministers of Britain and France—the notorious "Peace in Our Time"—providing for the annexation by Germany of the Sudeten province of Czechoslovakia. And just as was the case in the spring when Austria was swallowed by the Nazis, there is no evidence to suggest that the Munich agreement had any impact on Wojtyła, his father, or his colleagues.

The Spanish Civil War, underway since July 1936, was still being fought, and while leftist students at the university supported the Republicans against the Nationalists, backed in the field by Nazi dive-bomber aircraft and Italian army regiments, the group around Wojtyła demonstrated no particular interest in it, as far as is known. One of Wojtyła's contemporaries would say later that Poles, in Kraków and elsewhere, were so convinced of Poland's military prowess and of the vast French and British superiority over Germany that no one, and certainly not young people, realized the mortal danger they faced.

The "Polonists"—the Polish philology students—of the Philology Department dreamed, breathed, and lived poetry. It was among the most popular literary forms in Poland and particularly in Kraków during these interwar years; drama was another. Modern tendencies were highly appreciated by many, but romanticism, lyricism, and messianism were resurging as the most powerful strain in the writings of the new generation. It was back to Polish traditions—Norwid, Mickiewicz, Słowacki, and Wyspiański—and religiosity and spiritual content were very much present.

For Karol Wojtyła, the private person, literature released his pent-up emotions and sentiments—everything he had held back from friends and colleagues since high school in Wadowice (where Kotlarczyk of the Living Word was an exception). Now Karol threw himself into poetry and drama with all his mind and soul, with a prodigious outpouring of verse and prose.

In a broader sense, a knowledge of Wojtyła's early literary creation—even before he was twenty-one and before he became a priest at twenty-six—is absolutely crucial for the understanding of his philosophical, theological, political, and social thinking as pontiff of the Roman Catholic Church.

His remarkably powerful poetry of adolescence foreshadows his philosophical and theological conservatism through his mystical devotion and obedience to the most ancient teachings of the Church. It also reveals the depth of his Polish patriotism, which, in turn, defined his worldview when John Paul II became a significant player on the international scene. Among Wojtyła's dramas, *Brother of Our God,* written by him as a seminarian and freshly ordained priest between 1945 and 1950, points sharply to his advanced social doctrines, which would be transmuted into encyclicals from the very outset of his pontificate. Sadly, however, most of this exceedingly rich body of work is accessible only in Polish; only a fraction has been translated into other languages.

To write so massively, young Karol Wojtyła must have stayed up much of the night in the cramped basement on Tyniecka Street, his daytime hours being filled with his crushing academic load, his extracurricular activities, and his social life, all of which often spilled over into the evening (for a period during the war, Karol lived and wrote at the Kydryńskis' apartment). But he was already learning, with his extraordinary power of concentration, how to write—and pray—during every available moment day or night, sitting down, standing up, and even walking. This became a lifetime method and habit as student, priest, bishop, cardinal, and pope. He wrote while he prayed in his chapel, he wrote in the back seat of a car on ecclesiastic travel in Poland, and, later, he wrote as pope aboard airplanes over continents and oceans—always in longhand in Polish. He was blessed with amazing energy and strength—physical, mental, and spiritual—and this was already evident in his early Kraków days.

Wojtyła composed poetry over a span of more than forty years, since his student days in 1938, in Wadowice and Kraków, until his elevation to the papacy in 1978. He insists that he gave up writing poetry when he became pope, and revealed publicly that he was the author of scores of poems, many of them epics, dramatic plays, and articles published over long years in Kraków under at least four pseudonyms.

It is quite likely, however, that John Paul II was less than absolutely precise in affirming that he dropped poetry once he moved to the Vatican. There are very strong reasons to think that the last poem he is *known* to have written—"Stanisław," a hymn to the martyred bishop of Kraków with whom he so identifies—was actually completed after the start of his pontificate. Unlike most others, this poem carries no date of composition. It was made available by the pope to the Kraków Catholic monthly *Znak* (The Sign) in time for publication in the issue of August–September 1979, immediately after John Paul II's first pontifical pilgrimage to Poland. It appeared in *Znak* over the signature of Stanisław Andrzej Gruda, one of Wojtyła's pseudonyms, although a 1987 anthology, which includes "Stanisław," is presented as *Karol Wojtyła: Poems and Drama.* And interestingly, Wojtyła had picked "Stanisław" and "Andrzej" for the pseudonyms, the former being the murdered bishop's name and the latter that of St. Andrew Bobola, also much venerated by him.

It was a dramatic, even if private, gesture by Wojtyła, to choose "Stanisław" as his last published poem, completing it in its final form when he had already followed what he once described as the "straight line" from the tomb of St. Stanisław to the tomb of St. Peter. The penultimate papal poem is titled "Motherland." Marek Skwarnicki, a Kraków poet, literary critic, and the editor of the pope's poetry anthology, says that he has asked John Paul II whether "Stanisław" had indeed been finished at the Vatican, but "I obtained no answer." Skwarnicki also says that "we don't know if he stopped writing . . . he ceased to reveal his poetry when he became a pope."

In any case, the poem in blank verse is an arresting farewell presentation to the world of Karol Wojtyła's Polish Church, tradition, tragedy, and martyrdom—with Poland still under communist rule—as he leaves to become a pontiff:

I desire to describe my Church in the man
Who was given the name of Stanisław.
And the name, which King Bolesław inscribed with
his sword
In the oldest chronicles.
This name he wrote on the floor of the cathedral,
When streams of blood flowed over it. . . .
I desire to describe my Church, in which over
the centuries
Word and blood go together
United by the hidden sigh of the Spirit. . . .

And addressing the murderer-king:

My word had not converted you,
My blood will convert you. . . .

Before Wojtyła's election, only a handful of friends and editors knew the author's real identity. Few of the faithful in the Kraków archdiocese suspected that their bishop and then cardinal was an ardent poet as well. The bulk of John Paul II's literary output prior to the pontificate—the poems, plays, articles, sermons, and homilies—had been published in Polish by the late 1980s, with his permission. By his own admission, however, some of the very early poems have been "lost," and it is possible that he may have chosen to hold back others from public scrutiny.

Although he began writing poetry in his late teens, years before he committed himself to the priesthood, Wojtyła's entire poetic production has a clearly religious and philosophical character, often centering on reflection and death. And often it is difficult poetry. In retrospect, these early poems may stand as signposts pointing to his ultimate destiny. But there is no way of defining how conscious this poetic religiosity was when Karol still seemed determined to devote his life to literature and the theater. This is one of his private mysteries.

There is no known precedent of priests—let alone those who achieved the papacy—creating poetry on this scale. After John Paul II disclosed his secret poetic past, there was wonderment over how he could have reconciled dedication to God's greater glory with writing poetry, the sacred and the profane. According to Marek Skwarnicki, this was particularly true in Poland, given "the Polish psychology and respect for the attitude toward the Church hierarchy."

Wojtyła's own answer was that while priesthood is "sacrament and vocation," poetic creativity exists "in the function of talent," and both "touch on the personal mystery" that each author carries in him. On one occasion, he wrote a friend that "art . . . is a companion of religion and a guide on the road toward God: it has the dimension of a romantic rainbow—from the earth and the heart of man to Infinity." When he agreed to the publication of the collection of his poems, the pope remarked, in Polish, that "poetry is a great lady to whom one must completely devote oneself; I fear that I haven't been entirely correct toward her."

Skwarnicki, who is the foremost authority on papal poetry, suspects that Wojtyła actually began to compose while in high school. He says that there are "a few poems of the kind any high school graduate might write," among them a work titled "Ballads of the Beskidy" (after the mountain chain rising beyond Wadowice) and one or more about a highlander religious sculptor named Wowra whom Wojtyła knew and admired. But they cannot be located.

On Saturday, October 15, 1938, barely a few weeks after the start of his university studies, Karol read his poems with eight of his philology companions at a Literary Evening in the Blue Room of the Catholic House in Kraków. The evening was announced in newspapers and wall posters (it was paid admission) and Wojtyła's name appeared prominently.

The performance earned its participants eighteen złotys (roughly four dollars in those days), and the group marched from the Catholic House to the Old Town Market Square in search of a bar where the money could be happily spent. Karol, however, demurred, saying he did not feel well and had no stomach for alcohol or partying. As Jerzy Bober, one of the young poets, remembers the scene, "I handed Lolek two złotys, telling him in words brimming with sarcasm, 'Here, Lolek, for candy. . . .' And Karol, calm as he could be, brightened up, clutching the coin in his hand, and cried, 'So long boys! . . .'"

There is no record of the titles or contents of the poems Wojtyła read in the Blue Room, but it is probable that they were written in Wadowice simply because he would have not been in Kraków long enough to compose them in time for the October appearance. John Paul II himself said at a private lunch conversation in 1994 that the poems from his youth "have been lost or cannot be found."

But Karol kept composing inexhaustibly. Within a year, he wrote a cycle of poems known as *Renesansowy Psalterz* (Rennaissance Psalter), which was also called *Księga Słowiańska* (Slavonic Book), which includes "White Grave," in memory of his mother, and psalms, ballads, and sonnets. He wrote during that time a drama he titled *David,* in which the hero, as Karol put it in a letter to a friend, "wears Biblical attire" and Polish folk clothes. He added that *David* was a "cordial" play. This manuscript, too, has vanished.

The most impressive and inspired Wojtyła work of that period was the hymn "Magnificat," written during the spring and summer of 1939, just before the eruption of World War II. "Magnificat" is taken from the Latin version of the Song of Virgin Mary, "My soul doth magnify the Lord," and in it nineteen-year-old Wojtyła expresses in beautifully rhymed Polish his adoration of God, whom he calls "Father of Great Poetry," and his gratitude for poetry's "Happiness and Sorrow." He begs the "Blessed Holy Being, Slav and Prophet" to grant him compassion, and ends with this appeal:

> O Slavonic Book of longing! Toll 'til the end,
> Like the bronze music of the chorus of the
> resurrected,
> With a song holy, virgin, and poetry inclined,
> And with humanity's hymn—to the Lord's
> Magnificat.

On Thursday of Easter Week of 1939, Karol Wojtyła attended the ceremony of foot washing by Archbishop Sapieha at the Wawel Cathedral. A friend recalls that "afterwards, he stood for a rather long time, deep in thought, at the tomb of King Jagiełło. He prayed at length before the Most Holy Sacrament in Batory chapel."

In mid-May, Karol joined a pilgrimage of university youth to the shrine of the Black Madonna in Częstochowa.

But Karol was not all work—or prayer—and no play. In his own way, he was quite sociable. After completing the exams marking the end of their first academic year in June 1939 (Karol did superbly), the Polish philology class celebrated at a party at the home of the parents of one of the women students.

This is how another student, Maria Bobrownicka, remembered it: "There was some wine and we danced to the [music] of the record player. [Karol Wojtyła] danced like everybody else although he was more passionate about conversation than about dance." The occasion marked the second, and probably the last, time in his life that Wojtyła danced with anybody.

Also in June, Studio 39, the drama school, staged in the courtyard of the University's Collegium Maius eight evening performances of a musical comedy, the *Moon Cavalier*, in which actors played Zodiac-related roles. Karol played Taurus-the-bull (Taurus is his sign), wearing a huge papier-mâché mask and enjoying himself tremendously.

He spent the month of July in military uniform at the Academic Legion's camp in the village of Ożomla, not far from the eastern city of Lwów. Although Wojtyła had been exempted from regular military service, he was called to participate in occasional brief exercises and special summer projects. Ożomla was a Ukrainian-populated village, and the legion's men worked at building a school there to improve the traditionally hostile relations between Poles and Ukrainians. But Karol also found time to swim in a lake and play soccer "with great enthusiasm," according to his commanding officer. John Paul II still has photographs showing him in uniform, presenting arms, reporting to a noncommissioned officer, and having dinner. He also has a picture showing him at work on the school, bared to the waist, scapular around his neck.

Through the summer, Kraków and Poland still seemed strangely unaware of the approaching catastrophe. Oddly, there was no reaction among Cracovians—or in Karol

Wojtyła's circle—when the Nazis occupied Czechoslovakia in March. And Poland, now surrounded by the Germans on three sides, displayed its bravery by grabbing Czechoslovakia's Silesian region, adjoining its borders. Polish troops also moved into Lithuania.

On August 5 and 6, quite incongruously, the Polish army celebrated in Kraków the twenty-fifth anniversary of the formation of the first detachment of Marshal Piłsudski's legion. Marshal Edward Śmigły-Rydz, Poland's current strongman, presided over a military parade and received from "the children of Kraków" a wooden cannon and a doll in an army nurse's uniform. On both evenings, actors from Studio 39, including Karol Wojtyła as Taurus, were drafted to perform *Moon Cavalier* for the army's top brass.

On August 30, 1939, Wojtyła went to the headquarters of the Academic Legion in Kraków, as ordered, to return the military uniform he wore at summer camp. Summer was over and he would not need it, he was told.

CHAPTER 7

On the morning of Friday, September 1, 1939, Karol Wojtyła climbed the steep roadway to Wawel Cathedral to confess and to receive Holy Communion, as he did on the first Friday of every month. Several hours earlier, at dawn, German forces had entered Poland from the south, west, and north in a blitzkrieg attack that launched World War II. Nazi aircraft made their first bombing runs over Kraków during the morning, creating panic and chaos in the city.

As a result, Father Kazimierz Figlewicz, who lived in the cathedral compound, found it empty of priests, clerics, and staff. He feared he would not be able to celebrate Mass until he suddenly spotted Wojtyła in the church. Though the city was under air attack, Karol, in his imperturbable way, had crossed Dębnicki Bridge and walked over to the Wawel because, as Father Figlewicz put it, "he was rigorously observant in his religious commitments." Figlewicz was Wojtyła's confessor.

As they began celebrating Mass, Kraków suffered another air raid, and the priest wrote later that "this first wartime Mass, before the altar of the Crucified Christ and in the midst of the scream of sirens and the thud of explosions, has remained forever in my memory. . . . Does the present Holy Father still remember it?"

The Mass terminated, Wojtyła walked to the midtown

apartment of his friends, the Kydryńskis, to see if they were safe. It evidently did not occur to him that his father on Tyniecka Street might be in greater danger because Kraków's main radio transmitter, located in their Dębniki suburb, was a logical target. The Kydryńskis were fine, but Mama, fearing that their building would be destroyed in the bombing, decided that the family's most precious possessions, including bedding and warm clothes, should be moved to the Szkockis' Salwator villa on the Vistula embankment.

Juliusz Kydryński borrowed a handcart from a neighbor, and he and Karol started in the direction of the villa. Almost immediately, Nazi planes were bombing again, and they sought shelter in the carriage porch of a one-story building on Kościuszko Street. Kydryński related in a memoir after the war that "when we peeked over the entrance door, we could see in the cloudless, blue sky the silver Stukas [German dive-bombers] flying without interference over the city, dropping more and more bombs . . . soon, such hell broke loose that we no longer dared to open the door."

He went on: "We stood inside the house, as it trembled on its foundations, and Karol was absolutely calm, not showing the slightest fear. We weren't talking to each other, Karol against one wall and I against the other. We stood facing one another. But even if Karol was praying, he was praying in his soul, not even crossing himself. He stood there, very serious and calm." After a half hour, they returned to the Kydryńskis' building with the cart.

The next day, Karol and his father decided that Kraków would soon fall to the advancing German armies—they would occupy it on September 6—and that it would be wiser to flee east, where it was thought the Poles could consolidate their defenses. They could not guess that the Soviet Union would invade Poland from the other side on September 17, in fulfillment of the secret pact signed between Berlin and Moscow just three weeks earlier.

Along with tens of thousands of other refugees, the Wojtyłas journeyed by bus, truck, and horse cart about ninety miles to the town of Rzeszów, where they rested briefly. But before reaching Tarnobrzeg, the next town, and the banks of the San River, the father and son turned back. Karol explained in letters to his friend Mieczysław Kotlarczyk in Wadowice that they had returned to Kraków because "my father, small wonder, could no longer stand that hard trek. . . . He was enormously tired."

Back in Kraków, the Wojtyłas encountered the brutal reality of the Nazi occupation. The day the city was taken, the Nazi command ordered the detention of a group of distinguished citizens as hostages, threatening them with death if Kraków failed to show "obedience." The hostages included a bishop, two well-known priests, and two Jagiellonian University professors. And the Germans wasted no time making it clear what they had in mind for conquered Poland and conquered Kraków.

The western regions of the country were simply incorporated into the Reich on the grounds that they were really German because they had a significant prewar German ethnic minority. The rest of Poland—up to the line where the Soviet armies halted in their invasion—was designated as a protectorate under a governor-general with Kraków as his seat. As it happened, the Skawa River west of Kraków became the border between German territories and the protectorate, with Wadowice on the other side. Kraków and Wadowice thus suddenly found themselves in separate countries, as it were, with a tightly guarded frontier keeping them apart. Oświęcim was on the Wadowice side of the border and quite near.

Governor-General Hans Frank, who established his residence among the priceless paintings and tapestries of the royal castle on the Wawel, announced in a speech that "the Polish nation should be transformed into an intellectual desert." Reinhard Heydrich, the Nazi *gauleiter* in the region, warned that "nobility, priesthood and Jews must be liquidated." Albert Forster, another top Nazi official, declared that "because the voices of Polish politics were, above all, the clergy, the nobility, the teachers and other Polish intellectuals. . . . [they] must be removed immediately after the take-over of the country to make it impossible for them, from the very outset, to influence the masses."

The German master plan for Poland provided for the

gradual decay of Warsaw, where the population would be turned into slaves to produce for the Nazi economy, and for the postwar transformation of Kraków into a model German city. This was the reason for installing Governor Frank there along with numerous Nazi civilian and military institutions, and for transplanting German populations to Kraków. Within a year, over 20 percent of the city's inhabitants were Germans. Frank's policy was to eradicate intellectual and religious life in Kraków, Catholic as well as Jewish, and to use the population as slave labor in Germany whenever necessary.

On October 26, 1939, "public labor obligation" was imposed upon the entire Polish population between the ages of eighteen and sixty, except those engaged in "permanent, useful social labor." Those subject to "labor obligation," which was forced labor pure and simple, were to be sent to work on highways, railroads, and farms, being paid "wages considered just." Next, all the Jews, including children over twelve, were to be "directed to work indicated for them" for a period of two years as "an educational objective." Disobedience in general would be punished with fines of "unlimited sums" and prison; Jews would be punished with "heavy prison" and the confiscation of all their assets.

The Church was next on the list. Wawel Cathedral was closed to the faithful after Archbishop Sapieha was allowed to celebrate the last Mass there on October 29. Subsequently, the governor-general permitted Mass to be celebrated on Wednesdays and Sundays by only two priests—Father Figlewicz was one of them—but without worshippers. Figlewicz recalls that "we said Mass early in the morning before an empty church, under German guard." All the priests and cathedral staff who lived in the compound were expelled, except for Figlewicz and his colleague.

The theological seminary of the Kraków archdiocese, located directly below the Wawel, was closed and its buildings turned over to a special detachment of SS shock troops in charge of protecting the governor-general. When a delegation of Polish bishops called at the Wawel on Konrad Henlein, the leader of Czech Sudeten ethnic Germans now assigned to Governor Frank, to discuss the possible reopening of theological seminaries, they were told that "in Poland, the Church and the nation are one and the same. We must tear them apart. That is why we hit at both the Church and the nation in order to destroy you. You must disappear." Later, however, the Germans agreed to the reopening of some seminaries, provided that theology and other "university subjects" would not be taught. Only purely spiritual and liturgic teaching was tolerated, to prevent seminarians from being ordained as priests.

Many churches in Poland were closed down and priests, monks, and nuns deported to concentration camps. During the Nazi occupation of five and a half years, 1,932 priests, 850 monks, and 289 nuns were killed. In the meantime, the Nazis prohibited celebration of most Roman Catholic feasts as well as public prayers to the Black Madonna, the patron saint of Poland. And priests faced "severe punishment" for baptizing "persons of Jewish descent" as Catholics.

Finally, the Nazis turned to Polish culture, art, and education as they reverted to the *Kulturkampf* of the nineteenth century when Prussia ruled over its part of partitioned Poland. On November 6, the day the new academic year was to start, Kraków scholars and Jagiellonian University and Mining Academy professors were invited by the occupation authorities to a lecture by a visiting German scholar at Collegium Novum in the Old Town. All the 186 scholars and professors who came to the lecture were immediately arrested and deported to the Sachsenhausen-Oranienburg concentration camp in Germany. The university itself was closed down permanently.

Most of the professors were subsequently released when Lucjana Frassati-Gawrońska, the beautiful Italian wife of a prewar Polish diplomat, intervened on their behalf with Benito Mussolini, a personal friend. She had learned of the professors' fate during a visit to Kraków—one of her six trips to Poland from Rome on a Mussolini-approved Italian diplomatic passport—made secretly on behalf of the Polish resistance movement. Mussolini appealed directly to Hitler, but a number of professors died in the camp because of the brutal treatment they received.

For two years Mrs. Frassati-Gawrońska (whose brother was a monk whom Pope John Paul II would beatify in the

1980s) carried out an extraordinary mission for the Polish government-in-exile in London and the Polish underground. She delivered money, false passports, and military orders for the resistance fighters, and brought out of Poland under her personal protection endangered underground leaders and their families.

But Nazi war against Polish culture went on. The last Polish performance at Kraków's Juliusz Słowacki Theater was held on November 11. Afterward, the Germans used the theater for themselves.

On December 16, Governor-General Frank issued a decree ordering the seizure of all Polish art collections, including those in churches. In the case of Wawel, Frank had tapestries and Gobelins removed from the cathedral to his castle residence along with sacred objects, but the great panoramic sixteenth-century Flemish tapestries were smuggled out and taken secretly to Romania, then France and Canada. They were restored to the Wawel after the war.

Famous sculpted altars by the noted medieval sculptor Wit Stwosz were shipped from St. Mary's Church to Germany. From Polish museums and private collections, Frank acquired at least one Rembrandt and one Leonardo da Vinci; they were found after the war at his German family home.

In May 1940 Pope Pius XII confided in a private conversation to a senior Italian diplomat, Ambassador Dino Alfieri, that "terrible things" were occurring in Poland, adding that "we should say words of fire against such things." But neither he nor the Holy See pronounced such words—publicly condemning the Nazi crimes—at any time during World War II.

The Church's failure to speak out at its highest level become known as "the silence of Pius XII" and is one of the greatest moral controversies involving the papacy during this century. The pope's comment to Alfieri erases any doubt that he was fully aware of the situation in occupied Poland concerning persecutions against the Catholic Church as well as the Jews.

Kraków's Archbishop Sapieha for his part provided the Vatican's Secretariat of State with detailed information carried by trusted couriers, including Mrs. Frassati-Gawrońska. When Hitler invaded the Soviet Union in 1941, chaplains returning home from the eastern front via Kraków often carried Sapieha's secret messages to the Holy See.

In February 1942 the archbishop informed the Vatican that prisoners in Nazi concentration camps "were deprived of all human rights, handed over to the cruelty of men who have no feeling of humanity. We live in terror, continually in danger of losing everything if we attempt to escape, thrown into camps from which few emerge alive." On another occasion, Sapieha told a Knights of Malta chaplain who had stopped in Kraków and witnessed the deportation of Jews from the ghetto that "We are living through the tragedy of those unfortunate people, and none of us is in a position to help them anymore." He added: "And there is no difference between Jews and Poles." And the Vatican had had access to other channels as well. After the Nazis had occupied most of Western Europe, the Balkans, and parts of the Soviet Union, and their atrocities were widely observed and reported, Pius XII still kept his peace.

Karol Wojtyła, as student, seminarian, and factory worker in German-occupied Kraków, had no way of knowing what the pope was saying or thinking. In retrospect, however, the behavior of Pius XII raises fundamental questions affecting the moral authority of the papacy. Unquestionably, John Paul II today is completely familiar with the Vatican's wartime attitudes, and he must have drawn his own conclusions from them. While he would never publicly criticize a predecessor on the Throne of St. Peter, his actions during his own pontificate make it clear that he sees the responsibilities of the Church in a totally different light. He has protested loudly against the conflicts and atrocities in the former Yugoslavia, the former Soviet Union, the Middle East, Somalia, Rwanda, and other places, and against human rights violations, extreme nationalism, and anti-Semitism all over the world.

In a sense, the wartime travails of Pius XII were an education in the ways of the papacy for Karol Wojtyła, a man endowed with a superb comprehension of history. And, inevitably, their vastly different personal backgrounds must account for their actions. Whereas the ecclesiastic career of the aristocratic Eugenio Pacelli before his elevation as pope was almost entirely in the service of Vatican diplomacy, including as nuncio in Bavaria and Germany while Hitler was coming to power, and as secretary of state, Wojtyła's experience was pastoral and academic over long years—in addition to his humble origins, he was exposed to hard physical labor, the loss of his country to a foreign occupier, and the challenges of keeping alive both Polish culture and the Church under communist rule. Finally, their personalities could not have been more distinct.

To coin an expression, John Paul II believes in "aggressive tolerance," religious and political, starting with his readiness to denounce violations of human rights wherever they occur. He does not believe in compromise over principle, be it in his theological and moral positions or in his views of human rights and political freedoms. In fact, he holds that all these views form a comprehensive whole.

As young Karol Wojtyła was being confronted by the horrors of the Nazi occupation, Pius XII seemed prepared to live with the repugnant realities of German policies, in the name of what he perceived as the need to preserve Catholic unity at all cost. This stand apparently included a determination not to antagonize Hitler. Elected pope on March 2, 1939, Pacelli almost immediately sent a friendly letter to the führer. When the Nazis grabbed Prague and the rest of Czechoslovakia a few weeks later, Pius XII did not utter a single word to condemn this act even though Catholics were a significant segment of the Czechoslovak population. He said nothing when in 1940 the Nazis installed Monsignor Josef Tiso, a Catholic priest, as the puppet "president" of the "Republic of Slovakia" carved out of the defunct Czechoslovakia, and when murderous anti-Semitism and anti-Gypsy genocide swept Slovakia under Tiso's benevolent eye (the Slovaks hanged Tiso after the war).

The explanation offered for all these papal silences was that Pius XII subscribed to the doctrine of "impartiality" for the Holy See exercised by Pope Benedict XV during World War I. The doctrine, which Pacelli helped to draft as a ranking prelate in the Vatican's Secretariat of State, was based on the notion that since there were Catholics on both sides in the conflict, the Church should not support either warring party.

Notwithstanding the growing evidence of German atrocities in all the areas under Nazi control, Pius XII told Edoardo Senatro, a journalist for *L'Osservatore Romano*, the official Vatican newspaper, who had suggested gently that something critical should be said about them, that "you must not forget, dear friend, that there are millions of Catholics in the German army. Would you like to place them in the middle of a conflict of conscience?" (Pius XII evidently did not suspect that Hitler was planning in 1943 to kidnap him and occupy the Vatican.) Perhaps it was a matter of personal character. Cardinal Domenico Tardini, one of the Vatican's two undersecretaries of state, described his pope in a 1959 lecture in Rome: "Pius was, by natural temperament, meek and rather timid. He was not born with the temper of a fighter. In this he differed from his great predecessor, Pius XI, who rejoiced, at least visibly, in the contest. Pius XII visibly suffered."

As for John Paul II, to give one example, he risks antagonizing and even losing masses of Catholics worldwide in his battle against birth-control programs. It is a matter of principle for him, and he insists that no true conflict of conscience is involved. It is self-evident that birth control is evil, he affirms, and there are no two ways about it.

Andrea Riccardi, a highly respected Italian historian of the Church, points out in his book *Il Potere del Papa* (The Power of the Pope) that there was "no public protest" by Pius XII when the Vatican's sovereignty was violated by the Fascists, supported by German forces, in invading the Lombard Seminary and St. Paul's Abbey in search of Jews and other wanted persons hiding there. Riccardi recalls that "Jews were deported from a few hundred meters from the Apostolic Palace" and that the pope's attitude involved as well disregard of "the systematic destruction to which the Polish people, whose ties with the Holy See were profound, were submitted."

In sharp contrast, Monsignor Angelo Roncalli, then wartime apostolic delegate in Turkey, helped to save thousands of Jews throughout the Balkans by arranging for false Catholic baptismal certificates to be delivered to them and by intervening on behalf of Jews with Nazi-backed regimes in the Balkans and Eastern Europe. Roncalli became the successor of Pius XII as John XXIII and launched the liberalizing Vatican Council II. Karol Wojtyła, attending the council as a bishop, was one of the drafters of *Nostra Aetate* (In Our Time) Declaration, which included the affirmation that Jews must not be blamed for the killing of Jesus Christ.

In occupied Kraków, Wojtyła was impatiently awaiting the start of the new academic year, scheduled for November 6. In the meantime, he attended lectures on Polish etymology by Professor Kazimierz Nitsch, who had started them three weeks before the university was to reopen formally. Wojtyła said that Nitsch "began to fill again our young heads with national and Slavic honey." He was among the professors who would be deported to the German concentration camp on November 6.

In mid-September, theaters were still functioning in Kraków, and Karol not only went to the performances, but applied for work as an extra. He needed a job badly. After the collapse of Poland, his father no longer collected his military pension, their only income. However, there was no theater job for him nor work as a tutor at the university, and Karol, in good humor, tried to adapt himself to the harsh new conditions.

By October, the group of Polish philology students—the Polonists—came together again. At meetings at the Kydryńskis' apartment, Wojtyła and a half-dozen colleagues read aloud the great works of Polish literature, assigning themselves roles in Słowacki, Wyspiański, and Norwid dramas. Wojciech Żukrowski, another close friend, was back in town, staying five houses away from the Wojtyłas on Tyniecka Street, after escaping wounded from a German prisoner-of-war camp. He had fought in the Polish army in the first day of the war.

Karol wrote Kotlarczyk in Wadowice that *Vita*

Cracoviensis, "if you can imagine, consists of queues for bread and of rather rare expeditions for sugar . . . and of black nostalgia for coal . . . and of reading." He also did a lot of thinking about his country, now that it was lost, but looked ahead as well. In a November letter to Kotlarczyk (whom he addressed as "Brother Mieczysław at the Greek *Teatrum*"), he confessed bitterly that until then he had not seen Poland "in her real truth," having been unable to detect "the atmosphere of ideas that should have surrounded in dignity the nation of Mickiewicz, Słowacki, Norwid and Wyspiański."

It was nineteen-year-old Wojtyła's discovery of social injustice. He wrote: "Today, after reflection, I understand with full clarity that the idea of Poland lived in us, as a romantic generation, but in truth it did not exist because the peasant was killed and imprisoned for demanding his just rights from the government. . . . He was right and he had law on his side, [but] the nation was misled and lied to. . . ." Karol went on, charging that the sons of these peasants "were chased across the world by hostile winds, like in the days of the Partitions . . . so they would not rot in the motherland's prisons. . . ."

These were the same views that the idealistic young people on the left were developing simultaneously—that prewar Poland was unjust, oppressive, and Fascist-minded—and they were led to Marxism and communism. But Wojtyła approached it in another way. He told Kotlarczyk that "our liberation must be the gateway of Christ. . . . I think of an Athenian Poland, but of an Athens immensely perfected by the greatness of Christianity. Bards and prophets of the Babylonian slavery thought of such an Athens. [This] nation collapsed, like Israel, because it did not encounter the messianic ideal, its own ideal . . . that was not fulfilled."

This 1939 reflection about the unjust Poland was the foundation of Wojtyła's social and political philosophy as a young priest, Vatican Council bishop, and pope. He applied it in his struggle as bishop and cardinal against communism in Poland because communism, too, was oppressive and lacked the "greatness of Christianity," and in his thundering papal denunciations of "savage capitalism," for the same reason, after the collapse of the communist regimes in the late 1980s.

Karol and his father spent Christmas alone in their riverside basement. In a letter to Kotlarczyk, he described the holidays as "very sad." Although Kraków and Wadowice were separated by a frontier, Wojtyła and Kotlarczyk maintained their lively correspondence until Kotlarczyk and his wife could flee to Kraków in July 1941. Their letters were carried across the Skawa River border by friends who for family or professional reasons were occasionally allowed to travel between Kraków and Wadowice. Halina Królikiewicz, who lived in Kraków, was one of them. Kotlarczyk, older than Karol's other friends, was at that stage the most important person in his life, aside from his father, as an intellectual, cultural, and thespian mentor in whom he could confide all his ideas, plans, and dreams.

Despite Christmas sadness, joblessness, and the halt in his formal studies with the closing of the university, Wojtyła was more active than ever. He informed Kotlarczyk at the end of December: "I am very seriously busy. There are people that are dying of boredom now. But not me. I surround myself with books, I put up fortifications of Art and Learning. I work. Will you believe that I am almost running out of time? I read, write, learn, pray, and fight within myself. Sometimes I feel horrible pressure, sadness, depression, evil. Sometimes I almost glean the dawn, great lightness."

During the closing months of 1939 and during most of 1940, until he had to take a full-time job, Karol's literary production was phenomenal and of considerable erudition and quality. He composed countless poems, three dramatic plays, and translated Sophocles' *Oedipus Rex* from the Greek into Polish "in human language." The latter was suggested by Juliusz Osterwa, Poland's greatest actor and theater director at the time, who met Karol through Kydryński, taking an abiding interest in their dramatic work. Osterwa believed that all the great dramas, from *Oedipus* and *Antigone* to Shakespeare to Słowacki and Mickiewicz, should be presented in a way that "even women cooks can listen to with full understanding," and personally translated *Antigone* and *Hamlet* to meet his own standards.

Of Wojtyła's three dramas written during that period—all of them on Biblical themes—*David* was the first and probably the worst, and he may have destroyed the manuscript. The others, *Job* and *Jeremiah*, not only were preserved, but John Paul II, with pride of authorship, allowed their publication in Poland shortly after his election. Karol wrote them in longhand, painstakingly typing them later on a borrowed typewriter.

Job followed *David*, and Karol described it to Kotlarczyk as a "new drama, Greek in form, Christian in spirit, with the eternal contents, as in any drama, about suffering." He explained that *Job* was born from his "deep immersion" in the Old Testament, and his reading of King David's psalms and the Books of Job and the Prophets. The play's central message is that "suffering is not always punishment" and that Christ's sacrifice shows the "meaning of suffering." This is the mystical St. Stanisław theme Wojtyła had always emphasized in his teachings, invoking it after the assassination attempt against him and the serious illness and accidents he suffered as pope in Rome.

Karol informed Kotlarczyk that "people to whom I read it, liked it very much" because it "takes you by the heart, [and] is very dramatic and scenographic."

Jeremiah, he advised his friend, "was born like lightning, like a revelation during a reading of Jeremiah's prophecy." It is a three-act play whose heroic figure is the real-life Polish Jesuit priest Piotr Skarga, the great seventeenth-century court preacher, who had defied his own order during the Counter-Reformation and experienced his own "vision" of Poland.

But Wojtyła's Father Piotr, a bit heavy on pathos, is also modeled on Father Piotr in Adam Mickiewicz's drama *Dziady* (Forefather's Eve), a deeply mystical, religious, and patriotic work written feverishly after the defeat of the 1831 Polish uprising against Russian occupiers. Mickiewicz's priest reveals his "vision" in a monologue in his prison cell, a lengthy, emotional passage that is regarded as the source of the Polish literary tradition of messianism. It equates the martyrdom of Poland with the martyrdom of Christ and urges a moral revival. The "vision" of Karol's Father Piotr flows from Jeremiah's prophecy.

Wojtyła own nascent mysticism shines through the drama he composed when he was barely twenty. Again, John Paul II of today is the unchanged spiritual child of wartime Kraków.

CHAPTER 8

One of the most important moments in Karol Wojtyła's life came on a cold Saturday afternoon in February 1940, at the Salesian Fathers' parish church of St. Stanisław Kostka in Dębniki, a few blocks from his house on Tyniecka Street. It gave a wholly new dimension and understanding to his instinctive mysticism and, as much as any profound experience of his young years, it set him on the course toward the priesthood.

The crucial moment occurred when Karol met an unprepossessing forty-year-old tailor named Jan Leopold Tyranowski at a weekly religious discussion at the parish church. Almost instantly, Tyranowski became Karol's mentor in matters religious and spiritual, as Kotlarczyk was his mentor in theater and literature. Looking back at Wojtyła's life it is beyond question that, in addition to his father, Tyranowski and Kotlarczyk exercised the greatest influence on him. John Paul II has recognized it himself.

Father Mieczysław Maliński, a Kraków priest and writer who has known him well since the early days of the war, says that for Karol "it was a short way from Kotlarczyk to Tyranowski." He describes Kotlarczyk as "a visionary, a prophet obsessed with the idea of a 'great Poland,'" adding that "if Kotlarczyk taught Karol that good must be achieved through beauty, Tyranowski would tell him that 'priesthood is an even shorter way to make people good.' He convinced him, and then it was a straight road toward priesthood."

In a tribute to Tyranowski published in Kraków in 1949, after his death, Wojtyła—already a priest—depicted him as an "apostle" and as "someone really saintly." Nowhere in the lengthy text did he directly credit Tyranowski with guiding him toward the priesthood, but he made the point by remarking that "he had proved that one can not only learn about God, but that one can live through God." He taught Karol about faith and divine grace as no one had before.

Tyranowski, as both Wojtyła and Maliński acknowledge, was a strange person who at first invited rejection and suspicion. Short and gray-haired, he was physically unattractive by all accounts. He spoke in the cliché language of catechism, and his Polish was full of archaic turns of phrase that grated on the young men. The son of a Kraków tailor, Tyranowski was trained before the war as an accountant, but he decided to join his father and brother in the tailor shop in their dark walk-up second-floor apartment on Różana Street in Dębniki, a few streets away from the Wojtyłas' house on the river. He felt that working at home as a tailor, he had more silence and quiet, and more opportunity for concentration and prayer. Besides, he was a loner, convinced that his mission in life was to convey the idea of God and faith to others, especially to young people. Some of the latter referred to Tyranowski at first as a "religious bigot."

His great opportunity to bring God to his fellow man arrived when the Salesian Fathers at the Dębniki church gathered a group of local youths for a pre-Easter retreat in the first year of the German occupation, to try to keep alive their religious spirit. The retreat having proved successful, the Salesians requested a priest who lectured at Jagiellonian University to hold weekly theological encounters for twenty to thirty young people between the ages of sixteen and twenty-five, who had come to the original retreat. Tyranowski showed up at one of the first sessions, despite his age, demonstrating keen readiness to participate actively in the program. When the Salesians proposed the idea of organizing "Living Rosary" praying circles to link the youth even more strongly to church activities, Tyranowski volunteered to run them.

He conducted the recruiting for the circles so aggressively, stopping strangers on the street and asking very personal questions, that Father Maliński, for one, thought that this insistent, bizarre personage was a Gestapo agent. It had become a habit under the occupation never to answer searching questions from unknown persons, but this fact evidently never dawned on the inspired tailor. In any event, Maliński, who lived in the neighborhood and had been approached by Tyranowski in the street, joined the Living Rosary and was introduced by him to Karol Wojtyła.

It was at a Saturday Living Rosary meeting in February that Karol first came into contact with Tyranowski, and the instantly developed an intense personal relationship, master and pupil.

Karol wrote later that while the "truth" Tyranowski proclaimed was "already known from catechism, books and sermons," what he did best was "to work on our souls in the full meaning of this word . . . he wanted to bring out the resources he knew existed in our souls to reveal grace that becomes participation in the life of God." Evidently, it was a mystical experience that Tyranowski knew how to communicate and Wojtyła how to receive. Tyranowski himself, Wojtyła recalled, spent four hours a day in "reflection."

Lacking formal philosophical or theological training, Tyranowski had the gift of quiet, private preaching. Wojtyła remembers that "once in July, when the day was slowly extinguishing itself, the word of Jan [Tyranowski] became more and more lonely in the falling darkness, penetrating us deeper and deeper, releasing in us the hidden depth of evangelical possibilities, which until then we, tremblingly, avoided."

Karol, like other Living Rosary members, met individually once a week with Tyranowski, usually at the tailor's crowded apartment, in addition to the group encounters. The purpose was for the pupil and the master to review in detail the former's religious activities during the past week on the basis of notes he made every evening. Tyranowski believed that such discipline was required for the formation of character.

As their friendship grew, Tyranowski and Karol often walked along the Vistula embankment, discussing God, man, and religion. Later, when Karol found a job, Tyranowski accompanied him on the hour-long trek from home to work to talk even more. And Tyranowski occasionally visited the Wojtyłas at home, before the curfew, for joint reading of the Scriptures and more conversation.

Above all things, however, Tyranowski was a mystic and an ascetic. Wojtyła wrote that there were reasons to believe that he mortified his flesh. And he guided Karol toward the profound mysticism that would define for more than a half century the life of John Paul II. Tyranowski's own masters were St. John of the Cross and St. Theresa of Avila, the great Spanish mystics. "They were not only his masters," Wojtyła wrote, "but they literally allowed him to discover himself, they explained and justified his own life."

Wojtyła was, of course, describing his own experience in this fashion. His choice of St. John of the Cross as the theme of his first doctoral dissertation was undoubtly inspired by Tyranowski. The mystical behavior that suffering is a gift from God was dramatically displayed in the way Tyranowski died. At the age of forty-seven, he developed an infection that kept him in bed for a full year in excruciating pain, forced the amputation of an arm, and caused total deafness three days before he died in March 1947.

This was the death Tyranowski had desired, Wojtyła wrote, and for which he prayed. Notwithstanding the constant pain, Wojtyła added, his friend was "always bright and smiling, in fact radiant." Tyranowski had had the satisfaction of seeing Karol become a priest the year before, but his pupil was in Rome when he died.

Tyranowski's mystical legacy to Wojtyła was not only St. John and St. Theresa, but also the early desire to enter a monastery and lead a contemplative life. Though Karol was denied this destiny, monastic life always had a powerful attraction for him. As pontiff, Wojtyła established a cloistered convent within the walls of the Vatican, the first time a monastic institution was installed there. The convent, located in the Vatican Gardens "in the shadow of St. Peter's dome," was opened on May 13, 1994, to house eight Poor Clares from the Protomonastery of St. Clare in Assisi, Italy.

The inauguration date was the anniversay of the first apparition of the Virgin Mary at Fátima and, as the Vatican announcement put it, "has particular significance for the Holy Father, since it was on this day that he experienced Our Lady's motherly protection following the attack on his life in 1981." The founding statutes of the convent provide that "the specific purpose of this community is the ministry of prayer, adoration, praise and reparation so as to be a continual prayer in silence and solitude to support the Holy Father in his daily concern for the whole Church."

And in October 1994 John Paul II presided over the first synod of bishops dedicated to "the Consecrated Life," concentrating on male and female religious orders that have been shrinking dramatically over the past decades.

In wartime Kraków, Karol had to find a job to support himself and his father. In August 1940 he was hired as a delivery boy by a downtown restaurant. But the Nazis, having incorporated the city and the rest of the General Government into Germany in July, were now busy rounding up thousands of able-bodied Poles for forced labor. Strong and healthy at twenty, Wojtyła was a natural candidate for the next roundup. He was not safe running around Kraków as a messenger.

But friends came to his aid. The only protection against capture was the *Ausweiss,* an identity card indicating that the bearer was employed in a *Kriegswichtig* industry (that is, essential for the war effort). A Kraków industrial establishment that qualified for such an exemption was the Belgian-owned Solvay plant, taken over by the Germans and renamed "Eastern German Chemical Works," which produced caustic soda, an ingredient in explosives, from calcinated limestone.

The Solvay plant obtained limestone for calcination from a huge quarry in the village of Zakrzówek, an area directly south of Dębniki, and it was there that Karol became employed in September 1940 as a manual laborer. Big limestone blocks, pried loose with charges of ammoniacal explosives, were transported in iron carts over a narrow-gauge rail line to the plant in the industrial district of Borek Fałęcki, about five miles south of Zakrzówek.

Karol received the precious *Ausweiss* document, with its black eagle at the top, after being hired with a number of young intellectuals, including at least three of his close university friends, by Solvay's Polish general manager in Kraków, Henryk Kułakowski. The Germans had kept him in his post because of his expertise, and Kułakowski used it to provide protection for students recommended by his friends as part of the Polish resistance movement.

According to Edward Görlich, a Polish chemist who worked in the plant laboratory, another senior Solvay official named Föhl "paid off the Gestapo to close its eyes to the assemblage of young Polish intelligentsia in the Solvay establishment." The system worked, and Wojtyła spent four years in Solvay's employ.

He got the job after Jadwiga Lewaj, his friend and French language teacher, suggested Karol to Kułakowski, the general manager, whom she knew socially and who belonged to Kraków cultural elite circles. Wojciech Żukrowski, Juliusz Kydryński, and Tadeusz Kwiatkowski, who were his best friends, were hired at the same time as were Görlich, who was a professor at the Mining Academy, and a promising young pianist and museum curator. However, Żukrowski, whose grandfather had been a Solvay physician, claimed that he had arranged all these jobs, including his own.

Karol started at the quarry laying rail tracks between Zakrzówek and the plant and serving as a brakeman, assignments he did not seem to mind. He wrote to the Kotlarczyks in October that "I earn very well (relatively speaking, of course), and workers' 'supplements' are most welcome. . . . Most of my colleagues work like this. And it does us a lot of good."

The "supplements" were extra food rations supplied by the Germans to the *Schwerarbeiters* (hardworking personnel). Normal monthly rations at the plant included a piece of stringy meat, several kilograms of black bread, marmalade, cigarettes, and a liter of vodka. Karol traded the cigarettes and the vodka for lard to keep his strength. He was not complaining, but his life was exceedingly tough. It took him about an hour to walk from Tyniecka Street to the quarry, mainly across open fields, for the 8:00 A.M. to 4:00 P.M. shift. The winter turned out to be unusually severe that year, with deep snow on the ground and temperatures around thirty degrees Fahrenheit below zero.

Karol was rapidly losing weight, feeling bone-chilled and exhausted most of the time. Once a day, a few workers at a time were allowed to take turns spending fifteen minutes inside a quarry shack with an iron stove, where they gobbled their lunch of black ersatz coffee with saccharine and slices of black bread smeared with marmalade they brought from home. Żukrowski, also working at the quarry, remembers Karol "wearing a hat with frayed band, a jacket with bulging pockets, and mended pants covered with limestone dust and stiff from splashed oil." He also wore big wooden clogs.

But Wojtyła found time and energy to carry on with the theater. Usually during meetings at the Kydryńskis'—Juliusz and Karol often walked back together from work—the actors read classical Polish plays. Late in September, with Karol directing, they presented the recitation of a full act from a play by Stefan Żeromski before a handful of invited guests, and began preparing the performance of a Norwid play. From October on, the theater group congregated regularly every Saturday.

On Christmas Eve, Karol and his father crossed Dębnicki Bridge for the holiday supper, the Lieutenant's last. It was at the Kydryńskis'.

Karol Wojtyła Senior became seriously ill shortly after Christmas, and had to be confined to his bed in the basement apartment. He could no longer keep house, and Karol brought him dinner every evening in metal containers from the Kydryńskis' where he went after work to eat.

On February 18, 1941, a particularly bitter cold day, Karol and Maria Kydryńska, Juliusz's sister, took medicine and dinner containers to Tyniecka Street. It was late afternoon, and Maria was to heat the food for the meal. When they entered the basement, they found the Lieutenant dead.

Maria Kydryńska remembers the scene: "Karol, weeping, embraced me. He said through his tears, 'I was not present at my father's death.' He called a priest immediately." His father had died of a heart attack. He was sixty-two. Karol was not yet twenty-one.

He prayed all night on his knees before his father's body. Juliusz Kydryński joined him and, between prayers, they spoke in whispers on death. The next morning, Karol moved to the Kydryńskis' apartment for the next six months, unable to face the loneliness on Tyniecka Street. In Rome, in a private conversation in 1994, John Paul II reminisced briefly about the night of his father's death, saying softly, "I never felt so alone . . ."

The Lieutenant was buried on February 22, at Kraków's military cemetery, with Father Figlewicz, Karol's confessor, leading the prayer. At the Kydryńskis', Karol spent much of his free time praying, sometimes prostrate on the floor of the room he occupied in the apartment. It was a three-room apartment, and Karol slept in the middle room. He went to Mass every day. But Kydryński remembers that in addition to his work at the plant, his writings and religious occupations, Karol found time to pace up and down his room memorizing aloud French words from the private lessons and to help him shovel coal into the basement from the delivery truck.

His father's death was the most powerful and traumatic blow Karol had suffered in his life. Most of his friends believe that it was the determining factor in his ultimate decision to become a priest.

Father Maliński, who saw Wojtyła often, says that he went to the cemetery every day after work at the quarry, clear across Kraków, on the other side of the Vistula, to pray at his father's grave. Maliński worried that "something would happen" to Wojtyła because he was so distraught, but he thinks that Jan Tyranowski's influence helped to restore his equilibrium. He also says that "if it were not for Tyranowski, Wojtyła would not be a priest and I would not be a priest. . . . It does not mean that there was any pressure on his part. He simply opened a new way for us."

After his father's death, the tailor obviously became the most inspiring figure spiritually in Karol's life. It must be assumed that he spent long hours with Tyranowski in the aftermath of his final orphanage and that they discussed his future. But it would take another year and a half for the priesthood decision to mature in Karol's heart and mind.

Addressing seminarians in Kraków on March 8, 1962,

already a bishop, Wojtyła came the closest he had ever done publicly to an explanation of his resolve to become a priest. Recounting the wartime years, he said that "with pride and gratitude to God, I recall that it was granted to me to be a physical worker for four years. During that period, sparks were awakened in me concerning the most important problems in my life, and the road of my vocation was decided."

And he added: "I would be unjust if I did not mention at this moment Jan Tyranowski . . . who knew how to exercise an enormous influence on young people. I don't know whether it is to him that I owe my priesthood calling, but, in any event, it was born within his climate, the climate of the mystery of supernatural life."

Later John Paul II observed that "after my father's death . . . I gradually became aware of my true path. I was working at a plant and devoting myself, as far as the terrors of the occupation allowed, to my taste for literature and drama. My priestly vocation took shape in the midst of all that, like an inner fact of unquestionable and absolute clarity. The following year, in the autumn, I knew that I was called."

In the meantime, Wojtyła kept busy at his harrowing quarry job and at theatrical sessions with his friends. He also found time to retype at the Kydryńskis' the texts of his *Job* and *Jeremiah* dramas. He presented a set of each to Mrs. Kydryńska as a token of his gratitude for the family's hospitality.

In Kraków, the Nazi occupation increased in ferocity. On March 3, the Germans began rounding up Jews on a massive scale. The Jewish district of Kazimierz was turned into a sixteen-square-mile walled ghetto. A concentration camp for Jews was set up in the western suburb of Plaszów. In Wadowice, the synagogue and the Jewish cemetery were destroyed. The Jewish population was placed in a ghetto. Wojtyła heard that the family house of Jerzy Kluger, his Jewish schoolmate, was taken over for local Gestapo headquarters.

On May 23, the Gestapo raided the Salesian parish church in Dębniki, in Karol's neighborhood, arresting and deporting thirteen priests who subsequently died in concentration camps. Speaking at the Dębniki church as cardinal in the 1970s, Wojtyła said, "I shall never forget that day when we, young parishioners, learned that all, or almost all, the priests of the Dębniki parish and Salesian instructors were arrested and soon thereafter deported to concentration camps." Jan Tyranowski was in the church the day of the Gestapo raid, taking part in a choir rehearsal, but the agents overlooked the choir, deliberately or not, as they made the arrests.

As part of its war against the Church, the Nazis were deporting at that time a rising number of senior prelates. Archbishop Juliusz Nowowiejski of Płock died in a concentration camp in May 1941, followed by his suffragan bishop Leon Wetmański. Archbishop Michał Kozal of Włocławek was killed in Dachau. And the silence continued at the Vatican.

In the spring, Karol was shifted to an easier job at the quarry, thanks to the Zakrzówek manager, an ethnic German named Krauze who had grown up among Poles and tried to improve the lot of the young intellectuals working for him. The new job was assisting Franciszek Łabuś, an elderly foreman in charge of quarry explosions. Karol was responsible for placing the ammoniacal explosives and fuses inside holes drilled in limestone rocks. Łabuś ignited them. Then the two of them would hide behind an outcropping as the explosion shook the quarry and limestone blocks were hurled down to the ground below. One of the advantages of the new job was that Karol and his boss spent most of their time inside a shack. Not only was it warmer there, but Karol had a chance to read books—literature and, increasingly, religion.

Old Łabuś was very fond of Wojtyła. Many years later, he recalled that Karol "was so young when he came to work, and I was so sorry for him because he wasn't really any good [at this work]. . . . He had such delicate little hands. I thought it would be best if he went off to become a priest. . . . I told him once, 'You better be a priest,' and he just smiled. . . . Later, he reminded me that he *did* become a priest."

But the foreman also warned Wojtyła and his friend Wojciech Żukrowski, a quarry miner, that if even a "gram" of explosives was missing, "it would be Oświęcim . . . for you." The Germans kept careful track of the explosives to ensure that none was diverted to the underground movement.

Whether the old man knew it or not, Żukrowski was a member of the underground Armia Krajowa (Home Army), known as AK, and actually he did steal ammoniac and dynamite sticks from the site for the guerrilla units. Karol, according to Żukrowski, opposed participating in armed struggle against the Nazis, arguing that Poles did all they could in fighting the invaders in 1939, and that "the rest is in the hands of God—and Providence guides our destinies."

All the underground activities were highly compartmentalized for security reasons, and notwithstanding their friendship, Żukrowski never told Karol that he belonged to the military resistance organization.

Żukrowski and other anti-Nazi militants never regarded Wojtyła as a coward because he would not join the armed organization. They recognized—then and later—the importance of "cultural" resistance against the Germans engaged in their *Kulturkampf* against the Poles. This included the underground Polish theater in Kraków, in which Karol was deeply involved, and Żukrowski makes a point of emphasizing that "you could wind up in Oświęcim for participating in that theatre, too. . . . If he were caught with a briefcase full of theatrical notes, for example, they [the Gestapo] would say 'aha, you're a worker at the quarry, and you are conspiring with a secret theatre group'. . . ." And Wojtyła knew that young priests were serving as chaplains with underground AK detachments in the forests.

Wojtyła's experiences as a quarry worker remained engraved in his memory forever. In 1956, he described them—in his philosophical and religious reactions to his work—in a four-part blank verse poem, "The Quarry," published in a Kraków periodical. It is, in part, an ode to the beauty of hard labor: "All the greatness of that work resides within the man. . . ." It is a tribute to a dead "companion of labor": "His whole being was consumed by the white stone, and he became stone himself. . . . They put him, silently, down on his back on a sheet of pebbles.

Then comes his grieving wife and his son returns from school. . . ." And it is a hymn to his fellow workers:

> I know you, you splendid people, people without
> manners and forms.
> I know how to look into a man's heart without lies
> and pretense.
> Someone's hands belong to labor, someone's hands
> belong to the cross. . . .

The summer of 1941 brought two happy events for Karol Wojtyła. First, Mieczysław Kotlarczyk, his Living Word mentor, and his wife escaped from Wadowice to Kraków. Then, the Solvay management transferred him from the quarry to the main plant in Borek Fałęcki, a vast improvement in working conditions.

Karol invited the Kotlarczyks to come and live in his basement apartment on Tyniecka Street, and several months later he forced himself to come back there, too. Not only was he not alone there, but he had the company of his most intellectually and artistically stimulating friend. While Karol worked at the caustic soda plant—the day shift or the long night shift—Kotlarczyk earned a living as a tramway conductor.

Kotlarczyk's appearance in Kraków energized the young actors. At a meeting on August 22, at the apartment of the parents of two actresses, the underground Rhapsodic Theater was formally launched, functioning long past the war (when it emerged from hiding). Kotlarczyk, Wojtyła, Kydryński, Żukrowski, Halina Królikiewicz, Danuta Michałowska, and the rest of the hard core of the prewar theater lovers were on hand. They immediately began preparing a recitation performance of Słowacki's *King-Spirit,* in which Karol would play the tragic role of King Bolesław. The premiere was held at the same apartment on November 1.

Soon, the Rhapsodic Theater was linked with underground Unia. Unia was the cultural arm of the military resistance movement, with strong emphasis on "Christian thought." It had the active support of Archbishop Sapieha, who had a hand in all the underground operations.

Unia was created by Jerzy Braun, a well-known poet and playwright who represented the great tradition of Polish literary messianism. Along with others, Wojtyła joined Unia, taking a solemn oath of allegiance to "the union of man with man, union of nations with nations, union of all men with Christ."

These concepts matched Karol's nascent social philosophy. They were another foundation for the views he refined later as scholar, priest, and pontiff. Unia's ideas echoed traditional Polish sentiments against capitalism—though not in a Marxist context—and they have resurged after the collapse of communism in John Paul II's stinging pronouncements against the new era's runaway capitalism and consumerism. Karol accepted Unia's principle that "Christianity creates in a social way"—for the whole society.

Meanwhile, Karol's new job provided him with an extraordinary opportunity to study and pray in relative peace even though the plant was twice as far from home as the quarry. It now was nearly a two-hour walk each way. His assignment over the next three years was to hand-carry wooden pails of whitewash from limestone calcinating furnaces in the courtyard to the "laundry," as it was called, on the first floor of the building where impurities were washed out. Karol was also responsible for delivering samples of the liquid to the plant's laboratory. This was much easier and less exciting work than the quarry; for one thing, it meant being indoors most of the time. His friends, too, were transferred. Juliusz Kydryński was assigned to Solvay's reception office—the gateway to the plant for the workers—and Wojciech Żukrowski became a mechanic.

Wojtyła preferred the night shift (sometimes they would stay on for double shifts to spare themselves the long walks to and from the plant) because it was quieter, and he had more time for himself. On a night shift, Karol knelt at midnight on the factory floor to pray at length. His fellow workers remember him praying at every opportunity.

Devouring religious texts was another Wojtyła occupation during idle moments at Solvay. One of the first ones he studied there was the *Treatise on the Most Excellent Devotion to the Most Holy Virgin Mary,* written early in the eighteenth century by Louis Marie Grignon de Montfort, an ascetic Breton priest who was subsequently canonized by the Church. Apart from his childhood devotion to Mary at Kalwaria Zebrzydowska sanctuary near Wadowice, this blue-covered book was Karol's first serious introduction to Mariology.

As archbishop, Wojtyła once told a group of Kraków priests that before reading the *Treatise,* "I had difficulty in relation to the devotion of the Virgin Mary and to the worship of Lord Jesus. . . . So I struggled for a long time with this *Treatise* that so providently fell into my hand. I studied it back and forth, returning many times to different passages (I dirtied it considerably while doing it). . . . But after a few months of such study, something on this subject shaped up in me."

Another book Karol read with consuming interest was *Ontology or General Metaphysics* by Father Kazimierz Wais, a philosopher and theologian of note. This was Wojtyła's introduction to metaphysics, but because—in his word—he lacked adequate humanistic, philosophical, and literary preparation, it took him nearly two months to master metaphysical concepts. But it was a major breakthrough, leading him from "the world in which I lived in an intuitive and emotional fashion" to a world "justified by the most profound as well as the simplest of reasons."

Constant prayer was what kept Karol going, both in his inner life and emotional evolution and transition struggle and in his harsh daily endeavors. He prayed at the Dębniki neighborhood church on his way to work, he prayed at the plant, he prayed at the old, little wooden Borek Fałęcki church near Solvay on his way to the cemetery after work, he prayed at his father's grave, and he prayed at-home. Most of his co-workers regarded him with respect, admiration, and affection. They referred to him as "the student" or "our little priest," and often they would tell him to take a break during a shift, saying "you've done enough already . . . get some rest, read, eat or something. . . ."

Stefania Kościelniakowa, who worked at the plant kitchen, recalled that her supervisor once pointed to Karol, telling her, "this God-loving boy is an educated boy, very talented, he writes poetry, and now he writes about St. Theresa. . . . He has no mother . . . and he is very poor. . . . Give him a bigger slice of bread because what he gets at the plant is all that he eats." Mrs. Kościelniakowa said that "when I worked in the afternoon, I sliced the bread for the evening, and I always set aside a bigger piece for him."

And Wojtyła still found time for the Rhapsodic Theater, chats with Kotlarczyk and Tyranowski, and social get-togethers with other Kraków intellectuals. He was acquainted with most of the contributors to the *Literary Monthly,* the underground publication edited by Żukrowski and Kwiatkowski, which attracted Kraków's best writers. Among them was Jerzy Turowicz, a writer in his early thirties, with strong links to the Church. Their encounter was brief, but they would meet again after the war, and Turowicz would emerge as one of the very important personages in Karol Wojtyła's career.

CHAPTER 9

On Sunday, May 24, 1942, Karol Wójtyła, who had just turned twenty-two, arrived in Częstochowa as part of a two-day academic pilgrimage to the shrine of the Black Madonna, the Queen of Poland. He had participated before the war in mass pilgrimages to the Luminous Mountain, but the Germans now allowed only very small groups there. Wojtyła went with a dozen young men, including his friend Wojciech Żukrowski.

Two days earlier, Karol appeared in the lead role at the Rhapsodic Theater recitation performance of *Wesele,* a famous drama by Stanisław Wyspiański, held at a friend's apartment. He had breathed a sigh of relief during the first week of May when his close friend Juliusz Kydryński was released from a Kraków prison after a detention of three weeks. Karol Wojtyła was arrested at a downtown café during a mass roundup by the Gestapo even though he carried the *Ausweiss* card identifying him as a worker in a vital industry. In the end, the card freed him while most of the men arrested at the same time were deported to Oświęcim. On a sunny day in May, twenty-five of them were executed by a firing squad against the "Wall of Death" at the camp.

Now in Częstochowa, the group prayed in the chapel where the image of the Black Virgin was unveiled for their benefit (it is normally covered by a drapery). Unbeknownst to the Nazis, the students swore an oath to the Madonna, pledging that "on the eve of the inevitable confrontation with our enemy, which will end in their defeat, despite the maddened terror, we, the Polish academic youth, standing inflexibly in the defense of the [Holy] Spirit with faith in a better tomorrow, declare our oath on Luminous Mountain in wonderment over the judgement of Providence."

Returning to Kraków, Karol divided his time between the limestone plant and theater rehearsals and performances. One evening in September, after a rehearsal of a Norwid play in the basement apartment on Tyniecka Street, Wojtyła turned to Kotlarczyk, asking him not to cast him for future roles in Rhapsodic Theater performances. Karol went on to explain that he was planning to enter a secret theological seminary in order to become a priest.

Though Kotlarczyk must have been aware of Wojtyła's sentiments about religion, he spent hours attempting to dissuade him from taking this step. He invoked the sanctity of art as a great mission, reminding Karol of the Gospel warning against the waste of talent, and begging him to postpone his decision. Many years later, John Paul II remarked during a pontifical visit to Kraków that "Kotlarczyk believed that the Living Word and the theater are my calling, but Lord Jesus believed that it is priesthood, and somehow we agreed on that."

Father Maliński recounts that Wojtyła reached the final decision when he went to confession at the Wawel Cathedral early in September. Maliński says that he accompanied him uphill to the cathedral, then waited in an antechamber while Karol spent a long time with his confessor, Father Figlewicz. Coming out, Maliński adds, Wojtyła told him: "I want to tell you that I have decided to become a priest. I discussed it with Father Figlewicz."

Other historians doubt this version because Poles, except for priests with special clearances like Figlewicz's, were not allowed in the Wawel. In any event, Karol's desire to study for the priesthood was communicated immediately to Archbishop Sapieha, who was in the process of establishing a secret seminary of the Kraków archdiocese. This secret seminary tapped the resources of the faculty of the banned Theological Department of Jagiellonian University. It was headed by Father Jan Piwowarczyk, a well-known theologian, writer, and journalist. Wojtyła was one of ten candidates approved by Sapieha for the first academic year of underground studies.

The seminary began to function in October 1942. Except for Wojtyła, the students lived in the countryside, usually falsely designated as "parish secretaries," and traveled to Kraków for lessons at secret locations. They were taught individually, and in many instances they were unaware until the end of the war of one another's participation in the program. Simultaneously, an underground Jagiellonian University was created, reaching a total of eight hundred students in a variety of subjects taught by professors who had escaped deportation to concentration camps.

Although he was regarded as a cleric by the Church by virtue of his seminarian's status, Wojtyła's life did not change visibly. He continued work at the Solvay plant and he kept up his commitments to the Rhapsodic Theater for six months. At his request, Unia formally released him from his oath of membership in the underground organization as he prepared to enter the secret seminary.

The difference was that on top of all his other obligations, Karol had to study in the secret seminary at great risk. To be caught as a secret seminarian meant deportation to a camp or an execution squad. At least five youths studying theology illegally at a German-approved religious institution where only "practical" liturgical subjects were permitted were arrested in Gestapo raids and died in Oświęcim. A cleric named Szczęsny Zachuta, who belonged to an underground organization preparing Jews for Catholic baptism while he studied theology, was arrested and shot. And shortly after the secret seminary was born, its rector, Father Piwowarczyk, was detained on charges of printing illegal leaflets. He was released after several months in a Kraków jail.

As a cleric and candidate for priesthood, Karol was authorized to perform certain liturgical functions, ranging from administering baptism to the blessing of marriages, bringing Viaticum to the dying, and presiding at worship and prayer of the faithful. But because he was a secret cleric, he is not known to have performed any of these acts openly during his seminary period. Naturally, he did not wear ecclesiastic garb.

But soon Wojtyła was given an opportunity to participate directly in liturgy. Along with another seminarian, Franciszek Konieczny, he was invited to assist every morning at the Mass celebrated by Archbishop Sapieha in his private chapel. Karol and Konieczny had met in the past, but neither was aware that the other belonged to the secret seminary. This was the first time Wojtyła had seen the archbishop since the Wadowice high school graduation more than four years earlier, but Sapieha most evidently remembered him. Karol and Konieczny served at the Archbishop's Mass for two years, following which they had breakfast with Sapieha.

He rose at dawn to cross the river to the Archbishop's Palace on Franciszkańska Street for the 6:30 A.M. Mass, then raced to the Solvay plant for the day, visited his father's grave at the cemetery, and rushed home for his secret theological homework and theater planning with Kotlarczyk. Sometimes, Wojtyła went to the Archbishop's Mass after the night shift. And he had agreed to teach Latin to his friend Maliński, who also resolved to be a priest.

Late in November, Karol attended the commemorations of the four-hundredth anniversary of the birth of St. John of the Cross, the Mystical Doctor of the Church and the founder of the Order of Discalced Carmelites. The order was named after Mount Carmel. He was especially interested in St. John's poetry, borrowing his works from the Kraków monastery's Bibliotheca Carmelitana. Presently, Wojtyła called on Father Józef Prus, the provincial of the Discalced Carmelites in the region, conveying his hope and desire to join the order. But the Carmelites were not accepting novices under wartime conditions, and Father Prus doubted that a healthy young man like Karol would be allowed by the Germans to quit his strategic job to be a monk. He suggested gently that Karol might talk to him after the war.

Unperturbed, the next day Wojtyła played one of the lead roles in Mickiewicz's epic drama-poem *Pan Tadeusz,* a defiant, patriotic work. Just as he began to slowly recite the confession of Father Robak, the quiet in the apartment was shattered by a German loudspeaker installed across the street. Although the war was going badly for the Nazis, especially in the Soviet Union, the speaker was announcing new "victories." Tadeusz Kwiatkowski remembers that Karol "did not interrupt [the recitation], did not alter his tone. He spoke softly, calmly, as if he was not hearing the barking of the loudspeaker. . . ."

Wojtyła's farewell performance at the Rhapsodic Theater was in March 1943. From then on, his theological studies and work at the Solvay plant took up all his time. Serving at Mass every morning at the Archbishop's Palace brought him closer and closer to Sapieha.

Life for Wojtyła now settled down to a busy routine, and by 1944, optimism swept Kraków and the rest of Poland. The United States was in the war, the Allies had conquered all of North Africa and Egypt and were assaulting Italy, and the Soviets were smashing the Nazi armies the length of the eastern front. There was quiet sadness over the destruction of the Warsaw Ghetto in the Jewish Uprising of April 1943, and the underground organizations in and around Kraków strove to hide Jews from Nazi wrath.

On the afternoon of February 29, 1944, walking home from the Solvay plant after working two shifts, Wojtyła was struck by a passing heavy German army truck and thrown to the ground. Hitting his head against the sharp edge of the sidewalk, Karol lost consciousness. He might have died if Józefa Florek, a passenger in a tramway running along the empty street, had not spotted Karol lying on the pavement. She jumped out of the tramway and ran over to him, thinking he was dead. Just then, a German army command car halted there and an officer examined Wojtyła, discovering that he was alive. The officer instructed Mrs. Florek to bring some water from a nearby ditch to wash the blood from Karol's head and face, then flagged down a lumber truck, ordering the driver to take the injured man to a hospital. Wojtyła never learned the identity of the German officer. But he wrote a letter of thanks to Mrs. Florek.

At the Kopernik Street hospital, Karol was diagnosed as having suffered a brain concussion. It appeared, however, that he had remained unconscious for about nine hours, an unusually long time, which was potentially dangerous. Reminiscing about the accident fifty years later, almost to the day, John Paul II said he believed that "Providence saved me" in letting him live despite the lengthy period of unconsciousness. When a guest asked whether there was a parallel between the 1981 attempt on his life on St. Peter's Square and the Kraków accident, the pope replied, "Yes, it was Providence in both cases."

Wojtyła was released from the hospital after two weeks but was ordered to spend several more weeks convalescing. He moved to the new home of his old friend Irena Szkocka, whom he used to call Grandmother. The Germans had confiscated the Szkockis' villa across the Vistula, but they found a comfortable house, complete with a piano, on Szwedzka Street in Dębniki, just around the corner from Wojtyła's Tyniecka Street abode.

Karol spent his summer vacation in July with the parish priest in the small town of Raciborowice near Kraków, Father Adam Biela, also a Wadowice native. But as soon as he returned home, the great Warsaw Uprising erupted on August 1, 1944. On August 6, "Black Sunday," the German command, fearing an uprising in Kraków, launched a gigantic roundup operation throughout the city. At least eight thousand men and young boys were caught in the dragnet. Some were released later, others taken to prisons and concentration camps.

The Nazi sweep reached Dębniki and Tyniecka Street where soldiers and policemen invaded houses to grab the men and hurl them into canvas-covered trucks to be taken away. Karol and the Kotlarczyks were at home during the raid along Tyniecka Street, and Mrs. Kotlarczyk begged him and her husband to hide in the bushes in the garden. "But," she recalled, "my begging was in vain. Karol knelt and began to pray. Finally, the Germans broke into our two-story house. The upstairs apartments had to be opened. . . . I don't know how it happened, but they didn't enter our quarters in the basement. Karol still knelt in prayer, my husband sat motionless at the table."

The roundup convinced Archbishop Sapieha that his secret seminarians would be safer at his residence, and he sent out word for them to come immediately to the palace on Franciszkańska Street at the edge of the Old Town. To bring Wojtyła, he dispatched Father Mikołaj Kuczkowski, a young priest from Wadowice attached to the palace. Kuczkowski reached the Tyniecka Street house, then asked Mrs. Szkocka to walk back with him and Karol for extra security. It was a strange procession. The elderly Mrs. Szkocka marched ahead, watching out for German patrols, followed by Kuczkowski in his cassock and Wojtyła several meters behind. Karol, the last seminarian to report, entered the palace wearing his rough work trousers, a shirt opened at the neck, and his wooden clogs. He clutched two big notebooks under his arm. Mieczysław Maliński, Karol's friend who had also joined the secret seminary, was summoned to the palace at the same time.

The archbishop decided that the seminarians—seven of them—would stay at his palace until the end of the war. He ordered them to put on cassocks so that they would look like clerics. It was the first time Wojtyła wore priestly attire. Now the seminarians could study full-time. They slept on iron bedsteads in reception halls on the first floor of the vast palace, but they were forbidden to step into the street. The war was not over yet. Jan Tyranowski managed to slip occasionally into the palace to visit Wojtyła and his other seminarian friends. The last time Karol saw the tailor before he died was during such a clandestine visit.

Living at the palace, Karol no longer went to work at the Solvay plant, and the Nazis began looking for him, first with urgent letters addressed to Tyniecka Street, then with police visits. Archbishop Sapieha thereupon instructed Father Figlewicz to ask Solvay's general manager Kułakowski to remove Wojtyła's name from the workers' roll. It was illegal, but Kułakowski did it, remarking that "I would jump into the fire for the Archbishop. . . ."

On November 11, 1944, Sapieha personally celebrated the tonsure ceremony on Karol, at his request, in the private chapel. Tonsure, which is the shaving of the crown of the head, was a ceremony symbolizing the entrance into the clerical state (but it was formally abolished by Pope Paul VI in 1972, because it had fallen into disuse).

On January 17, 1945, Father Figlewicz celebrated the last

wartime Mass at the Wawel Cathedral. During the night, the Germans fled Kraków. On the morning of January 18, Soviet troops entered the city.

With the end of the war, the archbishop's seminary ceased to be secret. It moved to the buildings below the Wawel originally housing the Kraków Spiritual Seminary that the SS troops had commandeered in 1939. The seminary was again part of the Theological Faculty of Jagiellonian University. Karol Wojtyła now concentrated on his studies of St. John of the Cross, learning Spanish to read his works in the original. In April, he was named assistant instructor at the university's Theological Faculty—with a salary—conducting seminars on the history of dogma. He was just shy of his twenty-fifth birthday.

But Karol was also back to poetry. While living at the archbishop's palace during the fall of 1944, he composed an extremely long contemplative poem, *The Song About the Hidden God.* It was published, without a signature, in four sequential issues of the Carmelite monthly magazine, *The Voice of Carmel,* in 1946 and 1947—his adult debut in print. The first segment carried Wojtyła's name, but he insisted that it be removed, and the publisher had to recall the first press run.

The final strophe of the poem begs the Lord "not to reject my Adoration, which is nothing to you, because you are wholly within Yourself," but that for the poet this Adoration is "everything . . . a stream that tears the banks apart, before confiding its immense longing in the oceans. . . ."

The poem, not one of Wojtyła's easiest, is very much in the spirit of the mystical Carmelites. Karol returned to the order to apply again for the novitiate. Father Leonard Kowalówka, whom he knew slightly, was the superior of novices at the Carmelites' monastery at Czerna near Kraków, and Karol visited him in mid-1945 to make his request.

But Archbishop Sapieha had no intention of letting Wojtyła become a monk. He informed him that after all the wartime losses, the Church needed diocesan priests—and his favorite cleric remained in the seminary.

And he moved along in his progress toward full priesthood. He signed up for the fourth year of theological studies at the Seminary—the 1945–1946 academic year—taking on a very heavy load that ranged from pure theology and liturgy to canon law and a special moral theology course on "the right to live." Presciently or not, the choice of this particular course would serve him as one of the foundations during the most controversial years of his pontificate.

On December 21, 1945, Wojtyła received from the archbishop the minor orders of exorcist and acolyte (which would also be abolished in 1972). He ended the year spending Christmas with Father Stanisław Czartoryski, a friend, at a mountain parish. He had no family to join for the holidays.

While Karol Wojtyła's attentions were centered on his ecclesiastic future, newly liberated Poland was undergoing powerful political shocks. Polish communist leaders who had spent the war in Moscow had entered the country in the wake of victorious Soviet forces, which included a Soviet-commanded Polish army—one of whose young officers was Lieutenant Wojciech Jaruzelski, later Poland's communist president—and they were poised to assume political power. The bulk of the anti-communist Home Army underground was destroyed by the Germans in the 1944 Warsaw Uprising, and the pro-Soviet leadership did not face serious challenge.

Subsequently, the Yalta Conference in February 1945 forced the creation of a coalition government dominated by the communists, who held the presidency and the premiership of the nation. The ranking noncommunist was Peasant Party chief Stanisław Mikołajczyk, who was named deputy premier in the new regime after serving as prime minister of the London-based Polish government-in-exile. The destroyed Home Army took its orders from London.

The coalition government assumed power in Warsaw on June 27, 1945, and the process of communization was under way. The nation was polarized. Many young idealists supported the new order because they believed it would bring justice and economic development to Poland—somewhere along the lines of what Karol Wojtyła had outlined in his letters to his friend Kotlarczyk after the 1939 defeat, and what the Christian Unia group was advocating in the early 1940s. But, of course, they were not proposing Marxism-Leninism. In fact, Karol warned in a 1941 letter to Kotlarczyk against "the red banner and an unreal international humanism . . . that has nothing to do with Polishness, except for the language."

Kraków was regarded by the new authorities as a "black," "reactionary," and "clerical-landlord" city, and they were not altogether wrong. On May 3, 1946, a prewar patriotic holiday, Kraków students rioted against the government and the Polish Workers' Party (the euphemism for the communist party). Security forces fired on the students and some were injured.

There is nothing to indicate how Karol Wojtyła felt about the evolving political situation, although the Church, including Sapieha in Kraków—who had just been named cardinal—was cautiously moving into opposition against the regime.

The Vatican under Pius XII was obsessed with communism's threat to Europe, urging total confrontation. But the Polish episcopate, which had to live with the communists and needed to protect the Church at home, behaved more carefully and diplomatically—even after it was directly attacked. In September 1945, for example, the new authorities terminated the concordat between Poland and the Holy See on the grounds that during the war the Vatican, in violation of treaty provisions, had named a German as a bishop of a Polish diocese. Catholic publications had launched a heated debate about the social attitude of Polish Catholics.

Simply watching these unfolding events, Wojtyła was acquiring political experience and subtlety he would require in the years to come.

Meanwhile, Karol passed all his theological exams with flying colors and entered the final phase of his progress toward the priesthood. During spring 1946 he wrote a lengthy essay, "Analysis of Faith, According to St. John of the Cross—Faith as Means of Uniting the Soul with God." But it was thickly written, a problem that would always plague Wojtyła in his theological texts, and in a note he subsequently appended to it, he also recognized that "the analysis is faulty" and that "this analysis of the texts is insufficient . . . some of them cannot serve to demonstrate the validity of the thesis [that is] being propounded." Karol was capable of self-criticism.

On October 13, 1946, Cardinal Sapieha ordained Wojtyła as sub-deacon (an order also abolished by Paul VI) and a week later as full deacon. On that same day, October 20, Wojtyła formally requested his admission to the sacrament of priesthood, affiriming under oath that he was fully conscious of the obligations to be imposed upon him and that he was acting with "complete free will" in so doing.

On November 1, the Day of All Saints, Cardinal Sapieha ordained Karol Wojtyła in his private chapel as a priest of the Roman Catholic Church. On that date, Kraków was paying homage to the victims of the Oświęcim concentration camp, whose ashes were being brought to Rakowiecki Cemetery for burial.

Sapieha was rushing Wojtyła's ordination because he had chosen to send him to Rome for post-graduate studies—instead of assigning him to a parish as most new priests were—and wanted Karol to leave as soon as possible. Sapieha had an extraordinary eye and instinct for talent as well as a very long memory.

Karol was granted the special distinction of celebrating his first Mass at the Wawel Cathedral's Crypt of St. Leonard among the sarcophagi of Polish kings and heroes. Father Figlewicz was present as a witness. Karol said three "silent" Masses for the souls of his mother, father, and brother. They were held on November 2, and attended by all the members of the Rhapsodic Theater (he managed to attend a performance of *King-Spirit* that week). Later, there was a reception at the home of a friend. Father Wojtyła looked handsome and elegant in his Roman collar and cassock. His dark hair was neatly combed to the side.

He celebrated his next Mass at his neighborhood Dębniki church with a beaming Jan Tyranowski in attendance. He resigned his teaching post at the university. On November 11, he christened the daughter of his friends, the Kwiatkowskis, at their house; it was his first christening.

The records at St. Anna's Church show that the daughter was christened by "Carolus Wojtyła Neopresbyter."

On November 15, 1946, Father Karol Wojtyła, traveling with a cleric named Stanisław Starowieyski, boarded a train for Katowice, where they changed to the international train to Paris and then on to Rome.

It was an end and a beginning.

PART THREE

CHAPTER 10

For twenty-six-year-old Father Karol Wojtyła, the voyage from Kraków to Rome was a magic journey from Polish provincialism to the splendors of the legendary Eternal City, the seat of the Roman Catholic Apostolic Church, the fount of great spiritual learning, and a crucial center of postwar political intrigues and battles. This was clearly what the wise Cardinal Sapieha had in mind in dispatching his favorite protégé with such alacrity to embark on his studies abroad.

The year and a half he would spend in Italy was a most precious foundation for Wojtyła's future career. His road to the papacy began at the Belgian College at No. 26, Via del Quirinale, a stone's throw from Palazzo Quirinale where Italian presidents reside, just before Christmas 1946.

Most Polish theological students in Rome lived at the Polish College on Piazza Remuria, near the city's southern walls, but space there was restricted to those attending the Jesuits' Gregorian University. Wojtyła, on Archbishop Sapieha's orders, was to study at the Dominicans' Angelicum University because the conservative-minded old man was opposed to the more liberal Jesuits. This disparity was part of the continuing ideological and theological battle being fought throughout the Church on a variety of levels, including Kraków and Rome, and entering a new phase in the postwar period. The archbishop's preference for the Angelicum also matched Wojtyła's own developing attraction to the demanding Thomist philosophy taught by the Dominicans.

Wojtyła and Stanisław Starowieyski, his cleric friend, went first to the house of the Pallottine Fathers on Via Pettinari, just off Sisto Bridge on the right bank of the Tiber, after arriving from Paris at Rome's Termini railroad station toward the end of November. The Pallottine house was headed by Father Turowski, a Pole, who greeted them warmly. Wojtyła and Starowieyski spent nearly a month there, daily making the fairly long trek on foot to the Angelicum and delightedly discovering the beauty and charm of Rome.

It was the Primate of Poland, Cardinal Hlond, who at Sapieha's request arranged for them to be accepted as residents at the small Belgian College. Hlond was in Rome for an audience with Pope Pius XII, and he agreed to receive Wojtyła to discuss the problem. He then contacted Father Maximilien de Fürstenberg, a Belgian who was the rector of the Belgian College, on his behalf. That was the only meeting Wojtyła ever had with Hlond—an unusual occasion for a young priest—and he remembers very fondly "his great informality and cordiality."

The century-old Belgian College was then housed in a beautiful four-story building with a pleasant garden, hidden behind a wall and surrounded by trees (the building was sold in 1972, and the college moved elsewhere in Rome). It had only twenty-two student-priests and seminarians, including five Americans, who were served their meals by Belgian nuns. Wojtyła was able to improve his French with his Belgian colleagues and the nuns, all bilingual in French and Flemish, while beginning to learn Italian and English. He already spoke German and had taught himself Spanish back in Kraków. And Karol impressed his fellow residents with his prowess at the volleyball they occasionally played in the backyard.

Monsignor Robert W. Schiefen from Rochester, New York, was one of the Americans at the Belgian College. Schiefen and Thomas Larkin, now a retired bishop, had undertaken to teach Wojtyła English, and Schiefen recalls that when, as a lark, they taught him some "naughty" words, he would laughingly exclaim in English, "Oh, you're pulling my leg!" Schiefen says that Karol was so "avid" to learn the language that he listened to the Americans at meals with intensity that was "almost like eavesdropping."

As to the college, Schiefen describes it as having been "pure hardship." The building had no bathrooms until the British army installed them while using it after the liberation of Rome. When Wojtyła arrived there in 1946, the college had no showers; they were put in about a year later. "It was so cold in the winter," he recalls, "that I had a hotplate under my chair. In the summer, it was awfully hot." The residents each lived in a small room with only a bed, a desk, a chair, and a sink. And "the food was terrible."

The Belgian College was barely a quarter of a mile from the Angelicum, a perfect location. To reach it, Wojtyła walked down Via del Quirinale, past Villa Pia Park next door and the Jesuit church of St. Andrew, designed by the great architect of Rome, Giovanni Lorenzo Bernini, who, among his famous works, contributed the colonnades of St. Peter's Square. The Baroque church was important to Karol because it contains at its altar the relics of St. Stanisław Kostka, a Polish Jesuit saint who died there of malaria during his novitiate in 1568. This St. Stanisław is the patron of Polish youth, and Karol's neighborhood church in Dębniki in Kraków bears his name.

From the church, where he stopped to pray every day, Wojtyła marched several hundred meters down Via 24 Maggio to arrive at Largo Angelicum. The university stands on a hill rising above the square and the busy traffic of the surrounding streets. Piazza Venezia, where Mussolini delivered his fiery speeches just a few years earlier, is three blocks away.

Founded by the Dominicans in 1577, the university's official name in Wojtyła's time was Istituto Internazionale Angelicum. It has now the rank of a papal university, the St. Thomas Pontifical University, in homage to St. Thomas Aquinas. Its compound stands in the midst of a glorious garden. Atop the hill, the Dominicans' white-walled church is on the left, and the main academic buildings on the right. In a reddish terra-cotta color, the academic buildings, including faculty residences, were built during the Mussolini regime. A monastery-like inner courtyard is the center of the principal structure, with corridors leading from it to the classrooms and apartments. It is a serene place. Roman ruins run down a narrow street adjoining the Angelicum, and from the windows there is a splendid view of the Imperial Forum and the churches and palaces of downtown Rome.

Father Wojtyła instantly fell in love with the city. In a letter to Helena Szkocka, a daughter of his old friend Grandmother Szkocka, he wrote that "to begin to belong to Rome [is] a basic thing . . . a chapter that absolutely cannot be clarified in a few sentences. There are so many levels, so many aspects of this subject. One continuously relates to different details of it, and one feels richer all the time."

In 1979, shortly after his election, John Paul II spoke of "how alive is in my memory my first encounter with the Eternal City." He said: "It was late autumn of 1946, when, after I was ordained as priest, I arrived here to continue my studies. . . . I carried in me the image of Rome from history, from literature and from the entire Christian tradition. For many days, I crisscrossed the city, which then had one million inhabitants, and I couldn't fully find the image of that Rome I had brought with me. Slowly, slowly, I found it. It came to me especially after touring the catacombs—the Rome of the beginnings of Christianity, the Rome of the Apostles, the Rome of Martyrs, the Rome that exists at the beginnings of the Church and, at the same time, of the great culture that we inherit."

But Wojtyła has not mentioned publicly having met Pope Pius XII, who was then nearing seventy-one, at a private audience for Belgian College students arranged by Rector de Fürstenberg. The meeting probably did not last more than a few minutes, and chances are that Pacelli said nothing memorable to him during the ten or fifteen seconds of personal introduction. The pope was always ill at ease with visitors, and Wojtyła most likely did not do more than kiss the Ring of the Fisherman.

Still, it was uncommon for a young Polish priest to meet the pontiff at all at a private audience. And, above all, it was the first time Karol entered the inner sanctum of the Vatican, and one can only wonder whether it had occurred to him that one day *he* would be receiving and blessing visitors at the papal apartments and halls of the Apostolic Palace. The surroundings are simply unforgettable: the great silent halls and broad corridors filled with magnificent sacred art, the Clementine throne hall, the imposing Swiss Guards with their halberds, wearing the vertically striped black-and-yellow uniforms, the stern ushers in white tie and tails, and a deep sense of divine presence.

Meanwhile, Karol Wojtyła prayed almost every Sunday morning at the parish church in Garbatelli, a poor workers' district near St. Paul-Outside-the-Walls Basilica. In March 1947, immediately after Easter, he and Starowieyski drove to San Giovanni Rotondo, near Naples, to attend a lengthy, ecstatic Mass celebrated at a sanctuary there by the famous white-bearded Father Francesco Forgione Pio, a Capuchin monk with a miracle-maker reputation whose stigmata wounds on his hands, feet, and sides had been reappearing regularly since World War I.

Thousands upon thousands of worshippers lined up to confess before him at Casa Sollievo della Sofferenza (House of Relief of Suffering), and legend has it that Padre Pio, upon hearing Wojtyła's confession, knelt at his feet, predicting that he would be called to the Throne of St. Peter and be the target of an assassination attempt. Neither John Paul II nor the Vatican have ever commented on these reports.

But in 1962, as a bishop, Wojtyła supposedly wrote Padre Pio, asking him to pray for a Kraków woman scholar and mother of four children, suffering from cancer, and a week later to inform him of her sudden recovery and thank him for the prayers. Both letters are part of the dossier in the Vatican procedure toward the monk's beatification, now underway. On November 1, 1974, on the thirtieth anniversary of his priestly ordination, Wojtyła, then a cardinal, returned to San Giovanni Rotondo to celebrate Mass in the little church carved out in a rock in memory of Padre Pio and to spend three days there in prayer and reminiscences in the company of three Polish prelates personally the closest to him. Having encountered the Capuchin, Wojtyła had experienced a major mystical moment. And the

"Prophecy of Padre Pio" is nowadays an accepted part of papal lore.

After the 1974 visit to San Giovanni Rotondo, Wojtyła and Starowieyski went to Subiaco in the hills forty miles east of Rome, which is the site of the cave where St. Benedict of Nursia is said to have meditated in solitude for three years late in the fifth century before founding the Order of Benedictine monks. St. Benedict is one of the Church figures that John Paul II venerates the most, and, as it happens, Gregory the Great is the only authority for the known facts of the saint's life. In his *Dialogues,* Gregory describes Benedict as "conspicuous for [his] discretion," the term being used in the contemporary meaning of "humanism."

And Wojtyła took advantage of his time in Italy to visit other great sanctuaries, churches, monasteries, and museums, from Assisi of St. Francis to Monte Cassino of the Benedictines, Siena of St. Catherine, Capri, Naples, Florence, Milan, and Venice. After a year and a half, he had mastered Italy in its sacred aspects and vistas. He also discovered the monastery of Mentorella, established by Polish Resurrectionist Fathers, high up on Mount Guadagnolo in 1857, revisiting it within a few days of his papal election.

Karol Wojtyła's personal life has been punctuated by tragedy and suffering. In his public and ecclesiastic life, on the other hand, he has enjoyed the most extraordinary success from the very outset in forging links and friendships on the highest and most useful levels imaginable. Inevitably, year after year, one contact led to another, one friendship to another, until an impressive human network grew around him. His personality was vital in these relationships, but Karol also had the astounding good fortune of finding himself in the right place at the right time.

Cardinal Sapieha, of course, was his great patron until he died in 1951, having launched Wojtyła's career and supervised his progress through the archdiocese back home. In the course of a visit to Rome in 1947, when he was eighty, Sapieha found the time to visit Karol at the Belgian College.

The Belgian College and the Angelicum were the first

platforms for Wojtyła's lasting Church friendships. De Fürstenberg, the rector of the college, became a cardinal in 1967—at the same time that his former disciple Karol Wojtyła received the red hat from Pope Paul VI. Three of his conservative Angelicum professors—the Irishman Michael Browne, the Italian Aloiso Ciappi, and the Frenchman Pierre-Paul Philippe—also became cardinals. Wojtyła kept in touch with them long after graduating (but Wojtyła also attended lectures on metaphysics at the Jesuits' Gregorian University).

Father Marcel Uylenbroeck, a colleague at the Via del Quirinale residence, introduced him during their first summer vacation to a fellow Belgian priest, Joseph Cardijn, who after founding the Jeunesse Ouvrière Catholique (JOC) was named cardinal by Paul VI. To general surprise, Cardijn soared from plain priest to the purple in one jump. Uylenbroeck was already Cardijn's closest collaborator, and his Belgian connection proved to be extremely important to Father Wojtyła before too long.

Theologically, perhaps the most significant relationship developed by Wojtyła in Rome was with Father Réginald Garrigou-Lagrange, a white-robed French Dominican and professor of dogmatic and spiritual theology at the Angelicum. An authority on moral theology, an ascetic and mystic, Garrigou-Lagrange was regarded as one of the leading theologians of the century. He took Wojtyła under his wing—he was sixty-nine at the time (and would live to be ninety-two)—and became his mentor in the same profound sense that Jan Tyranowski had been his spiritual mentor in Kraków.

Known as "Réginald the Rigid," Garrigou-Lagrange was an outstanding authority on Thomism, refining Wojtyła's understanding of its multilayered philosophy and theology. Thomist teachings are the philosophy and theology as expounded by St. Thomas Aquinas. Thus Pope Leo XIII, a most enlightened pontiff, directed the clergy in his *Aeterni Patris* encyclical issued in 1879 to take the teachings of St. Thomas as the basis of their theological position. It was a response to "modernist" and free-conscience trends of the day. As a leading specialist in the mystical theology of St. John of the Cross, Garrigou-Lagrange was the "promoter" at the Angelicum of Wojtyła's doctoral dissertation on the Spanish saint, a theme that had fascinated Karol since he first met Jan Tyranowski. Garrigou-Lagrange had a formidable mind, and John Paul II considers him his greatest teacher. Another he remembers keenly from the Angelicum is the Polish Dominican Father Jacek Woroniecki, his metaphysics professor.

But as Wojtyła embarked on his studies, the Angelicum and much of the theological world was shaken by a great wave of spiritual and intellectual agitation, and he was rapidly drawn into it. Postwar politics and ideologies were its ingredients, too.

Rome and Italy had not yet quite recovered from the war when Father Wojtyła arrived from his ravaged country late in 1946. The city, which had suffered some damage from Allied bombing during the nine-month German occupation, had been liberated over two years before, but hunger and political chaos prevailed in much of the country. Now, the overriding issue was whether Italy would turn into a democracy or be conquered by her powerful communist party.

The Church under Pius XII was deeply engaged in this struggle, but it was also deeply divided between those in the Vatican who believed that communists could best be defeated by democratic political parties and those who saw salvation in a far-right Catholic party that could possibly lead to a rigid dictatorship. And, naturally, the whole dispute touched upon what role the Church should properly play in secular Italian politics.

For Wojtyła, who came from a country on the verge of falling under complete communist control, the Italian political battle over communism and the Church was enormously educational. In Rome, he could observe the postwar political struggle as it was developing on the world stage, in contrast with the specific situation in Eastern Europe where communism was triumphant principally because it was backed by Soviet armed power. The lessons learned in Rome would be useful before too long when, as bishop and cardinal back in Poland, Wojtyła would be a key figure in the complex confrontations between the Polish church and the communist authorities.

And, as he soon realized, the theological dimension was an exceedingly important element in the political controversy. It involved his mentor at the Angelicum and, in time, it involved him personally as he searched for solutions to the crises in a rapidly changing world. The interplay between theology and politics was an art and a reality, as Wojtyła learned in Rome in the mid-1940s. When he returned to Rome for good more than three decades later, he was able to demonstrate at once how well he had understood the theological-political dimension.

Watching Pius XII in action (or lack of it), Wojtyła spotted the pope's two principal character traits, learning the strengths and weaknesses of the papacy.

One of these traits was Pacelli's belief in total concentration of power. He had refused, for example, to name a new secretary of state, the second most powerful position in the Vatican, after Cardinal Luigi Maglione died in 1944. Maglione was much more in favor of democratic solutions in Italian and world politics than the pontiff, and he was attracted by some of the emerging new theological concepts that Pacelli saw as dangerously liberal.

For the next fourteen years, Pius XII functioned as his own secretary of state, a notion John Paul II would never entertain during his own pontificate. In the Holy See, the secretary of state is in charge of both internal Church affairs and foreign policy and diplomacy. At the same time, however, Pope Wojtyła knew everything about the advantages of a subtle and intelligent concentration of power, demonstrating it by his dislike of too independent-minded secretaries of state or prefects of Curia Congregations.

Pacelli's interesting trait was his proclivity for isolation. He rarely consulted his cardinals and archbishops, and detested meeting strangers. Such an attitude was wholly alien to Wojtyła. Moreover, Wojtyła understood the dangers in isolating top decision-makers—which popes are—and as bishop, arch-bishop, and cardinal in Kraków and as pontiff in Rome, he always surrounded himself with people who held views and ideas from which he could profit.

Wojtyła always was a superb listener and master of silences, blessed with the gift of making his interlocutors believe instantly that he was absolutely enthralled by their thoughts.

In the mid-1940s, the theological-political dimension in Church affairs emerged powerfully from the writings of French Catholic thinkers, creating considerable conflicts in Rome. Among the most captivating of these voices was Jacques Maritain, a lay Catholic philosopher of great renown, who became France's ambassador to the Holy See late in 1945, appointed by General Charles de Gaulle and remaining in Rome until 1948.

A Thomist and therefore theologically conservative, Maritain was politically liberal, strongly supporting new democratic trends in Europe, Latin America, and elsewhere. Just before the war, he wrote *Humanisme Intégral* to urge greater humanism in the Church, and *Christianisme et Démocratie* while in exile in the United States in 1943. Maritain proclaimed "New Christendom" in its political-theological dimension and was one of the fathers of the philosophy of Existentialism (long before Jean-Paul Sartre).

Maritain's New Christendom advocated a "Third Way" between Western liberalism and Soviet communism, an idea that had considerable appeal among Catholic intellectuals in the immediate postwar period. Karol Wojtyła's writings in the late 1940s, after his first exposure to the West, as well as after his return to Kraków and during his pontificate—and even after the fall of communism in the late 1980s—reflect many of the Third Way views, although he carefully skirts calling them by this name.

Archbishop Giovanni Battista Montini, the future Pope Paul VI, who was a close friend of Maritain and at the time a very influential Vatican undersecretary of state, was also quite sympathetic toward New Christendom. It fitted into his efforts to build a powerful Christian Democratic party in Italy, positioned between the extreme right and communism. He told Maritain on one occasion that the role of the Church in postwar reconstruction and world crises "must not be of a political force, but a spiritual force" that would guarantee "unity and liberty." He added that "the spiritual

Rome must be more open and move toward the international spirit," which clearly was not the case under Pius XII.

After his 1963 election, Paul VI became the Church's first determined voice in the defense of human rights worldwide—his immediate predecessor, John XXIII, having set the policy in motion—and he would later be a crucial supporter of Karol Wojtyła in his rise in the Church hierarchy. This was a perfect example of the linkage of theology and politics in the life of the Church.

Another powerful current coming out of France was the "New Theology," basically propounding a modernization of the Church's approach to world problems and to the relationship with its own faithful at a time of runaway secularization. The impulse toward New Theology was born, interestingly, among both Dominican Thomist scholars and Jesuit scholars. The leading Dominican Thomists in this movement were theologians Marie-Dominique Chenu, an Angelicum graduate, and Yves Congar, very distinct from the highly conservative Garrigou-Lagrange. The Jesuits were Henri de Lubac, a professor of fundamental theology, and Jean Daniélou, a wartime aviator and now a historian of the "Primitive Church."

Taken together, their ideas called for a greater involvement of priests with the people in their parishes and dioceses, and with their daily problems. They wanted the Church to become part of the contemporary reality and to retain (or attract) Catholics by direct engagement in their lives. The concept of worker-priests—priests with jobs of workers—then taking root in France and Belgium, was born from the New Theology. It appealed to Father Wojtyła and fascinated him.

What disturbed him at the same time, however, was that Garrigou-Lagrange, his mentor, had turned on the New Theology and New Christendom with uncontained rage. In an article published in 1946, shortly before Wojtyła entered the Angelicum, Garrigou-Lagrange denounced the four chief proponents of new Catholic thinking for distorting the ideas and philosophy of St. Thomas, for having referred to traditional Thomism as "theological imperialism," and for inviting Protestant and Eastern Orthodox theologians to a dialogue. As George Hunston Williams, an American Protestant Church historian and Harvard professor of divinity, wrote later, the onset of the new ideas "caused a vortex of consternation within the Angelicum."

Seventy-year-old Pius XII, whose most recent encyclical had been *Mediator Dei,* devoted to liturgy, sided with Garrigou-Lagrange's condemnation of the newfangled French ideas and criticized the worker-priest experiment. But Paul VI would appoint both Daniélou and de Lubac as cardinals. In a further twist in postwar Church zigzag history, these two Jesuits would subsequently join the conservative and authoritarian camp.

Of historical importance to the Church—and personally to Wojtyła—was Pius XII's decision immediately after the war to internationalize the Curia in terms of the College of Cardinals and major Congregations that until then had had a great preponderance of Italians. The pope, who had even considered naming Cardinal Francis Spellman of New York as secretary of state, created additional West European and U.S. cardinals, and opened the door to cardinals from the Third World, notably Latin America and Africa.

On July 3, 1947, Father Wojtyła passed summa cum laude the exams for his seminary teaching certificate, the equivalent of a master's degree. He received the highest possible grades from the four examiners in oral Latin-language tests.

Several days later, he and his friend Stanisław Starowieyski left by train for Marseilles, the first stop on their working vacation tour of France, Belgium, and Holland. Cardinal Sapieha instructed them to make the trip—and financed it—so that Karol could become familiar with "pastoral methods" in those countries, especially among Polish workers employed there. Starowieyski was still a cleric, but Sapieha wanted Karol to have company. As usual, he was directing Wojtyła's career like an unfolding battle plan.

In Marseilles, Wojtyła went to the docks to meet Father Jacques Loew, the French Dominican who was one of the founders of the "Mission de France" movement of worker-priests. A convert from Protestantism, Father Loew had first worked as a stevedore and now was the chaplain of

Marseilles dock workers. He made a huge impression on Karol, who was his guest at the Workers' Mission of St. Peter and St. Paul.

In an article printed on March 6, 1949, in Kraków's *Tygodnik Powszechny* (Universal Weekly)—his first published article, and front-paged at that—Wojtyła explained the phenomenon of Father Loew: "Father Loew came to the conclusion that the [Dominican] white habit by itself does not say anything anymore today. He decided to identify with his lambs. Living among workers, he decided to become one of them. After a time, he also became the pastor of his companions."

Wojtyła went on to tell his Polish readers that Cardinal Emmanuel Célestin Suhard, the archbishop of Paris, "wept after reading the bitter truth" about the critical situation of the French Church, which kept losing the faithful, in the book *La France, Pays de Mission?* by Father Henri Godin, the priest who inspired the worker-priest movement. To understand Wojtyła's immediate attraction to the worker-priest idea, it suffices to recall that only three years earlier he was a manual worker himself, praying on the factory floor and discovering the mysteries of the Gospel among limestone furnaces. Finding himself among the workers of Marseilles, meeting Father Loew, and repeating this experience in Paris, Brussels, and Charleroi, Wojtyła felt perfectly at home. It was a continuation of his Solvay quarry and factory life in Kraków, when he was the nearest thing to a worker-priest.

In Paris, where he stayed at the Polish Seminary on Rue des Irlandais, he went to see the suburban workers' parish of Father Michonneau, the author of *Missionary Community Parish,* another influential book in that field. In the Belgian coal region of Charleroi, Wojtyła spent several weeks as a visiting parish priest among Polish emigré miners. Starowieyski, who rejoined him there at the end of the visit, wrote that "Karol already felt at home with his 'parishioners' who gave him a very warm send-off." In Brussels, he called on his Belgian College companion, Father Uylenbroeck, who now was the secretary-general of the Jeunesse Ouvrière Chrétienne, especially active in Belgium.

After his exposure to the social experiments of the

Church in France and Belgium, Wojtyła concluded, as he put it in his Kraków article, that "apostolic work" of this kind is the correct way for the French Church "to reach its non-believers," because "Catholic intellectual creativity alone will not transform the society." His next conclusion, based on what he had observed on the trip, was that "it must be anticipated that in the near future a new type of apostolate will be inevitable in all milieus; in some to convert contemporary pagans, in others to prevent 're-paganization.'"

Consequently, he argued, liturgy must be adapted to these environments: "The liturgy of the suburban parishes of Paris or Marseilles is certainly not the liturgy of the great Benedictine abbeys. It must be understandable to the modern proletariat. It must convince him." But for the whole effort to succeed, Wojtyła added, "lay apostle-pioneers are essential," a requirement he would always emphasize, especially when he became pope.

Wojtyła's encounter with the worker-priest movement was another major turning point in his life. His attitude toward not only the relations between the Church and Catholic workers but, just as importantly, toward the social welfare of workers was vastly influenced by his experiences in France and Belgium—on top of his own Kraków worker years. They would define much of his social justice philosophy as part of the Church teachings and be reflected in his sermons and homilies, and later in his encyclicals.

Though John XXIII had banned, in effect, the worker-priest movement in the late 1950s, Wojtyła always had warm words for it. Reminiscing in the early 1980s about his French experiences, John Paul II said, "I brought back with me from all these visits and encounters a respect for the apostolic endeavors, and even a certain admiration for these priests who, with complete determination, search for de-Christianized milieus, and some act as worker-priests in order to be present in this fashion among the working class lost by the Church."

Wojtyła may not have realized it at the time, but among those observing the Mission de France experiment was the papal nuncio to France, Monsignor Roncalli, who would succeed Pius XII as pope in 1958. As John XXIII, he would summon Vatican Council II, which would address the social aspects of the Church in the modern world.

But much as Wojtyła was interested in his Roman studies and his foray into Western Europe, he always had Poland and things Polish on his mind—an attitude that would never change. In a letter from Brussels in October 1947 he informed his friend Kotlarczyk that "I read the Gospel in Polish every day, often aloud." Writing Helena Szkocka from Rome a few months later, Karol assured her that "I maintain incessantly my spiritual contact with the Motherland—through thought, prayer, reading—although I know very little about those close to me. About some, [I know] nothing. . . ."

Wojtyła and Starowieyski were back in Rome late in October, delighted with their tour. They learned and saw a lot. Aside from their discovery of the worker-priests, they had detoured to the shrine in Lourdes below the Pyrenees on their way from Marseilles to Paris for prayer and had visited the great museums of France, Belgium, and Holland for artistic inspiration. And they were treated like beloved guests everywhere they went. Starowieyski wrote with a touch of amazement that in Holland and Belgium "We didn't spend a cent on shelter or meals. . . . Our acquaintances and their great hospitality made this pilgrimage possible." In Paris, they slept at the Polish Seminary and dined at the Polish convent of Nazarethan Sisters.

During the first week of November, Wojtyła signed up for courses at the Angelicum for his second and last academic year there. It was heavy on mystical philosophy, including "Contemplation and Mystical Union with God" and "The Doctrine of St. Thomas on Beatitude," and metaphysics and "Religious Psychology." Father Garrigou-Lagrange was his professor of "Priestly Union with Priest Jesus," and his adviser on the doctoral dissertation on St. John of the Cross that Wojtyła was beginning to write.

On Christmas Eve 1947, Wojtyła and Starowieyski joined their fellow Belgium College residents in singing carols in French, Flemish, English, and German. Karol's baritone voice was loud and clear. And still true to his love of the theater, he presented a recitation of one act of *He Came to the Holy Land,* a play by Adam Bunsch, a Belgian author. The play's heroic figure is Brother Albert, a martyr about whom Wojtyła was already writing his own drama.

Thematically, the dissertation on St. John of the Cross and the play about Brother Albert, both martyrs, were close to each other (Karol was working simultaneously on the two). Both works were built on mysticism and on Thomist teachings, with special emphasis on "Thomist personalism," which appealed particularly to Wojtyła.

The essence of St. Thomas's teachings is that there are two sources of knowledge—the mysteries of Christian faith and the truths of human reason. But, according to him, Revelation, or Christian faith, is the more important of the two. And the chief characteristic of Revelation is that it presents humanity with mysteries, which are to be believed even when they cannot be understood. This concept is the foundation of Thomist mysticism that had so attracted Karol Wojtyła as his own spiritual thinking evolved under the influence of Jan Tyranowski and as part of his instinctive approach to the questions of life and death.

However, Revelation and reason, according to the writings of St. Thomas, are not contradictory, because in the end they rest on *one* absolute truth emanating from God. Thomism also accepts the metaphysics of Aristotle, whom St. Thomas regarded as his intellectual master, to explain the functioning of human reason. His final point is that Christian ethics must be the overwhelming consideration in human behavior and decision making between "natural virtues and vices," the virtues being based on faith.

As a contemporary example of this philosophy and theology, John Paul II holds that all artificial forms of birth control, let alone abortion, are "natural vices" that Catholics must reject as a matter of ethics stemming from faith and the *one* absolute truth. He insists that, in effect, faith goes beyond human reasoning—which, for instance, might claim that birth control is necessary for demographic equilibrium—and that Catholics must make decisions based on their conscience. They must make this choice, he teaches, because artificial birth-control acts are "vices" under "natural law" as extrapolated from the Scriptures. Thus there is no absolute freedom of conscience, and this point is forcefully implied in John Paul II's 1993 encyclical *Veritatis Splendor,* which may be his farewell theological summation, as St. Thomas's *Summa Theologiae* was his.

There have always been multiple Thomist interpretations and trends in theology, but Wojtyła, as he labored on his Angelicum dissertation, preferred Thomist personalism, remaining faithful to it all his life. In a 1961 lecture before philosophy students at the Catholic University in Lublin, Poland, he explained that "personal Thomism is based on the view that the individual good of a person must, as a matter of principle, be subordinated to the common good, but . . . such subordination cannot in any event erase and devaluate the person." Wojtyła stressed that "the freedom of conscience is the basic right of a person," but it must be linked to the Christian doctrine. However, as John Paul II's critics insist, it is the Church alone that reveals "common good" and the absolute truth, and that, indeed, Catholics are not allowed real freedom of conscience.

In Wojtyła's days, the Angelicum was famous for the teaching of the intellectual traditions of St. Thomas—the Aristotelian-Thomist philosophy and metaphysics in the context of reason and faith—but it also welcomed the mystical approach to theology. This was the approach Wojtyła was taking in his dissertation, "Questions of Faith in St. John of the Cross," under the great Garrigou-Lagrange, a specialist in mystical theology.

That St. John himself was a poet—*The Spiritual Canticle* and *The Living Flame of Love* are his most puissant mystical works—must have influenced Wojtyła toward the Spanish saint. In his five-part, 280-page dissertation, written entirely in Latin, he describes the "ecstatic agony" of the soul in search of faith and its "dark nights" of despair. He concludes that St. John of the Cross has shown that contemplation and prayer, as "a mystical experience," lead to true faith and "inner union with God." But Wojtyła remarks that faith alone is not sufficient to achieve "a psychological union of the intellect with God" because it must be faith "nourished by love and illuminated by the gifts of the Holy Spirit, especially of wisdom and reason."

It was not an easy theme. But Father Wojtyła, examined by Fathers Garrigou-Lagrange and Pierre-Paul Philippe, earned the acceptance of his dissertation on June 19, 1948, with the highest possible grades. It was formally confirmed in writing by Father Thomas Carde, the Magnificent Rector of the Angelicum. But Wojtyła was deprived of the title of Doctor of Sacred Theology. Under the Angelicum's rules, dissertations must be printed before the doctoral degree can be awarded. And Karol Wojtyła, the poor Polish priest, had no money for the printing.

Still, his sojourn in Rome had been like a dream. He had written Helena Szkocka that "my time vanishes with enormous speed. . . . I really don't know how a year-and-a-half has gone by. Study, observation, meditation—all act like a spur on a horse. Each day is tightly filled. It gives me the sense that I am serving God according to my possibilities and according to His will, which was indicated [to me] by my superiors. . . ."

On June 15, 1948, Karol Wojtyła returned to Kraków. As he departed Rome, he was leaving behind an optimistic Italy. The paralyzing fear of communism had receded after the Christian Democratic party, backed to the hilt by the Holy See (and the United States), had amply defeated the communist-socialist coalition in the historic elections of April 18.

But the Poland that Father Wojtyła found coming home was moving in a diametrically opposed direction, deeply affecting his work and life.

CHAPTER 11

By midcentury, Eastern Europe was sliding behind the Iron Curtain.

In Poland, the coalition government had come to a quick end, and Deputy Premier Stanisław Mikołajczyk, representing the democratic opposition, had to flee the country. The Polish United Workers' Party (PZPR), a merger of the Workers' Party and the Socialist Party, was formed in 1948, to capture total power. It was the new official name for the communists.

With the exception of Czechoslovakia, where the existing Communist Party had taken over the government in a bloodless coup in February of that year and kept its name, all the ruling communist parties in Eastern Europe were hiding behind euphemistic labels like PZPR. And all the communist-run nations had acquired equally euphemistic official descriptions: all became People's Republics.

In Warsaw, the PZPR was headed by Bolesław Bierut, an old-line communist who also functioned as the President of Poland. Hard-line communist regimes were installed as well in Hungary, East Germany, Romania, and Bulgaria. Yugoslavia under Marshal Tito had broken away from Soviet tutelage in 1948, but her communist government was not any less repressive.

Still, Poland was different from the rest of Eastern Europe. Even Polish communists, who acknowledge that

Poland was following her "own road to socialism," never implanted terror on the scale of the rest of the region, where mass show trials of fellow communists, along with democrats and rightists, were being staged by the regimes to eradicate the slightest form of opposition to their policies. Likewise the Polish regime did not attempt to collectivize the land, leaving most peasants alone.

In a unique fashion, some form of a dialogue or, at least, communication was always maintained between the rulers and the ruled. It reflected the peculiar nature of the Polish society, the nation's old political traditions, and, very importantly, the strength of Polish Catholicism. No other East European nation was as monolithically Catholic.

This applied to the regime and the Church as well. Their bizarre relationship, with each side desiring a dialogue notwithstanding their fundamental differences, was an extraordinary example of this very Polish state of affairs. Even in retrospect, it is astounding that this relationship worked as well as it did—all the way up to the election of John Paul II thirty years later. And what developed subsequently between the Polish pope and the Polish communists is equally astonishing in the history of politics and diplomacy.

When Karol Wojtyła returned to Poland from Rome in 1948, the Polish Church also was undergoing profound changes. Cardinal August Hlond, the Primate of Poland, died on October 23, at the age of sixty-seven, and on November 12, Pope Pius XII named forty-seven-year-old Bishop Stefan Wyszyński to succeed him in that post and as Archbishop of Gniezno and Warsaw. Historically, Gniezno, an ancient city in western Poland, and Warsaw formed a special archdiocese that was always headed by the primate. In the Polish Church, the primate is its lifetime head.

Wyszyński's advent as primate was much more than a generational change of guard. In the Church's own way, it represented the new Poland, too. Whereas Hlond was a typical prelate of the quasi-feudal prewar Poland who fled the country after the Nazi invasion, Wyszyński was a socially conscious scholar, an accomplished politician, and a war hero. He held a doctorate in canon law, lectured with frequency on social economy, and was involved with workers' movements as chairman of the Christian Workers' University and organizer of the Christian Union of Young Workers.

Like all Polish churchmen of the day, Wyszyński was violently anti-communist, just as he had been anti-Nazi and had always fought against extreme nationalism. Unlike most of his generation, however, he was highly critical of the excesses of capitalism, a powerful strain in the Polish Church that is expressed today by John Paul II.

Denouncing communism for "warping the view of the nature of society" and proclaiming "an idea of false liberation," Wyszyński nonetheless blamed its influence on the misdeeds of capitalism. He wrote: "They talk about the increase in Communism, and yet they do not want to believe that the reason for this growth is not so much Bolshevik propaganda as the lack of work, of bread, and of a roof over one's head." During the 1930s, Wyszyński published over one hundred essays and articles to press his social views.

Karol Wojtyła, who could not have known Wyszyński's writings at the time, expressed almost identical sentiments about social injustice in Poland in his "soul-searching" letters to his friend Mieczysław Kotlarczyk as a nineteen-year-old Kraków student in 1939.

It is worth noting that the notion of a Third Way between liberalism and Marxism goes back at least to Wyszyński. John Paul II's post-communism ideas are consistent with his intellectual and spiritual heritage, a point that may not be fully understood in the West—and notably the United States.

During the war, Wyszyński lived in hiding much of the time because of his anti-Nazi writings before the invasion and his growing links with the military underground. Arrested at least once by the Gestapo, he served as chaplain with armed partisan detachments in Polish forests, as professor at the secret university in Warsaw, and as priest at an institute for the blind near the city.

Two years later, Wyszyński was appointed bishop of Lublin, the seat of the Catholic University. At forty-five, he was the youngest Polish bishop (he was consecrated six months before Wojtyła was ordained as priest).

The regime's reaction to Archbishop Wyszyński's ascent to the office of primate underscored the ambiguities in its relations with the Polish Church. In December 1948, a month after his nomination, a top PZPR leader, Aleksander Zawadzki, charged in a speech that "a part of the clergy . . . are trying to take advantage of their clerical positions for anti-state political actions . . . individual priests and the religious are linked to the [anti-regime] underground. . . . We will be opposing that and only that activity which is damaging in the eyes of every progressive man." Obviously, there were priests who were doing exactly that, but the real purpose of the speech was to lay foundations for increasingly severe policies toward the Church.

Apart from minor police harassment, however, no serious effort was made to interfere with Wyszyński's ingress—solemn installation—in Gniezno and Warsaw, where huge crowds of the faithful welcomed him in the streets. The Church was faring considerably less well elsewhere in Eastern Europe.

In Yugoslavia, Archbishop Alojzije Stepinac was arrested in 1946 and sentenced to life imprisonment on charges of wartime collaboration with the Fascists. In Budapest, Cardinal Jozsef Mindszenty, the Primate of Hungary, was arrested on December 26, 1948—a month after Wyszyński became the Polish primate—and similarly given life in prison after a short show trial on trumped-up treason charges (he had spent a year in a Fascist prison just before the end of the war). Among the reasons for Mindszenty's imprisonment may have been his absolute inflexibility toward the communist regime; he would have no dealings with it whatsoever. Over one thousand monks, nuns, and priests would be arrested in Hungary in June 1950. In Prague, Archbishop Josef Beran was sentenced to fourteen years in prison after his arrest in 1949. Three bishops and thousands of priests, monks, and nuns were imprisoned in Czechoslovakia at the same time.

In Warsaw, Wyszyński wasted no time signaling to the regime that he was interested in negotiating some form of understanding—a modus vivendi—with it. His overriding concern was to assure reasonable freedom for the Church and the practice of religion in Poland, particularly in the light of mounting pressures and threats emanating from the authorities.

In March 1949, the regime had sent a communication to the Polish episcopate with the accusation that "there often occurred incidents in which priests patronize or engage in an outright cooperation with various criminal, anti-state groups which are agents of Anglo-American imperialism." Elsewhere in Eastern Europe, the charge of serving "Anglo-American imperialism" would have been followed by a wholesale purge throughout the Church establishment, but in Poland such matters were handled with greater delicacy for the time being.

In the meantime, the Holy See was making life even more complicated for the new primate. Pope Pius XII, continuing to act as his own secretary of state, unwisely wrote a letter to German bishops in February 1948, deploring alleged "injustices" suffered by the Germans after the war as well as the resettlement of twelve million German citizens from the regions east of the Oder and Neisse awarded to Poland by international agreements on the adjustment of postwar frontiers. Poland had lost *its* eastern territories to the Soviet Union, and most of the Polish populations were resettled in the former German lands.

The pope seemed to have retained a soft spot in his heart for the Germans, but his missive triggered loud protests in Poland and, inevitably, was grist for the mill of communist anti-church propaganda. Germany recognized Polish sovereignty over Oder-Neisse territories in a 1971 treaty, but until then the Holy See refused to appoint permanent Polish Church bishops in the ex-German dioceses, resulting in over twenty years of added tensions between the Church and the Warsaw regime.

Undeterred by all these problems, Wyszyński proposed the creation of a permanent "Mixed Commission" as a mechanism for the Church and the regime to resolve problems as they arose in the relationship. The regime accepted the idea with surprising alacrity although it had already set up the rival organization of "Patriotic Priests" to gain support among Catholics. A year was spent negotiating a Church-regime agreement regulating their relations, and the document was signed on April 14, 1950. The negotiations had been punctuated by the government's takeover of the Catholic Caritas relief organization and the arrest of three Jesuit priests.

It was the first such accord between the Church and communist authorities dealing as equals. In Hungary the same year, a completely one-sided agreement was imposed on the Church. The key phrase in the Polish agreement was that "the principle that the Pope is the competent and highest Church authority applies to matters of faith, morality and Church jurisdiction; in other areas the Episcopate will be guided by the Polish *raison d'état.*" The expression means "national interest." The agreement replaced, in effect, the concordat between Poland and the Holy See denounced by the regime in 1945.

Wyszyński was criticized, especially at the Vatican, for signing the agreement. But his rationale was that if the Polish Church was to survive—and with it pure Polish culture and identity—reality required a quid pro quo. Through thick and thin, this notion prevailed until the end of communist rule in Poland. The 1950 agreement served later as the basis for much of John Paul II's secret diplomacy. Even as bishop and cardinal, Wojtyła would use this document in his confrontations with the communists.

In exchange for support for permanent Polish Church jurisdiction in the former German territories (the regime paradoxally needed it to help assert Polish sovereignty there), a commitment to instruct the clergy that "their pastoral work . . . should foster respect for the laws and prerogatives of the state among the faithful," and begrudged willingness to sign Soviet-sponsored international "peace appeals," Wyszyński won what *he* considered to be vital concessions.

Thus the regime had agreed to allow the Catholic University in Lublin to continue functioning—it was the only Catholic university in continued existence in communist Eastern Europe—as well as to guarantee religious education in the schools, permit Catholic publishing activities, and refrain from interference in public worship, processions, and pilgrimages.

For the next four decades, there would be sharp conflicts between the two sides, considerable oppression of the

Church by the regime, and constant violations of the agreement by the communists. Amazingly, however, the link was never really broken, even when Wyszyński was arrested in 1953; and, gradually, the Church was able to extract more and more from the state.

Karol Wojtyła would become a master of this endeavor.

Back in Kraków from his Roman studies, Wojtyła returned to his basement on Tyniecka Street to await his first pastoral assignment, seemingly uninterested in the political situation in Poland. The pastoral orders came three weeks later, on July 8, 1948, after Karol had an opportunity to catch up with his friends.

The new assignment, personally approved by Cardinal Sapieha, was to serve as a vicar in the poor rural parish of Niegowici, some thirty miles east of Kraków, on the road to Tarnów and near the town of Bochnia. The parish, embracing thirteen villages on both sides of the Raba River, including Niegowici, was an ecclesiastic backwater although it is one of the oldest in Poland, founded in 1049. Its small wooden church, surrounded by tall birch trees, was consecrated in 1788 (an earlier church burned down in 1761), and Father Wojtyła's new home, where he arrived on July 28, was the tiny vicarage shack in Niegowici he shared with Father Kazimierz Ciuba, his co-vicar. Both worked under the parish priest, Father Kazimierz Buzała, concentrating on pastoral and teaching duties.

Niegowici had no running water, sewage, or electricity—kerosene lamps provided light for the inhabitants—and it was as primitive as any village in Galicja. Just before Wojtyła was assigned to the parish, the whole region in the Carpathian foothills was ravaged by a flood, severely damaging homes and country roads in and around Niegowici. In the eyes of most of his Kraków friends, the old cardinal had dealt Karol an incomprehensible punishment: to be sent to such a parish meant, they argued, a dead end in his priestly career when it had barely begun, particularly in the wake of his superb academic achievements at the Angelicum.

Wojtyła, however, never showed the slightest disappointment. He may or may not have known that Father Buzała, the parish priest, was held in the highest esteem by Sapieha, and that some of the most distinguished priests in the Kraków archdiocese had served in Niegowici. Clearly, it was the cardinal's idea of pastoral basic training. In any case, Karol threw himself with boundless energy and enthusiasm into parish work.

He was responsible for teaching rural elementary schools in four villages around Niegowici, celebrating daily morning Mass, serving at Sunday Mass, hearing confessions, visiting families and blessing their homes, calling on the sick, marrying couples, and christening babies. Together with his fellow vicar, he organized a Living Rosary circle. On his own, Wojtyła organized a drama circle and produced two plays with student actors at the village's Catholic House. And he twice took students to Kraków to the theater.

The day he first arrived in Niegowici, Father Wojtyła left at least one of his parishioners in a state of acute disenchantment. Driving his horse cart, this peasant was startled to come across a young priest walking down the dusty road in a frayed cassock and cracked boots, with a bulging old briefcase in which he carried his belongings. The man could not believe that the disreputable-looking priest making his way on foot from the railroad station in Kłaj, five miles away, was his new vicar.

But, as usual, Karol quickly attracted friends and admirers. He traveled by horse cart or on foot—in the rain or freezing cold, through mud or snow—from village to village, always available, always good-humored. Riding over bumps and potholes in a horse cart, he usually read a book. Walking, he prayed. When bedding was stolen from the home of an old widow, he took his bedding over to her and slept on a bare bedstead. In the timeless custom of the Polish countryside, Wojtyła responded gravely, "So be it!" to people who greeted him, as they did greet each other, with the words "Praise Him!" meaning Jesus Christ. The evocation of Christ was part of daily life.

Consulted by the parishioners as to how best to celebrate Father Buzała's fiftieth anniversary of priesthood, Wojtyła advised them to raise funds to erect a new church in Niegowici. They did so, and Wojtyła would consecrate the brick-and-mortar church late in 1958, as a freshly minted bishop, in the company of the new parish priest, Józef Gąsiorowski. They had been at the seminary together, and Father Gąsiorowski would preside in 1993 over a special Mass on the fifteenth anniversary of the pontificate of John Paul II. The wooden church had been moved to another village where there was none.

Above all, Wojtyła enjoyed contact with young people—as he would for the balance of his life. In the parish, he organized discussion encounters in orchards and classrooms, helped with the theater, and joined them in singing Christmas carols on cold December evenings.

His seminary friend Mieczysław Maliński, still a cleric, visited Wojtyła in Niegowici on several occasions, and remembers Wojtyła's description of a typical winter visiting day in the parish: "You go out in your cassock, your overcoat, your alb and biretta over beaten path in the snow. But snow will cling to your cassock, then it will thaw out indoors, and freeze again outside, forming a heavy bell around your legs, which gets heavier and heavier, preventing you from taking long strides. By evening, you could hardly drag your legs. But you have to go on, because you know that people wait for you, that they wait all year for this meeting. . . ."

Wojtyła went on warning Maliński about the danger that faced priests dealing day after day with the faithful: "When we talk about confession, the question has to do with the person kneeling before the grille. . . . You can't play at being woodpeckers, one pecking from one side, the other responding from the other side. You can't settle matters with a smooth word. You have to establish a dialogue and treat it seriously and from the heart. Confession is the crowning moment of our apostolic activity. . . . So the question is whether we can preserve the apostolic values. In the absence of deep inner life, a priest will imperceptibly turn into an office clerk, and his apostolate will turn into a parish office routine, just solving daily problems."

He observed that this phenomenon struck him in France, and that he was very impressed with the "sincere experiment" of the worker-priests he had encountered the previous summer there. In fact, he told Maliński, it was so much on his mind that he was writing an article about it, hoping to have it published.

On a day off, early in January 1949, Wojtyła took the train to Kraków, then made his way to Wiślna Street in the Old Town, just around the corner from the Archbishop's Palace. Climbing up the creaking stairs of the old corner building to the first floor, he entered the editorial office of *Tygodnik Powszechny,* the Catholic weekly, carrying his article neatly folded in an envelope under his arm. Jerzy Turowicz, the editor-in-chief, remembers the "thirtyish priest . . . who brought us that first article, about the Mission de France" (actually, Wojtyła was twenty-eight).

Turowicz and Wojtyła had met during the war at the home of a mutual friend among Kraków's intellectuals, but neither of them seems to remember it very clearly. But, Turowicz says, "we thought his article was very interesting, telling the story about the apostolate among workers, and we put it immediately on the front page." It was the beginning of thirty years of literary collaboration and a lifetime friendship.

Another Wojtyła errand in Kraków that winter was passing the exams, which he had requested, for a master's degree in theology at the Theological Faculty of Jagiellonian University. The university agreed to give him credits for attending the secret wartime seminary, then the restored Theological Faculty for a year after the war, as well as the Angelicum in Rome, and let him take the exams. Receiving top grades in Christian philosophy, history of philosophy, Old and New Testament studies, history of the Catholic Church, fundamental theology with liturgy, education, catechesis, and methodology, Wojtyła was awarded his master's degree.

A month later, the Theology Faculty awarded him a Doctorate in Sacred Theology on the basis of an expanded text of his Angelicum dissertation on St. John of the Cross, the degree that was denied in Rome because he lacked the money to print it. Kraków had no such requirements, and Father Władysław Wicher, a leading authority on moral theology who had survived imprisonment at the

Sachsenhausen concentration camp, praised Wojtyła for demonstrating "the psychological aspects of the experience of faith." He noted that "the author has a penetrating and meticulous mind, so meticulous that the reader is lost, not infrequently, in the forest of detail. . . ."

Father Wojtyła's own Christian morality was displayed in Niegowici early in 1949, when he refused to baptize a six-year-old boy named Hiller who had been taken to him by a woman parishioner from the village of Dąbrowa. The boy's secret, she explained, was that he was a Jewish child whom she had brought up as her own after his mother was killed by the Nazis in the Kraków ghetto. The mother begged her to hide the baby from the Germans, but now that the peril was over, the woman believed that he should be christened.

Under questioning by Wojtyła, the woman acknowledged that the boy had relatives in the United States, including a grandmother. Under the circumstances, he decided, it would be "disloyal" and amoral to baptize the child as a Catholic. The boy, he said, should be sent to his family in America. By the month of June, Hiller was sailing to New York aboard the Polish liner *Batory*.

On March 17, 1949, Karol Wojtyła was recalled from Niegowici after seven months in the countryside. Cardinal Sapieha had concluded that his protégé had completed satisfactorily his pastoral basic training, and that the time had come for the next step in his career.

During his service in the parish, Father Wojtyła had blessed the marriages of thirteen couples and christened forty-eight babies.

What the cardinal had in mind for Wojtyła this time was the post of vicar at St. Florian's Church in Kraków, five blocks north of the Old Town.

The church dates back to the twelfth century and is one of the five oldest in Kraków. When Wojtyła took up his duties there in late April, setting up household in a small, two-room rectory apartment, he found St. Florian's to be a fashionable church, with a large attendance by university students.

Sapieha thought that following the rural apostolate experience, Karol should now be exposed to a sophisticated urban religious environment. Because of his scholarly accomplishments, Wojtyła fitted well into an academic milieu, and the cardinal felt strongly that it was vital for the Church at this time of communization efforts by the regime to become a magnet and a home for students and intellectuals.

For Wojtyła, it was an ideal assignment: it combined his scholarly interests with his special rapport with young people, gave him precious freedom to pursue novel pastoral methods, and put him in touch with Kraków's cultural and intellectual elite. St. Florian's was an important step forward in the new phase of his career.

While the cardinal unquestionably attached great weight to the political aspects of attracting university youth to the Church and religion—and while Kraków's intellectuals were extremely political minded—there is nothing in Wojtyła's known writings, his public or even private remarks, or any of his actions to suggest that he was inclined toward any stand in politics. This was not necessarily unusual, and Wojtyła could certainly be accepted as principally a priest-scholar in Kraków society. At the same time, however, it formed part of a behavior pattern for a person who wished to be perceived as "nonpolitical," a pattern that in the foreseeable future would be quite useful. Wojtyła understood the art of political low profile.

The parish priest at St. Florian's was Father Tadeusz Kurowski, himself a scholar and Wojtyła's professor in the wartime underground seminary. Immediately after liberation in 1945, he had pioneered the concept of an activist students' apostolate. In his church, Wojtyła was the vicar dealing with university students and Father Czesław Obtułowicz was the co-vicar in charge of high school students. But Karol was clearly a favorite of Father Kurowski. Father Obtułowicz, who later worked closely with Wojtyła in the Kraków archdiocese, recalls that period well:

> The whole Kraków intelligentsia revolved around Father Kurowski who made good use of the arrival of the young priest from Rome. Because Niegowici was really a vacation after Rome. . . . In those days, it was most unusual to return to Kraków from studies in Rome.

> Polish graduates preferred to stay there, hoping for a post in the Curia. So Father Kurowski pulled Wojtyła in, that is, he invited him to meetings with different people, in different groups. . . . They were rather social encounters. Father Kurowski would invite Wojtyła so that he could talk to people about various things that interested them. . . . He wanted to present him right away to different people who were gathering around the Church, around the academic apostolate. . . . And in those days, after the war, there was great vitality, great intellectual movement in Kraków, now that everything could emerge from the underground. . . .

In close touch with intellectuals, artists, and students—the latter mostly from the nearby Faculty of Fine Arts and the new Polytechnic (Engineering Faculty)—the increasingly popular Father Wojtyła was able to weave around himself and St. Florian's an ever-growing network of friends and acquaintances. In time, it became known as the "Wojtyła milieu," very much alive even after his elevation to the papacy. They are the men and women who visit him at the Vatican and whom he greets warmly on his own pontifical visits to Kraków. From among them, John Paul II has selected a handful of exceedingly interesting people, priests and nuns and secular personages, who came to live in Rome in an official or private capacity. They are very important to the pope.

In a city where culture was a cult, the brilliantly educated, charming, and articulate twenty-nine-year-old priest was soon something of a celebrity. Full of energy, as Father Obtułowicz tells it, Wojtyła performed regular parish church duties along with his work with university students, which ranged from special sermons and homilies to lectures and discussions in St. Florian's sacristy and visits to students' dormitories and rabbit-warren apartments for late-night bull sessions. He took students to the theater and the movies, played chess with them, and led them on mountain hikes.

Wojtyła was in enormous demand, his co-vicar remembers, and hundreds of students of both sexes filled St. Florian's when he conducted pre-Easter retreats or delivered sermons on significant occasions. Having organized a choir to sing Gregorian chant, his efforts were crowned on May 5, 1951, when a full-scale *De Angelis* Gregorian Mass was sung at St. Florian's by men and women university students. The solemnly beautiful chant, usually sung by monk choirs, suddenly made best-seller charts worldwide in the 1990s, coinciding with John Paul II's pontificate.

During the two and a half years spent as a vicar at St. Florian's—before his superiors instructed him to move in still another career direction—Wojtyła seemed never to stop. He launched a program designed to draw the students' parents into Church affairs. The latter was Wojtyła's innovative idea, foreshadowing his rising concentration on problems of the family, marriage, and sexuality. As a vicar at St. Florian's, Father Wojtyła also christened 229 children.

Cardinal Sapieha, who was Karol Wojtyła's greatest patron and champion, died on July 23, 1951, at the age of eighty-five. Tens of thousands wept in the streets of Kraków as the funeral cortège advanced toward the Wawel Cathedral. Wojtyła was heartbroken. But the cardinal had evidently ordered Archbishop Eugeniusz Baziak, who had come earlier from Lwów to assist him and succeed him at the archdiocese, to assume the responsibility for Wojtyła's future.

Consequently, the archbishop, though running the archdiocese on a temporary basis, had the authority to do so. On November 11, 1951, Baziak instructed Wojtyła to take a two-year leave of absence from full-time priestly occupations to study for still another doctorate. Wojtyła requested permission to do both simultaneously—he did not want to lose touch with active priesthood and his other Kraków commitments—but Baziak forbade it. He told Wojtyła that he could undertake specific projects away from his studies only with special permission in every case. However, he allowed him to celebrate Mass at St. Catherine's Church and maintain contact with students at St. Florian's.

In his latest incarnation, Wojtyła was naturally free to use his own time in personal pursuits. At St. Florian's, he had resumed composing poetry, kept working on a new drama, attended Rhapsodic Theater performances still directed by his friend Kotlarczyk, and took private English lessons. He also began wearing glasses in public because of his shortsightedness; they were solid, horn-rimmed. There are thousands of photographs of Wojtyła wearing glasses when he was a Kraków priest, then bishop and cardinal. There are none of John Paul II wearing glasses, at least in the public domain.

From St. Florian's rectory, Wojtyła moved to the apartment of Father Ignacy Rózycki, a leading theologian and Jagiellonian professor, on Kanoniczna Street, just below Wawel Castle. That, too, had been recommended by Archbishop Baziak. He worked mainly at home on the new doctoral dissertation (it would take him over two years, as planned), finding time for his interests in literature and the theater. He discovered that he could keep up his intellectual friendships during brief vacations on joint skiing, hiking, and bicycle forays all over the Carpathian foothills and mountains.

Wojtyła's first major postwar poem, "Song of Reflecting Water," was published in May 1950 by his new friend Jerzy Turowicz in *Tygodnik Powszechny.* It was signed with the pseudonym of Andrzej Jawień, the first of his three pen names, and this was the first time he used it. Some of his friends believe that Jawień was taken from the name of several families in the Niegowici parish. But John Paul II has said in 1994 that it was "probably" borrowed from the name of the hero of the novel *Return to Life* by Jan Parandowski.

The poem is a blank verse lyrical prayer, singing of the search for God and faith in the depths of water in a reflecting well. It is based on John's citation of Jesus' words to the Samaritan woman at Jacob's well that "who drinks from the water that I shall give, will never feel thirst." It is very much in the spirit of Wojtyła's reflections on St. John of the Cross's "dark nights" of reaching for faith. In concludes with the discovery that the water in the mystical well reflects God, and on the cry that "I shall not be able to bring Thee wholly into myself, but I want Thee to remain in the well's reflection as leaves and flowers from above. . . ."

"Song of Reflecting Water" may well be one of Wojtyła's best and most inspiring poems in the simplicity of its smooth language. It must have met the high standards of Polish-language poetry to merit publication in a leading periodical in a city where every reader regarded himself as a literary critic. Another poem published in *Tygodnik Powszechny* in 1950 was a three-part work titled simply "Mother," a lyrical hymn to the mother who personifies the spirit of Our Lady.

Turowicz at *Tygodnik* was now publishing Wojtyła in both poetry and prose under different names. He was one of the few people who knew that the Jawień of poetry was the Wojtyła of the articles (the other pseudonyms followed later). After the Mission de France article in 1949, he published later that year Wojtyła's "Apostle" memoir about Jan Tyranowski, his mystical mentor.

In 1951, the weekly printed Wojtyła's long article "Mystery and Man," a rather difficult theological essay on the theme that "the historical fact of Jesus Christ looms in the eyes of faith as the mystery of the incarnation of God-Son." His conclusion was that only a believer can comprehend and appreciate the link between "the mystery of God-Man" and the realities of human life. The article was a good example of how Wojtyła often tends to sacrifice clarity for density of learned verbiage when writing about theology and philosophy. He is not—to this day—an easy prose writer. He does much better in poetry and drama in terms of creating very inviting language. And he is a magnificent extemporaneous speaker, immensely captivating when he sets aside the intricate prepared texts.

It was during the five-year period starting with his postwar Kraków seminary studies and his time in Rome and ending with the service at St. Florian's that Wojtyła composed his three-act drama *Brother of Our God*, by far his most interesting and socially and religiously important work. It was published only late in 1979, a year after he became pope, and it is generally unknown.

Wojtyła's long familiarity with the theater as actor and director turned him into a highly competent playwright. He has an ear for language, including colloquialisms, and the dialogue is smooth and natural. Stage directions, scenery descriptions, and scene transitions are perfectly professional. It makes the drama credible, and the story line, from the pen of a young midcentury Polish priest-philosopher, is rather surprising in its embrace of a violent social revolution.

A communist takeover, if not a social revolution, had already occurred in Poland—supposedly in the name of social justice—when Wojtyła was drafting his drama. He therefore evidently had in mind capitalism's oppression of the poor in the West and the Third World, and what he appeared to be proposing was a *Christian* social revolution.

Brother of Our God is the true story of Adam Chmielowski, a Kraków bohemian painter, trained in Warsaw and Munich, who around the turn of the century experienced a religious revelation and devoted himself to the poor and miserable of the city. Taking the name of Brother Albert, he founded a religious order of Franciscan Tertiaries—men and women—who became known as Albertine Franciscans, or just Albertine Brothers and Sisters, to run shelters for the poor and homeless.

Brother Albert (the Brother of God of the play's title) was a perfect subject for Wojtyła: not only was he a man of God, an intellectual and an artist, but a Polish patriot as well, having lost a leg at the age of eighteen fighting in the anti-Russian uprising of 1863. With his long white beard and wooden leg, Brother Albert was a familiar figure in the streets of Kraków in the early years of the century as he toured the city with a handcart, collecting old clothes and food for his "guests" at the shelter. Irena Szkocka, Wojtyła's friend, remembered seeing him around Kraków when she was a young woman.

He died in 1916 at the age of seventy-one, and was buried in the church of the Discalced Carmelite Fathers in Kraków. Wojtyła, who venerated Brother Albert, unveiled a plaque in his memory at the Carmelite church in 1963, when he was bishop. As pope, he canonized him in 1989. Adam the painter is now St. Albert.

In the play, Wojtyła portrays the painter first as opening his Kraków apartment-studio to the hungry and homeless, explaining to his artist friends that "we cannot allow a whole human mass to crowd night shelters, leading nearly animal lives, slowly losing all consciousness other than hunger and fear. . . ."

Divine revelation that he must devote himself to the destitute because of their right to minimal, decent life and self-respect—and *not* just mercy and compassion—comes to Adam in an encounter with an unnamed character after one of his many visits to a filth-infested municipal hovel for the homeless. He is bitterly derided there for the humiliating "mercy" of bringing them clothing and food. The unnamed character is unmistakably reminiscent of Jan Tyranowski, the mystic.

Another unidentified character berates the mere charity of the rich: "Aha, mercy! A coin here, a coin there, for the right of calmly owning millions—in banks, forests, farms, securities, stocks. . . . And with it, animal-like hard labor over 10, 12 or 16 hours for a red cent, for the hope of doubtful consolation, which does not change anything, and which over the centuries has been building up a powerful, splendid explosion of human anger, human creative anger. . . ."

The theme of "splendid human anger" now becomes recurrent in the play. A character identified as "The Speaker" tells the homeless in the shelter that "you have the right to have human rights."

He goes on: "I came here to awaken what sleeps inside you. I know that you all think what I think right now. But nobody dares to say it aloud. Why? Why don't you harness the strength that is within you? Why do you let yourselves be smashed by poverty and hold back your justified revolt? Why is your anger silent?

"DON'T BE AFRAID!" The Speaker exclaims, using the phrase John Paul II would use forty years later as the first words of his address to the world—the words of Jesus—after being chosen as pope. "Just provide the anger, and forces will emerge that will know how to shape it, use it and lead it!"

At the end of the play, many years later in the story, Brother Albert, known as Elder Brother to his fellow gray-robed monks, hears at their love-ordained shelter for the poor that in downtown Kraków "electricity and gas have been cut off, workers have abandoned their jobs to join demonstrations that are moving along the streets amid shouts . . . restaurants and shops are closing down . . . the police are everywhere. . . ."

"So! The powder was collected there," Brother Albert says, "and only a spark was needed. I knew about it for a long time. It had to happen. I knew about the anger! The great anger! The just anger! . . . You know that anger must explode, especially when it is so great! . . . And it will last because it is just! . . ." (It was not Brother Albert alone in the play who advocated "great . . . creative . . . just anger." John Paul II displayed it himself in an extraordinary emotional manner, without precedent in public papal pronouncements in modern times, when he marshaled all the resources of the Holy See and the Church worldwide in 1994 to battle against the proposed U.N. declaration on population that, in effect, accepted legalized abortion and other means of birth control.)

Wojtyła's emphasis in the drama is on Adam's religious experience of revelation. But it also is a powerful justification of revolutions with a Christian ethos. Writing *Brother of Our God* in the immediate postwar years, Wojtyła could not have foreseen that almost identical words and calls for revolutionary action in the name of God and social justice would be uttered a decade later by Roman Catholic priests in Latin America as they preached the new "Theology of Liberation."

As Pope John Paul II, he would come to fear what he thought were Marxist ingredients of this theology. But as a priest in Poland in the 1950s, he was quietly learning to fear the destruction of his Church by Marxist forces at home.

CHAPTER 12

On January 20, 1951, nine months after the signing of the agreement between the government and the Church, Bishop Czesław Kaczmarek of Kielce, a diocese in south-central Poland, was arrested by the secret police on vague treason and espionage charges. He would be held for two years, then tried and sentenced to twelve years in prison.

With Kaczmarek's detention, the regime had launched a campaign of persecution and intimidation against the Polish Church. But it never reached, even remotely, the dimensions of communist anti-Church terror (and terror in general) in the other East European countries. The campaign appeared to be aimed at controlling rather than destroying Church structures in Poland, and dialogue between the two sides was maintained even during the worst of times.

Thus Archbishop Wyszyński, the primate, was allowed to travel to Rome in February for an audience with Pope Pius XII—his first visit there since his appointment more than two years earlier. The regime regulated foreign travel by Poles, including the clergy, through the simple expedient of refusing to grant passports to those it did not wish to go abroad, which was the vast majority of the applicants.

Before leaving for Rome, Wyszyński conferred in Warsaw with President Bierut—it was the first time they ever met—and again on his return. Each meeting lasted three hours. In

April 1952 he sent his wishes to Bierut on the president's sixtieth birthday.

At the Vatican, the primate had the opportunity to inform Cardinal Dominici Tardini, the extremely conservative undersecretary of state, that he was wrong in accusing Polish bishops of being "soft on communism." He tried to explain to Tardini and the pope the realities of life behind the Iron Curtain and the accommodations that had to be made to protect the Church in Poland.

A year later, Wyszyński found it necessary to emphasize during a discussion with Catholic editors at home that "martyrdom is always a grace and an honor, but when I weigh the present great needs and demands of Catholic Poland, I want martyrdom only as a last resort." He added: "I want my priests at the altar, at the pulpit and in the confessional—not in prison." He had said exactly the same thing to Pius XII and Tardini in Rome.

At the same time, the regime did not interfere with most of the great processions and pilgrimages—such as those to the shrine of the Black Madonna in Częstochowa, where the primate delivered a sermon on human and Church rights on Assumption Day, August 15, 1952—nor with the freedom of worship.

In Kraków, Father Karol Wojtyła went freely about his pastoral duties with the students at St. Florian's and elsewhere even as the regime quickened its campaign to strengthen its controls over the Church through selective arrests of senior prelates. Among them was his friend Father Kurowski, the parish priest at St. Florian's. Wojtyła is not known to have protested publicly, from the pulpit or otherwise, this rising tide of persecutions of the Polish priesthood. The primate was denouncing it in Warsaw.

It is not entirely clear why the regime had ordered the campaign at that particular time, though it kept it within certain limits and preserved the relationship with the Church leadership. Some historians of the period believe that Bierut and his associates, including interior minister and security chief Jakub Berman, a Jew, felt that it was necessary to assuage the hard-liners within their own apparatus as well as the Soviet Union. *Pravda,* the official organ of the Soviet Communist Party, for example, was busy attacking Wyszyński. And the Korean War had erupted in June 1950, intensifying the East-West struggle.

In a country where the main players each had their own special agendas, the Bierut group may have concluded that by occasionally arresting bishops, it was paying the price for refusing to embark on a wholesale anti-Church crusade and for maintaining the dialogue with the primate and his advisers. They must have been aware that, given the strength of Polish Catholicism, a head-on collision with the Church would have been catastrophic. In a sense, each side's carefully crafted policies were the mirror image of the other side's politics. Bierut had to convince Stalin, and Wyszyński had to convince Pius XII.

In the meantime, the arrests and intimidation measures continued. Father Antoni Słomkowski, the Magnificent Rector of the Catholic University in Lublin, was arrested early in 1951, although the university itself was basically untouched. In the Włocławek diocese, where Archbishop Wyszyński had held his first postwar post, nine priests were put in prison in the spring of 1951.

And the situation worsened considerably in 1952. Now the Polish Church and the regime reached a total stalemate over the procedure for appointing bishops, with the dioceses in Kraków and Katowice in Silesia becoming the principal battlegrounds. The Church insisted on the pope's canon-law right to select bishops from lists submitted by the primate. The regime, desiring the power of veto for itself, finally had its way.

To deal with existing bishops of whom the authorities disapproved, the policy was to remove them, forcibly when necessary, and in some cases to arrest them. In Katowice, Bishop Stanisław Adamski and two auxiliary bishops were expelled. In November in Kraków, the regime actually arrested Archbishop Baziak and the auxiliary bishop, Stanisław Rospond.

To ensure the formal functioning of the archdiocese, in December the Kraków Church leadership elected Bishop Franciszek Jop from Sandomierz in the southeast to act temporarily in Baziak's place. The regime accepted it because the procedure followed its rules. The pope played no role in Jop's transfer. Archbishop Baziak's expulsion from the palace and his arrest shook Kraków's Catholic community. But Karol Wojtyła, working on his doctorate, said nothing publicly on the subject. Shortly thereafter Wojtyła went with friends to the Tatry for his first skiing expedition in the high mountains.

Now the regime turned its hostile attentions to Primate Wyszyński personally. On November 29, two weeks after the Baziak and Rospond arrests, Wyszyński was advised that Pius XII had named him cardinal, undoubtedly to strengthen the prestige of the Polish Church in the face of the communist onslaught (Poland had had no cardinal since Sapieha's death). But the regime refused to grant the primate a passport to travel to Rome to receive the purple from the pope's hands.

The authorities had been angered, among other things, by Wyszyński's firm opposition to the new postwar Polish constitution, drafted by communist legal experts. He had protested that the Church was not recognized as a public institution and was given no guarantees in the constitutional text for its free operations. Given the widely accepted principle of clear separation of church and state in most countries in the world, Wyszyński's position was legally unsound. But his responsibility was to fight for the Church's rights—he felt that the general language on freedom of worship in the constitution was not enough—and he used all the weapons at his command. But he could not accomplish much. *Tygodnik Powszechny,* for example, was barred by the censor from publishing the episcopate's memorandum on the subject. And Parliament approved the constitution on July 22, 1952, the anniversary of the birth of the People's Republic of Poland.

And the situation became even more ominous in 1953. In January, four priests and three lay workers of the Kraków archdiocese went on trial before a military court on charges of collaborating with the U.S. Central Intelligence Agency in spying and subversive activities against "People's Poland" and illegal trade in foreign currency. It was the first big show trial of the Polish clergy under the communist regime. In the way it was conducted, including attacks on the late Cardinal Sapieha, the impression was that the government was seeking an indictment of the Polish Church hierarchy for the benefit of domestic public opinion. It was also designed to back pro-regime Catholic organizations that were being busily activated, and to give them respectability at the expense of Wyszyński's hierarchy.

After a five-day trial, Father Józef Lelito, who headed the archdiocesan Women's Living Rosary Circle and the Catholic Association of Male Youth—activities very close to Wojtyła's own work in Kraków—and two of the lay workers were sentenced to death (though the sentences were not carried out). The others received long prison terms.

Stalin died on March 5, 1953, but things worsened for the Polish Church, instead of improving as many had hoped. In fact, Stalin's death led to a major controversy when *Tygodnik Powszechny,* which was financed by the Kraków archdiocese, refused to publish his obituary. Jerzy Turowicz and the other editors felt that if they could say nothing good about Stalin, it would be better to say nothing at all.

The regime's censors reacted by banning the weekly's publication until it agreed to praise Stalin, confiscating three successive issues. The third issue contained an interview with Primate Wyszyński by Turowicz, leading the editors to conclude that it was senseless to go on trying to publish the *Tygodnik* under the circumstances. And at the same time, the government demanded that Turowicz and an associate editor be fired as a condition of continued publication. After the editorial board turned down the demand, the secret police closed down *Tygodnik,* sealing its offices. Soon afterward, the weekly reappeared with its old name, the regime having turned it over to PAX, the pro-government Catholic organization linked to the also pro-government Patriotic Priests group.

PAX had its own newspaper and book publishing house, and for the next three years it would be the only authorized voice of Catholicism in Poland. Sadly, many Catholic intellectuals chose to write in PAX publications, justifying it with the explanation that it was better to be printed there than not at all. Tadeusz Mazowiecki, then a leftist Catholic figure and, in 1989, Poland's first post-communist prime minister, was a PAX member at the time, a fact that John

Paul II has never forgotten. When Mazowiecki ran for president in 1991, people in the Vatican chose to support Lech Wałęsa, the Solidarity chief, against him. Wałęsa won.

Karol Wojtyła, the author of many *Tygodnik* articles and poems, had abstained from writing for the weekly under the new management. His last appearances in print there were a long poem, *Thought Is a Strange Dimension,* and three long articles, "Instinct" and "Love and Marriage" in 1952, and "Religious Experience of Purity" early in 1953.

The poem is a metaphysical discussion of thought processes, which is quite a feat in blank verse, with the conclusion that reflection is aided by "silence and loneliness—loneliness [that is] possible in man because nobody is torn away from it by death." Silence, loneliness, and death remain Wojtyła's ever-recurring themes.

The two articles marked the start of his active preoccupation with Christian ethics of sexuality, a concern that would dominate his pastoral and papal attentions over the decades. In the first one, Wojtyła argued that "ethical purity" in sexual activity must establish clearly that the sex drive is directed toward "the transmission of life . . . and assures the existence of the human kind." In this sense, he wrote, it is ethically acceptable "to allow the sex drive to produce pleasure in the achievement of the right objectives" of procreation. Wojtyła's next central point was that "love" between man and woman is a prerequisite even for the ethically pure practice of sex, but that it must be sanctified by marriage. The second article affirmed that, for all these reasons, "purity . . . is such an important virtue in Christian religious life."

As the anti-Church campaign accelerated even more, on September 22, 1953, Bishop Kaczmarek was given his twelve-year prison sentence at a trial held two years after his arrest. And more was to come three days later.

Late in the evening of September 25, Cardinal Wyszyński was arrested by the secret police at the primate's residence on Miodowa Street in Warsaw on his return from St. Anna's Church, where he had preached a sermon on the anniversary of St. Ładysław, the patron saint of the capital. Plainclothesmen had broken into the residence to detain him, but one of them was bitten by Wyszyński's dog, Baca. The primate gave the agent first aid, then quietly entered the car that took him away from his duties as the head of the Polish Church.

After an all-night drive, Wyszyński was interned under police guard at the Capuchin Fathers' monastery in Rywałd in northwestern Poland. He was the first top Polish prelate to be arrested since the Prussians had imprisoned Archbishop Mieczysław Ledóchowski for twenty years in 1866, for opposing laws designed to eradicate Polish culture.

The evening the primate was arrested, Father Wojtyła was winding up a ten-day excursion with St. Florian students in the Carpathian Mountains, near Babia Góra peak. He had just inaugurated the practice of celebrating field Mass during the excursions. Earlier in September, Wojtyła had taken nine students on a five-day kayak trip down the Brda River.

In October 1954 the government closed down the Theology Faculty of Jagiellonian University in Kraków where Wojtyła was teaching after completing his latest doctoral dissertation. It was, instead, made part of the Theological Department of Warsaw University, a much more manageable institution as far as the regime was concerned.

While the Polish Church was struggling for survival against communist pressures and intimidation, a new phenomenon was emerging at the Vatican that would have a significant impact on Karol Wojtyła personally and loom large as a sharp controversy during the pontificate. It was the official approbation by the Holy See of Opus Dei, a novel religious organization spawned in Spain but beginning to expand around the world.

Opus Dei (Latin for "God's Work") was founded in Madrid on October 2, 1928, by Josemaría Escrivá de Balaguer y Albás, a twenty-six-year-old priest from Barbastro in northeastern Spain, as an organization of "apostolate" at the service of the Church. Its declared aim was to "open a channel for ordinary men and women living in the World to seek sanctity and carry out apostolate with a genuine and fully secular dedication."

Not a traditional religious order—like the Benedictines, Franciscans, or Jesuits—and much more ambitious than existent Roman Catholic lay associations (such as Catholic Action), Opus Dei was conceived as an unprecedented effort to combine the sacred and the secular in spreading and practicing the faith in a highly dedicated fashion. And from the outset, the idea was that Opus Dei be a compact, very motivated institution, whose members, clergy, and lay Catholics would be of spiritual and professional distinction. In the strict sense of the word—not pejorative—Opus Dei was meant to be an elite, never a mass movement.

As for Monsignor Escrivá, he was both a mystic in the great Spanish tradition of St. John of the Cross and St. Theresa of Avila, and a pragmatist who knew how to achieve extraordinary practical results for his organization. A pragmatic mystic, not at all a contradiction in terms in his case, Escrivá held doctorates in law and theology, and published extensively on spiritual matters. His fundamental work, *The Way,* first published in 1934 as *Spiritual Considerations,* is a collection of 999 "Thoughts"—or maxims or commandments—forming the "bible" of Opus Dei (over the next sixty years, *The Way* would sell four million copies in thirty-five languages).

As a pragmatic mystic, Escrivá clearly was another role model for Karol Wojtyła, who, as pope, would become the chief protector of Opus Dei, although it was Pius XII who first gave his and the Holy See's approval to the organization. Not the direct spiritual mentor that Jan Tyranowski had been to him, Escrivá nevertheless has exercised a powerful spiritual—and practical—influence over Wojtyła even though they never met. Wojtyła, of course, always had a penchant for the Spanish Church because of his allegiance to the traditions of St. John of the Cross.

During the 1936–1939 Spanish Civil War, Escrivá spent most of the time in areas held by the Nationalist forces of General Francisco Franco after fleeing Madrid, the seat of the Republican government. Priests, monks, and nuns were killed in great numbers in the Republican zones, and churches, monasteries, and convents were destroyed; that memory never left Escrivá.

Back in Madrid after Franco's victory, Escrivá requested the Bishop of Madrid-Alcalá in February 1941 to grant Opus Dei the formal status of a "Pious Society." Six weeks later, the bishop granted the request. From then on, Opus Dei was on its way to ever-rising Church prestige and power.

Now Escrivá decided that Opus Dei needed its own priests. Consequently, in May 1943 he dispatched Father Álvaro del Portillo, the secretary-general of Opus Dei, to wartime Rome to seek authorization from the Holy See. The following month Portillo was received by Pius XII, an unusual mark of attention, and Secretary of State Maglione, to outline Opus Dei's latest plans. He was evidently encouraged in these conversations, because Escrivá immediately applied to the Bishop of Madrid for the elevation of Opus Dei to the rank of a diocesan institution under the name of "The Priestly Society of the Holy Cross."

Matters moved rapidly. On October 11, 1943, the Holy See's Sacred Congregation for Religious and Secular Institutes (its name at the time), responsible for religious institutions and orders, issued its *Nihil Obstat* ruling in favor of Escrivá's proposed new society. (*Nihil Obstat* means that there are no obstacles in the way of a proposal.) On December 8, the Madrid archdiocese approved the creation of the society. It was the turning point in the history of Opus Dei.

With the war over, Escrivá concluded that the time had come for another step forward. In April 1946 he sent Portillo back to Rome with the proposal for the Holy See to grant Opus Dei and the Priestly Society of the Holy Cross the status of a pontifical institution. The pope received him at once. According to official Opus Dei historians, Pius XII "understood" that while the Priestly Society already was a Church institution, "it clearly was a new phenomenon" and Escrivá's request should be given consideration. In the meantime, the pope sent Escrivá his autographed photograph with "a special benediction."

Late in June, Escrivá, now formally described as "The Founder" (of Opus Dei), arrived for his first visit in Rome. The pope received him on July 16, assuring the Founder that he favored his proposal. Escrivá went back to Spain.

Having resolved to make Rome his new home and headquarters, Escrivá returned there the last week of November. That was the same week Karol Wojtyła arrived in

Rome to study at the Angelicum. It was one of those strange coincidences that seem to punctuate Karol Wojtyła's life. There is nothing to indicate that Wojtyła was aware of the existence of Escrivá and Opus Dei—they were not widely known at that stage—and there was no reason why the superbly connected Spanish prelate and the obscure Polish priest-student should meet.

On February 24, 1947, Pius XII signed the decree recognizing Opus Dei and the Priestly Society as a "Secular Pontifical Institute." This placed them under the pope's direct protection and granted them "universal juridical standing" and "convenient internal autonomy," in the words of Opus Dei historians. Papal protection, they wrote, served to "halt incomprehension and persecution from which Opus Dei was suffering."

But Opus Dei was able to report at the same time that it was expanding to the Americas and that its membership already included "physicians, lawyers, architects, military [officers], researchers, artists, writers, university professors and students." In May, Pius XII awarded Escrivá the title of papal "household prelate," a mark of personal friendship.

On June 16, 1950, in the course of the Holy Year, when over three million Catholics from all over the world made the pilgrimage to the Holy See, the pope further strengthened Opus Dei. A new papal decree proclaimed the permanent character of the new Pontifical Institute and approved its charter and statutes.

And Opus Dei was expending steadily—numerically, geographically, and qualitatively. From 1946, its membership had grown from 268 men and women to 2,954, including clergy, an impressive achievement considering that Opus Dei is extremely selective in its recruiting. It now had a college for men and a college for women in Rome, and over one hundred centers in Europe, the Americas, and Africa.

Very quietly, Opus Dei was acquiring influence all over the world in strategic points in Church establishments and, it appeared, very discreetly in political and business circles. And in February 1952 Pius XII added one more gesture toward the institute: he appointed Cardinal Federico Tedeschini as official "Protector" of Opus Dei.

The next great advance in the history of Opus Dei would come with the election of John Paul II.

In Kraków, Father Karol Wojtyła concentrated during the Polish Church's "Annus Terribilis" of 1953 on completing his doctoral dissertation, lecturing on matters of family and sexuality—his growing interest—and combining recreation with expansion of his scientific knowledge as it related to religion and philosophy.

On January 24, Wojtyła and two friends, both nuclear physicists, took the night train from Kraków to Poronin, a resort town in the Tatry Mountains. But as Professor Jacek Hennel, one of the physicists, recalled later, Wojtyła refused to travel first-class, telling them, "No, no, we go with the people. . . ."

Hennel had first met Wojtyła when, as a student, he attended his lectures and discussions on metaphysics at the Catholic Association of Male Youth some years earlier, and they soon became friends along with other young scientists and their wives or dates. It was the St. Florian's crowd. The railway trip to Poronin was intended as a test for Wojtyła, though he was not aware of it at the time. Hennel recalls:

> A few of us were planning a ski trip to last several days to a place named Gorce in the high mountains, and the suggestion was made to invite Father Karol Wojtyła, whom we knew and liked. But we were not sure about Father Wojtyła's skiing skills, so, without revealing our true intentions, we invited him for a weekend skiing excursion to Poronin, Bukowina and Zakopane. Our invitation was willingly accepted. But it was necessary to prepare the skis for him and to fit the bindings to the regular black shoes worn by priests. This was done by one of us at the workshop of the Physics Institute of Jagiellonian University.

He goes on:

> We arrived in Poronin, and Father Wojtyła went to church to say Mass. After lunch with the parish priest, we made downhill runs, then crossed several valleys.

> We spent the night in Zakopane. And in skiing, Father Wojtyła, who said he had not done it since high school, made great progress in a matter of hours. So I concluded that he was doing just fine at it. So, I am the first man in the world who has examined a Pope at skiing.

Professor Hennel subsequently invited Wojtyła to come along on the big Gorce trip, but his guest insisted on saying Mass every day, although it was explained to him that there were no adequate facilities in the mountains. Wojtyła's reaction, Hennel says, was, "I am a priest, this is my privilege, and I have no intention of giving it up." In the end, he had his way, first stopping at village churches along their skiing route, then celebrating Mass in the open air. Wojtyła, who wore normal skiing attire, carried his cassock in his backpack, donning it at the celebrations. He also had a collapsible chalice. Sometimes he said Mass at a peasant's home, other times in a barn, where Wojtyła and his companions erected an altar from straw, or on a mountainside with backpacks and tree branches made into altars.

The Gorce expedition was followed by more skiing trips, and it became a habit for Wojtyła to join his physicist friends on the slopes every winter. In warm weather, he went kayaking with other groups of young people on lakes and rivers. Hennel recalls that his friends were divided into "skiiers" and "kayakers," although some belonged to both sports groups. Most of the physicists, however, were skiiers.

These forays soon developed into more systematic occasions with Wojtyła leading students on excursions, which included Mass, discussions of religion and other serious themes along with fireside chats, singing, joking, and laughing. Wojtyła was always in sports clothes, sometimes in shorts and short-sleeved shirts, to avoid being recognized by the police wherever the groups went, and he was publicly addressed as "Uncle" or "Little Uncle" by the students for the same reason. It was forbidden for priests to shepherd youth groups around and, as Hennel says, "you could go to jail for celebrating Mass in a forest." For Wojtyła, the skiing, kayaking, bicycling, and trekking were part of his pastoral work, and he delighted in it.

In a 1957 article in the Kraków religious periodical *Homo*

Dei, Wojtyła (writing this time as "The Pastor") remarked that in pastoral youth group excursions, "all conversations need not necessarily be so-called fundamental conversations. One should be able to talk about everything—films, books, professional work, scientific research, and jazz-bands in a proper way. An excursion must be a well-prepared improvisation. . . ."

On skiing trips, Wojtyła always insisted that no remarks should be addressed to him during the first two hours in the morning, his time for reflection and contemplation. Afterward, Hennel recalls, "we would start talking, frequently about religious matters, and about theoretical concepts linked to metaphysics and morality."

Wojtyła had no background in science and physics, but Hennel says that in conversation he kept trying to relate scientific topics to moral and ethical ones. This was the approach Wojtyła would apply and develop as bishop, cardinal, and pope when he had to deal with such matters as cosmology or genetics in terms of Christian teachings.

During the summer of 1953, Wojtyła displayed amazing stamina. In August, for example, he led a sixteen-hour march into the mountains, carrying a forty-five-pound backpack filled with liturgical items for Mass. His longest hike in one day was twenty-six miles. At the end of 1954, Wojtyła was awarded a bronze medal by the Kraków Tourism Commission for covering 110 miles on foot, including sixty miles during the winter, over a five-month period of mountain trekking. His penchant for kayaking led him to enter an international kayak race on the Dunaj River, but his kayak sprang a leak and sank at the finish line, dumping him into the water. "Only the breviary did not get wet," he reported.

Working on his doctoral dissertation on Christian ethics and delivering sermons on special occasions at St. Florian's, Father Wojtyła still found time for discussions with students far into the night at the apartment where he lived on Kanoniczna Street. Hennel, his ski companion, remembers that "day after day, his students and friends stayed there until all hours. . . . It annoyed me because I knew the man had to get up the next morning at five or six to celebrate Mass, then go to work. And they just sat there until very late at night. . . ."

Wojtyła's doctoral dissertation with the formidable title of "An Assessment of the Possibility of Erecting a Christian Ethic on the Principles of Max Scheler" was presented in the form of a 175-page typewritten text and was unanimously approved by the Council of the Theological Faculty of Jagiellonian University on December 12, 1953. He could not, however, be awarded the doctorate because the Education Ministry in Warsaw refused to authorize Kraków University to do so. The regime was not keen on granting advanced academic degrees to priests.

The dissertation itself was an extremely difficult work on an exceedingly difficult subject. Max Scheler, whose philosophy Wojtyła had analyzed, was a German phenomenologist of mixed Jewish-Protestant parentage who died in 1928. He was a follower of Edmund Husserl, a Czech-born Jew and his contemporary, who is generally regarded as the father of phenomenology. Husserl's close collaborator was Edith Stein, a German-born Jewish scholar who converted to Catholicism and became a nun under the name of Theresa Benedicta of the Cross. She was killed at the Oświęcim concentration camp by the Nazis. Pope John Paul II would beatify her shortly after his election.

Wojtyła was introduced to phenomenology—a vaguely defined school of philosophy based on the study of physical and spiritual phenomena and experiences in human existence that has also led to existentialism—by his Jagiellonian University professor Roman Ingarden, who, in turn, had known Edith Stein. It was a curious coincidence that Wojtyła, attracted from adolescence by Christianity's Jewish heritage, now found himself so captivated by philosophers of Jewish origin, striving to determine whether their concepts, in this particular case, fit into Christian ethics.

As it happened, Wojtyła concluded in his dissertation that they did not. He wrote that although phenomenology itself was valid as philosophy—he regards himself as a phenomenologist—Max Scheler's ideas did not provide a sound basis for Christian ethics. He explained that despite his great respect for him, Scheler was not acceptable in this context because he had not recognized God explicitly as "the exemplary being" and failed to assign sufficient value to the role of conscience in man's morality.

In an encyclical forty years later—in 1993—John Paul II would place the greatest emphasis on the role of conscience in the entire sphere of Christian ethics and decision making by Christians in their lives. And it would be upon this foundation that the pope would launch his vehement campaigns in the 1990s—from his absolute rejection of *all* means of artificial birth control and abortion to priestly celibacy. An informed Christian conscience, he would insist, must be the ultimate guide in all such decisions, based on Christian "Natural Law." Wojtyła's philosophical contemplations in the 1950s were not a simple exercise in abstractions.

With the doctoral dissertation behind him, Father Wojtyła turned to full-time teaching and preaching literally the length and breadth of Poland while keeping up with his summer and winter "Uncle" excursions with his students. Except for his daily periods of prayer and meditation he seemed to be in perpetual motion.

After the regime closed down the Theological Faculty at Jagiellonian University in 1954, he agreed to teach Catholic social ethics regularly at seminars in Kraków, Katowice, and Częstochowa, and to lecture occasionally at Catholic University in Lublin as well as at St. Florian's and at the convent of the Ursuline Sisters in Kraków. It was travel, day in and day out.

At the 1954 pre-Easter retreat at St. Florian's, Wojtyła delivered before a large audience of students a seven-part "Lesson" on the concept of truth, the role of conscience in distinguishing between good and evil, the link between life and procreation, the perils of temptation, and the spirit of penance. He never cut corners in the teaching of ethics. In Lublin, Wojtyła spoke at length to a group of priests on the "Mother of God in the Life of a Pastor."

He was a most unusual teacher in every respect, to judge from the recollections of his students. Father Romuald Waldera, then studying at the Katowice seminary, remembers Wojtyła this way:

> He came to class in attire that certainly was not typical of a Kraków professor. Instead of a respectable black hat, he wore a leather aviator's cap. Over his cassock, he wore a dark-green overcoat made from fabric that must have been intended for a blanket. . . . During recess, he went upstairs to the chapel where he knelt on the hard floor although there were plenty of prie-dieux with pillows around. He lectured pacing up and down in front of us, then stopped and stared at us to make sure we had grasped what he was trying to expound. During exams, we had the impression that he was suffering. He took off his glasses, rubbed his forehead, asked one question, then another. He gave a grade after meditating for a long time. . . .

During 1955, Wojtyła kept up this pace. He went on at least three skiing expeditions between January and March, lectured in Kraków and Lublin in the spring, trekked in the mountains with students early in August, spent three weeks on the Drawa River with thirteen students aboard six kayaks in late August and September (they read C. S. Lewis on the trip), and made a bicycle pilgrimage from Kraków to the shrine of the Black Madonna in Częstochowa. Back home, he spent the autumn teaching social ethics and moral theology.

CHAPTER 13

The new year—1956—was a great turning point for Poland and for Karol Wojtyła.

It began with a classic Wojtyła adventure. Invited early in February to speak to novices at a convent in Szymanów, a small town in Galicja, Wojtyła advised his hosts that he would be arriving by train from Kraków at 6:30 P.M., and the sisters dispatched a horse carriage to the station to meet him. But winter temperatures suddenly plunged, and all trains were delayed; the rest of the story is told by the convent's Mother Superior:

> Having left the convent at 5:30 P.M., the horses came back at 11 P.M. with nobody. The priest, it turned out, was marching for miles at 2 A.M. in the dark, with temperatures 25 degrees centigrade below freezing, from the railroad station to the convent. Reaching the convent gate, he found it locked. For half an hour, he walked around the building, trying one door after another, until Sister Idalia in her cell happened to hear him. Because all the door locks at the rectory were literally frozen, she led our poor guest to his room through the attic from the adjoining house. Fortunately, our nice guest was not upset, and all went very well.

For the balance of the winter and through the spring, Wojtyła lectured, conducted discussions, skiied in the Tatra Mountains, and hiked with his students. He went kayaking when the weather turned warm.

He was in Kraków on June 28 when workers rioted in Poznań, the western industrial city, clashing with security forces in the biggest confrontation the regime faced since it first came to power. Demanding pay raises and better living conditions, tens of thousands of workers marched on downtown Freedom Square singing patriotic songs and religious hymns.

The police and the army fought the enraged crowd during the three-day rebellion, firing on the rioters. In the end, fifty-four people were killed and over two hundred injured. Polish "People's" security forces had never before massacred Polish working people, and Poland would never be the same again.

Between July and October, tensions mounted unbearably in Poland. Communist liberals were challenging the hard-liners in power with the support of opposition intellectuals, editors, professors, students, and much of the urban public opinion. In Poland, then and later, being a communist *liberal* was not an oxymoron. Indeed, the whole concept of communist rule was suddenly in question. And this, of course, meant challenging the armed might of the Soviet Union.

Bolesław Bierut, the country's president and PZPR first secretary, who had been excommunicated by the Holy See for imprisoning Primate Wyszyński, had died in March, being replaced in the party post by a non-entity named Edward Ochab. Emerging as the new political force on the Polish scene was Władysław Gomułka, a relatively moderate but controversial communist leader, who had lived under house arrest since his ouster from power eight years earlier. Communists were always settling accounts among themselves. Now bald, bullet-headed Gomułka was being hailed as the savior of the nation, and the great showdown began in mid-October.

After Moscow had threatened that it would not tolerate the hard-liners' replacement with Gomułka, Polish communist liberals succeeded in putting General Wacław Komar in command of special security forces, which included armored units. Komar, himself a communist liberal, had spent several years in prison, and he was raring to lead his troops into combat against the Soviets if an invasion was launched. This was a possibility Poles were taking with utmost seriousness, but patriotism was soaring again, and Komar had every reason to assume that most of the Polish armed forces would line up behind him.

On October 19, Nikita Khrushchev, the general secretary of the Soviet Communist Party, arrived in Warsaw with a retinue of his top military commanders to discover to his rage that Gomułka had just been returned to power. Shouting that Poland was "menacing the whole Socialist camp," Khrushchev clashed with Gomułka and his associates at a daylong meeting at the Belweder Presidential Palace, confirming reports that Soviet troops were advancing on Warsaw from bases in southwestern Poland, East Germany, and the Soviet Union, and that the capital was on the verge of being surrounded.

Gomułka, in turn, warned Khrushchev that he would not negotiate anything until the Soviets pulled out their troops—and that the Poles would fight. General Komar, meanwhile, maneuvered his units into blocking position. A Soviet armored column chose to halt sixty miles west of Warsaw when it came upon Komar's tanks. It must have finally dawned on Khrushchev that he would have a war with Poland on his hands, with the danger of a wider world confrontation. At two o'clock in the morning on October 20, he caved in.

Khrushchev flew home, Soviet troops were withdrawn, the Gomułka leadership was confirmed in power, and the only Polish concession was to allow the Soviets to maintain their bases in Poland and to remain members of the Soviet-directed military alliance. It was an incredible victory for the Poles—and the liberals—and Gomułka, the new hero, proclaimed that the communists were "taking their place at the head of the process of democratization."

Poland had now embarked upon the road that would lead in time to the emergence of the Solidarity movement fourteen years later, and the ultimate end of the communist rule.

The "Polish October," as these events were called, threw open the gates at prisons, restored liberal editors' and writers' freedom to publish, and convinced the ecstatic Poles that a democratic dawn had risen over the nation. The Church instantly shared in the new liberty.

On October 26, less than a week after the new leadership assumed power, Gomułka sent high-ranking emissaries to the convent of the Sisters of Nazareth in Komańcza to ask Cardinal Wyszyński to return immediately to Warsaw to resume his functions as primate and all his other ecclesiastic responsibilities. Gomułka urgently needed Wyszyński and the Church to help stabilize the fragile political and social situation in the country, recognizing once more the reality that Poland could not really be run without some form of collaboration on the part of the Catholic establishment and its faithful.

But even the men who had imprisoned him three years earlier had also been aware of it, never quite breaking the ties. Komańcza, in southeast Poland, was the fourth site of his internment since he was first taken to the Rywałd monastery in September 1953, and it was a great improvement on the previous locations. Wyszyński was moved there a full year before the Polish October as the communist authorities evidently began to realize that they had to end the battle with the Church in some fashion.

He was free to move around the small town of Komańcza and to receive letters, newspapers, and visits from his relatives and fellow bishops. At the convent, he had a "real" room, instead of the monastery cell, and the regime announced that henceforth the episcopate was in charge of his care. Bishops began visiting him to confer on Church matters, and on August 26, 1956, as the political crisis was deepening in the country, one million of the faithful had gathered at the shrine of the Black Madonna in Częstochowa at the great annual religious celebration. This alone must have impressed the communists with the fact that the strength of Polish Catholicism was unshaken.

Now Zenon Kliszko, Gomułka's second-in-command, and Władysław Bieńkowski, the new education minister, were at Komańcza to negotiate the primate's return. Wyszyński agreed to come back on the condition that all the imprisoned bishops and priests be freed, that bishops forced out of their dioceses be reinstated, and that the 1953 decree that had given the regime the power to appoint bishops be repealed. That last point would be of fundamental importance for the future of Karol Wojtyła.

The truly relevant fact about Polish communists and the Polish Church was that both always understood reality, and Gomułka and Wyszyński were no exceptions. Consequently, the primate's conditions were accepted overnight, and, on October 28, Wyszyński was back at his Warsaw residence, hailed by huge crowds filling Miodowa Street. And from the outset, Wyszyński counseled calm and moderation to all sides in the developing Polish situation.

On the same day, Cardinal Mindszenty was released from communist prison in Budapest by anti-communist rebels who had taken over the Hungarian capital. But, unlike in Poland, Khrushchev did not back down, and the rebellion was drowned in blood by Soviet tanks. On November 4, Mindszenty fled to asylum in the American legation, where he would remain for fifteen years.

In Kraków, Archbishop Baziak and Auxiliary Bishop Rospond were returned to their functions. *Tygodnik Powszechny* resumed publication with Jerzy Turowicz back in the editor's chair. The pro-regime PAX editors were out in the street.

Father Wojtyła was lecturing at Catholic University in Lublin during the October crisis, as always remaining publicly silent on matters of politics. The decisive week of the confrontation, he spoke on the subject of moral theology and matrimonial ethics. Two days after Khrushchev's capitulation, Wojtyła delivered a learned lecture titled "The Foundations of Perfectionism in Ethics."

Catholic University in Lublin (KUL) became Father Wojtyła's principal academic base late in 1956, just as Poland seemed to be headed toward new freedoms. He was named chairman of ethics, replacing Father Feliks

Bednarski, a Dominican and Thomist scholar, who had been appointed professor at the Angelicum in Rome.

The nomination was a great distinction. At thirty-six, Wojtyła was a senior member of the faculty of the most important Catholic philosophical and theological teaching center in Eastern Europe. Though Lublin was a quiet, provincial town, KUL, which had been founded in 1918, provided him with superb intellectual company as well as with recent bitter memories. The town had the tragic reputation of having had on its outskirts the Majdanek concentration camp. In 1944, Lublin served as the headquarters of the National Liberation Committee, which had arrived from Moscow as the forerunner of Poland's communist regime.

Wojtyła did not, however, sever his connections with Kraków, maintaining his home there and shuttling back and forth to Lublin on a savage commuting schedule. It was a twelve-hour overnight trip, and Professor Stefan Swieżawski, who taught medieval philosophy at KUL and often traveled with him, recalls that Wojtyła read or wrote before going to sleep, then, in the morning, stood motionless for an hour in front of the train compartment's window in silent prayer and contemplation.

He was an instant hit at KUL with the students and fellow professors. The students admired both his erudition and captivating teaching style—and his sartorial tastes. He usually appeared in a frayed cassock over olive green trousers and wearing "shapeless shoes," as a student put it in his journal. Classroom No. 33 at an old monastery where KUL was located at the time was always filled to the rafters when Wojtyła lectured. Students took benches and chairs, sat on windowsills and the floor, and lined the walls. They also seemed to feel they had a friend as well as a professor in him: he was always available for chats, for a small loan (no need to repay), and for the kind of confession they would not make before other priests. They too called him "Uncle."

Apparently, Wojtyła had the same effect on adults, including professors, as well. Jerzy Kłoczowski, a KUL historian (with whom Wojtyła endlessly discussed various theories about the martyrdom of St. Stanisław), recalls a situation involving a friend in the depths of a personal and emotional crisis. Finally, Kłoczowski says, "my wife and I concluded that only Wojtyła can talk with him. We couldn't think of anyone else. And, indeed, he and Wojtyła sat behind closed doors for an hour or two, and this man remembers to this day that it was a conversation that helped him enormously . . . in his enormous problems. I think it was his humanism, his ability to treat another person seriously. . . ."

Father Wojtyła divided his time during all of 1957 and the first half of 1958 between his chair of ethics at KUL and a series of exhausting lectures before physicians at the church of the Felician Sisters in Kraków. And, of course, he was working on articles, major poems, and a full-fledged book—and taking students trekking and kayaking.

Somewhere along the line, Wojtyła also produced what is regarded by scholars as an unusually important essay on the *Decretum Gratiani*, the compilation of Church laws by Franciscus Gratianus, the twelfth-century founder of the science of canon law. Although he lacked background in canon law, Wojtyła's study received high praise from specialists in Poland, France, and the Vatican. The work on Gratianus would lead him during the pontificate to personal involvement in the drafting of the new canon law. No topic seemed too far afield for Wojtyła, who seemed as if he were preparing himself for missions with limitless horizons.

Still, matters of ethics remained foremost on his mind as practical and just abstract theological considerations. As chaplain of health services of Jagiellonian University, Wojtyła addressed physicians on ethics on thirteen occasions between November 1957 and March 1958. The theme was the "contemporary mission of the contemporary physician" and his central message was that the Church "is continuously reborn" and that in this rebirth, laypeople must play a vital "autonomous role."

Again, seemingly looking very far ahead, Wojtyła stressed that because of its universality, "the Church lives in all the domains of life." He told his listeners that "the pope, for example, continuously turns to representatives of different specialties and discusses with them matters he has in his own workshop, trying to be competent [in these matters]."

Reporting on a national conference of two thousand

Catholic physicians in Częstochowa, which he had attended, Wojtyła discussed in depth how a physician should deal with problems of women seeking abortions and how a doctor and a priest in a community should cooperate in providing aid to women who went through with their pregnancies. That he urged the physicians to discourage abortions—widely practiced in the impoverished Polish society, where abortion on demand was legal—was normal for a Catholic priest. But novel in his approach, as a teacher of social ethics, was his sense that society had a further obligation toward the mother and the child if she chose to carry it to term. Wojtyła offered this example:

> A gynecologist from a small town in western Poland describes how in the course of his professional work he tries to dissuade by all possible means women who are one step away from the interruption of pregnancy from taking it. He uses all the arguments that medical knowledge, human experience, and finally faith offer him. Then he tries, in a very human way, to help the woman who, after rejecting [abortion], often is in need. . . . There was discussion [at Częstochowa] about the necessity of organizing help. The doctor must work together with the local priest, they must organize aid, including material aid, for mothers who, for so-called "social reasons," want to take the step [of abortion]. This is, of course, the seed of an idea, but undoubtedly a question of the future. . . .

Wojtyła went on to say that another responsibility of doctors is the preparation of young people for marriage because "we realize that it is too late to save an individual for whom everything has already burned. . . ." He appealed to physicians to conduct premarital courses because while priests are ready to help, "the priest is unable to teach young people competently in all the domains of married life. . . . In this way, medical work enters pastoral terrain. . . ."

Under the circumstances, Wojtyła said in one of his lectures, "physicians are increasingly an 'operational group' for the Church." He used the expression in the military sense. In the end, he concluded, the relationship between God and man was defined by Christ: "He who is not with me, is against me. . . ."

In November 1957, with the relaxation of regime pressures on the Church, KUL was authorized by the Higher Education Ministry to grant Wojtyła the doctorate for his dissertation on Max Scheler that Jagiellonian University was forbidden to do three years earlier. He was refused, however, a passport for travel to Belgium, France, and Switzerland where he had planned to familiarize himself with academic research there on the ethics of sexuality. The ministry had approved his application for the trip, but the security services would not issue him the passport.

In the course of 1957 and 1958, Wojtyła composed an essay, "On Love and Responsibility." Two years later, it would be expanded and issued in book form. This theme, along with questions of marriage and the integrity of the family, would gradually develop into the fundamental social doctrine of the pontificate of John Paul II.

Still in 1958, Wojtyła completed a 218-page typewritten teaching text, *Catholic Social Ethics,* published in *Tygodnik Powszechny;* an article signed Andrzej Jawień, "The Drama of Word and Gesture," about the Rhapsodic Theater; sixteen essays on "Elementary Ethics" under his own name; and an extremely lengthy mystical poem about Simon of Cyrene, who was forced to carry Christ's cross. Karol Wojtyła simply *had* to be the most prolific writer in Poland.

But now it was vacation time, and Father Wojtyła was spending the first part of July on an extended excursion with a group of friends and students in the mountainous Bieszczady area in the southeastern corner of Poland, near the confluence of frontiers with Slovakia and Soviet Ukraine. His last academic-year duty at KUL had been to preside over the evaluation of a doctoral dissertation by a woman student, "Friendship and Its Place and Value in the Aristotelian Ethical System." Mountain fresh air, exercise, and conversations with companions—a favorite pastime—were the rest and relaxation Wojtyła needed after an exhausting year of teaching, preaching, and writing.

In Castel Gandolfo, his summer residence near Rome,

Pope Pius XII—terribly aged, seriously ill, and immensely fatigued—had summoned his last ounce of energy for required Holy See paperwork. Among the documents on his desk were nominations for six new suffragans—auxiliary bishops—in Poland to help rebuild the Church after the communist oppression of the early 1950s. The pope was again free to name Polish suffragan bishops, but diocesan bishops and archbishops were another story.

One of the suffragan slots to be filled was in the Kraków archdiocese where Bishop Rospond, the old auxiliary bishop, had died in February. On July 8, 1958, Pius XII signed the nomination of Karol Wojtyła to be the titular Bishop of Ombia, an honorary title, and auxiliary bishop in Kraków. It is highly unlikely that the pope knew much about Wojtyła—suffragan nominations are usually signed on Curial advice and local episcopate recommendations—or that he remembered their brief meeting in 1946.

But the signing of this particular nomination fundamentally altered the future of Karol Wojtyła and of the Roman Catholic Church. It was Pius XII's last great historic act.

As a rule, the process of episcopal nominations is a tightly guarded Church secret because it involves personal rivalries among declared (and nondeclared) candidates and frequently requires very difficult choices within national episcopates. And in the case of Poland, it also touched on the delicate relationship with the regime.

The proposal to name Wojtyła a suffragan in Kraków had to be made by Archbishop Baziak, back from his three-year exile from the archdiocese, because it was his responsibility as the head of the Church there. But the rest of the story is a reconstruction based on the recollections and opinions of the few people with personal knowledge of these events who were still alive in the early 1990s.

Baziak's decision came as a surprise to the Kraków clergy. Much as Wojtyła was liked and admired for his scholarly achievements and preacher's talents, he lacked administrative experience of any kind (diocesan administration is part of the suffragans' duties) and had very little pastoral experience (only seven months in rural Niegowici and two years as a vicar at St. Florian's). Moreover, at thirty-eight he was very young to be bishop, especially in terms of the Polish tradition; Wyszyński was forty-five when he made it. But those who are familiar with Baziak's thinking believe that he was still carrying out the instructions given him by Cardinal Sapieha just before his death, to look after Wojtyła's future.

It is unknown what Sapieha had in mind for his protégé in terms of history. It probably defies credibility to suppose that he had a vision of Karol Wojtyła as pope, but it is entirely possible that he saw him as cardinal or even Primate of Poland. As for Baziak, who also admired young Wojtyła, he had already astonished the Kraków ecclesiastic establishment in 1951, when he pulled him out of the St. Florian's vicariate to force the young priest to take a two-year sabbatical to work on what would be his second doctorate. It did not seem to make much sense at the time, but evidently the archbishop was acting under a master plan for Wojtyła.

In any case, it was Baziak who unquestionably set Wojtyła on the course that would lead him to the papacy when he recommended him for the promotion to bishop. Stanisław Stomma, a very important and influential secular figure in the Polish Church who had known Sapieha, Baziak, and Wojtyła since the mid-1940s, says that he is absolutely convinced that Baziak "made Wojtyła." He remarks that "if Baziak hadn't picked him for bishop, Wojtyła would have spent the rest of his life as a distinguished professor at Catholic University in Lublin—he would never have been pope."

The next step was to obtain Primate Wyszyński's backing for Wojtyła. Proposals for bishop nominations must be forwarded to the Holy See by national episcopates in the normal course of events, and, naturally, the primate received more than one name (suggestions may come from anyone in the Church). In fact, as many as eight names may have been thrown into the hopper. Wyszyński presumably had heard about Wojtyła, who had a growing academic reputation in Polish Church circles, but it is almost certain that he had never met him, except in a group. Yet, Baziak's recommendation carried weight, and the primate, himself a scholar, may have been impressed by Wojtyła's credentials.

Though the regime's approval was no longer required for

suffragan nomination by local archdioceses—the government still had a veto over the appointment of archbishops—Wyszyński, as a matter of courtesy, informed the authorities of the names of the six proposed auxiliary bishops he was about to send to Rome. In an extreme case, the regime could have opposed a nomination through political pressure, but Wojtyła obviously presented no problems. He was regarded as wholly apolitical—just a nice, scholarly priest.

Karol Wojtyła, meanwhile, devoted the last week of July to a kayak trip with a youth group down the San River from Przemyśl, near the Soviet border, to Leżajsk, a fairly long row. He was back in Kraków on August 1 for a four-day retreat he conducted at the Benedictine Fathers' monastery in Tyniec, upriver from his old house on Tyniecka Street.

Monsignor Bolesław Filipiak, the primate's emissary, returned from Castel Gandolfo carrying the signed suffragan nominations just as Wojtyła, around August 5, was on his way to Święta Lipka, a vacation site on the Łyna River in the beautiful lake region in northern Poland. It was also a famous sanctuary in the cult of the Virgin Mary, second only in Poland to Częstochowa's Black Madonna. Wojtyła joined there a students' camping and kayaking vacation organized by KUL.

A student remembers him fit and happy, relaxed in shorts and sports shirt, but carrying a typed manuscript of his book *Love and Responsibility,* distributing a chapter to every member of the group, which "we discussed with him, sitting on the grass, on the lakeshore and on the edge of the forest."

On August 18, three days after the Feast of the Assumption—one of the most important for him in the Church calendar—Karol Wojtyła received at the Święta Lipka rectory a telephone call from the primate's office in Warsaw advising him of his nomination as suffragan bishop in Kraków and of Wyszyński's desire to see him at once.

There is no record of Wojtyła's reaction to the news from Warsaw that day. It was the moment for one of his deep silences. His students, caught between joy at his appointment and sadness at losing him as "Uncle" and teacher at

KUL, carried Wojtyła on their shoulders to the bus that would take him to Warsaw.

The next morning, deeply tanned and wearing a borrowed cassock, Wojtyła paid the call on the primate at the Miodowa Street residence. Then he booked passage on the night train to Kraków to pay his respects to Archbishop Baziak. But with time on his hands the rest of the day, Wojtyła made his way to the residence of the Ursuline Gray Sisters' convent on the boulevard along the Vistula River. He made the visit in his peculiar fashion. It was later described by one of his friends, Father Jan Zieja:

> It began . . . when an unidentified man dressed like a priest, therefore a priest, knocked in the early evening at the gate of the convent. "May I go to your chapel to pray?" he asked. He was led to the chapel and left alone. When he did not reappear after a long time, one of the Sisters looked inside the chapel. He was prostrate on the floor. The Sister withdrew in fear and respect. "He probably had important problems. Perhaps he is a penitent," she thought. After a time, the Sister looked again. The priest was still prostrate. But it was getting late. The Sister approached the praying man and asked timidly, "Perhaps Father would like to have dinner with us?" The unidentified man replied, "My train for Kraków doesn't leave until midnight. Allow me to stay. I have a lot to discuss with the Lord. Don't disturb me. . . ."

From Kraków, Wojtyła went back for a few days to the Święta Lipka camp. Although he had not yet been consecrated, he was invited to attend a meeting of the Polish episcopate conference at the Częstochowa monastery of the Black Madonna during the first week of September. He was assigned to the episcopate's permanent Commission on the General Apostolate. Awaiting the consecration ceremony, Wojtyła co-chaired a conference of professors of theology from all over Poland, delivering a lecture on social teachings at Polish seminaries. At the end of September, he prayed at a special retreat at the Tyniec monastery.

Karol Wojtyła was ordained as bishop on September 28, 1958, at a ceremony at Wawel Cathedral attended by as many people as could fit inside, with a crowd gathered in front of the church. As usual, he had his own ideas as to how it should be conducted, suggesting that the long and complex ceremony be explained by an announcer to the faithful in the cathedral as it proceeded. Archbishop Baziak, the consecrator and more of a traditionalist, vetoed the idea. Wojtyła also chose to wear a short mitre on his head rather than the more majestic tall one favored by most bishops.

Father Maliński, his seminary friend, caught a glance of Wojtyła in the cathedral just before the ceremony started: "He stood, with his head down, his face very tight, almost sad." But after swearing fidelity to the Scriptures and obedience to the pope, prostrating himself before the altar, being anointed with sacred oils, and receiving the laying on of hands and his bishop's ring, Wojtyła brightened up. He happily hailed his friends as he left the cathedral following the singing of *Veni Creator Spiritus.*

As bishop, Wojtyła chose as his official motto the Latin words *Totus tuus*—"All Yours"—taken from Louis Marie Grignon de Montfort, the Breton saint, in whose *Treatise* he had found divine inspiration, reading it on the floor of the Solvay factory during the war. Henceforth he placed the motto at the top of the page, in the right-hand corner, on every document and letter he penned the rest of his life.

In Rome, Pope Pius XII died on October 9, 1958, at the age of eighty-two. He had reigned for nineteen and a half years, the longest pontificate since Pius IX, who had been pope for thirty-two years, dying in 1878.

Cardinal Angelo Giuseppe Roncalli of Venice was elected pope, taking the name of John XXIII, on October 28, 1958, one month to the day after Karol Wojtyła's consecration as bishop. He would soon launch Vatican Council II, an important step toward the papacy for the thirty-eight-year-old Polish bishop.

PART

FOUR

CHAPTER 14

John XXIII wasted no time unveiling his plans for the Second Vatican Council—the announcement was made on January 25, 1959, three months after his enthronement—and late in May Bishop Karol Wojtyła in Kraków was invited by the Papal Ante-Preparatory Commission to submit his recommendations for the agenda.

Similar questionnaires went out to 2,594 Roman Catholic bishops and cardinals throughout the world who would be "Council Fathers"—an ecumenical council is an assembly of bishops under the chairmanship of the pope—and 76 percent of them responded.

Wojtyła, enthralled by the idea of the council, forwarded his comments to Rome on October 3, being among the first to do so as he prepared to play an active part in the sessions scheduled to open on October 11, 1962.

Nearly four years were required to ready the Church for the twenty-first ecumenical council in history, the first such undertaking in ninety years. The original was the Nicaea Council in A.D. 325. The Council of Trent was held between 1545 and 1563, under three successive popes, principally to deal with the challenge of the Protestant Reformation.

The next—and the last one—was Vatican Council I, in 1869 and 1870, under Pope Pius IX, which ended abruptly when King Victor Emmanuel II, the new Italian sovereign, occupied Rome and expropriated the Papal States. Pius IX declared himself a "prisoner" at the Vatican. Ironically, the best-remembered achievement of Vatican I under this unfortunate pontiff was to define for the first time the infallibility of the Roman pope in matters of dogma. His parting comment is said to have been that "the Council may have declared me infallible, but it also led me to bankruptcy."

Two world wars and almost a century later, it was the genius of the warm-hearted seventy-seven-year-old John XXIII to understand instantly upon his advent to the Holy See that an ecumenical council was urgent and essential to bring the Church into the radically changed modern world.

The new pope called the process *Aggiornamento,* the Italian word meaning "bringing up to date," and his great hope was that the Council would help to restore Christian unity in the ecumenical spirit of ending differences among Christian churches, promoting religious liberty worldwide, and inaugurating a fresh and truly human relationship between the Roman Catholic Church and its bishops and the masses of the faithful everywhere.

For young Bishop Karol Wojtyła, a product of World War II and an intellectual member of the militant postwar Church generation, full of ideas about how best to strengthen Catholicism's great moral teachings, Vatican Council II offered exciting prospects.

Working at his new office at the archbishop's palace on Franciszkańska Street, the seat of the Kraków Metropolitan Curia, and at his new bishop's quarters at No. 21, Kanoniczna Street, Wojtyła drafted his "Animadversiones"—comments—for the council agenda. His scholarly and unusual pastoral background along with his interest in everything from history and social ethics to marriage and sexuality placed him in a singularly advantageous position for participation in the forthcoming council. Unquestionably, he stood far above the intellectual level of the nearly three thousand bishops invited to attend the Vatican convocation. For the moment, however, he was totally unknown to the world Church hierarchy.

And for the first time, Wojtyła could work in comfort. His new home was spacious with unaccustomed elbow room after sharing the apartment in the building next door with Father Ignacy Różycki, his professor and friend. The bishop's apartment had its personal chapel, so welcome to a man as dedicated to prayer as Wojtyła, and Stefania Adelajda Wojtyła, his father's half sister, joined him to run his household. He was busier than ever before, adding a suffragan's duties to all his previous responsibilities, commitments, and interests, and, of course, trying to do more than any auxiliary bishop had ever attempted.

Indeed, Wojtyła was so busy that he brought upon himself the wrath of the communist authorities within six months of his elevation to the episcopate.

Since he had become bishop the previous September, Wojtyła kept up his normal activities—normal by his standards—but the regime, which had paid no attention to him in the past, suddenly discovered that he was an evil influence on Polish society.

Thus in October, he had celebrated Mass for lawyers in one church and for students in another, delivering meaty sermons on both occasions. In November, he celebrated solemn Mass at two churches close to his heart: St. Stanisław's in Dębniki in his old Kraków neighborhood near Tyniecka Street, and at the parish church in Wadowice. In his hometown, he called on his old parish priest, Father Leonard Prochownik, and visited the convent of his beloved Albertine Sisters and the Discalced Carmelites' monastery where, as a boy, he received the scapular he still wears.

Back in Kraków, he celebrated Mass to ask God for the beatification of Brother Albert, and a Mass for the editors of *Tygodnik Powszechny,* with whom he then discussed their problems with censorship. In December, he paid his first visit as bishop to Oświęcim, delivering a sermon at a students' retreat.

Early in January of the new year, Wojtyła brought up *Tygodnik's* problems at a meeting of the Apostolate Commission of the episcopate in Zakopane, raising at the same time the danger of influences exercised on the young people by "materialism, positivism, liberalism and existentialism." Later, he addressed nurses and physicians in sermons at separate Masses. In February he went to Catholic University in Lublin to give a lecture titled "Human Nature as

Ethical Basis for Man's Formation." In Kraków, in March, he met all day with *Tygodnik* editors, then inaugurated a lawyers' retreat, a physicians' retreat, and a science researchers' retreat.

It all seemed perfectly routine for a bishop, but the authorities perceived great peril in Wojtyła's continued contacts with so many professionals and students. It was one thing when he maintained these contacts as a simple priest, but apparently quite another when he became a bishop. Rather ludicrously, the regime decided to protest Wojtyła's activities.

On March 23, 1959, Wiktor Boniecki, chairman of the Kraków presidium of the National Council, an umbrella government political organization fronting for the communists, fired off a two-page letter to Archbishop Baziak charging that Bishop Wojtyła's "stand and activities" encouraged the clergy to "violate the law." The archdiocese, Boniecki wrote indignantly, not only fails to act against such violations, but "in some cases it participates in the activities of illegal associations."

Bishop Wojtyła, he claimed, was "an example" of the encouragement given the clergy law violators. "The proof of it," his letter said, "are 'meditation days' organized by him for lawyers, physicians, teachers and the youth. Organizing such occasions introduces an artificial division between believers and non-believers, violating at the same time the social and political unity of the local [Kraków] society."

The National Council letter also took exception to what "many preachers, among them Bishop Wojtyła," were saying to their audiences. "They try to analyze," it said, "the work of those in various [government] departments. . . . They do not stop at criticism of such work which, while in accordance with regulations of national authorities, does not meet the Church's views. On the contrary, the preachers' approval is given, not infrequently, to that which, from the standpoint of government regulations, should be condemned."

Then Boniecki acknowledged what really troubled him in Wojtyła's activities:

> Such activity deepens the division of citizens employed by state institutions into believers and non-believers. Besides, it weakens work discipline and the quality of [work] performance. . . . It distorts society's views, urging [people] to value more the opinion of a physician who is a practicing Catholic combating enlightened motherhood, or of a teacher who omits certain "sensitive" questions from government-approved textbooks, than the opinions of their non-believer colleagues.

The clincher in the letter was that "from the moment bishop Wojtyła assumed his post in the Curia, activities contrary to [official] regulations on the part of a certain segment of the Kraków clergy have grown, for which the Presidium holds bishop Wojtyła responsible."

Archbishop Baziak had turned the letter over to Wojtyła, who, displaying unsuspected combativeness, wrote back denouncing the National Council for attacking him. He wrote Baziak:

> I must state that this charge is baseless because there is no law forbidding bishops and priests to conduct normal pastoral work. My activity, or activities supported by me, that are mentioned in the letter are strictly and exclusively part of pastoral work. The cited "meditation days," which are routinely conducted for specific groups in a sacral site such as a church, chapel or monastery, have a strictly religious character.
>
> To claim that this creates an "artificial division between believers and non-believers" is entirely improper because both exist in society, and pastoral work is directed toward all who wish to take advantage of it. Those, I assume, are believers. In this case, don't they have the right to the fulfillment of their objective religious needs through pastoral activity? . . . The very same lay Catholics demand such pastoral work from us, and in its absence they accuse us of a lack of fervor and of not carrying out the duties of our calling.

He noted that even the communist-drafted Polish Constitution guaranteed the freedom of worship and conscience, and he charged that Chairman Boniecki's letter was "openly at variance with this constitutional principle." Wojtyła added:

> If this thinking is understood correctly, it appears that believers should not have the knowledge of Church teachings in fundamental questions of faith and morality. Thus, for example, they should know nothing about what concept of enlightened motherhood the Church recognizes as being consistent with natural law. . . . But if they will not know about it, and pastors will have no right to speak about it, how can one speak of freedom of conscience and worship?

Wojtyła concluded that the charge against him of criticizing those carrying out official policies is "a calumny."

The incident opened a new chapter in Wojtyła's attitude toward Poland's political situation. It made him a public figure, and henceforth he was ready to speak out and act on what he considered to be the sanctity of the rights of the Church and his fellow Poles. Strangely, the communists would misunderstand him again in the next phase of their relationship.

Just as the communists hurt Bishop Wojtyła's feelings with their accusations, he also experienced excruciating physical pain and illness during that month of March. Coming down with high fever, total exhaustion, and the swelling of neck glands, he summoned his physician and friend, Dr. Stanisław Kownacki. Worried, Archbishop Baziak urged the physician to give Wojtyła the best care possible (which, Kownacki said, he was doing anyway). A blood test showed that he had contracted mononucleosis, a contagious epidemic disease also known as glandular fever, caused by a virus. But to assure that no complications, particularly affecting the brain, were developing, Dr. Kowackni plunged a big needle into Wojtyła's spine to draw cerebrospinal fluid that would show whether he suffered from neurological diseases.

In the late 1950s, it was a complicated and painful procedure, with no adequate instruments available, and Wojtyła truly suffered. He later told Professor Swieżawski, his KUL friend, that "the virus disease was much worse, surgically, than the 'accident.'" It was a reference to the wounds he received in the assassination attempt in 1981. During the bone marrow extraction, Wojtyła sympathized with the doctor for having "to fight so hard trying to penetrate the hard bone with the needle."

The cure for mononucleosis, the bishop was told, was fresh air and exercise—at least two weeks in the summer and two weeks in the winter. He was, of course, delighted with his doctor's orders to go kayaking or skiing. When he could not take off two weeks in the winter, Wojtyła would go to the mountains for a day at a time, meticulously counting them to add up to fourteen. Father Maliński told him that it was "scientific justification" for the vacations he enjoyed taking anyway. And Wojtyła devoted a few minutes every morning to calisthenics in his bedroom—a practice he continued in the Vatican.

It is not clear when Wojtyła was finally cured. Records at the Kraków archdiocese indicate that he often missed days at work, and even trips, because of "illness." He was ill all of December 1961, and again in the fall of 1963. It also appears that he had an "iron constitution," and was capable of spending time in the heat of the lowlands and the cold of the mountains so that he could "speak to the people" as much as required.

And speak Bishop Wojtyła did, day in and day out, in Kraków and other cities, towns, and villages of the archdiocese. He became a familiar sight across the southwestern countryside, a slightly stooped figure wearing a purple biretta and frayed but clean cassock—he had that down-at-the-heels look, people said sympathetically—peering at priests and parishioners through his horn-rimmed glasses, asking questions, giving advice, and becoming involved in every aspect of parish life.

Father Kuczkowski, the former Curial chancellor, says that at first, parish priests deep in the rural areas had doubts whether Wojtyła, a scholar and bookworm, "will know how to establish contact with the people he will meet during a visitation." But soon, he recalls, "they become convinced that he knows how to talk to people, and that they will be able to understand him . . . they saw that he conducts the visitations in a very insightful way, but is very open to the people, and doesn't place a barrier between the bishop and the people. . . . And he was always courteous, polite, helpful."

Still, Father Kuczkowski says, "there was always an invisible frontier between him and the priests." Wojtyła was in their company during meetings and visitations, "joining them for lunch or dinner, chatting and joking, but there was one thing he didn't like . . . he didn't like to listen when something critical was being said about another priest."

Wojtyła did his homework in preparation for the visitations. Father Obtułowicz, who was co-vicar with him at St. Florian's and later the canon at the cathedral in charge of pastoral work, says that before each visit the bishop carefully studied parish reports sent to him beforehand by the priests. Then, "he looked around, comparing what he had read with what he saw . . . to see whether it corresponded to what was in the report."

Because Archbishop Baziak's age and poor health prevented him from travel, Wojtyła was responsible alone for parish visitations in the entire sprawling archdiocese. Father Obtułowicz emphasizes that the inspections were not only "parish after parish, quickly," but sometimes an extended stay, particularly in large urban parishes, to become really acquainted with the local situation. Sometimes, he says, Wojtyła would spend a whole week in one parish, participating "in all the activities the parish had."

The bishop also demanded that each priest in the archdiocese visit him in Kraków at least once a year to bring him up to date on the situation in his parish. He served them tea and cookies. The priests began at the same time to receive annual good-wishes cards on their name days, signed personally by Wojtyła. Every priest ordained by him receives a card, too.

Father Michał Jagosz, who knew Wojtyła well in Poland, believes that the way in which he conducted the visitations, and the number of people of all walks of life he met in the process, "made him more concerned about being understood by everyone, and that is why he became more communicative."

Even more importantly, Father Jagosz points out, "people realized that Wojtyła was turning into a defender of human rights, especially on behalf of people who wanted to be able to keep their jobs in government agencies even though they were believers, and to rest assured that there would be no repercussions if they took a child to Holy Communion or were married in church."

Wojtyła insisted that these were "normal rights" of the people, not a privilege, as were participation in great religious processions and other acts of public worship. Because the regime was reluctant to grant church-building permits in new parishes, Father Jagosz says, Wojtyła had made up his mind that it was wrong for him, for example, to celebrate Christmas Eve Mass in the warmth and comfort of Wawel Cathedral. He therefore proceeded to officiate on empty lots in the open air in the exact spots where he had petitioned the authorities for permission for the churches to be erected. He did not seem to mind the cold weather, and an umbrella was held over his head if it rained or snowed. With the faithful freezing along with him at these outdoor Masses in the darkness, Wojtyła was challenging as well as embarrassing the regime.

The bishop was a stickler for confrontational protocol. Priests in Poland, as elsewhere, are traditionally addressed as "Father," but the communists had instructed officials to address them as "Mister," at least in public. Wojtyła, for his part, ordered his priests to protest loudly whenever it happened. According to Father Jagosz, "sometimes it bore fruit and sometimes not, but it was a matter of principle to remind them that we won't accept everything that easily." Wojtyła had a very wide circle of cordial acquaintances among the clergy and laypeople, such as Father Maliński and Father Obtułowicz or *Tygodnik Powszechny* editor Jerzy Turowicz and some of his associates. But Wojtyła was always a very private person who reserved the notion of "friend" for very few people.

Wartime associates like Juliusz Kydryński, the writer, were still friends, but Wojtyła did not seem to see much of them. Among those close to him during that period were Jerzy Janik, the physicist and faithful ski companion, and his wife; an engineer named Jerzy Ciesielski, whose death by drowning with his two little daughters in the Nile near Khartoum in the Sudan in 1970 had upset Wojtyła greatly; and Wanda Półtawska, a physician, and her philosopher husband.

Father Tadeusz Styczeń, who was Wojtyła's student at KUL and more and more frequently a skiing companion, was a very special friend. A philosopher, Father Styczeń was noticed by Wojtyła as a most promising individual from the very outset in a way reminiscent of his own discovery by Archbishop Sapieha. To the extent that Wojtyła had a protégé, Father Styczeń was the only one. In 1963, Bishop Wojtyła presided over the evaluation of his doctoral dissertation on John Locke and scientific ethics.

Still at KUL as chairman of the Ethics Department in the mid-1990s, Father Styczeń may be the single most influential person, intellectually and spiritually, with permanent access to John Paul II, whom he visits quite frequently. And according to the pope, he was a key drafter of the 1993 *Veritatis Splendor* encyclical.

Karol Wojtyła is always perfectly willing to engage in massive overkill if he thinks it is in a good cause. He usually carries it off in high style.

In the early 1960s, a cause greatly on his mind was the sanctity of the institution of marriage, and he addressed it with an impressive literary tour de force by completing—among his other duties—the book *Love and Responsibility*, published in 1962, and composing the play *In Front of the Jeweler's Shop*. These were in addition to monographs and uncounted articles, lectures, and sermons on the subject.

Love and Responsibility is a relatively short work (255 pages in the Polish edition), dealing extensively with sexuality in the context of Christian ethics in chapters on sexual drive and its religious and "libido" interpretation, absorption of "sexual shame" by love, sexual psychopathology and ethics, and the concept of virginity. On marriage itself, the book discusses monogamy, "metaphysical analysis of love," and "the possession of one person by another," Wojtyła advocating the equality of man and woman in marriage. To be helpful to the male practitioner of sanctioned sex, he explains the rhythms of a woman's fertility, provides three tables of fertility periods, and describes the configuration of the female sex organ. Wojtyła is a master of theoretical research.

Remarkably, it became a best-seller, with hundreds of thousands of copies sold in Poland (a new edition in 1985, still under communism, had an initial printing of fifty thousand copies), and editions in English, French, Spanish (ten editions), Italian, German, Portuguese, Swedish, and Japanese. Most of the foreign editions appeared after Wojtyła was elected pope. Since 1985, Father Styczeń is listed as the publisher of the Polish edition under KUL's imprint.

In Front of the Jeweler's Shop, signed with the pseudonym of Andrzej Jawień and published in Kraków's monthly *Znak (Tygodnik*'s sister publication), carries the subtitle "Meditation on the Sacrament of Marriage, Turning Occasionally into Drama." It is a rather bizarre three-part theatrical construction, in which, instead of dialogue, the principal personages deliver narrative monologues, complemented by fragments of letters and the offstage voice of a chorus. It is not a religious work but a moral, inspirational, and slightly mystical one—with unexpected touches of sensuality.

The "Old Jeweler," who seems to be dealing only in wedding rings, is the symbol of the sanctity of marriage and the play's central personage. Sometime before the war, he sells a set of rings to a young couple named Andrzej and Teresa who are deeply in love. Teresa remembers that when Andrzej proposed to her, he did not ask, "Do you want to be my wife?" but to be "my life's companion." Andrzej remembers that he had always been looking for a woman who "really would be a second 'me.'" This underlines Wojtyła's view on equality in marriage.

The second part concerns a couple named Anna and Stefan whose marriage is on the rocks, and Anna decides to sell her wedding ring. But the Old Jeweler refuses to buy it after placing the ring on his scales and announcing that "it does not weigh anything . . . because a single ring has no weight, only the two together have weight." Anna is on the verge of striking up relationships with other men as a "casual woman" but is dissuaded by a mysterious wise personage named Adam (which is the real first name of Wojtyła's venerated Brother Albert).

In the third part, young Krzysztof and Monika come to the jeweler's shop to buy their wedding rings (it is after the war and they had met on a skiing trip). Krzysztof is the son of the happily married Andrzej and Teresa. Andrzej, however, was killed during the war and Adam, who had served in the same army unit, replaces him as Krzysztof's spiritual father (though Teresa had hoped he would propose marriage to her). Monika is the daughter of the unhappy Anna and Stefan. After Krzysztof and Monika are wed, Anna and Stefan find a "new . . . fulfilling love," and the play closes with an emotional happy ending.

After Wojtyła became pope, *Jeweler* was translated into Italian and made into a radio play. Then Hollywood bought it, producing the drama as a syrupy motion picture starring Burt Lancaster as the soulful Old Jeweler.

Back in real life, Bishop Wojtyła was increasingly at odds with the communist authorities. The Poland October of 1956 had turned into a false dawn as Party First Secretary Gomułka gradually transformed himself into a hard-liner fully obedient to Moscow. Most of the liberal gains had been gradually erased, and the regime resumed the pre-1956 campaign to control the Church, though in a more civilized fashion. Now it was nasty harassment instead of imprisonment and trials.

Wojtyła's strategy was finely tuned. He was not practicing fervent anti-communism publicly or privately—unlike many in the clergy who certainly did so behind closed doors—but he declined to accommodate the authorities. Quietly but aggressively, he stood for the rights of the Church as he had in his reaction to the 1959 letter from the National Council. He was prepared to compromise in specific situations on a commonsense basis, but he rejected compromises on matters of broad policy. This was the subtle difference between Primate Wyszyński and Bishop Wojtyła that would become more and more accentuated.

Consequently, Wojtyła pursued his own activities, ignoring the regime's warnings but not provoking it. In October 1959, for instance, he delivered a lecture and a sermon to Catholic intellectuals at the monastery of the Black Madonna in Częstochowa. In May 1960 he went to Wrocław in western Poland for a conference on pastoral work with "creative individuals." In July he became the "protector" of *Tygodnik*.

In the protector capacity, Wojtyła displayed openmindedness that surprised at least one visitor. Andrzej Micewski, a well-known leftist Catholic journalist and writer who once belonged to the pro-regime PAX movement, had come to seek the bishop's green light to be allowed to write for *Tygodnik*. Because of his leftist past, Micewski had not been welcome at the weekly, and as he recalls his visit to the archdiocese, Wojtyła asked him pointblank: "Have you stopped being a socialist?"

"I frankly told him, 'No, because I think that socialism can be reformed,'" Micewski says. "But Wojtyła tells me, 'You know, I have a different opinion, but I am pleased that you have told me honestly that you haven't entirely broken with socialism. And, yes, you will be able to write for *Tygodnik*.' . . . I think he really appreciated my honesty. . . ."

In September 1961 Wojtyła celebrated Mass at Wawel Cathedral on the twentieth anniversary of the Rhapsodic Theater, to which he had belonged during the war. Then he attended the opening of its production of *Forefathers' Eve*, the defiantly passionate patriotic play by Adam Mickiewicz that equates Poland's martyrdom with the Crucifixion—and was meant to be anti-Russian. The next day, he wrote an article about the play for *Tygodnik*, signing it with the initials "A.J."

In January 1962 Wojtyła spoke at St. Anna's Church on John XXIII's newly issued encyclical, *Mater et Magistra*, which dealt with Christianity and social progress, expanding and updating Leo XIII's *Rerum novarum* encyclical on the Church's social teaching. A week later, he was named by the episcopate to serve as national chaplain of "Creative

Intelligentsia." All of these activities were most carefully planned by Wojtyła, who was aware of the extraordinary importance of intellectuals in Poland's political life; he would remain closely allied with them over all the years of struggle and transition. He retained his ethics chair at KUL, although the best he could do for his students was to arrive breathlessly from Kraków three or four times a year to deliver a lecture lasting three or four hours, then race for the first train back.

The next turning point for Wojtyła came on June 15, 1962, with the death of Archbishop Baziak. The following day, the capitular chapter of the archdiocese elected Wojtyła as capitular vicar, which put him effectively in charge of the Kraków Church with the powers and prestige of an archbishop. Wojtyła had returned the day before Baziak's death from a trip to Warsaw that included his first flight aboard an aircraft.

With Baziak gone, Wojtyła no longer had a highly placed protector in Poland. The primate clearly was not interested in playing that role. But Wojtyła was now on his own, self-assured and enjoying his new authority. And he was ready to exercise it on behalf of the Church.

On August 28, three days after the authorities seized the building of the convent of the Sisters of Our Lady of Mercy, Wojtyła—who had been out of town—rushed there to assure the despairing nuns that although they had suffered "grave injury," all would be well.

In mid-September, the bishop was summoned back from a rural parish visitation when the regime attempted to seize the downtown buildings of the Kraków Seminary to turn them over to the Superior Teachers' College. Instantly, he had his driver take him to the regional headquarters of PZPR to confront the first secretary, Lucjan Motyka. This was the first time a Polish bishop had ever gone on his own initiative to see a communist leader.

But this head-on approach produced a compromise that the communists had never before accepted. Motyka and Wojtyła agreed that the teachers' college would occupy the third floor of the building while the seminary kept the rest of it.

It was Karol Wojtyła's diplomatic debut. But he added a

touch of theater to it: two weeks later, he led the seminary's faculty and students on a solemn, silent march to a seminary building around the corner to dedicate it to the Virgin Mary.

Next, he would turn to diplomacy and a very special form of theater at the Holy See.

CHAPTER 15

After fourteen and a half years, Karol Wojtyła was back in Rome, now a bishop, moral philosopher, and council father brimming with ideas he hoped to be able to contribute to the renewal of the Roman Catholic Church. It was also the first time since then that Wojtyła had left the confines of communist Poland for the refreshing intellectual and cultural air of Rome and the West.

Together with Cardinal Wyszyński, who, as Primate of Poland, led the Polish episcopal delegation to the Second Vatican Council, and ten fellow bishops, Wojtyła arrived in Rome by train from Vienna on October 6, 1962. In Vienna Wojtyła met Cardinal Franz König, one of the most influential and intellectually stimulating Church personalities in Europe. It was the start of an extremely important relationship in his ecclesiastic career.

Approximately twenty-five Polish bishops (of sixty) had applied for passports to travel to Rome, but fifteen were inexplicably turned down on this occasion. Wyszyński, as primate and the only Polish member of the council's Central Preparatory Commission, presumably could not be denied a passport.

But that Wojtyła was permitted to travel may have been a purely capricious act on the part of the UB (the secret police). On one hand, he had been annoying the authorities with his independence, but on the other he was the first bishop to have negotiated directly with a senior communist official, on his own initiative, and this may have intrigued the regime, which was always on the lookout for a chance to split the Polish Church.

While the Kraków bishop was the youngest of the Polish contingent, he was undoubtedly its most important member after Wyszyński, and arguably the brightest and the best prepared for the work of the council. And Wojtyła had also done his homework exceedingly well—with the aid of well-placed friends. Early in 1962, the Vatican had sent to Warsaw a secret document—a slim booklet listing over forty issues expected to come up for discussion. It had been refined by the Ante-Preparatory Commission from three volumes of replies to the questionnaires that had been sent out to the 2,594 bishops in 1959. Its distribution was limited to senior figures in national episcopates.

In the case of Poland, the document was to be delivered only to Cardinal Wyszyński, Archbishop Baziak in Kraków, and four bishops who belonged to the Polish preparatory commission. Wojtyła, still a suffragan, was not entitled to receive it. But in the mysterious fashion his network of friends operated, a copy turned up one day on his desk. It was of immense help in getting ready for the council.

In Rome, Wojtyła and the other younger bishops were assigned lodgings at Istituto Polacco (Polish Institute), a five-story raw-amber-colored corner building on the narrow Via Pietro Cavallini, a block from the Tiber and near Cavour Bridge on the west bank of the river. It is an affluent, middle-class neighborhood, not far from the Vatican.

Cardinal Wyszyński and other senior Polish prelates were staying at Collegio Polacco (Polish College), a large residence surrounded by cypress trees on Piazza Remuria on elegant Aventino Heights on the other side of the Tiber. At the Istituto, Wojtyła occupied a small apartment overlooking Via Pietro Cavallini and its shops.

It is a fairly short, pleasant walk from Wojtyła's lodgings at the Istituto to the Vatican, where the council sessions were held at St. Peter's Basilica, and, taking his long strides, he could cover it in fifteen minutes or so. Leaving the building at No. 38 Via Pietro Cavallini, he would stroll two blocks to the large Piazza Cavour, past the majestic Palace of Justice on his left, then along Via Crescenzio to Piazza Adriana and around the moated Castel Sant'Angelo, and into the broad Via della Conciliazione, which led directly to St. Peter's Square. Wojtyła enjoyed the walk, was delighted to be back in Rome, rediscovered pizza, and celebrated the new moment in his life by discarding his eyeglasses, at least in public.

During his long absence, Rome had become prosperous again, certainly around the Vatican, with the harsh postwar period long forgotten. Poverty reigned only where workers lived. Via della Conciliazione was filled with impatient, honking traffic, tourist buses, and crowds of pilgrims making their way to the square before the area was sealed off for the seven-week period of the first session of the Second Vatican Council.

Awaiting its inauguration, Wojtyła spent his first week in Rome consulting with his friends—all of them influential and very well informed—and beginning with the help of his Polish friends to establish contacts with personalities in the Curia and other bishops arriving from the five continents. His Italian was still fluent, and his French, English, Spanish, and German more or less serviceable. Very few other bishops had Wojtyła's full command of Latin, so it could not quite be lingua franca among the Church dignitaries.

On October 8, he was received along with the rest of the Polish episcopal group by Pope John XXIII at the papal apartments at the Vatican. Wojtyła had now met two popes, briefly, but still most unusual for a young Polish priest.

In Rome, Wojtyła was lucky in finding his old friend Father Andrzej Maria Deskur in a strategic position as the council's press secretary. Deskur (himself a cardinal many years later) had worked in Rome since 1952, but they had known each other since the autumn of 1945, when both were students at the Kraków Seminary; it is a friendship that has endured for over a half century.

Deskur, four years younger than Wojtyła, was the scion of an old wealthy aristocratic family of remote French origins (the name, he says, was Descourt when his ancestors came to Poland centuries earlier), and he was as superbly connected in Rome as he was in Poland. He had a law degree, a theological doctorate, had attended the Pontifical Diplomatic Academy, was multilingual, and was a natural guide for Wojtyła through the thicket of Curial politics.

With Deskur in a key spot at the council, Wojtyła had some guidance in his last-minute preparations. Deskur recalls strolling with him in the Vatican Gardens during the pre-inauguration week as they discussed "what great problems are emerging and what trends may come out of the Council." And it was Deskur who discreetly spread the word among power-wielders of the Curia that Wojtyła was a new person worth knowing.

"So, all my friends wanted to meet this Bishop Wojtyła," Deskur recalls. "In Rome, you must remember, lots of people knew old Cardinal Sapieha and wanted to meet his successor, which, in effect, Wojtyła already was."

Among them was the aging, partially blind Cardinal Alfredo Ottaviani, the Prefect of the Holy Office (later the council modernized its name to the more palatable appellation of the Congregation for the Doctrine of the Faith), the all-powerful theological and ideological watchdog of the Vatican (and once the seat of the Holy Inquisition). Ottaviani was by far the most conservative senior figure in the very conservative Curia, and he would loom during the council as the chief foe of any meaningful change in the structure, appearance, or policy of the Church in any realm. Romans joked that when Ottaviani once instructed a taxi driver to take him "to the council," the man asked, "You mean Trent?"—a reference to the sixteenth-century ecumenical council called to battle the Protestant Reform.

Deskur recalls that Wojtyła's reputation spread so rapidly that "when we were preparing membership lists before the Council, all the commissions kept asking for him." He says that Wojtyła and Father Jean-Marie Lustiger, the future archbishop of Paris, were the most sought after by the commissions and subcommissions. (Lustiger, of Polish origin and a convert from Judaism, would be named cardinal by John Paul II seventeen years later.) Thus from the outset, Wojtyła found himself in an extraordinary position at the Vatican Council for an obscure young bishop from a faraway country.

Wojtyła made a new Polish friend—Monsignor Władysław Rubin, rector of the Polish College and one of the secretaries of the council's Ante-Preparatory Commission. He, too, was an excellent guide and adviser, and a close friend until his death in the 1980s, as a John Paul II cardinal. Professor Swieżawski, his philosopher friend from KUL, was in Rome as a council *perito,* a lay expert.

Among old friends, Wojtyła immediately called on his favorite Angelicum teacher, Father Garrigou-Lagrange, a "consultor" to the Council, who provided him with further insights into the approaching debates. And he kept meeting new people every day—and every night.

Harvard's Professor Williams, who attended the council as an invited Protestant "observer," recalls that Wojtyła had visited him and fellow Americans at San Angelo boarding house, near Sant'Angelo Castle, after they had asked the Polish delegation to send one of its members for a discussion of the Church in Eastern Europe. Though Wojtyła's English was still rather wobbly in those days, Williams remembers how impressed he was with the Kraków bishop. In 1978, Williams predicted in the Harvard *Crimson* that Wojtyła would be the next pope.

On the eve of the council, Rome's atmosphere was electric. Everyone knew that great changes were coming, even those who feared and opposed them. The council fathers were divided among conservatives, progressives, and moderates, though all these terms were essentially misleading, meaning different things to different bishops, varying from theme to theme, and often defined by their national, political, racial, cultural, educational, age, and theological backgrounds.

At the start of the council, Wojtyła, as on so many other occasions, defied classification. Professor Williams described him as a "progressive conservative," which probably is as accurate a term as could be applied to him. Wojtyła's public attitudes at the council also underlined that he is not single-minded on every issue, a fundamental fact about him.

In Rome in the 1960s, he was conservative in some dimensions and progressive in others—just as he is in the pontifical mantle—but he tended strongly toward more progressive and social justice positions. Studied thirty years later, his stand at the council also indicates that he has always been absolutely consistent on all issues. It is therefore a myth that Wojtyła was more progressive (or "liberal") as a council father than as pope.

At the council, he gravitated toward progressive-minded Church theologians, intellectuals, and reformers rather than toward the hard-line conservatives of Cardinal Ottaviani's persuasion. The scholars who impressed him the most were the *periti* (experts), ranging from the German Jesuit Karl Rahner and French Jesuit Jean Daniélou, the French Dominican Yves Congar, and the Swiss theologian Hans Küng. This was perhaps because Wojtyła was attracted to thinkers and intellectuals in the first place. As pope, however, he would break with Küng because he would not tolerate Küng's growing dissent with the Church teachings he preaches.

Throughout the Vatican Council, which opened with pomp and solemnity on October 11, Bishop Wojtyła shone through his hard work. But, as usual, he found time for extraordinary extracurricular activities.

The day began for him at 6:45 A.M. with Mass at the Istituto. Then he walked to St. Peter's Basilica where the sessions began with a solemn Mass at 9:00 A.M. With 2,860 council fathers in attendance (plus over 150 auditors, experts, and observers), a two-thousand-square-meter section of the huge basilica was turned into a conference hall.

On each side of the broad central passage, tall stands with ten rows of seats were erected to accommodate the 108 cardinals, 9 primates, 5 patriarchs, 543 archbishops, 2,171 bishops, 129 Fathers Superior of religious orders, and 93 abbots. They sat in green velvet chairs with prie-dieux and lap writing desks in accordance with rank and seniority. The cardinals were on the lower levels and the bishops higher above, toward the rafters, but all nationalities were mixed. It was the biggest and the most varied gathering of men of the cloth in the history of the Roman Catholic Church.

Wojtyła's seat was near the entrance to the basilica, and from there he could observe on the opening day the arrival of John XXIII borne on a *sedes gestatoria*, an ornate sedan chair, in the dying Vatican tradition, and watch bearded Cardinal Eugène Tisserant, the head of the College of Cardinals, celebrate the inaugural Mass.

For nearly seven weeks, Wojtyła could also listen to the daily drone of speeches delivered in Latin, mostly execrably spoken Latin (especially by the Anglo-Saxons), before his turn to speak for the first time came on November 7. *His* Latin was excellent because of the Polish educational system under which, as Deskur once remarked, "we had to memorize Horace's Odes, but some of the 'Council Fathers' could not understand the Latin translations of the texts of their own speeches." The Basilica also echoed with the discussions and conversations of the nearly three thousand council fathers and lay participants filling the area.

Usually stopping to pray at one of the side chapels or altars before reaching his seat, Wojtyła then proceeded to display quietly his amazing powers of concentration as he wrote poetry in longhand on the lap desk while listening intently to the speeches. Back in Kraków, he had already earned a legendary reputation at the archdiocese for his ability to read his mail with utmost attention, often going through a whole stack of letters, as he listened to a discussion over which he was presiding. At the end, he would surprise those present by summarizing with absolute precision the debate of the previous two or three hours, not having missed the slightest nuance, and announcing his decisions or recommendations. Ursuline Sister Emilia Ehrlich, whose father was a Polish Jew and university professor and mother an Englishwoman, and who taught him English at the archdiocese, was astounded that Wojtyła closely followed lessons while writing a speech or sermon. (She is now one of his confidential secretaries at the Vatican.)

During the seven weeks of the council's first session in 1962, Wojtyła composed a seven-poem cycle under the overall title of simply *The Church*. These poems described for the most part what he saw and heard in the basilica—one is called "The Wall," another "The Floor," and a third "The Crypt"—but the most intriguing is the nine-line

poem "The Negro." It is the only poem in the cycle deali with a specifically identified human being, whereas in t other ones "man" is mentioned as a generality.

Wojtyła speaks in it to "My Dear Brother" in whom h feels "the immense continent in which rivers sudden break off . . . and the sun burns the body like ore in a mi furnace." He tells him that "I sense in you a simila thought, but even if it does not run in the same way, it sti separates truth from error by its very weight." And h concludes with the sentiment of "happiness of weighing o one scale the thoughts that so differently flicker in your eye and mine—though they contain the same meaning. . . ."

"The Negro" seems to convey Wojtyła's discovery, spirit ually and sociologically, of people of other races and, in a sense, of the Third World. Though nobody in Africa was likely to read it, it was meant as a message of friendship. Father Maliński, who often accompanied him at the council sessions, noted that Wojtyła had many conversations with African bishops.

"The Negro," then, marks the beginning of his intense interest in Africa in particular and the Third World in general, demonstrated by the papal globetrotting and even earlier voyages. The African Church, of course, is one of the oldest in Christendom, and, in the 1990s, John Paul II saw in it the future of Catholicism, engaging in vast efforts to evangelize the continent.

At eleven o'clock, there was a morning break in the session and most of the fathers congregated at coffee bars in the basilica, but Wojtyła rarely left his seat. Apart from poetry, he used the time there to draft speeches he would make in the Polish service of the Vatican Radio, prepare KUL lectures, and work on a new book. On the way out of the basilica, however, he would again be sociable, chatting with fellow bishops and meeting more and more of them. Among them was Polish-descended Archbishop John Krol of Philadelphia, later a cardinal and lifetime friend to whom John Paul II may, in part, owe his papacy.

Back at the Istituto Polacco, Wojtyła would have a short nap, then study council texts or write a speech of his own or a lecture or a sermon. In the late afternoon and evening, he

attended meetings of council commissions and subcommissions to which he belonged. He dined at the institute or as the guest of other bishops or religious orders, ending the day with a stroll on the terrace, with the floodlit St. Peter's cupolą clearly visible.

The council was shaken during the first month of its deliberations by the Cuban Missile Crisis, when the Soviets deployed nuclear weapons in the Caribbean island, bringing the world to the brink of a global war. John XXIII appealed to President John Kennedy and Nikita Khrushchev on October 25 to do everything in their power to save the peace.

Bishop Wojtyła is not known to have offered public comment on the crisis, nor was he expected to do so. But he was already deeply involved in work on one of the council's basic documents—"The Church in the Modern World"—which touched on the great issues of peace and war. They would become preeminent in his pontifical concerns.

For personal peace and serenity, Wojtyła favored the sanctuary of Mentorella in the mountains some forty miles east of Rome. It is one of the oldest sanctuaries in Italy, and, since 1857, it has been under the care of Polish Resurrectionist Fathers. The sanctuary, the church, and the small monastery—nowadays only four fathers live there—are atop strikingly beautiful Mount Guadagnolo. Wojtyła was brought to Mentorella for the first time by his friend Deskur during the Second Vatican Council.

It became one of his preferred hiking areas, and the fathers remember Wojtyła arriving by bus to the village below—he could not afford even to rent a car in those days—then climbing about nine miles along a paved road to reach the sanctuary, his trousers rolled up to the knees. When he returned to Mentorella as cardinal, the father superior, Jan Mika, told him at dinner that "the Italians are saying that the next pope will be Polish." Wojtyła demurred, but he drove to the sanctuary to pray there on October 7, 1978, nine days before his election. He returned by helicopter two weeks after becoming pope.

At the Vatican Council, a major step on his road to the papacy, Wojtyła addressed the fathers twice during the

October–December 1962 session and submitted two written texts for their consideration. Again, he demonstrated his wide-ranging interests: he spoke on complex matters of liturgy, while his written presentations dealt with "means of Social Communication," which meant the media, and on the organization of the Church. Even as a young bishop living behind the Iron Curtain, Wojtyła understood the overwhelming importance of using the media for the Christian message.

The question of liturgy that Wojtyła addressed on November 7 was as political as it was theological. The draft document on liturgy urged, against firm conservative opposition led by Cardinal Ottaviani, basic changes in the rite of the Mass, simplifying it in order to make religion accessible to the faithful. It was not only a matter of Mass being said in the vernacular and not in Latin and of having the priest face the congregation instead of turning his back to the worshippers, as tradition demanded, so that his eyes could be centered on the altar. Much more important in the changing world was how to adapt Catholic liturgy to non-European churches.

This had aroused Wojtyła's interest. It was a religious Third World issue over what is now known as "inculturation." African bishops in particular were insisting on the freedom of allowing certain traditional and more expressive forms of worship to coexist with the Roman model of the Mass. To forbid such cultural regionalisms, as the conservatives desired, could drive the faithful away from the Catholic Church because African traditions were so deeply embedded.

Thirty-two years later, inculturation on a much broader scale, including the acceptance of tribal marriages along with Church weddings, faced John Paul II at the 1994 African Bishops Synod in Rome. Most of them argued in favor of inculturation as a precondition for successful evangelization by the Catholic Church in rivalry with Islam and Pentecostal Protestant sects, both of which were rapidly advancing in Africa.

Speaking on November 21, on the draft document "Sources of Revelation," concerning the interpretation of the Scriptures as the source of the faith, Wojtyła stepped into a theological hornets' nest. Immensely controversial and emotional, the matter could not be settled. The language supported by Wojtyła was defeated by a vast margin.

The council's first session ended on December 8, and Wojtyła was back in Kraków the following week to face Polish realities. Among them, as 1963 began, was the question of naming an archbishop to replace the late Baziak. Wojtyła had been acting archbishop, in effect, in his capacity as capitular vicar, but it was by no means certain that he would win the permanent appointment. It was an exceedingly complex and delicate question involving the Kraków Church, Primate Wyszyński, the communist authorities, and the Holy See—in that order.

It also related to Wojtyła's long-range future. But, in the meantime, he played host to a visitor who would be equally involved in that future. The visitor was Vienna's Cardinal König, whom Wojtyła had met briefly on his way to Rome the previous October.

After being refused a Polish visa several times, presumably because he was both a liberal and very active in promoting new policies toward the Soviet Union and Eastern Europe, König finally was granted one, and he advised the Polish episcopate that he would be arriving in Poland on May 29. He was driving from Vienna through Czechoslovakia and would enter the country through the border crossing point at the Polish city of Cieszyn.

Because Cieszyn was in the Kraków archdiocese, Wojtyła was informed simply as a matter of jurisdiction in case König required some form of assistance. But Wojtyła motored to Cieszyn to welcome the Austrian cardinal to Poland.

König remembers the occasion very clearly. He says that after crossing the frontier in his car with the "Vienna 25" license plate—the cardinal's official car—"I noticed a young priest in the crowd gathered there, and I asked, 'Who is that priest?' He seemed so shy. . . ." The cardinal had forgotten meeting him the previous autumn.

Wojtyła greeted him formally, but König thinks that the bishop was "a bit uncomfortable . . . his self-confidence was terrible. . . . He still felt like a young priest . . . and he didn't speak German well. I think we spoke in French." König spent two nights at the Kraków archdiocese *sede vacante*, chatting at some length with Wojtyła, then went on to Warsaw to visit Primate Wyszyński. Being resented by the Polish authorities, and even by some groups in the Polish Church, König appreciated Wojtyła's courtesies toward him. As a friend put it later, "that was when König acquired a debt toward Wojtyła, repaying it fifteen years later."

König and Wyszyński had been friends for many years, but König says that Wojtyła outshone the primate at the Vatican Council because the older man was distracted. He thinks that what mattered the most to Wyszyński at that stage was the one-thousandth anniversary of Christianity in Poland—it would fall in 1966, and he liked being called "the Primate of the Millennium"—and foremost in his thoughts was the possibility of a papal visit for the occasion. No pope had ever visited Poland before.

"So," König explains, "Wyszyński just didn't care very much about the Council. To him, it had to do only with the western world, and he was thinking, 'well, far more important is the other side of Europe . . . Eastern Europe. . . .' "

This is how Wojtyła became, for all practical purposes, the spokesman for the Polish episcopate throughout most of the Second Vatican Council. But the Wyszyński factor, perhaps unbeknownst to him, was hovering in the background as his own future came under scrutiny, intrigue, and manipulation.

CHAPTER 16

The Kraków archdiocese had been a *sede vacante,* an "unoccupied seat," since Archbishop Baziak died in June 1962. It could not be run forever by a capitular vicar, and Karol Wojtyła himself was uncomfortable under this temporary arrangement. But it was up to primate Wyszyński to select a successor.

According to the existing procedure, the primate was to submit a list of at least three names to the regime. In turn, the authorities could accept or reject any of the nominees. Once a name was approved Wyszyński would send it to the Vatican for a final decision.

Despite the myth, both in Poland and abroad, of the father-son relationship between Wyszyński and Wojtyła, there is virtually unanimous agreement among those familiar with the situation that the primate did not wish to see the latter as archbishop in Kraków. Fifteen years later, he would be horrified over the possibility that Wojtyła might be elected pope; in fact, he never believed it would happen.

The truth concerning these events is extremely important because it establishes beyond doubt that the communist regime in Warsaw, wholly misunderstanding the realities of the Polish Church and its personalities, was directly responsible for Wojtyła's appointment as archbishop. This, in turn, led to his cardinalcy and his eventual elevation to the pontificate. The ultimate historical irony was, of course, the decisive role played by John Paul II in the negotiations resulting in the demise of communist rule first in Poland and subsequently elsewhere.

Wojtyła experienced a number of fortunate occurrences in his life, ranging from Cardinal Sapieha's tutelage over his career to Wyszyński's almost casual act of making him auxiliary bishop—another irony. But the real turning point was the secret maneuvering during 1963 involving the primate and the communists over the Kraków archbishop's seat. It was something of a blindman's buff.

It is important to emphasize in this complicated and immensely delicate affair that there never was open hostility between the two men. Wojtyła may not have even known at the time that Wyszyński was arrayed against him. In any event, Wojtyła always displayed absolute loyalty and respect toward the primate, even—and especially—after he became pope.

Following Wyszyński's return from the initial session of the Second Vatican Council, it became obvious that seven months after Baziak's death he could no longer temporize. He finally did act, preparing names of candidates for the regime's consideration, to be presented one at a time. Wojtyła's name, however, was proposed only at the very end, and it would take a full year to resolve the problem. But why did the primate try so hard to keep Wojtyła down?

First, they faced a generational problem, Wyszyński being nineteen years older than Wojtyła and having been born under Russian occupation during the partition of Poland. As Andrzej Micewski, the writer who served on the primate's Privy Council, has remarked, "Wojtyła did not grow up in captivity. He grew up in a normal Poland and for him, unlike for Wyszyński, the national question was not the central one. For Wojtyła, the central question was universal Catholicism." Micewski's point was that the primate was still consumed with fears about Poland's actual *existence* whereas Wojtyła was concerned about what *kind* of Poland there would be—and how the Church fared at home and abroad.

This perception went a long way to explain why Wyszyński, fearful that the Soviet Union might intervene in Poland under some pretext and again erase her independence, believed all along in compromise rather than confrontation with Polish communist authorities. When Wojtyła as bishop was forced to adopt a political attitude, he developed a strategy of confrontation *and* compromise, according to the circumstances. But Wyszyński doubted that Wojtyła would be as accommodating in his dealings with the regime as the primate had been from the start.

Stefan Swieżawski, the philosophy professor and Vatican Council *perito* (expert), remarks that "Wyszyński always strove for some compromise and the building of bridges between the state and the Church," and that "he subordinated his views [on the Polish situation] to things with which he often didn't agree."

Wyszyński also tended to resent Wojtyła intellectually and, in the words of a prelate who knew them both well, "perhaps he was afraid of him." Though the primate was a canon lawyer and a Church scholar with a fine record on social justice, he was suspicious of the more progressive breed of younger intellectuals, in and out of the Church, who dabbled in poetry and theater, of which Wojtyła was a prime example.

Stanisław Stomma, a member of the *Sejm* (Parliament) representing the left-of-center but Church-linked Catholic group Znak, the nearest thing to opposition tolerated by the regime, believes that Wyszyński "had no trust in intellectuals, no trust in literary figures." And Wojtyła, he says, was "too politically literary."

Stomma remarks that "Wyszyński considered that [rural] people are the salt of the earth in Poland, and, as he told us many times, he wanted an Episcopate along those lines." The primate also feared that Wojtyła could be "manipulated" by different forces because of his inexperience.

A Kraków priest familiar with the events put it even more bluntly: "The primate had the notion that the people he named to high posts should be mediocrities, and Wojtyła clearly was not a mediocrity."

This was the state of affairs when Wyszyński finally submitted nominations for the post of Archbishop of Kraków to the Department of Religious Denominations in the Polish government. The accepted procedure was that the authorities had three months to reply in each case. If in that time they had no objections the nomination was assumed to have been accepted. Otherwise, another name had to be forwarded.

The primate therefore submitted a name at a time, six of them being rejected in succession. These names remain secret. Wyszyński, finally, proposed Wojtyła, and this recommendation was in time forwarded to the Vatican as well. Stanisław Stomma, who as Znak deputy was acting as an unofficial intermediary between the episcopate and the regime, thinks that the primate, who was running out of plausible options, had come under increasing pressure from the Kraków Church and Catholic intellectuals to recommend Wojtyła. He says that many of the Polish bishops were very impressed with Wojtyła after the first session of the Vatican Council, and this, too, had an impact. Professor Swieżawski was among those who urged Wyszyński to propose Wojtyła.

Stomma recounts that at the start of the negotiations he was summoned by Zenon Kliszko, the speaker of the Sejm and the number two man in the Polish communist establishment, who was in overall charge of relations with the Church. Kliszko, who met frequently with Stomma, asked him who would be the best candidate for Kraków.

"I told him, firmly and categorically, that Wojtyła was the best and the only choice," Stomma says. Kliszko informed him that there were a number of candidates, without revealing the names, but that he knew Wojtyła would be at the bottom of the primate's list. According to Stomma, what Kliszko did was "to wait out Wyszyński and force him to come up with Wojtyła."

Why did the communists settle on Wojtyła? Stomma suggests that the overriding reason was that Kliszko wanted "bishops who were not politically hostile. . . . He imagined that Wojtyła was apolitical, that he didn't like politics, that he would not get mixed up in them, and that he would stick to pastoral work." The authorities seemed to have forgotten the accusations they had lodged against Wojtyła in 1959, but Stomma believes that they were favorably impressed with his visit to the communist leader in Kraków in September 1962 to negotiate the problem of the seminary.

Kliszko also hoped to play Wyszyński against Wojtyła on the general principle of dividing the Church whenever possible.

As it turned out, the communists commited a fatal error in approving Wojtyła. Stomma says that "when Wojtyła took over in Kraków, he emerged as a tough archbishop, strongly defending the sovereignty of the Church" and that Kliszko was "disappointed and annoyed" that he had not lived up to the regime's expectations.

Father Andrzej Bardecki, a Church historian and a *Tygodnik Powszechny* editor, is convinced that two men opened Wojtyła's road to the papacy: Archbishop Baziak in 1958, by naming him auxiliary bishop, and Zenon Kliszko, the communist leader, in 1963, by approving him for Kraków archbishop. Otherwise, Wojtyła would never have become cardinal and certainly not pontiff.

Karol Wojtyła was named Metropolitan Archbishop of Kraków by the pope on December 30, 1963. He was solemnly installed at Wawel Cathedral on March 3, 1964. He was forty-three.

Pope John XXIII had died on June 3, 1963, six months after issuing his *Pacem in Terris* ("Peace on Earth") encyclical, which was the first significant move by the Holy See to bring an end to the East-West Cold War. In March he had received Alexis Adzhubei, Khrushchev's son-in-law and editor of the Soviet government newspaper, in the first public contact between a pope and a senior Soviet official. It resulted in the release of Archbishop Josef Slipyi of the Ukrainian Catholic Church from a Siberian labor camp, a Soviet gesture toward the Holy See and a matter of special interest to the Polish Church next door.

Cardinal Montini, the sixty-seven-year-old archbishop of Milan, who once served as a Vatican diplomat in Poland, was elected to the papacy on June 21, 1963, taking the name of Paul VI. It was he who signed Wojtyła's nomination as archbishop. The new pope would pursue and expand the Vatican's *Ostpolitik*—the policy of opening toward the communist east—setting on a course John Paul II would carry to its ultimate conclusion. In the meantime, Paul VI would become Wojtyła's new and most important protector.

Wojtyła was back in Rome for the second session of the Vatican Council on October 7, 1963, because a bout with mononucleosis had made him miss the opening day on September 29. Wyszyński and twenty-three Polish bishops had gone ahead (but Kraków's auxiliary bishop Julian Groblicki was denied a passport). Wojtyła met Paul VI for the first time on October 16, during an audience for the Polish delegation, but it was purely ceremonial. Wyszyński, on the other hand, had several private meetings with the new pope during the autumn.

Though he spoke only once at the basilica during the 1963 session, on October 21, Wojtyła made a significant contribution to what emerged later as the *Lumen Gentium* (Light of All Nations) Declaration on the Dogmatic Constitution of the Church. Dealing with the modernization of the Church and its liturgy, it was the most important document of Vatican Council II. Specifically, he convinced his fellow council fathers that the chapter on "People of God" should precede the one on the hierarchy, suggesting in his beautiful Latin that people are what the Church, in the end, is all about. It was a fundamental statement of the renewed Church philosophy and theology.

The 1963 session ended on December 4, with the approval of declarations on Sacred Liturgy and Social Communications, Wojtyła having special interest in the latter. He had even greater interest in ecumenism—the unity of Christian churches—and religious freedom, submitting a written commentary on the two linked subjects. They would be among the top priorities of the John Paul II pontificate.

The next day, Wojtyła left for the Holy Land with a group of bishops for a ten-day visit, a deeply emotional experience that left a lasting impact on him and influenced much of his papal thinking and policymaking in the Middle East. The group flew from Rome to Cairo, then on to Jerusalem, landing at the airport on the Jordanian side of the divided city and moving on to Israel. This was the first time Wojtyła had left Europe.

He described the voyage in a most detailed letter to the priests of the Kraków archdiocese, stressing that "we felt that working at the Council on the renewal of the Church, we must address ourselves directly to Lord Christ [in the places] where He was born, lived, taught, acted, then suffered, died on the Cross, was resurrected and entered the heavens."

In classical Wojtyła style, the letter was a biblical travelogue, relating the sites he visited to the history of Christ and the Church, starting with Egypt and the exodus of the "Chosen People" to the Promised Land. He described flying "in beautiful, sunny weather" over the Old Testament route of "the Egyptian desert to the Shores of the Red Sea . . . the mountains of Sinai, and again the desert." The first night was spent in Bethlehem in the crypt where Jesus was born, celebrating Mass from midnight until 5:30 A.M., when the Polish group had to make room for the Greek Orthodox priests, the custodians there, and *their* daily early-morning Mass.

Characteristically, Wojtyła noted that at Grotta Lactis (Milk Grotto), the Mother of God had nourished Jesus with milk from her breast when a drop of maternal milk fell to the ground, according to the legend, and that "from time immemorial, women lacking milk in their breasts, Christian and Moslem alike, make pilgrimages to the grotto asking for 'Mary's intercession.'"

He went to the Wall of the Temple in Jerusalem, "a holy place for us, Christians, because Lord Jesus had called it, 'the home of His Father.'" Then, the bishops visited the shores of the Dead Sea, the Sea of Galilee (where "fishermen pull in their nets as in the time of Lord Jesus"), and the land of Galilee, spending a night atop Mount Tabor.

Back in Jerusalem, Wojtyła and his companions followed the Way of the Cross (where he found a "Polish" archaeological-biblical museum maintained by Polish Elizabethan Sisters at the Third Station), placing their bishops' insignia on the spot where the Cross stood on Golgotha. He noted pointedly that the Golgotha Basilica was under the joint care of Roman Catholics, Russian and Greek Orthodox, and Armenians, "which does not offend [one] at first sight though it is known that the fact of the split of

Christianity, so much against the wish of Jesus, hides behind it."

At home, Archbishop Wojtyła spent much of his time in 1964 explaining the work of the Vatican Council to priests and the faithful before returning to Rome for the next session. At a meeting at the Kalwaria Zebrzydowska sanctuary, Wojtyła firmly told a priest who had raised the question, that "the Roman Curia does not rule over bishops; they are governed by the pope who uses the Curia in the governance of the whole Church." This foreshadowed the tough, monarchical approach he would apply toward both the bishops and the Curia during his pontificate.

The third session of the council opened on September 14, and Wojtyła displayed breathless activity during its seven-week period. And as archbishop, he was moved to a seat closer to the altar in the basilica. He delivered addresses to the council on ecumenism, religious freedom, the lay apostolate, and the draft declaration on the Church in the modern world. The latter, to become known as *Gaudium et Spes* (Joy and Hope), would be as important as *Lumen Gentium* among the accomplishments of the council.

However, Wojtyła considered that the original draft of the document was inadequate because it sought to impose "authoritatively" on Catholicism—and on nonbelievers—sets of values to be observed in human relations. In his view, the Church had to "reason" with people. Addressing the council fathers, Wojtyła had the first opportunity of presenting his social philosophy before a world forum: "The modern world," he said, "is new in good and it is new in evil. It contains new values, but also new crises. It is a world of new closeness between people and nations, but, at the same time, a world that is threatening and dangerous in a new way for each person and entire societies. It is a world of progress and luxury, in which the majority of humanity suffers simultaneously from hunger."

Again, Karol Wojtyła was faithful to his principles; the theme of the 1964 speech would resound in papal encyclicals and addresses of the 1980s and the 1990s. On behalf of the Polish episcopate, he proposed basic changes in the *Gaudium et Spes* document. The council named him to membership in the Central Sub-Commission dealing with the declaration, and he found himself in the company of some of the most distinguished progressive theologians in the world. Among those who counted in the Church, Wojtyła now became one of the best-known council fathers. And the circle of his friends and acquaintances was widening daily.

Wojtyła was also the only speaker at the council to address a speech in the basilica to "Venerable Fathers, Brothers and Sisters," recognizing the presence of women auditors there. The controversy over his stand on the equality of women in the Church would erupt much later.

After the third session of the council ended on November 21, Wojtyła made a quick trip to Sicily with several Polish bishops and paid a second visit to the Holy Land. Back in Rome, he had his first private audience with Paul VI on November 30. It marked the birth of a long and very special relationship. The pope reminisced about his youthful days in Poland, nearly forty-five years earlier, then told Wojtyła that "our principal pastoral duty as bishops is toward priests, workers and students." Wojtyła informed Paul VI that he had been a worker for several years before studying theology, and, he recounts, "I saw that the pope was pleased that I had been a worker." Paul VI sent him a pallium, a circular band of white lamb's wool that is worn by archbishops around the neck on special occasions; it was a great distinction and a sign of personal warmth on the part of the pope.

Returning to Kraków, the archbishop delivered a Christmas sermon at St. Szczepan's Church on religious freedom, one of his favorite themes: "There must be a climate of religious freedom in society, a climate of respect for the human conscience, for human convictions. . . . For the Church, the problem of religious freedom is a sign of progress. . . ."

Consumed by the work of the council, Wojtyła commuted between Kraków and Rome during the winter and spring of 1965. He was committed to the drafting of the "Church in the Modern World" document. On September 14, Wojtyła was in St. Peter's Basilica for the fourth and final session of the Second Vatican Council, remaining until the end, on

December 8. He was gone from Kraków this time for nearly three months. His only break from Council duties was a one-day trip in mid-October to Paray-le-Monial in France for a special pontifical Mass.

The final session of the council was a battle royal between progressives and conservatives over religious freedom and, in particular, over the Church's relations with non-Christian religions, notably the Jews. Austria's Cardinal König and Germany's Cardinal Augustin Bea led the offensive for religious freedom, with Archbishop Wojtyła acting as strategist, drafter, and floor manager. Cardinal Ottaviani of the Holy Office was the chief opponent, charging dramatically that "truth and falsity cannot be treated as equal and they cannot have the same rights."

But religious freedom declarations were approved, including the *Nostra Aetate* (In Our Time) document on relations with non-Christian religions. Its Paragraph Four affirmed, in a historical breakthrough for the Church, that Jesus' Crucifixion "cannot be blamed on all the Jews living without distinction, nor upon the Jews of today." Wojtyła was one of the authors, and he applied it subsequently to justify all his gestures toward the Jews and the state of Israel, before and during his pontificate.

Most interestingly, Wojtyła was among the bishops who helped to defeat a proposal calling upon the council to issue a formal condemnation of communism. He shared the view that great ideological conflicts in the world cannot be solved through condemnations, and that new ways must be found to achieve lasting solutions.

It was about the same time that Paul VI set in motion his far-reaching *Ostpolitik* toward Moscow and the communists in Eastern Europe. Such was the complexity and subtlety of this situation that Wojtyła, as a Polish archbishop, could favor an improved relationship with communism as a matter of constructive, long-range diplomacy while squaring off with communist authorities at home over the treatment of the Church there. It was a state of affairs that the West never understood. Nor, for that matter, was it understood that the most interesting young personality in the Church emerging from the Second Vatican Council was a Polish archbishop named Karol Wojtyła. This is why, perhaps, the advent of John Paul II would be such a surprise.

Even before the Vatican Council ended, Wojtyła found himself embroiled in a most painful public controversy. Along with Archbishop Bolesław Kominek and Bishop Jerzy Stroba, he drafted an appeal addressed to the German episcopate that concluded with the words "We forgive and we beg forgiveness." The document, prepared during the council in Rome in collaboration with several German bishops, also reviewed the tragic history of Polish-German relations and expressed comprehension of the sufferings endured by the Germans.

Issued on November 18, 1965, in the name of the Polish episcopate, the bishops' appeal set off a firestorm. Polish communist authorities did not allow its text to be published, but they launched a violent campaign against the bishops under the slogan "We shall not forget and we shall not forgive."

On December 22, however, Kraków newspapers published an open letter to Wojtyła from workers of the Solvay chemical plant where he had worked during the war, declaring themselves "deeply shocked" by the bishops' appeal. The letter expressed their "astonishment" at the archbishop's participation in drafting it, adding that "nobody had granted the Polish bishops a mandate to take a stand on matters properly in the care of other institutions." It went on to remind Wojtyła that "thousands of Polish priests" had been killed at Oświęcim and that the Germans had undertaken "bestial measures of biological destruction" against Poland. The letter closed with words of "deep disappointment" over the "anti-citizen act" on the part of Wojtyła, their wartime work companion.

Whether or not the letter had been written by the communist authorities, as seems likely, it was grist for the mill of anti-Church propaganda. Two days later, a saddened but indignant Wojtyła penned a lengthy missive to the workers—not published in the Kraków press—suggesting that "you could not have written [your letter] if you had familiarized yourselves with the text of the appeal and the reply of the German bishops."

The archbishop told the workers that the appeal was based "on the deepest principles of Christian ethics" and that the German bishops, in turn, "had asked God and then us for forgiveness for the sins of their nation." And he showed his anger: "I am answering your letter . . . as an injured party. I am injured because I have been accused and calumniated publicly, without any effort [by you] at learning the facts and motivations. When we worked together during the occupation, we had much in common—and, in the first place, respect for man, his conscience, his personality and his social dignity. I had learned this in great measure from Solvay workers—but I do not find this basic principle contained in your letter."

On December 26, Wojtyła went to preach on the subject of the appeal at a Kraków church, reading and analyzing all the letters. He would not be trifled with.

But he also received some good news before the year was over.

In Rome, Paul VI had created the Synod of Bishops as a collegial institution to meet periodically in the spirit of the Vatican Council, naming Bishop Rubin, Wojtyła's friend, as secretary-general. Now the Kraków archbishop had a direct line to the heart of the Roman Curia.

In Poland, where communist policies remained undecipherable and the party split internally, the authorities had unexpectedly granted permission for the erection of a church in the Kraków suburb of Nowa Huta, the center of the steel industry in the region. The permit was issued nine years after the initial petition was made; in the meantime, a small chapel served a parish of twenty thousand faithful. Wojtyła had been fighting for the Nowa Huta church since he first became bishop.

During July 1965 Wojtyła had conferred for the first time with Zenon Kliszko, the communist official who had approved his candidacy to be archbishop. And Wojtyła's amazing literary production continued. After the cycle of poems composed during the Vatican Council's first session, he came up with an inspirational essay, "Reflections About Fatherhood," in 1964; a poem about his pilgrimage to the Holy Land in 1965; lengthy reportage-like letters from Rome to *Tygodnik Powszechny* on the council (he was, in a way, covering his own activities journalistically); a thick volume on the accomplishments of the council under the title *At the Sources of Renewal,* and, naturally, scores of sermons and homilies.

The millennium of Christianity in Poland was celebrated throughout 1966, leading to renewed tensions between the Church and the communist authorities. Though there was no interference with the great pilgrimages to the image of the Black Madonna in Częstochowa—millions of Poles made them—the police harassed the Church by preventing a framed copy of the image from being festively paraded across Poland.

Primate Wyszyński had hoped that Paul VI would honor Poland with a visit for the millennium, but the regime turned the idea down. A papal presence in the country during the height of religious and patriotic fervor was the last thing the communists needed. Had the pope come, he would have been invited to celebrate the great Mass of Jubilee at Częstochowa. In his absence, the Polish episcopate selected Wojtyła to do so on Sunday, May 3. Wyszyński delivered the blessings sent by Paul VI.

In addition to the May Mass, Wojtyła celebrated 53 solemn millennium Masses from one corner of Poland to another in the course of the year (including in his hometown of Wadowice). He also published a seven-part poem for the Easter Vigil—included in it were a "Conversation with God," a "Conversation with Man," and an "Invocation to a Man Who Became the Body of History."

It was also in 1966 that Wojtyła formed a lifetime association with the man he trusts on a personal basis above all others. He is Monsignor Stanisław Dziwisz, now private secretary to John Paul II, with whom he has spent close to thirty years, first in Kraków, then at the Vatican. A highlander from the small town of Raba south of Kraków and a master skiier, Dziwisz was ordained in 1963. He served as vicar in the mountain village of Maków Podhalański, then was sent to study in Kraków where he also worked at the seminary library. Wojtyła spotted him there, naming Dziwisz as his personal chaplain despite his youth. When he was elected to the papacy, he brought Dziwisz along.

A quiet man with a keen intelligence, phenomenal memory, and a pleasant sense of humor, Dziwisz is closer to Wojtyła than any other person. Rather incredibly, John Paul II has virtually no personal office staff—Dziwisz is *it,* with assistance from an elderly Vietnamese monsignor, Vincent Tran Ngoc Thu, who also has the title of private secretary (but speaks no Polish). The Papal Household Office handles ceremonies and logistics. Dziwisz's title of private secretary is nominal: in real life he is the pope's right hand, adviser, and confidant. John Paul II relies totally on his loyalty and discretion to run his hands-on papacy on a day-to-day basis. They also skied together in the Italian mountains until Wojtyła's 1994 hip fracture put an end to his days on the slopes.

Dr. Joaquín Navarro-Valls, a Spanish psychiatrist and journalist who is the pope's official spokesman and director of the Holy See Press Office, is another frequent companion. John Paul II is personally fond of the chainsmoking Spaniard who has permanent access to him. During summer vacation mountain hikes, Dziwisz and Navarro-Valls are often the only ones with the pope (other than security agents).

Archbishop Wojtyła was received by Paul VI in private audience on April 20, 1967, when he traveled to Rome for a week of meetings at the Pontifical Council for the Laity. The pope had established the council in January, naming Wojtyła as a consultant. This was the second time they talked alone (in Italian).

Paul VI had been accelerating his *Ostpolitik,* having received Nikolai Podgorny, the chairman of the Supreme Soviet, on February 2. Late in February, the pope had dispatched to Poland a personal mission composed of Monsignor Agostino Casaroli from the Vatican Secretariat of State and Monsignor Deskur, Wojtyła's old friend.

Both the Holy See and the Warsaw regime had been thinking of the possibility of establishing diplomatic relations, which would be a first for a communist country (except for Cuba, which had them continuously since before Fidel Castro's revolution). Casaroli and Deskur came on a fact-finding mission, meeting with Polish officials and spending a lot of time with Wojtyła. Poland and *Ostpolitik* were the subject of the April conversation between Wojtyła and Paul VI.

Poland may have wished diplomatic relations with the Vatican, but the regime was again being ornery toward the Church. Thus primate Wyszyński was refused a passport in May to attend the Bishops' Synod in Rome. In solidarity with him, Wojtyła, also a synod member, declined to go although he had a valid passport. And, inexplicably, the authorities closed down the Rhapsodic Theater of Mieczysław Kotlarczyk, Wojtyła's oldest surviving friend in Poland. The archbishop's appeal to Culture Minister Lucjan Motyka, his Kraków sparring partner over the issue of the seminary, to let the theater remain open went unanswered.

On May 29, eleven days after his forty-seventh birthday, Wojtyła was notified that Paul VI had named him a cardinal. The nomination came as a surprise in Poland. Though Wyszyński was the only Polish cardinal, there was no pressure on the Holy See to appoint a second one immediately. Moreover, other Polish archbishops were older than Wojtyła. Clearly, Paul VI regarded him as a favorite.

On June 26, 1967, Karol Wojtyła was invested by the pope along with twenty-six other cardinals at the Sistine Chapel in one of the great ceremonies of the Roman Catholic Church. John Krol of Philadelphia, whose parents were born in a Polish village, was among the new cardinals. The next afternoon, the twenty-seven freshly minted cardinals joined Paul VI in concelebrating a solemn Mass on St. Peter's Square as the sun was beginning to set over the Vatican.

CHAPTER 17

In 1967, at the young age of forty-seven, Karol Wojtyła seemed to have reached the top of his ecclesiastic career.

The cardinalate is a lifetime appointment although cardinals, under rules established by the Second Vatican Council, must retire from governing, pastoral, or administrative activities at seventy-five. But they remain members of the College of Cardinals, being most pleasantly pensioned off, and they can vote in a conclave for a new pontiff until the age of eighty.

For Cardinal Wojtyła, this meant, in practical terms, that he was guaranteed full-time occupation and great Church and political power for the next twenty-eight years. Because he was the governing Metropolitan Archbishop of Kraków, which is a function independent of the cardinalate title and prestige, he was the second most powerful and influential Church leader in Poland after Primate Wyszyński, and many churchmen believed that in fact Wojtyła had more quiet influence.

Wojtyła was, of course, deeply engaged in policymaking in the Polish episcopate and he was increasingly drawn by Pope Paul VI into Holy See matters. He was a Kraków-based Polish celebrity. Still, there were limitations on what he could do and say. His admirable and absolute loyalty to Primate Wyszyński, notwithstanding Wojtyła's deep but silent reservations about the man and his ideas, was the principal limit—self-imposed—on his freedom of action and speech, aside from the observance of normal hierarchical deference.

Did Karol Wojtyła ever think that he might be pontiff of the Roman Catholic Church?

Obviously, he had heard the idea—or hope—mentioned on innumerable occasions, from Father Pio in Italy in 1947, to a little girl in the town of Ludźmierz six weeks after he was anointed cardinal. A friend described the event in a memoir preserved in the archives of the Kraków archdiocese: "A little girl, welcoming the cardinal, recited a poem in which the final words expressed the expectation that he would now become pope. This caused general merriment. The Cardinal did not laugh. He leaned down gravely and kissed the little girl on the forehead."

As a practical matter, papal prospects for him were dim at that stage, except for reasons of age. Though longevity has characterized popes in this century—both Pius XII and John XXIII died in their eighties—Paul VI was already seventy when he named Wojtyła cardinal in 1967. Even if he, too, lived past his eightieth birthday (which he would), Wojtyła would still be extremely young by pontifical standards.

The real problems were that the idea of a non-Italian pope was still very farfetched (although Paul VI had mentioned it once) and that, at least when measured in 1967, Wojtyła had not yet acquired the necessary stature to be a plausible conclave candidate notwithstanding the excellent reputation he had acquired during the Second Vatican Council. He would use well the eleven years of cardinalate that lay ahead to augment this stature.

For the nonce, Cardinal Wojtyła had turned the Kraków archdiocese into something of a "minipapacy," although, of course, nobody ever used that term.

There are no scientific measurements to define the activities of cardinals, or the quality of their achievements, but it is hard to imagine any other cardinal at that time being as insatiably active and busy as Wojtyła. Certainly no example comes to mind. And the diversity of his concerns and interests was astounding.

It is probably irrelevant historically whether the Wojtyła phenomenon stemmed from the force of his personality or from a plan for the future, or both. The fact was that his phenomenon existed to an impressive degree. His increasingly frequent visitors from abroad were very much impressed with Wojtyła's style and operation. And soon he began broadening his horizons further with global voyages.

The cardinal worked around the clock, or so it appeared to his associates and assistants, to strengthen his Kraków minipapacy through an unending chain of innovative ideas and projects. He was turning the archdiocese into a unique Church establishment, surely by Polish standards, and personally playing a commanding and highly visible role in every conceivable endeavor.

His top priority, inevitably, was to find novel ways of spreading the faith, encouraging worship and religious teaching, and to create a powerful structure in Kraków. At the same time, he spared no effort to make the archdiocese a major intellectual and cultural center. There was nothing like it in Poland.

This had to be done, however, against the background of continuing pressures by the regime against the Polish Church. In the contest with the communist authorities over the rights of the Church and the faithful, Wojtyła sought to avoid open conflict. But while he preferred—whenever possible—to achieve his objectives by negotiation and even selective compromise, he never abandoned his principles nor ceded on the essentials.

His strategy was to wear down the communists with personal or written protests over any violation of what he considered to be Church rights, or human rights in general, including the freedom of Catholic education and catechism. Wojtyła thundered at church sermons and drowned the authorities in streams of petitions and requests for the building of churches and seminaries; permits for processions, pilgrimages, and parades; and ceaseless complaints over the drafting of seminarians for military service.

Curiously, the communists had a very different idea of what Karol Wojtyła represented when he attained his position of power in the Church in 1967. Though he had been bishop and archbishop for nine years, they still seemed unable to understand and assess him correctly. Consequently, they embarked on an ill-conceived campaign to drive a wedge between him and Primate Wyszyński, not really convinced they would succeed.

The regime's view of Wojtyła was expressed in a top secret document of the UB, the Polish secret police, dated August 5, 1967—five weeks after he became cardinal—and titled "Our Tactics Toward Cardinals Wojtyła and Wyszyński." The five-page document was discovered in the archives of UB headquarters after the end of the communist rule. It provides fascinating insights into the mentality of the regime. Some excerpts:

> In evaluating the two cardinals, it is necessary to consider their character traits, the social environment from which they came, degrees of career in Church hierarchy. . . .
>
> Cardinal Wyszyński was brought up in a traditional family of Church servants. In the opinion of the clergy, this is an inferior type of people, and this stigma weighs on him to this day. . . . On many occasions, "getting even with the clergy" was [for him] the Freudian "principle of compensation." . . . His extreme clericalism and [cult of] Marianism was born in the climate of his family home. . . . He built his "scientific career" on anti-communist activity and anti-communist writings, which, in 1948, were decisive in his advancement [to bishop]. . . .

The document went on about the primate:

> On the one hand, the Vatican needed a banner for an anticommunist crusade in Poland, and on the other hand reactionary forces in the country and in exile needed to create a legal opposition, and there was no candidate with greater experience. . . . The stigma on his personality was also maintained by his continued presence and activity in provincial towns like Włocławek or Lublin. . . . During the "cold war," his position becomes greater—he is the standard-bearer of the anti-communist front. . . . In the final period of the

> Pius XII pontificate, he was the "expert" on questions of establishing relations between the Church and socialist countries. Poland at the time was the "testing ground" for such matters. . . . John XXIII's pontificate and Vatican Council II resulted in the diminution of his position, which was then maintained artificially. . . . But it all led inevitably to the drop in his prestige. . . .

Turning with contempt to Wyszyński's politics, the document said:

> He represents the view that it is useful to make "arrangements" with the authorities on specific questions, but he conducts feuds and organizes clashes because it augments interest in the Church and draws people to the defense of its "endangered interests." . . . His concept of shallow, emotional and devotional Catholicism is correct and profitable from the viewpoint of the Church's immediate interests [for some years]. . . . His treatment of the intellectual elite, Catholic intelligentsia and laity as "uncertain elements" has its roots in Polish realities. The correctness of his reasoning is justified by facts: shallow, traditional and devotional religiosity is the religiosity of the Catholic masses. Thoughtful religiosity, on the other hand, is peculiar to a thin layer of the intellectual elite. The strength of the Church in Poland has resided for centuries not among the elites, but in the Catholic masses.

Cardinal Wojtyła enjoyed much more respect on the part of the secret police:

> The tenth successive Kraków cardinal, he comes from a family of intelligentsia—from a religious but not devotional environment. He studied at Jagiellonian University, and had contacts with leftist youth. . . . During World War II, he was a worker in a Kraków chemical plant, which possessed considerable traditions of workers' movements. . . . He rose in the

Church hierarchy not thanks to an anti-communist stance, but thanks to intellectual values (his works on Catholic morality and ethics, such as *Love and Responsibility,* have been translated into many languages). . . .

And the UB had more secret compliments for Wojtyła:

> It can be safely said that he is one of the few intellectuals in the Polish Episcopate. He deftly reconciles—unlike Wyszyński—traditional popular religiosity with intellectual Catholicism, knowing how to appreciate both of them. . . . He has not, so far, engaged in open anti-state political activity. It seems that politics are his weaker suit; he is over-intellectualized. . . . He lacks organizing and leadership qualities, and this is his weakness in the rivalry with Wyszyński. . . .

This was the conclusion of the secret police:

> The model of Catholicism and coexistence with socialist countries proposed by Wojtyła . . . corresponds to the future line of the Vatican. His model of Catholicism is "open Catholicism" toward the problems of contemporary Poland. He has support in intellectual and reformist Catholic circles in the Vatican and the French, German, Dutch and Italian episcopates. . . . The cardinal's secular life style brings him closer to the circles of the young intelligentsia and students (for example, participation in camping, kayaking, tourist excursions). . . . He is under an overwhelming influence of forces and pressure groups completely different from Cardinal Wyszyński. Independent of his wishes, these forces will draw him into conflict with the Primate. . . .

Next, the police document discussed recommended tactics toward Wojtyła:

> Both cardinals will guard the interests of the Church although their differences in perceiving these interests

> will deepen. To expect a break-up in the unity of the Episcopate is utopian. It is necessary to concentrate on softening up and dulling the edge of its political opposition. Wojtyła will not go for open struggle with Wyszyński and he will not let himself be pushed into it. In an eventual struggle, he can count only on forces inside the Church. We must risk the approach that the less he [Wojtyła] is pushed by us, the sooner a conflict will develop. Sooner or later, these two trends must clash . . . on many fronts.

The UB analysts predicted that Wojtyła "wishes to make the Kraków archdiocese independent, at least in part, of interference by the Warsaw cardinal, and we should help him." They wrote that Wyszyński had received Wojtyła's elevation to cardinalate "with clear resentment." Therefore, the document suggested, "we should act positively on matters of prestige that would improve Wojtyła's self-esteem," but "he will be irritated by any attempt, no matter how innocent, to push him into conflict with Wyszyński."

These were the final police recommendations on how to deal with Wojtyła:

> We must observe and study every manifestation in the relations between the two cardinals, and conduct an elastic policy, according to changing circumstances. . . . We must use diplomatic channels to determine whom the Vatican is the most likely to support and see whether Wojtyła has in the future real chances of becoming the head of the Polish Episcopate. We must not hit the archdiocese too hard—although we must occasionally apply "administrative measures"—in order to remove suspicions toward Wojtyła on the part of groups at home and abroad [who are] not sympathetic toward him. . . . We must encourage Wojtyła's interest in the overall problems of the Polish Church, and assist him in problems concerning his archdiocese. For this reason, we should initiate high-level meetings between Wojtyła—for example, with Premier Cyrankiewicz and with Kliszko—to discuss general questions. . . . And we must continue to demonstrate our ill-will

toward Wyszyński at every opportunity, but not in a way that would force Wojtyła to show solidarity with Wyszyński. . . .

Evidently unaware of the communists' assessment and their game plan, Wojtyła stepped up his battle for Church rights when he became cardinal, publicly fighting the regime an inch at a time.

In a sermon in Sandomierz, an old southeastern town, on June 8, 1968, a year after he received the purple, Wojtyła chose to remind his listeners of the Russian occupation of Poland during the great partitions of the nineteenth century, an extremely delicate topic. The occasion was the 150th anniversary of the Sandomierz diocese, and the cardinal had this to say: "During that difficult period, the Catholic Church played a significant role in the Polish lands when it came to the preservation of the unity within the nation. . . . Bishops and priests never allowed the Church to become Russified. . . . The unity of the Church with the nation always had, and still has, a fundamental meaning for both the Polish nation and the Church."

Wojtyła's words had particular impact because three months earlier, in March 1968, a major conflict had erupted in Warsaw between the government and university students. It began with a theater performance of Adam Mickiewicz's patriotic—and anti-Russian—play *The Forefathers' Eve* (a Wojtyła favorite), leading to riots in the streets and on the university campus.

It was followed by a frantic anti-Semitic campaign launched by Gomułka, the party's first secretary, for wholly incomprehensible reasons, considering that the Jewish population of Poland had dwindled down from the prewar three million to less than thirty thousand at that stage. Virtually all the Jews were fired from government and teaching jobs, and most sought safety in exile.

But the March event marked the beginning of the end for the Gomułka regime. Fully identified with Soviet policies, he dispatched Polish troops to Czechoslovakia in August 1968 as part of the invasion designed to end the liberal Marxist "Prague Spring" experiment—"Marxism with a

Human Face." Polish regiments had been included in the "Fraternal Assistance" operation by the Soviet-let Warsaw Pact military alliance with forces from five countries.

Gomułka's own end came in December 1970, when the army and security troops clashed with rioting workers in Gdańsk, the port city on the Baltic, who demanded better living conditions and protested against a sharp pre-Christmas rise in food prices. It was the repetition of the 1956 Poznań confrontation that had brought Gomułka to power as a "liberal savior." Tanks fired on the workers and scores were killed. The communist establishment responded in the usual fashion, throwing out the boss and his friends. Gomułka was replaced with Edward Gierek, a career party official who had worked as a coal miner in France and Belgium, and was a much more moderate and modern leader.

Wojtyła learned about the changes on December 20, at a Kraków hospital while visiting a sick priest. They listened together to a radio news broadcast reporting them, the cardinal remaining silent for a long while. Then he said, "Strange are the ways of God. . . ."

In sermons at two New Year's Eve Masses, Wojtyła denounced the Gdańsk bloodshed in no uncertain terms. "The measure of the tragedy of the recent days," he said, "is the fact of Polish blood spilled by Poles." He demanded "the right to bread, the right to freedom . . . a climate of real liberty . . . of freedom from fear over what may happen if one does this or that . . ." as conditions for social peace.

The Gierek era failed to reduce meaningfully the communist pressures on the Church, although the climate was improving somewht. And Wojtyła was increasingly successful in his contest with the authorities.

In 1958, the year he became suffragan bishop, for example, they had authorized the erection of only two churches in the Kraków archdiocese to replace structures that had burned down. In 1973, as cardinal, Wojtyła petitioned for the building of seventy-seven churches, and sixteen of the requests were granted. In a 1976 letter to the chairman of the Kraków presidium of the National Council, the cardinal remarked that "it cannot be considered normal that

Catholic citizens must fulfill their religious obligations over long years under the open sky, freezing and being drenched. . . ."

The regime's insistence on drafting seminarians greatly irritated Wojtyła. The 1950 Church-State Agreement, still legally in force, guaranteed them deferment until they completed their studies. But in the late 1960s and the early 1970s, the government began drafting seminarians, especially in Kraków because, as an official remarked, "your cardinal is so inflexible." Wojtyła responded, intervening directly by letter on at least two occasions with Poland's new premier, Piotr Jaroszewicz, and deferments were granted to around one half of those called up. Seminarians who were not deferred were seen off at the Kraków railway station by the cardinal and groups of worshippers singing religious and patriotic songs while the police watched passively.

Addressing a conference of priests at the archdiocese in May 1973, he said that "the rights of citizens do not exist to be manipulated at will. They exist so that citizens may have a certain sense of security in terms of their actual rights. . . . Kraków is particularly endangered [by violations] because here we mainly have giant parishes where catechizing runs into hundreds of hours weekly."

Speaking on the Feast of Our Lady of Częstochowa on August 26, 1973, the cardinal expressed his concern about "the liberty of the Polish soul" as a result of a government education reform law that "does not say a single word about the Christian society, about the contribution of Christ, Church and Christianity to Polish education. . . . In the name of the [international] convention signed by our government on combating discrimination in education, we demand absolute freedom to teach religion in the context of catechizing. . . . We also demand that no threats be made against the majority of parents who desire that their children be taught the truths of faith and moral Christianity. . . ."

Wojtyła's quiet toughness toward the regime contrasted with the attitude of much of the Polish Church establishment, often including the primate, who tended to cooperate more fully with the authorities—a fact the secret police failed to grasp fully in its 1967 assessment of the two cardinals.

Wyszyński believed until the end that the Church must be supportive of the government in maintaining "social peace" in the country, a stand he would maintain even when the Solidarity trade union movement was in full rebellion in the summer of 1980. Wojtyła was much more restrained in his attitudes, presumably sensing that a fundamental change would come sooner or later.

The differing behavior within the Polish episcopate, and among the clergy at large, during the communist period is an important part of national and Church history. With records made available after the collapse of communism, it is increasingly clear that the impression the Polish Church was a monolith, a "fortress," and a fighting force is simply a myth. In terms of Wojtyła's behavior, as cardinal he was entirely consistent in pursuing his two-track policy of negotiation and compromise, when convenient, and toughness, when indicated.

This point was made in a broad way in a 1994 article in Kraków's *Tygodnik Powszechny* that discussed what it called "Opposition and Accommodation" on the part of the Church during the communist years. The article acknowledged that the Church "defended not only itself, but the values linked with every person and with Poland's spiritual culture."

But, it said, "there was accommodation, too." It cites a highly embarrassing speech delivered on December 17, 1953, by Bishop Michał Klepacz, who served as the head of the Polish episcopate after the September arrest of Primate Wyszyński, but never before published.

Addressing Deputy Premier Józef Cyrankiewicz and other top communist officials on the occasion of a declaration of allegiance by the bishops to the regime, Klepacz said:

> through our oath [today] we affirm our faithfulness to the People's Republic of Poland and promise that we shall do everything to contribute to the development and strengthening of its power and security. . . . As the Polish Episcopate, we affirm that this oath is an expres-

sion of the ancient Christian teaching about social and national obligations of every Catholic. . . . The Catholic clergy sees as its mission and patriotic duty to participate in the collective effort of the whole nation to improve the well-being, the security of the country and the excellence of our motherland, which is, at the same time, the guarantee of the rejection of any attempts to take advantage of the religious sentiment for anti-Polish objectives.

CHAPTER 18

During the 1970s, Cardinal Wojtyła made great strides in developing his minipapacy not only in terms of political defiance, but in highly creative institution building as well.

Religious education on all levels was always one of his top priorities, and from the outset he came up with the most imaginative ideas. With the teaching of religion in schools banned early in the communist years, though partly restored in 1956, the Church had sought alternatives through instruction in churches and special catechesis centers, but, by and large, these were uncoordinated efforts.

In Kraków, Wojtyła moved quickly as cardinal to set up an effective system of religious education for children outside schools, relying both on Church and laypersonnel. The authority for this undertaking flowed from the Pastoral Synod of the Kraków archdiocese convoked by the cardinal in 1971 for a seven-year period to implement the teachings and decisions of the Second Vatican Council. In fact, Wojtyła turned the synod into a quasi-permanent institution (it ceased functioning after he left town to become pope) to supervise all his major projects and modernize the functions of the archdiocese. It was the only such institution in the Polish Church.

The synod and a Priests' Council, also created by Wojtyła, were hands-on operations. Bishop Tadeusz

Pieronek, then the cardinal's special assistant, says that "the boss . . . was extremely interested in it." If he could not attend a session of the synod, Pieronek recalls, "he inquired about it immediately . . . so he was always up-to-date about everything. He did not run the Synod directly, but he frequently instructed it on all the fundamental points."

Using the synod and the Polish Episcopate's Commission on Lay Apostolate, of which he was chairman, Wojtyła harnessed all the resources available for catechesis. Soon, he had 250 nuns teaching religion along with lay instructors at a variety of locations. When the government forbade the renting of commercial premises as "catechesis houses," Wojtyła encouraged the teaching at private homes. The regime responded with threats against cooperating homeowners and raised their taxes, whereupon the cardinal took it upon himself to write personal letters to every one of them. He thanked them for their help and urged them not to give up. It was a Wojtyła habit, before and during the pontificate, to intervene personally—and loudly—in any situation of importance.

Where no facilities of any kind were available in a parish, the cardinal ordered the priests to hold a "pastoral hour" for children in their churches.

As for university students, Wojtyła launched in 1969 the "Sacrosong Movement," an experiment in sacred or religious music played outside the church in a modern fashion, as a form of catechism to bypass regime strictures against religious education. "Sacrosong" appears to be a word coined in Poland, although the idea is based on similar experiments in the West and the Third World in the use of youth music and folklore in pastoral work.

Poland had a tradition of old-fashioned religious singing on a variety of occasions involving young people—Wojtyła himself led songs on excursions and summer camps—but this time the Kraków cardinal authorized the Church to seek inspiration in rock music (still called "beat music" in Poland). The difference in Sacrosong between Poland and the West was, of course, that the Poles used it to beat communist restrictions. A music lover, Wojtyła (who brought Gregorian chant to Kraków churches fifteen years earlier), described Sacrosong as "a new expression of the Gospel."

Accordingly, he helped to organize nationwide Sacrosong festivals and contests, including the funding of an interdiocesan silver cup in the shape of the tower of Kraków's Marian Basilica that would pass annually from winner to winner like a soccer championship cup. In 1975, the Kraków Dominican Fathers' Theater presented performances of a Polish version of the rock opera *Jesus Christ Superstar.*

Leaving no stone unturned, Wojtyła organized pastoral work aimed at the blind and the deaf and mute. A center for the blind at the Kraków church of the Franciscan Fathers, serving about one hundred persons, owned a collection of records and tapes with recordings of around one hundred well-known works of religious literature. Pastoral centers for the deaf and mute were established in Kraków and three provincial areas. Catechism was conducted in sign language, and a special class for instructors was set up at the seminary. On at least one occasion, Wojtyła preached a sermon at a retreat for the deaf and mute, interpreted into sign language.

To educate future priests, Wojtyła, still as archbishop, organized in Kraków the Papal Theological Academy to take the place of the Theological Faculty of Jagiellonian University, closed down by the regime in 1954. He expanded it as cardinal. The academy grew out of the theological section of the Kraków Seminary, which was legal, and Wojtyła decided to transform it into a small, independent university with theology, philosophy, and history departments. The academy was legal because the authorities decided to let it function.

Father Michał Heller, a scientist and philosopher who helped Wojtyła set up the academy together with Father Józef Tischner, another member of their group of philosopher friends, remembers that they would sit around the table in the cardinal's apartments at the Curia palace, planning the creation of the philosophy department. Wojtyła, Heller says, was determined that the department would not imitate other philosophy faculties, "but develop its own style and philosophy," such as "a philosophy of physics, a philosophy of mathematics. . . ."

Both Heller and Pieronek remember Wojtyła's love for conversations and discussions when they worked with him during the cardinalate. Heller recalls the lengthy talks about the Papal Academy, pointing out that "the cardinal was never in a hurry. . . . He always seemed to have all the time in the world."

Pieronek remembers daylong conversations during walks in the hills in the countryside "where we would change into walking boots and a sports blouse, and talk for hours about everything of relevance: the Academy, the Synod, or diocesan matters." Later, Pieronek joined the cardinal and Father Dziwisz, his chaplain, on skiing excursions during which there was endless conversation, too. He says that "you could say anything you wanted to Wojtyła, argue, quarrel a bit, but, in the end, you found yourself accepting the thoughts he was propounding."

Wojtyła always regarded himself as a teacher, first and foremost, and as cardinal in Kraków he invested a massive amount of time holding forth on Christian ethics and morality, including sexuality and vice, as he interpreted them. He inveighed in sermons and homilies against abortion, artificial means of contraception, alcoholism, and atheism. He continued to do so as pope in Rome at every public opportunity—and he created many of them.

The cardinal established an Institute of the Family in Kraków to coordinate teaching and advice pertaining to all these matters. Then he set up an operation named "S.O.S. Cardinal Wojtyła" to assist materially mothers who had chosen to forgo planned abortions. It was a home for unwed mothers where they could remain as long as a year after giving birth.

Humanae vitae, the encyclical issued by Paul VI on July 25, 1968, and one of the most controversial Church documents to appear since World War II, was among Wojtyła's preferred preaching topics. Actually, Wojtyła was a drafter of the encyclical at the outset of his cardinalate, a fact that has never been publicly disclosed.

Meaning "Of Human Life," *Humanae vitae* is essentially

the papal condemnation of abortion and artificial means of contraception, such as birth-control pills. It forbids them as a violation of Christian teachings. The ban on contraceptive devices is the most controversial aspect of the encyclical, placing before Catholics the dilemma of disobeying Church teachings or risking acquiring larger families than they wish or can afford (sexual abstinence is not an alternative favored by many). Though it is statistically unprovable, it is assumed, even at the Vatican, that the majority of Catholics do not observe the ban on artificial contraception.

The encyclical was the product of seven years of intensive deliberations by a papal "Birth Control Commission" (it wasn't actually called that, except colloquially) of senior churchmen and lay experts, named by John XXIII to determine whether in the light of new situations in a changing world—notably huge population increases—the Church should not rethink its negative position on artificial contraception.

The last word on the subject from the Vatican had been a 1951 speech to midwives by Pope Pius XII, on marital chastity, indignantly rejecting contraception through artificial means. The only form of limiting births permitted by the Church is the so-called rhythm method, which suggests that couples avoid intercourse during the woman's fertile period. At best, it results in a spacing of pregnancies, a course consistent with current Church teachings.

Paul VI had inherited the birth-control problem from John XXIII, and on June 18, 1966, the commission's majority submitted its final report to the pope, asserting that Catholic opposition to artificial contraception "could not be sustained by reasoned argument." It was stressed that there is nothing in the Bible opposing birth control.

The majority had reached its decision on June 3, but Wojtyła, a member (and an archbishop at the time), did not attend the crucial meeting. The accepted version is that out of solidarity with Primate Wyszyński, who had been denied a passport to go to Rome, he chose to stay home, too. But the passport incident did not occur until the end of September, and there is no explanation why Wojtyła chose to be absent when the vote was taken.

Paul VI agonized for two years over the recommendations until resolving in mid-July 1968 to reject them, overruling the findings on the basis of his pontifical authority. Wojtyła, along with Cardinal Ottaviani of the Holy Office (who, in distinction from Wojtyła, was the strongest conservative voice at the Second Vatican Council), played decisive roles in influencing Paul VI to do so.

It is likely that Wojtyła's book on sexuality, *Love and Responsibility*, which argued that artificial contraception degraded women, was either read by the pope or summarized for him after the French- and Italian-language editions were published late in 1965. Wojtyła was received in private audience by the pope on April 20, 1967, shortly before he was named cardinal, but it is not known whether they discussed the birth-control recommendations or Wojtyła's book.

Wojtyła met again with the pope on July 3, 1967, immediately after becoming cardinal. He was back in Rome in February 1968 to assume his titular assignment as Bishop of the Church of San Cesareo in the suburb of Palatio, first erected in the seventh century, the time of Gregory the Great. (All cardinals receive "titular" sees.) On February 19, he had a late-morning meeting with Paul VI. That was the last time they conversed before the pope issued *Humanae vitae* in July 1968.

Wojtyła had been working quietly in Kraków on the draft of the encyclical at least since returning home as cardinal a year earlier. He organized his own Kraków commission on birth-control matters, which prepared materials for *Humanae vitae* and forwarded it directly to the pope. He said later, "We had sent some materials to the Vatican." A Polish theologian who worked with Wojtyła on this matter says that "about sixty percent of our draft is contained in the encyclical."

Eleven years later (two months before he was elected pope), Wojtyła confirmed, almost casually, his role in preparing *Humanae vitae*. Reminiscing about his contacts with Paul VI, he remarked that because "unfortunately" he had been unable to attend the June 1966 meeting of the commission, "I sent my opinions in writing to the Holy Father."

For Paul VI, Wojtyła's assistance with the encyclical and his unconditional support in what must have been the most difficult moment of his pontificate unquestionably represented the turning point in his relations with the Polish cardinal, to whom he displayed gratitude and appreciation for the rest of his life.

In Kraków, Wojtyła went public with his support for *Humanae vitae*, praising it three weeks after its issuance in an Assumption Day sermon at the Marian Basilica on Old Town Square. "If it poses great demands on a person in the moral realm," he said, "these demands [still] must be met. . . ." Speaking at the start of the academic year of his Institute of the Family, the cardinal said that the encyclical "is the expression of the unchanging truth, always proclaimed by the Church. . . ."

Next, he founded "*Humanae vitae* Marriage Groups" as an institution with strict regulations, designed to assure that married couples, not just either the husband or the wife, make the "commitment" to the requirements of the encyclical and the rejection of artificial birth-control methods. The regulations left up to the couples the decision as to whether they choose to practice sexual "purity"—abstinence—presumably during even the wife's nonfertile periods. But they urged the couples to engage in "apostolic" work in this context to persuade others to respect *Humanae vitae* obligations.

Wojtyła's own commitment to *Humanae vitae* never flagged. In fact, it grew with the passing years as a deep moral belief.

Cardinal Wojtyła pursued his teacher's role with the 1969 publication of *Person and Act*, a book on phenomenology so difficult that his own Kraków priests joked that if one of them is sentenced to Purgatory, he will be sprung free upon reading the entire text. The story extracted the nearest thing to a belly laugh from the cardinal.

Twenty-five years later, he explained in his latest book that he had originally intended *Person and Act* as a response to Marxist polemics against religion and the Church, but that his attention shifted to the central question of "man with his morality" inasmuch as "interest in man as a person was present in me for a long time."

He wrote: ". . . It was inevitable that I would arrive at

this theme from the moment I crossed the boundary into the field of questioning the nature of human existence—questions asked by men not only in our time but in every time. The question of good and evil never leaves man. . . ."

Wojtyła's interest in man—and his religion—was demonstrated again when he visited the synagogue in Kazimierz, the Jewish district of Kraków, on February 28, 1969. Nobody in Poland had ever heard of a cardinal visiting a synagogue, but Wojtyła insisted on doing it as a gesture of friendship and because he had fought so hard for the Vatican Council's declaration removing the blame for Christ's death from the Jews.

Honoring the request by the chairman of the Kraków Jewish community, Maciej Jakubowicz, the cardinal and the parish priest from a neighboring church entered the synagogue on Szeroka Street with their heads covered, according to the Jewish custom. It was Friday and the faithful were praying at the temple. Wojtyła, who wore a black cassock, conversed at some length with Jewish community leaders outside the building before joining the congregation. Then he stood silently in the back of the synagogue, listening to the service. At the second synagogue in Kazimierz, Wojtyła found only a solitary worshipper at prayer.

That same year, fascinated as ever by Polish history and Church history, Wojtyła ordered the restoration of the Wawel Cathedral, then in its seventh century, and of the graves of kings and queens buried there. It was one of his first acts as cardinal.

When restoration experts discovered the grave of Queen Elżbieta, the wife of King Kazimierz the Great, which had been buried for centuries under a mass of rubble, the cardinal authorized them to open the coffin and remove her remains for reburial. Next, the king's grave was opened in Wojtyła's presence: it contained the king's bones, his scepter, a leather orb, an iron sword, a cloth cover with silver thread, and a gold ring with a turquoise. Given the cardinal's scientific-historical curiosity (he had St. Stanisław's skull examined by forensic experts some years earlier), microbiological tests of the interior of the royal crypts were undertaken at his direction.

Presiding over his Kraków minipapacy, Cardinal Wojtyła wove an increasingly intimate relationship with the papacy of Paul VI.

He was a member of three Congregations of the Curia—the Congregations are like superministries in a government—and a member of the Synod of Bishops established by the pope in 1969 as a permanent organ to implement the decisions of the Second Vatican Council. The three Congregations were for the Clergy, for Sacraments and Worship, and for Catholic Education—all of them important. Each Congregation is headed by a prefect, and all the members are cardinals. Wojtyła also served as a consultant to the Council for the Laity.

He had attained the highest levels of the Holy See in terms of personal influence, prestige, and access all the way to the top, and his network of friends reached deep into the Curia. The expertise he now needed the most was in world affairs, his presence at the Vatican Council having been confined principally to Church questions.

Respected and competent in that field, Wojtyła was still in a sense a provincial figure from remote and isolated Eastern Europe. He continuously invited foreign cardinals and bishops to Krakó—especially from the Third World—but this served chiefly to enlarge his world Church ties.

Concentration on foreign policy in Rome and international travel would remedy this. Paul VI, whom he saw again in mid-March 1969, was a wise counselor who had spent much of his life in Vatican diplomacy, and he encouraged Wojtyła to broaden his experience. If Paul VI ever considered Wojtyła seriously as a potential successor, he had to help him acquire international grounding through discreet exposure to the work of the Secretariat of State and through contacts overseas.

By the time Wojtyła called on him in the spring of 1969, Paul VI was already a seasoned globetrotter, "the first modern pope," as his biographer, Peter Hebblethwaite, called him. He had traveled more than any previous pope, possibly because his pontificate happened to coincide with the advent of speedy and comfortable jet airliners. He had been to the Holy Land—Israel and Jordan—as well as to India, Turkey (where he embraced Ecumenical Patriarch

Athenagoras of the Eastern churches), Portugal (in pilgrimage to the shrine of Our Lady of Fátima), Colombia (to attend the Latin American Eucharistic Congress in Medellín), and Uganda and Tanzania. He had flown to New York to address the United Nations General Assembly. And he was engaged in quiet peacemaking in the Vietnam war.

Another important mentor in foreign affairs was Cardinal König in Vienna, whom Wojtyła saw regularly on his trips to and from Rome. In the late 1960s, König was already deeply engaged in *Ostpolitik*, mainly on the pope's behalf, and his knowledge covered situations in Eastern Europe of direct interest to the Kraków cardinal. König also served as president of the Vatican's Secretariat for Non-Believers, founded by Paul VI in 1965, to deal with much of the world outside the Vatican walls.

Archbishop Casaroli, whom Wojtyła had met earlier in Poland, worked closely with König on Eastern Europe. An outstanding Vatican diplomat, Casaroli would become exceedingly important to Wojtyła in many fields in the future. But, in the end, what the cardinal from Poland needed most was to see the world.

Karol Wojtyła's first grand voyage—to North America—happened, however, by accident. Polish communities in Canada and the United States had extended an invitation to Cardinal Wyszyński, but the primate refused to go. He was a timid soul, he spoke no English, and he was horrified by the prospect of holding press conferences. The invitation was then made to Wojtyła.

On August 26, 1969, Wojtyła flew to Rome and on to Montreal on the first leg of his inaugural transatlantic expedition. Father Dziwisz, his chaplain, and his friends Bishop Franciszek Macharski from Kraków and Father Szczepan Wesoły, based in Rome, accompanied him. They spent nearly three weeks in Canada, touring Montreal and Québec City, where Wojtyła was at ease speaking French, then the Anglophone cities of Ottawa, Toronto, Calgary, Edmonton, Winnipeg, and Hamilton and London, Ontario.

It was an exciting trip, but it is doubtful that Wojtyła learned much about Canada during his stay there. He met Polish-Canadian clergy, celebrated Mass in Polish at Polish churches, socialized with Polish-Canadian communities at lunches, receptions, and dinners, and held perfunctory meetings with Canada's Primate Cardinal Maurice Roy and leading Canadian bishops.

On the other hand, Wojtyła learned a lot both in Canada and then in the United States about the techniques of social life. Father Wesoły (now an archbishop) recalls that "he discovered the institution of the cocktail party, which he didn't like at first, realizing that it was a good idea to be able to stand with a glass in your hand, whether you drank or not, while chatting with hosts and fellow guests. . . . It was different from Polish parties at home where people just down their vodka. . . . Wojtyła also got to like dinners and banquets because they offered an opportunity for conversation around the table, even if there were speeches. And he acquired a taste for press conferences as his English kept improving en route."

Leaving Canada, Wojtyła visited Niagara Falls and crossed to Buffalo for the start of a two-week trip around much of the United States. Wesoły says that Wojtyła was advised that he should visit every American city where cardinals had sees, and, consequently, he went to Detroit, Boston, Washington, D.C., Baltimore, St. Louis, Chicago, Philadelphia (where he knew Polish-descended Cardinal Krol), and New York. He did miss a few American cardinals in the cities he did not visit, and visited cities that had no cardinals.

Again, he learned more about Polish-Americans and their churches and institutions than about the United States. In Michigan, Wojtyła was taken to the Polish-American Seminary at Orchard Lake. From Philadelphia, Cardinal Krol flew him by helicopter to the sanctuary at Doylestown, Pennsylvania, known as "American Częstochowa." It was Wojtyła's first helicopter flight and he loved it.

Then Wojtyła rushed back to Rome to spend most of October at an extraordinary session of the Synod of Bishops. Reporting over the Polish service of Vatican Radio on his Canadian and American trips, the cardinal—who was the first Polish cardinal ever to visit North America—emphasized their "religious character" and explained that Poles abroad were able to maintain their spiritual link with

Poland through the Church. He said he was received "surprisingly well" by American bishops and cardinals, and saw how well second- and third-generation emigrants had done for themselves in the United States.

Given the strong opinions that John Paul II now holds about the United States—many of them far from favorable—it is unfortunate that he did not take advantage of the relatively relaxed and informal travel as cardinal to become somewhat better acquainted with American realities. His 1976 visits to Philadelphia for the Eucharistic Congress (the year of the Bicentennial) and to Boston (where he spoke at Harvard about "alienation") and Washington, D.C. (a lecture at Catholic University) were not learning experiences, either. And the breathless ceremonial papal trips, of course, are not fact-finding missions; as John Paul II, he returned to the United States three times between 1979 and 1993.

Wojtyła's attendance at the Philadelphia Eucharistic Congress had, on the other hand, the advantage for him of mixing again with the flower of the Church's hierarchies.

Back in Poland, the cardinal offered a curious comment about the United States in an interview with *Tygodnik Powszechny:*

> The question of belonging to a nation of fathers and forefathers reaches deep into the conscience of man, requiring truth about himself. Not accepting this truth, man suffers a basic need and is condemned to some kind of conformism. . . . This is a real problem in the structure of the American society. The extent of this problem is demonstrated today by the so-called "Black Question." I have not noticed any average American—even of the WASP type—express the words "American Nation" with the same conviction that an average Pole in Poland speaks of the Polish nation.

Cardinal Wojtyła had crossed the globe in 1973, spending the full month of February in Australia, New Zealand, and Papua New Guinea (with a stop in the Philippines). The Eucharistic Congress in Melbourne had been the ostensible reason for the trip, and Wojtyła had the opportunity of making a splendid impression on the cardinals and bishops, and making new ecclesiastic friends.

But he had been bitten by the bug of global jet travel during the North American trip four years earlier, and in his restless way he was raring to go. Visiting Polish missionaries and emigrant communities in the region, particularly in mysterious New Guinea, justified the long journey. He traveled with Father Wesoły and Father Dziwisz.

Presumably because he could not tolerate the idea of even minimal idleness in the course of long intercontinental flights and occasional free hours on the ground, Wojtyła produced a diary the size of an average-length book.

Overall, Wojtyła was impressed at the Melbourne Eucharistic Congress by its "ecumenical emphasis," including an "Aboriginal Mass" celebrated there. He met Mother Teresa for the first time, and was exposed to discussions about "population and ecology" and the Theology of Liberation. It had also been Wojtyła's first exposure to the Third World. In August 1975 it had been followed by visits to Kraków by Cardinal Paul Zoungrana of Upper Volta (now Burkina Faso), the first black cardinal to set foot in Poland, and bishops from New Delhi, and Moeya, Tanzania.

Cardinal Wojtyła had become a familiar figure at the Vatican and in the papal apartments. Not only was he frequently in Rome attending meetings of his Congregations and the Bishops' Synod, but he was a regular visitor to Paul VI's private study. In the course of three years—1973 to 1975—he was received eleven times by the pope in private audiences, probably a record for nonresident cardinals (prefects of important Curia Congregations met with the pope on business every week). In May 1970 Wojtyła had brought 260 Polish priests, survivors of Dachau and other Nazi concentration camps, to meet Paul VI.

If there were any doubts that Wojtyła was Paul VI's special favorite, they were dispelled by the sudden invitation to him, in February 1976, to conduct the Roman Curia's Lenten Retreat in the presence of the pope. This was as high a personal and theological honor as can be granted a prelate by the pontiff, but Wojtyła was given only three weeks to prepare his presentation—"Meditations"—for the weeklong retreat held behind closed doors in St. Matilda's Chapel in the Vatican.

Arriving in Rome on March 2, Wojtyła first went to pray at the Mentorella sanctuary in the nearby mountains—it was an important spiritual site for him—then entered the chapel for the week of meditation. The retreat ended on the morning of March 13, with Wojtyła's "Meditations," and Paul VI received him at noon for a private audience.

Wojtyła's "Meditations," later published as a book under the title *A Sign of Contradiction,* was not simply confined to theology and the rejection of the "God is dead" concept then in vogue in intellectual and philosophical discussions around the world. Instead, it was a ringing manifesto defining the Church's morality and ethics, and Wojtyła's view of the world caught between the evils of Marxism and excessive capitalism.

He had expressed these ideas many times before, but now they were offered as a fundamental statement of policy before men who would be decisive in choosing the new pope. Paul VI, who listened to the "Meditations" wearing a penitential hair shirt and thorns against his flesh beneath his papal robes, was seventy-nine years old and in very poor health. All those at St. Matilda's Chapel knew they were witnessing the end of the pontificate. But they did not know that Paul VI had suggested that Wojtyła speak in Italian, rather than Latin, so that the cardinals would become aware that he could function very well as pope. Wojtyła had selected the Gospel theme of the "sign of contradiction" to apply explicitly to Paul VI for his having been rejected, as Christ had been in His teachings, for his defense of man's dignity in *Humanae vitae.* The pope, he said, had been opposed because of the encyclical "in apparently Christian and 'humanistic' circles linked with certain Christian traditions"—thus becoming a "sign of contradiction," in the words of Luke.

Having issued two years earlier unprecedented formal appeals to the faithful and the priests of the Kraków archdiocese to combat abortion, Wojtyła returned to the topic in the Lenten "Meditations," denouncing "campaigners in favor of abortion" and announcing that "we are in the front line in a lively battle for the dignity of man."

Communism was still very much entrenched in 1976, or so it seemed, but Wojtyła was prepared to condemn both Marxism's "autocracy" and capitalism's "exploitation . . . and economic imperialism." The Third World, he observed, would not be saved by "liberation" from the First World nor by Marxist influences from the Second World. Readers of the *Sign of Contradiction* in Washington, Western Europe, and elsewhere (if there were any) should not have been surprised hearing John Paul II making exactly the same points in crescendo throughout his pontificate—before and after the fall of communism.

Meanwhile, Marxism was faring worse and worse in Poland. In June 1976 the Gierek regime repeated Gomułka's 1970 mistake of suddenly raising food prices. Workers rioted at the huge automotive plant in Ursus, near Warsaw, and in other urban centers. Railwaymen declared a general strike. But Gierek had learned the lesson from four years earlier: he and Defense Minister General Wojciech Jaruzelski refrained from using force, and the price rise was canceled.

The Polish Church, with Primate Wyszyński and Cardinal Wojtyła concurring, urged the workers to return to their jobs, appealed for social peace, and pressed the government not to punish the workers and rioters. Calm returned, but the June crisis led to the birth of KOR, the Polish acronym for the Committee for the Defense of Workers.

Led by intellectuals like Adam Michnik and Jacek Kuroń, most of whom once were ideological leftists, KOR created for the first time in Polish history a functioning political alliance between intellectuals and workers. KOR and the regime would battle each other for the next four years, though on a relatively low-intensity scale. The Solidarity trade union movement, emerging in rebellion in 1980, probably would not have survived without KOR's advisers.

Wojtyła quickly established close ties with KOR, which already was linked with the Catholic Intellectuals' Clubs (KIK), and the so-called progressive wing of the Church, politically identified with the cardinal, played a significant role in the great events to come in Poland. Interestingly, Adam Michnik, a Jew, is a historian specializing in the

Polish Church and an advocate of dialogue between a "modern Polish Church" and left-of-center intellectuals.

In a Christmas sermon, Wojtyła alluded to the June events, remarking that "when people are injured and suffering, the Church comes to their aid without any political motivation—only from motives of Christian love, Christian solidarity."

But in a New Year's Eve sermon, he sounded a cautionary note lest people forget the presence next door of the powerfully armed Soviet Union while standing up for their rights. He said: "One may not be a thoughtless Pole: our geographic position is too difficult. Thus every Pole has the obligation to act responsibly, especially at the present time. . . . But we had to fight for the fundamental right of defining, 'Who is the nation? Who is the state?' as we did during the first months of this year. . . ."

Wojtyła, as he later confirmed, was already developing the sense that Poland was witnessing the beginning of the end of an era. And Gierek, for his part, began moving closer to the Church.

On May 15, 1977, Wojtyła had the enormous satisfaction of consecrating the new church in the workers' suburb of Nowa Huta, the most famous modern church in Poland, after long years of struggle with the regime. Nowa Huta had been built by the government as a "socialist city," which was one reason it took such a dim view of allowing a major church to be erected there. Although the permit for the construction had been issued in October 1967, immediately after Wojtyła became cardinal (and the secret police urged support for his "self-esteem"), it took ten years to build the church because of steady harassment by the authorities.

And in December, Gierek was received by Paul VI, the first Polish communist leader to be granted a papal audience. Wojtyła had met with the eighty-year-old pontiff in September.

Karol Wojtyła called on Paul VI on May 19, 1978. It was one day after his fifty-eighth birthday. It was the last time he saw him.

Wojtyła took a long vacation during the summer, visibly tired and not in the best of health. He had been ill for nearly three weeks in April 1977, and for two weeks in February 1978. And he suffered from migraines.

He was resting on the shores of a lake not far from Rome when he was notified on the morning of August 7 that Paul VI had died the previous evening at his summer residence in Castel Gandolfo. Death had come at 9:41 P.M. from a massive heart attack. At that precise moment, the little alarm clock the pope had bought in Poland nearly sixty years earlier, and that had never left his side, went off with a loud buzzer.

On August 12, two Polish cardinals—Wyszyński and Wojtyła—arrived in Rome for the papal funeral and the conclave that would elect Paul VI's successor.

Cardinal Albino Luciani, the Archbishop of Venice, was chosen on August 26, taking the name of John Paul I. Wojtyła's name had been mentioned a few times during conclave conversations inside the locked Sistine Chapel, but he was not a serious candidate, not even in his own mind. He knew that Paul VI had wanted him to be the first *non-Italian* pope, but the moment had not quite arrived because there was at least one acceptable Italian candidate—Luciani. Wojtyła had a private audience with the new pontiff on August 30, one of few cardinals to be honored so quickly.

On September 28, Wojtyła celebrated the twentieth anniversary of his consecration as bishop by officiating at the opening of the Wawel Cathedral museum.

At the Vatican, Pope John Paul I died within the same hour.

His death was announced early the following morning, and it was Józef Mucha, the cardinal's driver, who had heard the news on the car radio and rushed to the Curial Palace to inform Father Obtułowicz, the chancellor. Obtułowicz recalls that Wojtyła was at breakfast when he brought him word of John Paul I's death. He sat in silence for a moment, then said: "God works in mysterious ways. . . . Let us bow our heads before them. . . ."

But he went on with his own work. He took part later that morning in a meeting at the Council of the Theological Department, then left by car for Złote Łany for a two-day inspection of the new parish there. Returning to Kraków on

September 30, Wojtyła asked the driver to stop at the edge of woods near the Kalwaria Zebrzydowska sanctuary.

He sat in the car for a time, busily writing letters on his lap desk, then had Mucha take him home. At the palace, he instructed an assistant to have the letters typed. As the assistant remarked later, "It was as if he wanted to wind up all his affairs here, not leaving behind him anything undone."

On October 2, Wojtyła traveled to Warsaw for a meeting of the General Council of the Polish episcopate. He was relaxed and unhurried.

At 7:30 A.M. on October 3, 1978, Karol Wojtyła and Primate Wyszyński flew to Rome.

PART

FIVE

CHAPTER 19

If Karol Wojtyła had a premonition about his own future when he returned to Rome early in October for the second conclave of 1978 he behaved over the next two weeks in a remarkably businesslike fashion, just another cardinal preparing to elect a new pontiff.

And if a Wojtyła candidacy was beginning to emerge in quiet Roman conversations during this interregnum, the Kraków cardinal had no visible part in it. With or without his knowledge, the matter was in the hands of his friends and potential supporters. Though the Holy Spirit may inspire the cardinals in their choice, as the Church says, a papal election has always been an exercise in exquisite politics. The October conclave and the days preceding it were no exception.

Installed at the Polish College on Piazza Remuria in Aventino Heights (Primate Wyszyński was staying at the Polish Institute on the Vatican side of the Tiber), Wojtyła went within hours of his arrival in Rome to pray at the body of John Paul I laid out in state at St. Peter's Basilica. The next afternoon, he joined his fellow cardinals at the pope's funeral. The balance of his time prior to the start of the conclave was taken up with daily sessions of the General Congregation for Cardinals—this body governs and administers the Holy See together with the *camerlengo* (the cardinal chamberlain, who, in effect, serves as acting pope until a new pontiff is chosen)—and with solemn Masses, visits with Polish friends, and quick excursions to the Roman countryside.

Much of Wojtyła's time was spent with his old friend Bishop Deskur, a powerful political-minded and superbly connected bridge-playing prelate, and another friend, Bishop Rubin, the secretary-general of the Bishops' Synod. Both were splendidly informed about preconclave politics and intrigues, whether they discussed them or not with Wojtyła. It is hard to imagine that Wojtyła had shown no scintilla of interest in conclave gossip—after all, he, too, was a natural politician and a papal elector.

Deskur, who was attending and organizing scores of political dinners and meetings around town with ecclesiastic dignitaries, drove Wojtyła to Lake Vico, a scenic spot some fifty miles from Rome, on Sunday, October 8. The previous day, Wojtyła had gone to his favorite mountaintop sanctuary of Mentorella. Then he visited Castel Gandolfo, the site of the lakeside papal summer residence in the hills above Rome.

The week before the conclave, Wojtyła stepped up his social-political activities. Deskur hosted events for him with Italian Cardinal Nasalli Rocca and Archbishop Luigi Poggi, a top Vatican diplomat with experience in Poland, and with Chicago's Cardinal John Cody, whose parishioners included great numbers of Polish-Americans. Wojtyła already knew well Cardinal Krol of Philadelphia, himself a Polish-American, but he realized the importance of widening his contacts in the important U.S. contingent. The preconclave period grew more and more like a secular political convention, and Wojtyła was attracting increasing attention among his peers. His name kept popping up in the accelerating maneuvering by the cardinals.

Naturally, Wojtyła was saying nothing about his possible candidacy—public humility and modesty are conclave requirements—but Deskur is convinced that he already knew that he was destined to be elected. He recalls that during a walk they took in the Vatican gardens a few days before the conclave began, "It was very clear to me that somewhere inside his mind and his soul and his heart Wojtyła knew that he would be pope."

Still, a conclave is always a mystery. Moreover, the electoral political situation at that stage was extremely complex and wholly unpredictable.

Two main questions faced the 111 cardinals assembled in Rome to choose the new pontiff. One was whether there was a viable and acceptable Italian candidate to maintain the tradition of Italian popes, which was by no means certain, and the other was whether the Church was ready to name a non-Italian pope for the first time in 456 years (Adrian VI, a Dutchman from Utrecht, had been elected in 1522, reigning for just over a year). This was the first time in four and a half centuries that such a prospect had even arisen, and the next step, it was feared by the Italians, might be to decide *who* such a non-Italian should be, a daunting task.

However, the Italians themselves had created a situation that threatened to impose another foreign pope on the Holy See when Cardinal Giuseppe Siri of Genoa and Cardinal Giovanni Benelli of Florence emerged from the outset as the two principal rival candidates. Their confrontation deadlocked the conclave even before it started.

Siri, seventy-two, had been a protégé of Pius XII and was identified with the most conservative wing of the Church, the group that believed the reforms of Vatican Council II had been a dreadful mistake. Benelli, fifty-seven, had been one of the closest associates of Paul VI as the *sostituto*—deputy secretary of state—and generally represented progressive post-conciliar views. In their rivalry, the future of the Church seemed to be at stake. And no compromise between them was possible.

Siri was a strong candidate for the papacy in the August conclave—in fact, he was ahead after the first ballot—but he was quickly blocked by Benelli's forces. After only one day of voting, Benelli's candidate, Cardinal Albino Luciani of Venice, had been elected pope, a moderate in the tradition of John XXIII and Paul VI, whose names he combined to become John Paul I.

In October, however, there was no Italian Luciani-type compromise candidate, and the battle was joined as soon as the cardinals had gathered in Rome for John Paul I's funeral. Within a week, Siri had built so much strength that it was being taken virtually for granted that he would be the next pontiff. At that point, Benelli jumped again into the fray, almost a declared candidate supported by a loose coalition of West European and Third World cardinals who feared a return to the precouncil past if Siri won.

With the internationalization of the Curia instituted by John XXIII and Paul VI, power had shifted significantly from the Italians in the College of Cardinals to other Europeans and, especially, to the Third World, where the Church saw its long-range future. Now, for example, the secretary of state was the Frenchman Jean Villot (who also served as camerlengo), the first foreigner ever to hold that post. There were as well a half-dozen highly influential Latin American cardinals and at least two key Africans.

The makeup of the College of Cardinals had changed, too, in favor of the Third World, then extremely progressive-minded. Whereas fifty-five out of the eighty cardinals who had elected Paul VI in 1963 were Europeans, there were only fifty-six Europeans among the 111 cardinals preparing to vote in October 1978.

The Roman Curia—the permanent Church establishment—had only twenty-eight cardinals in the college, not enough to be decisive in a final faceoff (Siri, of course, was the Curial candidate). Moreover, Paul VI had decreed that cardinals over the age of eighty could not vote at all; this removed nine presumably conservative votes from the college whose authorized total strength stood at 120. An entirely unprecedented political situation had materialized, opening the doors to a non-Italian.

Wojtyła had taken notice of the new state of affairs in a Vatican Radio Polish-language broadcast on September 4, ten days after John Paul I's election, remarking that "such a rapid choice had not been generally expected." Rather, he said, "it was thought that the conclave would last longer, considering especially the number of cardinals present—the largest ever." But Wojtyła also noted that the outcome of the election had vindicated Paul VI's "blessed decision" to enlarge the College of Cardinals and that the other decisive factors had been "the numerous contacts in the Church throughout the world stemming from the [Vatican] Council, Bishops' Synods and other meetings." As it happened, few cardinals could match Wojtyła's numerous contacts.

Wojtyła, in the meantime, remained publicly passive, confining himself to the occasions arranged by Bishop Deskur—who was a potential "popemaker" backstage without even being a cardinal or an archbishop—and cordial social contacts with many cardinals he had known and cultivated over long years.

On the evening of Sunday, October 8, after returning from Lake Vico with Deskur, Wojtyła conferred with Cardinal Benelli's private secretary at the Polish church of St. Stanisław on Via Botteghe Oscure, his Roman political headquarters. It was run by his friend, Bishop Szczepan Wesoły, who normally looked after Polish pilgrims in Rome. Ostensibly, Benelli's secretary had come to solicit Wojtyła's backing for the Florentine, but, in retrospect, he may well have been assessing the Polish cardinal as a fallback candidate if Benelli himself could not prevail.

Intrigue thickened on Wednesday, October 11, three days before the conclave. Approximately fifteen West European and Third World cardinals met quietly during the evening at the French Seminary on Via Santa Chiara, an imposing building in midtown Rome, to plot anti-Siri strategy. Among them were two French cardinals, two Italians, two Canadians, an Englishman, one Belgian, two Brazilians, two Africans, and a Korean. All of them were extremely influential in the college.

But this group was not yet thinking of a non-Italian. They were prepared to go with Benelli or, as alternatives, with Italian Cardinal Ugo Poletti, the Vicar of Rome, or Cardinal Giovanni Colombo, the Archbishop of Milan. They were not yet ready to break with the Italian tradition. But two key cardinals, who had not attended the French Seminary session, were already cogitating about a non-Italian pope and, specifically, about Karol Wojtyła.

They were his old friends Cardinal König of Vienna and Cardinal Krol of Philadelphia, the sons of Poles (both names happen to mean "king"). Though their politics differed—König was a "progressive" and Krol a "conservative"—they were in agreement that Karol

Wojtyła was the man for the season. König believed that the point had been reached in history when the Church could be saved only by the European "East" because Western civilization was in decay—a view he shared with Wojtyła—while Krol was hugely impressed by the Pole's youthful energy and deep spirituality.

Reminiscing in 1993 about the conclave, Krol pointed out that many foreign cardinals, including himself, were deeply disturbed about the political situation in Italy, including specifically the financial and government scandals surrounding the mysterious P2 Masonic lodge. The scandals had tarnished top Italian leaders and brushed the Roman Curia.

Therefore, Krol said, "some of the cardinals thought that a non-Italian [pope] would be better off. . . . They felt that a non-Italian would be an asset for the Church. And, actually, it turned out in such a way." Krol, as far as is known, is the only cardinal to acknowledge publicly that the P2 lodge issue had influenced the ultimate decision of the foreign cardinals in favor of a non-Italian—and the foreigners now had the majority in the college. It was one of the great conclave secrets.

In any event, it was at that juncture—in the days immediately preceding the conclave—that Wojtyła's undeclared candidacy gradually began to take shape. And, unquestionably, König and Krol were the chief architects of the campaign. The Viennese could bring along the West European progressives and many of the Third Worlders. Krol could (and did) bring along the Americans.

On the morning of Friday, October 13, the cardinals congregated at the Vatican for the selection of the cells each would occupy in the Apostolic Palace next to the Sistine Chapel for the duration of the conclave. Under canon law, the cardinals must remain sequestered inside the sealed area until they elect a pope. They may have no contact with the outside world—even the outer windows of their cells are nailed shut—and they can talk only to each other. Wojtyła drew Cell No. 91.

A few minutes later, Wojtyła was informed that Bishop Deskur had suffered a paralyzing stroke. It was a tremendous emotional blow to him—particularly on the eve of the conclave—and he rushed to the Gemelli Polyclinic across town to see his friend. Nobody was closer as a personal friend to Karol Wojtyła than Deskur, and he remembered now how the bishop had met him at Rome's Fiumicino Airport two months earlier to take him to St. Peter's Basilica to pray before the body of Paul VI, his beloved protector. That, too, had been a moment of trauma for Wojtyła.

On Saturday, October 14, the opening day of the conclave, Wojtyła concelebrated at 7:15 A.M. a Mass at the Polish College, where he was staying, in prayer for Deskur's recovery. Later in the morning, he was at St. Peter's for the Mass for the election of the pope celebrated by Cardinal Villot, the secretary of state and camerlengo. At 3:00 P.M., on his way to the Sistine Chapel for the start of the conclave, Wojtyła was driven over to the Gemelli Polyclinic to check again on his friend.

Once more, Karol Wojtyła's life was punctuated by tragedy, suffering, and martyrdom. He would mystically stress fifteen years later in his *Veritatis Splendor* encyclical that martyrdom is "the highest witnessing of moral truth, to which relatively few are called."

From the polyclinic, Wojtyła's Polish monk driver took him directly to the Sistine Chapel, where the cardinal barely had time to drop off his battered little suitcase in Cell No. 91 before Cardinal Carlo Confalonieri, the eighty-five-year-old Dean of the College of Cardinals, called the conclave to order.

Wojtyła went to his assigned seat near the altar on the left-hand side of the chapel in the second of the two raised rows there, right behind Cardinal König—the seating is by seniority of cardinals—just as the college rose to intone *Veni Creator.*

The reason the cardinals are sequestered inside the Sistine Chapel compound until they elect a pope is to assure absolute secrecy about the proceedings—the outside world is never to know how the decision is made—and to shield them from any outside influence during the conclave. They sleep and eat in the compound, holding morning and afternoon sessions of speech making and balloting (usually two ballots per session), and spending ample time during meals and between plenary meetings to consult, gossip, and cut deals.

Sitting inside the Sistine Chapel, the cardinals find themselves in, arguably, the world's most magnificent structure. Inaugurated by Pope Sixtus IV in 1483, the chapel is a relatively small rectangular construction that adjoins St. Peter's Basilica on the north and today forms a part of the Vatican Museums complex. The Apostolic Palace and the papal apartments are immediately to the north of the chapel. The basilica, the chapel, the palace, and the apartments are linked by passages. Sixtus IV, one of the great popes of the incredibly creative *Quattrocento,* had also built the famous Vatican Library next to the chapel.

It is impossible to imagine a more inspiring site than the Sistine Chapel for the cardinals of the Church to choose their pontiff. On the north wall, behind the altar, they see *The Last Judgment,* which Michelangelo completed in 1541. Conceived as a Dantesque vision of the universe beyond the grave, it is one of humanity's greatest artistic creations. Lifting their eyes to the ceiling, the cardinals discern Michelangelo's *The Creation,* with God extending His hand to Adam, another peerless creation.And along the walls, they may admire biblical works by Botticelli, Perugino, Ghirlandaio, Rosselli, and Signorelli: *The Rescue of Moses, The Story of Genesis, Nativity, The Last Supper, The Twelve Apostles,* and images of twenty-eight popes.

The Sistine Chapel is the ultimate demonstration of Christendom's artistic inspiration and the power of its religious art. It is there, as John Paul II affirmed, that the Holy Spirit acts to guide the cardinals in determining who should be the Successor of Peter.

On Saturday afternoon, October 14, the cardinals departed from the chapel after the singing of *Veni Creator.* They returned on Sunday to concelebrate Mass at seven o'clock in the morning, and began the first day of their deliberations. In their two rows on raised platforms on either side of the chapel, the cardinals were face-to-face across the central aisle. The altar and *The Last Judgment* were to their side. Each cardinal had a desk in front of him. Each had a pencil and a pad. They were to write the last name of the candidate of their choice on a slip of paper, first carefully double-checking the spelling, then place it in an urn. The ballots are always unsigned to protect their secrecy. The votes are read out, one by one, by three vote-counter cardinals supervised by three poll-watcher cardinals. The votes are called aloud so that the cardinals may write them down and have an immediate sense of who is (or is not) running ahead.

However, at the end of the first day, October 15, nobody was clearly ahead in marshaling the required two-thirds-plus-one-vote majority in order to be elected. After the four Sunday ballots—two in the morning and two in the afternoon—the conclave was deadlocked between Siri and Benelli, with neither of them even approaching the minimum seventy-five votes of the III cardinals.

Siri, originally the favorite, had been badly hurt when an interview highly critical of Vatican Council II reforms that he had granted earlier that week to *La Gazzetta del Popolo,* to be published *after* the conclave, appeared mysteriously on Sunday morning as the cardinals gathered to deliberate. The article was immediately photocopied and smuggled into the Sistine Chapel, costing Siri precious uncommitted votes.

An effort by the conservatives to shift support to Cardinal Pericle Felici, the hard-line head of the Pontifical Commission for the Interpretation of Second Vatican Council Decrees, made no headway. But Benelli could not command sufficient support, either. As the cardinals adjourned for dinner, France's Cardinal François Marty, the Archbishop of Paris, told his colleagues that "a day had been wasted."

Each time a ballot failed to produce a winner—four times on Sunday—black smoke streamed out of the chimney protruding from the corner window on the left side of the Sistine Chapel. It was the time-honored method of advising the huge crowd in St. Peter's Square and beyond that no pope had been chosen on the last try. White smoke, on the other hand, would signify election—and this was the sign that the throng below awaited so eagerly.

The smoke is produced by burning humid hay in a stove

located in the left-hand corner of the chapel, in the back section behind a tall partition. It then goes up a pipe to the sixth window, from which it is released through the chimney into the air for the crowds to see. Chemical additives to the hay render the smoke white or black. Cesare Tassi, the saturnine-looking Sistine Chapel official in charge of papal election arrangements, says that "yes, we *do* worry very much about not making a mistake in picking the correct additive in sending out the smoke signal. . . ."

Overnight from Sunday to Monday, more and more cardinals began to realize that no Italian candidate had a chance to be elected and that they had no choice but to turn to a foreigner. König, Krol, Belgium's Leo Jozef Suenens, Spain's Vicente Enrique y Tarancón, and Brazil's Aloísio Lorscheider took it upon themselves to convince their fellow cardinals of this reality during dinner and at chats in small groups in the cells and in the corridors of the Apostolic Palace.

It became evident at the same time what the qualities were the new pope should possess, a subject the cardinals had not really defined beforehand.

First of all, they concluded, the Church needed a "pastoral" pontiff, with considerable experience in the apostolic work of running parishes, dioceses, and archdioceses. This was particularly important in the aftermath of the Vatican Council, when the entire Church structure had to be reorganized. In fact, there had been no pastoral popes since Pius X, who died in 1914. Benedict XV, Pius XI, Pius XII, John XXIII, and Paul VI were intellectuals who had spent most of their careers in Vatican diplomacy. John Paul I was a pastoral pope, but he had lasted only thirty-three days.

As Cardinal Enrique y Tarancón, the archbishop of Madrid, who had known Karol Wojtyła for at least five years before the 1978 conclave, explained immediately after the election, "We wanted a pastor more than an intellectual, and with his Polish pastoral experience, his pastoral way of being, his direct contact with the masses, Wojtyła was the man we had sought. . . . It was very healthy psychologically for the Church to have a humanist as pope, someone close to the people." Enrique y Tarancón said that this was the message he was imparting among his colleagues that Sunday night—evidently successfully. The remaining plausible Italian candidate—Benelli—was a lifetime diplomat and Holy See bureaucrat, although Paul VI had named him Archbishop of Florence and cardinal in 1977.

The other consideration was age and health. Pius XII, John XXIII, and Paul VI had all died in their eighties, and this time the Church needed a younger pontiff, one who perhaps could lead it into the Third Millennium. Thus, even at seventy-two, Siri seemed too old. That John XXIII suffered from cancer when he was elected in 1958 was a closely kept secret, and he died within five years (he spent his final months in isolation under the official version that he could not hold audiences because he was in "religious retreat"). Paul VI's health was extremely fragile in the last decade of his reign, and he was less and less in charge as the years elapsed. John Paul I clearly was seriously ill when—with hesitation—he accepted his election the previous August. He then declined to keep Paul VI's commitment to attend the Latin American Eucharistic Congress in Puebla, Mexico, the following January.

So now the cardinals looked for a youngish, robust pope who would combine pastoral experience, intellect, personality, dedication to the Vatican Council, and a solid understanding of world diplomacy. It was a very tall order.

Monday, October 16, the first order of business (after the morning Mass) was for the non-Italians to persuade the College of Cardinals that the time had come for a foreign pope. And Wojtyła supporters, now in growing numbers, had to make it plain—delicately—that he was the man.

Cardinal König rose at the morning plenary session to make the basic case before his fellow electors. This is how he remembers the occasion: "I recall that before the previous conclave, I got several letters from unknown people in Italy, saying, 'please vote for a non-Italian because our country is in such a mess, and it would help us if a non-Italian becomes pope.' A very curious argument. So, at the beginning, in my opinion, the reason [for the opposition to Wojtyła] was that he was young, and, much more than that, a non-Italian coming from an Eastern country."

König was making the point that while the cardinals

realized that a younger pope was desirable, Wojtyła, only fifty-eight at that time, seemed too young to many. This view was shared by Primate Wyszyński who, at seventy-seven, embarrassed some of his friends by suggesting during Sunday night Sistine Chapel conversations that *he* would be the "natural" foreign pontiff—if it came to that. Actually, the primate, who always had very mixed feelings about Wojtyła, believed, rather surprisingly, that the next pope should be an Italian. His biographer recounts that Wyszyński "thought that tradition would be respected in the election of another Italian pope. . . . What is more, he regarded such an outcome as fitting: not only did he think the Romans should have an Italian bishop, but he also feared the consequences of violating a 455-year-old tradition."

Such, then, was the resistance König and his allies had to overcome. As he recalls the Monday morning session, "I defended my opinion openly before the conclave. I said that 'it's time to change the system and to vote for a non-Italian. That is my opinion.'"

After two ballots Monday morning, there still was no pope and, once more, black smoke poured out the chimney of the Sistine Chapel to the disappointment of the tens of thousands of the faithful in St. Peter's Square. Having no idea what was happening inside, the crowd was growing increasingly tense and worried. But as they sat down to lunch, the cardinals had finally made up their minds that they would pick a foreigner. Still, the question was, "Who?"

As the Monday afternoon session opened, it was obvious that there were only four plausible foreign candidates: Wojtyła, who had received a few votes even on Sunday afternoon; König, who definitely did not want the job; Cardinal Eduardo Francisco Pironio of Argentina (who was fifty-eight); and Cardinal Johannes Willebrands of the Netherlands, sixty-nine, who had earned much respect for his work in the realms of religious liberty and ecumenical unity among Christian churches. Willebrands, in fact, received twenty votes Monday morning before shifting his own support to Wojtyła.

Cardinal Enrique y Tarancón recalled that "at noon of

the second day I realized that it would be Wojtyła." He added that "the first day—Sunday—after four ballots, the cardinals were a bit disoriented, but on Monday morning we felt it would be Karol Wojtyła. We had seen on the first day that it couldn't be an Italian, so we had to search for a new way, and on the second day it was clear where we were going."

Belgian Cardinal Suenens said that "on the second day, there wasn't too much discussion. It became the language of mathematics. And Karol Wojtyła was the most evident name."

But the first ballot Monday afternoon—the seventh of the conclave—did not produce Wojtyła's victory. He was still short of the magic seventy-five votes. More black smoke. Cardinal Krol had brought around the Americans, and Cardinal Joseph Ratzinger, the conservative German theologian, delivered the votes of the Germans, who in the morning declined to go for the Pole. Brazil's Lorscheider, Argentina's Pironio, and Benin's Bernardin Gantin mobilized Latin American and African votes. But most of the Italians were still denying Wojtyła their twenty-five votes, and the outcome remained in doubt as the cardinals got ready for the afternoon's second vote.

The problem was to make Wojtyła fully acceptable to all the Church factions and, evidently, this required a formidable last-moment effort. As Cardinal Enrique y Tarancón put it, "We were not looking for a conservative or a progressive, but someone 'sure' in line with Vatican Council II. It was not in ideological terms. Besides, Wojtyła was a pastoral bishop, which was vital."

Cardinal Villot, the Secretary of State and camerlengo, called for the eighth ballot shortly after 5:00 P.M. The tension inside the Sistine Chapel was unbearable; many feared an unbreakable deadlock over the Italian question, which would plunge the Church into a profound crisis. König said that "there was enormous tension the whole time."

Then the break came. Cardinal Sebastiano Baggio, the powerful Italian Prefect of the Congregation for Bishops, decided to back Wojtyła, followed by just enough recalcitrant Italian cardinals. As votes were called out by the counters, the cardinals wrote down the numbers on their pads. König, who sat directly ahead of Wojtyła, recalls that "when the number of votes for him approached one-half [of the needed total], he cast away his pencil and sat up straight. He was red in the face. Then he was holding his head in his hands."

König went on to say: "My impression was that he was completely confused. Then the final majority number turned up. He had two-thirds of the votes plus one. . . ."

As the ballot reached ninety-four for him—seventeen cardinals refused to accept him—Wojtyła leaned down over the desk and began writing furiously.

At 6:18 P.M., Cardinal Villot announced in the chapel that Karol Wojtyła of Kraków had been elected pontiff of the Roman Catholic Church. Cardinal Villot approached Wojtyła to ask in Latin: "In accordance with the canon law do you accept?"

Wojtyła had no hesitation. "It is God's will," he replied. "I accept."

The cardinals broke out in applause. Cardinal Enrique y Tarancón summed up later what had just happened in the Sistine Chapel: "God forced us to break with history to elect Karol Wojtyła."

In the back of the chapel, Cesare Tassi's stove spewed out white smoke to the world. It announced that a pope had been chosen, but his identity was not made known at that moment. Suspense gripped St. Peter's Square as night fell.

Taking the name of John Paul II—out of respect for his predecessor—Karol Wojtyła became the 263rd successor of St. Peter, the 264th pope of his Church, and thereby head of seven hundred million Roman Catholics, the single largest and oldest religious institution in the world.

As pope, he also became "The Bishop of Rome, the Vicar of Jesus Christ, the Successor of St. Peter, Prince of the Apostles, the Supreme Pontiff who has the primacy of jurisdiction and not merely of honor over the Universal Church, the Patriarch of the West, the Primate of Italy, the Archbishop and Metropolitan of the Roman Province, the Sovereign of the State of Vatican City, Servant of the

Servants of God." He was to be addressed as "His Holiness the Pope" or, more informally, as "Holy Father."

At the age of fifty-eight and a half years (almost to the day), the rugged, athletic Polish cardinal, standing five feet ten and a half inches, was the youngest pope since 1846, and, of course, the first foreigner since 1523. And John Paul II wasted no time demonstrating to the cardinals and then to the rest of the world that he would be a very different kind of pope.

As soon as Karol Wojtyła accepted the papacy, Cesare Tassi, the Sistine official, led him out of the chapel through a small door to the left of the altar, below *The Last Judgment,* to a whitewash-walled narrow room to don the white papal vestments awaiting the new pontiff (actually, the room held three sets of vestments on portmanteaus: in small, medium, and large sizes, to fit whoever was chosen).

Returning to the chapel, Wojtyła found an armchair placed in front of the altar where, according to tradition, he would sit to receive the cardinals' vows of obedience. But, as Cardinal Enrique y Tarancón recalled, Wojtyła had other ideas.

"When the Master of Ceremonies invited the pope to sit down," he said, "Wojtyła replied, 'No, I receive my brothers standing up. . . .'" One by one, the cardinals came to Wojtyła to be embraced by him. The longest embrace was for Primate Wyszyński. Then the cardinals sang the *Te Deum.* The ceremony in the chapel lasted nearly one hour (the paper ballots were burned at the same time to assure eternal secrecy over the election proceedings).

Next, Wojtyła left the Sistine Chapel through the back door, past the partition, leading the papal procession across the vast Regal and Ducal Halls of St. Peter's Basilica to the Loggia, the central balcony overlooking the vast darkened square filled with over two hundred thousand faithful—Italians, foreign pilgrims, and tourists.

Cardinal Felici was the first to step out on the balcony at 6:44 P.M. as the great cross on the facade of the basilica lit up and the Swiss Guards marched into the square, the band playing and the huge papal flag unfurled. In sonorous Latin, Felici shouted: "I announce to you a great joy. . . . We have a Pope!—*Habemus Papam!*"

As the first roar of the crowd died down, Felici identified him: "Carolum Sanctae Romanae Ecclesiae Cardinalem Wojtyła . . . Ioannem Paulum Secundum!"

Silence swept St. Peter's Square. Wojtyła was a totally unknown name to the multilingual crowd. People looked at one another questioningly, wondering who was this Wojtyła? An African? No, someone said, "He's Polish!"

Now John Paul II, red chasuble over his white robe, the papal cross over his chest, and a happy smile over his broad face, moved forward to bestow his first "Urbi et Orbi" (City and World) blessing. It was 7:20 P.M. But first, departing from custom, he delivered a brief address in Italian:

> May Jesus Christ be praised! . . . Dearest brothers and sisters, we are still grieved after the death of our most beloved Pope John Paul I. And now the most eminent cardinals have called a new bishop of Rome. They have called him from a distant country, distant but always so close through the communion in the Christian faith and tradition. . . .
>
> I do not know whether I can explain myself well in your—our Italian language. If I make a mistake you will correct me. And so I present myself to you all to confess our common faith, our hope, our confidence in the Mother of Christ and of the Church, and also to start anew on this road of history and of the Church, with the help of God and with the help of men.

It was, in effect, his acceptance speech—his bid to be accepted as a non-Italian pope in Italy—and he had drafted it in the Sistine Chapel after the cardinals' votes for him had exceeded seventy-five. And John Paul II found that he was accepted in Italy and across a fascinated world with extraordinary speed and ease. He also imposed himself instantly upon the Church and the Roman Curia.

As he faced the great Roman crowd in St. Peter's Square, Monsignor Dziwisz, his chaplain and secretary, scurried across the city to bring the pope's meager belongings from his Polish College apartment on Piazza Remuria to the temporary lodgings in the Apostolic Palace where he would spend the first night as pontiff.

John Paul II concentrated on what were for him four immensely important activities on Tuesday, October 17, his first full day as pope.

In the morning, he concelebrated solemn Mass at the Sistine Chapel with all the cardinals, again bestowing the "Urbi et Orbi" blessing.

In the afternoon, he was driven in the black Mercedes papal limousine to the Gemelli Polyclinic to visit his paralyzed friend, Bishop Deskur. "He taught me how to be pope," John Paul II said as he walked into Deskur's room. A crowd had gathered in the clinic's corridors for a glimpse of him, but the pope had to be reminded that they expected a blessing. Smiling sheepishly, he made the sign of cross, remarking, "I'm not used to it yet. . . ."

In the late afternoon, John Paul II received Polish friends at an informal ceremony he called "Farewell to the Motherland" in a room behind the stage of the Paul VI Auditorium next to the basilica. Each friend was summoned individually over a loudspeaker to come to greet the pope. Jerzy Kluger, Wojtyła's Jewish friend and classmate from Wadowice high school, and his English wife were the first to be called.

In the evening, Wojtyła gave orders for his cardinal's red zucchetto—skullcap—to be placed at the altar of the Polish Virgin of Ostrabrama in Vilnius in Soviet Lithuania. It had to be smuggled there.

That was how the pontificate of John Paul II began.

CHAPTER 20

Sentimental and emotional as John Paul II might have been about his Polish roots and connections—as demonstrated during the first moments of the pontificate—the pope assumed power on October 22, 1978, armed with a tough and precise agenda concerning the governance of the Church and an aggressive conduct of the Vatican's foreign policy.

It was clear at once that Karol Wojtyła was not an "accidental pope" who would improvise as he went along, but one who came fully prepared to run the papacy with both compassion and hard-eyed determination. As his friend Cardinal Deskur (who received the purple from him in 1985) put it recently, "Everything the Holy Father endured in his life, prepared him for what he had to be. Just as an arrow is readied for the shot from the bow, God prepares the proper people, He prepares his arrows. . . ."

With the Church wallowing in deepening internal crisis—losing the faithful massively and losing influence among Catholics—John Paul II moved immediately to impose strict discipline over the Roman Curia and the entire Roman Catholic institution worldwide. He followed the rigid concepts and ideas he had refined over the decade of his Kraków cardinalate and through his very considerable involvement in the activities of the Holy See during the reign of Paul VI, from *Humanae vitae* anti-contraceptive strictures to the ban on theological dissent. He insisted that priests and nuns wear religious garb at all times.

To the surprise of many Catholic experts, John Paul II restored, in effect, the ancient monarchic and absolute model of the papacy, seemingly abandoning the principles of collegiality instituted, with his participation, by Vatican Council II. Yet his basic approach to his new task was in character: he was not a man who accepted compromise. Under the cheer, the charm, and the charisma, there was pure steel.

In terms of international relations, John Paul II became the first modern pontiff to turn the Vatican into a full-fledged player in world affairs. He thus ended more than a century of division between the Church's spiritual and temporal endeavors. In the words of a Church historian, the pope "unified the religious and the social-political dimensions" of the Church in an unprecedented fashion. He made the Vatican into a modern nation-state with ever-expanding diplomatic ties around the globe. Though the Holy See had signed the Helsinki Final Act of the Conference on Security and Cooperation in Europe (CSCE) in 1975 (which, among other goals, undertook to guarantee the inviolability of postwar frontiers), its role was rather muted until the advent of John Paul II.

As an extraordinary innovation in the attitudes of the Vatican, the new pope's decision to engage in the active practice of foreign policy was aimed first and foremost at the situation in his native Poland and the rest of Eastern Europe, and even in the Soviet Union. From the outset, however, John Paul II displayed intense interest and involvement in peacekeeping—including his diplomatic intervention in defusing a threatened war between Argentina and Chile in 1979, and his opposition to the Persian Gulf War in 1991—in social justice in the Third World, and in religious freedom and observance of human rights everywhere.

Given the rising tension in the communist world in general and in Poland in particular—and considering his powerfully assertive Polish national identity—it was inevitable that his attention would be centered instantly on the land of his birth.

This reality, of course, came as a tremendous shock to the rulers in Warsaw and Moscow, representing a potential fundamental political challenge to regional communist stability. Karol Wojtyła's election had been a complete surprise.

But as the communists, especially in Poland, gradually understood that John Paul II was not about to launch an all-out anti-communist crusade, pure and simple, the initial reaction was transformed into a new era in East-West relations. The pope played an immensely complex and discreet, but crucial, role in it. From the beginning, John Paul II had subtly accelerated the *Ostpolitik* of contacts with the communist world initiated by Paul VI.

In the meantime, Warsaw and Moscow had to devise plausible responses to this new and frightening state of affairs, at least as perceived by the Soviets. However, as was probably astonishing to outsiders—both East and West—the reaction of the Polish regime was not at all hostile, once it recovered from the Wojtyła surprise. It was a fact directly derived from Polish history and nationalism, and overriding the last vestiges of Marxist-Leninist ideology. The national reaction, naturally, was pure joy.

Edward Gierek, the first secretary of the PZPR, the euphemism for the Polish communist party, learned about Wojtyła's election that Monday evening as he lay in bed at home nursing a bad back; he received a call from Stanisław Kania, a senior member of the Political Bureau. As he recalls it, he turned to his wife, saying: "A Pole has become pope. It is a great event for the Polish people and a great complication for us.

"I needed not listen to church bells to know how the news will be received [in Poland]," he went on. "I immediately issued instructions to the press and all the mass media to act in tune with the mood of exaltation sweeping Poland. And I thought right away that a visit by him to Poland will take place."

Gierek, who had come to power in 1970, in the aftermath of a massive workers' rebellion against the regime, in which scores were killed by the security forces, was not about to underestimate Polish sentiments for *their* pope. He knew that any display of hostility by the regime toward John Paul II would have catastrophic consequences, and he had no choice but to put the best face on an impossible situation.

The next day, therefore, Gierek, Polish President Henryk Jabłoński, and Prime Minister Piotr Jaroszewicz signed a lengthy telegram to the new pope expressing "cordial congratulations" and "best wishes" on his election "in the name of the nation and the highest authorities of the Polish People's Republic."

Almost gushingly, the telegram declared that the choice by the conclave had created "great satisfaction in Poland," but the signers could not resist a touch of ideological propaganda:

> For the first time in ages, a son of the Polish nation—which is building the greatness and prosperity in its Socialist motherland in the unity and collaboration of all its citizens—sits in the papal throne . . . [the son] of a nation known throughout the world for its special love and peace and for its warmest attachment to the cooperation and friendship of all peoples . . . a nation, which has made universally recognized contributions to the human culture. . . . We express our conviction that these great causes will be served by the further development of relations between the Polish People's Republic and the Apostolic Capital.

The phrasing of the Polish congratulatory telegram was presumably intended to please the very nervous Soviets. But in his response sent two days later, John Paul II chose to ignore the political discourse and to concentrate—most warmly—on the future of the relationship.

> I have accepted with special gratitude the congratulations and wishes, full of courtesy and cordiality, sent to me by the highest authorities of the Poland People's Republic. On the occasion of the choice of a son of Poland for the capital of St. Peter, I am [identified] with all my heart with my beloved Poland, the mother-

> land of all the Poles. I earnestly hope that [Poland] will continue to grow spiritually and materially, in peace and justice and in respect for man. In the spirit of the dialogue undertaken by my great predecessors, whose names I bear, I hope, with God's help, to achieve all that is useful to the well-being of the beloved nation whose destiny has been linked for a thousand years with the calling and the service of the Catholic Church.

Both messages, worded with extreme care, were designed to create a positive relationship between the Polish pope and the Polish communist regime. Gierek and his associates had emphasized their recognition of the greatness of the Church's decision to elevate a son of Poland to the papacy, while John Paul II had made a point of referring to the regime as the "Polish People's Republic," legitimizing, in effect, its political existence—a matter of enormous importance to Warsaw.

The diplomatic ballet had started and a new chapter opened in East European history.

On October 22, during the ceremony of John Paul II's inauguration before the two hundred thousand faithful massed in St. Peter's Square and carried live on Polish television, the delegation of the Polish People's Republic, headed by President Jabłoński, sat in the front row, facing the altar. The next day, Jabłoński had a private audience with the pope, informing him that the Polish authorities had arranged for five thousand of the faithful to be flown to Rome for the ceremony.

Moscow, considerably more reserved, took cognizance of the Wojtyła election in a congratulatory telegram from Leonid Brezhnev, the general secretary of the Soviet Communist Party, and it did send a delegation to the papal inauguration. (President Jimmy Carter dispatched a low-profile delegation led by House of Representatives Speaker Thomas P. O'Neill and including Polish-born National Security Adviser Zbigniew Brzeziński.)

The Kremlin was naturally disturbed by the creation of the Polish pope, but it was anxious to see whether and how John Paul II would pursue *Ostpolitik.* Foreign Minister Andrei Gromyko had first conferred with Paul VI at the

Karol Wojtyła's parents, Karol Senior and Emilia, on their wedding day in 1904. Karol Senior is wearing his uniform as a noncommissioned officer in the Austrian army.

The Wojtyłas with Karol's older brother, Edmund.

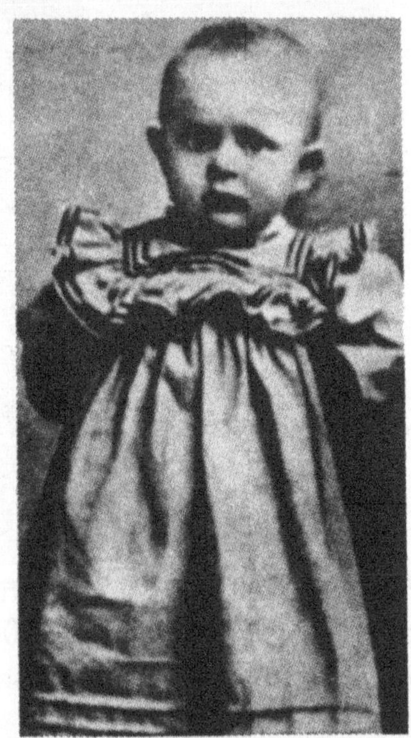

Karol Wojtyła before his first birthday.

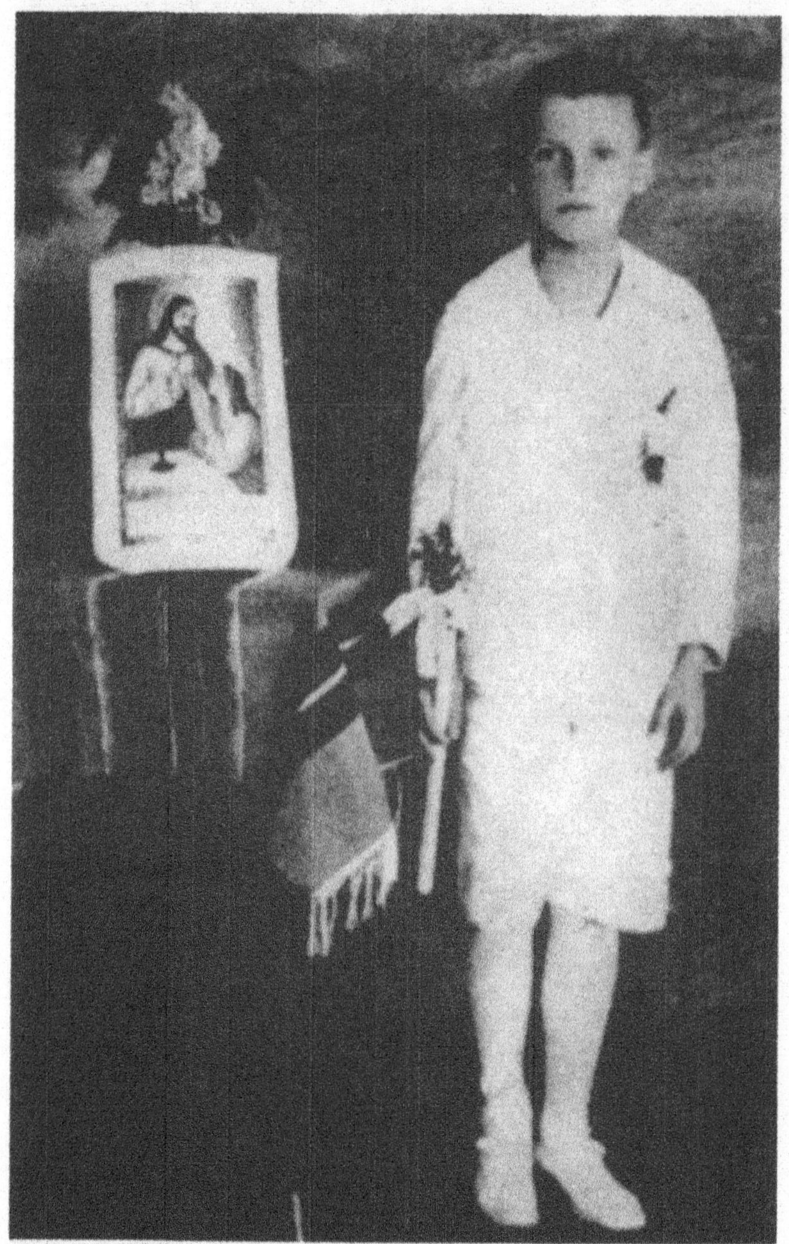

Karol Wojtyła at his First Communion.

Karol Wojtyła at the time of his high school graduation—Wadowice, 1938.

The Kraków house on Tyniecka Street where Karol lived from 1938 to 1944.

Danuta Michałowska, Karol's fellow performer in underground wartime patriotic plays.

Karol Wojtyła as a university student in Kraków, fall 1938.

Karol Wojtyła, first on the right, at his Academic Legion military training, July 1939.

Karol Wojtyła as a wartime quarry worker.

Karol Wojtyła as vicar at Niegowici parish, near Kraków, 1948.

Bishop Karol Wojtyła (second row, right) attending the Second Vatican Council at St. Peter's Basilica, Rome 1962.

Bishop Karol Wojtyła at the Vatican, 1962.

Bishop Karol Wojtyła visiting a village parish in Kraków archdiocese, June 1963.

Pope Paul VI placing the cardinal's ring on Wojtyła's hand during the consecration Mass, 1967.

Cardinal Karol Wojtyła presiding over a doctorate examination at Catholic University in Lublin, Poland, 1967. Next to him is Dr. Teresa Ryłska, another examiner.

Cardinal Karol Wojtyła walking in the Carpathian foothills at a religious ceremony with Polish highlanders in folkloric costume, 1968.

Cardinal Karol Wojtyła presiding over the placing of a cornerstone at the church of Nowa Huta, a suburb of Kraków, May 1969. Behind, to his left (without glasses), is Monsignor Stanisław Dziwisz, then his chaplain, now his private secretary at the Vatican.

United Nations in New York in 1965, and four more times at the Vatican, and Soviet President Nikolai Podgorny had called on the pope in January 1967. Now Gromyko arranged to fly to Rome in January 1979, to be received by John Paul II three months after his election in order to keep alive the dialogue between the Holy See and Moscow. The pope assured him of the Church's continued interest, stressing the importance of assuring religious freedom in the Soviet Union.

Curiously, most of the outside world paid little attention to all these contacts involving the Holy See and the communists. The conventional wisdom was that, by definition, a pope—especially a Polish pope—had to be militantly anticommunist in word and action and that the Kremlin had to be on the warpath with the Vatican.

A very special relationship already existed between Poland and the Vatican even before Karol Wojtyła reached the pontificate. Gierek had met with Paul VI in December 1977, and meetings between him and Primate Wyszyński had become virtually routine. The Polish Church was enjoying its greatest freedom in communist history at the time of John Paul II's election, at which time there were 19,913 priests (197 more than it would have in 1991, two years after the fall of communism) and 5,325 students in the seminaries. A record number of 569 priests were ordained in communist Poland in 1978, the highest ratio of priestly vocations to population in the world.

But the Polish pope established a whole new dimension: Polish pride.

Mieczysław F. Rakowski, then a liberally inclined party magazine editor and member of the Central Committee, and later its first secretary and Poland's last communist prime minister, put it this way:

> The news of Wojtyła's election was received by us—in the party and in the government—as an extraordinary event. In fact, we received it simply with pride. You see, a Pole became pope! For a Pole—and it is not important if this Pole is an agnostic, atheist or communist—the pope is that person in the world that

ennobles the nation from which he hails. In my opinion, this Polish pope had valorized everybody in Poland—in the national sense of Poland's position in the world—from a peasant to the parish priest, bishop, Primate, First Secretary of the party, the prime minister and all the members of the party.

Rakowski continued:

> The point is that a sense of defeat and of lesser importance among other nations is encoded in the national conscience. And this had been happening over many centuries. Once, in our history, Poland was truly a European power, from sea to sea. . . . Then came the Partitions, and for 123 years Poland was absent. . . . Thus an inferiority complex developed over the centuries. And, suddenly, a Polish pope appears. A Pole is elected pope. So, finally, we have been recognized in the world . . . that we can produce the Successor of God on earth. That's why it was received so positively. . . . There really was a feeling of pride that a Pole was chosen Successor of St. Peter. And ideology played no role in it. It was a collective, national intoxication. . . .

John Paul II himself instantly reasserted his own identity with Poland and the linkage between the Polish Church and the papacy, thereby defining the policies he would follow in the years to come. In a message to "My Beloved Countrymen" on October 23, the day after his inauguration, the pope said:

> In recent decades, the Church in Poland had acquired a particular significance in the dimensions of the Universal Church and the dimensions of Christianity. It had also become the object of great interest because of the special set of relationships, which, in the search that contemporary humanity and different nations and states are undertaking in social, economic and civilizing domains, offer a great meaning. The Church in Poland has acquired a new expression,

> become the Church of special witnessing . . . upon which are turned the eyes of the whole world. Our nation, the contemporary generation of Poles, lives in this Church and speaks through it. Without accepting this fact, it is difficult to understand that today it is a Pope-Pole who addresses you. . . . It is difficult to understand that this choice was not met with resistance, but with understanding and a cordial acceptance. . . .

John Paul II went on:

> I speak to all my countrymen without exception, respecting the viewpoints and beliefs of all, without exception. Love of the Motherland unites us and must unite us above all the differences. It has nothing to do with narrow nationalism or chauvinism. It is the right of the human heart. It is a measure of human nobility, a measure tested frequently in the course of our not-so-easy history. . . . It is not easy to give up the return to the Motherland. . . . But I ask you to oppose everything that violates human dignity and diminishes the habits of a healthy society, often threatening its very existence. . . . My Beloved Countrymen: whenever you receive the blessing of Pope John Paul II, remember that he came from among you and that he has a special right to your hearts and your prayers. . . .

As Party First Secretary Gierek had correctly predicted, the moment he learned of Karol Wojtyła's election, the Polish pope's pilgrimage to Poland was the next inevitable historical event with which the communist regime simply had to live, whether it liked it or not.

The idea was foremost in John Paul II's mind from the instant of his choice in the Sistine Chapel. He mentioned it to President Jabłoński and Primate Wyszyński in separate audiences on Inauguration Day, and pledged it in his October 23 message to Poles, saying that "I very much want to come to you on the 900th anniversary of St. Stanisław. . . . I trust that this jubilee will bring a renewal of our faith and Christian morality because we see in St. Stanisław the patron of moral order in Poland and hierarchic order for nearly one thousand years. . . ."

St. Stanisław's anniversary falls on May 8, and that was the date the pope had chosen for his first pontifical voyage to Poland the following year—seven months hence. But he had to reckon with the defense mechanism of the communist regimes in Warsaw and Moscow.

The anniversary, the centerpiece of his devotion to martyrdom, had been a bone of contention between Wojtyła and the authorities for long years, from the time since, as cardinal, he had fought for the right to hold citywide processions across Kraków in homage to the saint. The authorities always suspected that the Church wished to use these occasions to equate the regime with the tyrant king who had ordered the bishop's murder in 1079. As pope, John Paul II had now reopened the whole question.

Thus, much as the Polish regime respected the pope and his desire for a May homecoming, it still had to cope with political realities both at home and in Moscow. And the Soviets kept complaining to Warsaw about "excessive" courtesies toward the new pope.

While Rakowski, the former prime minister, believes that the Gierek leadership had not detected a "strategic danger" to itself in the first flush of pride over the election, the prospect for a Wojtyła visit to Poland—and especially his insistence on commemorating St. Stanisław's anniversary in Kraków on May 8—had changed this attitude. But what was the extent of such "strategic danger," and could it even be defined at that early time?

The first decision by the regime was to announce that John Paul II would be welcomed in Poland, a statement required to keep domestic public opinion quiescent and to look reasonable internationally—even though the problem of dates was an increasingly serious one for Gierek and his allies. Thus on the same day as the pope issued his message to Poles—hinting at a St. Stanisław anniversary visit—Kazimierz Kąkol, the Cabinet minister in charge of the Bureau of Religious Affairs, said in a formal statement that "if the Pope comes to Poland, it is a matter of certainty that he will be warmly welcomed by the state authorities as well as by the people." But he added that "the choice of the date and the duration of the journey are obviously conditioned by circumstances having a mutual and many-faceted nature."

In the meantime, John Paul II had plunged into frenetic activity on all fronts.

He set the spiritual and political tone for the pontificate in his Inauguration Day sermon in Italian with the urgent appeal to Catholics "to fear not to receive Christ and to accept his authority." His voice rising, the pope said: "Fear Not! . . . Open wide the doors to Christ and His authority of salvation! Open the frontiers of states, [of] economic and political systems, of broad domains of culture [and] civilization [and] development! Fear not! Christ knows what lives within man. . . . Only He knows!"

Alluding to the fact that Paul VI had been the last pope to be crowned—with a triple tiara—John Paul II said that, like John Paul I, he had not wished to be crowned because "this is not the time to return to a ritual which, certainly unjustly, might be perceived as the symbol of contemporary papal authority.

"Absolute authority," the new pope emphasized, "is no more than the service to the people of God. . . . It is sweet and gentle. . . . It never speaks the language of force, but it is expressed in the love of brethren and in the truth."

In this manner, John Paul II affirmed his unquestionable moral authority over his Church, at a time of disarray, on the model of Gregory the Great. Yet, at the same time, he was the first in memory to try to humanize the papacy, to bring it down to the people from the mystical heights of the past when, still in this century, popes were borne in a *sedes gestatoria,* a sedan chair, above the faithful.

He displayed the sweetness of authority when he rose from his throne at St. Peter's Square's altar on the first day to kneel and embrace Primate Wyszyński around his knee just as the aging cardinal attempted the same embrace of the pope in the ageless gesture of obedience. The image of the two Polish men of the Church frozen in their eternal embrace may be the best-remembered scene of John Paul II's inauguration, at least to the Poles who watched it on television and in the vast Roman square.

Afterward, the pope mingled with hundreds of journalists in an impromptu, happily chaotic news conference in the Hall of Benedictions of the Apostolic Palace—the first one ever held by a successor of St. Peter—answering questions in a half-dozen languages. He plucked out of the crowd Jerzy Turowicz, his old editor at Kraków's *Tygodnik Powszechny,* for a special embrace. Six days later, he flew by helicopter to the Polish Fathers' hilltop sanctuary of Mentorella for an hour's private prayer and meditation. It was his first papal helicopter flight.

To accentuate in turn his identity as head of the Italian Church and as the Bishop of Rome (he also acquired an Italian passport along with a Vatican passport), John Paul II went to pray at the shrines of St. Francis—one of his favorite saints—in Assisi and St. Catherine in Siena.

One of few popes ever to take seriously the title of Bishop of Rome, he made it a practice from the very outset to visit Roman parish churches (there are 323 of them, and he would visit over 233 of them in fifteen years). At least once a month (unless he was ill or away), John Paul II was driven to a parish, often in the remote industrial suburbs, to concelebrate Sunday Mass at 9:00 A.M., first meeting parishioners, including children. He also instituted the custom of inviting the priest whose parish he was about to visit to a meal at the Vatican earlier that week to learn about the congregation's problems. It was a continuation of the Kraków pastoral tradition.

Thirty years after his graduation from the Angelicum, John Paul II returned in November to the ancient Dominican university in midtown Rome on a sentimental journey. He was always tempted to remember and relive the past, never breaking with it. He spent an hour there, reminiscing about the old days of quiet learning on Angelicum Hill.

It dawned very quickly on the Roman Curia that it had a restless and informal pontiff on its hands. Not only was he ready to leave the walls of the Vatican on the shortest possible notice on a foray in Rome or beyond, but he constantly demanded information on every topic of Church affairs and international life. Unlike his predecessors, John Paul II believes that meals should be used for conversations—as well as for bodily nourishment—which means that guests are invited to virtually every lunch and dinner (seldom more than two or three persons at a time), served the Vatican brand of Polish-Italian food, and given decent Italian red and white wine. The meals are not considered papal audiences, and the guests are never listed in the daily report on official visitors published in *L'Osservatore Romano.* Often the guests are simply personal friends, usually Poles.

While his mind remained very much on the pilgrimage to Poland in the spring of 1979, John Paul II left Rome on the morning of January 25 on a voyage in another direction that would be his baptism of fire in the complexities of religious-political diplomacy he proposed to carry out in his pontificate. This was the trip to Puebla, a city in Mexico, for the conference of the Latin American episcopate that Paul VI had promised to attend.

It was his first papal journey abroad, his first exposure to Latin America, and his first encounter with the Theology of Liberation, a concept with which John Paul II could never quite come to terms, religiously or politically. This theology also was a major intellectual challenge to the priest from Poland who believed profoundly in social justice, but feared—on the basis of his Polish experiences under communism—that its exercise could fall under Marxist control. For one thing, Fidel Castro had now been running his "socialist" revolution in Cuba for twenty years, and the pope presumably shared Western fears of its export to other parts of Catholic Latin America.

Before leaving the Vatican, John Paul II had read all the works by the Reverend Gustavo Gutiérrez, the Peruvian priest and philosopher who is regarded as the father of the Latin American theology of militant social protest. But reading Gutiérrez was not a substitute for understanding Latin America's harsh realities, and the pope left many of the bishops in Puebla with the impression that he preferred that the Theology of Liberation—which argues for cooperation, when required, with leftist forces in the pursuit of social justice—be abandoned in favor of a more traditional Church "Option for the Poor."

Quite a number of bishops were heartbroken, but the decision fitted John Paul II's notion that the central Church must never lose control over its component parts or persons. Under his definition of the Holy See's jurisdiction over hearts and minds, the sacred and the profane were increasingly coming together.

Theology apart, however, the pope's first trip was an unqualified success personally in terms of Latin American and world public opinion. It was greatly aided by television, which was becoming one of the most powerful instruments of John Paul II's papacy. He was a natural on television. In Mexico, which at the time had no diplomatic relations with the Holy See, millions filled the streets to cheer him, forgetting the old Mexican anti-clerical tradition.

When the pope's Italian airliner (with a full press contingent aboard) first landed in Santo Domingo—the oldest city on the island of Hispaniola, where Christopher Columbus had touched on his first voyage of the discovery of the Americas—John Paul II, a saintly figure in white, stunned the watching world by kneeling on the airport tarmac to kiss the ground. He would do it every time he visited a new country, as long as he physically could, as a spiritual hallmark of papal travel. Columbus having been first in 1492 to bring Christianity to the Americas (at least by his presence as a Christian), John Paul II was reaffirming this missionary act 487 years later.

A month after his return to Rome, on March 4 John Paul II issued his first encyclical, *Redemptor hominis* (Redeemer of Man), in which he set forth his fundamental views on human dignity, human rights, social justice, and the moral teachings of the Church. He had begun to draft it in longhand in Polish immediately after his October election, and it was the fastest a pontiff had ever issued an encyclical after assuming office.

Even then, John Paul II was a man in a hurry, forcing events to happen and anxious to establish his stamp upon the Holy See. *Redemptor hominis* served this purpose, proclaiming principles he always held true and from which he would never depart through his pontificate. It was a classic Wojtyłan blend of social progressivism and theological conservatism—a blend not always comprehended in and out of the Church—and John Paul II would forever be faithful to it. He is the most consistent of men.

But now it was time for Poland.

CHAPTER 21

Historical reality is sometimes a product of creative political fiction. Such was the case with the breakthrough journey to Poland by John Paul II in June 1979.

The fiction was that the pope was coming as the invited guest of the Polish episcopate, and not as the guest of the Polish government, and it was the perfect, dignified, face-saving solution for all concerned. Inasmuch as the pope is the head of state of the Holy See, a political entity, Poland theoretically could invite him in that capacity. Had the regime chosen, however, not to let the pontiff make the visit at all (as happened with Paul VI at the Polish Christianity millennium anniversary in 1966), the device of presenting the Polish episcopate as the official host would have been irrelevant.

The formula was ironed out jointly by the Polish Church, the Polish regime, and John Paul II, the Vatican's chief hands-on negotiator working together with Archbishop Agostino Casaroli, whom he had named pro-secretary of state (acting secretary of state) on April 28, 1979. Casaroli, who was given the acting title because he was not yet a cardinal, replaced French Cardinal Villot, deceased a few weeks earlier. (Casaroli was made cardinal two months later at John Paul II's first consistory.) The pope wanted to waste no time in moving ahead with his East European policies.

The Holy See's leading diplomatic expert on Eastern

Europe and the Soviet Union, the sixty-five-year-old Casaroli was a superb choice. He had conducted sensitive Vatican diplomatic business in Eastern Europe since the early 1960s (when he first met Wojtyła), had visited Moscow, and was greatly respected throughout the communist realm. Villot himself had told friends that the pope would allay some of the Soviet fears about him if he were to appoint Casaroli to the post.

In allowing the Polish episcopate to invite John Paul II, the Gierek regime made it appear to its own ideological constituency—and especially to Moscow—that it was simply deferring to the wishes of an overwhelming majority of its population to welcome the pope in Poland. It was obviously transparent, but there was no alternative. The Vatican was delighted with the idea and it had saved Warsaw embarrassment.

At that point, something of a de facto partnership was emerging among the three principals who wanted the papal trip to be smooth and peaceful. John Paul II would be received by the Church and the Polish faithful as the Roman Catholic pontiff and by Poland's authorities as a head of state, thus satisfying diplomatic protocol.

As a practical consideration, the episcopate was willing and ready to assume the formidable organizational tasks of the visit, including the assignment of its own volunteer order and security services, which spared the regime the unpleasant necessity of deploying its hated, high-visibility riot police all over the country to assure public peace. The pope's own contribution was to drop his insistence on commemorating St. Stanisław's anniversary in May, delaying the visit until June. Still, Polish censorship banned the publication of John Paul II's Christmas messages to Poles in *Tygodnik Powszechny*. The messages were intended to mark the start of St. Stanisław's jubilee year and to remind the faithful that the martyred bishop had "defended society from the evil which menaced it."

In Moscow, the more Leonid Brezhnev thought about the pope's impending visit to Poland, the more alarmed he became. Brezhnev may have wished to improve the Soviet Union's relations with the Vatican, even under a Polish pope, but he was the man who did not hesitate to order the military invasion of Czechoslovakia in 1968, to do away with the liberal experiment of "Marxism with a Human Face" there, and he was increasingly uncomfortable with developments in Poland, even before Karol Wojtyła's election.

In Brezhnev's opinion, Polish underground opposition groups were emerging without adequately devastating counteraction by the regime, the government was openly flirting with the Church, and now the leadership was prepared to tolerate an incursion by the Polish pope. To Brezhnev, this was a real "strategic danger," and he felt the time had come to bring his Polish comrades back to their senses.

Early in 1979, even before the Polish episcopate had issued the formal invitation to John Paul II, Brezhnev telephoned First Secretary Gierek in Warsaw. This is how Gierek remembers what surely was an exceedingly bizarre conversation, even by communist world standards:

> Brezhnev said that he had heard that the Church had invited the pope to Poland. "And what do you say to that?" he asked me. I answered: "We shall receive him with dignity." Brezhnev said, "I advise you not to receive him because it will cause you much trouble." I replied: "How can I not receive the Polish pope since the majority of our compatriots are of Catholic faith, and for them the election was a great feast. Besides, what do you imagine I can tell the people? Why are we closing the barrier to him?" Brezhnev said: "Tell the pope—he is a wise man—that he could announce publicly that he cannot come because he has been taken ill." I answered: "Comrade Leonid, I cannot do that. I must receive John Paul II." Then I heard this [from Brezhnev]: "Gomułka was a better communist because he would not receive Paul VI in Poland, and nothing terrible has happened. The Poles have already survived one such refusal, so they will survive it again if you do not let this pope in." I stated that "political sense, however, dictates to me the necessity of letting him in." Brezhnev said, "So do what you want, so long

as you and your Party do not regret it later"—and he terminated the conversation.

Gierek chose "for obvious reasons" not to tell Cardinal Wyszyński about his exchange with Brezhnev when the primate called on him on January 24 to open discussions about the papal journey (that same week John Paul II was receiving Soviet Foreign Minister Gromyko at the Vatican). But Wyszyński, as Gierek puts it, "was too intelligent and too familiar with Poland's postwar realities not to suspect that this would be a visit our allies would not greet with enthusiasm."

The January meeting resulted in a joint communiqué, describing the meeting as a "continued exchange of views on the most important affairs of the nation and the Church, which are important for the establishment of appropriate relations and cooperation between Church and state for the sake of national unity in the task of creating the success of the Polish People's Republic and strengthening its position in the world." At that stage, relations between Gierek and Wyszyński were at their best—in fact, the best ever between the communist regime and the Church—reflecting the extent of their mutual dependence.

Gierek now needed the support of the Church, at least tacitly, as Poland's economic and social situation deteriorated rapidly. Wyszyński and the episcopate had been helpful to the regime in June 1976 when, following spreading food riots, it had appealed to the workers to return to their jobs while urging the government not to punish the rioters. The Church did not believe that a social explosion was a solution to Poland's problems.

That was the turning point in their relationship, both men agreeing that notwithstanding their ideological differences, peace had to be preserved in the country. Neither wished to see blood again in the streets of Polish cities, and Wyszyński, along with John Paul II, believed that a slow evolution toward greater freedom was inevitable.

On Wyszyński's part, this judgment represented a change in his views. Prior to 1976, he was basically content with the status quo and an ongoing dialogue with the authorities to assure that the rights of the Church were respected. He assumed, as many others did, that communism was here to stay, and accommodation was needed.

In Kraków, Wojtyła had increasingly tended to challenge the regime although he was not expecting, either, an end to communism soon. But now, as pope, he was formulating a more sophisticated vision of relationships between the Church and communism through *Ostpolitik* initiatives, beginning with Poland, and Wyszyński represented this policy in dealing with the regime.

Moreover, John Paul II attached considerable importance to the political potential of KOR, the Committee for the Defense of Workers, formed after the 1976 riots, which for the first time in Polish history had brought together workers and intellectuals. By 1979, KOR had become a serious oppositionmovement, complete with an underground press and a book publishing industry, enjoying backing from left-of-center Catholic intellectuals. Most of the latter were closer politically and personally to Wojtyła than to Wyszyński.

As for the Church, it required Gierek's cooperation in preparing the papal visit, and it pushed for more and more concessions from the regime. Early in 1979, for example, at least a dozen churches were under construction in Warsaw alone (in all, there were 13,000 churches in Poland, compared with 6,700 before the war). Naturally, Wojtyła's election had dramatically altered the Church-state relationships. This was why it had been so simple to create the fiction of the episcopate's invitation as the framework for John Paul II's approaching pilgrimage.

Finally, on March 2, the episcopate announced that "the Primate of Poland . . . sent Pope John Paul II an official letter in the name of the Episcopate on February 22, expressing gratitude for his readiness to visit Poland and our Church."

Simultaneously, a government communiqué stated that President Jabłoński, "in the name of the highest national authorities, has expressed satisfaction over the invitation sent by the Polish Episcopate and over the declarations by

Pope John Paul II that he wishes to visit his Motherland, the Polish People's Republic."

It added that "the first son of the Polish nation to exercise in ages the highest dignity in the Church, will be received cordially by the authorities as well as by the society." But the regime felt compelled to speak of the "conviction" that the pope's visit "will favor the unity of all Poles and deepen the cooperation of the Church with the Socialist nation in a further development of relations between Poland and the Apostolic Capital, in the name of preserving peace in the world, restraining the forces of aggression and war, and strengthening cooperation and friendship among nations."

John Paul II, the communiqué said, will visit Warsaw, Gniezno, Częstochowa, and Kraków between June 2 and 10. That same week, the censors allowed *Tygodnik Powszechny* to publish the full text of the highly outspoken *Redemptor hominis* papal encyclical. It all was beautifully orchestrated.

Then Gierek flew to Moscow, Prague, and Budapest to consult with the comrades. Two weeks later, Archbishop Casaroli was in Warsaw to check up on the arrangements.

The impact, repercussions, and consequences of the papal visit were, of course, wholly unpredictable, making it exciting, promising, and potentially dangerous to all concerned. Looking ahead, however, the more thoughtful among analysts and observers on both sides were centering on the long-term political effects rather than on the actual events during the nine days in June.

In the final phase before the pope's arrival, Primate Wyszyński flew to Rome for a last-minute audience with John Paul II, then called on Gierek at Warsaw's Parliament building. He thanked the Polish authorities, a government communiqué announced, "for their help and efforts in preparing for the Pope's visit."

A week before leaving for Warsaw, John Paul II named two Polish cardinals as part of the group of the fifteen new Princes of the Church in his first consistory. The Poles were Franciszek Macharski, replacing Wojtyła as cardinal in Kraków, and Władysław Rubin, the secretary-general of the

Synod of Bishops. Both happened to be John Paul II's old personal friends. Now Poland had three cardinals, including the primate.

The new pope seemed to be accomplishing more on all fronts in a half year than most of his predecessors had in two or three years. For example, in the middle of intense preparations for the Polish trip—late in March—he signed both a Holy See document denouncing racism and pledging the Church's participation in the struggle against it, and a Vatican commitment to support a proposal for a worldwide referendum on disarmament. Addressing forty thousand pilgrims in St. Peter's Square, John Paul II urged prayers for the Camp David agreement between Israel and Egypt, just brokered by President Carter, to turn into "a decisive impulse in the dynamic process of peace." Along with the future of Eastern Europe, the Middle East—the cradle of the three monotheistic religions (Jewish, Christian, and Muslim)—was a top priority for the pope.

He found time to deliver a lengthy message to a group of Jewish organization leaders during an audience in the Throne Hall of the Apostolic Palace on the history of Jewish-Catholic relations in the aftermath of Vatican Council II.

"As a sign of the understanding and fraternal love already achieved," John Paul II told his Jewish visitors, "let me express again my cordial welcome and greetings to you all with that word, so rich in meaning, taken from the Hebrew language, which we Christians also use in our Liturgy: Peace be with you . . . Shalom, Shalom!"

Then he left for Poland.

John Paul II landed in Warsaw on the morning of June 2, 1979, eight months to the day after he had left as Cardinal Wojtyła for the Vatican conclave, and from the moment he knelt to kiss the Polish ground at Okęcie Airport, he lived nine days of national ecstasy.

At least ten million Poles (of a population of thirty-five million) saw him in person in the nine cities, towns, and sanctuaries where he appeared, prayed, and spoke before the masses of humanity. The country had exploded in color:

white-and-red Polish flags and white-and-yellow papal flags were everywhere, and portraits of a smiling Wojtyła decorated with papal pennants seemed to be in every window along the routes of his motorcades. His appearances drew the biggest crowds in Polish history.

Others watched him on Polish state television although the ever-zealous party officials had ordered their cameramen to keep the lenses on John Paul II in tight shots and avoid showing the huge throngs in attendance at Mass and other events. It was foolish totalitarian behavior because every citizen knew that millions had turned out to cheer the pontiff and intone the ancient song, "We want God!" Poles spoke of "our nine days of freedom."

The pope set the tone for his visit—his second foreign papal trip—with admirable diplomatic deftness, again blending the spiritual and the temporal in defining his Polish mission as well as his overall policies. Responding to airport welcoming remarks by President Jabłoński, John Paul II announced that "my visit is dictated by strictly religious motivation" although "I earnestly hope that [it] will serve the great cause of closeness and cooperation among nations . . . mutual understanding, reconciliation and peace in the contemporary world . . . [and] the internal unity of my compatriots. . . ."

He had thus made it clear from the outset that he had come to Poland as a Polish pilgrim, head of the Roman Catholic Church, and a world statesman. John Paul II may have agreed to forgo presiding over the May commemorations of the anniversary of St. Stanisław's martyrdom—a burning political theme of which every Pole was by now aware—but he did not let him be forgotten.

Starting with the explanation in his departure speech at the Rome airport that the occasion for the trip was "the jubilee of St. Stanisław, bishop and martyr," the pope obstinately mentioned the saint at almost every opportunity in his speeches, homilies, and prayers across Poland, including a meeting with young people in Kraków at the site of the bishop's murder. Speaking at St. John the Baptist Cathedral in Warsaw's Old Town, his first stop after the triumphal motorcade from the airport, John Paul II reminded the faithful that St. Stanisław was one of the capital's patron saints, and "therefore I begin right here to venerate him on the first leg of my jubilee pilgrimage."

And so it went for nine days, with the regime resignedly realizing that it was impossible to outmaneuver Wojtyła on his own Polish turf, though *Trybuna Ludu,* the party daily newspaper, commented bitterly that "it is hard to tell where pastoral work stops and politics begin."

Apart from the silliness of its television coverage, the authorities helped rather than hindered the papal tour. They provided John Paul II with Polish national airlines helicopters to fly him from place to place, kept the security forces out of sight at a decent distance, and made no effort to prevent the millions of Poles from witnessing the pope's presence in what was an amazing display of crowd self-discipline. Every diocese and parish visited by the pontiff had supplied volunteer marshals wearing white-and-yellow armbands to direct traffic and assure order.

As Mieczysław Rakowski, the party editor of *Polityka* observed, "It was still the fascination with Wojtyła . . . it was the continuation of that national pride." Besides, he noted, John Paul II had disarmed the leadership with his remark, in the speech he addressed to Party First Secretary Gierek at Belweder Presidential Palace on his first day in Warsaw, that he wished to express "my thanks and my respect for you and for all your efforts aimed at the common good of our compatriots and at the deserved significance of Poland in international life."

Gierek and his associates took it as an explicit gesture of legitimizing their regime. John Paul II, thinking in terms of a future Polish solution, was subtly co-opting them, a most innovative approach for a churchman dealing with old-line communists, and one that was not widely understood at the time.

Religion and patriotism always went hand in hand in Polish history, and the pope elevated that sentiment to magnificent heights on Jasna Góra—the Luminous Mountain—at Częstochowa, the shrine of the Black Madonna, the Queen of Poland. He went there after appearances in Warsaw and Gniezno, the see of the oldest Polish diocese. Spending three days in the Częstochowa-Jasna Góra area, John Paul II spoke *twenty-three* times—surely a record in papal annals—before audiences ranging from sealike crowds at solemn Mass to groups of fathers and mothers superior of male and female religious orders, the Polish Episcopal Conference, young people, and the sick and the infirm.

And the pope's homilies and speeches from the most hallowed ground in Poland were not the usual sort, pious exhortations to which worshippers there were accustomed. Some were lengthy and complex essays on Polish history in the context of Częstochowa's salvation by the Madonna from besieging Swedish armies in the seventeenth century—but moving into the modern age as well—or in the context of St. Stanisław, his martyrdom, and human freedom. Others were lectures on the state of the Church following the Second Vatican Council. As an American reporter wrote from Częstochowa: "Every papal gesture, every deft historical reference had political connotations in this setting."

Thus John Paul II had come back to Poland as preacher and teacher, historian and patriot, philosopher and theologian. It was his greatest tour de force to date, and he was only halfway through the Polish pilgrimage.

But the most personal and emotionally charged part of Wojtyła's Polish homecoming was the return to his archdiocese: Kraków, Kalwaria Zebrzydowska, Wadowice, Oświęcism, Nowy Targ. . . .

And adoring throngs turned out to welcome him home, filling every square foot of the sprawling, triangular Błonia Meadow, just east of Jagiellonian University and the Old Town, where he spoke lovingly to his fellow Krakowians, calling the city "this Polish Rome." He talked nostalgically about his Kraków youth, the university, the Nazi occupation, his work at the stone quarry and the Solvay plant, his priestly calling, and his years as bishop and cardinal. His every word was heard in reverent silence, then shouts and applause would soar to the blue spring sky like cannon salvos.

The next day, June 7, John Paul II followed his sentimental memory route to his favorite Kalwaria Zebrzydowska sanctuary and its Stations of the Cross, reminiscing about his childhood and adult visits there, always drawing inspiration from them. He also recalled that his grandfather and his great-grandfather had served as guides to pilgrims at the sanctuary.

Two hours later, the pope was *really* home—in Wadowice. His old religion teacher and parish priest Edward Zacher greeted him tearfully, and Karol Wojtyła loved every moment in his town, recognizing every person in sight, embracing quite a few, shaking many hands. He praised the local band that played for him, but remarked that "before the war, as we oldsters remember but the young know nothing about, we had the superb band of the Twelfth Infantry Regiment. . . ."

After the jokes and laughter of Wadowice came the sorrow and sadness of the Oświęcim-Brzezinka concentration camp later that afternoon. Wojtyła had gone there many times in the past, but, as he said during the Mass he celebrated at the camp, "This is a very special sanctuary, and I couldn't have failed to come here as pope." And, once more, John Paul II mentioned St. Stanisław, the nation's first martyr.

Walking slowly along the paths of the camp, preserved intact by the Poles as an eternal memory of the Holocaust, the pope knelt before a stone tablet inscribed in Hebrew, a tablet inscribed in Russian, and a tablet inscribed in Polish. The Hebrew words, he said, "bring to mind the memory of a nation whose sons and daughters were condemned to total extermination. This nation has its beginning with Abraham, who is 'the father of our faith.' . . . And this nation, which received from God Jahwe the Commandment, 'Thou Shall Not Kill,' has itself experienced killing in a particular manner. . . . Nobody may walk past this tablet in indifference. . . ."

A Mass at the market town of Nowy Targ at the foothills of the Carpathians and three more breathless days in Kraków completed John Paul II's Polish pilgrimage. At churches, the Jagiellonian University, and meetings with bishops, theologians, monks, nuns, the young, and the sick, the pope kept up the drumbeat of his message of religious faith and patriotism—and of his devotion to St. Stanisław.

In the end, he had had his way, spiritually and politically, in this virtuoso management of his journey.

President Jabłoński bid him farewell graciously at Kraków Airport on June 10, not omitting his side's political point: "Your Holiness' words dedicated to human labor and the dignity of the people of labor were heard with special attention in the entire nation. . . . We see in it a convergence with the thought which underlies the foundation of our Socialist system: freedom of labor, social justice, an overall respect for human rights. . . ."

How, in its immediate aftermath as well as in retrospect, should John Paul II's pilgrimage to Poland be judged in terms of history? Was Brezhnev right in warning Gierek that the papal trip would cause the party to "regret it later"? Did his presence jump-start the national revolt that led to the demise of East European communism, as some of the more superficial commentators claimed after the fact?

The truth appears to be that, quite regardless of Wojtyła's election and his 1979 visit, the situation in Poland had become so critical—socially, economically, and politically—that the country was again on the verge of explosion. Communist economic mismanagement, government corruption, and political repression had created the climate that had resulted in the bloody crises of 1956, 1970, and 1976. And matters were even worse in 1979, when John Paul II returned to his homeland and the entire European communist structure was beginning to crumble.

In other words, Polish political dynamics did not really require an external stimulant. At the same time, however, such a stimulant in the person of a Polish pope in the midst of his fervently devout Catholic compatriots unquestionably played a part in accelerating the march of events, at least in terms of the national psychology.

This state of affairs was understood equally well by John Paul II and the Warsaw regime, and both sides behaved accordingly.

The pope had a clear interest in strengthening the morale of Polish society and bringing it hope for what he saw as tough years ahead. But he certainly was not anticipating a communist collapse in the foreseeable future, and the last thing on his mind was precipitating a rebellion conducive to an unmeasurable tragedy.

Instead, as his public attitudes and pronouncements in Poland indicated, John Paul II was counting on an evolutionary process toward a peaceful transition to democracy—someday. Rather than confront the regime, he chose to try to push it toward such an evolution, without challenging its legitimacy for the time being. The traditional blend of faith and patriotism—plus an invigorating dose of St. Stanisław martyrdom inspiration—were the elements he considered essential to keep alive the national morale.

Bishop Tadeusz Pieronek, secretary-general of the Polish episcopate, who was among the organizers of the 1979 papal visit, says that what John Paul II accomplished was to "awaken the Polish society that was quite disoriented" at that time. Pieronek points out that the pope had never planned to do more during the first pilgrimage. On each of his four visits to Poland—between 1979 and 1991—he applied different political criteria according to the prevailing situation, the bishop says.

Marek Skwarnicki, John Paul II's poetry editor, friend, and occasional travel companion, wrote fifteen years after the first voyage that Poland's "freedom shock" and euphoria came during the pope's presence, between June 2 and 10, 1979, rather than when communist rule finally ended a decade later. "It was," he wrote, "an intoxication with the crowds' freedom to live in a 'human Poland,' to pour out into 'their' streets in towns and villages not controlled by 'them.'"

On the other hand, Skwarnicki noted, John Paul II had no intention of overthrowing the regime when he came to Poland. "If the Church, the bishops and the pope really wanted to threaten it with force," he wrote, "only a few words of encouragement at that moment would have been sufficient to set off the explosion of a new national uprising in Poland." Skwarnicki added, "I had the same thought being with the pope in Manila [in 1981], where the Marcos dictatorship was in power, and when one papal word would set the Philippines on fire."

The Warsaw regime, for its part, assumed from the very beginning a nonconfrontational approach toward John Paul

II and his trip. Aside from a few face-saving devices and overzealousness (censoring the papal Christmas message and manipulating television coverage), the Polish authorities began—ironically—to hope that the pope's visit would shore them up in the face of their growing difficulties. They were frankly looking for a dialogue. But the situation had to be understood as a very special Polish phenomenon, which foreigners often found difficult to grasp.

An editorial in *Polityka,* the independent-minded weekly publication of the party's Central Committee (another Polish communist peculiarity), put it squarely after the pope's voyage was announced:

> While relations between the Socialist state and the Catholic Church never were and never will be idyllic for reasons of basic ideological differences—and the pope's visit to Poland will not remove them—this visit must not be examined from the viewpoint of rivalry. . . . The Party's policy toward the Church and the faithful is not aimed at confrontation and it does not contain any element of struggle against religion. . . . The Catholic Church possesses serious means of influencing the minds of the faithful and the shaping of moral and patriotic attitudes in tune with Poland's national interest.

Therefore John Paul II's "Nine Days in June" do not seem—in retrospect—to have fundamentally altered the situation in Poland, except in a general psychological sense. But, more subtly, they laid the foundation for the pope's brilliantly creative diplomacy when the true moment of crisis arrived some years later. His equally careful and courageous attitudes during martial law in Poland in the early 1980s and subsequently were part of the same policies that allowed him to act as a highly credible player at the decisive stages of the liquidation of communism in Eastern Europe.

Mieczysław Rakowski, the last communist prime minister, has concluded—analyzing fifteen years later John Paul II's first visit from the regime's standpoint—that the great Polish rebellion of 1980 would have occurred in any event.

In fact, he points out, the birth of the Solidarity trade union movement came more than a year *after* the pope's visit, stemming from a series of local labor disputes and strikes fueled by general national discontent.

Rakowski says that

> the workers' rebellion would have happened even without the pope because our system, in which I functioned, collapsed not under the influence of any external forces—although they may have been helpful—but under the contradictions that tore asunder that system and transformed the working class into a directing force, a demiurge of history.
>
> I am not prepared to share the view that the Polish pope accelerated the process, which already existed in the late Seventies. The rebellion of the Polish proletariat in Gdańsk, on the Baltic coast, in 1970, took place during an Italian papacy.

And, like many other Polish analysts, Rakowski attributes a much greater importance to the emergence in 1976 of KOR, the underground opposition alliance of workers and intellectuals, without which the subsequent Solidarity movement might have foundered.

While the communist regime in Warsaw digested John Paul II's visit to Poland with relative equanimity, alarm bells sounded loudly in Moscow, and the Soviet leadership ordered a top secret worldwide campaign on an unprecedented scale against the new pope, the Vatican, and their policies.

The campaign was triggered not only by the pope's Polish visit—against which Brezhnev had warned Gierek in January—but also by what the Kremlin perceived as "dangerous" and "aggressive" activities of the Roman Catholic Church in all the communist countries, including the Soviet Union, and elsewhere under John Paul II's command.

According to documents obtained in mid-1994 from the archives of the Central Committee of the Soviet Communist Party in Moscow—and never disclosed before—the Secretariat of the Central Committee approved on November 13, 1979, a six-point "Decision to Work Against the Policies of the Vatican in Relation with Socialist States." The Secretariat was the party's principal operational organ. All the Soviet political organizations and agencies, ranging from the party's Central Committee Secretariat's specialized departments to the Foreign Ministry, the KGB (the Committee on State Security), the Academy of Sciences, the Tass news agency, and Soviet state television and radio were given specific assignments in the anti-Wojtyła campaign.

The "Decision" was originally drafted at a November 5 meeting of an eight-man working group of the Secretariat, which included Victor Chebrikov, then deputy chairman of the KGB under Yuri Andropov, Pantaleymon Ponomarenko, a veteran diplomat in charge of the Secretariat's Information Department, and Leonid Zamyatin, Tass director general.

The final "Decision" document was signed a week later by nine members of the ruling Politburo under Brezhnev. Among them were Konstantin Chernenko and Mikhail Gorbachev, who, successively, became general-secretaries of the Soviet Communist Party after Brezhnev's death (Andropov was Brezhnev's short-lived immediate successor), chief party ideologue Mikhail Suslov, and Andrei Kirilenko, an old-line Politburo member. Ten years later, Gorbachev would meet John Paul II, establishing a warm and lasting contact with him.

The first point of the "Decision" provided for the "mobilization" of the communist parties of Lithuania, Latvia, Ukraine, and Byelorussia (Soviet republics with significant Roman and Greek Catholic populations) and of Tass, Soviet state television, the Academy of Sciences, "and other organizations . . . of the Soviet State" to launch "propaganda against the policies of the Vatican."

The second point called for an "exchange" of information and propaganda concerning Vatican policies with the communist parties of Austria, Argentina, Belgium, Ireland, Italy, Portugal, France, and West Germany—all these countries having large Catholic populations.

The third point instructed the Ministry of Foreign Affairs "to enter into contact with those groups of the Catholic Church engaged in work for peace" in foreign countries "and to explain to them the policies of the Soviet Union in favor of world peace."

The fourth point ordered the Foreign Affairs Ministry and the KGB to "improve the quality of the struggle against the new Eastern European policy of the Vatican."

The fifth point was addressed specifically to the KGB. It instructed the secret service agency "to publicize in the Western countries [the fact] that Vatican policies are harmful" and "above all, to show in the Socialist states that Vatican policies go against the life of the Catholic Church." The KGB was directed to "show that the leadership of the new pope, John Paul II, is dangerous to the Catholic Church." This was to be accomplished "through special channels in Western countries" and through publications in the socialist countries.

The sixth point urged the Academy of Sciences "to improve the study of scientific atheism" and to pay greater attention "to the study of the activities of churches and religious associations" everywhere. The academy was "to inform the Central Committee of the Soviet Communist Party about the activities of the churches and, above all, about the efforts of the churches to ameliorate their influence in Socialist lands."

Related documents in the Central Committee Secretariat archives discuss Soviet concern over the advent of John Paul II. They indicate that different departments of the Secretariat had been analyzing all the speeches, statements, and interviews by the pope as well as studying his impact among Roman Catholics in Lithuania, Latvia, and Byelorussia, and Greek Catholics in Ukraine (the latter are in communion with the Holy See despite liturgical differences).

One of the documents declares that "the problem now is that . . . they [the Vatican] now use religion in the ideological struggle against Socialist lands . . . through new methods [and they] try to increase religious fanaticism against the political and ideological principles of the Socialist societies. The Vatican, above all, applies this new propaganda, which constitutes a new policy."

It goes on to say that "after the change of leadership in the Vatican, the characteristics of Vatican and Catholic Church policies in different regions of the Soviet Union have become more aggressive—above all in Lithuania, Latvia, western Ukraine and Byelorussia." The document then notes that John Paul II had been frequently addressing Catholics in the Soviet Union, inspiring the activity of "disloyal priests."

The "Decision" of the Central Committee Secretariat emphasized that "to organize the struggle against Vatican policies, it is necessary to know the specific conditions of the Catholic Church in different Socialist lands and to know the complex processes occurring inside the Catholic Church." It declares that "we must stimulate the tendencies in the Catholic Church that are opposing the anti-communism of the Vatican policies" as well as to clarify "for the young generation the activities of the churches and religious organizations that are against Soviet law."

Finally, the Foreign Affairs Ministry was exhorted to keep the Soviet Communist Party informed about "the Vatican's activities in international relations." The Academy of Sciences and the Council on Religious Affairs were told to inform the party "about the influence of the new Vatican policies on the Catholic Church in the Soviet Union."

The extent of the Kremlin's fear of the influence of John Paul II and the Catholic Church in the Soviet Union, where Roman Catholics were a small minority except in the western republics, had never been suspected in the Vatican. And, indeed, as reflected in the 1979 documents of the Central Committee Secretariat, it verges on the irrational as—surprisingly—the Kremlin devoted virtually no attention to Poland and the rest of Eastern Europe where John Paul II's growing popularity could pose a serious problem.

At that point, however, Brezhnev was clearly given to misjudgments. A month later—at Christmas 1979—he ordered the invasion of Afghanistan, which, in the end, undermined the destiny of the Soviet Union vastly more than John Paul II could ever have hoped to accomplish.

CHAPTER 22

Inheriting a world in crisis at the end of the 1970s, John Paul II responded with imagination, flexibility, generosity, and the grand gesture.

Inheriting a Roman Catholic Church mired in internal crisis, the new pope responded with dogmatic rigidity, absolute theological inflexibility, and, in the view of many critics, a startling lack of imagination in dealing with old and new generations of Catholics, both in industrialized countries and in the misery-stricken Third World.

These two seemingly contradictory strains defined from the very first day the John Paul II papacy.

He never deviated from the principles he had laid down at the start of his pontificate, tolerating no public dissent within the Church on matters of Catholic morality and ethics, faith and interpretation. Banning all open discussion within the church on theological issues in dispute, the pope made his own the old Latin adage *Roma locuta, causa finita est* (When Rome speaks, the matter is closed). He took the position that only the application of strict discipline could save the Church and resolve its crises.

At the same time, however, John Paul II became the world's most forceful apostle of social justice in rich and poor nations alike, being as critical of the excesses of capitalism as he was of the shortcomings and political repression of Marxism-Leninism.

In fact, the pope has argued that communism had been born from wide-spread social inequalities—which he sees worsening everywhere after the communist collapse—and that in its present form "radical" capitalism and consumerism are a menace to humanity. He also holds them responsible for the breakdown of family life and for what he calls the "culture of death."

Within less than three years of his pontificate, in September 1981, John Paul II turned to the question of social justice in his encyclical *Laborem exercens* (On Human Work), charging that "millions today live in conditions of shameful and unworthy poverty," and demanding "relief and hope" for them. He returned even more insistently to this theme in the *Sollicitudo Rei Socialis* (On Social Concern) encyclical in December 1987, and in *Centesimus Annus* (The Hundredth Year) in May 1991. In the latter, the pope warned against the dangers of "radical capitalistic ideology."

However, John Paul II's fervent advocacy of social justice and human rights was not at all incompatible with his rejection of theological liberalization in the Church. Pope Leo XIII, who had launched contemporary Catholic social justice teaching with his 1891 *Rerum novarum* (Of New Matters) encyclical, viewed liberalism as a "deadly plague" and insisted on unquestioned papal authority.

The great novelty of John Paul II's reign was his dedication to religious liberty and tolerance, and to an ecumenical unity of Christian churches—stronger even than Paul VI's—but that, too, brought criticism from the conservative camp.

Inevitably, John Paul II soon emerged as a highly controversial figure in the Church. A man of extraordinary intellectual power and knowledge, he was also completely self-assured in the execution of his decisions. His old editor friend, Jerzy Turowicz, remarked after three months of the pontificate that "Wojtyła became Pope with such ease as if he had been born to be Pope." Unlike Paul VI, he never appeared to be torn by inner conflicts or hesitations, though, being a most private human being, greatly given to deep prayer and meditation, he remained an enigma.

And perhaps the most striking contradiction of John Paul II's reign was that he always commanded unique personal popularity in his time, among Catholics and non-Catholics, but could never gain the universal religious allegiance he sought within his own Church. He evoked the deepest loyalty among those close to him and bitter hostility among many others.

All of this, of course, perpetuated the Church's internal crisis, far beyond the situation he had encountered upon his 1978 election.

That crisis had been brewing almost since the end of the Second Vatican Council in 1965, reaching exceedingly disturbing proportions in the late 1960s, and seriously threatening the unity of the Catholic Church worldwide by the time John Paul II assumed the papacy. Over the past decade or so, protests against Rome's excessive authority and charges that the "renewal" and the collegial spirit of Vatican II were being violated had been mounting through Western Europe, the United States, and Latin America. Under ever-hesitant Paul VI, however, the situation had been allowed to drift, and the crisis went on deepening.

Church historians believe that the post-council crisis was vastly more menacing to the Roman Catholic institution than even the so-called Modernist Crisis between 1890 and 1910, which, in turn, had been the most dramatic one since the Reformation of the sixteenth century. Even Cardinal Ottaviani, the former head of the Congregation for the Doctrine of the Faith, admitted it publicly in 1969. Some theologians compare it to the Great Schism of 1054, which divided the Church between the East and the West.

The Modernist Crisis was essentially a clash over Rome's centralized authority and power of judgment over the rest of the Church, although the roots of the crisis went back to the Enlightment and the French Revolution of 1789, both of which were long regarded as an abomination (and still are by today's ultraconservatives). Leo XIII, the social thinker, who is widely regarded as one of the great popes, maintained this attitude.

And it is astounding how little truly changes in the history and conflicts of the Church. Writing in 1994 about the Modernist Crisis a century ago, a leading American theologian observed that at the time "two principal models were at loggerheads: the monarchic and the democratic. The papacy and its supporters identified with the monarchic model, while liberals and Modernists identified with the democratic."

There is no better definition of the crisis wracking the Church in the second half of the twentieth century. The confrontation over the issue of authority—which, most importantly, includes the question of the voice and participation in major Church matters by others than the pope alone—was reignited after Vatican Council II, with the addition of several specific new issues. It has continued unabated as a fundamental crisis well into the 1990s, under John Paul II.

The rebellion broke out in full in 1967, when progressive-minded West European churchmen and lay Catholics, chiefly intellectuals, accused the Holy See, in open letters signed by thousands, of failure in moving ahead with the implementation of the council's decisions on collegiality (that is, participation in policymaking) and of not showing proper respect for fellow Catholics. The Church in the Netherlands published its own Catechism along progressive lines, ignoring the Vatican's strictures and engaging in its separate crisis with the Holy See. The post-conciliar reality was that while inspiring texts had been approved by the Church fathers, the traditionalist, hard-line Vatican establishment simply dug in its heels against the innovations (from Mass in the vernacular to religious tolerance).

Paul VI, highly intelligent, quite moderate, but endlessly self-tortured, was unable to provide the leadership required to help resolve the crisis. Instead, speaking to a group of priests in Milan in 1969, he remarked sadly that "the Church today is in a time of unrest, self-criticism, [and] one could say, almost auto-destruction."

His *Humanae vitae* encyclical on family life, which banned all forms of artificial contraception, served to escalate the crisis alarmingly when it was issued in July 1968, after much indecision, and it haunted his pontificate until his death a decade later. The main criticism within the Church was that it had not been a "collegial" decision.

The crisis over the *Humanae vitae* issue was magnified even more under John Paul II, one of the encyclical's anonymous authors, who, notwithstanding the advent of educated new Catholic generations, has remained absolutely inflexible on that subject. He has maintained this posture despite his undoubted awareness that uncounted millions of Catholics across the world simply ignore the ban on contraceptives. To him, it is a matter of moral principle, as is his war on abortion.

From the dawn of his papacy, John Paul II has added fuel to Church controversies and to the underlying crisis by emphasizing his inflexibility on other sensitive issues: his iron opposition to the ordination of women as priests and his denial of "first-class citizenship" treatment to women in the Church, such as nuns; his unbending insistence on priestly celibacy; and his refusal to allow priests to marry (although nothing in the Scriptures prohibits it).

Given his firm belief that only total discipline and control can save the Church from secularization and destruction, Pope Wojtyła has created his own controversies. He has battled Church progressives in Latin America, so vital to Catholicism, over the Theology of Liberation, which he suspected of being a Marxist disguise, and over the priests' right to be directly involved in politics. He forbade priests worldwide to run for elected office or exercise executive office, such as cabinet minister, and ordered priests already holding legislative seats not to seek reelection. And, intolerant of public dissent, he has barred outstanding European, American, and Latin American theologians from teaching altogether at Catholic institutions if they depart from his views.

Desiring absolute papal control over all these fundamental issues, John Paul II took a series of controversial political and theological decisions early in the pontificate that altered considerably the balance of power in the Church. Thus, almost simultaneously, he drastically weakened—or attempted to weaken—the influence of the Society of Jesus—the Jesuits—and bestowed great power and autonomy on Opus Dei.

Although collegiality and shared policymaking was one of the central innovations of the Second Vatican Council—

with the notion that the Synod of Bishops, created in 1965, would be a legislative body "permanent by nature" co-governing with the pope—John Paul II took a dim view of this idea. Indeed, he approached in a "prudent" way his commitment in his inaugural speech to "the most exact execution" of the council's decisions.

Shortly after the election, Cardinal Villot, then secretary of state, had asked the pope whether he had considered "giving the council of the synod a permanent presence?" The council is the synod's senior body.

"No," John Paul II replied. "That would have been a synod in the manner of Oriental churches. The pope remains the supreme and sole legislator. . . . However, it would be useful to broaden the responsibilities of the synod, consulting it more on specific problems, but not to turn such consultation into law."

The Vatican Council had defined collegiality in these words: "The bishops of the Church, in union with the pope, have supreme teaching and pastoral authority over the whole Church." But, of course, such collegiality can be cumbersome for an activist pontiff. The full synod now meets on the average of once a year, though "particular" synods (such as the 1994 African Synod) may be called more often.

John Paul II's attitudes on matters of Church policies, moral teachings, freedom of thought within the institution, and his love of discipline have been the subject of intense debate throughout his pontificate, since the first moment when he surprised his constituency by his toughness and determination to rule alone. Because of his intellect, his sense of history and politics, his life under Nazi and communist repression, and his instinctive closeness to people, especially the young, Wojtyła had been expected to be more of a "modern" pope, more attuned to the changing times, and more flexible in his posture albeit without sacrificing principle.

Why, then, did John Paul II turn out so differently?

The best answer seems to lie in his own writings and pronouncements. His absolutist approach to the question of Christian morals flows from the rigid teachings of Aristotle and St. Thomas Aquinas, and his own Thomist academic background. His mystical and messianic approach to life and faith come from the great Polish tradition in which he was steeped from childhood and from the influence of St. John of the Cross. These strains, too, are absolute, leaving no room for compromise. And so is the sense of mission, John Paul II's most powerful driving force.

Upon assuming the papacy in 1978, John Paul II was surely familiar with the extent of the Church crisis and the global condition of the institution. Official Church statistics were available to further enlighten him.

And the fact was that while the world population was soaring, the Roman Catholic Church was shrinking in absolute as well as relative numbers, although with eight hundred million faithful it was still the largest Christian religion. Ordination of priests is obviously a crucial indicator of how well the Church is faring, and John Paul II could see that their number worldwide had fallen from 4,380 in 1974 to 3,824 in 1978, a considerable drop. Europe accounted for the worst decline—from 2,273 to 1,774. In North America, the decline was from 848 to 697.

The number of diocesan priests globally had fallen in four years from 392,609 to 251,856, with the greatest loss in Europe. In North America, it went down from 68,540 to 42,579. Deaths and retirement accounted for the loss, and new ordinations were not even beginning to make up for them. Baptisms had risen from nearly sixteen million to nearly seventeen million between 1970 and 1978, but with Catholics representing nearly 20 percent of the world population, this increase was well below the natural growth of Catholic populations.

John Paul II was clearly facing a disturbing and significant trend. His immediate challenge was to arrest and reverse it, but it was questionable whether his policies would achieve this goal—or result in a continuing crumbling of the institution. Naturally, there was much more to it than statistics: it was impossible to count Catholics quietly abandoning the Church, or those simply ignoring its basic moral teaching.

Though he is supreme pontiff, John Paul II has to rule within the Church hierarchy and, most particularly, with the Roman Curia to accomplish his objectives. But the human quality at the highest level of the Curia inherited by the new pope was rather dubious, enhancing Wojtyła's natural inclination to govern alone.

The Curia, mainly anchored in the 109 acres of territory constituting the sovereign state of the Holy See (though some of it spills out into Rome proper), consists of the Secretariat of State, which is the equivalent of both the office of prime minister and foreign ministry—which would deal in 1994 with a record 164 foreign ambassadors—plus a full apparatus of clerical government. It includes nine Congregations concentrating on the various aspects of religious life, twelve pontifical commissions, three judiciary institutions, and nineteen commissions, committees, and administrative offices, plus libraries and museums, the Vatican Radio and *L'Osservatore Romano* newspaper. The pope has his own household and liturgical staffs.

But John Paul II was slow in making changes in the Curia, first attempting to master the intricacies of its complex bureaucracy, which in many ways resembles a medieval royal court, where gossip and currying favor reign supreme. Nowadays, virtually everybody has a personal computer, producing computerized gossip and keeping a memory of favors done and owed.

An early example of Curial sycophancy came on March 4, 1979, when the pope announced to the bishops and cardinals gathered in an Apostolic Palace hall the issuance of the *Redemptor hominis* encyclical marking "The Beginning of His Papal Ministry." The churchmen broke into loud applause, but John Paul II, peering at them through his contact lenses (which he had just begun to wear), calmed them down. "This is not the time to clap," he admonished smilingly. "Clap when you have read it. . . ."

The pope spent several months visiting the Congregations and commissions before making up his mind about Curial appointments and policy shifts. Archbishop Paul Marcinkus, an American who was the pope's financial adviser, advance man, and guardian on domestic and foreign trips during the first years of the pontificate, concluded after a short time that John Paul II was "theoretically a fast learner . . . who listens and asks questions, but not a man for detail." Marcinkus, who said he understood that Wojtyła had not been "a great administrator in Kraków," remarked that it would have been better if the pope knew more "what each office does" in the Vatican.

John Paul II's choice of Cardinal Casaroli as secretary of state followed Cardinal Villot's death, and in him he found an excellent foreign policy adviser, although, in the end, he always formulated his own policies, often keeping them close to his chest. Archbishop Achille Silvestrini (later cardinal), a world-class diplomat, was Casaroli's deputy in charge of international affairs; he was de facto foreign minister of the Vatican. Cardinal Roger Etchegaray, the archbishop of Marseilles, became the global troubleshooter.

The pope maintained Cardinal Johannes Willebrands, the archbishop of Utrecht in the Netherlands and one of the most outstanding Church personalities, as president of the Pontifical Council for Promoting Christian Unity in order to advance vigorously the ecumenical cause of reuniting Christian churches—one of Wojtyła's top priorities.

In 1981, John Paul II named Cardinal Joseph Ratzinger, then fifty-four, to replace Croat Cardinal Franjo Seper as prefect of the Congregation for the Doctrine of the Faith (Seper had replaced the nearly blind Ottaviani). Ratzinger is a white-haired, soft-featured German theologian and Scripture scholar with a brilliant intellect and the relentlessness of the Inquisition four centuries earlier.

The pope had known Ratzinger since the Vatican Council, when Ratzinger, then a liberal, attended as a monsignor and advisor, and the German is his most trusted counselor, to the extent that anyone in the Curia enjoys that status. John Paul II has no identifiable Curial favorites. The preservation of theological purity, fully in tune with the pope, is Ratzinger's responsibility. He sees the pontiff privately the most often of all the prefects of Congregations—several times a week—and he is unquestionably the most important senior figure in the Holy See; he has been there the longest under John Paul II. Ratzinger runs his Congregation from the massive, dark, forbidding-looking edifice, once known as the "Holy Office" and just as feared today, that overlooks St. Peter's Square from the south.

The whole question of the Theology of Liberation has been one of the most significant controversies of John Paul II's reign, involving, as it does, the matter of dissent and authority within the Church, among other aspects. Ratzinger, who had been working closely with the pope for two years before becoming prefect, has played a key role in it.

The political and theological handling of the delicate matter of the Theology of Liberation was not the Church's finest hour. Perhaps it is best depicted in terms of the life and death of Archbishop Oscar Arnulfo Romero of El Salvador, a martyr of the Church.

In a sense, Romero's story begins in Mexico, where he went in January 1979 to attend the decennial meeting of the Latin American Episcopal Conference (CELAM) and where he saw and heard John Paul II for the first time. Held in the city of Puebla, eighty miles from Mexico City, the CELAM conference was designed to review the situation of the Church in Latin America ten years after it had issued its "Medellín Declaration" (named after the Colombian city where the bishops had met with Paul VI in 1968, which had launched the concept of the Theology of Liberation).

There is no precise definition of this theology, mainly because it has various modalities and has been evolving over the last three decades. But Harvey Cox, professor of divinity at the Harvard Divinity School and a leading authority on the subject, has put it this way:

> From the outset, Liberation Theology was principally and basically a religious movement with political and social implications. But it was not a fundamentally political movement with religious overtones. It was a religious movement springing from a religious, spiritual revival in Latin America among the Latin American poor. The vision underlying Liberation Theology . . . is to try to understand the meaning of Christianity, the

Bible and the Gospel from the perspective of the poor, the marginalized, the outsiders, the broken-hearted.

Dr. Cox, who is a Baptist, says that

> the original impetus of Liberation Theology was the Latin American bishops saying that "we cannot really play the role of arbiter between the wealthy and the poor, between the landowners and the peons. . . . We have to bring our resources and our way of teaching and our personnel into the service of the majority." And they did it. All over the continent people did that; they actually began to re-deploy Church resources.

Apart from Liberation Theology priests' and religious orders' direct and personal involvement in the social and economic problems of the faithful, the new movement created "Base Ecclesial Communities." These are self-ruling groups of priests, brothers, and nuns working together with Catholic laypeople, both to strengthen the faith and to improve the human condition in their cities, towns, and villages.

The Base Communities, Dr. Cox says,

> constitute one of the most energetic and vital forces in the whole Church in Latin America, and by definition not controllable by the traditional means of clerical control. They are not eucharistic communities in which the priest has to preside; laypeople, sisters, women and other people lead these communities. They are communities of celebration and song and discussion and Bible studies, and prayer and service. . . . So you have to see Latin American Liberation Theology as being not just an intellectual movement, but a Christian renaissance or revival of spirituality with very strong populist overtones.

The late Penny Lernoux, an American Catholic writer, has noted that

> the appeal of Liberation Theology in Latin America lies in its integration of religious and political liberation. If religion previously served as a repressive politi-

> cal tool, it can also be used as a means of political liberation. . . . In Latin America, Catholicism is the cultural starting point for everything else. Latin Americans do not have to change their basic religious beliefs—their culture—to achieve liberation, but only their perspective.

One man to whom the Theology of Liberation appealed powerfully was Archbishop Romero, whose country, El Salvador, had been caught up for years in a savage civil war between rightist military regimes and Cuban-supported leftist rebels of the Farabundo Marti National Liberation Front (FMLN). The sixty-two-year-old Rome-trained prelate was a quiet and non-political bishop from a remote mountain village in eastern El Salvador who was named archbishop—and head of the Salvadoran Church—in February 1978 precisely because he was not controversial.

But Romero was converted to political militancy when, three weeks after his installation as archbishop, pro-regime gunmen shot and killed his close friend, Father Rutilio Grande, a rural Jesuit priest who was active in organizing Base Ecclesial Communities and protesting against attacks on Church people preaching the Theology of Liberation. Instantly, the meek Romero became an enraged and outspoken advocate of human rights and protector of peasants, an attitude that earned him the hostility of several fellow bishops and the military rulers.

At Puebla, Romero was assigned to a CELAM committee preparing the Liberation Theology section of the document the conference was to issue. But it was also there that he became aware of John Paul II's emotional opposition to the movement and to the direct involvement by priests in political situations in their countries—even in defense of the poor and of the lives of priests and lay Catholic activists.

The pope's attitude appeared to be derived from his own unfamiliarity with Latin America, which he had never visited, and the opinion of his advisers that the Theology of Liberation was essentially a pro-Marxist movement—or very close to it. Though he had recently read Gustavo Gutiérrez's books on the subject, he accepted the judgment that this theology was dangerous (he was told by one adviser that Gutiérrez was "an ecclesiastic excuse for violence") and he went along with recommendations that Puebla should "correct the mistakes of Medellín."

Warning John Paul II against the spirit of Medellín were principally Ratzinger; Cardinal Sebastiano Baggio, the Italian prefect of the Congregation for Bishops; and the Colombian Archbishop Alfonso López Trujillo, the forty-four-year-old secretary-general of CELAM. Strongly conservative, they took the position that innovations like Base Ecclesial Communities threatened the authority of the bishops and Rome, and therefore should be forbidden (this attitude was still prevalent in the Holy See in 1994).

But with the pope committed to his lifetime devotion to social justice, considerable confusion developed in planning and drafting his speeches in Mexico. The main speech, in fact, was rewritten, aboard the airliner en route to the Americas, from what was said to have been a "banal text."

In the end, compromise prevailed. The pope and the "Puebla Declaration" refrained from criticizing directly the Theology of Liberation or the Base Communities, but John Paul II found language to discourage Church justice-seekers from going along with social revolutions. He said that "the idea of Christ as a political figure, a revolutionary, as the subversive man from Nazareth," goes against the New Testament. Other biblical scholars, of course, have different interpretations about the "historical Jesus."

Nothing was settled at Puebla in a formal fashion—CELAM's declaration repeated that the Church favored "an option for the poor"—but the mood had shifted away from the dynamism of Medellín. It left many bishops, including Romero, highly disappointed. And what disappointed them even more was that John Paul II had failed in his Mexican speeches even to allude to widespread murders and tortures practiced by dictatorial regimes throughout the Americas against their opponents, among them priests and nuns. In contrast, Latin American churchmen like Brazilian Cardinals Paulo Evaristo Arns and Aloísio Lorscheider had loudly denounced for years political violence and oppression in their countries.

The vagueness of Puebla strengthened the position of bishops like Baggio and López Trujillo in their campaign against the "Marxism" of the Theology of Liberation, and soon Romero, who kept speaking against violence and political murders in El Salvador, became himself one of the targets. As priests were being killed and assaulted in his country, the Vatican imposed an Apostolic Visitator over Romero to replace him, in effect, in the running of the Salvadoran Church, which was split between the archbishop and the more conservative bishops.

Now Romero was being accused of being a subversive. As he noted in his diary on August 11, 1979, his meetings with the Salvadoran bishops were "dominated by the prejudice that there is Marxist infiltration in the Church. It was impossible to overcome the prejudice, in spite of my trying to explain that many priests are persecuted because they want to be faithful to the spirit of Vatican II, translated for Latin America by Medellín and Puebla. This was understood very little. Rather, the blame was laid on the instruments of Marxism, which, according to them, the Church is serving."

But Romero found little solace from John Paul II. After waiting in Rome for six weeks for the audience he had requested, the archbishop was finally received on May 7, 1979. The purpose of his visit was to convince the pope of the need to protest against the murders of priests and others by Salvadoran death squads, and Romero brought along thick files on seven of the most recent assassinations of priests.

This was John Paul II's response as recorded by the archbishop in his diary:

> He acknowledged that pastoral work is very difficult in a political climate like one in which I have to work. He recommended great balance and prudence, especially when denouncing specific situations. He thinks that it is better to stay with principles, because there is a risk of making errors or mistakes with specific accusations.

The pope's words depressed Romero. He wrote:

> And I left, pleased by the meeting, but worried to see how much the negative reports of my pastoral work

> had influenced him, although deep down I remembered that he had recommended "courage and boldness" but, at the same time, tempered with the necessary prudence and balance.

On January 30, 1980, Romero was again received by John Paul II, and again it was discouraging. He wrote in his diary that the pope

> received me very warmly and told me that he understood perfectly how difficult the political situation of my country is; that he was concerned about the role of the Church; that we should be concerned not only with defending social justice and love of the poor, but also with what could result from a score-settling effort on the part of the popular Left, which could also be bad for the Church. . . . At the end, he gave me a very friendly embrace and told me that he prayed every day for El Salvador.

A few minutes after 6:00 P.M. on Monday, March 24, 1980, Archbishop Romero was killed with a single shot to his chest as he celebrated Mass for the mother of a friend at the chapel of the Divine Providence Hospital in San Salvador, the capital. He was assassinated on the orders of the military intelligence command.

Oscar Arnulfo Romero, the Church's latest martyr, was the St. Stanisław of El Salvador.

The Vatican campaign against the Theology of Liberation became a pretext, at least in part, for the purge of the Society of Jesus by John Paul II in the early 1980s. The linkage was the Jesuit participation in Theology of Liberation activities of a segment of the Catholic clergy throughout Central America, including Romero's El Salvador, where the civil war went on unabated, and Nicaragua, where the Marxist-oriented Sandinistas won power in mid-1979 after overthrowing the dynastic dictatorial regime of the Somoza family.

Founded in 1540 by the Basque Ignatius Loyola to stem the decline of the Church in the face of the Protestant

Reformation, the Society of Jesus was in the 1980s the world's single largest religious order, with nearly thirty thousand Jesuits, and great schools, scholars, and universities as well as missionaries around the globe. But it was perceived by the new pope as too progressive, "liberal," and not sufficiently responsive to his theological and political leadership in such situations as Central America. It therefore had to be disciplined. The inside story of "defanging" the Jesuits, as some of them call these events, or, more politely, "the intervention of the pope," has remained largely unpublicized over the years.

Surprisingly, the disciplining first took the form of John Paul II's refusal to allow the Jesuits' Rome-based Superior General, the Basque priest Pedro Arrupe, to convoke the order's General Congregation in 1981, at which he had planned to present his resignation. The seventy-three-year-old Arrupe, who had served as Superior General since 1965, wished to retire for reasons of health and age. But after they met in the spring of 1980, when the Holy See and the Jesuits were embroiled in disputes over Central America (where the Jesuits wished to be even more active in the context of the civil war), the pope wrote him that "I don't want you to call this meeting and to resign, for the good of the Church and the good of your own Order."

Many informed Jesuits suspect that John Paul II wanted to prevent Arrupe's resignation and the planned election until he had time to investigate the order thoroughly. In any case, he would not receive Arrupe again until almost a year later—an unusually long time to keep the head of a major order waiting—when he once more turned down his resignation request. At an audience in April 1981 the pope and Arrupe pursued this question.

Meanwhile, John Paul II was shot the following month, and Arrupe suffered a severe stroke in August 1981, rendering the matter of his future moot. Arrupe then appointed Father Vincent O'Keefe, one of his assistants general and former president of Fordham University in the Bronx in New York, as the order's vicar general. O'Keefe, an American, thus became the acting head of the Jesuits. But two months later, John Paul II carried out his coup d'état against the order.

On October 6, Secretary of State Casaroli delivered a letter from the pope, addressed to the ailing Father Arrupe, suspending the Jesuit constitution in order to prevent an immediate election of a new Superior General and, meanwhile, deposing O'Keefe as vicar general. To replace him, John Paul II named eighty-year-old Father Paolo Dezza, an Italian Jesuit (and later cardinal) as his personal representative to run the society with the aid of Father Giuseppe Pittau, the Jesuit provincial superior in Japan. Pittao was given the right of succession to Dezza.

The pope did not allow the Jesuits to hold their Congregation until September 1983—two years later—when they elected Father Peter-Hans Kolvenbach, a highly respected Dutch scholar and Middle East specialist, as Superior General. But, by then, the Jesuits had lost much of their influence, at least visibly.

The explanation offered by John Paul II for his unprecedented "intervention" in the Society of Jesus was, in the words of a Jesuit historian, that "we were causing confusion among the people of God by what we were writing, by what we were teaching, and by some of the counsel we were giving. And that in these things, we were writing or counseling or advising people against the teachings of the Church."

The other charges were said to include that "some of our men had crossed from the religious dimension that would be benefitting priests and the religious into the social and political order—and so we were involved in politics. Then [the pope] said that there were a lot of secularizing tendencies going on in our Order, and he was concerned about the formation we were giving our young Jesuits . . . that our formation was too liberal, and we were not giving them enough of a traditional formation. . . . Look at Central America, look at what you are doing there. You Jesuits, you have an influence on the other orders. So if you do it, these other orders will feel they can do it, too."

(The Holy See became extremely annoyed when the late Father Timothy Healy, then president of Georgetown University in Washington, D.C., a Jesuit institution, had refused in 1979 to drop the plan to award an honorary degree to Archbishop Romero of El Salvador. The request had been made to Father Healy by Cardinal Gabriel Marie

Garrone, the prefect of the Congregation for Catholic Education.)

But, of course, nothing is black and white in the Vatican. The Jesuits continue to run the great Gregorian University in Rome (where Father Pittau was magnificent rector in the early 1990s), Vatican Radio, and the intellectually influential *La Civilitá Cattolica* bimonthly magazine, and there are many of them in key Curial posts, even in Cardinal Ratzinger's Congregation. In 1983, John Paul II named Carlo Maria Martini, the intellectual Jesuit archbishop of Milan, to be cardinal. Martini is one of the highest regarded cardinals.

The Vatican's war against the Theology of Liberation did not cease, however. In August 1984 Ratzinger's Sacred Congregation for the Doctrine of the Faith issued an "Instruction" designed to "draw the attention of pastors, theologians and all the faithful to the deviations, the risk of deviation, damaging to the faith and to Christian living, that are brought about by certain forms of liberation theology which use, in an insufficiently critical manner, concepts borrowed from various currents of Marxist thought." On December 21, John Paul II declared in a year-end address to the cardinals of the Curia that the Church, while committed to helping the underprivileged, must protect the poor from "illusory and dangerous" ideologies.

Though Marxism-Leninism has all but vanished from the international scene, the Theology of Liberation goes on. But the Holy See has not yet addressed the issue in its new dimension. Poverty in the Third World, of course, keeps increasing.

John Paul II's offensive against the Theology of Liberation was launched at the start of his pontificate simultaneously with a Holy See ban on theological dissent on the part of Catholic scholars.

As early as December 1979, Hans Küng, a Swiss theologian who taught at the University of Tübingen in Germany (and whom Wojtyła once admired), was deprived by Ratzinger's Congregation of his license to teach Catholic theology because of his questioning of the doctrine of papal infallibility (proclaimed by Vatican Council I in 1870). The

Küng matter became a cause célèbre, triggering massive protests from episcopates around the world, but John Paul II did not relent, insisting in a 1980 statement that the action against him had been "responsible." Father Jacques Pohier, a French Dominican, was equally punished at the same time as Küng for raising questions about Christ's resurrection.

In 1986, the blow fell on Father Charles E. Curran, a professor at the Catholic University of America in Washington, D.C., when he received a letter from Cardinal Ratzinger that he could "no longer be considered suitable nor eligible to exercise the function of a Professor of Catholic Theology." It was a "definitive judgement," personally approved by John Paul II, and it was based on Father Curran's public opposition to the anti-contraception *Humanae vitae* encyclical. Curran had taken a defiant view that "a person could dissent in theory and in practice from the condemnation of artificial contraception in the papal encyclical . . . and still be a loyal Roman Catholic."

Looking back at his experience in a broader perspective, Curran says that "some things are more core and central to faith than others, and therefore . . . all of the Catholic faith is not of the same significance. . . ." And he adds that "contraception is not a practical problem for people in the Catholic Church today. . . . Married couples have made up their minds long ago. The only reason why contraception is an important issue today is because it has become symbolic. Because if you change on contraception, you're going to have to recognize that you're going to have to change on other things as well."

Küng, Pohier, and Curran have lost their right to teach at Catholic institutions, and other leading theologians with dissenting ideas have suffered inquisitory treatment at the hands of Cardinal Ratzinger's Congregation. Among them are Belgium's Edward Schillebeeckx, Germany's Bernhard Häring, Peru's Gustavo Gutiérrez, and Brazil's Leonardo Boff, a Franciscan who finally left the priesthood altogether.

In 1993, John Paul II vigorously reaffirmed his original ban on priestly involvement in politics, presumably because, among other considerations, it could lead to new dissent as well as to the questioning of absolute papal authority in the political realm. Ironically, this most political of popes does not wish his priests to partake of politics.

Quoting from the new *Catechism of the Catholic Church* (the first since the Council of Trent in the sixteenth century), he said in an August statement that "it is not the responsibility of the Church's pastors to become directly involved in political action and social organization. This task pertains to the vocation of the lay faithful." The pope then warned that "the priest . . . will keep in mind that a political party can never become the object of absolute loyalty."

John Paul II, however, was evenhanded theologically in disposing of dissent. In 1988, he excommunicated the ultraconservative French Archbishop Marcel Lefebvre, who, rejecting Vatican Council II reforms, had ordained his own priests and bishops. After Lefebvre's death in 1991, at least a half million Catholics remained loyal to his teachings.

Coincidentally or not, the purge of the Society of Jesus fairly converged with the elevation by John Paul II of the Sacerdotal Society of the Holy Priest and Opus Dei to the rank of a "personal prelature." The pope's decision was announced on November 27, 1982, and Monsignor Álvaro del Portillo, president general of Opus Dei, was named the first prelate of the organization and later was ordained bishop.

There is no precedent in Church history for a personal prelature, which represents considerable autonomy for Opus Dei. Composed of priests and lay Catholics—over 80,000 of them (including 1,500 priests) in 1994—Opus Dei now reports directly to the Congregation for Bishops in Rome and to the pope. Its national units (there were thirty-seven of them in foreign countries in 1982) are subordinated to Rome rather than to local diocesan bishops, although they are instructed to work with the latter as required by the circumstances.

It was John Paul II's personal decision to bestow such power and recognition on Opus Dei, although he consulted at length with Curial and foreign bishops (Spanish bishops disliked the idea) before authorizing the personal prelature.

Though he has never discussed publicly the reasons for his attraction to Opus Dei, the pope certainly has never made a secret of his deep interest in it.

Interestingly, John Paul II had never met Monsignor Josemaría Escrivá de Balaguer y Albás, the founder of Opus Dei. On a visit to Rome in the mid-1970s, when he was cardinal, Wojtyła had requested a meeting with Escrivá, but the Spaniard's schedule was too full and he could not receive him.

Escrivá died on June 26, 1975, but Wojtyła often thought about the man who conceptualized Opus Dei. Through personal connections among Opus Dei priests and lay members, he became quite familiar with the society and quickly became one of its admirers. What appears to have impressed Wojtyła about Opus Dei was its emphasis on laity's engagement in apostolic work—one of his own basic concerns—and its immense internal discipline and sense of obedience. He also recognized the high professional attainments of its people, many of whom are leading politicians, corporate executives, scientists, academicians, and senior military officers.

The interest was reciprocated, and Opus Dei began quietly supporting the Kraków archdiocese in a variety of material ways, including travel funds. Unlike Third World religious groups preaching the Theology of Liberation—and, Wojtyła thought, flirting with Marxism—Opus Dei was unconditionally anti-communist.

Wojtyła demonstrated his empathy for Opus Dei and his respect for the memory of Escrivá when he flew to Rome in October 1978, to attend the conclave summoned in the aftermath of the death of John Paul I. One quiet afternoon, just before the conclave, he was driven to Opus Dei headquarters in the Parioli section of the city to pray at the tomb of Escrivá at the church there. After Bishop Portillo died in 1994, John Paul II returned to the Opus Dei church to pray before his body as it lay in state.

John Paul II has become the great protector of Opus Dei, and the organization has responded by placing itself entirely at his orders, with all of its very considerable resources. In 1989, the moment communist rule collapsed, Opus Dei launched its apostolic and educational activities in Poland, opening pastoral centers for men and women and cultural associations. Later, Opus Dei provided funds and personnel, including priests, to help establish an effective Roman Catholic Church in newly independent Kazakhstan of the former Soviet Union.

On May 17, 1992, John Paul II beatified Escrivá, just short of seventeen years after his death, at a ceremony before a quarter million people in St. Peter's Square. It was one of the most rapidly completed processes of beatification.

PART SIX

CHAPTER 23

The fate of Poland dominated the attention of John Paul II over the entire decade of the 1980s, the duration of the great Polish crisis, along with the Holy See's breakthrough in relations with the Soviet Union, and his travels in the five continents. The common denominator in all these endeavors was the effort to assert the pope's role as both a world statesman and spiritual leader, seeking to influence Christians and non-Christians alike in favor of humanity's great causes.

The decade was the apogee of John Paul II's pontificate. It was the richest and most productive period in every realm—diplomatic, scientific, and religious—but it also brought danger, tragedy, and grief.

The pope's discreet but enormously effective personal management of the Polish crisis, which was the touchstone in the ultimate process of the disintegration of communism, has surely earned him a distinguished place in history. His two visits to Poland in the course of 1980s were crucial in affecting the march of events, as John Paul II displayed the keenest instinct and judgment about the situation there. And he did so in dealing with the Soviet Union where, in the end, Mikhail Gorbachev became one of his principal diplomatic partners.

In a sense, John Paul II deliberately became the "Pilgrim

Pope," as he often called himself, because he understood that modern technology—the jet airplane, the helicopter, satellite television, and the limitless uses of computer resources—made it possible for him to reach *in person* huge masses of the globe's population. This, in turn, created new opportunities for the success of the "New Evangelization" apostolic, ecumenical, and peacekeeping missions. To put it another way, John Paul II succeeded in bringing the Roman Catholic papacy to the world in an unprecedented manner. His own captivating personality was, of course, a vital factor in achieving it.

John Paul II used his first pontifical year to establish his presence firmly both in the Vatican and on the international scene. By the end of 1979, he had his Curia team well in place, leaving no doubt that he was absolutely in charge of everything at the Holy See. Internationally, his jet travel centered on his top priorities.

First, it was Santo Domingo and Mexico to stake out his claim to undisputed religious leadership within a half year of the death of Paul VI. It was followed by the issuance of the *Redemptor hominis* encyclical, defining his theological, social, and philosophical views. Next came Poland to affirm his religious and patriotic ties to the homeland, a mission that was supremely political in its essence.

Then, a short stay in heavily Catholic Ireland en route to the United States for a week's visit—the first of three there as pope—and a peace exhortation and social justice speech at the United Nations General Assembly in New York. In Washington, D.C., John Paul II was exposed, probably for the first time, to a public complaint, delivered by an American nun—Sister Theresa Kane—about the inferior treatment of women in the Church. Curiously, this highly intelligent pontiff never grasped the reasons for Catholic women's rising unhappiness with the Church.

Finally, the pope undertook in late November a three-day journey to Turkey, a secular nation with a 98 percent Muslim population but also the seat in the Phanar district of Istanbul of the Greek Orthodox patriarch. For John Paul II, who welcomes challenges, the Turkish experience was particularly rewarding.

With a tiny Roman Catholic minority living in the country, for whom he celebrated solemn Mass, the pope's principal interest on the trip was in making it clear to the Islamic world that the Holy See was not its enemy. Early in 1979, the Ayatollah Khomeini's fundamentalist Muslim revolution had achieved power in Iran, and there was much loose talk in the world about religious conflicts erupting from Mediterranean shores to the coast of the Persian Gulf.

Equally important for John Paul II was the reaffirmation of the rapport established in the 1960s by Paul VI with Greek Orthodox Patriarch Athenagoras, the first such contact between these Christian churches since the Great Schism of 1054. Patriarch Dimitrios, who had succeeded Athenagoras, greeted the pope as "Holy Brother" at their encounter at St. George's Church in Istanbul, and John Paul II was encouraged by what he saw as another step toward ecumenical unity. Then he made time to fly east into Asia Minor to pray at the House of Mary on Mount Ephesus, one of the holiest shrines in Mariology.

Still, the pope could not stay away altogether from world politics, making hopeful allusions in his speeches to the possibility of improved relations between Turkey and Greece, military anti-Soviet allies in the North Atlantic Treaty Organization (NATO) but political and religious enemies in their own region. Turkish forces had invaded Cyprus, a predominantly Greek-populated island, in mid-1974 to form a separate Turkish Cypriot state in the north, and NATO kept worrying about an open Greek-Turkish war.

The great crisis in Poland erupted in July 1980 while John Paul II was spending two weeks in Brazil, the country with the world's largest nominally Roman Catholic population, as part of a hugely ambitious globetrotting schedule that year. He visited nine countries on three continents, trips fully covered by live television everywhere.

The tour started with a ten-day foray into Africa early in May, taking the pope to Zaire, Congo, Kenya, Ghana, Upper Volta, and the Ivory Coast (the site of the world's biggest Roman Catholic cathedral, bigger than St. Peter's Basilica in Rome), crisscrossing the African continent.

Africa, which he had never visited, represents in John Paul II's mind the last frontier of Roman Catholicism, perhaps its last fortress in a world where he so greatly fears secularization, and it would be the region most often visited by him during his pontificate (in 1978, all of Africa had fewer priests—around eight thousand—than Central America and Mexico).

Though the African Church is one of the oldest in Christianity, the existing Roman Catholic communities, which he hopes to see expanded, struggle in sharp competition with traditional animist religions, the rise of Islam across Africa, and the penetration by well-financed Protestant sects, mainly from the United States. On the first African voyage, however, the pope seemed not to be fully aware that the Church's resistance to inculturation, the absorption of certain African cultural traditions into Catholic worship (such as the acceptance of tribal marriages alongside church marriages), was a serious obstacle to his evangelization plans. It would be only at the African Bishops' Synod in Rome in 1994 that inculturation began to make headway under pressure from the African bishops.

From May 30 to June 2, John Paul II was in the more familiar environment of France ("The Oldest Daughter of the Church," but increasingly unfaithful), where he spoke emotionally to young people and addressed UNESCO on the importance of preserving cultures and civilizations.

The pope arrived in Brazil on June 30, the day before strikes over food price rises, suddenly announced on July 1, began breaking out in Polish cities, starting in Lublin (the home of Wojtyła's Catholic University) and spreading, on July 16, to the railroad system in the Lublin area. But neither the communist authorities and the Church in Poland nor John Paul II in faraway Brazil—nor, most probably, the workers themselves—had the slightest inkling at that juncture that this was the dawn of a historic upheaval.

As Edward Gierek, then the first secretary of the PZPR, the ruling communist party, acknowledged later, Poland's social and economic situation had been deteriorating rapidly in the second half of the 1970s—the 1976 food price riots were an example—and he was concerned about stability in the country. The past winter had been the harshest in a century, playing havoc with the economy. However, Gierek chose to blame his own security services for not estimating correctly the Polish potential for explosion, or informing him about it.

Meanwhile, Gierek and Primate Wyszyński had been steadily improving the relations between the authorities and the Church. Indeed, Gierek recalls, he was a target of strong criticism within the party's leadership that he had gone "too far in his concessions to the Catholics" in the aftermath of the papal visit. But, he adds, "the balance of power in Poland for years had made it necessary to take seriously the voice of the Catholic hierarchy."

The Lubin railwaymen's strike became a major worry to the Kremlin because Soviet troops in East Germany, about one half million men, were totally dependent on the railroad link across Poland—and across the Lublin area—for all their supplies, including fuel, food, and munitions. On July 27, therefore, Gierek flew to Brezhnev's summer vacation villa in Crimea to assure him, in what he called "a rather unpleasant conversation," that the rail strikes had ended and the situation was well in hand. He stayed on in Crimea, taking his own vacation there. Several key Polish Politburo members were vacationing on the Black Sea in Bulgaria.

By the time John Paul II was back home from Brazil at his summer residence in Castel Gandolfo, strikes in Poland were spreading to Warsaw, Poznań, Kraków, Bydgoszcz, Gdańsk, and a number of heavy-industry centers throughout the country. They were spontaneous local work stoppages for lower food prices and higher wages rather than a national movement, chiefly because no organization existed yet to set one in motion. KOR, the center of intellectual dissidents, for example, was not a mass-opposition organization. But a mood of rebellion was clearly rising throughout Poland.

The pope was kept informed in detail of these events through the Polish Section of the Vatican Secretariat of State as well as directly through the episcopate in Warsaw and other Church channels. But he did not seem to be unduly alarmed yet.

Gierek, who had convinced himself that the Lublin

strikes were an isolated episode, rushed back to Poland in mid-August, finally realizing the gravity of the situation. Strikers at the big shipyard in Gdańsk (where workers and security forces had had their bloody clashes ten years earlier) were now demanding the creation of independent labor unions—side by side with the regime-controlled unions—and Gierek noted that this demand plus the appearance of "political slogans" had introduced "a completely new reality."

Thursday, August 14, 1980, marked the turning point in the Polish crisis—and in the history of Poland and communism.

In the small hours of the day, workers arriving for the morning shift at the Lenin Shipyard in Gdańsk declared an "occupation strike," locking the gates behind them and forming a strike committee to act as their leadership. An occupation strike meant that the workers would not leave the premises but would not work. It had the advantage of massing thousands of workers within the shipyard perimeter to keep the protest going, but shielded them from the security forces. Nobody thought that the Gierek regime would order the riot police or the army to storm the shipyard to dislodge the workers. The bitter memories of the 1970 Gdańsk confrontation were still very much alive on both sides.

Although the strike leaders on that first morning had belonged since the early 1970s to a small, illegal free labor union movement, the occupation of the shipyard was virtually improvised overnight. It did not have a defined political goal. The initial demands were the reemployment of a woman crane operator, a free labor union activist who had been transferred to a job outside Gdańsk in January because of her militancy, and a relatively modest across-the-board wage rise. The crane operator's fate seemed to be of primary concern at the outset, as the original strike leaders had brought with them six thousand copies of a leaflet clamoring for her reinstatement.

But, as it often happens in history, events were decisively altered by the actions of a single individual. In this case, it was a thirty-seven-year-old heavily mustached unemployed electrician named Lech Wałęsa, who in mid-morning jumped the fence of the shipyard to join the strikers there—and became their undisputed leader. Wałęsa had been involved in the free union movement since the 1970s, having been fired from the shipyard and several subsequent jobs for political activity and having been arrested innumerable times. He was certainly well known to the workers.

Now the Lenin Shipyard strike became a major national event. Other Gdańsk shipyards joined it later in the day, as did shipyards and factories in nearby Gdynia and Szczecin, along the Baltic coast, and Elbląg just northeast of Gdańsk. An Inter-Factory Strike Committee—its Polish acronym was MKS—was organized and its appeals to the national labor force for solidarity with the shipyard strikers led to the birth of a countrywide free labor organization—Solidarity. Inevitably, Solidarity turned into a political movement.

But it was a movement with powerful Roman Catholic overtones. Though there is nothing to indicate that either the Polish episcopate as such had played any role in precipitating the Gdańsk events, Solidarity immediately identified itself with Catholicism. Given the Polish patriotic-religious traditions, this was not necessarily surprising, but its spontaneity was unexpected.

Wałęsa, the father of six children, was a deeply devout Catholic who during the strike wore an image of the Black Madonna of Częstochowa on his coat lapel. But he was not preaching religion as he went on organizing the workers for what already loomed as a long confrontation, in one form or another, with the authorities. Solidarity's religious sentiment thus seemed to flow naturally from the men and women locked inside the shipyard. A wooden cross was erected in front of the shipyard's entrance at the spot where riot policemen had killed four workers in 1970. On Sunday, August 17, Father Henryk Jankowski, the parish priest of St. Brygida Church in Gdańsk and Wałęsa's friend, celebrated Mass for the strikers in the shipyard's courtyard, an uplifting experience for them.

John Paul II had done nothing to trigger or encourage the crisis that summer—he remained publicly silent most of the time on the subject—but overnight his portraits and white-and-yellow Holy See flags appeared on the gates of the Lenin Shipyard. It is impossible to establish precisely a cause-and-effect linkage between his 1979 visit to Poland and the birth of Solidarity fourteen months later, but such actual linkage seems to exist. It is nevertheless true that the presence of the Polish pope in Rome had given the workers a special sense of assurance and even protection once the protests had erupted as a result of long-pent-up national resentments against the ruling system.

The sense of being protected by John Paul II, both as a perception and a reality, during the long decade of the Polish crisis was vital, psychologically and politically, in keeping the opposition movement alive and going. At the same time, the pope began to weave his quiet but intricate diplomacy on a separate back-channel track, seldom visible to either the opposition or even to the Polish episcopate, sending and receiving emissaries on confidential missions between Rome and Warsaw, and Rome and Moscow. His patience and long-term perspective were the great assets of his diplomacy.

On Monday, August 16, the Solidarity command announced a sixteen-point list of demands. The most important was the demand for free unions: "After the end of the strike is proclaimed, the MKS will not dissolve but will carry through the execution of the demands; it will organize free trade unions, acting as the district council of free unions." However, the strikers were not seeking the abolition of the regime-run unions. Later in the week, Wałęsa and his associates were joined by advisers from KOR with political and legal experience, mostly Catholic intellectuals from Warsaw and Kraków. The list of demands grew from sixteen to twenty-one, with the addition of points covering the abolition of censorship, freedom of speech, Solidarity's access to national media, and the right to strike.

Now Gierek was faced with the choice of negotiating with the strikers over what was obviously the political future of Poland or using force. He chose negotiation, and he did not use his security services to interfere with the activities of Solidarity and the KOR leadership. It was a historic decision on the part of Gierek, who, having come to power in the aftermath of the 1970 Gdańsk bloodshed, was determined to refrain from using lethal force in putting down rebellion on his watch. He presumably might have had KOR leaders arrested and have stormed one or more shipyards or factories on strike, but he had concluded that it could have led to tragedies on a grand scale.

Gierek was supported in his decision to deal peacefully with the strikers by General Wojciech Jaruzelski, the defense minister and a Politburo member. This, too, was crucial because it served to assure the workers that the Polish army, still among the most respected institutions in the country along with the Church, would not turn its firepower on them. It was now too late for the riot police or the security services alone to handle the threat posed by Solidarity.

As for Jaruzelski, he was a dedicated communist army officer with an unusual family and religious background that, quite possibly, influenced his behavior then and later. Descended from a small-gentry family, before the outbreak of World War II the general had attended a Warsaw high school run by the Order of Marist Fathers. The family fled east ahead of the advancing Nazi armies only to be deported to the Soviet Union after Stalin moved his troops into Poland two weeks later. Jaruzelski joined the Soviet-sponsored Polish army, which was part of the Soviet armed forces, and fought with it all the way to Germany. Afterward he made an exceptional communist party and army career. But, as he acknowledged later, the impact of his Christian upbringing never left him altogether, becoming an important personal element in the relationship he would develop in time with John Paul II.

Negotiations with the Gdańsk strikers continued through all of August, and Gierek came under mounting pressure from Brezhnev to do *something* about the situation, which the Soviets felt threatened the entire communist system in Eastern Europe. Hard-liners within the Polish party turned on him, too, demanding a food blockade of the Baltic coast cities to "starve out" the strikers and their families.

At one point, Gierek recalls, Brezhnev telephoned him

from Moscow to warn about the dangers to socialism in Poland and "to assure that we can always count on them" (the Soviets). Brezhnev told him, "You have a *kontra* on your hands and you should grab them by the snout. . . . We shall help!" *Kontra* was the communist shorthand for counterrevolution. Gierek says that he replied, "There is no *kontra* here and the strikes result from economic causes," and "I assured him again that we are fully in control of the situation and we absolutely need no help. I underlined this several times."

Boris Aristov, the Soviet ambassador in Warsaw, visited or telephoned Gierek almost daily to insist on the Kremlin's concerns about Poland. In Moscow, Brezhnev set up a special top-level "Crisis Staff" to deal with the Polish problem, which became known among Soviet officials as the "Polish Club." It included Defense Minister Dimitri Ustinov, KGB Chairman Andropov, chief ideologue Suslov, Foreign Minister Gromyko, and Politburo members Chernenko and Gorbachev. The latter was still a hard-liner.

Thus far John Paul II had maintained a studied silence about the Polish events. At a General Audience on August 20, however, he allowed himself the careful comment that "in connection with news reaching us from Poland, I wish to recite two prayers in your presence: . . . 'that religion would always enjoy liberty and our motherland enjoy safety. . . .' Let these prayers show how much we, now present in Rome, are united with our compatriots in the motherland."

The same day, the pope dispatched a letter to Primate Wyszyński to assure him that

> in the course of the recent difficult days, I am especially close [to you], and in my prayers and in my heart I participate in the trials through which—once again—my motherland and my compatriots are living. . . . News on this theme does not leave the front pages of the press and television and radio programs. . . . I pray that the Polish Episcopate, with the Primate at its head, may also this time help our nation in the hard struggle for daily bread, social justice and the assur-

ance of the inviolability of its rights to its own life and development.

Late in August, John Paul II wrote a private letter to Brezhnev, the first of at least two such missives, assuring him that the unrest in Poland was no threat to the Soviet Union. The letter was hand-carried to Moscow by Monsignor Hilary C. Franco, an American who is a senior official of the Congregation for the Clergy, as were other items of secret correspondence between the Vatican and the Soviets. Monsignor Franco will not specifically confirm that he had carried letters from the pope to Brezhnev and that on each occasion had to wait a number of days for replies, but he acknowledges being in Moscow in August 1980, "jogging along the Kremlin" to while away the time.

For its part, the United States wanted John Paul II to know that it shared his concerns about Poland—he was obviously an engaged party—and President Carter wrote him a private letter to that effect.

In Warsaw, Gierek, looking for understanding and support, turned to Wyszyński. Late in August, they held a four-hour conference at night at Gierek's villa outside Warsaw. This is how Gierek recalls the occasion:

> Toward the end of the second week of the strikes on the coast, I decided to secure the help of the Church in order to avoid a conflict. . . . I recognized that in order to reach an agreement with the strikers, the help of the Church was necessary because, in my opinion, to continue leaving it [the Church] on the sidelines threatened incalculable consequences for the country. . . . I informed [the primate] that heavy pressure is being placed on us and on me personally, but that I had no intention of capitulating . . . and as long as I keep my post, I shall not allow the use of force against the workers on the Coast.

Gierek believes that as a result of their conversation, Wyszyński "took our side" in a sermon delivered at the shrine of the Black Madonna in Częstochowa on August 26, the day of her feast. The primate called for "national and civic maturity," urged Poles to return to work although there were faults on both sides, and warned that protracted strikes menaced the future of the nation. Like Gierek, the strikers—and public opinion—interpreted the sermon as advice to the coast workers to end the strikes on what essentially would be the regime's terms. Many Poles bitterly concluded that once more the elderly primate was making concessions to the regime at the expense of the people to assure social peace at all costs and, with it, more privileges for the Polish Church.

Wyszyński and the episcopate responded by insisting that the meaning of his sermon had been "twisted" by Polish television through the broadcast of only selected parts of the text. They said they had done no more than to urge the pilgrims at the shrine to resume normal work after the ceremony. Striving to limit the damage, the episcopate's Steering Committee issued a communiqué asserting that the freedom to form independent labor unions was a precondition of social peace. But Wyszyński had lost personal credibility with many of his fellow Catholics.

John Paul II was appalled by the primate's performance. A report on the sermon had been given to him at his Castel Gandolfo residence the next morning, and the pope reacted with immense anger. When the topic came up a few days later at breakfast with two visiting Polish priests, both personal friends, Wojtyła exclaimed, with deep pain reflected in his face: "Oh, this old man. . . . This old man!"

The pope, who himself preferred negotiation to confrontation whenever possible, is said to have remarked that Wyszyński did not understand the situation that had developed in Poland, that as "an old man" he no longer had "a sense of orientation" about the events.

Though the Warsaw government and the strikers' leadership finally signed an agreement in Gdańsk on August 31, recognizing the principle of free labor unions, John Paul II remained silent to avoid complicating further a situation that was still fraught with great danger. (Wałęsa signed the accord for Solidarity with a huge felt-tip pen with an image of the pope on it.) On September 5, the party's Central Committee fired Gierek as first secretary—presumably because it needed a scapegoat after giving in to the strikers on the question of free unions—and named Stanisław Kania, the Politburo member in charge of security, in his place. Gierek did not attend the session because of what he described as a worsening heart condition.

During the rest of autumn, the regime and Solidarity went on negotiating the next step in the ever-quickening evolution in Polish life—the granting to Solidarity of an official status as an independent labor union. It was a tough negotiation, with Moscow leaning heavily on Kania and the party leadership to resist Solidarity. And, again, the authorities needed support from the Church. At their request, the Joint Government-Church Commission met on September 24, for the first time in more than a decade. On October 11, Kania and Wyszyński discussed the Polish situation, and three days later the primate flew to Rome to review the state of affairs with John Paul II.

The primate stayed in Rome for over two weeks as the negotiations at home entered a critical phase, and, as some in the Polish episcopate believed, it was preferable for Wyszyński to be absent from the scene during that period. John Paul II thought that it was extremely important for the Church to present an absolutely clear position concerning all these events. Bishop Bronisław Dąbrowski was given the authority to speak for the Church in the primate's absence.

When the Supreme Court in Warsaw granted Solidarity its official registration on November 10, the pope took it upon himself to be the spokesman. The registration was an act of extraordinary importance because for the first time ever a communist regime had abandoned its monopoly of control over the working class. It clearly opened the way to even more basic political changes.

Addressing Polish pilgrims at the end of his weekly General Audience at the Paul VI Auditorium in the Vatican on November 12, John Paul II said he wished "to express my joy over what has been accomplished in our motherland in recent days, over this wise and mature understanding reached between the authorities and the new independent professional unions, which are starting their activities based on the registration of their statutes." He said that he wished to send "blessings from all my heart" to the new unions, "which bring together such an enormous number of my compatriots, people of physical as well as intellectual occupations."

Thinking in terms of the future, John Paul II then offered this evenhanded comment, for the benefit of both sides: "I hope at the same time, that the maturity that over the past months has characterized the behavior of our compatriots, the society as well as the authorities, will continue to prevail." The pope had become convinced that a long process of fundamental political transition had begun, but that it could be achieved only through the cooperation of all the forces in the nation. In the meantime, he felt relaxed enough about Poland to leave for West Germany on a five-day trip on November 15.

The Kremlin, on the other hand, felt less than pure joy about the new Polish agreement. Starting late in November, photography by U.S. satellites disclosed menacing movements by Soviet combat units toward Polish frontiers. Great concern developed in the West over the danger of a military intervention to smash the Solidarity experiment.

By December 1, the Soviet deployments became ominous. East Germany sealed the Polish border. Poland was now confronted by Soviet armor and mechanized divisions massed in western Ukraine, East Germany, and Czechoslovakia. Remembering the Soviet invasion of Czechoslovakia in 1968, the United States and its NATO allies feared the worst. Accordingly, they launched a diplomatic and propaganda campaign designed to dissuade Brezhnev from an act of folly. The presumption in the West (as well as inside Poland) was that Poles, unlike Czechoslovaks twelve years earlier, would fight the invaders, and that a wider war might ensue. The Soviet ambassador in Washington, Anatoli Dobrynin, was summoned by Secretary of State Edmund Muskie to be warned of (unspecified) consequences of a Soviet invasion. President Carter sent a private warning to Brezhnev, and West European governments bombarded Moscow with similar messages.

John Paul II and the Holy See kept quiet in public because of the pope's judgment that any comment on their part in a situation of such extreme sensitivity might polarize it even further. But emissaries traveled discreetly between the

Vatican and Moscow, delivering private letters. On December 15, after the tension had abated, Vadim Zagladin, a ranking member of the Secretariat of the Central Committee of the Soviet Communist Party, met with John Paul II for a very private discussion on Polish affairs. Reports circulated subsequently that the pope told Zagladin that he would have rushed to Poland to be with his people in the event of an invasion, but John Paul II has denied these.

It may never be known whether the Soviets had really planned to invade or whether their ostentatious show of force was designed to scare both Solidarity and the Warsaw regime into halting the "counterrevolution." Zbigniew Brzeziński, who was Carter's national security adviser, wrote later that the Soviets drew back at the last moment because of the U.S. pressure, but he may have overstated the importance of the American role. For one thing, Washington had already applied economic sanctions against the Soviet Union for the previous year's invasion of Afghanistan, so short of the unlikely option of a military response, the United States did not have much leverage.

Communist analysts believe that, as much as anything else, Soviet military failures in Afghanistan had persuaded Brezhnev that he did not need a simultaneous second war on his hands. Mieczysław Rakowski, the last communist prime minister, has written that "though I have no foundations for questioning [Brzeziński's] activities in this affair, it should be mentioned, to respect historical truth, that [Party First Secretary] Kania held a fundamental and dramatic conversation with Brezhnev [on December 5], which had a decisive influence on the leadership of the Soviet Communist Party in abandoning the plans, which had been loudly disseminated around the world."

Kania had flown to Moscow after presiding over an emergency session of the Polish party's Central Committee on December 2 and 3, which produced an appeal and a warning to the nation that "the fate of our motherland . . . is in the balance. The persistent unrest is pushing our nation to the brink of economic and moral annihilation."

The appeal had a cooling effect, and on December 5, just as Kania and Brezhnev were meeting in Moscow, Solidarity announced that there was not a single strike underway anywhere in Poland. The following day, Brezhnev chaired a hastily called Warsaw Pact summit conference, with Kania present, and the danger of an invasion was dissipated, at least for the time being. Brezhnev left on a scheduled visit to India on December 8 (on December 7, not realizing that the crisis had ended, National Security Adviser Brzeziński had telephoned the pope at the Vatican to inform him that the invasion was still imminent).

In Poland, the three principal political forces—the regime, the Church, and Solidarity (now accepted as a virtual partner)—joined in efforts to restore social peace. With John Paul II's approval, the Polish episcopate issued a pastoral letter on December 14 titled "Polish Bishops Ask for Christian Responsibility in the Homeland." This time, the Holy See had made sure that the episcopate did not go overboard in supporting the regime as Wyszyński had done on August 26.

On December 16, Church, Solidarity, and government officials gathered in front of the great cross at the Lenin Shipyard in Gdańsk to commemorate the victims of the 1970 clashes between the security forces and rioting workers. Kania had said earlier in his Central Committee speech that these events were a memory "which does not divide but unites."

The first great chapter in the Polish crisis of the 1980s was now closed.

On November 30, John Paul II issued his second encyclical, aptly named *Dives in misericordia* (Mercy's Wealth). On December 30, he published a pastoral letter, *Egregiae Virtutis* (Of Outstanding Virtue), devoted to St. Cyril and St. Methodius, the Christian missionaries known as the "Patrons of Europe." Then he began working on his Japanese pronunciation in preparation for his forthcoming trip to Japan and the Philippines; he was determined to deliver at least a few speeches in Japanese.

The new year—1981—started for John Paul II with a visit by a Solidarity delegation led by Lech Wałęsa that arrived on January 13. They met twice.

"The son went to see his father," Wałęsa said when the pope received him in the late morning of January 15. They spent a few minutes alone in the papal private study, then were joined by Wałęsa's wife, Danuta, and the other thirteen members of the Solidarity delegation. It included Father Jankowski, who had celebrated Mass in the shipyard during the strike, Tadeusz Mazowiecki, the erstwhile leftist Catholic intellectual who was a Solidarity adviser during the Gdańsk negotiations, and Anna Walentynowicz, the crane operator whose firing had precipitated the strike.

It was a happy occasion for John Paul II, who appeared as a Polish patriot, head of the Church, and a fervent advocate of free labor unions. Over thirty years earlier, he had written ecstatically about French unions and worker-priests in the first article he had ever published, and now he treated the Solidarity delegation and the press gathered in Consistory Hall to a lengthy treatise on the rights of workers.

He urged Solidarity to practice "social morality" in the dealings between workers and employers—a constant theme in the pope's approach to questions of labor—but, still conciliatory toward the authorities in Poland, he stressed that there should be "no contradiction between this kind of self-governing social initiative of the working people and the structure of a system that considers human labor as a fundamental value in social and national life."

John Paul II also desired to explain publicly to the Soviets, without naming them, that the rise of Solidarity was a "strictly internal affair of all the Poles." He said that the efforts "of the autumn weeks were not directed against anyone" and that "every society, every nation has the right to undertake such efforts. . . . We know that over the centuries, Poles were deprived many times of this right by force. . . . It is in the interest of peace and international order that Poland enjoy this right fully."

This was his signal to all concerned that he had every intention of remaining engaged in the cause of Polish freedom as a new era seemed to dawn. And three days later, John Paul II emphasized his devotion to this cause as he invited Wałęsa and his companions to the seven o'clock Mass in his private chapel and breakfast in his private dining room.

In Poland, General Jaruzelski was named prime minister on February 9, appointing Rakowski, the reform-minded party magazine editor, as deputy prime minister and putting him in charge of negotiations with Wałęsa and Solidarity about further changes in the functioning of labor unions. Among contentious issues was the demand for legal status for Rural Solidarity, a free union of farmworkers.

Simultaneously, the Joint Government-Church Commission embarked on what would be nine years of continued negotiations over every aspect of religious and political life in the country, including future visits by John Paul II.

And on February 23, the pope dispatched another private letter to Brezhnev, also hand-carried by Monsignor Franco, admonishing him about respecting the sovereignty of Poland and the rights of Solidarity.

The Church had become a full-fledged player in the shaping of Polish politics and history.

John Paul II spent the second half of February 1981 traveling to the Philippines and Japan, both visits evoking the terrible events of World War II in which the two countries were mortal enemies. The predominantly Roman Catholic Philippines, occupied by the Japanese during the war, was now experiencing an unending leftist rebellion and the surge of an Islamic movement.

In Japan, the pope chose to visit Hiroshima and Nagasaki, the targets of American atomic bombs in 1945, in addition to Tokyo, and he made a deep impression on his mainly non-Christian audiences. Father Pittau, the Magnificent Rector of Rome's Gregorian University, who accompanied John Paul II on the Japanese tour, recalls the pope's appearance in Hiroshima:

> It was one of the most beautiful and moving speeches. He approached it in terms of a prayer: "Lord, hear me! It is the voice of the mothers who have lost their children. It is the voice of the children who have lost their mothers and their fathers. . . . Never again Hiroshima! Never again Oświęcim!" He pronounced a part of it in Japanese, and I could see people crying. . . . And when he saw the Museum of the Atomic Bomb in Hiroshima, he was really moved. You could see in his face this kind of sorrow.

John Paul II, Father Pittau says, spoke in Japanese from a text

> written in our alphabet, but in Japanese, with all the accents. He practiced it with a Japanese priest. And under the Japanese text he would have the translation into Italian or English so that he understood what he was saying. . . . The Japanese could understand him. And the people saw his respect for the Japanese culture. . . . In Tokyo, a policeman told me, "I have been in the service for security of so many important people, but this is the first time that I see a very important man who understands and respects our culture and uses our language!"

Departing Japan, the pope left behind one set of horrors. Returning to the Vatican, he soon encountered horror of another kind.

CHAPTER 24

The horror was the pistol shot fired at John Paul II from less than twenty feet in St. Peter's Square on the afternoon of Wednesday, May 13, 1981, in an assassination attempt by a Turkish terrorist.

The bullet from the powerful 9mm Browning Parabellum penetrated his abdomen, shattering the colon and the small intestine, and went through the sacral vein system. Miraculously, in the words of attending surgeons, the projectile passed a few millimeters from the central aorta. Had it hit the aorta, John Paul II would have died instantly. The bullet missed other vital organs, such as the iliac artery and the ureter, and even nerve centers near them went untouched.

Still, it was touch-and-go during the five hours and twenty minutes of surgery at the Agostino Gemelli Polyclinic, twelve minutes by screaming ambulance from the Vatican. The pope was rushed there from St. Peter's Square within minutes of being struck by one of the two bullets fired by Mehmet Ali Agca in the midst of twenty thousand pilgrims and tourists at the weekly General Audience (the second bullet missed the pontiff altogether). John Paul II had been standing in his open jeep, and Agca had to fire at an upward angle from the pavement.

John Paul II lost consciousness as he reached the hospital, and Monsignor Dziwisz, his private secretary, who was with him during the attack, decided to administer the sacraments of Extreme Unction before the surgery began. When Dr. Francesco Crucitti, the chief surgeon, opened the abdomen, he found it filled with blood, some six pints of it. The sacral system was pouring out blood, the pope's pressure was down to 70 and falling, the pulse had nearly vanished, and Dr. Crucitti realized that his patient had already lost three quarters of his blood.

Stanching the hemorrhage and starting a massive transfusion, he discovered deep lacerations in the colon; it had to be sewn up and twenty-two inches of intestine had to be cut away. Finally, the doctors had to treat the injury to the pope's right shoulder and a finger of his left hand caused by the bullet as it exited his body (two American women tourists standing nearby were badly wounded by the same bullet). And a tooth had been broken during anesthesia.

Monsignor Dziwisz remembered that John Paul II, in great pain after being shot, whispered a short prayer in Polish, "Mary, my mother . . . !" before losing consciousness. He said that the pope later told him that while still conscious, he was certain that his wounds were not fatal and that he would survive. And just a month after the shooting, John Paul II received at his Vatican apartments a Rural Solidarity delegation from Poland, encouraging the farmers in their free trade union struggle and blessing their loaves of bread. His robust constitution and his excellent physical condition helped to speed his recovery.

At his first public appearance in St. Peter's Square after four months of convalescence, John Paul II explained to the crowd of pilgrims that the assassination attempt had been a "divine test" for which he was grateful to God. In his own mystical way, the pope said that "during the last months God permitted me to experience suffering, and the danger of losing my life. He also allowed me to understand clearly . . . that this was one of his special graces for me as a man and at the same time . . . for the Church."

His suffering included a return to the hospital late in June for the treatment of a dangerous cytomegalovirus infection—most likely transmitted with blood during the emergency transfusion—and a second surgical intervention. It was necessary to reverse the colostomy performed as part of the original surgery so that the pope could resume his natural gastric functions. The doctors had wanted to delay the second operation well into August, fearing a cytomegalovirus relapse if done prematurely, but John Paul II insisted on August 5, the Feast of Our Lady of the Snows, in order to be back at the Vatican on August 15, the very important Feast of the Assumption.

The pope had his way, the stitches were taken out on August 13, and he went home the next day. After Assumption, he flew by helicopter to the Castel Gandolfo summer residence to convalesce.

A man who wrote 462 speeches in his first 257 days of papacy (then he slowed down a bit), John Paul II could not stand idleness, even in the hospital with his insides ruptured, and he wasted no time. He met daily with Secretary of State Casaroli to discuss and decide a multitude of matters, worked on the galleys of the *Laborem exercens* encyclical (which would be published on September 14), celebrated Mass in his room, and taped messages to the faithful to be played in St. Peter's Square, starting with the first one on May 18, the fifth day after the shooting and his sixty-first birthday.

In it, John Paul II said: "I am praying for the brother who wounded me and whom I sincerely forgive."

The pope's health was soon fully back to normal, but the assassination attempt raised a host of canon law, spiritual, political, police, and intelligence questions that have never been adequately answered. As usual with Karol Wojtyła, there was a touch of the mystical and extraterrestrial about events involving him. And this time, his suffering was moral and emotional as well as physical.

The day after John Paul II was shot in Rome, a medical communiqué in Warsaw announced that Primate Wyszyński was dying of stomach and lymphatic cancer. The two men had had deep if well-concealed differences, but they also had very much in common concerning their country and their Church, and the pope, ever loyal to him, felt a sentimental attachment to Wyszyński. To millions of Poles, of course, the virtually simultaneous news about both their principal religious leaders being on the brink of death was devastating, and millions prayed across the land.

John Paul II was informed of Wyszyński's condition as he began his own recovery, and on May 24, he telephoned from his bedside to the primate's residence in Warsaw. However, the telephone cord did not reach Wyszyński's bed, and the pope had to give up the call. When the cord was lengthened the following day, Wojtyła repeated the call and they had a brief farewell conversation, bed to bed.

Primate Wyszyński died on May 28, two months short of his eightieth birthday. In Rome, Polish Cardinal Władysław Rubin and 101 priests con-celebrated Mass in his memory at Santa Maria in Trastevere, Wyszyński's titular bishop's church, where Cardinal Hozjusz, who could have been the first Polish pope centuries ago, is buried.

And there was bad news on another front. While John Paul II lay in the hospital, Italian voters chose overwhelmingly in a referendum to maintain the legality of abortion. On an issue of fundamental importance to him—an issue he addressed heatedly for months as Primate of the Italian Church—only 32 percent of the predominantly Catholic voters cast their ballots against abortion. It was not a reflection on the pope personally, but he was enormously disappointed. He always has had difficulty in accepting societal realities freely expressed.

Never mentioned publicly in the aftermath of the assassination attempt—and during John Paul II's entire recovery—was the matter of governance of the Holy See and the Church worldwide in the event of a prolonged or permanent incapacitation of a pope. Provisions exist under canon law for temporary governance by the camerlengo and the General Congregation for the College of Cardinals between the death of a pope and the election of his successor—a finite period—but none if a pontiff becomes ill, physically or mentally, and remains indefinitely in such condition.

In John Paul II's case in 1981, the question was irrelevant because his recovery was so swift in terms of his ability to function and govern even from his hospital bed. In fact, the Vatican was anxious to show to the world that, despite his wounds, the pope was, relatively speaking, in good shape.

Thus on his birthday, five days after the shooting, Arturo Mari, the Vatican's official photographer, was allowed to take a picture of John Paul II in bed, his face wan, bandages on his shoulder and hand, a bottle of mineral water on the bedside table. That evening, Italian television broadcast the photograph, showing that the pope was recuperating well. This was a first, and what had clearly prevailed was Wojtyła's excellent sense of public relations.

Still, the 1981 experience failed to suggest to the Curia—or to John Paul II himself—that canon law ought to be amended to allow for a situation in which the pope's recovery is unexpectedly slow or he has been incapacitated. This *could* have been the case with Wojtyła, given the gravity of his wounds. But nothing has been done about it even though a new code of the canon law was personally reviewed and approved by John Paul II in 1983, just two years after his skirmish with death. In fact, at this writing nobody knows how and by whom papal incapacitation may be defined.

Political terrorism was rampant in the world when John Paul II became its victim on that sunny May afternoon in 1981. It was sweeping Western Europe (Italy's Prime Minister Aldo Moro had been kidnapped and murdered in Rome in 1978 by the Red Army Brigade), the Middle East, Asia, and Latin America. The United States had experienced the political assassinations of John and Robert Kennedy and the Reverend Martin Luther King, Jr., and President Gerald Ford was attacked twice. President Reagan was shot and seriously wounded in Washington, D.C., two months before the pope by an insane youth with no political motives. But no Roman Catholic pontiff had been murdered in many centuries, and the two attempts to harm Paul VI were committed by nonpolitical, demented individuals.

On February 16, 1981, a grenade had exploded at a sports stadium in Karachi, Pakistan, where John Paul II was about to arrive to celebrate Mass. He had stopped in Karachi en route home from Japan. A man was killed in the explosion, but there was nothing to indicate that the pope had been the intended target.

Coincidentally or not, John Paul II addressed himself to the perils of terrorism a week before the attempt on his life.

On May 6, not quite three months after the Karachi incident, the pope greeted a new contingent of Swiss Guards with these words: "We pray to the Lord that violence and fanaticism may be kept far from the walls of the Vatican."

The twenty-three-year-old Mehmet Ali Agca became the unquestioned symbol of violence and fanaticism in the Vatican the moment he fired his heavy pistol at the smiling figure in white robes blessing the pilgrims from his "Popemobile" open jeep in St. Peter's Square during the Wednesday afternoon General Audience on May 13. What remains in question fourteen years later, however, is *who* is Agca and *why* did he try to murder John Paul II?

In many ways it is a mystery comparable to that of John Kennedy's assassination, both in the wealth of theories and in the absence of wholly convincing answers. John Paul II, for one, has chosen not to search for them, accepting the events as divine will and having forgiven Agca both in his first public statement three days after the shooting and then personally when he visited the Turk in his Rome prison cell at Christmas two years later.

Yet, the circumstances surrounding the shooting are so extraordinary and the role and behavior of governments and intelligence services so strange—even after so many years—that these events form part of contemporary history.

One must begin with Agca himself. Born in a village of eastern Turkey, Agca has been described in all the subsequent police reports as "intelligent and lucid," though he would become irrational in prison. Since his youth, he was linked with the "Turkish Mafia," engaging in the smuggling of arms, drugs, and cigarettes to and from neighboring Bulgaria, earning "lucrative sums." Agca's other connection was with the Gray Wolves, the military wing of the National Action Party and the leading extreme rightist terrorist organization in terror-ridden Turkey. He was said to have been professionally "trained" in Syria as a terrorist, although Syrian camps usually trained Middle Eastern leftists.

On February 1, 1979, Agça participated with others in the

murder of Abdi Ipekci, the liberal editor of the most important Istanbul newspaper, *Milliyet*. He was arrested in June but escaped from the Kartal-Maltepe military prison on November 25, supposedly with "outside help." The next day, Agca sent *Milliyet* the following letter:

> Western imperialists, fearful that Turkey and her sister Islamic nations might become a political, military, and economic power in the Middle East, are sending to Turkey in this delicate moment the Commander of the Crusades, John Paul, disguised as a religious chief. If this visit . . . is not canceled, I will without doubt kill the Pope-Chief. This is the sole motive for my escape from prison. . . .

John Paul II arrived in Turkey on November 28, three days after Agca's escape, but there was no attempt of any kind on his life. Agca's announcement of his plan to kill the pope was as bizarre as everything else related to his activities then and afterward. If, as Agca claimed, he was a right-wing Gray Wolves member (which Italian investigators subsequently accepted), he would be unlikely to denounce "Western imperialists" and call the pope "their chief." It is a matter of political jargon. Agca's explanation to the Italians after shooting John Paul II that the Istanbul letter had been intended to distract the Turkish police from hunting for him after his escape from prison the previous November was not plausible. The Turkish authorities would have concentrated all their resources on protecting the pope during his three days in the country regardless of Agca's threat; he was less important for the moment.

If Agca had shot John Paul II in the service of the Soviet and Bulgarian secret services—as he later claimed along with a great many other contradictory things—to paralyze the rise of the pope-blessed Solidarity movement in Poland, then his original threat made absolutely no sense. John Paul II was in Turkey in November 1979, but Solidarity was not born until August of the following year. But, as in most cases of political assassinations (or assassination attempts), this sort of "evidence" tends to be manipulated by all interested parties to suit their purposes. Agca's own past therefore clarifies nothing about the motives for his 1981 act of violence.

Eighteen months elapsed between Agca's Istanbul threat and his actual attack on John Paul II in the Vatican. According to Italian government investigators, he had gone to Sofia, Bulgaria, in July 1980, where he was reportedly put in touch with agents of the Durzhavna Sigurnost, the Bulgarian secret service. They were said to have hired Agca to assassinate the pope in the spring of 1981, to do away with Solidarity. He was to be paid $400,000.

Again, however, the dates do not jibe with reality. At the time of the alleged plotting between the Bulgarians and Agca—at the end of July 1980—Solidarity did not yet exist. The Gdańsk strikes erupted in mid-August, followed by the emergence of the name "Solidarity," and the signing of the pact with the government on August 31.

Agca used the next nine months traveling around Western Europe, spending much time in Rome, and visiting Zurich, Vienna, Palma de Mallorca, and finally Milan, where the Browning pistol was delivered to him by a "Gray Wolf" agent. He obviously had plenty of money at his disposal. Agca was back in Rome on May 10, 1981. During the afternoon on May 13, before the weekly General Audience began, Agca, two Turks, and two Bulgarians drove to the Vatican area, according to the Italian authorities' report, to check on St. Peter's Square's crowd-distribution arrangements. Agca was unfamiliar with it.

Agca and his closest Turkish friend, Oral Celik, remained there, awaiting the start of the General Audience at 5:00 P.M. (nowadays General Audiences are held in the morning to save on overtime to Vatican employees and the police, who have to be paid when they run late in the afternoon).

Agca fired at John Paul II at 5:17 P.M. as the white jeep passed slowly among rows of pilgrims. This was almost to the minute the time of day of the pope's 1978 election.

The Turk tried to flee but was grabbed by a Franciscan nun who was standing nearby, and he was wrestled down to the ground by the crowd and turned over to the police. Italian investigators assert that Bulgarian agents had arranged to drive Agca away from the area of the square, then smuggle him out of Italy in a truck with diplomatic seals, but his instant capture had made it impossible. Likewise, Agca's associates, if indeed he had any, could not kill him to keep him silent.

Agca confessed to the crime immediately and was sentenced to life in prison on July 22, at the end of a three-day trial.

But this was not the end of the story. Agca embarked on a new series of confessions in May 1982, implicating by name Bulgarian and Turkish confederates after insisting at first that he had acted alone. He also told the Italians of a plot to murder Lech Wałęsa, who came to Rome the third week of January 1981 to be received twice by John Paul II. The Polish leader was to be killed with a car bomb at his hotel, but Agca explained that the plan was abandoned because there were too many police there.

Investigations and trials related to the papal assassination attempt went on for years without producing convincing conclusions concerning suspected conspiracies by Soviet and Bulgarian security services or explaining Agca's motives beyond any doubt. Neither did documents obtained in the 1990s, after the fall of the communist regimes, from the secret archives of the Soviet and Bulgarian intelligence agencies. And as late as 1992, a new study by the Central Intelligence Agency confessed the CIA's inability a decade after the fact to come up with satisfactory answers. It also confessed that the agency had been deeply split over the available "evidence."

In retrospect, it appears that all the major intelligence agencies behaved in the strangest of ways from the moment John Paul II was shot and nearly killed by Mehmet Ali Agca. And other strange things kept happening throughout the 1980s in the context of the assassination attempt.

KGB headquarters in Moscow was alerted to the political repercussions of the shooting in a top secret cable from its Rome station sent that same evening. According to documents released in 1992 by the new Russian government, the cable said: "John Paul II was wounded by an unknown assailant. The crime was perpetrated while the Pope was driving through a crowd of the faithful in an open automobile. . . . Early reports connect this attempt on the life of John Paul II with the complex political situation in the country [Poland]."

The wording of the cable suggests that either the KGB Rome station was not informed about the anti-pope plot, which is entirely possible in the compartmentalization of intelligence work, or that the Soviets really had nothing to do with it, which is also possible (as the CIA would point out later). In any event, the cable adds nothing to the knowledge about the assassination attempt.

U.S. intelligence agencies responded slowly—and disconcertingly—to the May 13 event. It took the National Security Agency (NSA), the most secret of all U.S. agencies, at least four days to make the association between the attempt on John Paul II and the fact that coded cable traffic between the Bulgarian embassy in Rome and the Sofia headquarters of the Durzhavana Sigurnost had accelerated markedly during March and April.

The NSA's function is to intercept open and coded radio, telephone, microwave, and telex traffic of friend and foe around the world—known as SIGINT (Signal Intelligence)—and in this instance it involved routine monitoring of the Rome-Sofia intelligence flow. The NSA, which is very accomplished in cracking codes, tried during those days to pick up all communications between communist countries' embassies abroad and their home offices.

Normally, the eavesdropping is conducted automatically, but when the NSA finally realized that a connection might exist between the pope's shooting and the traffic of the Bulgarian embassy in Rome, it began a massive computer retrieval operation. Studying the decoded cables, the NSA came upon references to names, "teams," a "safe house," "points of entry," passports and other travel documents, money transfer routings, and the mention of a car "ten minutes away." But it also discovered that the Bulgarian traffic had abated greatly during the first two weeks in May, the period before the assassination attempt. After the shooting, cables from Sofia inquired about the "exfiltration of the team."

It is not known what, if anything, NSA headquarters at

Fort Meade, Maryland, just outside of Washington, made of this jumble of intercepts, and, more to the point, whether it shared its information with the CIA and other U.S. government agencies. No account of the NSA intercepts of the Bulgarian traffic has ever been made public before, and declassified CIA internal documents on the assassination attempt suggest that the agency was not even aware of any "Bulgarian Connection" until November 1982, when Agca began openly linking the Bulgarians to the attempt.

The first full-fledged internal CIA study of the 1981 Vatican events—"A Review of the Record"—was not produced until May 1983 because other agency priorities had pushed it to the back burner. That study showed "a tendency to cast doubt on Bulgarian complicity." A new study, titled "Agca's Attempt to Kill the Pope: The Case for Soviet Involvement," was issued only in April 1985 after CIA Director William Casey had expressed his personal conviction that Agca was a killer employed by the Bulgarians at the behest of the KGB. But this review likewise failed to provide hard conclusions that Moscow was behind the assassination attempt.

Testifying before the Senate Select Committee on Intelligence in September 1991, Robert Gates, former CIA deputy director and a leading Soviet specialist, acknowledged that "particularly in the first several years after the attempted assassination, CIA moved very awkwardly and slowly in trying to deal with the problem." He added that "it is fair to say that at least at the outset" the CIA had been moving so slowly because of "a mindset that accepted the idea that a lone gunman was responsible."

In fact, the first internal CIA reference to the shooting in St. Peter's Square was circulated only five days after the event. It said: "Turk who tried to assassinate the Pope has told the Italian police very little . . . no information from him or other sources on his organizational ties . . . press allegations of links with far-right Turkish groups still unconfirmed."

But the most interesting reason for the CIA's top analysts (including Gates) to reject the Italian authorities' scenario that the Soviets had ordered the Bulgarians to kill John Paul

II to smash Solidarity in Poland was that they were convinced that Moscow had "no incentive" whatsoever to do it.

The Senate Intelligence Committee stated on October 24, 1991, in its report on the Gates hearing on his nomination to be CIA director—which was the occasion for his testimony on the subject, among others—that "the attack was unanticipated by the Intelligence Committee although analysts, as early as 1978, had foreseen the problems that a Polish Pope might have for the U.S.S.R. However, by 1981, analysts had become convinced that Moscow had a working arrangement with the Pope to moderate Polish unrest in return for Soviet promises of non-intervention. The general view was that the Soviets would have little incentive to destroy this relationship."

A "Note" to the CIA deputy director for intelligence from the agency's Papal Task Force on July 12, 1985, reported that "after the assassination attempt, analysts tended to conclude that John Paul II's role as an aggravating force in the Polish crisis was outweighed by his moderating role and that Moscow had little to gain from removing him, particularly given the risk of detection. . . . Killing the Pope would not have solved Moscow's Polish problem but could instead have exacerbated it by causing further unrest."

This was an exceedingly perspicacious and sophisticated assessment, and, as it turned out, a correct one. John Paul II's private contacts with the Soviets since the December 1980 visit to him by Vadim Zagladin, the high official of the Soviet Communist Party's Central Committee, and the letters between the Vatican and Moscow secretly carried by Monsignor Hilary Franco early in 1981, had indeed given the Kremlin the sense that he was striving for moderate evolution—and not confrontation—in Poland.

As for the Reagan administration, it too behaved most cautiously in this area although the president was still referring to the Soviet Union as the "Evil Empire." In the absence of ascertainable facts, the administration pointedly refrained from accusations against Moscow concerning any involvement in the attack on the pope. It was aware that unfounded accusations might preclude for a very long time negotiations with the Soviet Union on disarmament or any other topic in which the United States had an active interest.

The Warsaw regime, for its part, displayed concern over the health of both John Paul II and Primate Wyszyński. When the Joint Government-Church Commission met on May 15, two days after the Vatican shooting, Deputy Prime Minister Kazimierz Barcikowski opened the session with the remark that "the month of May has begun badly for Poland." Bishop Dąbrowski nodded and told him that the pope's first question concerned Poland: "How is the Primate? What is happening in Poland?"

In June 1984 the Italian state prosecutor had formally charged three Bulgarian officials and five Turks—in addition to Agca—with conspiracy to assassinate John Paul II. But on March 30, 1986, a Rome court acquitted the eight men because it said it lacked sufficient firm evidence to convict them. Agca had already been serving his life prison term for nearly five years. In court to testify against the men, he insisted that he was Jesus Christ.

Still, the case was not closed. The eight men were acquitted "for lack of proof," but the court chose not to declare them innocent, an acceptable procedure under Italian law. *La Civilitá Cattolica,* the authoritative Jesuit journal whose articles are reviewed before publication by the Vatican's Secretariat of State, published an editorial in June 1986 that the acquittal was a "disconcerting sentence" and that it appeared that the attack on John Paul II was the result of "an international plot" that could not be proved.

A retired senior American official, fully familiar with all the CIA investigations on the subject, concurs with the view that neither Brezhnev nor KGB Chairman Andropov would have ordered the pope's assassination because it would have boomeranged against the Soviets in the form of a popular explosion in Poland. He finds it plausible, however, that the Bulgarian secret police may have set a conspiracy in motion out of overzealousness and a desire to please the Kremlin.

Given the recent discovery of the Soviet Communist Party Central Committee Secretariat's secret 1979 "Decision" to launch a campaign against the Polish pope, it is entirely possible that top Bulgarian officials had interpreted it as a license to kill him, and proceeded accordingly. On Politburo orders, the key parts of the "Decision" were communicated to communist parties in Eastern Europe so that they could act to implement some of the proposed anti-Wojtyła measures. But in the end, the shooting in St. Peter's Square may remain a mystery forever—at least publicly.

John Paul II is not disturbed by this possibility. Nobody knows, of course, what (if anything) Agca had revealed when the pope visited him in his cell in Rome's Rebibbia Prison on December 23, 1983. His intent was to offer the Turk his forgiveness personally, but the two men spent twenty minutes conversing intensely as they sat in chairs facing each other, often whispering into each other's ears. They spoke in Italian, which Agca had learned in prison. Agca kissed John Paul II's hand when he entered and when he left the cell, and then the pope took Agca's hands in his several times. In 1987, the pope received Agca's mother, Muzeyen Agca, in audience.

The heavily bearded Agca, who frequently grants prison interviews to newspapers, has said that "the pope knows everything." Archbishop Mario Rizzi, the papal nuncio in Sofia, told journalists in November 1992 that John Paul II "certainly knows the whole truth though I believe that he is not anxious to throw light on that entire background. John Paul II is convinced that his life was saved miraculously. . . ."

More specifically, the pope believes that his life was saved, as "a real miracle," by the Virgin of Fátima, whose feast day is on May 13, the date of the assassination attempt. Her shrine in Portugal, north of Lisbon, is one of the holiest in the world, and her fame is traced back to that day in 1917 when the Virgin appeared on the first of six occasions to three shepherd children. She is said to have made three prophecies, two of which have come true: that Russia would be "reconverted" after spreading "errors" in the world, and that two of the three shepherds would die young. The third prophecy is a terrible secret, which, it is said, popes may know—or not.

John Paul II went to Fátima on the first anniversary of Agca's attack to thank the Virgin for saving him and to place the bullet that had struck him on her altar. It was later fitted alongside diamonds in the golden crown worn by the statue of the Virgin, who is formally known as Our Lady of the Rosary. The bullet-pierced and bloodstained sash the pope had on when he was shot has been sent to the Black Madonna in Częstochowa.

In Fátima, John Paul II met Lúcia de Jesus dos Santos, the seventy-five-year-old Carmelite nun who was the survivor among the shepherd children. The others, Francisco Marto and his sister Jacinta, died in 1919 and 1920, respectively. And while at the sanctuary, John Paul II was saved again: Juan Fernández Khron, a thirty-three-year-old Spanish priest, lunged at him with a large knife but was seized in time by security personnel.

Returning to Fátima on the tenth anniversary of the assassination attempt, the pope thanked the Virgin "for the unexpected changes that restored confidence to nations that had long been oppressed and humiliated." That was the fulfillment of the second prophecy, he said. But John Paul II warned on that 1991 visit that after the collapse of communism, Europe seemed "tempted by a vast, theoretical and practical, atheistic movement that appears to seek a new materialistic civilization." It was in Fátima that he first so fully expressed his somber vision about the world's post-communist future, a message of pessimism that he now constantly voices.

In his prison cell, meanwhile, Agca has developed both an obsession with and fear of the Virgin of Fátima, having heard that she had saved the pope from his bullet and the Spanish priest's knife. When John Paul II visited him in 1983, the Turk begged the pope to reveal "the mystery" of Fátima and the Virgin's third prophecy. According to Joaquín Navarro-Valls, the Vatican spokesman, "Agca is fascinated by Fátima."

There is one more strange twist to the Agca story, a subject that Vatican people are most loath to discuss with outsiders.

In June 1983, Emanuela Orlandi, the fifteen-year-old daughter of a Vatican employee named Ercole Orlandi, disappeared from the family house. According to private accounts, Cardinal Casaroli, the secretary of state, received soon thereafter a telephone call informing him that the girl had been kidnapped but would be returned alive if the pope intervened with Italy's President Sandro Pertini to pardon Agca and release him from prison.

John Paul II, who was instantly advised about the call, found himself confronted with a terrifying dilemma. That evening after dinner, as they were going up in the private papal elevator to the terrace of the Apostolic Palace, John Paul II is said to have mentioned the dilemma to a visiting friend, a Polish priest. The friend volunteered the opinion that under the circumstances the pope should indeed request presidential pardon for Agca and to make the matter public.

John Paul II was spared making a decision, however, because the next day Agca announced in a television interview that he did not wish to leave prison. Asked whether Emanuela had been kidnapped to free him, Agca replied, "She was kidnapped for my freedom. But it wasn't an intelligent action and therefore it has failed."

It has been said that the reason Agca had asked to stay in prison was his fear that he would be assassinated by the person or persons who had persuaded him to shoot the pope—so that there would be no living witnesses. Another account stresses that Agca fears that the Virgin of Fátima will take revenge on him if he is freed.

Dr. Navarro-Valls, the Vatican spokesman, denied forcefully in 1994 that Agca feared retribution from the Virgin, pointing out that the Turk had been claiming in recent years that he had already served enough time in prison and should be released. But Agca had been contradicting himself on every possible subject, also describing himself as Christ and the Messiah. On the thirteenth anniversary of the assassination attempt, in 1994, he said in an interview that "it's pointless to keep speculating and looking for secret plans and plots. The truth is that on that day not even I knew why I shot. . . . I might have done it to make history."

Emanuela Orlandi was still missing eleven years after her disappearance. In January 1994, a Rome monthly magazine with strong ties to the Holy See, *30 Giorni,* reported that a magistrate in charge of the Orlandi case had told them that he would not exclude the possibility of submitting questions to the Vatican in search of information that might be useful in his investigation.

John Paul II's year of horror and miracle—1981—was not confined to the assassination attempt and its direct consequences. Next, his beloved Poland would be struck from within.

CHAPTER 25

At dawn on Sunday, December 13, 1981, exactly seven months after the failed attempt to assassinate John Paul II, the Polish armed forces imposed martial law over the country, smashing Solidarity and imprisoning thousands of opposition leaders and militants.

For Poland, it was the greatest trauma since the end of World War II. For the Polish pope, it was a dramatic test of his political sagacity and diplomacy.

Ironically, the blow aimed at Solidarity soon resulted in the emergence of the Polish Church as the communist regime's most important political partner in Poland and of John Paul II as the "Great Mediator."

The pope's convalescence coincided with the dramatically worsening Polish crisis, including ominous new threats of intervention by Soviet and Warsaw Pact armies. But he remained in close contact with the situation, guiding the policies of the Polish episcopate from Castel Gandolfo and the Vatican, where he consulted with Church as well as regime emissaries.

His personal reaction to the implementation of martial law was instant. Addressing Polish pilgrims in St. Peter's Square after the Angelus prayer at noon that same day, John Paul II declared that "the events of recent hours force me once more to turn to you with a request for prayer in the cause of our common motherland. . . . Polish blood must not be shed because too much of it has been shed, especially during the last war. Everything must be done to build in peace the future of the motherland."

Next evening, addressing a huge crowd praying for Poland in St. Peter's Square, the pope said that "the solidarity with the Polish nation serves to confirm the values and principles, which are inviolable rights of man and rights of a nation. . . . To protect these principles means to defend and develop justice and peace in today's world. . . ."

Aside from exhortations, however, the Church in Poland had to address the new realities, and the pope was fully aware and supportive of it.

Astonishingly cordial relations had developed between the Warsaw regime and the Church in the aftermath of John Paul II's trip to Poland in 1979, and they were reflected in relations with the Holy See as well. This was particularly important after the 1980 birth of Solidarity, even though the Church openly supported the free union movement while the government increasingly regarded it as a threat and a foe.

When the tensions between Solidarity and the regime became unbearable in the autumn of 1981, and as the danger of a Soviet-led invasion grew daily, the Church became the institution to which the moderates on all sides turned in the hope of a solution to the rapidly deepening crisis. By then, however, it was too late.

In Warsaw, meanwhile, the meetings of the Joint Government-Church Commission held since 1980 in the Parliament building were not just friendly and generally constructive but often even jocular. Deputy Prime Minister Barcikowski and Director of the Office of Religious Affairs Jerzy Kuberski, representing the government, and Kraków's Cardinal Franciszek Macharski and Bishop Dąbrowski, the secretary of the episcopate, representing the Church, were getting along famously.

John Paul II's "revolutionary" play, *The Brother of Our God,* had finally been authorized to be performed at the request of a Kraków theater (*In Front of the Jeweler's Shop* had been performed earlier). In the spring of 1981, the commission was discussing prospects for a papal return to

Poland in August 1982, and the question of the Church's access to radio and television for broadcasting Mass as well as programs containing moral teachings.

On July 7, the pope, who returned to the hospital for the treatment of his infection, named Bishop Józef Glemp, a canon law professor from Warmia diocese, to be Primate of Poland, succeeding Wyszyński. It was believed that Glemp had been Wyszyński's choice. Three weeks later, Glemp and Cardinal Macharski, a personal friend of John Paul II, visited him in his hospital suite, discussing Polish affairs at length. In September, back in Castel Gandolfo, the pope received in audience two Soviet cosmonauts. Fascinated by cosmology and space, he plied them with questions about life without the pull of gravity. But it was also a gesture toward Moscow.

In Poland, it was clear by mid-October that the situation was entirely out of hand. Both the PZPR, the ruling communist party, and Solidarity were divided into hard-line and moderate wings. The center had collapsed, and nobody seemed to be in control of the country. Economic activity was paralyzed by hundreds of strikes, from heavy industry to urban transport, called by local or regional Solidarity leaders. There were riots and clashes between the police and the population.

General Jaruzelski, the defense minister and Politburo member, had been named prime minister in February 1981—he had the reputation of being a moderate, and the armed forces still remained the most trusted institution in Poland—and he, in turn, appointed Mieczysław Rakowski, the liberal-minded party magazine editor, as deputy prime minister. Rakowski's principal assignment was to negotiate with Wałęsa on labor and political issues, but their talks finally broke down in the autumn. The gulf separating Solidarity and the regime was too wide to bridge. In October, Jaruzelski replaced Stanisław Kania as party first secretary, concentrating the reins of power in his hands. It was a decision of the Central Committee, supported by the military.

Cardinal Glemp, the new primate, whom Jaruzelski had met several times earlier in the year, was visiting John Paul

II at the Vatican when he learned about the general's elevation. "God bless him," he said. Wałęsa, on a trip in Paris, remarked that "though it's hard to say what will happen tomorrow, I'm sure we can reach an understanding as Pole to Pole, especially because thus far I've had good conversations with General Jaruzelski."

This encouraged Jaruzelski to try to establish what he called a "National Unity Council" formed by the regime, the Church, and Solidarity. Primate Glemp, whom he consulted on October 21, liked the idea (as, of course, did the pope). Wałęsa agreed as well. Consequently, Jaruzelski, Glemp, and Wałęsa met in the evening of November 4 at the prime minister's modest official residence in Warsaw. It was an unprecedented meeting in communist history, and after long hours of discussion, the three men decided to go ahead and form the council.

John Paul II's direct involvement in the Polish crisis was growing daily. On October 13, he conferred for two hours in Castel Gandolfo, where he was still recovering, with Józef Czyrek, the Polish foreign minister and a Politburo member, who had been anxious to present the regime's assessment of the crisis. Czyrek recalls that the pope had questioned him closely about the danger of collapse of the Polish economy and the likelihood of a Soviet intervention. John Paul II then told the minister that he supported Solidarity as a "positive social movement," and that the Church would stand behind all the efforts aimed at a dialogue and Solidarity's new accords with the authorities.

On November 5, the pope met again with Primate Glemp, who had rushed back to Rome to report on his session with Jaruzelski and Wałęsa the previous evening. Though John Paul II's mind was very much on Poland, he found time on November 29 to appeal to the U.S. and Soviet governments to seek an agreement in the new round of SALT (Strategic Arms Limitation Talks) starting in Geneva the following day. He wanted to have a voice in international policymaking.

But in Poland, there were no prospects of any agreement, and Jaruzelski was now under powerful pressure from Moscow and other East European communist capitals to liquidate Solidarity—"or else." During November, there were 105 strikes of indefinite duration, and 115 additional strikes were being planned. As Jaruzelski wrote later, Poland in 1981 was "coming apart as a socialist state, hardening the resolve of other Warsaw Pact countries against any changes [in the system]."

Soviet Marshal Victor Kulikov, commander-in-chief of Warsaw Pact forces, had been visiting the Polish capital continuously during the autumn, demanding personal meetings with Jaruzelski to persuade him to move against Solidarity. And it was Kulikov who made it clear that the Warsaw Pact countries would no longer tolerate the kind of changes that were developing in Poland. At a December 3 secret meeting of pact defense ministers in Moscow, Kulikov said that "the growing political struggle [in Poland] is having negative influence on the Polish Army, and this had led to concern among Warsaw Pact members. Polish communists may count on the support and aid from friendly countries. . . ."

Later that day, Defense Minister Ustinov read the Soviet riot act to General Florian Siwicki, the Polish acting defense minister attending the Moscow session:

> You cede all the time before the arrogant assault of the counter-revolution. Foes of socialism are increasing their demands and, in fact, [they are] defining the development of the situation. They are taking the state apart. Tomorrow they will take power away from you, and you just look. Remember, we shall never agree to the removal of the Polish People's Republic from the defensive system of the Warsaw Pact, and to its further weakening. Poland occupies a key strategic location in the European Theatre. . . . This is no longer your problem alone. . . . Bear in mind that we shall never allow interference with the vital interests of our alliance. . . .

That same day in Radom, a city in central Poland, Solidarity held an emergency national meeting to announce a general strike for December 17, should Parliament grant Jaruzelski the power to rule by decree for the balance of the winter in order to stabilize the economy. One of the many anomalies of the Polish communist dictatorship, particularly during that period, was that the hand-picked and usually docile Parliament could reject government proposals. And in this case, the Church joined Solidarity in opposing Jaruzelski's plea for full powers.

Now the die was cast. Jaruzelski concluded that Solidarity's extreme wing, dominating the organization, was out to capture power in the country. Wałęsa has written in his memoirs that at the Radom meeting he had lost control over events. "In Radom," he acknowledged, "I took a hard position, against my convictions, in order not to be isolated."

Jaruzelski knew that he had only two choices left—and that time was running out. One was to launch a military coup d'état and implement martial law (actually, it was called "state of war" because the Polish Constitution did not provide for martial law) and the other was to risk a Warsaw Pact invasion that would have been inevitable if he did not act. Several Soviet combat divisions were permanently stationed in Poland, and scores of Warsaw Pact divisions stood poised along all her frontiers.

On December 7, Brezhnev telephoned Jaruzelski to tell him that "counter-revolution is on your back. It will be too late unless you undertake the necessary measures; this is a matter that concerns all of us."

Primate Glemp met with Wałęsa and his top advisers on December 5, 7, and 9, and speaking with the approval of John Paul II warned them that "you have exceeded through your [political] actions the mandate given you by the working people. If you want to conduct a clean political game, set up a committee alongside Solidarity's leadership, but do not involve the entire union in your game."

Kulikov was back in Warsaw on Friday, December 11. On Saturday, the twelfth, Jaruzelski decided to give the green light to "Operation Z," the code name for the planned coup that he had prepared in absolute secrecy long in advance.

In the predawn hours of Sunday, December 13, the armed forces, the uniformed militia (the police), and the security services struck in perfect coordination. In effect, they occupied the country, severed all communications and transportation within Poland and with foreign countries, and set up a military junta headed by General Jaruzelski to run Poland under the "state of war."

Despite the massive display of power, fatalities were confined to nine miners killed at the Wujek coal mine in the southwest in a clash with the militia. But within twenty-four hours, over five thousand opposition leaders, Solidarity activists, artists, actors, and intellectuals were rounded up and placed in internment camps. According to Jaruzelski, who later said that the mass arrests were an indefensible "idiocy," the total of all those detained during the state of war was 10,554. This number included Gierek, the former party first secretary, and other former top officials, because Jaruzelski had pledged in announcing martial law on December 13 that there would be no return to the political situation and corruption that existed prior to the 1980 Solidarity-government accords.

In the meantime, however, Poland was a political no-man's-land and a "vast concentration camp," in the words of John Paul II as he commented privately within days of the coup. On Christmas Eve, the pope lit a candle in his Vatican apartment window as a sign of solidarity with "suffering nations."

Neal Ascherson, a British writer and keen observer of the Polish scene, summed up the December events well when he wrote that "what is clear is that this crisis of late 1981 in Poland overcame the very limited resources for mediation and compromise that were available in the Polish system—even the resources of the Church."

General Jaruzelski wrote subsequently that the decision to declare martial law "was taken in Poland, in a group composed exclusively of Poles. I take the responsibility for it." He described the coup as a "lesser evil," remarking that "with any other solution, Poland might have lost everything. During the 'state of war' it has lost a lot. But it was not deprived of [future] chances. We opened [these chances] ourselves later."

John Paul II and General Jaruzelski began exchanging private handwritten letters five days after the event, with the pope initiating the correspondence.

Possessed of a fine sense of history and fully grasping

Polish realities, John Paul II shared Jaruzelski's judgment—though he never acknowledged it publicly—that the "state of war" was a "lesser evil" than a civil war or a Soviet-directed invasion. For his part, Jaruzelski knew from the outset that without the cooperation of the Church and the pope, even given tacitly, he could never find a way out of the crisis. The "state of war" obviously could not be a very prolonged affair, and the country had to start functioning again and to reform its obsolete and ossified economy.

First, however, a secret Polish emissary from New York took it upon himself—apparently with success—to bring the Pole in Rome and the Pole in Warsaw closer together at this time of intense crisis.

He was Bogdan Lewandowski, undersecretary-general of the United Nations, who had represented the secretary-general, Kurt Waldheim, at John Paul II's inauguration in 1978. Lewandowski is a Polish citizen and, under U.N. regulations, had been recommended for his high-ranking post by the Warsaw regime. In this sense, he was wearing a U.N. hat and a Polish hat on a mission that had resulted from an urgent White House call.

The call to Lewandowski at his New York apartment was made late Saturday evening by Richard Pipes, the Polish-born Harvard historian and a leading authority on the Soviet Union, then serving on the staff of the National Security Council in the Reagan administration. It was already dawn in Poland, and the White House Situation Room had just received through the State Department a flash from the American embassy in Warsaw that army tanks were occupying the capital. Pipes wondered whether Lewandowski knew anything about the background of the coup (which the undersecretary did not), and hinted that the White House would be happy to learn whatever it could through him.

Pipes's call inspired Lewandowski to embark on a self-appointed mission to Rome and Warsaw (though both Waldheim and Pipes knew about it) to see whether he could be helpful in some way to all parties concerned. A professional diplomat, the white-haired Lewandowski had instant access to the highest levels in both cities, and it had occurred to him that, as a senior U.N. official, he could serve as a safe conduit between the pope and Jaruzelski if other channels had been blocked by the Warsaw coup.

Lewandowski arrived in Rome on Tuesday, December 15, and was invited to dine with John Paul II and Monsignor Dziwisz, the papal private secretary, in a private capacity, first meeting in the pope's study. Lewandowski recalls that the pontiff appeared tense and saddened though he did not seem surprised by the events in Poland. He thinks that John Paul II feared a "holocaust" with Poles killing one another. When Lewandowski indicated that he was en route to Warsaw, the pope told him that Jaruzelski should be apprised of his concerns.

Arriving in Warsaw on Wednesday, December 16, via Vienna, Lewandowski was received by Jaruzelski the following day at his prime minister's office. In the course of their two-hour conversation, Lewandowski conveyed John Paul II's views to the general. Jaruzelski responded with assurances that bloodshed would be avoided and that there would be no further victims. He said that it was most important that the pope fully understand the Polish situation, and especially the fact that the regime proposed to proceed with major economic and social reforms initiated before the coup. With the general's knowledge, Lewandowski taped the conversation.

Back in Rome at the week's end, Lewandowski joined John Paul II for breakfast after the morning Mass in the papal chapel, passing on to him Jaruzelski's comments (having given the tape to Monsignor Dziwisz). He recalls that the pope asked him many questions about KOR's intellectuals, who had served as Solidarity's advisers.

On December 18, John Paul II penned an appeal to Jaruzelski with copies addressed to Primate Glemp and Wałęsa (who was under house arrest in a villa near Warsaw, but was handed the letter). The appeal, couched in general terms, expressed the hope that no blood would be spilled, that political prisoners would be released, and that Poland would return to normalcy. On December 22, the pope received Bishop Dąbrowski, the secretary of the Polish episcopate, to hear the Church's version of what was happening back home.

Jaruzelski's reply was delivered to John Paul II on January 5, 1982, by Kazimierz Szablewski, chief of the Mission of the People's Republic of Poland for Permanent Contacts with the Holy See. In Warsaw, the Vatican had a Mission of the Holy See for Permanent Contacts with the Polish Government, headed by Archbishop Luigi Poggi, a top specialist in East European affairs, who commuted between the two capitals. These were de facto embassies, and traffic between the Holy See and Warsaw (except for secret traffic) was conducted through them.

The general recognized in his letter to the pope that the imposition of martial law had been a "shock to our society," adding that "many people feel disappointed in their hopes, crushed by circumstances, embittered." But he assured John Paul II that the country would not return to pre-Solidarity days and that he was prepared to work with all groups and persons, regardless of their views, who were ready "to cooperate to lift the nation out of its difficulties."

John Paul II wrote back expressing his fears that the sentiments of the people to whom Jaruzelski had alluded not only existed, but were deepening as a result of conditions "stemming from the prolongation of the state of war, such as the growing difficulties in procuring food because of . . . [high] prices." The pope told the general that the "shock" triggered by martial law was also a result of the "internment of thousands of leading Solidarity militants, including Lech Wałęsa, along with a number of painful sanctions in relation to the worlds of labor and culture. . . . It is not only necessary to remove the shock, but, above all, to rebuild trust."

But the most important thing was that the pope-general contact was never broken (even though very few people knew it existed) and that the Church and John Paul II were able to play "the role of mediator," as former Prime Minister Rakowski put it, after the declaration of martial law, seeing to it that "Polish tensions did not reach the boiling point of an active volcano." And, Rakowski added, it was "John Paul II who sponsored the activities of the Church."

The 1982 correspondence between the pope and Jaruzelski marked the start of a very special and subtle relationship that at the end of the decade would render possible the historical transition from communism to democracy under the benevolent eye of Mikhail Gorbachev, the pontiff's new friend, and lead to fundamental transformations throughout Eastern Europe. In history's strange ways, the martial law period and subsequent readjustments, closely monitored by John Paul II, were the necessary bridge to the big change. But in 1981, the communists were not ready to surrender or even share power.

However, the Reagan administration could not comprehend this state of affairs when, ten days after the fact, it responded to the martial law proclamation with harsh economic sanctions against Poland. Believing that it was defending Polish democracy, it was, in effect, punishing the victim—the Polish people. Reagan had also sent a letter to Brezhnev protesting against Soviet pressures on Poland and applying additional sanctions against the Kremlin (already penalized briefly two years earlier for invading Afghanistan).

Washington, to be sure, was not aware of the John Paul II—Jaruzelski back channel, and it was genuinely surprised when the pope endorsed a declaration by Polish bishops opposing the American sanctions on the ground that it would penalize the people without changing the situation. Even more surprising to the administration was the communiqué issued on January 18, 1982, by the Joint Government-Church Commission after its first session under martial law that "in the difficult situation of the country, economic sanctions applied against Poland strike at the interest of the nation and, to an important degree, render more difficult [the efforts] to overcome the crisis, halting the return to the full exercise of the process of renewal in the spirit of [our] social agreements." The language had been approved by Primate Glemp.

Earlier, John Paul II had sent Reagan a personal letter, simply thanking him for his support for Poland, without mentioning the sanctions, but the White House announced publicly that the pope had expressed his gratitude for the sanctions. In the end, the Vatican issued a denial.

Actually, the Reagan administration's behavior in the context of the Polish crisis was perplexing in many ways.

Most strangely, it failed to warn Solidarity of the Jaruzelski regime's plans to destroy it through the imposition of the "state of war," although it was in the possession since mid-November of detailed plans for "Operation Z," including the approximate date.

The United States had obtained the plans from Colonel Ryszard Kukliński, a highly trusted officer of the General Staff of the Polish Army, who happened to be a CIA agent, a mole of long standing. Kukliński had been feeding precious intelligence to the CIA all along, but he was able to deliver "Operation Z" material only when he fled Poland in the middle of November. American officials lamely explained later that a warning to Solidarity might have led to a civil war or a bloody uprising. It is not a convincing explanation.

Meanwhile, initial U.S. misunderstanding of John Paul II's attitude on Poland led to further confusion. When Reagan visited the pope on June 27, 1982, spending two hours with him, he offered the Holy See financial and intelligence "collaboration" to support Solidarity's underground activities in Poland. John Paul II, according to persons familiar with this conversation, thanked the president politely. He said that, naturally, all assistance would be welcome, but that the Vatican had no need or desire for such "collaboration" inasmuch as it had its own channels to help Polish causes.

Nevertheless, the myth was spawned in Washington that John Paul II and Reagan had formed a secret "holy alliance" that resulted in the ultimate collapse of communism in Eastern Europe. This fabricated version of history annoyed the Holy See—and the Poles—when it first surfaced publicly in the United States, but now it simply amuses them. Andrzej Micewski, the Polish writer who served as personal adviser to the Primate of Poland during that period, has written that "only people who have very sparse knowledge of the Catholic Church could suppose that matters pertaining to financial channels would be discussed or settled on a pope-president level."

The truth is that the Holy See did provide limited financial aid to Solidarity and other opposition groups in

Poland through Church and other conduits. Some of these funds came from the Institute for Religious Works (whose Italian acronym is IOR), the principal Vatican financial institution that became embroiled in the early 1980s in scandals involving a number of private Italian banks with which it worked. The IOR's problem was that it had issued what amounted to letters of guarantee to some of these banks, which, in turn, engaged in shady operations leading to collapse and great losses to depositors. Roberto Calvi, the head of one of these banks, died under extremely strange circumstances.

That the IOR had found itself in such a predicament is a serious blemish on John Paul II's reputation as an administrator. Extremely trusting but impatient with detail, the pope had left the Vatican's financial matters in the hands of Archbishop Paul C. Marcinkus, the American from Cicero, Illinois, who was the president of the IOR in addition to his duties as organizer of papal travel. Marcinkus, for his part, has claimed inexperience and naïveté as reasons for his gullibility in dealing with the Italian banks, and, of course, was quickly replaced at the IOR. He lives in retirement in Sun City West, Arizona.

Unfortunately, however, the IOR affair coincided with the Polish crisis, and charges were made that John Paul II used the IOR to transfer millions of dollars of unclear origin to Solidarity and other anti-communist organizations in Poland in the context of the alleged "holy alliance" with Reagan. The actual transfers from IOR were small, but for a decade this whole question has been part of fairly savage Vatican and Italian politics, including suggestions that the infamous P2 Masonic lodge was also involved in it in some fashion. The Holy See also completely mishandled the public relations aspects of the situation, adding fuel to the accusations with its dignified silence. The pope learned a valuable lesson, and Vatican finances are now under the most strict controls. Quietly, the Holy See transferred $240 million to the Italian government to compensate Italian banks for possible losses.

In addition to funds provided by the Holy See to Solidarity, other monies as well as printing and communications equipment came from the AFL-CIO in Washington and West European labor unions (the equipment was mostly smuggled through Scandinavia). And there is no question that funds from the CIA were directly channeled to Solidarity through the agency's Warsaw station and through Polish-American churches in the United States to Polish priests with whom they had contacts. Quite incidentally, the Vatican had asked the Reagan administration at about that time to abandon the CIA practice of disguising its operatives in Central America as priests.

Solidarity leaders explained later that the organization's survival during and after the "state of war" never hinged on great sums of foreign money, but on the moral and political support it received when, for example, John Paul II returned to Poland in 1983, conducting a publicized meeting with Lech Wałęsa, whom the regime had been treating as a nonperson. And his 1987 visit shored up Solidarity at a critical moment of transition. At home, the Church collected money and food directly from the population for the families of thousands of interned opposition militants.

While no "holy alliance" ever existed, liaison and cooperation between Washington and the Holy See functioned in other ways. Among these were the fairly frequent private briefings on world political, diplomatic, and military situations provided to John Paul II on the administration's behalf by the multilingual Lieutenant General Vernon Walters, a former deputy director of the CIA who was serving at the time as ambassador-at-large.

When on one occasion Walters showed him maps of the Soviet Union and Eastern Europe produced from high-resolution satellite photography and pointed out detailed locations of Soviet nuclear launchers and troop concentrations, the pope asked whether satellite maps could also show where Gulag prison camps were located. Walters obliged a day or two later with detailed maps that he brought rolled and gift-wrapped. (The suspense of wrapped presents has always been one of Karol Wojtyła's great delights.)

Among the results of Reagan's visit to John Paul II was the establishment of full diplomatic relations between the United States and the Holy See, long a desire of the Vatican.

Because of the law passed by Congress in 1867 denying funds for diplomatic envoys to the pope, the only U.S. representation at the Holy See was the personal representative of the president, who paid his own expenses. It was a concept devised by Franklin Roosevelt during World War II. But, at Reagan's request, Congress changed the law in 1983, and there have been full-fledged U.S. ambassadors to the Holy See ever since (invariably political appointees). What John Paul II did not know, of course, was that the National Security Agency was secretly monitoring his and the Holy See's telephone communications with the Polish episcopate. It is doubtful that even Reagan was aware of it.

With the Holy See's growing involvement in world affairs under John Paul II, the Vatican volunteered mediation between NATO and the Warsaw Pact in negotiating an agreement on halting deployment of tactical nuclear weapons in Europe, then a major Cold War issue.

And in a gesture presumably designed to please the pope as well as pro-life groups at home, Reagan ended in 1985 all U.S. financial contributions to the United Nations Fund for Population Activities (created as an American initiative during the Nixon administration) and the International Planned Parenthood Federation because they funded abortions in countries where the procedure was legal. William Wilson, the first American ambassador to the Holy See, named by Reagan, was quoted as saying at the time that "American policy was changed as a result of the Vatican's not agreeing with our policy."

President Clinton would reverse the new policy in early 1993, resulting in the first of many public attacks on him by the Vatican over population-control issues.

In the ecumenical realm of American-Vatican relations, Billy Graham, the Protestant evangelist, came to Rome in 1982 to meet John Paul II. The two men liked each other and have kept in touch in the ensuing years.

Reagan and John Paul II shared the dubious honor of having been targets of assassins. When Reagan was shot in Washington on March 30, 1981, the pope sent him a telegram expressing his satisfaction over the president's survival. Reagan reciprocated on May 13. And on October 6, John Paul II signed a telegram to the widow of Egypt's

President Anwar el-Sadat, shot that day by religious fanatics.

Nineteen eighty-one was the year of assassins.

And, as John Paul II was completing the recovery from his wounds, 1982 turned out to be the year of war, engaging him directly and personally in three regions.

In Poland, the "state of war" continued during the entire year, and the pope devoted much time to the orchestration of Church policies there while keeping actively alive his contacts with General Jaruzelski and his regime. In fact, he had instructed the episcopate in Warsaw to start negotiating a visit from him in August to preside over the commemoration of the six-hundredth anniversary of the date the icon of the Black Madonna was brought to Częstochowa.

In the South Atlantic, Argentina and Britain had been waging a war since April over the Falkland Islands, a British possession that Argentina called the Malvinas and claimed as rightfully theirs. It was the first war in the South American region since the conflict between Peru and Ecuador in the 1940s, and John Paul II had concluded that he must use his influence to try to help bring about peace.

In the Middle East, a part of the world with special spiritual significance for the pope, high- and low-intensity warfare still plagued Jews and Arabs, Christians and Arabs, and Arabs and other Arabs. Though Israel and Egypt had signed the United States-brokered Camp David Accords, other Arab states and Palestinian organizations still battled the Israelis. Iraq and Iran were fighting a murderous war along the Persian Gulf, and a religious civil war was now devastating Lebanon, where Christians and Muslims had lived in harmony for centuries. The pope's intent was to use the Holy See's considerable diplomatic resources in the search for peace throughout the Middle East.

It was to Africa, however, that John Paul II traveled first on February 12, 1982, resuming the world voyages interrupted by the assassination attempt. It was his first foreign trip in a year, but the second to Africa during the pontificate, emphasizing again his belief that the future of the Catholic Church lay there.

Fulfilling the commitment he had made the previous year

for this African trip—it was canceled after he was shot—the pope went to Nigeria, where a large Christian minority lives alongside the Muslim majority (not always peacefully), to Benin (the homeland of Cardinal Bernardin Gantin, whom he would soon name prefect of the powerful Congregation for Bishops), and to the former French and Spanish colonies of Gabon and Equatorial Guinea. It was a punishing weeklong trip, but John Paul II appeared to have regained completely his health and boundless energy.

But it was the next travel commitment that brought to the fore John Paul II's inventiveness and tact in a spectacular way. The Catholic Church of England and Wales had invited him for a visit at the start of May 1982, and Queen Elizabeth II added her invitation when she called on the pope in October 1980. The trip was to have an ecumenical aspect as well with a planned Canterbury meeting with the Anglican primate, Dr. Robert Runcie.

The problem whether to go to Britain arose two weeks before the trip when Argentine forces attempted to conquer the Falklands, and Britain dispatched a sea and air armada to defend them. The dilemma perceived by the Roman Curia was that John Paul II would be visiting a largely Anglican country at war with a predominantly Catholic country. Moreover, the conflict also had anti-colonialist aspects that the pope could not ignore, given his advocacy of Third World causes. And Protestant extremists in England were loudly opposed to a papal presence as a matter of principle.

It was a diplomatic nightmare, but, in the meantime, Wojtyła flew to Portugal on May 12, to thank the Virgin of Fátima for saving his life the year before, and to meditate en route about the British situation. John Paul II's closest advisers urged him simply to postpone the visit indefinitely—it had already been delayed by the Falklands War—although Cardinal Basil Hume and Cardinal Gordon Gray had rushed to the Vatican to plead with the pope not to disappoint their faithful.

The pontiff, however, had a better idea. He invited the two English cardinals and all three Argentine cardinals along with other Church dignitaries to concelebrate a "Reconciliation Mass" with him at St. Peter's Basilica on May

24. It was a moving spectacle, and at the end of the Mass the pope announced that he would go to *both* Britain and Argentina. Next, he sent identical messages to Prime Minister Margaret Thatcher in London and President Leopoldo Galtieri in Buenos Aires, exhorting them to halt the fighting.

It was a novel chapter in the history of cautious Holy See diplomacy, but John Paul II felt that he had an obligation to intervene—having successfully mediated between Argentina and Chile to defuse a conflict in 1979—if his peacemaking was to be taken seriously. Having proclaimed at the St. Peter's Mass that "peace is an obligation, peace is a duty," the pope flew to Britain on May 28 for a five-day visit and an enthusiastic welcome.

On the evening of June 10—three days after receiving President Reagan at the Vatican—John Paul II left Rome for a thirty-hour overnight stay in Buenos Aires, shortly after Argentina's defeat in the Falklands hostilities. Actually, the pope spent more time aboard his airliner flying to and from Buenos Aires (with refueling stops only in Rio de Janeiro) than on Argentine soil, but he made his point about evenhandedness in peacekeeping as he prayed in downtown Plaza España with 120 Latin American bishops and 1,700 priests. It was a peace pageant.

Still, John Paul II's visit to Argentina presented other risks. President Galtieri, the army general who conceived the ill-fated Falklands invasion, was the latest in the string of military dictators engaged in a lengthy "dirty war" of tortures, killings, and disappearances of thousands of political opponents. In view of the pope's stand on the question of human rights, he was presumably content to spend as little time with him as possible. John Paul II was criticized for not speaking out in Buenos Aires in defense of human rights, but he had determined that it was neither the time nor place for it.

Forty-eight hours after returning to Rome from South America, the pope raced to Geneva for a day to attend an international labor conference. Now he was happily in his element of quasi-perpetual motion, having visited eight countries on three continents between mid-February and mid-June.

In the Middle East, John Paul II had to confine himself to traditional diplomacy, yet he displayed both initiative and political courage. On January 7, he had received at the Vatican Israeli foreign minister Yitzhak Shamir, the Polish-born future prime minister, in his first encounter with a senior official of the Jerusalem government. He had wanted to learn something firsthand about the Arab-Israeli conflict while demonstrating at the same time his sympathy for Jewish causes. In February 1981 the pope held a meeting with Rome's chief rabbi, Elio Toaff, at a local parish church, the first time a Bishop of Rome had ever conversed with a Roman rabbi; the two men have seen each other periodically over the ensuing years.

Between his trips to Argentina and Britain, the pope became increasingly concerned over the rising violence in the civil war in Lebanon. On June 8, he sent a telegram to Lebanese President Elias Sarkis to express his preoccupation. With the Middle East still very much on his mind, John Paul II received on September 15 Yasser Arafat, the chairman of the Palestine Liberation Organization. At that time Arafat was treated as an international pariah and terrorist, and the pope came under violent criticism for bestowing legitimacy on him. But Wojtyła had the knack of being far ahead in making correct political assessments. The criticism, he told associates, did not bother him in the slightest.

The Polish "war" naturally consumed a great deal of John Paul II's time and attention during 1982. In the course of the year, he conferred five times with Primate Glemp, twice with Cardinal Macharski, who led the Church delegation at the sessions of the Joint Government-Church Commission, and twice with Bishop Dąbrowski, the secretary of the Polish episcopate, in addition to meetings with scores of bishops from different Polish dioceses. He remained fully informed about the evolution of the situation, both through these Church channels and through the steadily improving contacts with the Warsaw regime.

It is clear in retrospect that John Paul II believed in the possibility of a rational solution for the Polish crisis that would allow the lifting of martial law and a considerable degree of political and economic liberalization in a gradual fashion. This evaluation defined his broad policies toward the Warsaw regime. He certainly did not anticipate that communist rule would vanish in the foreseeable future.

Meanwhile, the episcopate and the regime in Poland worked toward the same general objective through their increasingly productive contacts in the joint commission, which now met almost every month. At the same time, the Church complained about militia attacks on young demonstrators in Kraków, and the government complained about what it regarded as instances of the Church's anti-communist propaganda, but it was all done in an off-hand manner. Inevitably, the Church was criticized by its purists for having "sold out" to the regime and Jaruzelski by his hard-liners for being "soft" on the Church.

So much progress in the relationship had been made in the immediate aftermath of the military coup that Monsignor Alojzy Orszulik, a member of the episcopate delegation, was allowed to discuss Poland's political situation with Lech Wałęsa at the villa where he lived under house arrest. Stanisław Ciosek, a Cabinet minister, also called on Wałęsa to debate the future of labor unions in the country. These meetings, of course, were kept strictly secret, as were the deliberations of the joint commission during which, for example, a Church delegate would remark that Wałęsa "lacks the intelligence to formulate his own ideas" and a government delegate would reply that "there haven't been serious conversations with him."

All in all, it was a classically Polish surrealistic state of affairs, which, in the end, made the breakthrough possible. And it was an environment in which John Paul II felt very much at home—though from a distance.

At the Vatican, efforts were made to reciprocate the regime's courtesies toward the Church. When Jerzy Kuberski, the former education minister and the head of the Office of Religious Affairs, was appointed as the new chief Polish diplomat at the Holy See early in June, he was immediately received by Cardinal Casaroli, the secretary of state, and Archbishop Silvestrini, who was de facto foreign minister, as a mark of special attention. Kuberski's actual title was rather unimpressive (though it was the longest in the Vatican diplomatic list)—he was Minister-Counselor, Director of the Group for Permanent Working Relations Between the Government of the Polish People's Republic and the Apostolic Capital—but he carried more weight than most ambassadors.

In July 1982 Kuberski accompanied Foreign Minister Czyrek to a meeting with John Paul II at Castel Gandolfo to decide the date of the pope's trip to Poland. Czyrek told the pope that the situation was still too volatile and the government preferred that the visit be postponed until the middle of 1983. John Paul II already knew about the regime's concerns and, careful not to upset the delicate political balance, agreed to wait a year.

Soon thereafter the Polish episcopate and the government signed a framework agreement on organizing the papal journey. A secret study by the communist party's Central Committee, weighing all the pros and cons of the visit, concluded that it was worth the risk. It made the assumption that John Paul II's arrival in Poland after the disappearance of Solidarity would again legitimize the regime, a judgment that demonstrated how decisions can be made to fit wishful thinking.

In Moscow, Leonid Brezhnev died on November 10. John Paul II sent a telegram of condolence and appointed a Vatican delegation to the funeral to be led by Professor Giovanni Battista Martini Betolo, a member of the Papal Science Academy.

In Warsaw, Lech Wałęsa was released, and General Jaruzelski announced on December 31, 1982, the suspension but not the formal lifting of the "state of war" in Poland.

An era had ended. And an era was about to begin.

CHAPTER 26

John Paul II and General Wojciech Jaruzelski, the prime minister of Poland, met for the first time at Belweder Presidential Palace in Warsaw on Friday, June 17, 1983, the day after the pope's arrival on his second Polish pontifical visit.

Their meeting launched what would become a crucial personal relationship over the ensuing years; it marked a major turning point in Poland's postwar history. If there was any "holy alliance" at all, it engaged the Polish pope and the Polish communist army general. Jaruzelski affirms that "the role of the pope was enormous in the transformations that occurred in Poland and, following in Poland's footsteps, in the whole [communist] bloc."

And this pope-general relationship would also lead in time to a direct rapport between John Paul II and the Soviet Union's Mikhail Gorbachev, with Jaruzelski playing a unique secret "mutual friend" role in its development.

This is how General Jaruzelski remembers that first meeting:

> For me, it was a deep personal experience. I am a non-believer, but, you know, something remains in the genes from one's youth. So the pope, this figure in white, it all affected me emotionally. Beyond all reason. . . . I was deeply moved by that encounter. I

> was even nervous. . . . It was our first conversation, a get-acquainted conversation, but, at the same time, very important in substance. . . .

Jaruzelski, who freely reminisces about his childhood family and school Catholic background, admits that "I was aware that my legs were trembling and my knees knocking together" when he first found himself in the presence of John Paul II. Attentive viewers had observed it in a quick television close-up shot, and the general had no qualms about confirming it in a conversation ten years later. John Paul II has told friends that he had "certainly" noticed it, but "only in the beginning did his knees tremble."

> In that first encounter [Jaruzelski goes on], I had the subconscious sense that this is something special, that I am in the presence of greatness. Especially after I had seen those crowds, these millions falling on their knees. I have seen people, bishops, writers kneeling, kissing his hand. So it is a contagious mood. Of course, I am rationally very, very sober in such situations, and I have the consciousness of his human dimension. . . . But it was a very deep experience for me. And when you add his personality, his charisma, you can imagine the impression. . . .

John Paul II and Jaruzelski may have seemed at first sight, even to each other, as improbable partners in a relationship of remarkable closeness. The general has a somewhat forbidding appearance: he is reserved, he stands ramrod stiff because of a corset he wears due to a back injury, and he wears glasses with dark-tinted lenses to protect his extremely sensitive eyes. The pope, on the other hand, is outgoing, gregarious, and immensely attractive. Ideologically, they cannot be further apart, something both were acutely aware of when they first met.

Yet an astonishing feeling of liking and trust soon developed between them. The pope had sensed that the general was an emotional person with high moral standards, and he held him in high esteem. When during a meeting with Polish bishops at the Vatican in the late 1980s a participant made a critical remark about Jaruzelski, John Paul II interrupted to say, "Please, do not say anything critical about the general in my presence. He has put an enormous sack of stones on his back." And the pope went out of his way to meet with Jaruzelski in Warsaw during his 1991 visit to Poland, after the general had returned to private life, and to receive him privately at the Vatican in 1992.

For Jaruzelski, the central fact about John Paul II was "the pope's Polishness." He says that "he belongs to the generation, as I do, for which the memory of Poland living in slavery for well over one hundred years was still present. He always comes back to it in conversation. He would say to me, 'General, I always have in my mind that terrible tragedy our nation had suffered . . . the Great Partitions.'" The second fact about the pope that attracted him, Jaruzelski says, was "his intellect, his knowledge. . . . In every conversation, there would be a citation from Norwid or Wyspiański. . . . His pragmatism lives surrounded by romanticism, this very emotional approach to our history. . . ."

Actually, as Jaruzelski recalls, his first conversation with John Paul II was not too easy in the beginning. "I could feel the reserve, a certain constraint, an official coolness."

The pope had arrived in Warsaw on June 16, for a weeklong visit, at a time when the Polish situation was still tense. The "state of war" had been suspended on December 31 but not formally lifted, there still were a great many political prisoners (Jaruzelski says there were exactly 147 of them that week) although Lech Wałęsa had been released the previous November, and heavy restrictions still regulated travel and other activities.

Though John Paul II's second Polish pilgrimage was essentially religious in nature, it inevitably carried powerful political overtones. In March that year, the pope had toured Central America and Haiti—his first voyage in 1983—and it was just as political in its own way. In Nicaragua, the Marxist Sandinista regime was engaged in open warfare with American-organized contra rebels. John Paul II was interrupted by hostile hecklers as he was delivering the homily at Mass at the Managua cathedral, and he roared back, "Silence!" In El Salvador, he found the military regime in the midst of an unending civil war with Marxist revolutionaries (he prayed at the tomb of Archbishop Romero, martyred three years earlier).

After landing at Warsaw's Okęcie Airport, John Paul II defined the character of his visit as he kissed the ground, and said in his arrival speech that "this is like a kiss on the hand of a mother—because the motherland is our earthly mother. . . . Poland is a special mother. Her fate was not easy, especially in recent centuries. She is a mother who has suffered a lot and still suffers. This is why she has the right to special love. . . . *Pax vobis!* Peace with You, O, Poland, my Motherland!"

The pope's first day in Warsaw was filled with High Mass at the Old Town cathedral and a meeting with nuns. The second day was frankly political, with the encounter at Belweder Palace its business highlight. His official hosts in Poland were President Jabłoński, whose functions were purely ceremonial and whom the pope had met twice before, and Primate Glemp. Jaruzelski attended in his capacity as prime minister.

Because of the political nature of the meeting, John Paul II and Jaruzelski took over the hour-and-a-half conversation, with Jabłoński and Glemp silently listening. The general, recalling that he had already sent the pope three extensive letters earlier in the year, says that "I presented the circumstances of the proclamation of the 'state of war,' all the problems connected with it, and our plans for change, reconstruction and renewal."

As the conversation with John Paul II gradually became more relaxed and "warmer," Jaruzelski says that he felt at ease in explaining to the pope how "indignant" he was over President Reagan's demands that Poland enter into a dialogue with Solidarity and the Church as a condition for lifting the sanctions.

> I told the pope that for the time being we are not establishing contacts with Solidarity, but that the dialogue with the Church was never interrupted. On the contrary, it gets stronger. . . . I reminded him that his [the pope's] plays are being performed in ten cities, in

> eleven theatres . . . that the circulation of Catholic publications and bulletins had gone up from 800,000 to 1.9 million. . . . I spoke very personally about the burden I had assumed on December 13, in the awareness that I shall carry this burden until the end of my life, that I shall be fought by many people. . . .

The general also mentioned to John Paul II his childhood, his wartime exile in Siberia with his family, his military service, and that "I always tried to serve the nation."

The pope, Jaruzelski says, "is a man who knows how to listen calmly even when he disagrees completely with what he hears. . . . This touched me very much. . . . Every meeting I have had with him brought us closer together in a purely human sense—not only in an intellectual format, but with warmth. . . ."

Nevertheless there were disagreements and problems during the papal tour that took John Paul II to the sanctuary of the Black Madonna in Częstochowa, the western cities of Poznań and Katowice, and Kraków—and to a secluded valley in the Tatry Mountains. At the Belweder meeting, the pope told Jaruzelski that the regime's cancellation of Solidarity's official registration as a trade union under the "state of war" was even more painful to him than the martial law itself. He argued about the importance of free labor unions in democratic societies, one of his favorite social themes.

Jaruzelski had begrudgingly agreed to allow John Paul II to meet Wałęsa after the Holy See had presented it as a matter of principle for the pope. John Paul II believed that as a publicly declared supporter of Solidarity, he must see Wałęsa, especially as the latter was no longer under detention. Under heavy pressure from party hard-liners, the general had resisted this request but finally decided to let the stubborn pontiff have his way. The pope had let it be known that he would not come to Poland if this visit was denied, and Jaruzelski concluded that the political damage would be greater if the threat was carried out.

Wałęsa was back at home in Gdańsk, but the shipyard where he had led the great strike of 1980 refused to let him return to his job, in a cheap gesture of bureaucratic petulance. The regime's policy was to turn him into a "nonperson," reasoning that Solidarity could not function without his prestige, but, as it soon discovered, this was a spectacular miscalculation.

The compromise worked out by the Holy See and the government was that the pope and Wałęsa would meet privately, away from the press and television cameras. There are, however, differing versions of the encounter.

Wałęsa's own version is that he had written John Paul II in mid-May to request an audience, saying that "we refuse to live in the past, to founder in misery and regret. Our faces are turned toward our country's future. It is in the name of my country, Holy Father, that I permit myself to ask you for an audience."

Strangely, Wałęsa's account is limited to two paragraphs in his autobiography, revealing virtually nothing about the meeting:

> What I remember most . . . was the atmosphere of openness and simplicity—his words were like an invitation to remove the daily mask one wears to cope with life. One curious thing struck me during that meeting. I suddenly noticed the Pope's large feet, and I watched how he walked. Surprisingly, his steps were steady, measured and confident. They seemed to give me back my strength.

The regime had selected a villa in the Chochołowska Valley in the Tatry Mountains for John Paul II to see Wałęsa, probably unaware that it had been one of Karol Wojtyła's favoring skiing sites in his Kraków days. It was chosen because the meeting would occur during the pope's stay in Kraków, whence he was flown by helicopter.

Wałęsa arrived by helicopter from Gdańsk in the company of Bishop Tadeusz Gocłowski, who had been charged by the Polish episcopate with the responsibility for his safety. According to the bishop, they had been told that Wałęsa would be received by the pope in Kraków, but, suddenly, they were landing in a beautiful, remote mountain valley.

Bishop Gocłowski has written that the meeting "lasted

probably forty minutes" and the conversation "naturally concerned the situation in the country, the mood among the working people, and prospects for Solidarity's activities." He added that he was struck during their meeting by the "certainty of the victory of the ideal, which had so dominantly spread across Poland. They were in full agreement that difficult as it may be, facts were irreversible."

Jaruzelski's version is totally at variance with the bishop's. He says that Wałęsa, his wife, and children were awaiting John Paul II at the villa, and that the meeting was "very short, I think fifteen minutes. . . . There were no conversations one could call political—they were rather paternal. The pope patted the children on the head, asked how they were, if they were studying well. . . ." Wałęsa wore the image of the Virgin Mary in the lapel of his jacket, and brought gifts for John Paul II, which the papal aides forgot to take along on the return flight to Kraków.

The pope thinks that this visit, which was suddenly publicized after the fact, saved Wałęsa from political oblivion after his release from internment, although "nothing of substance" was said between them. John Paul II's reasoning was that he would strengthen Solidarity by resurrecting Wałęsa, who, in his opinion, was no longer regarded seriously by communists and non-communists. Jaruzelski thinks that "if it were not Wałęsa, then someone else would have reanimated and guided this movement although it was obviously important from Wałęsa's personal view."

The ultimate irony was that four months later, in October 1983, Wałęsa was awarded the Nobel Prize for Peace, which made his prestige soar even higher. But he still could not get a shipyard job.

Oddly, John Paul II and Jaruzelski firmed up their relationship as a result of a series of incidents that threatened to jeopardize the success of the pope's visit. Jaruzelski recalls that as the pontiff traveled triumphantly across Poland

> we, the authorities, began to discern certain disturbing things, which might destablilize the situation [in the

> country]. . . . The pope, of course, never said anything that might have actually created a controversy with us. But he knows how to speak so splendidly, to modulate the mood, and to create perceptions in such a way that a word spoken at random could open the way to a situation that might be hard to control.

At that juncture, the pope was in Częstochowa, and Jaruzelski dispatched a senior official there to broach his concerns delicately with the papal entourage. John Paul II responded with a proposal for a meeting with Jaruzelski in Kraków, although no second encounter between them had originally been planned.

This time they met alone, spoke very frankly, and set the foundations for future collaboration on a scale that neither of them anticipated at the moment. Jaruzelski remembers it as a "cordial meeting," with both men spelling out their concerns in detail. The general says that John Paul II was

> in a very difficult position, under pressure from the crowds that almost expected him to lead them to the barricades. I appreciated that. On the one hand, as our guest, he did not wish to do anything that might have disturbed peace and stability. He did not want to awaken any premature hopes. On the other hand, he felt convinced inside that he must support this movement [Solidarity] and all these national and social aspirations, that he must keep them alive, and reinforce this hope in some fashion, but without crossing certain frontiers.

The two men discussed at length the question of labor unions, social justice, and political trends, and, at one point, Jaruzelski says that John Paul II told him, "General, please do not feel insulted, but I have nothing against socialism—I just want socialism to have a human face." The Kraków session, he recalls, "ended on a very constructive note."

Quite aptly, as it happened, the high point of the pope's visit to Kraków was Mass at which he beatified Father Rafał

Kalinowski, a Carmelite, and Brother Albert—the artist named Adam Chmielowski who founded the Albertine Order and about whom Karol Wojtyła had written his play *The Brother of Our God.*

John Paul II returned to Rome on June 23. General Jaruzelski ended the "state of war" on July 22, the national holiday of the Polish People's Republic. On November 10, Jaruzelski received a furious letter from Yuri Andropov, the general secretary of the Communist Party of the Soviet Union, the KGB chairman who had succeeded Brezhnev exactly a year earlier.

Unlike Brezhnev in 1979, Andropov had not attempted in 1983 to persuade the Poles to keep John Paul II away. But, as Jaruzelski puts it,

> our closeness to his Church disturbed our allies more and more. It was not only the Soviet Union, but especially Czechoslovakia, Hungary and East Germany, where they knew that this would have an impact on the situation between the state and the church in their countries. Thus they exercised great pressures on Brezhnev and then on Andropov. [Hungarian Party First Secretary Janos] Kadar once told me that "the Poles are flirting with the Church too much."

In his secret letter to Jaruzelski, Andropov wrote that "I want especially to speak of the Church. During the crisis, it received the greatest benefits and very seriously strengthened its political positions and its material-financial base." Andropov went on:

> Today, the Church is a powerful opposition force against socialism, appearing in the role of patron and defender of the underground and defender of the idea of Solidarity. The Church is reanimating the cult of Wałęsa, gives him inspiration, and encourages him in his actions. This means that the Church is creating a new type of confrontation with the [Communist] Party. In this situation, the most important thing is not to make concessions, but to establish firmly a line of

> restricting the activity of the Church to the [Polish] constitutional framework, and narrow the sphere of its influences on the social life. We understand that this is not a simple problem, that many factors must be weighed, that one blow will not solve it—but time must take care of it. . . .

Unfazed, Jaruzelski moved to reinforce further his ties with John Paul II, writing him in a letter on December 19 that he still was "under the impression of [our] conversations" during the papal visit. "It gave me the opportunity of meeting the pope—a Pole," he wrote, adding that he thought often about their talks because, "regardless of understandable differences in assessments, they were full of heart-felt concern for the fate of our motherland and the wellbeing of man." The general then informed the pope that the Polish authorities were doing everything in their power "to avoid the most acute dangers" and that "the situation in the country is stabilizing." And he wished John Paul II a happy New Year.

The Kremlin kept up its protests about the Poles' growing friendship with the Church when Konstantin Chernenko became general secretary of the Soviet Communist Party in 1984, succeeding Andropov, who died after eighteen months in power. In mid-April, Jaruzelski was summoned to a top secret meeting with Defense Minister Dmitri Ustinov and Foreign Minister Andrei Gromyko that was held in a railway parlor car on the Soviet side of the border in Brest and resulted in "a very difficult conversation."

On April 26, Chernenko presided over a session of the Soviet Politburo to discuss, among other things, the Polish situation and the Brest meeting between Jaruzelski and Ustinov and Gromyko. According to a transcript of this closed meeting (as were all important Soviet Communist Party meetings), Chernenko said that

> Jaruzelski informed us for three hours about the situation [in Poland]. . . . Concerning the attitude of the Polish Church, he described the Church as an ally, without whom progress is impossible. He did not say a word about a determined struggle against the intrigues

of the Church. Therefore Jaruzelski's position was, above all, a justification of everything that is presently happening in Poland.

Gorbachev was already a full member of the Politburo, and the secret transcript quotes him as remarking during the session that "this Jaruzelski must be thinking about some kind of pluralism. . . ." He and Jaruzelski had not yet met.

Speaking of the pressures on him during 1984—perhaps the worst year of the transition—Jaruzelski says,

> You can't imagine what I had to live through. . . . Not quite half-a-year after Andropov's letter, there is more pressure on us [from Moscow], critically assessing our policy toward the Church. And we were caught in the middle. From one side, the West was attacking us, applying sanctions. And from those [in the East] whom I was asking for economic assistance, they were refusing it. They were attacking us over our relations with the Church.

But matters became still worse for Jaruzelski. In September, he was convoked to another railway-car border meeting with Ustinov and Gromyko to receive another tongue-lashing over Warsaw's relationship with the Church. And absolute disaster struck on October 19, when rogue Polish secret service agents and militia officers kidnapped and murdered Father Jerzy Popiełuszko, a young and greatly popular priest who was the chaplain of the Huta Warszawa steel works in the suburbs of the capital and a resident vicar attached to the St. Stanisław Kostka Church, a Solidarity stronghold.

Popiełuszko, whose assassination was never properly investigated by the Polish authorities, instantly became a Church martyr in the great Bishop Stanisław tradition. His death probably did more to galvanize Poles in their support for Solidarity than any event since John Paul II's visit almost a year and a half earlier, much more than anything men like Wałęsa could achieve through underground conspiracies.

Jaruzelski says that he was "shattered" by the news of the priest's murder. But he adds that "one must respect the Church" for its role in that emergency. "For the pope and for Glemp, every martyr strengthens the Church. But they did not take advantage of it to create any kind of destabilization."

On December 13, exactly three years after he had proclaimed the "state of war" in Poland, Jaruzelski received a "brutal" letter from Chernenko, charging that "all the hostile elements are receiving support and protection from the Church." Chernenko wrote that "gaining strength and finding no serious counter-action on the part of the authorities, the Church is now directly defying the Socialist state. It organizes disorders. . . . It is preparing a counter-revolutionary army in the full sense of the word. And it prepares political and spiritual ground for a social upset [of the system]. . . ."

Poland was a constant preoccupation for John Paul II, but he also concentrated on running and reorganizing the Universal Church as well.

On February 2, 1983, the pope named eighteen new cardinals in the second consistory of his pontificate. He had named eleven cardinals at his first consistory on June 30, 1979, but that was essentially an emergency operation within nine months of his election to bring up to strength the College of Cardinals.

The 1983 consistory—like the one on May 25, 1985, when he would appoint twenty-seven cardinals—reflected to a remarkable degree the diversity that John Paul II wished to bring to the Church, placing in many cases a greater premium on a prospective cardinal's intellect than on his conformity to the pope's views (although a number of ideological allies were named, too).

Among the most interesting choices in 1983 was Jean-Marie Lustiger, then fifty-six, who had been serving as Archbishop of Paris since 1981. Born in Paris to Polish-Jewish parents who had emigrated to France after World War I (his father was a shopkeeper), Lustiger converted to Catholicism as a teenager. He survived the war and the Nazi occupation in the care of a Catholic family after his parents were deported to Germany; his mother died in the Oświęcim concentration camp in 1943. Lustiger was ordained a priest in 1954, spending many years thereafter as a chaplain to university students before being named Bishop of Orléans. Widely regarded as one of the Church's most brilliant intellects, Lustiger says that he hardly knew John Paul II when he received the red hat of the cardinalate. This fact, he says smilingly, "takes care of the charges that I'm part of the pope's Polish mafia." Over the years, the two men would grow very close.

The other significant choice was Archbishop Martini of Milan, the Jesuit, who was fifty-five years old at the time. He is a noted biblical scholar, former magnificent rector of the Gregorian University in Rome, and one of the Church's outstanding intellects.

John Paul II also made selections of political and geographic significance, both in 1983 and 1985. From the communist world, he had named Primate of Poland Glemp (cardinalate is not a prerequisite to be Primate); Archbishop Henryk Roman Gulbinowicz of Wrocław, Poland; Franjo Kuharic of Croatia (then still Yugoslavia); Jozef Tomko of Slovakia (then Czechoslovakia); Julijans Vaivods of Latvia (then part of the Soviet Union), who was eighty-seven years old; and Ivan Miroslav Lubachivsky of the Ukraine (then also in the Soviet Union).

From the Middle East, the pope chose the Maronite Patriarch Antoine Pierre Khoraiche of Lebanon. From the Third World, he selected Bernard Yago from the Ivory Coast, Francis Arinze from Nigeria, Paulos Tzadua from Ethiopia, Michael Michai Kitbunchu from Thailand, José Ali Lebrun Moratinos and Rosalio José Castillo Lara from Venezuela, Alfonso López Trujillo from Colombia, Miguel Obando y Bravo from Nicaragua, and Ricardo Vidal from the Philippines. And from the United States, he named Joseph L. Bernardin of Chicago, Bernard F. Law of Boston, and John J. O'Connor of New York.

In April 1984 John Paul II reorganized the Roman Curia in a drastic fashion. The appointment of Cardinal Gantin of Benin as prefect of the Congregation for Bishops was the most important change. The prefect of the congregation proposes all new bishops for nomination by the pope—

except for bishops from mission territories—and this was the first time an African had attained such a position of power in the Vatican. But Gantin also is a man of rare personal charm.

And once in a while, John Paul II enjoyed some special fun, too. In 1984, for example, he went skiing in the *summer* high in the Italian Alps. The site was the eternal snows of the eleven-thousand-foot Adamello glacier, where on July 16 the pope flew aboard a military helicopter with Italy's President Pertini, a nonskiier, and Monsignor Dziwisz, the papal secretary and a champion skiier. Wearing navy blue ski trousers, a gray-green shirt, and a navy blue windbreaker, John Paul II, then sixty-four years old and three years after surviving the assassination attempt, spent nearly four hours on the steep slopes the first day and a few more hours on the second before flying home. At dinner at the Adamello shelter, John Paul II toasted President Pertini, announcing that "this is the first time I've ever gone skiing in July!"

CHAPTER 27

On March 11, 1985, the Central Committee of the Soviet Communist Party elected Mikhail Gorbachev as general secretary, succeeding Chernenko, who had died the previous month. He was the fourth general secretary in three years.

John Paul II received the news at the Vatican, as unaware as everybody else of the changes Gorbachev's election portended, exactly one month after returning from his third South American and his twenty-fifth papal journey. He had visited Brazil, his first exposure to South America, in 1980, and Argentina ever so briefly in 1982. This time he had gone to Trinidad and Tobago, Venezuela, Ecuador, and Peru, winning an enthusiastic welcome all along the route, observing the extent of Latin American misery in the cities and villages, and hearing more than he wished about the Theology of Liberation.

Already in the course of the Brazilian visit the pope had encountered how this new theology had divided the Church. Also in Brazil, he had a dramatic encounter with Third World poverty when he toured Rio de Janeiro's Favela do Vidigal mountainside slum. It was there that Father Stanisław Starowieyski, his companion of the Kraków underground seminary and Roman studies, had died of disease as a missionary to the poorest of the poor of Brazil.

John Paul II donated his papal ring to the Favela do Vidigal community.

Traveling in Peru in 1984, the pope knew that Father Gustavo Gutiérrez, the father of the Theology of Liberation, lived in a similar urban slum in Lima, the capital, but there never was any possibility of John Paul II meeting him. The pope continued to regard this theology as being Marxist-tainted, or worse.

With Gorbachev's advent, John Paul II's and the Holy See's interest in Marxism and its possible mutations turned fully to the Soviet Union and Eastern Europe as the realization gradually dawned that a completely new climate was developing under perestroika, the Russian word meaning "restructuring." It was Gorbachev's term for his new policies. Immediately and inevitably, Gorbachev and perestroika affected the political situation in Poland, a fact that General Jaruzelski and Primate Glemp, his Church "ally," grasped at once and proceeded to act upon accordingly.

Coincidentally or not, Foreign Minister Gromyko called on John Paul II in late March 1985, within weeks of Gorbachev's election, on a mission that the pope found to be unclear but intriguing. The veteran Gromyko, who served every Soviet leader since Stalin, seemed to be probing in various directions, even hinting that the Kremlin might be interested in diplomatic relations with the Holy See.

And also coincidentally or not, John Paul II issued on June 2 his new encyclical, *Slavorum Apostoli* ("Apostles to the Slavs"), which was interpreted as a gesture toward an ecumenical dialogue with the Eastern churches, including the Russian Orthodox in the Soviet Union. The encyclical commemorated the thousandth anniversary of the apostolic mission in the Balkans and Eastern Europe of St. Cyril and St. Methodius, and the pope noted that they had led the nations of those regions to join those elsewhere in Europe that had already accepted Christianity.

Superbly aware that history is an instrument of proselytism as well as of politics, John Paul II remarked cheerfully as he presented the encyclical that "you will all understand how cordially this anniversary is shared by the first son of the Slav family summoned after nearly two thousand years to the apostolic capital of St. Peter in Rome."

In Poland, meanwhile, Jaruzelski personally instructed the party's Central Committee in July to disseminate to its key officials throughout the country a study by its Social Sciences Academy on the attitude of party members toward religion. Based on sociological research in "socialist and capitalist countries," the study found that for many years Poland had had "the highest percentage of persons [in the world] declaring themselves as believers and participating in religious practice."

These were the study's main conclusions:

> Since the mid-1970s, an increase in religious attitudes has been observed. It reached the apogee after the election of K. Wojtyła and during the social-political crisis of the 1980s. This phenomenon emerged particularly acutely among the intelligentsia, especially among persons with higher education. This is indicated in the results of studies in 1978 [before the election of K. Wojtyła] and in 1983. . . . An example is the attitudes of persons with higher education: private prayer at home was declared to be 25 percent in 1978, and 51.2 percent in 1983.

Accepting these realities, Jaruzelski (if not all his top party associates) also accepted the related fact that both religiously and politically the Church and John Paul II personally would be a permanent feature of Polish life. Accordingly, the Joint Government-Church Commission, in which the pope had considerable influence through the Polish episcopate, busied itself late in 1986 with plans for a Consultative Council to be formed by leading public and professional figures, regardless of political persuasion, to advise the government on broad national policies. This was Jaruzelski's idea and the regime made it clear that it would encourage the participation of opposition intellectuals, writers, and economists though the door remained officially shut to identifiable Solidarity personalities.

In this sense, the Church became the government's full-fledged partner in preparing Poland's ultimate peaceful transition from communist rule. At that stage, neither side could anticipate how swiftly events would start to occur. But the planning for the Consultative Council turned out to be the foundation for the creation two years later of the "Round Table" format of negotiations that would lead to Polish democracy. Many of the persons connected with the Consultative Council project had close links with the Church. Indeed, the Joint Government-Church Commission was shaping up as a "holy mini-alliance," as one of the bishops remarked privately.

Unquestionably, Mikhail Gorbachev, knowingly or not, had provided additional impetus for the new Polish experiment when he announced in Prague in 1987 that "the entire framework of political relations between the socialist countries must be strictly based on absolute independence" and that "every nation is entitled to choose its own way of development, to dispose of its fate, its territory, and its human and natural resources."

This meant the formal demise of the Brezhnev Doctrine of the "defense of socialism" that had been invoked to justify the 1968 Soviet invasion of Czechoslovakia and would have been invoked had Soviet and Warsaw Pact troops marched into Poland in 1980 or 1981.

In Poland, at least, Gorbachev's words were interpreted, certainly by the Church and the opposition—if not yet by Jaruzelski—as a green light for seeking basic changes in the political structure of the country. At the Vatican, John Paul II noted that he was being proven correct in his belief that an evolutionary process of change in Poland, which he had been encouraging since his 1979 visit, was inevitable. And there was no question that the communist apparatus was rotting within, with the party split into more and more factions.

The pope's periodic pilgrimages to Poland, as he called them, were now being taken for granted by the regime. Consequently, the Joint Government-Church Commission began preparing his next trip, scheduled for June 1987, at the same time it debated at its meeting in November 1986 the formation of the Consultative Council. All the pieces were falling into place.

And Soviet attitudes had become so relaxed, relatively

speaking, that Primate Glemp was able to visit Byelorussia and Moscow twice in 1986, to meet with Catholic and Russian Orthodox clergy and Soviet scholars and officials. It was the first time a Polish cardinal had ever traveled to the Soviet Union.

On January 13, 1987, John Paul II and General Jaruzelski conferred alone for eighty minutes in the papal study in the Apostolic Palace in what both "great Poles" later publicly described as a "historical visit."

Jaruzelski had come to the Vatican in preparation for the pontiff's forthcoming pilgrimage to Poland, and their conversation was a crucial breakthrough in the Polish process of evolution as well as in the cementing of their personal relationship. Moreover, it served to lay the cornerstone for the "John Paul II-Jaruzelski-Gorbachev Triangle" that the Polish general helped to construct in absolute secrecy.

It was the pope's and Jaruzelski's first meeting in three and a half years, since the Kraków emergency session in June 1983, although they had maintained vigorous private correspondence in the intervening period.

Jaruzelski thought that the timing of their Vatican conference was excellent because the Consultative Council that the Church had helped the government to hammer together was already functioning, many domestic reforms were underway, and, as he puts it, "we could already discern on the horizon what would be the 'Round Table.'" As for John Paul II, he felt that Jaruzelski had fulfilled all the promises he had made him in Poland in 1983: the "state of war" had been lifted, political prisoners had been released, and most of the restrictions on the population had been removed. Thus the pope welcomed the general most warmly to his study.

As Jaruzelski recalls the conversation across the pope's narrow desk, "I found that he had a complete understanding of the processes through which we were living." And John Paul II, he says, "accepted with great attention and approval the concept that we [Poland] are positively influencing the changes happening in the East.

"I concluded," Jaruzelski goes on saying, "that the pope saw in the trends and changes occurring in Poland a significance well beyond the Polish framework . . . that they are, to a great extent, an impulse for the changes occurring in the other countries, especially in the Soviet Union."

It was in the course of that conversation that Jaruzelski first mentioned Gorbachev to John Paul II. This had followed Jaruzelski's discussions with Gorbachev about the pope. The pontiff and the general would return to the subject when John Paul II came to Poland five months later, in June 1987. Jaruzelski had met Gorbachev for the first time in April 1985, about a month after his election as general secretary, and they had remained in close contact ever since. During their initial five-hour session, Jaruzelski recalls, they talked about the Polish Church and the pope.

As Jaruzelski sums it up, "I flatter myself in thinking that I was the one who, for the first time, brought the pope and Gorbachev together though without their physical presence. . . . Because I was the one who knew Gorbachev well."

The general's account of his secret "mutual friend" dealings with John Paul II and Gorbachev is so extraordinary—it has never before been revealed publicly—that it is best told in his own words:

> It simply flowed from the position I occupied in politics at the time that I became, as it were, an informal conduit and the carrier of certain opinions from Gorbachev to the pope and from the pope to Gorbachev. I was able to speak to each of them about my assessment of their respective personalities in the most constructive aspect. I told the pope what I knew about Gorbachev and what role Gorbachev was playing, what were his intentions, what difficulties he faced, how important it was to support him, how to understand him, and what a great chance this was for Europe and the world—even if everything was not happening as smoothly as one may desire. And when I spoke with Gorbachev, I tried to convey to him the opinions of the pope, in which he was very much interested.

According to Jaruzelski, it was Gorbachev who originally broached the subject of John Paul II during one of their meetings in 1986. This is how the general remembers it:

> Gorbachev asked me what the pope was like, how he thought. And I, in turn, tried to communicate to him the sense of the personal dimension of the pope and, at the same time, his positive role. I pointed out that he was the first pope to become so greatly committed to the cause of peace, and not only verbally, but through his great participation in many activities. He was the first pope who had emphasized so strongly the question of social justice and whose social teachings were rather close to some concepts of socialist and communist ideology, as you prefer. I told him that this was a Slav pope who sensed better than others the realities of our region, our history, our dreams.
>
> I like to think that in my conversations with Gorbachev I was able to improve his view on the pope and the Roman Catholic Church. I said that the pope is a man of universal thought who was not at all uncritical about capitalism, in which he detected certain illnesses, and that he talked openly about it. . . . But the pope wanted to pursue an "eastern policy" of rapprochement. And I think this had a certain influence on Gorbachev's thinking. . . . In a sense, I was becoming an intermediary between them.

Jaruzelski says that he had told the pope from the outset about his conversations about him with Gorbachev—and told Gorbachev about discussing him with the pope. John Paul II has confirmed that he was fully aware of the emergence of this "triangular" situation and that he was "very much interested" in Gorbachev.

When John Paul II was asked in 1994 about Jaruzelski's role in establishing the contact between him and Gorbachev, he said, "Yes, he was an intermediary, but, of course, not an official one. . . ." He said he liked Jaruzelski because "he is an intelligent man."

Jaruzelski says,

> In my conversations with the pope in 1987, both at the Vatican and in Warsaw, I spoke very forcefully about Gorbachev's way of thinking—Gorbachev was

> calling it the "new thinking"—and with Gorbachev I spoke very forcefully about the pope. Afterwards, they met, conducted correspondence. . . . In my last conversation with the pope [at the Vatican in 1992], he affirmed that Providence had sent us Gorbachev.

The general emphasized that in his talks with Gorbachev, "I said that the Church in Poland has played a noble role, both historically and contemporaneously, and that in such a situation there must be a place for the Polish pope who remains a Polish patriot."

Primate Glemp had also acted as an emissary in the nascent relationship between John Paul II and Gorbachev that Jaruzelski was orchestrating. Jaruzelski says that through his frequent conversations with Glemp,

> I tried to convey [to the pope] my assessment of Gorbachev and *perestroika,* and that he should be supported. . . . So my contact with the pope was not only through our direct talks. The contact was permanent. Glemp traveled all the time [to Rome] and had contacts with the pope. And I felt from Glemp's reactions that Gorbachev's efforts were watched with great interest and sympathy [by the pope]. And that, as far as I was concerned, my information and my suggestions in this matter were received with understanding and approval.

The general believes that Glemp also acted as "a kind of an emissary" of the pope to the Soviet Union when he visited there, particularly on ecumenical matters in terms of the Russian Orthodox Church. Gorbachev was kept informed about it, Jaruzelski says, "and this was quite important for him because it offered him an entrance to the Catholic world and to the West in general."

John Paul II was back in Poland on June 6, 1987, for a week-long visit on his third pontifical pilgrimage. Earlier that year, he had traveled to Uruguay, Chile, and Argentina and to Germany. Since his 1983 Polish visit, he had been twice to Asia, four times to Latin America, and once to Africa, in addition to a trip to Canada, one to India, and six to West European countries.

Although his presence in Poland ceased to be a novelty, it was still cause for a national explosion of enthusiasm, especially because Poles felt that the nation was on the eve of the *fin de régime.* Solidarity was functioning almost openly, and the government made no effort to discourage John Paul II from spending an hour with Wałęsa and his family at a diocesan residence near Gdańsk. This time they did discuss Poland's political future.

Earlier that day, the pope told hundreds of thousands of workers in his homily at Mass in Gdańsk that the 1980 accords between Solidarity and the government had their roots in the bloody 1970 events there and that "they will remain in the history of Poland as an expression of the growing consciousness of the working people concerning the entire social-moral order on the Polish soil."

The pope and Jaruzelski met twice in private and, as the general recalls, he had the satisfaction of informing him that for the first time in postwar history bishops and party first secretaries in all the regions of Poland had met to plan together the papal activities during this visit. Similar meetings had been held on the town and village level between parish priests and party officials, and Jaruzelski said he hoped Church and party representatives would henceforth meet on a regular basis.

When the conversation turned to Gorbachev, the general told John Paul II that "he must not lose and he will not lose," and that "he must be helped." It was thanks to Gorbachev, he said, that Poland was now enjoying relative sovereignty within the Warsaw Pact.

Afterward events in Poland moved rapidly—always under the pope's and the Church's watchful eyes. Gorbachev visited Warsaw and Kraków in July 1988, receiving the first warm and spontaneous reception any Soviet leader had ever received from Poles. A wave of strikes during 1988 and rising demands by the opposition for power sharing and Solidarity's return to a legal status convinced Jaruzelski and the party leadership that the time had come to begin negotiating changes in Poland's basic political structure.

Jaruzelski, who had given up the office of prime minister to assume the post of President of Poland—with full executive powers—named Mieczysław Rakowski, earlier a deputy prime minister, as the transition prime minister in charge of negotiations with the opposition. By late 1988, all sides had agreed on round table talks in which every political group, including Solidarity's leaders (although Solidarity as such was still illegal), would be represented. In fact, Wałęsa was invited to confer with General Czesław Kiszczak, the interior minister who had placed him under detention in 1981.

The episcopate and the government were the midwives of the round table undertaking, which was to lead to the creation of a coalition cabinet with the inclusion of ministers with direct links to the Church. And among Prime Minister Rakowski's initial acts was to call on Cardinal Glemp. They reviewed the political situation and Glemp told Rakowski that it was essential to support Gorbachev's policies in the Soviet Union—as John Paul II was already doing discreetly at his end.

Less felicitous was Rakowski's plan to shut down the Lenin Shipyard in Gdańsk, the birthplace of Solidarity but a vast drain on the country's financial resources. The shipyard, obsolete and losing considerable money, still employed twelve thousand workers; John Paul II came to the rescue. Speaking to Polish pilgrims in the Vatican during the first week of November, the pope declared that "again, we have cause to be worried about the Gdańsk community, and especially about the Gdańsk shipyard. We have always tried to offer our solidarity to 'Solidarity.' At this moment, too, we are expressing this solidarity." That was the end of attempts to do away with the shipyard.

On February 6, 1989, round table negotiations began at the palace of the Council of Ministers in Warsaw. In preparation for the talks, Rakowski led a government delegation to discuss with Cardinal Macharski and the episcopate the possibility of holding parliamentary elections in 1989, six months ahead of the normal schedule, because of the impending structural changes. It was the first time that the regime and the episcopate held a policy meeting on such a high level, but the Church was now an equal partner in the management of Polish affairs.

On April 6, the round table announced the agreement to reshape Poland through parliamentary democracy and reforms in the economy, ending its subordination to government decisions and control. It was the end of communism in Poland, an extraordinary event, achieved peacefully and serving as an example for the rest of Eastern Europe. Solidarity regained its official status, and on April 20, Wałęsa and five of his top associates flew to Rome to thank John Paul II for his efforts on behalf of Polish democracy and Solidarity.

As a result of parliamentary elections held early in June—the first free elections in Poland in over forty years—Solidarity won power overwhelmingly. Parish priests at Mass across the land had urged the faithful to vote for Solidarity candidates and defeat the communists. Tadeusz Mazowiecki, the Catholic intellectual who had been one of Wałęsa's advisers during the great strikes in 1980, became the new prime minister. As part of the round table agreements, General Jaruzelski remained as president for two more years.

On July 17, Poland and the Holy See established formal diplomatic relations, symbolizing and capping the amazing accomplishments of the alliance between the Polish pope and the Polish communist army general.

Many years later. John Paul II was asked whether he thought that the negotiations about Poland's future might have collapsed and a "tragedy" occurred if instead of Wojtyła, Jaruzelski, and Gorbachev, the papacy were held by a non-Slav and the Polish and Soviet leaders were old-fashioned communist apparatchiks. The pope pondered the question, and replied that he could agree with such a hypothetical interpretation. The pope also indicated that the Polish situation had been much more complicated than elsewhere in Eastern Europe where, after the events in Poland, the communist regimes had simply collapsed. The Polish case had required much diplomacy and acumen.

But the Polish pope, increasingly impressed by Mikhail Gorbachev, now had his eye on the Soviet Union. His interest was in expanding religious freedom there, establishing diplomatic relations with Moscow, and cooperating with the Soviets on a whole range of international problems. Starting in the late 1980s, roughly about the time Jaruzelski had begun to act as the "informal intermediary" between him and Gorbachev, John Paul II instructed Holy See diplomats to try to establish a dialogue with the Soviet Union.

An opportunity to do so was actually supplied by Gorbachev himself. Russian Orthodox Patriarch Filaret of Kiev, who had always been close to the Kremlin, was instructed by Gorbachev in the spring of 1988 to invite the leaders of all the world religions to come to Moscow to commemorate one thousand years of Christianity in the Russian lands. The invitation itself was an unprecedented gesture on the part of the Soviets, following an announcement by Yuri Kashlev, the Soviet delegate to a Conference on Security and Cooperation in Europe (CSCE) meeting in Venice early in February, that the Leninist religious policies of the past seventy years would no longer be applied in the Soviet Union.

In what Vatican officials describe as "one of the most crucial decisions at the end of the Cold War," John Paul II, fresh from the Jaruzelski briefings and messages, decided to send not just one but two Holy See delegations. He had hoped to be able to visit the Soviet Union himself for the Christian millennium, but as recently as March, Patriarch Filaret had declared that the pope would not be invited. John Paul II's special desire was to come to the Ukraine, the home of as many as five million Catholics of the Byzantine-Ukrainian Rite (often called Uniates), who are in communion with Rome and accept the pope's authority.

The Moscow invitation fit perfectly, however, into the pope's long-range strategy for the Soviet Union. Imaginative as ever, John Paul II named a "religious delegation" formed by Cardinal Johannes Willebrands, then president of the Pontifical Council for Christian Unity and the Vatican's camerlengo, and Bishop Pierre Duprey, the secretary of the council, and a separate "political delegation" consisting of Secretary of State Casaroli and Vatican

Spokesman Navarro-Valls. It was the highest level representation the Holy See could dispatch; moreover Casaroli was the Vatican's leading authority on the communist countries.

Casaroli carried a six-page letter from John Paul II to Gorbachev, with instructions that it be handed personally to the Soviet leader. The existence of the letter and its contents have never been made public, but in it the pope urged Gorbachev to agree to full freedom of religion in the Soviet Union for people of all creeds—especially for Roman Catholics in Lithuania, Latvia, and Byelorussia, and Uniates in the Ukraine—and to have, in effect, proposed the establishment of diplomatic relations between Moscow and the Holy See.

The Vatican representatives attended a solemn Christianity millennium session at the Bolshoi Theater along with 250 religious leaders from all over the world, including Moscow's Russian Orthodox Patriarch Pimen, the Dalai Lama, and Billy Graham. Gorbachev was represented by his wife, Raisa.

Though Casaroli and Navarro had informed the Foreign Ministry that they had a letter from John Paul II to Gorbachev, they were kept waiting four days, including the weekend, at the Sovietskaya Rosyia Hotel luxury suite, for an invitation to deliver it. Then they were informed that Gorbachev would receive them at the Kremlin the next day, June 13. Casaroli and Navarro were driven there in a KGB car and taken to Gorbachev's private office, a floor above where Lenin's had been.

Gorbachev and Foreign Minister Eduard Shevardnadze received them with great cordiality, each making a point of telling the Vatican visitors that they had been baptized at birth (subsequently, as president of independent Georgia, Shevardnadze was rebaptized). Casaroli handed Gorbachev the papal letter and a "very pleasant, polite conversation" ensued. Gorbachev, however, had no letter and no message for the pope, and fourteen months would elapse before he was ready to reply formally.

But John Paul II was pleased when Casaroli and Navarro reported to him that Gorbachev had spoken to them at some length about the future of the young people in the

Soviet Union—the future of the world's youth is another of the pope's favorite topics—and that the two Soviet leaders had chosen to mention their childhood baptism. He read it as a "signal" from the Kremlin, showing interest in further dealings with the Holy See.

Gorbachev sent another such "signal," or so the Vatican thought, when he visited Kraków's Wawel Cathedral, where Karol Wojtyła had been consecrated as bishop thirty years earlier, during his July visit to Poland. Then followed a long silence from the Kremlin.

Suddenly, in the last week of August 1989, a Soviet emissary appeared at the papal summer residence in Castel Gandolfo with a letter from Gorbachev to John Paul II. The pontiff had just returned from Santiago de Compostela in northern Spain where he had presided over the celebrations of World Youth Day.

It is unclear what precisely had impelled Gorbachev to write John Paul II after such a long delay, but the entire political situation in Eastern Europe had changed dramatically since the pope had written to him the previous year. In Poland, the June elections had handed Solidarity its smashing victory, and Mazowiecki was now the new prime minister. And communist regimes elsewhere in Eastern Europe were beginning to unravel.

In any event, Gorbachev's seven-page letter (never released publicly) praised John Paul II's writings—"I know what you have written," Gorbachev wrote—and stressed that he had been particularly impressed with the pope's *Sollicitudo Rei Socialis* (On Social Concern) encyclical, issued on December 30, 1987.

In it, the pope declared that "We present to the Blessed Virgin difficult individual situations, so that she may place them before her Son, asking that he *alleviate and change* them. But we also present to her *social situations* and *the international crisis* itself, in their worrying aspects of poverty, unemployment, shortage of food, the arms race, contempt for human rights, and situations and dangers of conflict, partial or total." Gorbachev wrote John Paul II that he, too, was preoccupied with human beings, first and foremost.

But the key phrase in Gorbachev's letter was that "We must meet." Though he had proposed no date, Holy See and Soviet diplomats in Rome (the Soviet embassy in Italy had a senior official in charge of Vatican contacts) went to work immediately and in the deepest secrecy on preparing the encounter. When Gorbachev and President Bush agreed to confer aboard the Soviet liner *Maxim Gorky* in Marsaxlokk Bay in Malta on December 2 and 3, the Vatican meeting was set for December 1.

Gorbachev and his wife arrived in Rome on November 30, and the Soviet leader set the tone for the next day's session with the pope in a speech he delivered before the Rome City Council, declaring that perestroika had radically changed the Soviet attitude toward religion, "whose values could serve, and already served, the cause of renewal in our country." He said that "our attitude has changed toward problems that we treated, and I do not want to hide it, in a simplistic way, such as, for example, that of religion."

When Gorbachev entered the papal apartments on the late morning of December 1, he was the first general secretary of the Soviet Communist Party ever to meet with a pontiff though he also was the Soviet head of state, for which he had a precedent. Pope Paul VI had received Soviet President Podgorny in 1967, but Podgorny was little more than a figurehead.

White-robed John Paul II welcomed Gorbachev and his wife warmly in the parlor of the papal apartments before the two men adjourned to the adjoining study for their private conversation. Gorbachev was wearing a dark suit and Raisa was in a short red dress. (Vatican protocol officials acknowledged later that they had told the Soviet embassy that she could wear "whatever she likes to" when an inquiry was made about proper attire. "We should have known better," they said.)

The pope and the general secretary spent about twenty minutes alone—they sat on either side of John Paul II's small antique desk—conversing in Russian (the pope using his Polish version of Russian). The pontiff sat in his armchair and Gorbachev on a straight-backed chair. Then they were joined by interpreters for the delivery of their formal speeches.

Replying to the pope's greetings, in which he recalled the "painful events of the past" and expressed his hope for "renewal," Gorbachev described their meeting as "an event of extraordinary importance." Then, departing from his prepared text, he proposed that diplomatic relations be established between the Holy See and Moscow, and invited John Paul II to the Soviet Union.

Discussing the visit that evening at dinner with his closest aides, the pope indicated that he was "exalted" and pleased by it. He said that Gorbachev had told him that he was prepared "to go all the way on religious liberties and other freedoms." Asked what he thought of Gorbachev, John Paul II replied, "He is a man of principle. He is a person who not only believes in principles, but he is ready to accept whatever unpleasant consequences of his acts may occur." He did not find "typical communist mentality" in Gorbachev, and he was "very much interested in where he got all those new ideas for reforming and changing the whole organization of the Soviet Union."

General Jaruzelski believes that the crucial "factor" in creating a basic understanding between John Paul II and Gorbachev was the Soviet leader's commitment in their conversation to grant formal recognition to the Greek Catholics in the Ukraine—the Uniates, who accept the pope in Rome as their head—as a separate church and to return its confiscated properties.

The Holy See's interpretation of Gorbachev's attitude and remarks was that he needed support for perestroika from religious institutions, notably from the Russian Orthodox Church, and that he regarded John Paul II as his "natural ally" because he enjoyed "great moral authority." Gorbachev had also conveyed the notion that the Soviet Union could do business with the United States only in the context of American strategic interest, but he believed that the pope had no "geopolitical objectives" in dealing with the Soviets and therefore is a "natural ally."

As a result of the John Paul II–Gorbachev meeting, diplomatic relations were established in 1990 between the

Holy See and Moscow. The Roman Catholic Church was authorized to function openly in the Soviet Union (though it already did to some extent in Lithuania and Byelorussia), and the pope named Archbishop Tadeusz Kondrusiewicz, a Pole, as Apostolic Administrator for Moscow and the western Soviet Union, and separate apostolic administrators for Siberia and Kazakhstan.

The relations between the Vatican and the Soviet Union became so close that in 1990 Secretary of State Casaroli advised a senior American diplomat at the Vatican that he could be of instant assistance in the event of a major crisis between the Soviets and the United States. But, as Casaroli would learn only years later, Czech secret service agents, operating with the KGB, had installed concealed listening devices in his office. KGB agents had also infiltrated the Pontifical Oriental Institute where Russian Orthodox and Ukrainian Uniate priests were trained.

A year and a half after his meeting with John Paul II—in August 1991—Gorbachev was ousted from power after a coup that failed (he was made to pay for it), communism collapsed in the Soviet Union, and the country came apart. The pope was visiting Budapest at the time of the coup, and he immediately sent a telegram of support for Gorbachev, but it was too late.

To this day, Gorbachev is received with great cordiality by John Paul II whenever he comes to Rome as a private citizen. And his admiration for the pope was expressed in an article written in 1992: "Everything that happened in Eastern Europe in these last few years would have been impossible without the presence of this Pope and without the important role—including the political role—that he played on the world stage."

In his 1994 book *Crossing the Threshold of Hope,* John Paul II offered an answer to the question posed to him as to the reasons for the death of communism. Referring to the three Portuguese shepherd children from Fátima "who suddenly, on the eve of the outbreak of the revolution in October, heard 'Russia will convert'" when the Virgin appeared to them, the pope wrote: "They could not have invented those predictions. They did not know the history of the geography, and even less were they familiar with social movements and ideological developments. And nevertheless it happened as they had announced."

But, John Paul II added, "in a certain sense Communism as a system fell by itself . . . as a consequence of its own errors and abuse."

PART SEVEN

CHAPTER 28

With the demise of communism in Europe, John Paul II, ever the uncompromising fighter and champion of moral causes, turned his full firepower in the 1990s on the "culture of death" in the capitalist world, which he regards as a menace to civilization equal in the long run to the defeated Marxism-Leninism.

Defying life-threatening abdominal surgery and crippling accidents that repeatedly forced him to the hospital, the pope entered the new decade determined to prepare humanity—Catholic and non-Catholic alike—spiritually as well as politically for the approaching new millennium of the Christian era. The sacred and profane blended as he preached his credo in an urgent crescendo from the altar of St. Peter's Basilica in Rome to the hills of Sicily and from a field Mass near Denver, Colorado, to the ancient halls of the University of Riga in Latvia, one of the Baltic republics freshly liberated from Soviet dominance.

And just as forcefully, John Paul II plunged into peacemaking and activist diplomacy from the Persian Gulf to the former Yugoslavia and from the Middle East and the Holy See's formal recognition of Israel to the African tragedies of Somalia, Liberia, and Rwanda, where he begrudgingly approved the use of an international military force for humanitarian purposes.

Because this tough Polish pope acts in absolutist terms,

his outspoken stances on the issues both of Catholic discipline and social behavior in general—from birth control and the role of women in the Church to excessive Western consumerism—have touched off swirling controversies. The controversies skyrocketed in the early 1990s as the pontiff embarked on his new crusades with unprecedented intensity, seemingly racing against time.

A man of unshakable principles and lifelong consistency in his fundamental views, John Paul II never cared to be "politically correct," before or after this expression was coined in the West, preferring frank speech and paying no attention whatsoever to criticism rising inside and outside the Church, particularly in the United States.

In the course of what is clearly the final phase of his breathlessly assertive pontificate, he has voiced his opinions and prohibitions in very explicit encyclicals in 1991 and 1993 (he has issued ten of them in fifteen years, compared with six written by Paul VI during a comparable period), scores of Apostolic Letters, several thousand speeches and homilies, and—in 1994—an internationally best-selling book covering a wide range of religious, temporal, and personal themes. And despite disruptions caused by health problems, he has kept up an exhausting travel schedule.

John Paul II, who issued an Apostolic Letter on the Christian sense of suffering (*Salvifici Doloris*) in 1984, less than three years after barely surviving an assassination attempt, was not spared pain and suffering in the 1990s. But believing that suffering is a form of grace granted by God, he has never complained.

On July 15, 1992, surgeons at Rome's Gemelli Polyclinic removed a precancerous orange-sized tumor from the pope's colon in a potentially life-threatening four-hour operation. John Paul II had been taken to the hospital after reporting considerable stomach pain. When X rays showed that he had a tumor in the sigmoid flexure of the colon, the pope, then seventy-two years old, was informed of the seriousness of his condition. As in 1981, he received the Last Sacraments before surgery began because "he wanted to be prepared to die," in the words of his official spokesman, Dr. Navarro-Valls, a physician by training.

To reach the tumor, the surgeons reopened the scar left

from the 1981 surgery, which runs from below his chest almost to his groin, rather than make a fresh incision. While inside, they discovered that the pope had gallstones and decided to remove his gallbladder as well. After the three-inch-long tumor was excised, a biopsy indicated that it was turning cancerous. As Dr. Navarro-Valls put it, the tests had shown "proliferating cells which were losing their benign characteristics to take on those of a malign degeneration without, however, showing invasive behavior."

Again, John Paul II's rugged constitution helped him to recover well from the operation—he was convinced that God still had a mission for him and would not keep him from fulfilling it—and there have been no subsequent signs of cancer. In October, he flew to the Dominican Republic for the five-hundredth anniversary of the arrival of Christianity on the island of Hispaniola and a meeting of the Latin American Bishops' Conference (CELAM). During the Christmas period, the pope spent six hours skiing in the mountains near Rome.

On November 11, 1993, John Paul II dislocated his right shoulder and suffered a slight fracture in its socket when he tripped over the hem of his robes and fell on the steps in the Hall of Benediction in the Apostolic Palace after an audience with officials of the U.N. Food and Agriculture Organization (FAO). The pope was treated under general anesthesia, and his arm and shoulder were immobilized with a sling. He wore it for about four weeks, joking that he could bless just as effectively with his left hand. Less than three months later, John Paul II went skiing, quietly disobeying doctors' orders.

Much more serious was the accident on April 28, 1994, when, around 11:00 P.M., he slipped in the bathroom of his apartment. Having suffered a complete transcervical fracture under the head of the right femur, the pope underwent two hours of surgery for hip replacement with the implant of a prosthesis. His activities were considerably curtailed (spring trips to Belgium and Sicily had to be canceled), and John Paul II had not fully recovered by the end of the year despite an August vacation in the northern mountains.

Throughout the autumn of 1994, the pope was visibly in serious pain, walking slowly and carefully—almost shuffling—and carrying a cane publicly for the first time. During a mid-September visit to Zagreb in the former Yugoslavia, he had great difficulty walking, and a long-scheduled trip to the United States in October had to be called off for health reasons, though he traveled on overnight visits to the south of Italy and Sicily late in the fall. His overall physical appearance—great fatigue, a weak voice, and trouble with his leg—set off rumors and speculations about the state of his health. (And on November 27, he smashed his right pinkie in the door of his limousine as he was getting out at St. Peter's Basilica to celebrate Holy Mass. He had to wear a little bandage.)

John Paul II has grown increasingly emotional and confrontational in his vision of the world and its ills as he progresses through the eighth decade of his life. He turned seventy on May 18, 1990. His old Kraków friends say that he had never before displayed such emotionalism, but they believe, as do many observers in Rome and elsewhere, that his attitudes and rhetoric reflect accurately the concerns of many others in the world over the condition of contemporary society.

In this sense, the pope's instincts may be very much attuned to global trends and fears, especially among the young people, and his message may fit well into the context of the time toward the end of the century and millennium even if his tone often tends to be messianic, apocalyptic, and verging on hyperbole.

On the mercilessly hot morning of August 15, 1993, the Feast of Assumption, John Paul II summed up his own distress over the present state of the world as he addressed a half million young people gathered at Cherry Creek State Park near Denver for World Youth Day:

> A "culture of death" seeks to impose itself on our desire to live and live to the full. There are those who reject the light of life, preferring the "fruitless works of darkness." Their harvest is injustice, discrimination, exploitation, deceit, violence. In every age, a measure of their apparent success is the death of innocents. In our own century, as at no other time in history, the

> "culture of death" has assumed a social and institutional form of legality to justify the most horrible crimes against humanity: genocide, "final solutions," "ethnic cleansings," and the massive taking of lives of human beings even before they are born or before they reach the natural point of death. . . . Vast sectors of society are confused about what is right and what is wrong, and are at the mercy of those with the power to "create" opinion and impose it on others.

The evening before, during the prayer vigil at the park, the pope expressed grave warnings to his audience:

> Christ, the Good Shepherd . . . sees so many young people throwing away their lives in a flight into irresponsibility and falsehood. Drug and alcohol abuse, pornography and sexual disorder, violence: these are grave social problems which call for a social response from the whole of society, within each country and on the international level. . . . In a technological culture in which people are used to dominating matter, discovering its laws and mechanisms in order to transform it according to their wishes, the danger arises of also wanting to manipulate conscience and its demands. In a culture which holds that no universally valid truth is possible, nothing is absolute. Therefore, in the end—they say—objective goodness and evil no longer really matter. Good comes to mean what is pleasing or useful at a particular moment. Evil means what contradicts our subjective wishes. Each person can build a private system of values.

World Youth Days, established by John Paul II in 1986 as formal biennial gatherings to enhance the Church's efforts in pastoral work among young people, have been held, prior to Denver, in Rome, Buenos Aires, Santiago de Compostela in Spain, and Częstochowa, each time in his presence. But the pope has succeeded in making them into joyful occasions rather than simply venues for collective prayer and ominous warnings. At the Colorado state park, for example, there were soloists and combos and a symphony orchestra on the huge stage where John Paul II sat for long hours in an armchair, smiling, waving, and tapping his foot to the music, and occasionally joking into the microphone. Giant closed-circuit television screens above the stage magnified his figure manyfold for those in the vast crowd too far away to see him in person. The mood had seized the audience, there was rhythmic applause, there was the wave.

Colorado being fairly bilingual, a group began chanting, "Juan-Pablo-Segundo: Te-Ama-Todo-El-Mundo!" (John Paul the Second: The Whole World Loves You), which rhymes in Spanish, but the pope interrupted with a mock severe admonition, also in Spanish: "No, no, aquí se habla inglés!" (No, no, English is spoken here!), to the delight of the young crowd.

With the Denver visit as the centerpiece, 1993 had been a particularly busy year for John Paul II. In addition to the Youth Day activities, he had met President Clinton for the first time, for a long discussion of foreign policy.

In February, the pope had gone to Benin, Uganda, and Sudan on his latest African tour. The one-day stop in Khartoum was a daring penetration into a stronghold of Islam, the world's fastest-growing religion, with which the Roman Catholic Church is in open competition on the African continent. The unending Sudanese civil war pits northern Muslims against southern Christians and animists. John Paul II expressed his hope that *shari'a,* the Muslim law, might someday be changed to allow conversions from Islam to Christianity, but he found no encouragement among his Muslim fundamentalist hosts.

In April, the pope flew for one day to Albania, once Europe's most savage dictatorial communist state, which he described as being "like the tomb in which the Jews buried Christ, putting the stone against its entrance. . . . [But] the tombstone was rolled away and a period of changes began." Concern about a suspected assassination plot had forced him to go by helicopter, instead of by road, from Tirana, the capital, to the town of Shkoder to embrace its archbishop, Frano Illia, who had served a prison sentence of twenty years at hard labor. In June, John Paul II went to Spain, one of his favorite countries, to encourage a revival of the Spanish tradition of missionary evangelism.

En route to Denver in August, the pope had stopped in Kingston, Jamaica, and Mérida on Mexico's Yucatán Peninsula. Speaking to Indians at high noon in a village an hour away, with the sun beating down on him, he assured them that the Church had cared for their welfare from the first day the *conquistadores* had set foot in Mexico. But five months later, when Indians rose in revolt against their landlords and the government in Chiapas, in Mexico's Southwestern region, the Vatican was busy trying to remove the local bishop, Samuel Ruíz, the friend and champion of the poverty-stricken peasants.

After resting for less than three weeks from the North American foray, John Paul II traveled to Lithuania, Latvia, and Estonia, his first visit to the former Soviet Union. The three days in Lithuania, which has long historical ties with Poland and where Polish is still widely spoken in Vilnius, the capital (a Polish city before the war), were a "very emotional experience . . . it was very important for me," as the pope put it later. The first evening in Vilnius, he prayed at the altar of Our Lady of Ostrabrama, also a patron saint of Poland. He had revisited Poland itself in 1991, on his fourth quadrennial pilgrimage.

John Paul II's inflexibility on issues of moral, ethical, and religious principle, and the emotionality attached to it, were displayed more markedly than ever during 1994, which also turned out to be his personal *annus horribilis* of illness, physical disability, and bitter disappointment over canceled foreign trips.

The most overwhelming issue for him in this field—perhaps the most important of the entire pontificate—dealt with birth control. In anticipation of a September meeting in Cairo, John Paul II launched a "spring offensive" on a scale unprecedented in papal diplomatic history to prevent the United Nations Conference on Population and Development from adopting a policy document that in his eyes would legitimize internationally both abortion and artificial contraception.

Inasmuch as this whole question touched on government policies as well as on moral and religious beliefs, it became a nightmarish tangle of political and spiritual controversies and considerations for all the concerned parties: the pope, President Clinton, the 170 governments planning to be represented in Cairo, nongovernmental organizations, population control and anti-abortion lobbies, churches of all persuasions (in Muslim countries governments and Islamic groups and institutions hold varying views on population matters), and millions of Catholics and non-Catholics holding individual views. And the language used by the Holy See in this "spring offensive" was truly astonishing.

The opening gun was fired on February 23, when *L'Osservatore Romano,* the Holy See's official organ (its editor is appointed by the pope and its editorial offices are located inside the Vatican walls), devoted nine full pages to the text in Latin of John Paul II's "Letter to the Family." The newspaper's pages are wider than those of the *Wall Street Journal,* and the issue included a booklet with the text in Italian. Subsequently, it was disseminated around the world in *L'Osservatore*'s half-dozen weekly foreign-language editions, from English to Polish.

As 1994 was the U.N.'s and the Church's International Year of the Family, and the pope's "Letter" addressed itself to the sanctity of family life, including the protection of the life of the unborn. Though the Church believes that life begins at conception, *L'Osservatore* the same day carried an article by its moral theologian, Franciscan Father Gino Concetti, declaring that even the use of the anti-conception pill is a reason for excommunication because it is morally tantamount to abortion, an offense calling for such punishment. It must be assumed that Father Concetti was conveying the views of John Paul II. Many theologians, however, dispute this idea (apart from the practical impossibility of enforcing the punishment).

The "Letter to the Family" announced that the doctrine of the Church on abortion and contraception would never change, which meant at least during the lifetime of John Paul II. What the next pope might do on contraception is, of course, a matter of conjecture. Paul VI might have changed the doctrine on contraception in 1967, if Cardinal Wojtyła of Kraków had not, in effect, talked him out of it. But no pope is likely to budge on abortion.

John Paul II is serenely indifferent to opposing attitudes, even on the part of the most respected fellow Catholics. This was illustrated by the 1981 visit to him by President Valéry Giscard d'Estaing, who vainly sought to explain the reasons for continued legality of abortion in largely Catholic France. Giscard wrote in his memoirs that he had told the pope:

> I am a Catholic, but I am president of the Republic of a lay state. I must not impose my personal convictions on my fellow citizens, but I must see to it that the law corresponds to the real condition of the French society so that it will be respected and observed. I understand fully the view of the Catholic Church and, as a Catholic, I share it. I judge it to be legitimate that the Church demand that those who practice its faith respect certain interdictions. But this may not be imposed through penal sanctions by civil law on the entirety of the social body. . . . I was not seeking to justify myself in [his] eyes, but to make [him] see the dilemma that was mine and that I had to resolve in my conscience.

In 1994, the "Letter to the Family" set the stage for the great population battle that John Paul II had resolved to wage and direct, fully engaging his personal prestige and that of the papacy. The pope henceforth took every opportunity to raise the question publicly with greater and greater force and emotion. That winter and spring, he pounded the theme in homilies at Sunday morning Mass at Rome's suburban parish churches and at noontime Angelus prayers—often turning red in the face from anger—and in virtually every speech to visiting foreign bishops, groups of pilgrims, and delegations of secular organizations. The population battle seemed to overshadow most other Vatican concerns.

On March 19, John Paul II escalated the campaign with a personally signed letter to all the heads of state in the world and to U.N. Secretary General Boutros Boutros-Ghali urging them to reject at the September Cairo conference a draft document on population control that had been principally authored by the International Planned Parenthood Federation. The document called for massive global contraception programs to stem massive population growth and introduced the concepts of "reproductive health" and "reproductive rights," which the Vatican regarded as the enshrinement of abortion on demand in international law.

In his letter, the pope said that the draft of the final document for Cairo came as "a disturbing surprise" to him. He declared that in the light of the "innovations" it contained, "there is reason for fear that it could cause a moral decline resulting in a serious setback for humanity, one in which man himself would be the first victim."

The pope also noted that "the idea of sexuality underlying this text is totally individualistic to such an extent that marriage now appears as something outmoded." The words harked back thirty years to Karol Wojtyła's first book, *Love and Responsibility*.

The sense of drama pervading the Vatican on this whole matter was illustrated by a front-page editorial in *L'Osservatore Romano* that compared John Paul II's population missive to the warnings to humanity on the eve of World War I by Pope Benedict XV and the eve of World War II by Pope Pius XII. It is impossible to determine whether this interpretation and comparison was suggested by John Paul II himself or by overzealous advisers who largely control the Holy See's public relations and may have wished to please him disproportionately.

But the pope himself introduced a highly political and divisive note in his letter when he commented that the document "leaves the troubling impression of something being imposed: namely a life-style typical of certain fringes within developed societies which are materially rich and secularized." He then asked: "Are countries more sensitive to the values of nature, morality and religion going to accept such a vision of man and society without protest?"

This was an allusion to the belief held by some in the Third World that population control programs are the genocidal conspiracy by the wealthy nations to keep down poorer societies by preventing them from growing. John

Paul II appeared to be endorsing this conclusion, noting in his letter that in the draft document "the theme of development . . . including the very complex issue of the relationship between population and development, which ought to be at the centre of the discussion, is almost completely overlooked."

The Holy See takes the position that the dangers stemming from natural population growth—such as the inability to feed, house, clothe, educate, and employ the new generations and to provide health care for them—can better be faced through great economic development programs rather than birth-control programs. It has protested, for example, the proposal in the U.N. document that population control funds be increased from the current $5 billion to at least $13 billion by the year 2000, arguing that the money could be spent more productively on economic development.

Most specialists in Third World problems reject this approach on the grounds that money is limited and that no infrastructure can be created in the foreseeable future to meet the demands for even a minimal decent existence for a world population projected to expand from 5.7 billion estimated in 1994 to ten billion within the next two decades. U.N. experts have urged efforts to stabilize the number at 7.2 billion by the year 2050.

But the reasoning adduced by John Paul II for investment in greater economic development instead of birth-control measures also fits into his over-all advocacy of vastly improved wealth distribution between the rich nations and the Third World. It is part of his critique of "savage capitalism." In fact, the pope's letter to the heads of state was followed by a sixty-six-page study issued by the Pontifical Council for the Family charging the developed world with "contraceptive imperialism."

On April 22, John Paul II telephoned President Clinton in Washington to request his personal intervention to modify the U.N. document after a preparatory commission, meeting in New York, had adopted the "reproductive health" concepts of the original draft, overwhelmingly voting down the objections of the Vatican delegation. Actually, those concepts were placed inside brackets, meaning that they would be subject to discussion in Cairo. Still, the pope was so alarmed that he decided to involve Clinton personally in the dispute, notwithstanding the administration's pro-choice position on abortion and contraception. At that juncture, the pope moved toward open confrontation with the United States.

The dispute, muted by diplomatic courtesy (and the fact that the two men genuinely like each other), continued when President Clinton conferred for forty minutes with John Paul II at the Vatican on June 2, at the start of a European tour. The pope was still convalescing from his April hip surgery, but it did not slow him down.

The Cairo conference dominated their meeting, and Clinton reported that John Paul II had urged him not "to be insensitive to the value of life or appear to be advocating policies that would undermine the strength of the family." As for him, the president explained, he had a "genuine disagreement with the pope on birth control in relation to rapid population growth. . . . We do support active and aggressive family planning efforts; we do have differences over contraception."

Moreover, the Vatican seemed determined to ignore disclaimers by Clinton and Vice President Al Gore that the United States' support for the *availability* of abortion for women in poor countries is not equivalent to support for abortion on demand or abortion as a method of family planning. The pope's stand was absolutist: he would not tolerate any reference to the *permissibility* of abortion in the U.N. text, no matter how qualified.

And on the day of Clinton's meeting with John Paul II, *L'Osservatore Romano* commented in an editorial that the time had come "to become liberated from an ideological interpretation of the problem of natural [population] growth . . . and to approach these problems in a deeply ethical way because they concern the right and dignity of the human being and of the family and the sovereign rights of developing nations." The Vatican newspaper also offered the reminder that along with political and economic imperialism, there is "anti-conception imperialism." Uncannily, the Vatican rhetoric was beginning to mimic that of the recently defeated Eastern Europe.

* * *

But John Paul II's emotionalism was not limited to the population controversy. It had begun to develop earlier. Thus at the close of an outdoor Mass in Agrigento in Sicily, a stronghold of the Mafia, on May 9, 1993, the pope exploded in true rage against the mobsters in an attack without precedent for the Italian Church, which (with a few exceptions) had always looked the other way.

"God once said, 'Don't kill!'" John Paul II shouted, departing from his prepared text, his voice trembling. "Man, any man, any group of men, the Mafia, can't change and trample this most sacred law of God! . . . Those who have on their consciences the weight of so many human victims, must understand—must understand!—that they can't be allowed to kill innocents. I say to those responsible, 'Repent!' One day the judgement of God will come . . . !"

The pope's outburst caused a sensation, and Mafia retaliation as well. Shortly after his Sicilian visit, powerful bombs damaged two ancient Rome churches, including John Paul II's cathedral church, San Giovanni in Laterano. In September, an outspoken anti-Mafia priest, Father Giuseppe Puglisi, was shot dead in Palermo. And, stunningly, Italian investigators announced in July 1994 that the Mafia had struck to punish the Church for violating, through the pope's attack on it, the "nonaggression pact" it believed it had always had with the ecclesiastic institution.

But when John Paul II returned to Sicily early in November 1994, he was not resuming the Church's old silence—he still was the fighting pope. Addressing a crowd in the cathedral square of Catania, he said that most Sicilians "wish to leave behind them the corruption exercised by the few to the detriment of the many. There is no time or room for sitting silently by or [for] fearful mediocrity. At the present historic moment, there can be no room for fearfulness or inertia." (That morning, a Catania priest found on his doorstep a lamb with a slit throat, and a note warning, "Watch out! The same may happen to you.")

The pope's fists and voice were raised in anger during a pre-Christmas Sunday homily addressed to the crowds in St. Peter's Square on December 18, 1994, when he demanded an end to the fighting in the former Yugoslavia. "Stop! Stop! Stop!" he shouted.

Speaking on Christmas Eve, John Paul II told members of the Vatican Curia in the course of the annual reception that social injustice in the world had acquired much greater proportions than in the past, crossing national and continental boundaries.

Full of emotion, the pope denounced the "brutal extermination . . . of vagabond children, those forced into prostitution . . . the commerce of children by organizations dealing with transplants of organs, child victims of violence and war, and . . . those manipulated for the traffic and sale of drugs or other criminal activities."

The pope's 1994 "spring offensive" kept gaining momentum as the Cairo conference approached. On June 14, 114 cardinals summoned to Rome to discuss plans for commemorating Christianity's third millennium passed a resolution (proposed by New York's Cardinal O'Connor) warning that the measures in the U.N. draft would legitimize "abortion on demand, sexual promiscuity and a distorted notion of the family" and that they reflected "cultural imperialism." It appeared that O'Connor had been chosen to propose the resolution because much of the draft language opposed by John Paul II had been inspired by American feminists. All signs were that the United States and the Holy See were divided by a cultural barrier of understanding. In other words, the feminists' push for the "empowerment" of women in general in terms of participating in family planning was perceived at the Vatican as nothing less than an attempt to legalize abortion on demand.

The papal campaign soon became worldwide. National conferences of bishops in the United States, Canada, Latin America, and much of Europe urged their governments to support the Vatican position at the Cairo conference. In Manila, Cardinal Jamie L. Sin brought out 200,000 Catholics into the streets to express their support for John Paul II in his battle for humanity. And papal emissaries turned for additional backing to Muslim governments, hoping to take advantage of the fact that some Islamic groups interpreted the Koran as opposing birth-control measures. Archbishop Jean-Louis Tauran, secretary for the Holy See's relations with states (the Vatican's foreign minister), visited Libya and Iran, apparently asking their backing, greatly annoying the United States, which regards the two countries as international pariahs.

Three days before the Cairo conference opened on September 4, Vatican spokesman Navarro-Valls found it necessary to make an unusual personal attack on Vice President Gore, who was to lead the U.S. delegation, over his denials that Washington was attempting to legalize abortion internationally. In a press statement, Navarro-Valls said that "Mr. Al Gore . . . recently stated that 'the United States has not sought, does not seek and will not seek to establish an international right to abortion.' The draft population document, which has the United States as its principal sponsor, contradicts, in reality, Mr. Gore's statement."

In Cairo, the seventeen-man Vatican delegation stalled the conference for days over the language on abortion and contraception in the proposed final document, the "Program of Action" for the next twenty years. Increasingly, however, the Vatican found itself isolated and criticized for "obstructionism," and John Paul II personally instructed the delegation to look for a political compromise without abandoning the Holy See's basic moral principles.

President Clinton, dreading an up-and-down vote that would threaten a damaging split between the United States and the Vatican, likewise instructed his delegation to go for a compromise. In the end, everybody gained and everybody lost.

The final language of the "Program of Action," approved by unanimous consent and signed by all the delegations (including the Holy See's), was a gain for John Paul II in that it provided that women have the right to "methods of their choice for the regulation of fertility" rather than the original provision that they should have the right to "fertility regulation," which the World Health Organization interprets as meaning abortion. The pope's loss was that the hated word "abortion" did, after all, appear in the text, although the reference was softened to say that abortion should be "safe" where it is "not against the law."

In a way, John Paul II had the last word. Archbishop Renato Martino, the Vatican's chief delegate, announced that "nothing is to be understood to imply that the Holy See endorses abortion or has in any way changed its moral position concerning abortion." Likewise, he said, it has not changed its opposition to contraceptives or sterilization or the use of condoms in AIDS prevention programs. Then the delegation issued a two-page list of written reservations to the final text, underlining that the "Program of Action" was still tainted by an "individualistic understanding of sexuality," not properly emphasizing mutual love in married life, a traditional Wojtyła view of man-and-woman relations.

Was it worthwhile for John Paul II to have become engaged so ferociously in the population battle?

His conviction is that, despite wide criticism, the answer is resoundingly affirmative. He believes that if he had not fought, with all his energy and skill, the U.N. conference would have made abortion *on demand* part of international law—and that it was therefore worth the risks.

In his Christmas Eve speech to the Curia, the pope insisted that the original draft of the U.N. document was "absolutely unacceptable, attempting to include abortion in ambiguous language, among other means of birth control." But, he said, "the Church made its voice heard . . . to awaken the consciences," then quoted Mother Teresa of Calcutta, his favorite nun in the world, in her comment that "not the mother, not the father, not the doctor, not an agency, not a conference, not a government, has the right to end a life—only God who has created it."

Moreover, the Cairo disagreements had no damaging impact on the relations between the Holy See and the United States. In fact, President Clinton proposed in a letter to John Paul II early in December 1994 the establishment of formal cooperation between the U.S. government and the worldwide network of Roman Catholic relief and welfare agencies to assure that American aid reached its intended recipients abroad. Such an arrangement, meant especially for disaster situations, would be unprecedented in the relations between the United States and any global religious institution. Clinton said in his letter "that by working together more closely and better coordinating our responses to humanitarian crises we could alleviate the suffering" resulting from natural disasters and wars. "We would like to share information, including field reports, on a more systematic basis," the president wrote the pope. John Paul II accepted the proposal.

Clinton also broke new ground in U.S.-Vatican diplomacy by suggesting to John Paul II that they cooperate "in the areas of crisis prevention and mediation." Given the Holy See's public and private access virtually all over the world—and its diplomatic and church networks—the Vatican could, indeed, be a crucial partner for the United States in peacemaking everywhere.

Sadly lost in the abortion controversy in Cairo was the Holy See's proposal that the families of Third World migrants working in developed countries be allowed to join them. It was one of John Paul II's human rights and "human decency" ideas, his strongest suit as an international statesman, but Western Europe, to which the proposal mainly applied, had no appetite for hundreds of thousands of Third World wives and children.

In the broadest dimension, the pope's attitudes and policies in the 1990s are anchored in his sense of universal moral values and his concern that they are collapsing everywhere. The questions of sexuality, abortion, and contraception naturally are a crucial part of it for him, but he basically casts himself as a champion of family values at a time when the traditional institution of family is crumbling in much of the world, and therefore, he believes, undermining society in general.

This was the meaning of John Paul II's "Letter to the Family," intended to establish him as the world's principal authoritative voice on moral issues. And the pope, more outspoken on "taboo" subjects than most statesmen and politicians, is entirely at ease discussing publicly, for example, sexuality in all its aspects as it affects family and society.

In his struggle for morality, John Paul II believes that strict discipline is vital, particularly in the Roman Catholic Church, the rampart from which he directs his campaigns and battles. But the price he pays for maintaining this discipline is the mounting controversy within the Church itself. And a powerful case in point is the question of the role of women, another matter of principle for the pope.

The issue is whether women may be ordained as priests (as they are as ministers in several mainstream Protestant denominations), and it is probably the most divisive in the Church alongside *Humanae vitae*'s ban on artificial contraception. John Paul II is absolutely opposed to the ordination of women and, moreover, he has formally prohibited debate on this theme within the Church.

He did so in the Apostolic Letter *Ordinatio sacerdotalis* (On Ordination of Priests) addressed to "the bishops of the Catholic Church," issued on May 22, 1994, and designed to put an end to the rising internal pressure for ordaining women. Not only was the letter the most explicit justification of his opposition to women priests, but it also constituted a ban, unprecedented in modern history, on free discussion within the Church. The publication of the letter has set off waves of protest among women and many theologians, spawning added controversy over freedom of speech in the Church, but John Paul II is inflexible on such matters.

In the Apostolic Letter, the pope first quoted from a 1975 declaration on the subject by Paul VI:

> [The Catholic Church] holds that it is not admissible to ordain women to the priesthood, for very fundamental reasons. These reasons include: the example recorded in the Sacred Scriptures of Christ choosing his Apostles only from among men; the constant practice of the Church, which has imitated Christ in choosing only men; and her living teaching authority which has consistently held that the exclusion of women from the priesthood is in accordance with God's plan for his Church.

John Paul II then cited from his own 1988 Apostolic Letter *Mulieris Dignitatem* (On Dignity of Women):

> In calling men only as his Apostles, Christ acted in a completely free and sovereign matter. In doing so, he

> exercised the same freedom with which, in all his behavior, he emphasized the dignity and the vocation of women, without conforming to the prevailing customs and to the traditions sanctioned by the legislation of the time.

Finally, he added the thought that

> the fact that the Blessed Virgin Mary, Mother of God and Mother of the Church, received neither the mission proper to the Apostles nor the ministerial priesthood clearly shows that the non-admission of women to the priestly ordination cannot mean that women are of lesser dignity, nor can it be construed as discrimination against them. Rather, it is to be seen as the faithful observance of the plan to be ascribed to the wisdom of the Lord of the Universe.

But what triggered the greatest indignation among the pope's critics was his statement that because this whole matter was "at the present time in some places . . . still open to debate" despite the teaching that priesthood is to be reserved to men alone, he had decided that "in order that all doubt may be removed regarding a matter of great importance . . . in virtue of my ministry of confirming the brethren, I declare that the Church has no authority whatsoever to confer priestly ordination to women and that this judgement is to be definitively held by all the Church's faithful."

L'Osservatore Romano made it even clearer that John Paul II's words closed the subject when it explained that the question of ordaining women "does not belong to matters freely open to dispute . . . and to teach the contrary is equivalent to leading consciences into errors."

This ban on further debate in the Church raises the question of whether John Paul II was leading the institution back to the period before the Second Vatican Council thirty years earlier. Theologians recalled that while Pius XII had declared in his 1950 *Humani generis* (On Human Species) encyclical that when the pope pronounces on a question, even in his ordinary "Magisterium" (Teaching Office), the matter is no longer open to free debate, the Church fathers at the Council chose not to include this language in the text of the Dogmatic Constitution of the Church, its basic document.

Vatican Council I had proclaimed in 1870 the infallibility of the pope. John Paul II came close to it in alluding to his "ministry" as justification to shut off debate.

Father Avery Dulles, a conservative Jesuit theologian at New York's Fordham University, explained the pope's action by writing that although John Paul II had refrained from "proclaiming a new dogma," he has confirmed "by his apostolic authority a tradition that he takes to be already binding." He observed that in his letter the pontiff had designated "the kind of assent that is owed to irreversible Catholic teaching."

Commonweal, a New York religious Catholic publication, spoke for the critics when it warned in the title of its editorial on the ban on women's ordination, "Don't even think of it!"

A month after signing his Apostolic Letter, John Paul II seemed to be attempting to placate women by declaring in a speech that "their dignity must be respected." He said that

> the Church considers the movement, described as the emancipation, liberation or promotion of woman, in the light of the revealed teaching on the dignity of the human person, on the value of individual persons—men and women in the Creator's sight, and on the role attributed to woman in the work of salvation. The Church therefore holds that the recognition of woman's value really has its ultimate source in the Christian awareness of the value of every person.

It is unlikely, however, that this "recognition" has done much to console women who believe that, apart from ordination, they should be given more voice and authority in the management of the Church's affairs. Thus at the Bishops' Synod on "The Consecrated Life and Its Role in the Church and in the World" held in Rome in October 1994, which dealt with religious orders, women's presence was extremely limited—59 out of 348 participants from the orders—even though throughout the world there are 615,000 nuns and only 224,000 fathers, brothers, friars, and monks.

While Cardinal Ratzinger, the prefect of the Congregation for the Doctrine of the Faith and the Vatican's chief theologian, had written in a commentary published in June that "a woman, very likely an Abbess, or a Mother General, or a nun of great holiness or expertise . . . could be named soon to a Curial post in Rome," the October synod confined itself to the vague statement that "consecrated women should participate more in the Church's consultations and decision-making as situations require."

And, according to rulings issued by Cardinal Ratzinger during 1994, women outside the Church were not accorded any new concessions or exemptions.

In August his Congregation declared that a woman whose damaged uterus could pose a severe threat to her health in a future pregnancy is not permitted to have a hysterectomy or a tubal ligation. The question had been raised by American bishops on behalf of Catholic hospitals in the United States, but the Congregation decided that such surgical interventions were not "morally acceptable."

In September, Ratzinger signed a letter to the world's bishops stating that divorced Catholics in unsanctioned second marriages cannot receive Communion (unless they renounce sex), a second marriage being sanctioned only if Church courts find the first marriage null. The letter was a response to a 1993 pastoral letter issued by three leading German bishops—including Bishop Karl Lehmann, president of the German Episcopal Conference—suggesting that divorced people who had remarried could receive Holy Communion if they were persuaded in conscience that their first marriage had been invalid (the following year, Lehmann was pointedly bypassed when the pope named new cardinals).

All these rulings carried the personal approval of John Paul II. He does not anticipate in his time any relaxation in the severe observance of the Church's traditions and dogmas. When during his 1987 visit to the United States an American priest asked him at a symposium when there might be women priests and married men priests, the pope smilingly but puzzlingly answered in the words of a popular British World War I song: "It's a long way to Tipperary. . . . It's a long way to go. . . ." (He omitted the next line: "To the sweetest girl I know.")

The relations between the Vatican and the generally more open-minded Catholic Church in the United States—never free of tensions—were dealt unusually severe blows by both the papal letter on the ordination of women and, six months later, another power play by Cardinal Ratzinger on the issue of gender.

In November 1994, Ratzinger's Congregation for the Doctrine of the Faith overruled the Congregation for Divine Worship and the Sacraments in an unprecedented fashion by suddenly vetoing new translations into English of the New Revised Standard Version (NRSV) of the Bible and texts of the psalms in the New American Bible—the Psalter—because of their introduction of "inclusive language." This is usage that removes masculine gender words from the liturgy, turning to such sex-neutral terms as "humanity" instead of "mankind" (although God remains "He"). "Exclusive language" preserves the masculinity of biblical terms.

The new translations were based on a 1990 statement by the U.S. National Conference of Catholic Bishops that "some segments of American culture have become increasingly sensitive to 'exclusive language,' that is, language that seems to exclude the equality and dignity of each person regardless of race, gender, creed, age or ability. . . . The word of God proclaimed to all nations is by nature inclusive, that is, addressed to all peoples, men and women. Consequently, every effort should be made to render the language of biblical translation as inclusive as a faithful translation of the text permits."

The bishops voted 195 to 21 in favor of the inclusive language version, the translations were approved by the Congregation for Divine Worship and the Sacraments in 1992, and the Church in the United States and Canada proceeded to print millions of copies. Without explaining publicly the reasons for its action, Ratzinger's Congregation then moved unexpectedly to suppress the texts as unsuitable for use in liturgy.

There was no known reaction to this Curial humiliation on the part of the prefect of the Congregation for Divine Worship and the Sacraments, Cardinal Antonio María Javierre Ortas, a Spaniard who is a leading authority on ecumenism. Evidently Ratzinger carries more weight with John Paul II, who had to authorize the veto, than Javierre Ortas.

American bishops, too, were humiliated because the Holy See placed into question their teaching authority, which they regard as their fundamental right, especially in the light of the Second Vatican Council decrees on collegiality. Prior to this latest controversy, the English-language translation (from the original French) of the *Catechism of the Catholic Church*, the first in four and a half centuries, was delayed two years in 1992, to render it into exclusive language.

Notwithstanding smoldering anger in their ranks and denunciations in much of the U.S. Catholic press, American bishops chose to avert an open confrontation with the Holy See on gender-related matters. They chose what amounted to silence. At their annual conference in November 1994, they expressed in a "pastoral reflection" their approval of John Paul II's ruling against the ordination of women and further debate on the subject as "a clear reaffirmation of Catholic teaching as a pastoral service to the whole Church and we accept that it be definitely held by all the faithful."

Having failed in 1992 to marshal enough votes for a full-fledged pastoral letter on the concerns of women (although it had been in the works for nine years), this time the bishops declared that "we need to look at alternative ways in which women can exercise leadership in the Church." This was to be a substitute for ordination, and the bishops noted with some satisfaction that "one recent study shows that eighty-five percent of non-ordained ministerial positions in parishes are now held by women."

But Sister Theresa Kane, who addressed the pope on the problem of women in the Church during his 1979 American visit, does not quite share this satisfaction. She says that "about seventy percent" of American Catholics favor the ordination of women.

There is no question that important numbers of American Catholics are increasingly alienated by the ever-stricter Holy See attitudes toward their lives and form of worship. They wonder whether John Paul II, in his concerns over the "culture of death," overlooks or disregards other vital aspects of the American culture—and whether the gulf will go on deepening between them and the Holy See, if not the pope himself.

John Paul II's relentless conservatism on matters of the Church and faith does not prevent him, however, from being remarkably open-minded and forward-looking concerning the relationship between religion and science. He has, in fact, been courageous and innovative in leading a new approach toward establishing historical truth in this realm.

Thus within a year of his election—on November 10, 1979—John Paul II commemorated the centennial of the birth of Albert Einstein, the century's greatest mathematician and physicist (and a Jew), by proposing that the Church reexamine the case of Galilei Galileo. Although the Church had, in effect, admitted as far back as 1741 that the Italian astronomer had been right in his belief that the earth revolved around the sun (and not the other way around) by granting an imprimatur for the publication of his writings, it had never acknowledged that *it* had been wrong in 1633 in trying him in court for his theories.

However, John Paul II, who had been fascinated by science since his early Kraków days (and his friendship with Polish scientists), was the first pope to conclude that, in terms of historical truth, the Church owed Galileo more than a tacit acceptance. In his speech to the Pontifical Academy of Science on the Einstein anniversary, the pope remarked that

> the greatness of Galileo is, by any standard, like Einstein's; but the difference is that the former, unlike the latter, had to suffer much—we cannot hide it—

> from men and organs of the Church. . . . I submit that theologians, men of science and historians, in a spirit of sincere collaboration, should deepen the examination of the Galileo case . . . to honor the truth of the faith and of science and open the door to their future collaboration.

In 1983, a special Galileo Commission was established by John Paul II in a message issued on the 350th anniversary of the publication of Galileo's original *Dialogues,* stressing that through "humble and assiduous study" the Church should undertake "to disassociate the essentials of faith from the scientific system of a given age." A year later, the Vatican admitted in a formal statement that "Church officials had erred in condemning Galileo."

In its report, the commission acknowledged that

> the philosophical and theological qualifications wrongly granted to the then new theories about the centrality of the sun and the movement of the earth were the result of a transitional situation in the field of astronomical knowledge and of an exegetical confusion regarding cosmology. Certain theologians, Galileo's contemporaries . . . failed to grasp the profound, non-literal meaning of the Scriptures when they describe the physical structure of the created universe. . . . It is in that historical and cultural framework that Galileo's judges, incapable of disassociating faith from an age-old cosmology, believed quite wrongly that the adoption of the Copernican revolution . . . was such as to undermine Catholic tradition, and that it was their duty to forbid its being taught.

Galileo's vindication after three and a half centuries was an unprecedented breakthrough in the history of the Church, but to John Paul II it represented only the first step in a much broader effort to establish a dialogue between religion and modern science. Father George Coyne, a Jesuit astronomer who is the director of the Vatican Observatory in Castel Gandolfo (and whose office adjoins the pope's apartment on the top floor of the small summer palace), says that the Galileo case served "to do away with the myth that the Church, the culture of faith and the culture of science are intrinsically opposed to one another."

This fact is extremely relevant at this juncture, Father Coyne believes, because the ever-quickening scientific progress in areas ranging from the origin of the universe to biogenetics raises fundamental theological and ethical questions that the Church must evaluate to avoid a Galileo replay. Consequently, John Paul II sponsored in September 1987 a "Study Week" at the Vatican Observatory on the three-hundredth anniversary of Sir Isaac Newton's *Principia Mathematica,* a basic work of science, on the "relationship among theology, philosophy and the natural sciences."

When the Vatican Observatory published the results of the Study Week in a series of essays, the pope wrote Father Coyne a lengthy letter on June 1, 1988, setting forth his views on the subject. Now regarded as the basic Church pronouncement on science and religion, the papal letter declared that

> the Church and the Academy engage one another as two very different but major institutions within human civilization and the world culture. We bear before God enormous responsibilities for the human condition because historically we have had and continue to have a major influence on the development of ideas and values and on the course of human action. . . . We have come into contact often during these centuries, sometimes in mutual support, at other times in those needless conflicts which have marred both our histories. . . .
>
> By encouraging openness between the Church and the scientific communities, we are not envisioning a disciplinary unity between theology and science like that which exists within a given scientific field or within theology proper. As dialogue and common searching continue, there will be growth toward mutual understanding. . . . What is important is that the dialogue should continue and grow in depth and scope. In the process, we must overcome every regressive tendency to a unilateral reductionism, to fear, and to self-

> imposed isolation. . . . Both religion and science must preserve their autonomy and their distinctiveness. Religion is not founded on science nor is science an extension of religion. . . . While each can and should support the other as distinct dimensions of a common human culture, neither ought to assume that it forms a necessary premise for the other.

As a practical proposition, the pope encourages the Church to learn more about science and become involved in it. He supports the training of priests in science and helping them to become researchers if they so desire. And he stands behind the modernization of the Vatican's own research in various fields.

Since 1582, when Pope Gregory XIII required astronomical data for the reform of the calendar (now known as Gregorian), the Vatican has been immersed in cosmology. Leo XIII founded the Vatican Observatory on a hillside behind the dome of St. Peter's Basilica, and Pius XI moved it to Castel Gandolfo because Rome's city lights made observation of the sky extremely difficult. But in the 1980s, Rome's lights had become too bright even for Castel Gandolfo, and John Paul II authorized the observatory to build the Vatican Advanced Technology Telescope on Mt. Graham near Tucson, Arizona, one of the world's best observation sites.

The observatory also published in 1993, with the pope's encouragement, a 450-page book on *Quantum Creation of the Universe and the Origin of the Laws of Nature,* which, according to Father Coyne, "discusses the relationship of modern scientific ideas about the beginning of the universe and the theological notions of God creating the universe." John Paul II, says Father Coyne, believes "in the need for the absolute, complete independence of scientific research and theological research. There are two independent approaches to the truth, and one cannot dictate to the other."

To keep up personally with scientific advances, the pope plays host every other year to a three-day seminar at Castel Gandolfo, attended by leading scientists. He spends his entire time at the seminar, listening during the sessions and conducting discussions during meals.

John Paul II's interest in science and medicine also extends to psychiatry, a field long regarded with suspicion by the Church, which fears, among other things, that psychoanalysis aspires to replace confession. On January 4, 1993, he received at the Vatican a delegation of the American Psychiatric Association for a meeting that its president, Dr. Joseph English, has described as "a watershed in relations between religion and psychiatry."

The admission of error over Galileo has opened the way to further reconsideration of Church history. Already busy planning the "Jubilee of the Millennium" for the year 2000, in May 1994 John Paul II sent a twenty-seven-page letter to all the cardinals outlining a series of areas where the Church may rethink other historical errors, from religious wars that he said had inexcusably allowed great violence in the name of faith to the tribunals of the Inquisition.

On November 14, he issued a sixteen-thousand-word Apostolic Letter to Catholics telling them that the Church "cannot cross the threshold of the new millennium without encouraging her children to purify themselves, through repentance, of past errors and instances of infidelity, inconsistency, and slowness to act." He wrote that the Church must atone for "acquiescence" in human rights abuses by totalitarian regimes of this century. In what was one of his major policy statements, John Paul II demanded that the Church publicly repent for sins committed by Catholics across the centuries in errant, overzealous defense of their faith. If all his plans are carried out, it would be a monumental project, almost on the scale of the Second Vatican Council. Cardinal Roger Etchegaray, the pope's roving foreign affairs emissary, was named to oversee this enterprise. *L'Osservatore Romano* the following week proclaimed John Paul II "the Moses of our time."

CHAPTER 29

John Paul II's vision of the post-Marxist world is aggressively anti-conservative and anti-capitalist when he sees capitalism acting "savagely."

Having played a central role in helping to bring about the demise of communism, he now predicts a coming conflict of civilizations between the affluent West and poverty-stricken Eastern Europe and the Third World—unless the West awakens to the realities of intolerable social and economic inequities. This is John Paul II's end-of-the-millennium message to humanity.

The teachings of the Church on social justice go back at least a century. In Karol Wojtyła's case, his writings since wartime have firmly established his personal philosophy on the subject, including his article on French worker-priests and his play *Brother of Our God,* written when he was a young priest. His experiences with Marxism in Poland in his prepontifical days and his subsequent contacts with both the developed and underdeveloped worlds through his constant travel and meetings with thousands of bishops (there were 4,196 of them in the world at the end of 1991) calling on him on quinquennial *ad limina* ("on the threshold") visits have provided the pope with special insights into social justice problems.

John Paul II had already outlined much of his social thought in the *Redemptor hominis, Laborem exercens,* and

Sollicitudo Rei Socialis encyclicals. But he formulated these concepts as actual Holy See policy in the *Centesimus Annus* encyclical issued on May 1, 1991, on the hundredth anniversary of Leo XIII's *Rerum novarum* encyclical, which had pioneered the Church's social doctrine. During his twenty-five-year reign, Leo XIII had also issued less-known encyclicals: *On the Evils of Society, On the Abolition of Slavery* (in Brazil), *On the Nature of Human Liberty, On Italian Immigrants in America,* and *On Social Conditions in Belgium.*

When John Paul II published *Centesimus Annus* (the date he picked was May Day, the world labor feast, although *Rerum novarum* had come out on May 15), communism had already collapsed, and he was addressing concrete new situations in the world.

A critique both of defunct Marxism and triumphant capitalism, the encyclical proffers a plague-on-both-your-houses conclusion: "The historical experience of the West shows that even if the Marxist analysis and its foundation of alienation are false, nevertheless alienation—and the loss of the authentic meaning of life—is a reality in Western societies too."

Not an admirer of present-day Western culture, John Paul II charges that alienation

> happens in consumerism, when people are ensnared in a web of false and superficial gratifications rather than being helped to experience their personhood in an authentic and concrete way. Alienation is found also in work, when it is organized so as to ensure maximum returns and profits with no concern whether the worker, through his own labor, grows or diminishes as a person, either through increased sharing in a genuinely supportive community or through increased isolation in a maze of relationships marked by destructive competitiveness and estrangement, in which he is considered only a means and not an end.

Next, the pope raises the question of whether after the failure of communism "capitalism is the victorious social system, and . . . should be the goal of the countries now making efforts to rebuild their economy and society?" He asks, "Is this the model which ought to be proposed to the countries of the Third World which are searching for the path to true economic and civil progress?"

Applying his answer to the former communist nations as well as to the Third World, John Paul II comes up with a harsh analysis:

> If by "capitalism" is meant an economic system which recognizes the fundamental and positive role of business, the market, private property and the resulting responsibility for the means of production, as well as free human creativity in the economic sector, then the answer is certainly in the affirmative, even though it would perhaps be more appropriate to speak of "business economy," "market economy" or simply "free economy." But if by "capitalism" is meant a system in which freedom in the economic sector is not circumscribed within a strong juridical framework which places it at the service of human freedom in its totality, and which sees it as a particular aspect of that freedom, the core of which is ethical and religious, then the reply is certainly negative.

The pope notes that while "the Marxist solution has failed . . . the realities of marginalization and exploitation remain in the world, especially the Third World, as does the reality of human alienation, especially in the more advanced countries." And he announces that "against these phenomena the Church strongly raises her voice!"

Observing that "vast multitudes are still living in conditions of great material and moral poverty," John Paul II writes that "the collapse of the communist system in so many countries certainly removes an obstacle to facing these problems in an appropriate and realistic way, but it is not enough to bring about their solutions."

Then he sums up the post-communist situation with this warning: "Indeed, there is a risk that a radical capitalistic ideology could spread which refuses even to consider these problems, in the *a priori* belief that any attempt to solve them is doomed to failure, and which blindly entrusts their solution to the free development of market forces."

Because papal encyclicals are not widely read in the world outside of the Church and a relatively small circle of scholars and commentators, John Paul II's concepts have been distorted to a disturbing degree by ideological advocates in different camps.

Conservative and "neo-liberal" commentators, especially in the United States, have heralded the notion that the pope's anti-communism is equivalent to an uncritical pro-capitalist stance, and that it was his championing of the "market economy" (in which he never engaged) that had brought Marxism to its knees in the Soviet Union and Eastern Europe.

Others, largely in the Third World, claim that John Paul II is opposed to private property even though the encyclical emphasizes that "ownership of the means of production, whether in industry or agriculture, is just and legitimate if it serves useful work." But the pope does stress that such ownership

> becomes illegitimate . . . when it is not utilized or when it serves to impede the work of others, in an effort to gain a profit which is not the result of the overall expansion of work and the wealth of society, but rather is the result of curbing them or of illicit exploitation, speculation or the breaking of solidarity among working people. Ownership of this kind has no justification, and represents an abuse in the sight of God and man!

John Paul II is careful to affirm that "the Church has no models to present" because "models that are real and truly effective can only arise within the framework of different historical situations, through the efforts of all those who responsibly confront concrete problems in all their social, political and cultural aspects." But his list of "don'ts," particularly addressed to Western capitalism, makes it fairly clear what sort of society the pope would like to see emerge in the post-Marxist world. And he says that "the Church offers her social teaching as an *indispensable and ideal orientation.*"

The pope chose Riga, the capital of Latvia, which until two years earlier was a Soviet republic, to unveil what can only be described as his Post-Communist Manifesto. He did it on September 9, 1993, in a speech at Riga University in the course of the Baltic journey that marked his first visit to the former Soviet Union, with Moscow's troops still in the country.

Addressing the Latvians, tens of thousands of whose Jewish citizens had been killed by the Nazis and tens of thousands of others deported as slaves to the Soviet Union as World War II washed back and forth across their territory, John Paul II, himself personally affected by the war, noted that "behind us we have bloody unprecedented tragedies . . . without, however, having arrived at that world of peace for which we all long. . . .

"We are thus living in the most sensitive period of the history of Europe and the world, troubled by senseless conflicts, against an overall background marked by thousands of contradictions. . . . None of us can foresee the future!" the pope said, his voice rising on the ominous note of an Old Testament prophet.

Then he set forth his views on the post-communist society in the context of the Church's teachings and his own assessments of the new state of affairs to define how "just" nations should be organized.

> Catholic social doctrine is not a surrogate for capitalism. In fact, although decisively condemning "socialism," the Church . . . has always distanced herself from capitalistic ideology, holding it responsible for grave social injustices. . . . I, myself, after the historical failure of communism, did not hesitate to raise serious doubts on the validity of capitalism. . . .

As to Marxism, John Paul II went on,

> The needs from which that system had historically arisen were real and serious. The situation of exploitation to which an inhuman capitalism had subjected the proletariat since the beginning of industrialized society

> was indeed an evil which the Church's social teachings also openly condemned. This, basically, was Marxism's kernel of truth which enabled it to present itself as an attractive reality to Western society. However, the solution it offered was destined to fail. . . . In the name of the "class," or of presumed benefit for society, individuals were oppressed or even eliminated.

While the pope insisted that "the Church's social teaching is not a third way between capitalism and communism" and "its task is not to draw up a 'system,'" he offered her services "to indicate the impassable limits and suggest possible ways so that the various political and economic policies formulated in the concrete history of peoples in relationship to an infinite number of variables may be worthy of man and in conformity to the moral law."

And these, according to John Paul II, are the requirements for societies in the *real* new world order:

> A balanced concept of the State which emphasizes its value and necessity, while protecting it from every totalitarian demand; a State conceived, therefore, as a service of synthesis, of protection, of orientation for civil society, with respect for it, its initiatives and values; a State based on law together with a social state which offers everyone the legal guarantees of an orderly existence and assures the most vulnerable the support they need in order not to succumb to the arrogance and indifference of the powerful. . . .
>
> The value of democracy understood as participative management of the State through specific organs of representation and control in the service of the common good; a democracy which, above and beyond its rules, has in the first place a soul made up of the fundamental values without which it easily turns into open or thinly disguised totalitarianism.

John Paul II, unlike his twentieth-century predecessors, is a foreign policy activist and the chief guide of Vatican diplomacy. He demonstrated this in a quiet but remarkable fashion in the early 1990s, when, turning his attentions from Eastern Europe to the Middle East, he set in motion the process leading to the Holy See's diplomatic recognition of Israel, forty-five years after its birth. It marked the Vatican's return to an active involvement in Middle Eastern affairs and renewed influence there after a long lapse.

The inside story of the pope's guidance of a new policy toward Israel begins in November 1991, on a note of urgency upon the arrival in Rome of the new Israeli ambassador to Italy, Avi Pazner, a veteran diplomat who had previously served as special adviser to Prime Minister Yitzhak Shamir. Even before he could present his credentials to the president of Italy, Pazner received a call from Emanuelle Scammacca del Murgo y della Agnon, the Italian ambassador to the Holy See, inviting him to lunch at his residence. This was highly unusual before the presentation of credentials to the host government, and Pazner pointed it out. But Scammacca insisted, and the lunch took place within days.

To Pazner's enormous surprise, the fellow lunch guest was Monsignor Luigi Gatti, one of the highest-ranking Holy See diplomats, who was responsible for Middle East policies. Ambassador Scammacca then excused himself, leaving Pazner and Gatti alone for what turned out to be an absolutely confidential two-hour conversation in which the Vatican diplomat immediately raised the question of "formal talks" to resolve outstanding problems between the Holy See and Israel, such as Church property and taxes.

Pazner, who has no doubt that Gatti's approach was on direct instructions from John Paul II through the secretary of state, replied that under standing Israeli policy, no formal talks were possible in the absence of diplomatic relations. When Gatti commented that the Holy See could not establish them pending the final definition of Israel's borders, Pazner replied, "Well, you do have relations with other countries whose borders are not totally defined." But the two men agreed to "keep this conversation going." Prime Minister Shamir, apprised of the unexpected lunch meeting, instructed Pazner to be responsive to future Vatican initiatives, if any.

The Holy See clearly did not wish to waste time, and early

in 1992, Pazner was received by Secretary of State Sodano and Archbishop Tauran, the "foreign minister."

The Middle Eastern situation had changed radically in the previous year with Iraq's defeat by the allied coalition in the Persian Gulf War. U.S. intervention had been forcefully opposed by John Paul II on the ground that it was not a "just" war. The pope, who had sent fervent appeals to President Bush and President Saddam Hussein to discourage the fighting, had taken the view that the Western powers had not adequately attempted to negotiate a peaceful solution with Iraq after its invasion of Kuwait in August 1990 before launching Desert Storm.

But in the aftermath of the war, when the United States was able to persuade Israel, Jordan, Syria, Lebanon, and the Palestine Liberation Organization to participate in a Middle Eastern "peace process" negotiation for the first time, the pope concluded that it was now appropriate for the Holy See to become an active participant in the diplomacy of the region.

Pazner was also fully aware of John Paul II's frequently displayed sympathies toward the Jews and their cause. On April 12, 1986, for example, he became the first pope ever to visit the Rome synagogue, across the Tiber from the Vatican, conversing at length with Chief Rabbi Elio Toaff. The rabbi later remarked that while the distance between the Vatican and the synagogue was only a few kilometers, it had taken "two thousand years" to be covered by a Roman pope.

Pazner also knew that John Paul II had intervened personally several times to solve the bitter dispute between Jewish organizations and Polish Carmelite nuns over the latter's installation of a shrine in a chapel adjoining the site of Oświęcim concentration camp. The Jews considered the shrine a violation of the memory of those who died there. In April 1993 the pope would finally and directly order the nuns to move their shrine in fulfillment of an accord reached in Geneva between a delegation of cardinals, representing the Church, and Jewish representatives.

After Pazner's contacts with Sodano and Tauran, the conversations seemed to stall in the winter of 1992, over the basic relationship between the Holy See and Israel. Concerned, Pazner let it be known that he would welcome an opportunity to meet with John Paul II to present his case for the establishment of full diplomatic relations.

Inasmuch as Pazner had no official diplomatic status at the Holy See, a special formula had to be devised for this most unusual situation. But following the precedent when popes received Israeli prime ministers and foreign ministers at private audiences, Polish-born Pazner and his Argentine-born wife were invited to an audience for April 26, with the understanding that he would be free to conduct diplomatic business with John Paul II.

Pazner recalls that he had prepared himself for the meeting with the most meticulous care, studying the entire diplomatic and political history involving Israel and the Holy See, realizing that he had only "one chance" to argue his brief.

John Paul II received the Pazners in his study, sitting down behind his desk after the greetings. They spoke French, their best common language. Pazner and his wife sat across the desk "like students." Pazner took a deep breath and after ten minutes of "small talk" to create a rapport between them, he embarked on a "respectful but firm argument in favor of Holy See diplomatic relations with Israel," explaining "maybe for twenty minutes" that Israel sought peace, that full relations would be in their mutual interest, and that most nations have recognized Israel.

Pazner recalls that the pope "listened with enormous attention, enormous concentration" to his presentation, but said nothing. Ten seconds, thirty seconds, a full minute had elapsed in silence, and Pazner remembers that "I had that terrible feeling that I had made a horrible mistake, that I had played it wrong, that I had overstated my case, that the pope would flatly say, 'no,' and throw me out."

But "after that terrible minute," John Paul II glanced pleasantly at Pazner and said, "Well, so you think that we are the worst ones in the sense that we have not recognized Israel?" Pazner, mortified, protested that, of course, he had not meant it that way, that Israel certainly did not regard the Holy See as being the worst.

"Ah," the pope said with a smile, "in our religion it says

that often the last is the best!" Pazner then understood that John Paul II had decided to move ahead with the diplomatic relations. The rest of the time was spent in pleasantries, the pope addressing Mrs. Pazner in her native Spanish and trying Polish on the ambassador, who had forgotten the language because he had been brought up in France.

In July 1992, three months after Pazner's meeting with John Paul II, a special Holy See–Israel Bilateral Commission was formed to negotiate establishment of diplomatic relations. It was slow going because there were many difficult unsettled issues. Israel, for example, would not discuss the ultimate status of Jerusalem—it affirmed that it was the capital and would never be a subject of any negotiations—although it was prepared to assure access to the holy places there. But, little by little, progress was made.

The Labor Party won the June elections in Israel and Shamir was replaced by Yitzhak Rabin as prime minister. Pazner, whom the new government had asked to remain as ambassador to Italy, suggested that Shimon Peres, the new foreign minister, should pay a courtesy call on John Paul II in the context of the continuing negotiations. The audience took place on October 23, and Pazner, who accompanied Peres, remembers the occasion:

> We sat across the desk from the pope. At the beginning of the conversation, Peres formally invited the pope to visit Israel. The pope did not respond, and general conversation continued for ten or fifteen minutes. Peres then thought that perhaps John Paul II had not heard him correctly, so he repeated the invitation, clearly and distinctly, making it absolutely clear that this was a formal invitation to visit Jerusalem. There was a moment of silence, and I saw tears in the pope's eyes, the tears slowly streaming down his cheek. He was terribly, terribly moved and touched. He thanked us for the invitation. . . . It was a Shakespearean moment. . . .

But a year elapsed before an agreement was reached on establishing diplomatic relations. The pope was busy with extensive travel during most of 1993, and Pazner believes that the final decision to sign an accord could have been taken only by him personally. Meanwhile, on September 13, 1993, Prime Minister Rabin and PLO Chairman Arafat had signed their agreement at the White House in Washington on partial Palestinian self-rule in the Occupied Territories, and this seemed to give new life to the Holy See–Israel negotiations.

On September 21, John Paul II received in Castel Gandolfo the chief Ashkenazi rabbi of Israel, Meyer Lau, who had attended an interdenominational religious conference in Milan (at which Mikhail Gorbachev was the keynote speaker), and told him, "Today, my visit to Jerusalem is nearer than ever." John Paul II had visited Jerusalem as bishop, but his great dream is to visit it as pope, as Paul VI had done. This is why he became so emotional when Foreign Minister Peres had extended the invitation to come to Jerusalem. The Israelis took the pope's remark to Rabbi Lau to mean that diplomatic relations would come soon so that the pope could make an official trip to Jerusalem as head of state (when Paul VI went there, East Jerusalem was still under Jordanian control, and it was not considered a visit to Israel).

On December 30, 1993, Israel and the Holy See signed an agreement in Jerusalem establishing full diplomatic relations. Archbishop Giovanni Celi, a senior Vatican official, qand Foreign Minister Peres toasted their achievement with champagne. Ambassador Pazner is convinced that it all happened because John Paul II had wished it to be so.

Afterward the pope explained his decision:

> It must be understood that Jews, who for 2,000 years were dispersed among the nations of the world, had decided to return to the land of their ancestors. This is their right. And this right is recognized even by those who look upon the nation of Israel with an unsympathetic eye. This right was also recognized from the outset by the Holy See, and the act of establishing diplomatic relations with Israel is simply an international affirmation of this relationship.

John Paul II had also wished for a unique and unprecedented moment in the history of the Roman Catholic Church, which occurred on Thursday, April 7, 1994, when six candlesticks of the menorah were lit and the Kaddish prayer for the dead recited in his presence at the Vatican.

It was the fiftieth anniversary of the Warsaw Ghetto uprising, and the pope chose to honor the memory of the Jews who died in the name of freedom and their dignity—as the Church had never done before.

On a blustery Roman morning, John Paul II first met with a hundred or so survivors of Nazi concentration camps and their families at the Consistorium Hall in the Apostolic Palace. "We are very honored by the presence here today of the survivors of the Holocaust," the pope said softly to his guests. Then he appealed for the end of anti-Semitism and all nationalisms.

Rising from his armchair, the pope stood for well over a half hour greeting the survivors and their kin one by one, shaking hands, and asking them in Polish where they were born. When a grandmotherly woman said she was from Kraków, he brightened and told her, "Oh, I know Kazimierz [the Jewish District] so well. Are you from there?" To a grizzled man who replied that he was from Warsaw, John Paul II remarked, "So you were in the ghetto and you lived through the uprising. . . ."

The pope was unhurried, relaxed and visibly moved, seeming to dispose of endless time to make each visitor feel very welcome and very much part of the occasion. Many of the Jews wept openly. Many had tears in their eyes. Many heard their voices crack.

In the late afternoon, the survivors and their families and hundreds of invited guests, including twenty cardinals, filled the Paul VI Auditorium next to St. Peter's Basilica for the concert commemorating Shoah—the Holocaust. London's Royal Philharmonic Orchestra and its American guest conductor, Gilbert Levine, a Jew, who had helped to organize the concert together with Monsignor Dziwisz, the papal secretary, were on the stage. Levine knew the pope since his days as principal conductor of the Kraków Philharmonic in the late 1980s (in December 1994 Levine became the fourth Jew in history to be knighted by the pope in the Equestrian Order of St. Gregory the Great).

After John Paul II, Rome's Chief Rabbi Toaff, and Italy's President Luigi Scalfaro took their seats side by side in armchairs placed in the center aisle facing the stage, the ten-year-old daughter of a Polish camp survivor lit six of the seven candlesticks of the menorah, one each for each of the six million Jews who had perished at the hands of the Nazis. It was the first time in memory that a menorah was lit inside the Vatican, in the presence of the pontiff.

Then Gilbert Levine raised his baton to open the Holocaust concert with Max Bruch's *Kol Nidrei* prayer (the prayer for the eve of Yom Kippur, the Day of Atonement), for violoncello and orchestra. The Third Movement of Beethoven's Ninth Symphony and Schubert's Ninety-second Psalm followed. Next, Richard Dreyfuss, the American actor and a Jew, recited the narrative to Leonard Bernstein's Symphony No. 3, the *Kaddish* (Prayer for the Dead), and the orchestra completed the program with Bernstein's Chichester Psalms. John Paul II told the audience, "This must not be forgotten!" and walked up to the stage to shake hands with the conductor, the soloists, and several members of the orchestra.

It was an extraordinary Vatican scene. After the concert, the survivors, many of them wearing striped blue-and-white scarves from the concentration camp clothing material and black skullcaps, mingled and chatted with the cardinals in their red skullcaps. Cardinal Lustiger of Paris, who was born a Jew, proudly introduced around his cousin, Arno Lustiger from Frankfurt, who remains a Jew. (Earlier in the year, the pope had urged support for a half-billion-dollar hospital center to be built in Warsaw in the memory of Poles who had saved Jewish lives in wartime.)

On September 29, John Paul II received the credentials from Shmuel Hadas, the first Israeli ambassador to the Holy See. He welcomed him, declaring that the Holy See and Israel "are linked in respect for the right to freedom of religion and conscience. . . . They have joined forces to oppose every form of intolerance, in whatever way it is expressed. Most particularly, they are vigilantly working together to oppose all anti-Semitism, aware that we have recently been forced to observe some deplorable manifestations of it."

The incomprehensible happens at the Vatican, too. Early in August 1994 it was announced there that a month earlier Archbishop Donato Squicciarini, the papal nuncio in Vienna, had discreetly decorated former Austrian president and former U.N. Secretary General Kurt Waldheim with the Knight's Cross of the Order of Pius IX in recognition of his efforts for peace.

For reasons he never considered necessary to explain publicly, the Polish pope, who had lived under Nazi occupation, has repeatedly brushed aside the international controversy over Waldheim, who had held "positions of increasing responsibility and sensitivity" as an intelligence officer in the German army in regions of Yugoslavia "where notoriously brutal actions were undertaken by the Nazi forces in which he served."

Waldheim had become something of an international pariah when his wartime past was disclosed in the early 1980s (he is, for example, barred from entering the United States), but John Paul II received him at the Vatican in 1987, and again in Vienna in 1988, during a pastoral visit to Austria.

For John Paul II, the year 1994, the sixteenth year of his pontificate, was a time of Church history making, far-reaching diplomacy, and personal heartbreak.

Despite his failing health and strength, he presided over two major Bishops' Synods in fields of deep importance to him—Africa and religious life—leaving his personal imprint on them. For Africa, he urged faith in diversity, but avoided detailed recommendations in his opening speech. For the religious orders, he recommended dedication and iron discipline. He named thirty new cardinals, a record number for a single consistory. He brought fresh controversy to his Church with his hard-line edicts against debate on priesthood for women and for liturgical conformism. And he laid the plan to welcome the third millennium of the Christian era.

John Paul II's personal diplomacy addressed itself that year to all the great issues facing the world. He engaged his prestige in quiet negotiations to bring an end to the savage wars raging in the former Yugoslavia, dispatching secret emissaries to deal with Serbs, Bosnian Muslims, and Croats. The intensity of military actions around Sarajevo in September forced the pope to cancel at the last moment a flying visit to the besieged city where he had planned to pray for peace with Catholics, Muslims, and the Serb Orthodox. The inability to go there pushed him into deep depression.

But he did fly to Zagreb to pray with Croat Catholics, displaying publicly for the first time the extent of his physical suffering in the aftermath of the April hip replacement surgery. Watching John Paul II stubbornly fulfilling all the obligations of a pastoral visit there—sometimes flinching in pain and walking slowly with a cane—provided moments of quiet drama.

Having established diplomatic relations with Israel, John Paul II extended them to Jordan and the Palestine Liberation Organization (PLO) as well. But in the Middle East, too, the pope had to face sharp disappointment when the recrudescence of terrorism in Lebanon—a Roman Catholic church was bombed early in the year—kept him from a scheduled visit in May.

And on December 27, 1994, four Roman Catholic priests—three Frenchmen and a Belgian—were killed by Islamic fundamentalist terrorists in the Algerian town of Tizi-Ouzou, sixty miles east of Algiers. The priests, members of the Marist Order, thus became the latest Church martyrs.

Throughout the first part of the year, the pope began his battle against the U.N. population document. He agonized over his helplessness in the Rwandan civil war in which thousands where massacred inside Roman Catholic churches, and hundreds of thousands across the country, where nearly one half of the population are Catholics, were killed by fellow Rwandans. He had visited Rwanda in September 1990. And he sent envoys to Georgia, once part of the Soviet Union, to help resolve the civil war there.

Worried about new wars, civil and international, John Paul II had instructed his Pontifical Council for Justice and

Peace, a separate but very important foreign policy arm of the Holy See, working directly with the pope, to study the world commerce in arms. After eight years of research, the council issued its report in June 1994—*The International Arms Trade: An Ethical Reflection*—with the finding that the world arms industry, estimated at $20 billion annually in trade, had "grown out of control." It concluded: "Never before has our earth known so many armed conflicts, fed by a proliferation of arms which is often simply taken for granted. At the same time, the trafficking of arms, as venal as it is cynical, evades all moral consideration."

For John Paul II, then, the year closed in a mood of political pessimism and personal suffering. But his sense of humor and his determination to perform his mission were intact. Walking across St. Peter's Basilica to inaugurate the October Bishops' Synod, he waved his cane and exclaimed, "Eppure, si muove!"—"Yet, it moves!" These were the words muttered by Galileo in Italian as he left the church where the tribunal had forced him to recant his thesis that the earth revolves around the sun. Indeed, the earth was moving and so was the pope.

CHAPTER 30

At the age of seventy-five and in the seventeenth year of his pontificate, John Paul II is unquestionably the world's best known public figure and religious leader. But the Roman Catholic Church over which he presides is going through one of the most profound crises in its history, notwithstanding the pope's "New Evangelization" crusade, as it approaches its third millennium.

John Paul II and his Church must be situated, however, within the broad context of the astonishing phenomenon of religiosity—an exploding hunger and search for faith, spirituality, and religion—sweeping the globe in the 1990s in a manner that is unprecedented, at least in this century. Only in this way is it possible to interpret the problems of Roman Catholicism in the religious mosaic in the world.

Accounting for roughly one fifth of humanity, the Catholic Church is its single largest *organized* religion, but it is increasingly challenged by Protestant evangelical sects, such mainstream denominations as the Mormons, and by Buddhism and Islam. Muslims, too, constitute one fifth of the world's population, but theirs is not a centralized religion.

Significantly, the challenge is not aimed in hostility at John Paul II's Church. It is part of the wider religiosity phenomenon and a quest for opinions. It is a new dimension in the life of our religions, and the Polish pope is well aware of it.

* * *

Naturally, there is no scientific or statistical explanation for the global surge of religiosity. However, religion and politics often blend and converge in much of the world, sometimes turning against one another, and this represents another aspect of the new phenomenon.

There are rival and frequently murderous agendas pushed across the former Soviet Union, the former Yugoslavia, the Middle East, and Africa, with probably more to come. John Paul II and the Holy See, banking on their moral authority, have therefore striven to help quell this strife through vigorous secret and open diplomacy, though with mixed and occasionally contradictory results.

A moralist and trained philosopher, John Paul II believes that both the strife and the religiosity phenomenon derive from a fundamental breakdown in the structure of families, societies, and nations, as capitalism seeks to replace Marxism as a global ideology (he thinks that "radical capitalism" *is* an ideology) and that new confrontations are in the making. In the meantime, the pope sees a dangerous void developing, with people everywhere losing optimism and hope.

Apart from the correctness of his interpretation of the state of affairs in the post-communist world, facts bear out John Paul II in demonstrating that, indeed, there is something inherently flawed in the present human condition, and that the more we witness violence and instability, the greater is the thirst for salvation through religion and faith. Occasionally, all these strands crisscross to create the chaos, confusion, and mayhem of the 1990s. In any event, the pope is determined to be heard as a moral voice of reason among worshippers of all faiths, and the fear of religious wars has become one of his central preoccupations in this decade.

And, of course, religious warfare in multifarious shapes is more rampant today than at any time during the twentieth century and suggests, among other conclusions, that the marvels of advanced technology seem now to be as much at the service of war as of peace, notwithstanding the end of the great East-West confrontation. John Paul II is alarmed to see military technology soaring out of control in the new generation of conflicts.

This technology is available, for example, in the former

Yugoslavia where the Serb Orthodox are locked in mortal combat with Bosnian Muslims and Croat Catholics. In the Balkan wars of the 1990s, religion is as much a factor as blind nationalism and territorial greed. This is why John Paul II had been so desperately anxious to go to Bosnia-Herzegovina with his message of peace and prayer—and so frustrated by his inability to do so because of advanced Serb missiles hitting Sarajevo and its airport and threatening incoming aircraft.

Prayer in Sarajevo might not have been the perfect answer to the grief and despair of the population, but in the four years of genocide, carnage, and "ethnic cleansing" nobody has had a better idea—not the United Nations, not NATO, and not the United States.

In Israel, in the Israeli-occupied Palestinian territories and in liberated Gaza, irredentist Hamas guerrillas of the Islamic Resistance Movement—attacking the Israelis as well as their rivals of Yasser Arafat's PLO—are both Islamic fundamentalist religious fighters and political power challengers. They appear to hope to create an Islamic Palestinian theocratic state fashioned after the Iran of the late Ayatollah Ruhollah Khomeini, their principal patron state.

Islamic fundamentalists in Algeria and Egypt are battling the secular regimes in their countries to achieve the same result. Sudan has already become an Islamic fundamentalist state at war with the Christian and animist minority in the south.

To the extent that he might exercise any influence in defusing a full-fledged civil war in Algeria, John Paul II acted in November 1994, to charge discreetly Rome's Sant'Egidio Community, a private Catholic group often working as his surrogates and with a remarkable record of achievements in peacekeeping (including the settlement of the Mozambique civil war), with mediation between the military regime and the fundamentalist Islamic Salvation Front (FIS).

In Egypt, there is no room for papal mediation, in part because Islamic radicals of the Muslim Brotherhood there have no unified political command similar to Algeria's FIS. But the pope did go to Sudan in 1993, to try to convince the

Arab fundamentalist regime in Khartoum to end the southern war with black Christians. Archbishop Tauran, the Vatican's foreign minister, paid a quiet visit to Libya and Iran in 1994, to discuss regional peace.

If nothing else, John Paul II hopes to help keep dialogue channels open. He remembers that Islamic fundamentalists killed Egypt's President Sadat in 1981 (in Gaza, the chant in the streets in 1994 was, "O Arafat, the jihad killed Sadat!"), and he cannot exclude religious motivations in the assassination attempt against him by the Turk, Agca, the same year. In Gaza, jihad, which means "holy war," is used as well to describe armed fundamentalist movements. (When he visited Manila in January 1995, a man identified as Abdul Basid Abdul Ramin, an Iraqi implicated in the 1993 bombing of the World Trade Center in New York, was suspected of being behind a frustrated plot to kill the pope during his stay in the Philippines.)

There is a powerful religious ingredient in the ongoing war between Christian Armenia and Muslim Azerbaijan, the former Soviet republics, over the Nagorno-Karabakh enclave. Oil-rich Azerbaijan adjoins Iran. In the unending Afghanistan civil war, Muslims are killing Muslims at a horrifying rate as they do in Tajikistan, a former Soviet republic, next door. The runaway Russian Caucasian republic of Chechnya also wishes to become an Islamic state, and it was still resisting Russian armed attacks in February 1995.

Cyprus has been divided since 1974, between the majority Greek Orthodox south and the Turkish Muslim north, with U.N. peacekeeping forces preventing the renewal of hostilities on that Mediterranean island off the coast of Turkey. Turks have vandalized Greek Orthodox churches in the north and the Greeks have done violence to mosques in the south.

It may be hard to believe that in the twilight of the twentieth century, at the peak of technological civilization, conferences on religion and peace are still necessary. But the World Conference on Religion and Peace held a "World Assembly" at the Vatican early in November 1994, and John Paul II appeared before the delegates to sound the warning that "as old barriers fall, new ones arise whenever fundamental truths and values are forgotten or obscured, even among people who profess themselves to be religious.

"Today," the pope said in one of his most important post–Cold War pronouncements, "religious leaders must clearly show that they are pledged to the promotion of peace precisely because of their religious belief. Religion is not, and must not become, a pretext for conflict, particularly when religious, cultural and ethnic identity coincide. . . . Religion and peace go together: to wage war in the name of religion is a blatant contradiction."

And since 1986, interdenominational peace prayers have been sponsored by John Paul II in Assisi, the home of St. Francis.

The Roman Catholic Church and Islam are the world's two largest religions, and, significantly, each preaches a high degree of discipline in theology and lifestyles, according to their respective lights. In this age of yearning for order and direction, this may be one of the reasons why they keep a hard core of believers, in the case of the Church, and attract new converts, especially among Muslims. On a numerically smaller scale, this is also true of Protestant fundamentalism and Judaism (although Jews do not proselytize).

Unlike the time of the Crusades, there is no open confrontation today between Roman Catholicism and Islam, and no lethal battles over the faithful and the "infidel." They are nevertheless the two great religious rivals in the world—peaceful ones so far—with Islam surging as the world's fastest growing religion (including its rise among African-Americans in the United States) as part of the global religiosity phenomenon.

Turkey, an overwhelmingly Muslim nation, has lived as a secular society since Mustafa Kemal Ataturk established the Turkish republic in 1923, on the ruins of the Ottoman Empire. Today, however, Muslim fundamentalists, led by the fast-expanding Islamic Welfare Party, are challenging the secular state—thus far peacefully—as they seek to transform the country into something akin to a theocracy. The Islamic Welfare Party already controls 10 percent of the votes in the Turkish parliament and holds the mayoralties of the principal cities, including Istanbul and Ankara, the capital.

A Turkish swing toward Islamic fundamentalism would alter all the political relationships in that strategic region of Asia Minor. It would most likely influence the destiny of the former Soviet Central Asian republics with their majority Muslim populations, and create a fundamentalist Islamic arc stretching from the Bosphorus, the strait dividing Europe from Asia, to the Middle East, the Persian Gulf, the Indian subcontinent, Indonesia, and the western borders of China (which also has large Muslim populations).

John Paul II's instinct convinced him within a year of his pontificate to visit Turkey as a high priority (it was his only visit there), and he has maintained cordial personal relations with Islamic scholars and leaders. But the pope realizes that the Church is virtually helpless in this situation, and he is careful not to antagonize the Muslims.

It is in Africa, however, that John Paul II sees a much more promising future for Roman Catholicism—perhaps the most promising in the world— and there the Church frankly competes with Islam. On ten separate trips, the pope has visited thirty-eight African nations, some of them more than once, making the continent the region to which he pays the most attention. He is planning to visit South Africa in late 1995, having refused to do so in the era of apartheid (when his plane was forced to make an emergency landing in Johannesburg during an African tour, the pope avoided all contact with South African authorities).

In terms of religious leadership, John Paul II carries universal moral authority no other spiritual figure can match. Islam, which is a religion without central hierarchy, lost one of its great leaders when Mohammad Ali Araki, the grand Ayatollah of Iran and head of Shiite Muslims, died in the holy city of Qom late in November 1994, at the age of 100. The late Ayatollah Khomeini had been one of his students.

Perhaps the most influential Islamic leader today is Sudan's Sheik Hassan Turabi, a theologian and a scholar as well as a radical, whom John Paul II met in Khartoum and later received at the Vatican. He is also the commander of the new, twenty-thousand-man Popular Defense Force, which late in 1994, had spearheaded the offensive against the rebel Sudan People's Liberation Army in the south inhabited by Christians and animists. In June, he had supported the Islamic fundamentalist forces in North Yemen in defeating the secular government in South Yemen.

Among the pope's other scholarly Muslim interlocutors is Professor Fatah el-Sheik, the rector of Cairo's al-Ahzar University, which is the leading Islamic theological authority in Egypt and beyond. As theologians, John Paul II and Fatah el-Sheik understand each other very well—just as they understand the phenomenon of religiosity pervading the world.

And religiosity is spreading everywhere very much, including the United States where, according to a 1994 Harris Poll, about 95 percent of Americans believe in God and 90 percent believe in heaven (and slightly more than three fourths of the Christians believe in the devil and hell). A November poll by *Newsweek* magazine reported that 58 percent of Americans said they felt the need to experience spiritual growth, and a third of surveyed adults claimed to have had a mystical or religious experience.

Americans have always been quite religiously inclined and God-fearing, a tradition harking back to the Pilgrims, but the turn toward God and religion in public life—and its tie to politics—became especially accentuated in the mid-1990s. It affected all religions and generations, cutting across political party lines, presumably as a response to the catastrophic weakening of the societal fabric that John Paul II had been warning about from the Vatican. It was deeper and much more complex than, for example, a simple turn to conservatism, as at the polls in the 1994 mid-term elections.

Similar tendencies have been developing in Europe, Asia, and Latin America in the wake of the vast political, economic, and social changes and tensions during the century's last decade. As John Paul II has often repeated in recent years, "uncertainty" and disorientation swamped people everywhere, and to his mind it was logical and natural that they were seeking solace and answers in religion, if not always in the ways (or in the churches) that he would have preferred. It was a vindication of his tireless campaign in the defense of family values.

Thus late in 1994, principal leaders of opposing political parties in the United States addressed themselves publicly to religion and spirituality in a manner not heard in a long time.

Hillary Rodham Clinton, a traditional liberal and "old-fashioned Methodist," agreed to discuss her religious views in an unusual magazine interview, summing them up in this reply to a question: "I think God is omnipotent and omniscient. I think that because of the fact that I am a child of my tradition and have developed as I have over time, I think of God more in a Father sense." Mrs. Clinton also told the interviewer that she believed in "the Father, Son and Holy Spirit," in the "atoning death of Jesus," and "the resurrection of Christ."

President Clinton, of course, is a southern Baptist who studied at the Jesuits' Georgetown University in Washington, D.C., and is an instinctive preacher. His speech about the fate of children before black ministers at a Memphis, Tennessee, church in November 1993 was a classical sermon, which moved John Paul II considerably when he read it some months later. In general, the Clintons are regarded as the most openly religious First Couple in this century, even more than the Carters.

Even before the November 1994 elections the Republican leadership announced that they would push for a constitutional amendment that would allow organized school prayer, the Supreme Court having ruled in 1962 that such prayer violates the First Amendment's prohibition against the establishment of religion. The proposal created great political controversy, but it illustrated well the religious mood in the country.

Inevitably, religion has spilled over into American politics in the mid-1990s in a manner many Americans regard as disturbing. In the 1994 elections, conservative Protestants, also known as the "Religious Right," solidified their considerable political strength for the first time in American history. The Christian Coalition, headed by Pat Robertson, the preacher (and onetime presidential candidate), and thirty-three-year-old Ralph Reed, its chief strategist and executive director, were instrumental in nominating and electing Republicans to Congress in their November landslide victory.

Protestant ministers in churches across the country urged worshippers to vote for anti-abortion and other conservative candidates unpolluted by liberal backgrounds, and the Christian Coalition distributed thirty-three million voter guides the week before the election. Exit polls suggested that up to 33 percent of all voters were white evangelicals, up from 18 percent in 1988.

The Roman Catholic Church also became engaged in the election campaign, using diocesan newspapers and other channels to influence voters in the balloting on state propositions against abortion, euthanasia, and homosexual rights. Many diocesan newspapers also published surveys of candidates' stands on controversial issues, with the implicit nod for those in favor of Church-sanctioned policies.

There is no likelihood of permanent political coalitions between the Protestant Religious Right and the Catholic Church—they disagree too deeply on many social issues—but there have been (and will be) tactical alliances on specific questions. In the early 1990s, for instance, they joined forces in New York City to defeat school board members who favored abortion, the distribution of condoms, and sex education. Elsewhere, "Family Councils" of pro-life Catholics and conservative Protestants have sprouted as local activist political groups. In Oregon, Baptists, Buddhists, Jews, and Muslims joined the Catholic Church in unsuccessfully opposing an assisted-suicide measure on the ballot; the Catholics raised nearly $1 million for the campaign from Sunday service collections.

With baby boomers turning to religion along with those of other generations anxious about the approaching millennium, spirituality seemed to touch everything in America in the mid-1990s. During the summer months in 1994, the New Catholic Catechism sold an astonishing two million copies in hard cover. In October, John Paul II's *Crossing the*

Threshold of Hope, an essay on faith and the Church with some autobiographical strokes, became a runaway best-seller in the United States as it did in all its twenty-one-language editions (the pope's share of the profits will go to his personal charities although the State of the Vatican had a $22 million deficit that year).

Other spiritual books were selling extremely well, too. M. Scott Peck's inspirational *The Road Less Traveled* had been on the *New York Times* paperback best-seller list for a record eleven years as of late 1994, and was still going strong. All in all, the religious and inspirational book market in the United States generated sales of over $1 billion that year, and it was certain to rise even higher.

John Paul II, who has a fine singing voice, was also breaking worldwide sales records with a CD presenting his monthly Saturday night Rosary chant in Latin, against a background of Handel (his favorite composer) and Bach. Nearly three million copies of a CD of Gregorian chant (once resurrected by Karol Wojtyła as a young Kraków priest), sung by Benedictine monks, have been sold in the United States.

At American campuses, students have begun to publish periodicals discussing "biblical Christianity," and attendance has been very high at Catholic and Protestant retreats across the country.

In Rome, *L'Unità,* the daily newspaper of the Communist Party (now known as the Democratic Left Party), climbed aboard the bandwagon when in late 1994 it started publishing the first six books of the New Testament, immediately selling two hundred thousand copies. A smiling John Paul II received in audience *L'Unità* editor Walter Veltroni to thank him for this propagation of faith.

In South Korea, people began to turn en masse to religion after a series of lethal accidents in 1994, ranging from airline crashes and the sinking of an overloaded ferry with 290 passengers to the collapse of bridges in Seoul. President Kim Young Sam, who is a Presbyterian in a still predominantly Buddhist nation (though it also has a sizable Catholic population), was forced to show to the press that a large stone statue of the Buddha still stood behind his official residence. Koreans had been afraid that the Buddha was avenging a reported removal of his statue by causing the accidents. But Christians in South Korea have grown from 1.2 million in 1957 to 14 million in 1994, in a total population of 44 million.

(Buddhists everywhere were offended by John Paul II's description of Buddhism in his 1994 book *Crossing the Threshold of Hope* as "an atheistic system." In Sri Lanka, where the pope went in January 1995 to beatify a Catholic priest who had converted from the Brahman faith in the seventeenth century, the Catholic Bishops Conference issued a public apology, saying that John Paul II had not intended to hurt the feelings of Buddhists.)

In Beijing, forty thousand worshippers attended Christmas Eve midnight Mass in 1994 at the fourteen Roman Catholic churches in the Chinese capital, and hundreds of policemen were summoned to control the crowds. The Beijing churches are administered by the communist regime's Patriotic Catholic Association, which does not recognize the authority of the pope in Rome. China is the only country in the world where Mass is still officiated in Latin rather than in the local language, even though the Second Vatican Council had recommended that Mass be said in the vernacular.

In Latin America, Mormons have grown from 700,000 in 1980 to 2.7 million in 1994.

In Russia, the fall of communism has resulted in an explosive revival of the Russian Orthodox Church, in rivalry with a returning Roman Catholicism and an invading army of Protestant evangelical missionaries, mainly Americans (including Billy Graham). The number of Orthodox monasteries in Russia, a country rich in mystical traditions, has soared from sixteen to three hundred in three years.

How successfully does the Roman Catholic Church under the leadership of John Paul II ride the crest of the global wave of religiosity in terms of its own position among its faithful and in relation to other robust religions? How can the Polish pope go about asserting the primacy of this largest single organized church against external dangers and internal erosion? And, finally, what does John Paul II's Church stand for at this time of uncertainty and anxiety on the eve of the new millennium, and of its own great crisis?

Because these questions relate to John Paul II's stewardship, all judgments and measurements are confined to the span of his pontificate. Projections for the future are extrapolated from the performance of the Church under his guidance, to the extent that it is prudent to attempt them in this age of constant change.

Though statistics are one way of measuring the present condition of the Church, they are essentially unreliable. The number of baptized Catholics, for example, offers no insights into the observance of the Church's teachings and, for that matter, into continued membership in the Church. The number of baptisms of infants and children does not indicate whether they remain Catholics in adolescence or adulthood. Figures on the number of priests and seminarians provide a better idea of the state of the church because they touch on the basic matter of vocations.

Moreover, the danger exists in the case of John Paul II, vastly more so than in any other papacy of the twentieth century, of equating—or confusing—the person of this immensely popular and enormously controversial pontiff with his ecclesiastic institution. Pius XII and Paul VI, for instance, were easily identified with their Church. Karol Wojtyła of Kraków is much too complex and independent a human being to be so defined.

And this may be one of the Church's greatest problems at this juncture. He may be loved and admired as a person, but not necessarily followed or obeyed as the head of his Church.

(If commercialization reflects popularity, then John Paul II has no rivals in what has become the worldwide exploitation of his image, often vulgar and too frequently sanctioned by the Church to generate income. Aside from his book best-seller triumphs, the pope appears on millions of portraits and photographs sold in Rome and wherever he visits abroad, on T-shirts, calendars, and mugs. When he visited Germany, huge pope lollipops—"pope sicles"—

went on sale. In shops in the narrow streets adjoining the Vatican, fancy certificates of blessings for individuals or families—with names to be filled in by the purchaser—are sold with assurances that they were personally blessed by John Paul II. They cost $15, and the Vatican has not questioned the assurances. Clearly, John Paul II is a commodity in very high demand. Television networks everywhere are prepared to pay high fees for a papal interview, but he does not grant them.)

Nevertheless it is useful to glance at the statistics to freeze the frame on at least some of the aspects of the Church.

First, the total world baptized Catholic population. At the end of 1991 (the last year for which figures are available), it stood at 944,578,000, having increased by sixteen million from the previous year. This meant that the percentage of Catholics held steady at roughly 18 percent of the global population, indicating that the Church had ceased to grow in relative terms, while other religions, notably Islam, were making much more headway both in births and conversions.

Since it is commonly known, though it cannot be quantified, that the Church has been losing more and more of its faithful to the Protestant sects in the United States, Latin America, and even Africa—a fact that John Paul II has acknowledged through public warnings against such sects—then the inescapable conclusion is that the Roman Catholic Church is shrinking.

It is even losing believers to santería—voodoo-like cults—in the Caribbean, South America, and Florida (the home of many Cuban exiles), and to vodun in Africa. Vodun is spirit worship, which was transplanted with the slaves as voodoo or macumba to the Caribbean and Brazil. As the pope discovered during a 1993 visit to the village of Ouidah in Benin in Africa's West Coast, Christianity and vodun blend and co-exist there—the local church was across the road from a temple dedicated to the cult of sacred pythons and tended by a Christian—much to the dismay of the Holy See, which still finds it hard to accept syncretism and inculturation.

Again, statistics are not very helpful, but the ultimate

irony that may well face John Paul II is that Catholicism is receding because of fewer births in Catholic families that increasingly disregard his strictures against artificial forms of contraception and against abortion.

There is abundant anecdotal evidence that this is so both in the industrialized countries (in Italy the population growth rate is zero) and in the Third World. There, local priests are the first to admit that "my flock loves the Shepherd [the pope] but they are not going to have twelve children to please him," as a Mexican prelate put it in a whispered aside during Mass celebrated by John Paul II in Mérida in August 1993. In the United States, in the words of a New York priest, Catholics "purchase his book, then buy condoms."

Is the pope aware of this reality, does he agonize over it as he sees one of his most sacred principles violated, or does he accept it as one more act of suffering imposed on him by the Lord? A supremely private person, John Paul II is more likely to keep the suffering to himself while, remaining inflexible, he goes on battling the challenges to his moral teachings, no matter what it will cost him or the Church. His entire life trajectory has prepared him for this final drama, of which the most punishing truth may be that his insistence on moral principle may chase even more Catholics away from the Church.

In the United States, Archbishop Rembert Weakland of Milwaukee, one of the intellectually most respected American prelates, admits to the worry that "we may be forcing people to leave and dividing the Church." Weakland, who has been in charge of the Wisconsin archdiocese since 1977 (Wisconsin's population is 30 percent Catholic), says that there as well as elsewhere in the United States, "the church attendance is going way down, it's going down rapidly. There is a kind of disillusionment with the Church, that it isn't moving rapidly enough."

The archbishop believes that "one-fourth of those we lose go into the Pentecostal or evangelical churches . . . the other three-fourths disappear into the woodwork. They just feel that 'the Church is moving too slowly, it's not relevant to life, there's nothing there for me.' . . ." Among

Hispanics, whose numbers are growing in Wisconsin, about one half of those who arrive stay attached to the Church, according to Weakland, and about 25 percent "go over to the Pentecostal groups."

With the passage of time, John Paul II's lifelong sense of mysticism seems to grow. The pope has always applied it to his own suffering and to the great moral causes he defends, but he appeared to be taking a giant new stride when he delivered on November 16, 1994, a catechesis on the mystery of the Church, concentrating on "chastity for the sake of the kingdom of God."

Citing Jesus' praise of voluntary celibacy by men even in marriage, he went on to quote His words: "For there are eunuchs who have been so from birth, and there are eunuchs who have been made eunuchs by men, and there are eunuchs who have made themselves eunuchs for the sake of the kingdom of heaven. He who is able to receive this, let him receive it."

John Paul II often returns to the theme of celibacy of priests—another major Church controversy, most recently spotlighted by the disclosure of priestly pedophilia on a large scale—as a fundamental tenet of the ministry. Whether this stance influences priestly vocations cannot be precisely determined, but in this case statistics do throw significant light. Thus since 1978, the year of John Paul II's election, the number of priests worldwide has dropped from 416,329 to 404,031 at the end of 1991, which is alarming to the Church, given the natural increase in the Catholic population over this twelve-year period. In North America and Central America, the drop was from 114,522 in 1974 to 82,018 at the end of 1991, roughly 25 percent. The number of male religious orders' members worldwide has gone down from 74,792 in 1978 to 62,184 in 1991. In the women's religious orders, the drop during his pontificate has been from 984,782 to 875,332.

Even more disturbing to John Paul II must be the decline in the ordinations of priests in the United States and Canada, a crucial area for the Church, from 697 in 1978 to 568 in 1991. That same year there were 15,613 students of theology preparing themselves for both diocesan and religious clergy, but it is impossible to estimate how many of them actually attain priesthood.

In 1994 a study on "The Image of Ministry: Attitudes of Young Adults Toward Organized Religion and Religious Professions" presented to the Religious Studies Association has concluded that the Roman Catholic Church, which does not ordain women, is the only major religious denomination in the United States projecting "a significant clergy shortage" in the first decade of the next century.

If money is any measure, American Catholics give less of it to their Church than other Americans do, being at the bottom of contributors despite their relatively high incomes. For instance, according to a 1993 study, households of Assemblies of God members, an evangelical denomination, gave an annual average of $2,985 while Catholics gave $819.

In terms of Catholic religious practice, the number of baptisms rose from 16,979,094 worldwide in 1978 to 18,139,392 in 1991, a very slim increase in twelve years and well below the natural increase in Catholic populations. Catholic marriages totaled 3,790,181 in 1978, and only 3,514,812 in 1991, again a big loss as calculated in terms of growing Catholic populations.

Why is the Catholic Church under John Paul II losing in numbers and influence despite his continuing personal popularity, at a time when Islam and Protestant evangelical churches are expanding, carried forward by the new current of religiosity?

Much of the answer is found in Archbishop Weakland's discovery in his Wisconsin constituency of the feeling that the Church is not "relevant to my life," a judgment voiced throughout the United States. John Paul II's theological severity and conservatism, which, if fully accepted by the faithful, would affect their lives in a direct and intrusive fashion—such as the whole range of his moral teachings on sexuality—is unquestionably another factor in the movement away from the Catholic Church.

But the success of the Protestant sects in challenging the Catholic Church in its strongholds is equally important in assessing the problem increasingly facing John Paul II. Evangelical groups, often U.S.-financed, have been proselytizing in Latin America (and, to a lesser degree, in Africa) for long decades, establishing important bridgeheads in Brazil, the Andean countries, and the Central American isthmus. They first came to Brazil from the United States in the nineteenth century, after the Civil War. After World War II, Protestants organized "flying missionaries" to reach Indians in the Ecuadorean jungle with their single-engine aircraft. In Peru, American missionaries created linguistic institutes to study Indian languages. In Columbia, they had missions all over the country. They were often denounced by the Catholic Church in all these nations as CIA agents.

In the last twenty years or so, the evangelicals made extraordinary progress, posing a serious threat to the spiritual monopoly the Church had maintained in Latin America since the days of the sixteenth-century Spanish and Portuguese conquest. Theoretically, at least, Latin America still is the Church's largest single domain.

Both Brazil and Guatemala each have had two Protestant presidents, though their democratic credentials left much to be desired. The idea of Protestant presidents in Latin America would have been unthinkable in the first half of this century. In nominally Catholic and supposedly communist Cuba, Protestant churches have tripled their membership in the last three years.

At the risk of generalizing, it could be said that the ever-rising appeal of the Protestant groups, especially Pentecostal, is derived from the freedom of religious practice they offer the faithful, without the doctrinal demands and the hierarchical regimentation of the Roman Catholic Church. The evangelicals dispense a participatory religion, directly involving the worshippers, who are free to hold whatever political or theological views they choose although they place an emphasis on high spirituality ("praying in the Spirit") and prayer healing. But they have a rigid moral code.

There are Assemblies of God or other Pentecostal ministers in charge of evangelical congregations, but there are no bishops, archbishops, cardinals, or any other form of centralized power—there is no evangelical equivalent of

Rome—and this seems particularly attractive to Latin American Christians fatigued by centuries of the strict "dos" and "don'ts" imposed by the Catholic clergy. That the Protestants do not force believers into tough moral choices on birth-control issues—apart from abortion—is naturally a critical factor in their competition with the Catholic Church. But does this freedom mean that Protestants are less acceptable as Christians than their communist ecumenical brethren?

For a large segment of the Catholic clergy in Latin America the answer is that the Protestants are perfectly good Christians, and, consciously or not, they have attempted to imitate them on the grounds that the Church would be richer with involved, freedom-minded believers than with men and women simply going through the motions of being Catholics.

This was the experiment, pioneered by young liberal Brazilian bishops in the 1960s and 1970s, with the Base Ecclesial Communities (CEB), designed to be essentially self-governing religiously active local Catholic organizations. They often functioned without priests, whose numbers in the country kept dwindling. Attracting considerable support, the CEBs were never meant as defiance or challenge to Rome or the pope, but the Holy See saw them as a pernicious influence and, in effect, banned them. Cardinal Eduardo Francisco Pironio, an Argentine who was on the papal "short list" at the 1978 conclave and now serves as president of the Pontifical Council for the Laity, believes that initially the CEBs were probably a good idea, but that the Church could not risk their potential threat to the authority of the bishops.

Unlike in the years that immediately followed the Second Vatican Council, liberal Latin American prelates, including cardinals, are not overly popular at the Holy See these days. Cardinal Paulo Evaristo Arns of Saõ Paulo, Brazil, who defended the opposition against the military regime tortures and was an advocate of the CEBs, saw his huge archdiocese split in five parts, with only one remaining in his hands. Pironio himself had been demoted by John Paul II from the more powerful post of prefect of the Congregation for Institutes of Consecrated Life and Societies of Apostolic Life, which runs the religious orders. The Theology of Liberation remains on the Vatican black list even after the demise of Marxism, and this, too, discourages Catholic intellectuals. In the last decade new bishops and cardinals named in Latin America—as in the United States and Europe—are almost invariably of conservative persuasion. Opus Dei is much in favor among them.

John Paul II has, of course, devoted great attention to Latin America, starting with his 1979 presence at the Puebla conference and visiting all the Latin American countries—except Cuba, even though that country never severed diplomatic ties with the Holy See—in the course of ten voyages there. He went to the predominantly Protestant Jamaica, Trinidad and Tobago, and the Bahamas. Everywhere in the Western Hemisphere the pope has preached his New Evangelization gospel and has been received, almost invariably, with overwhelming popular enthusiasm. Crowds fought to be near him, to touch his hand or his garments.

There is no sign, however, that John Paul II's pastoral missions have arrested or reversed the trend toward Protestant denominations and away from the Catholic Church in Latin America. This fact dramatizes the great difference between the respect and even personal adulation accorded John Paul II and the virtual rejection of many of his teachings and the Church's doctrines on the part of millions of Latin American Catholics. In this sense, the future of his Church in Latin America may be rather bleak, certainly for the balance of the present pontificate. John Paul II is too much a man and bishop of principle to alter his policies in the slightest to regain backing for the Church. As a professor of ethics, he would regard such behavior as unethical.

Because the Latin American trends of moving away from the Catholic Church exist everywhere—notably in the United States and Western Europe—the question arises as to the character and nature of the Church developing in the closing phase of John Paul II's reign and afterward, into the new century and millennium.

A most insightful critique of this pope's Church was offered in 1994 by an internationally respected senior Roman Catholic churchman, personally devoted to John Paul II, and very familiar with the Holy See as well as Europe, the United States, and the Third World. He spoke candidly but anonymously:

> In the next five years, there is going to be a lot of tension in the Church. I expect that there will be tension because it involves so many aspects of Church life, and I expect the tensions will be constantly increasing, not just from the United States, but also from other parts of the world. And I expect Latin America to be a constant problem.

The churchman expressed the fear that "some of the people around the pope are accepting the idea that even if we go down in numbers tremendously, as long as we are faithful and remain faithful, it is going to be all right . . . that even if the Church in the United States is reduced from 59 million Catholics to 15 million faithful Catholics, that's all right." He said that "this kind of thinking is very dangerous. That is part of the problem that we all face in the leadership today. We don't want to be put in a situation of forcing people to leave and dividing the Church. I must admit that I worry about that very much."

Speaking of the Holy See's growing choice of conservative bishops under John Paul II, the prelate remarked that

> the fear people have is that it is becoming a kind of ideological selection. But more than that—and the Holy Father has to be very careful about it, like any person in power—is the fact that he surrounds himself with people who think too much alike. That's a very great danger because you don't get new ideas and creative ideas if you surround yourself constantly with people who have the same ideas. I perfectly agree on the question of loyalty. I think you need a staff that is very loyal. But if that staff cannot contradict you, then you've got problems. And the Holy Father doesn't have

> the breadth around him that he would need, and that worries me a great deal.

Furthermore, the churchman said, John Paul II seems to reject the view held by England's Cardinal John Henry Newman, one of the great nineteenth-century cardinals, that "a tremendous dynamic" exists between "the learning Church and the teaching Church." Newman, he observed, has said that "the teaching Church could make a false statement, but you would gradually begin to refine the teaching" if "you are listening and there is a dialogue." But, according to the churchman, "the present Holy Father would not like that aspect of Newman's teaching. I think that he feels that the Church—that is, the hierarchy of bishops—have the truth and they are to teach it, and that's it." He went on:

> I think the Holy Father likes the idea of a very active, committed, obedient group that is very loyal, that is trying to transform the world. I have always said that the theology of Opus Dei, I like. The practice, I hate. The theology is vindicated by Vatican II. It's a lay movement of laypeople who are taking the Gospel into the world. What bothers me about Opus Dei is the way in which it is highly clerical in its control. It bothers me the way in which the chaplains control the lay. I get nervous when I see it in action. What influence that has on the Holy Father in practice, I am not sure. But I think that in theory he likes it.

(In December 1994 John Paul II conferred still a greater honor on Opus Dei when he elevated the Spanish bishop Julián Herranz Casado, a member of Opus Dei, to archbishop and named him president of the Pontifical Council for the Interpretation of Legislative Texts. The sixty-four-year-old Spaniard is the first Opus Dei archbishop and the first Opus Dei member to hold a senior position in the Curia. The council's presidency had been traditionally held by a cardinal, and, under the circumstances, the new archbishop may become in time the first Opus Dei cardinal.)

Margaret O'Brien Steinfels, the editor of *Commonweal,* the Catholic cultural and intellectual journal, had addressed herself to the problems faced by Catholics seriously dissenting from present Church teachings and the freedom of conscience they wish to have in making their choices. She cites John Paul II's words in his 1993 *Veritatis Splendor* encyclical that "dissent, in the form of carefully orchestrated protests and polemics carried on in the media, is opposed to ecclesial communion and to a correct understanding of the hierarchical constitution of the people of God," but disagrees with him over what constitutes responsible dissent.

Mrs. Steinfels writes:

> The position held by many of us Catholics, that *Humanae Vitae* and the present pope are tragically mistaken in considering every act of contraceptive sex by married people inherently evil, is dissent. . . . [The] consumer culture has given us terms like cafeteria Catholicism, supermarket Catholicism, pick-and-choose or mix-and-match Catholicism. I think such images are an insult to those Catholics who had made conscientious decisions after serious prayer, reflection, and anguish that a specific church teaching does not deserve their adherence. But I also think that such terms do name a reality, and one that is obviously at odds with both communion and serious dissent.

The recurrent theme in all the discussions of John Paul II's pontificate is the perceived contradiction within the Church between his theological conservatism and his firm commitment to progressive policies of social justice. And this contradiction appears to grow deeper as the pope himself becomes more and more theologically rigid while the evolving world situation forces him to be increasingly assertive in the defense of the rights of the oppressed.

Ironically, this commitment to the cause of the poor pits the Church against victorious political conservatism wherever it occurs. The U.S. Catholic hierarchy, which in many ways mirrors the views of John Paul II, found itself at odds with the Republican-dominated Congress, in the immediate aftermath of the 1994 election, over proposed social cutbacks.

A month after the elections, a Catholic commentator wrote that

> while the [U.S.] bishops may be increasingly conservative on ecclesial issues, they remain unshakable supporters of Catholic social teaching, particularly their own, as it affects the poor, the oppressed, the immigrant, the threatened, the uneducated and the sick. . . . It will not be just "those liberal Catholics" who will be opposing "conservative" national politics. The U.S. bishops will be leading the charge. They well know about the violence and the poverty and the needs their social teaching confronts. Whether a rural bishop or a metropolitan area cardinal, they can recite horror stories of oppressive poverty, taking examples from their own streets, parishes and social service agencies. . . . This concern for the poor is a hallmark and a rallying point for practically all U.S. Catholics. . . . Popular opinion has turned against the poor. Catholics, however, belong to a church that does not court popularity on such matters. . . . If we are faithful, it could be a very fine hour in the annals of U.S. Catholicism.

This attitude, naturally, is not confined to American Catholics. In Western Europe, and most notably in France and Germany, the Church has confronted the governments to defend the rights of immigrants, most of them from the Third World, and to protect them from deportations. John Paul II has raised the subject of migrations repeatedly in recent years. And this is perfectly consistent with his and the Church's broader activism in human rights issues worldwide.

With a few lapses, the Church under John Paul II has an impressive record on human rights, and the pope's voice has the greatest moral authority in this realm (in which, indeed, there are very few authoritative voices). And he has used his global travel to preach the human rights message.

Starting an African trip in April 1989, John Paul II told his audience in Tananarive, Madagascar, that he could not visit South Africa because "even if the pope shows due respect to the local authorities of one government or another, he must be respected in his functions as someone who says the truth—the truth in faith and the truth in moral order and in social and political spheres. Socio-politically speaking, we all know very well what the moral problems are in this sphere in South Africa."

In October 1989 John Paul II went to pray on a field in Dili in East Timor where Indonesian troops had killed as many as two hundred thousand East Timorese when Indonesia annexed that former Portuguese colony in 1974. East Timor is a Roman Catholic enclave in Muslim Indonesia, but the pope did not dwell on religious differences when he told his listeners that "for many years now, you have experienced destruction and death as a result of conflict. You have known what it means to be victims of hatred and struggle. Many innocent people have died while others have been prey to retaliation and revenge."

John Paul II was the first world leader to visit East Timor after its occupation by Indonesia fifteen years earlier, and he has retained active interest in its fate.

President Clinton became aware of the East Timor problems when he visited the Indonesian capital of Jakarta in November 1994 and found demonstrators holed up in protest on the grounds of the American embassy. Clinton, however, had nothing to say about East Timor even though according to the province's Roman Catholic bishop, Carlos Felipe Ximens Belo, thousands more people had been killed after the annexation. Bishop Belo said that "after interrogation, people were tortured and beaten and condemned without a just and formal trial."

With John Paul II's support, the Church throughout the Third World had been confronting dictatorships and human rights violations—in most places—continuing a tradition developed after World War II. In the Philippines, Cardinal Jaime Sin was among the leaders of the revolt against the Marcos dictatorship. In Central America, the Church had been denouncing right-wing government death squads for over two decades of conflict there (even though

John Paul II was less than an admirer of the martyred Archbishop Romero). In 1994 in Guatemala, the Church's human rights office was the principal organ for the monitoring of the rising number of political killings under the military regime.

John Paul II has also deployed discreet emissaries in human rights missions around the world. Vatican diplomats initiated quiet discussions with the Myanmar (formerly Burma) military junta three years before the United States had tentatively decided to do likewise. Cardinal Etchegaray, the president of the Pontifical Council for Justice and Peace and the pope's principal roving envoy, went to China in 1993, to discuss human rights as well as the future of the Catholic Church, believing that the most important thing is to open channels of communication and dialogue. But in 1994, Beijing resumed arresting Roman Catholic priests not identified with the regime's religious organizations.

Etchegaray, who first visited Fidel Castro in Havana in 1992 (they got along splendidly), returned to see him in November 1994 on a four-day visit to discuss help for Cuba's poor and to establish a Cuban Justice and Peace Commission to promote human rights. This was a breakthrough of sorts because Etchegaray had told friends in 1993 that the Holy See would not become engaged in any form of mediatory diplomacy in Cuba if it threatened the Church's credibility. The Cardinal had evidently judged that the time had come for the Holy See to involve itself in the problems of the island's approaching political transition; the Church's concern is the avoidance of a bloody transition at the end of Castro's long rule.

But there was no Holy See interest whatsoever expressed in the transition in Haiti that was forced by the U.S. military intervention in 1994. The Vatican had taken a dim view of Jean-Bertrand Aristide when he was elected president in 1991, because he was an ordained priest—a violation of the new canon law's ban on priests running for elective office—and, perhaps even more so, because he was an outspoken populist and advocate of the Theology of Liberation (about which he had written a rather unremarkable book).

When Aristide was overthrown by the Haitian army, the

Holy See became the only state formally to recognize the new military junta. Strange as it may sound, there were no Vatican protests against massive human rights violations, including numerous political killings, during the junta's rule, and not a single public word of support for Aristide's restoration to office. Subsequently, Aristide applied to the Holy See to allow him to leave the priesthood altogether.

Apart from such startling incongruities, John Paul II has staked out an unassailable position for his Church in the fundamental areas of social justice and human rights. When papal history of his reign is written, it is quite conceivable that these achievements will outweigh his theological conservatism and severity. He may be best remembered for his quintessential human decency.

In the meantime, John Paul II has been directing Church affairs on a truly heroic scale. He was the Church's principal architect, strategist, and public performer on the international scene. Without his commanding personality and his flair for the spectacular, even the best ideas might have foundered—and, of course, he seemed to have a grand new idea daily.

The greatest spectaculars—in scope and solemn drama—were John Paul II's lengthy journeys, the pope having concluded from the outset he would be the best emissary of the New Evangelization, imaginatively utilizing the combination of jet travel and local and satellite television. Close to fifty journalists, Italian and foreign, always traveled on the papal aircraft (at first-class fares) to provide experienced press coverage. The whole operation worked with military precision.

In the course of sixteen years of the pontificate—between January 1979 and September 1994—John Paul II had visited 110 foreign countries on sixty-two separate trips to all the five continents. He covered 580,000 miles in the air (plus uncounted thousands in "popemobile" motorcades on the ground), spending a total of 420 days—one year and fifty-five days—engaged in travel, which is roughly one sixteenth of his entire tenure as pontiff. He liked long flights because they gave him the opportunity to read, write, and pray over long stretches of time without the interruption of the daily Vatican schedule of audiences and meetings.

The pope's longest trip was to Asia in November 1986, covering 32,615 miles in thirteen days, six hours, and fifteen minutes. His shortest trip was by helicopter to the Republic of San Marino, an enclave in the center of Italy, lasting exactly five hours. During the sixty-two foreign trips, John Paul II delivered 2,026 long and short speeches and homilies in dozens of languages (usually reading from a text in a given language with the assurance of a trained actor). He also made 118 trips in Italy, usually to Catholic sanctuaries or provincial churches, traveling by plane, helicopter, or car. No statesman in history is known to have traveled so much and spoken to so many audiences around the globe.

Sainthood, according to the official definition, is the highest form of honor the Church can accord persons "who died as martyrs and/or practiced Christian virtue to heroic degree, and are now in heaven and worthy of liturgical veneration and imitation by all faithful." Hence the expression, "going to heaven." The Church has venerated saints—"holy persons"—from its earliest years. During its almost two millennia, it has designated close to three thousand persons as such, though the list is now being gradually revised and updated while new saints are being added.

The process of "making saints" is known as canonization. It is completed by an infallible declaration by the pope that a person has been found worthy, through painstaking investigation, of the honor of sainthood. Canonization is preceded by the preliminary step of beatification when the pope decrees that "the Servant of God may be called *Blessed* and be honored locally or in a limited way in the liturgy." Only a small percentage of the beatified are canonized as well.

Beatifications and canonizations were presumably intended from the outset to honor deserving persons as well as to humanize the Church by identifying it with individuals—men, women, and children—to whom prayers could be addressed (and candles lit) for their intercession with God. The saints and the blessed are to be role models to the faithful. The accounts of their heroism or martyrdom are made known, becoming part of the lore of the Church.

But it took the imagination of John Paul II to realize the full potential of the saints-making institution for the strengthening of the Church. From the beginning, he approached it on a heroic scale, beatifying and canonizing candidates in numbers that have vastly exceeded the totals of all his twentieth-century papal predecessors. Sainthood does enhance the Church's image of holiness in a way that is immediately communicated to the faithful (today by color satellite television).

Beatification and canonization are exhaustive processes, sometimes lasting scores (and even hundreds) of years of studying the candidates' lives, writings, and heroic practice of virtue, and, except in the case of established martyrdom, seeking to certify at least one miracle worked by God through a candidate's intercession. Gregory the Great, the sixth-century pope who "never rested," was named a saint as well as a "Doctor of the Church."

So monumental is the saints-making enterprise that a major Curial institution—the Congregation for the Causes of Saints—is exclusively devoted to this task. John Paul II wasted no time, however, in energizing the Congregation so that it could process an unprecedented number of beatifications and canonizations. He waived, for example, Canon 2138 of the new canon law that required proof of two miracles to canonize—now one miracle will do.

It is the pope who presides over beatifying and canonizing ceremonies on St. Peter's Square or inside the basilica (although some have been performed elsewhere), and they are extraordinary Roman extravaganzas of pomp and solemnity, sometimes attended by hundreds of thousands of the faithful massed in and near the square. The ceremonies attract attention to the Church, bring throngs of pilgrims to Rome (more and more of the new saints and blesseds are non-Italians), and make for great television.

In slightly over seventeen years, John Paul II has created 272 new saints (among them 117 Vietnamese, 103 Korean, and 15 Japanese martyrs, the Asians having been canonized as separate groups). During his fifteen-year pontificate, Paul VI declared 72 new saints (among them a group of 40 English and Welsh sixteenth-century martyrs and 22 Ugandan nineteenth-century martyrs). Thus John Paul II elevated almost four times as many saints as his immediate predecessor in a comparable period.

All the popes in the twentieth century prior to John Paul II had created a total of 158 saints.

The beatification figures in this pontificate were even more impressive. Through the end of 1995, John Paul II declared 731 persons to be blessed (24 during that year alone). The first persons he had beatified were the Dominican friar Francis Coll and Pauline brother Jacques Laval, both on April 29, 1979.

Paul VI had beatified thirty-one persons. All the popes of the century before John Paul II had beatified a total of seventy-nine "Servants of God." John Paul II went them almost eight times better.

Another grand effort of historical importance by John Paul II in 1994—the year of two Bishops' Synods, two group beatifications, the anti-abortion "spring offensive," and great physical suffering caused by his broken hip—was his consecration of thirty new cardinals on November 26.

It was one more Vatican spectacular in terms of the gathered crowds of the faithful, but in a real sense John Paul II had opened with the new appointments the doors to the papal succession, whenever it occurs. Twenty-four of the thirty new cardinals were under the age of eighty, and therefore legally able to vote for a new pope in a conclave, bringing the number of electors in the College of Cardinals up to its official top limit of 120, for the first time since the late 1960s.

The move did not suggest that John Paul II had premonitions of impending death. The college had been considerably under strength for some time through attrition, and it was the pope's duty to rebuild it as an advisory institution as well as a potential electoral body. It was the sixth time John Paul II had named cardinals in his pontificate, and now 83 percent of the electors were his choices; the balance were surviving Paul VI cardinals.

While it would be entirely erroneous to conclude that in this fashion he has assured the election of a favored successor—conclaves, as history and Karol Wojtyła's own election have shown, are absolutely unpredictable—the college now reflects the two main features of his papacy. It is theologically more conservative than it was in the aftermath of the Second Vatican Council, and it is much more international.

Naming new cardinals from twenty-four countries, John Paul II carried on Paul VI's policy of internationalizing the Curia, making it less Romecentric and Eurocentric. As the first non-Italian pope since the sixteenth century, he obviously understands that to survive in a world in which the demographic power has shifted to the Americas and the Third World, the Church must become truly universal. It is not quite that—yet—but John Paul II, the globetrotter, has moved it in the right direction.

Because geography is a vital part of conclave politics, the new college raises the distinct possibility that John Paul II's successor will also be a non-Italian. Italians, who represented 35 percent of the college when Paul VI was elected, are now down to 17 percent. With twenty electors, they still are the largest single group, but the power has definitely shifted away from them and from Western Europe (most Italians would be perfectly happy with a new foreign pope: only the old Roman aristocratic families resent John Paul II as a "foreign occupier" because he has paid them scant attention).

After the 1994 consistory, the United States, Latin America, Africa, Asia, and Eastern Europe together control 59.5 percent of the college (the United States, with ten electors, including two new ones, has the second largest single bloc after Italy). Theoretically, therefore, the next pope could be a cardinal from the Third World, but it is idle to try to predict future alignments and coalitions.

More interesting perhaps is that one half of the new electors are under the age of seventy, a fairly young group. John Paul II, who was elected at fifty-eight, named three cardinals under sixty: Vinko Puljic of Sarajevo, forty-eight; Jaime L. Ortega y Alamino of Havana, fifty-eight; and Jean-Claude Turcotte of Montreal, also fifty-eight (Wojtyła made it at forty-seven). Pierre Eyt of Bordeaux, France, an interesting, strongly conservative personality, is sixty. Juan Sandoval Iniguez of Guadalajara, Mexico, is sixty-one. William H. Keeler of Baltimore is sixty-three. Because it is a given that the college would prefer a pope for the new millennium with considerable longevity and one attuned to the thinking of new generations, it is quite conceivable that John Paul II's successor may emerge from this group. The immensely popular Cardinal Carlo Maria Martini of Milan, a Jesuit scholar who claims that his "liberal" Church reputation is exaggerated, is sixty-eight, and he cannot be ruled out. He was made cardinal by John Paul II in 1983.

It is, of course, a matter of conjecture how John Paul II assesses his stewardship of the Roman Catholic Church amidst the swirling controversies.

But it is no secret that one of the great disappointments of his pontificate was the failure of all the ecumenical efforts to bring closer together the world's Christian churches. These are the Western Church of Rome and the Orthodox churches of Eastern Rites that became separated as a result of the Schism of 1054, as well as other Christian churches that broke away as long as fifteen centuries ago (such as the Assyrian Church of the East), and the Protestant churches born from the sixteenth-century Reform in Europe.

The Roman Catholic Church obviously does not expect all the Christian churches to return to communion with Rome—that is, to accept the authority of the pope—but since the Second Vatican Council in particular, meaningful efforts have been made to assure at least greater unity and dialogue. The Pontifical Council for Promoting Christian Unity, first established as a "preparatory secretariat" by John XXIII and later directed by Cardinal Willebrands, is one of the busiest and most highly regarded Curial institutions. John Paul II has deep personal involvement in the ecumenical project.

Very little, however, could be achieved during the present pontificate because in its own way Christian unity is one of the most intractable and sensitive religious problems, with deep suspicion and much hostility on all sides, despite the goodwill of many leaders of respective churches. It was much easier for the Roman Catholic Church to improve its relations with Judaism in the wake of the Vatican Council II declarations than with sister Christian churches; for one thing, Jews and Catholics are not religious rivals.

But rivalry and resentments persist among the Christians. In the case of the Holy See and the Anglican Church, Paul VI and Archbishop Michael Ramsey announced in 1966 their intention "to inaugurate between the Roman Catholic Church and the Anglican Communion a serious dialogue .... which may lead to that unity for which Christ prayed." John Paul II and Archbishop Robert Runcie reaffirmed it in 1982 and 1989. The entire effort collapsed, however, when the Anglican Church voted in 1992 to ordain women as priests. The Holy See declared the situation to be intolerable and unacceptable, and quietly watched many Anglican priests and laymen joining the Roman Catholic Church.

Paul VI and Orthodox Ecumenical Patriarch Athenagoras I, the spiritual head of Eastern Orthodox churches, held cordial meetings in 1965 and 1967. Their successors, John Paul II and Patriarch Dimitrios I, did likewise in 1979 and 1987. But other than expressions of hope for continued dialogue and subsequent gestures of friendship, nothing concrete has occurred to indicate that the Great Schism will be overcome in the foreseeable future.

Rome's relations with the Russian Orthodox Church plunged after the fall of communism in the Soviet Union, largely because the Holy See moved too fast to start rebuilding the Roman Catholic presence there. Russian Orthodox leaders, many of whom had collaborated with the Kremlin, resented the activities of the minority Roman Catholics, seeing them as interlopers and hostile rivals. Patriarch Alexei II of Moscow and All the Russias turned down John Paul II's invitation to attend a religious meeting in Rome in 1992.

When Archimandrite Joseph Poustooutov of the Moscow patriarchate addressed the Bishops' Synod in Rome in October 1994, he announced that "the mission in Russia is primarily the task of the Russian Church, which has been present in this country for over 1,000 years. . . . The Holy Church in Rome can help in carrying out this task, but this aid must particularly avoid proselytism, which is foreign to the nature of our fraternal relations as apostolic Churches. . . ."

The Jesuit periodical *America* commented in a 1994 article that thirty years after the promulgation of the "Decree on Ecumenism" by the Second Vatican Council, "it is not clear that the ecumenical promise of Vatican II has permeated the day-to-day workings of the Roman Catholic Church, nor that the optimism engendered by the council has been perpetuated even after so many fruitful postconciliar dialogues. . . . Younger Christians tend to be blissfully unaware of their achievements."

But nothing seems to discourage John Paul II in his determination to go the distance to fulfill the vision he holds of his God-entrusted mission—not his health, not the ravages of war and violence, not his failure to make ecumenism advance and abortion to be abolished.

With his astounding capacity for physical and mental recovery from absolute exhaustion, John Paul II seemed to be catching a new breath, after a year of personal suffering, canceled travel, and political and theological disappointments. In a World Day of Peace message issued on December 8, 1994, he announced that "at the beginning of 1995 . . . my gaze [is] fixed on the new millenium now fast approaching."

But there are reasons to suspect that the hip-replacement surgery performed on him in Rome in April 1994 was somewhat less than fully successful and that the pope remains in constant pain when he walks. It has also been said that the Holy See had declined informal offers from American and French bishops to send specialists to Rome to examine him and consider further remedy. And nothing has been said about a "revision" surgery to correct the April operation.

People close to John Paul II say that it is inevitable that henceforth he will have "good days" and "bad days," but they also point out that the pope is actively looking ahead, anxious to preside over the millennium Jubilee in the year

2000, when he will be eighty years old (a year younger than Paul VI at his death). His good humor seemed to be returning when he flew to Sicily late in November 1994 and joked about his newly acquired walking cane with a group of young people in Siracusa.

"Are you pro-cane or anti-cane?" he asked. "Some say it makes me look older. Others, that it rejuvenates me. . . . Ah, I see you are pro-cane! . . . I'm preparing to go to Manila with my cane. I'll get there and I think my cane will, too."

And, true to his word, the pope spent eleven days in January 1995 attending the World Youth Day celebrations in Manila and stopping in Australia, Papua New Guinea, and Sri Lanka. In Manila, John Paul II was greeted by close to five million people attending a field mass, the largest crowd he had drawn in his entire papacy. Then he scheduled a quick trip to Prague, the capital of the Czech Republic, two days after his seventy-fifth birthday on May 18.

Though making small concessions to his own comfort as a result of the hip injury, John Paul II was not even contemplating slowing down. Until recently, his routine was to rise at 5:30 A.M., but now he gets up at five o'clock sharp for two hours of prayer and meditation in his private chapel. Then he celebrates Mass in the presence of invited outsiders, sits down at breakfast with guests in his dining room, walks over to his study to work alone—reading and writing—until 11:00 A.M. For the next two hours or so, John Paul II receives groups and individuals in private audiences (some publicly announced and some kept confidential).

Lunch with guests starts shortly before 2:00 P.M., then the pope rests for a half hour. When his hip does not bother him too much, he likes to stroll for a while on the roof terrace of the Apostolic Palace. He is back at his study for solitary work until 6:30 P.M., when he receives prefects of Curial congregations and other high Vatican officials. He tries to squeeze in a few Polish pilgrims before his 8:00 P.M. dinner, always with guests, then he goes back to work and pray. He seldom is in bed before midnight.

Much prayer is interwoven into his daytime and evening hours, and, on certain days, John Paul II goes to confession at his private quarters before his personal confessor, a Polish priest of long acquaintance.

On August 21, 1978, two weeks after Paul VI died, Cardinal Karol Wojtyła reminisced in a talk in Polish over the Vatican radio, in a strangely prescient way, about the last time he had met the pope, on May 19 of that year: "I always knew about his weak health, his inadequacies with his legs, his difficulty in walking. At the same time I admired the unaffected functioning of the mind—and the undaunted will to live."

Theologians, philosophers, and historians—and just plain people around the world who have been touched by John Paul II in some fashion—will debate for years, if not decades, his merits and failures as pontiff of the Roman Catholic Church.

Some will argue that the Polish pope was a great world leader, morally and politically, but that he had failed as the head of the Roman Catholic Church. Others will offer differing interpretations as perspective on his papacy lengthens and more insights are gathered into his work and thought.

In the end, events will define his role as the supreme pastor of his Church and provide judgments of his guidance of Catholicism into the third millennium of the Christian era. There is no question, however, that this man of broad smiles, brooding silences, steely stamina, and endless tenderness for the young, the sick, and humanity will have left a profound impact on our world. There has been no one quite like him in our time.

To know John Paul II, even slightly, is sufficient to sense that he is at peace with himself, his God, and his world in a very simple human fashion.

When he left Kraków for Rome in 1978, with a premonition of the future, Karol Wojtyła observed quietly that a straight line leads from the tomb of St. Stanisław, the martyred Polish bishop, at Wawel Cathedral to the tomb of St. Peter in the basilica in the Vatican. The same straight line leads back from Peter to Stanisław. Wojtyła has never forgotten it.

He always looked homeward.

AFTERWORD

In 1999 the late Tad Szulc was asked to write an obituary in anticipation of the Pope's eventual death. The following is an overview and update to 1999 from the original 1995 publication of this book. Mr. Szulc himself died in 2001.

It was the most natural thing in the world for Cardinal Karol Wojtyla of Krakow, Poland, to find himself elected Pope of the Roman Catholic Church, a turn of history for which he had prepared himself, consciously or subconsciously, all his life. In the end, his absolute self-assurance made him both immensely popular and extremely controversial. The world was taken by surprise when Cardinal Wojtyla was chosen as pontiff, but the smiling Polish prelate was ready to forge ahead.

After the College of Cardinals voted by secret ballot on October 18, 1978 to anoint him as the 264th successor of St. Peter at the unusually young age of fifty-eight, John Paul II—the name he had selected for himself—assumed the papacy with extraordinary ease, courage, joy, good humor, unprecedented informality, and an iron determination to run and reshape the Church according to his own uncompromising counsel. Unlike many past popes, John Paul II displayed no questions, doubts, hesitations, modesty (false or otherwise), or uncertainties from the moment of his election as the first "foreign," that is non-Italian, pontiff in 456 years.

AFTERWORD

Wasting not an instant, the new pope threw himself into the maelstrom of global ecclesiastic, liturgical, political, and diplomatic activity that never stopped—and hardly slowed down in his final years, notwithstanding age, and increasingly fragile health.

A friend inquired about his health in the late 1990s, when Wojtyla shuffled rather than walked, and the pope responded with a mischievous gleam in his eyes, "I'm fine—from the head up!" His mind and intelligence remained perfectly clear—alert and brilliant until the last day.

Throughout the longest pontificate of the twentieth century, and one of the longest ever, continuing into a third decade and into the new century, John Paul II never really changed in terms of his religious devotion, fundamental philosophy, ideas, and relationships with people. His absolute faith in his own wisdom—some called it stubbornness or worse—and his astounding activism in all imaginable realms, sacred and profane, left a profound impact on the affairs of the Church and much of the world beyond it. He had an impressive vision of history, becoming a key diplomatic player. But in many ways, he always was a man of mystery: friendly, but unpredictable in his actions and indecipherably private.

Future historians will weigh and assess this pontificate with the benefit of perspective, hindsight, and materials that are certain to come to light at an appropriate time. What is already clear, however, is that John Paul II was one of the most remarkable and fascinating popes in the two millennia of Church history, reminiscent of Gregory the Great, his role model, who reigned in the sixth century. It is, of course, premature today to proclaim John Paul II as a "great pope" though millions of his admirers thought of him as such—while others took quite an opposite view, both from the right and the left of the political spectrum of which the Church is so very much a part.

What made John Paul II so interesting were, first and foremost, his powerful intellect and cultural acumen, his deep religiosity, and his unique background of having lived both under the Nazi occupation of Poland and postwar Communism. So were his experiences as a laborer, parish priest, academic adviser, professor, and writer on ethics. He held two doctorates, and was a poet, playwright, actor, multilinguist, outdoorsman, athlete, skier, globetrotter, a supremely talented politician, and a diplomatic peacemaker who helped to end the Cold War.

No pope in recent history nor any of his rivals at the time of the 1978 election held such amazing credentials. And he was handsome in his Slavic way, charismatic and charming.

But John Paul II was extremely controversial because he espoused unshakable views and opinions that gratified great segments of the world's one billion Catholics and offended others on matters ranging from abortion, artificial contraception, and priestly noncelibacy to women's ordination as priests in the area of the Church—all of which he violently opposed.

Normally, John Paul II sought no advice, but theology was an exception, and he was unquestionably influenced by Cardinal Joseph Ratzinger, a German who served as Prefect of the Congregation for the Doctrine of the Faith and was the Vatican's chief theologian. The pope had known the unforgivingly hardline Ratzinger for decades and had absolute confidence in his judgments on theology. The cardinal's views were so rigid and quasi-medieval that Vatican insiders referred to his Congregation as the "New Inquisition Office." Still, the pope's door was open to Church and secular liberals and moderates: he needed to know what *everybody* thought.

On the world scene, John Paul II was a tireless advocate and defender of political democracy, human rights, and social justice and an outspoken critic of "unbridled" capitalism that he regarded as "no real improvement on Marxism." He deplored materialism, drug addiction, and alcoholism, warning the West against its "culture of death." He was no fan of the United States as a society.

Religious liberty everywhere was among John Paul II's principal concerns and he manifested it at every opportunity. Thus for the Jews, he was the best pope ever, preaching against anti-Semitism with angry fervor. Referring to the Jews as "our elder brethren," he kept reminding his audiences that the Vatican Council II in the mid-1960s had proclaimed Jewish innocence in the crucifixion of Christ and he thundered that it was anti-Christian to be anti-Semitic. He prayed on many occasions at the Auschwitz concentration camp, not far from his Polish hometown, in memory of the millions of Jews and others murdered there by the Nazis as part of Hitler's "Final Solution."

John Paul II was the first pope in history to cross the Tiber River to visit the Rome synagogue and meet the Grand Rabbi, an acquaintance that lasted until his death. Wherever there were Jewish communities, he met with their representatives on his foreign trips.

If John Paul II made peace with the Jews, he could not achieve it with his fellow Christians. One of the greatest disappointments of his pontificate was his inability to bring unity to Christian churches after the schism of 1054 and the Reformation. The pope maintained a dialogue, but not more, with Protestant denominations. And he could make no headway with the Russian Orthodox Church whose patriarch, Alexei II, steadfastly refused even to meet him. Relations with other Orthodox churches, such as the Greek, were polite. Outside of Christianity, John Paul II had rather limited success in winning converts in Africa—the last frontier—in rivalry with Islam. Somewhat inexplicably, he was a critic of Buddhism.

Overall, John Paul II was often accused of being contradictory in his positions—he was considered conservative or downright reactionary by some and progressive by others—but he always insisted, when queried, that he was absolutely consistent. This dualism was a matter of faith as well as intellectual pragmatism to John Paul II, and he was critical of Catholics who accepted some of his tenets while rejecting others. He called it "boutique Catholicism," where one could choose what one liked.

As a rule, John Paul II tolerated no dissent and no debate of his decisions in questions relating to the Church and his interpretation of religious dogma, coming closer than any of his predecessors to the invocation of papal infallibility proclaimed by the Vatican Council I in 1870, when the world was so very different. He punished Catholic theologians and teachers who publicly disagreed with his interpretations by banning them from Catholic educational institutions. John Paul II was tough, opinionated, often unforgiving, and often incapable of loyalty to old friends, priests or not, who dared to disagree with him, even privately. But he was loyal and devoted to old school chums from his native town of Wadowice in southern Poland and to fellow actors in the wartime underground theatre in Krakow.

Admittedly, John Paul II was the most popular pope in history—his face was certainly the most seen on earth—thanks to television, which he used with the superb instinct of an erstwhile actor, and to the jet aircraft that flew him to over seventy countries (most often to Poland and the United States, where he went many times) on all the continents. One of his great regrets was that he had never been invited to visit China or Russia though he did travel to three Baltic nations that were once part of the Soviet Union.

And John Paul II was a man of enormous patience and courtesy, often driving his scheduling and security staffs to despair. Rather than disappoint his audience, he tended to remain at a site long past the appointed time, tarrying on and on, asking questions of the worshippers and hearing them out at what seemed to be impossible lengths.

At home in Rome—and even at his summer retreat in Castel Gandolfo on Albano Lake—John Paul II seemed to work virtually around the clock, immersed in Church and world problems, studying papers and reports on every conceivable subject, his curiosity and interests being limitless, and receiving visitors practically every day at audiences, breakfasts, lunches, and dinners in his small, private dining room at the Apostolic Palace or at the retreat. Lunches with him and his Polish private secretary, Bishop Stanislaw Dziwisz, usually consisted of Italian-type food cooked by Polish nuns and served with excellent Italian wine (the pope watered his white wine) and were stimulating, informal affairs, free exchanges of ideas wholly lacking in protocol, especially if the guest was Polish and John Paul II could converse in his native language with which he was most at home. Indeed, his personality and body language changed to be more intimate when he began speaking Polish. The pope was a superb listener, as he was a superb speaker, whether on a one-to-one basis or at a microphone facing multitudes.

From these meetings and encounters over the years, John Paul II, who was both dogmatic and open-minded, developed new attitudes for the Church—some revolutionary by Rome standards—as he sought to bring it into the modern age in myriad ways while preserving the dogmas and traditions of the past. His decision to rehabilitate Galileo more than three-and-a-half centuries after a Church tribunal had condemned him for insisting that the earth was round and revolved around the sun was an example of this fresh approach to science though it took a special commission appointed by the pope to reach that conclusion. To celebrate the new century, a special high-level commission of cardinals listed other faults committed by the Church as well as its offenses against humanity, including religious wars.

John Paul II was also a devotee of technology, far beyond television and the jet plane. The Vatican today is fully computerized, it has an Internet website (inaugurated personally by the pope), and the Holy See has issued CDs and CD-ROMs of religious chants—including some in the pontiff's own voice

It was all part of the pope's desire and determination to bring the world to the Church and the Church to the world as it had never been done before. Believing that he and the Church had to use their moral authority to pre-empt war and violence and to fight for peace and justice, John Paul II engaged the Holy See and himself in international affairs in an unprecedented fashion.

During the 1980s, the pope played a historical role in negotiating, in effect, a peaceful transition from Communism to democracy in Poland, his homeland, in a series of private meetings with General Wojciech Jaruzelski, the Polish Communist president, and Mikhail S. Gorbachev, the Soviet Union's new leader. Poland had already been aroused by the birth of the opposition Solidarity workers' movement, and John Paul II built skillfully upon all these opportunities through classic secret diplomacy. The success in Poland led to the collapse of Communism elsewhere in Central and Eastern Europe, and, ultimately, to the dismantling of the Soviet Union herself. In this sense, the pope contributed greatly to the demise of the Cold War. He maintained pleasant personal relations with Jaruzelski and Gorbachev in subsequent years.

John Paul II held strong views on international relations, including his public opposition to economic sanctions against countries the United States regarded as hostile: Cuba,

Libya, Iran, and Iraq. He believed, obviously correctly, that sanctions made no difference to the regime itself while the populations, notably children, suffered. In 1999, the pope demonstrated his stubborn streak—and his principles—by resisting powerful but quiet American pressure to cancel his planned pilgrimage to the birthplace of Patriarch Abraham in Ur in Iraq to celebrate the start of the Third Millenium. The American fear was that John Paul II's presence, though very brief and wholly religious in character, would "legitimize" Saddam Hussein. The pope thought this was nonsense and he so informed American diplomats.

Finally, John Paul II engaged the Vatican in all great international conferences on economic and social themes, sending delegations led by respected experts in their fields to United Nations global meetings on subjects ranging from population to economic development in the Third World and human rights in under-privileged nations.

There is no doubt that when history is written, John Paul II will loom as an extraordinary presence on the global stage, but he may be judged differently as the spiritual shepherd of his Catholic flock and head of the Church. The question, in fact, will be how actually *faithful* may these faithful remain in the aftermath of his reign, policies, and actions, and what will be the future of the Church in the twenty-first century. This is a point of deep controversy within the Church which, at least in numbers, has been shrinking in adherents and in priestly vocations.

The shrinkage—and the parallel loss in authority and influence—is a phenomenon predating John Paul II's accession because of the changing nature of societies everywhere as well as growing competition from other religions, chiefly Protestant Pentecostal denominations and Islam. But many Catholic observers and scholars, secular or not, believe that John Paul II was directly responsible for the acceleration in the losses suffered by the Church.

If this was the case, and, evidently there is no empiric way of determining it, the Polish pope brought this state of affairs about as a result of his conviction that in order to survive in the decades and centuries ahead, the Church must become highly disciplined and obedient under his stewardship.

And John Paul II made it crystal clear very quickly that absolute and unquestioned authority resided in his hands in a way that harked back at least to Pope Pius XII whose death in 1958 coincided with the emerging trends toward a dilution of power in the Church. He chastised the independent-minded Society of Jesus, depriving the rather worldly Jesuits of much of their power as a religious institution and a subtle political force. From the start of his reign, he displayed a preference for Church conservatives in his choices of bishops and cardinals (only the pope has the authority under canon law to name bishops), a policy evidently consistent with his wish to guarantee the Church's disciplined character. This is where, however, John Paul II created a monumental problem for himself—and *his* Church.

One of the most crucial decisions of the Vatican Council II, in which he had participated as an impressive and articulate young bishop, was that the Church should be governed through a "collegiality" of bishops. This meant that the pope, who also is the bishop of Rome, should rule in consultation with some three thousand and five hundred bishops from all over the world rather than alone—as in the past.

In practice, the idea was that the pontiff would deal with representatives of regional bishops' conferences, Curial bishops, and heads of important dioceses. But John Paul II chose to disregard, in effect, the notion of "collegiality," replacing such in-depth consultations with periodic regional synod assemblies of bishops, which turned out to be essentially ceremonial affairs with virtually scripted discussions in his presence and pre-determined policy outcomes. His other form of contact with bishops were the quinquennial *ad limina* ("Threshold") formal, fifteen-minute, individual visits. Thus among the most serious charges leveled against John Paul II was that he had violated the "collegiality" spirit and precept of the Vatican Council.

In Latin America, and to a lesser extent in the United States, the local authority of the bishops was diminished by the pope, affecting in particular the more liberal ones named by his predecessors, to assure that everything was controlled centrally from Rome. As a consequence tens of thousands Latin American CEB members converted to Pentecostal denominations to preserve the community spirit in their impoverished towns and villages. The defections were very high in Brazil, Chile, Colombia, and Guatemala.

John Paul II's irrevocable prohibition of abortion and all forms of artificial contraception (except for the rhythm method) had the inevitable effect in the Third World—and in the industrialized countries as well—of forcing uncounted millions of Catholics simply to ignore his injunctions and thousands of priests to look the other way.

In the United States, even Hispanic populations were turning away from the Church and gravitating toward Protestant denominations. In Washington, D.C., late in 1999, thousands of Hispanics, mostly immigrants, held the first gathering of Hispanic Protestant churches. In Florida, thousands were abandoning the Church for Pentecostal or charismatic Protestant denominations as well as for the ancient African *santeria* rites. In Wisconsin, the Milwaukee archdiocese, one of the most liberal in the United States, was staggered by its losses among Hispanics.

The Polish pope was, of course, aware of the Church's losses as a result of his policies. But he appeared to have concluded that a smaller, but highly disciplined and obedient Church was preferable to one mired in open controversy, defiance and even chaos that he foresaw. It was both a dogmatic and intellectual choice—John Paul II was far too intelligent not to appreciate the risks and dangers of his stance—and only the future will tell whether he was right in terms of his Church.

In the pursuit of a "New Evangelization," as he called it, John Paul II was reminiscent of the Fathers of the Church at the dawn of Christendom and of his hero, Gregory the Great, concentrating on young people and children through the special attention he always paid them. He had invented such mass events as the biennial World Youth Days, held in his presence in the U.S., France, the Philippines, and other countries. To him, the young were the future of the Church. And he sought to enhance the prestige of the Church by beatifying and canonizing more persons than any pope in history. He showed special favor to organizations of priests and lay apostolates such as Rome-based *Opus Dei* that contributed remarkable intellectual and political power in his support along with very considerable financial resources for the Church. In fact, he beatified the Spanish founder of *Opus Dei* shortly after the latter's death.

Looking back at the extraordinary character, life and career of Karol Wojtyla, even non-believers are inclined to accept that he had been predestined to become a pope, indeed a very special pope, and that in the mysterious ways in which history progresses, it was eminently natural for him to reach the apex of his Church. By the same token, John Paul II drew his strength and courage from his profound spirituality and unflagging faith, even at the worst moments of his life. He was a man who in his youth had aspired to lead an existence of quiet contemplation and prayer as a Discalced Carmelite monk, and to the end of his life prayed seven hours a day, alone in his bedroom or chapel, at meals, at work behind his desk, and in the course of his sweeping world travels.

ACKNOWLEDGMENTS

This biography could be written only with the extraordinary cooperation of scores of people in Europe and the United States who gave generously of their time and memories in formal interviews and private conversations with me. Most of them are listed below, with my profound gratitude. Some men and women preferred to speak anonymously, and their wishes are respected here though my appreciation is not any less for that.

In the first place, my heartfelt thanks go to His Holiness Pope John Paul II, who not only spared me some of his precious time, but whose interest in my project greatly facilitated access to others. He was most gracious both in terms of this book and of the interview he granted me in February 1994 for *Parade* magazine, the only interview ever accorded a U.S. publication.

I am especially grateful to Monsignor Stanisław Dziwisz, the pope's private secretary, for his exquisite courtesy, patience, trust, friendship, and support during the entire period of my research for the biography of John Paul II.

My very special thanks go to Dr. Joaquín Navarro-Valls, the Spokesman for the Holy See and Director of the Press Room of the Holy See, for his vital support and advice in setting in motion my undertaking, for sharing with me many of his recollections concerning the Holy Father and the policies and initiatives of the Holy See.

I am grateful as well to members of Dr. Navarro-Valls's staff who made my work at the Vatican and my world travel with the pope smooth and easy: Deputy Director Monsignor Piero Pennacchini, the Reverend Sister Giovanna Gentili, Victor Van Brantegem, and Mrs. Elisabeth Fouquet Cucchia.

As noted earlier, this is not an authorized biography, and the manuscript was not perused at the Vatican before it went to press.

The following list of acknowledgments does not imply any order of priority in my gratitude to the men and women to whom I had the privilege of listening, most avidly, for over two years.

In the membership of the College of Cardinals in Rome, I interviewed Cardinal Bernardin Gantin, Dean of the College of Cardinals and Prefect of the Congregation for Bishops; Cardinal Andrzej Maria Deskur, one of the pope's closest Polish friends; Cardinal Roger Etchegaray, President of the Pontifical Council for Justice and Peace and President of the Pontifical Council Cor Unum, and diplomat extraordinary; Cardinal Eduardo Francisco Pironio, President of the Pontifical Council for the Laity; Cardinal Jean-Marie Lustiger, Archbishop of Paris; Cardinal Achille Silvestrini, Prefect of the Congregation for the Oriental Churches; Cardinal Johannes Willebrands, President Emeritus of the Pontifical Council for Promoting Christian Unity; and Cardinal Rosalio José Castillo Lara, President of the Pontifical Commission for the State of Vatican City and President of the Administration of the Patrimony of the Holy See.

In Vienna, I met with Cardinal Franz König, President Emeritus of the Council for Dialogue with Non-Believers and Archbishop Emeritus of Vienna; in Philadelphia, I interviewed Cardinal John Krol, Archbishop Emeritus of Philadelphia; in Kraków, I conversed with Cardinal Franciszek Macharski, who succeeded Karol Wojtyła as Archbishop of Kraków. During a 1987 visit to Warsaw, I interviewed Cardinal Józef Glemp, the Primate of Poland. In the course of reporting for a magazine article on the new pope in 1979, I interviewed in Brussels Cardinal Leo Jozef

Suenens, Archbishop Emeritus of Mechelen-Brussels, and in Madrid, Cardinal Vicente Enrique y Tarancón (who died in 1994), then Archbishop of Madrid. Also in 1979, I interviewed the late Archbishop Władysław Rubin (later Cardinal), a close friend of John Paul II. In Santo Domingo in 1993, I interviewed Cardinal Nicolás de Jesús López Rodríguez. I learned a great deal from these sixteen cardinals.

In Rome in 1993 and 1994, I interviewed Archbishop Justin Rigali, then Secretary of the Congregation for Bishops, now Archbishop of St. Louis, Missouri; Archbishop John P. Foley, president of the Pontifical Council for Social Communications; Archbishop Jean-Louis Tauran, Secretary for Relations with the States in the Secretariat of State (the de facto foreign minister of the Holy See); Archbishop Tadeusz Kondrusiewicz, the Apostolic Administrator for Russia (with his see in Moscow); Archbishop Szczepan Wesoły, of the Polish Church of St. Stanisław at Botteghe Oscure, who looks after Polish pilgrims in Rome and who traveled around the world with Cardinal Wojtyła; Bishop Michael Louis Fitzgerald, Secretary of the Pontifical Council for Interreligious Dialogue; Father Michael Thomas of the same council; Bishop Pierre Duprey, Secretary of the Pontifical Council for Promoting Christian Unity; Bishop Javier Echevarría, the new Prelate of Opus Dei, and his predecessor, the late Bishop Álvaro del Portillo; Monsignor Diarmuid Martin, Secretary of the Pontifical Council for Justice and Peace; Monsignor Iván Marín-López, Secretary of the Pontifical Council Cor Unum; Monsignor Hilary C. Franco of the Congregation for the Clergy; Monsignor Stanisław Ryłko of the Secretariat of State; Father Leonard P. Boyle, Prefect of the Vatican Library; Father George P. Coyne, Director of the Vatican Observatory; Father Martin F. McCarthy, Astronomer, Vatican Observatory; Father John F. Long, Rector of the Pontifical Russian College; Father Edward Kaczyński, president of the Mater Ecclesiae Superior Institute of Religious Science at the St. Thomas Aquinas Pontifical University; Father Giuseppe Pittau, Magnificent Rector of the Pontifical Gregorian University; Father Gianpaolo Salvini, Editor, *La Civilitá Cattolica;*

Father Robert Graham, *La Civilitá Cattolica;* and Father Czeslaw Drażek, editor of the Polish-language edition of *L'Osservatore Romano.*

Also in Rome: the Very Reverend Peter-Hans Kolvenbach, Superior General of the Society of Jesus; Father John O'Callaghan, General Assistant of the Society of Jesus; Father Adam Boniecki, Superior General of the Congregation of Marians of the Immaculate Conception, who is the author of *Kalendarium* and *Roman Notebooks,* the most fundamental works on the life of John Paul II from birth until the midpoint in the pontificate; Father Michael Jagosz, Director of the John Paul II Documentation Center at the Polish House in Rome, whose assistance was invaluable in preparing this biography; Father Konrad Hejmo, who looks after Polish pilgrims in Rome; and Father Feliks Bednarski, who was replaced by Father Wojtyła as Chairman of the Department of Ethics at the Catholic University in Lublin and sent to Rome to be attached to the Santa Maria Maggiore Basilica in Rome.

And my very special gratitude goes to my friend Marjorie Weeke of the Pontifical Council for Social Communications, who taught me patience and gave me all the right advice on how to work my way through the Vatican, about which she knows more than most people.

And also in Rome: the Honorable Raymond Flynn, American Ambassador to the Holy See; Louis John Nigro, Jr., Deputy Chief of Mission at the U.S. Embassy to the Holy See, and his predecessor, Cameron Hume; Israeli Ambassador to Italy Avi Pazner, an old friend; Chief Rabbi of Rome Elio Toaff; Professor Andrea Riccardi, the most outstanding contemporary Church historian and a new friend; Adriano Roccucci, a collaborator of Professor Riccardi; Jas Gawronski, personal friend, author, journalist, former European Parliament deputy, who has known John Paul II for a very long time; Jerzy Kluger, Karol Wojtyła's high school classmate and still a close friend, and his wife, Renée; Curtis Bill Pepper, old friend, author, former *Newsweek* bureau chief in Rome, and his wife, Beverly, who are a priceless asset for visiting reporters; and Professor Stanisław Grygiel, a philosopher and member of the Pontifical Council for the Family.

ACKNOWLEDGMENTS

My professional colleagues in Rome: William D. Montalbano of the *Los Angeles Times;* Victor Simpson of the Associated Press; Philip Pullella of Reuters; Alan Cowell of the *New York Times;* Agostino Bono, John Thavis, and Cindy Wooden of the Catholic News Service; Luigi Accattoli of *Corriere de la Sera,* the best writer on Vatican matters; Father Antonio Pelayo of *Ya* of Madrid; Dominique Chivot of *La Croix;* Dominik Morawski, a Polish writer about the papacy; and Werner Kaltefleiter of German television.

Mario Tizzan of Hotel Sant' Anna made me feel at home in Rome.

In Poland, the following persons have earned my eternal gratitude:

Halina Kwiatkowska, a distinguished actress in Kraków who played opposite Karol Wojtyła in amateur theater in Wadowice and Kraków, and remains his friend to this day: she gave me a guided tour of Wadowice on the fifteenth anniversary of John Paul II's pontificate; the late Juliusz Kydryński, fellow writer and fellow Kraków wartime factory worker; Wojciech Żukrowski, a fellow writer and fellow factory and stone quarry worker; Dr. Karol Poliwka of Warsaw, a classmate of Karol Wojtyła; Father Mieczysław Maliński, who was Karol Wojtyła's colleague at the Kraków Seminary, has written very helpful books about him, and had the patience and courtesy to guide me to every spot in Kraków where the pope had lived, studied, and worked; Professor Jacek Hennel, a Krakó physicist and Wojtyła's skiing companion; Jerzy Turowicz, editor of *Tygodnik Powszechny,* who has published Karol Wojtyła since 1950, has remained his friend, and has been a friend to me for twenty years; Jacek Woźniakowski, head of the Znak publishing house and first post-communist mayor of Kraków; Marek Skwarnicki, a writer and authority on the poetry of Karol Wojtyła; Adam Michnik, old friend and publisher of Warsaw's *Gazeta Wyborcza;* Jacek Żakowski, *Gazeta* religious specialist and a fine one; Andrzej Micewski, author, journalist, and a specialist on the Polish Church; and Stanisław Stomma, a writer and adviser to the primate of Poland.

Also in Poland: General Wojciech Jaruzelski, former

President of Poland and First Secretary of the Polish United Workers' Party (communist), with whom I spent long hours in Warsaw listening to his recollections of his contacts with John Paul II; Mieczysław Rakowski, former Prime Minister of Poland and First Secretary of the party; Jerzy Kuberski, former Polish Ambassador to the Holy See and head of the Religious Affairs Office in the Jaruzelski government; and Bogdan Lewandowski, former Undersecretary General of the United Nations, who met with John Paul II and General Jaruzelski within a week of the imposition of martial law in Poland in 1981.

I received valuable assistance from Bishop Tadeusz Pieronek, Secretary of the Polish episcopate; Archbishop Bronisław Dąbrowski, former Secretary of the episcopate; Bishop Józef Życinski of Tarnów; Professor Jerzy Kłoczowski at the Catholic University in Lublin; Father Tadeusz Styczeń, Chairman of the Department of Ethics at the Catholic University in Lublin and a close collaborator of John Paul II; Professor Stefan Swieżawski in Warsaw, a historian of philosophy who was the examiner of Karol Wojtyła's doctoral dissertation; Father Mikolaj Kuczkowski, who was Karol Wojtyła's first gradeschool religion teacher, then parish priest of the famous steel-mill town church in Nowa Huta built under Cardinal Wojtyła's supervision; Father Czesław Obtułowicz, who was Wojtyła's co-vicar at St. Florian's church in Kraków; Father Józef Gąsiorowski, who was Wojtyła's seminary companion and now is parish priest at Niegowici; Father Michal Heller, a Kraków scientist who works closely with John Paul II; Father Tadeusz Fedorowicz of the Laski Center for the Blind, who has known Wojtyła since his early days; Father Stanisław Musiał, who dealt with the problem of the Carmelite nuns at Oświęcim; Father Andrzej Bardecki, a friend of Wojtyła and a *Tygodnik Powszechny* editor and writer; and Michael Hornblow, Chargé d'Affaires at the U.S. Embassy in Warsaw and, earlier, Chargé d'Affaires at the U.S. Embassy to the Holy See, an enormously knowledgeable diplomat. In Kraków, Alicja Furgała of the United States Information Service was of vast help in locating sources.

Henryk Jagielski, an old friend, drove me across Poland on this project as he had driven me in the course of earlier

Polish projects over the last twenty-two years. In Warsaw, Mrs. Ernesta Jagielska Jekiel transcribed all my Polish-language interviews with amazing speed and accuracy.

In the United States, I received crucial encouragement and advice from Father Vincent O'Keefe, now Religious Supervisor of America House in New York City, earlier President of Fordham University, and General Assistant of the Society of Jesus in Rome; Monsignor George G. Higgins in Washington, D.C.; and Monsignor Bryan Walsh in Miami.

Much knowledge and information came from interviews with Archbishop John R. Roach of St. Paul and Minneapolis; Archbishop Rembert G. Weakland of Milwaukee; Bishop Mark J. Hurley of San Francisco; Monsignor Robert W. Schiefen of Venice, Florida, who was Father Wojtyła's colleague (and self-appointed English teacher) at the Belgian College in Rome in 1946; Father Thomas J. Reese of the Woodstock Theological Seminary in Washington, D.C., and a chronicler of the Church; Father Avery Dulles at Fordham University; Father Charles E. Curran, formerly of Catholic University; and Sister Theresa Kane of the Sisters of Mercy in Dobbs Ferry, New York.

I had important interviews and conversations with Dr. George Hunston Williams, Harvard Divinity School Professor Emeritus and the author of *The Mind of John Paul II,* the first major work on this aspect of the pope, whom he had met at the Second Vatican Council in Rome; Dr. Harvey Cox of the Harvard Divinity School and an authority on the Theology of Liberation; Harvard historian Dr. Richard Pipes; Dr. Joseph T. English, former President of the American Psychiatric Association, who led the first delegation of psychiatrists ever to meet with a pope; Lieutenant General Vernon C. Walters, U.S. Army (Ret.), former Deputy Director of Central Intelligence, Permanent Representative to the United Nations, and American Ambassador to West Germany, who used to brief John Paul II on the Cold War; the Honorable David Walters, former American Ambassador to the Holy See; Rabbi James Rudin of the American Jewish Committee; Maestro Gilbert Levine of New York, who conducted the 1994 Holocaust Concert at the Vatican in the presence of John Paul II; Werner Fornos, president of the Population Institute in Washington, D.C.; Professor Krzysztof Michalski of Boston University and the Vienna Institute for Human Sciences; Kenneth L. Woodward, Religion Editor of *Newsweek;* Flora Lewis of the *New York Times;* the late Peter Hebblethwaite, the biographer of Pope Paul VI; and George Volsky of Miami, an old friend and transplanted Krakowian.

At the United States Catholic Conference in Washington, D.C., I am grateful for advice and assistance from Monsignor Francis J. Maniscalco. Director of the Office of Media Relations; William Ryan and Sister Mary Anne Welsh from the same office; Thomas E. Quigley; Father George Sarauskas; and Father Anthony Czarnecki.

William A. Schmitt, Director of Communications of the Prelature of Opus Dei in New York, provided important guidance concerning the prelature in Rome.

At the library of Woodstock Theological Seminary, I was assisted by Ms. Adoreen McCormack and Ms. Nora Callahan.

In Montreal, Monsignor Neil E. Willard, General Coordinator at the archdiocese, familiarized me with the problems of the Church in Canada.

William Nylen in Miami performed miracles in transcribing thousands of pages of interviews: my interviewees spoke in English with every imaginable foreign accent, but they could not outwit Bill. Beata Wróblewski in Washington, D.C., efficiently transcribed additional Polish-language interviews. Cristina Jaramillo in Miami coped very well with Spanish-language interviews from Rome and Santo Domingo. In New York, Christine M. Olszer typed at demonic speed the entire manuscript, complete with Polish diacritical marks over and/or under almost every Polish name or word.

All this interviewing required much world travel, and my transcontinental and transatlantic voyages were brilliantly organized (it takes brilliance to travel well these days) by Amy DeVos of the Waters Travel Service in Washington, D.C. But she has been doing this for me for many years, and my constant changes in plans never seem to perturb her.

It was a joy to work for the third time on a book with my favorite editor, Lisa Drew, who now is also my publisher under her own imprint at Scribner. Katherine Boyle at Scribner has won my admiration for making it all work without a hitch under a truly tough production schedule. John Fontana designed a magnificent jacket for *Pope John Paul II: The Biography* and Grzegorz Gałązka in Rome, who has been photographing the pope for years, came up with the beautiful picture that graces this book.

Anne Sibbald, of Janklow-Nesbit Associates, my agent and friend, deserves immense credit for making me finish the biography on time, not succumbing to literary and other distractions.

Now in my family: my wife, Marianne, served for the eighteenth time as my first editor on a book as well as critic, researcher, supplier of normally unobtainable vital literary materials, and household generalissimo. My son-in-law, Wladimir M. Sachs, made a very long and complex seven-language bibliography take shape in the blink of an eye.

Finally, my deepest thanks go to my *manual* portable Underwood typewriter for surviving one more book under my heavy two-finger-typing creative method. . . .

NOTES ON SOURCES AND CHAPTER NOTES

Trillions of words have been written in every imaginable language (including Esperanto) about John Paul II in treatises, books, essays, and magazine and newspaper articles. The pope himself is the author of books, dramatic plays, poetry, essays, articles, and thousands of sermons and homilies.

Only a very small percentage of this massive body of material, however, throws much light on the personal story of Karol Wojtyła, the Polish pontiff, and, consequently, the reading list used by a biographer must be supplemented and enriched with detailed interviews with those who have known him, more or less well, at different stages of his life, from Wadowice to the Apostolic Palace at the Vatican.

In preparing this biography, I have relied heavily both on the literature, including John Paul II's own prepontifical writings, most of which is available only in Polish (but is listed here in the bibliography that follows), and on scores of in-depth interviews at the Vatican, in Rome; Warsaw, Kraków, and smaller Polish cities and towns; Vienna; Paris; Madrid; Brussels; Santo Domingo; New York City; Philadelphia; Washington, D.C.; Miami; Dobbs Ferry, New York; and Montreal (the interviewees are listed in the acknowledgments).

In terms of the literature, I have found that a study of the pope's writings is absolutely indispensable in any attempt to try to understand his complex personality. In most cases, exact citations and references are identified in the text of this book.

About a dozen other books were equally indispensable in working on John Paul II's biography.

For the prepontifical period, the most basic work is Father Adam Boniecki's *Kalendarium* of the life of Karol Wojtyła, virtually a day-by-day account of his activities from his birth on; it includes important texts and documents as well. *Kalendarium* is well fleshed out in *Rodowód* (Origins) of John Paul II's life by the late Józef Szczypka. Both are available only in Polish. Father Mieczysław Maliński, the pope's seminary colleague and Kraków neighbor in wartime, has written several books about him, and his very useful *Pope John Paul II: The Life of Karol Wojtyła* has been translated into English.

Wojtyła's youthful and adult years are covered in Polish-language collections of reminiscences by friends, *Młodzieńcze Lata*, edited by the late Juliusz Kydryński, and *Moje Spotkania z Janem Pawłem II*, edited by the Reverend Wiesław Niewęgłowski (see bibliography). Some of the pope's own recollections of childhood and adolescence are contained in André Frossard's *"Be Not Afraid!"* (available in English) and his *Portrait de Jean-Paul II*, only in French.

Harvard School of Divinity Professor George Hunston Williams's *The Mind of John Paul II: Origins of His Thought and Action* is first-rate and "must" reading. Peter Hebblethwaite's excellent biography of Pope Paul VI provides significant insights into Wojtyła's politics as bishop and cardinal—and the pope's protégé. Professor Andrea Riccardi's superb *Il Potere del Papa* traces the evolution of the papacy from Pius XII to John Paul II; it is another must, but is available only in Italian.

The pontifical period is also rather inadequately covered in serious literature. However, the three volumes of Father Boniecki's *Notes Rzymski* (Rome Notebooks), only in Polish; Frossard's *"Be Not Afraid!"*; Riccardi's *Il Potere del*

Papa; Dominik Morawski's *Pomost na Wschód* (Bridge to the East), only in Polish; Kenneth L. Woodward's *Making Saints;* and Wilton Winn's *Keepers of the Keys* are the most important in this realm.

Relations between communist Poland and the papacy of John Paul II are best described in the memoirs of General Jaruzelski, former Prime Minister Rakowski, and former Party First Secretary Edward Gierek, and Aneks Publishers' transcripts of secret discussions between the Polish Church and the regime, *Tajne Dokumenty, Państwo Kościół*—all in Polish (but listed in the bibliography).

Material in this book derived from my own interviews, most of which are listed in the Acknowledgments, is identified either in the text or in the Chapter Notes (except when anonymity was requested). His Holiness Pope John Paul II's comments in conversations with me are not quoted directly because they were informal chats, but are conveyed in such phrases as "the pope believes," and are clearly in context.

All of the pope's public pronouncements and texts signed by him have been published in *L'Osservatore Romano*—this is the official version in all languages—and are identified in the Chapter Notes as OR. Material from other publications is fully identified in the Notes.

CHAPTER 1

3–7: In this section, as elsewhere, the principal sources are Oscar Halecki's and M. K. Dziewanowski's histories of Poland (see bibliography).

7–9: Adam Boniecki's *Kalendarium* and Józef Szczypka's *Rodowód.* Remarks about St. Stanisław are from *Kalendarium,* from close friends, and from the pope's private conversation with the author. Descriptions of his activities are from the author's observation and from close friends. The Kraków comments on prayer are in *Kalendarium.*

10–15: OR is the source for the pronouncements on population, etc.

NOTES

14: The material on Gregory the Great is from the two-volume biography by F. Homes Dudden.
15: Author's observations.

CHAPTER 2

17–22: Halecki, Dziewanowski.
22–24: All quotations are from OR or persons cited directly, or conversations with the author.
25–30: The material on Stanisław and martyrdom is from *Kalendarium,* Dziewanowski, Szczypka, and private conversations with the author. The contemporary martyrdom references—Peru and Sicily—are from the *New York Times.*

CHAPTER 3

32–34: Halecki, Dziewanowski.
35–36: *Kalendarium,* Szczypka, *Młodzieńcze Lata.*
36–45: Halecki, Dziewanowski, *Kalendarium.*

CHAPTER 4

49–51: Entry on St. Augustine, *Encyclopaedia Britannica,* eleventh edition, 1910.
53–62: *Kalendarium,* Szczypka, author's interviews with Halina Kwiatkowska (nee Królikiewicz), Jerzy Kluger, author's visits to Wadowice.

CHAPTER 5

63–83: *Kalendarium,* Szczypka, author's interviews with Father Mikołaj Kuczkowski, Kluger, Halina Kwiatkowska, and Dr. Poliwka; *Młodzieńcze Lata, Spotkania,* Frossard's *"Be Not Afraid!";* Beer interview in North American Newspaper Alliance (NANA), 1979; the pope's reference to the 147th Psalm was in the *Parade* magazine interview with the author in 1994. Accattoli is quoted in Riccardi's *Il Potere.*

CHAPTER 6

84–100: *Kalendarium,* Szczypka, author's interviews with Halina Kwiatowska, Father Mieczysław Maliński, the late Juliusz Kydryński, *Młodzieńcze Lata, Spotkania;* material on the poem "Stanisław" is from the author's interview with Marek Skwarnicki in Kraków. Kraków descriptions are from the author's visits.

CHAPTER 7

101–106: *Kalendarium,* Szczypka; Kydryński, Maliński interviews.

105–106: The story of Lucjana Frassati-Gawrońska is from *Tygodnik Powszechny* in Kraków, 1994, and from the author's interview with her son, Jas Gawroński.

106–108: Most of the material on Pius XII during the war is from Riccardi's *Il Potere.*

109–114: *Kalendarium,* Szczypka; Maliński, Kydryński interviews; *Job* by Karol Wojtyła (in *Collected Poetry and Drama,* in Polish; see bibliography); *Dziady* by Adam Mickiewicz (in Mickiewicz's *Dzieła Poetyckie* [see bibliography]).

CHAPTER 8

115–123: *Kalendarium,* Szczypka, *Młodzieńcze Lata, Spotkania,* author's interviews with Maliński, Kydryński, Wojciech Żukrowski. Karol Wojtyła wrote about Jan Tyranowski in an article—"Apostoł"—in *Tygodnik Powszechny* in issue No. 35 in 1949, reprinted in *Aby Chrystus się Nami Posługiwatł* (see bibliography).

122–123: The address to seminarians is in *Kalendarium.* John Paul II's reminiscences after his father's death are in Frossard's *"Be Not Afraid!"*

122–129: *Kalendarium,* Szczypka; Maliński, Kydryński, Żukrowski, Halina Kwiatkowska, Jerzy Turowicz interviews. *The Quarry,* in Polish, is in *Collected Poetry and Drama.*

CHAPTER 9

130–141: *Kalendarium,* Szczypka; Maliński, Kydryński, Żukrowski, Halina Kwiatkowska, and Father Kuczkowski interviews. John Paul II himself spoke in a 1994 conversation with the author about the wartime accident with the German truck.

CHAPTER 10

145–162: *Kalendarium,* Szczypka; author's interviews with Monsignor Schiefen and Magnificent Rector Father Edward Kaczyński of St. Thomas Pontifical University (Angelicum) in 1994; the material on Pius XII and Paul VI is in Riccardi and Peter Hebblethwaite, *Paul VI;* Wojtyła's comments on Thomism are in his collected lectures, *Wykłady Lubelskie,* issued by the Catholic University of Lublin (see bibliography).

CHAPTER 11

163–181: *Kalendarium,* Szczypka, *Spotkania.* Most of the material on Primate Wyszyński is from Andrzej Micewski's biography (see bibliography). Wojtyła's Kraków and Niegowici period is based in part on the author's interviews with Father Czesław Obtułowicz, Father Kuczkowski, Jerzy Turowicz, Father Gąsiorowski, Father Maliński, and Marek Skwarnicki. Texts (in Polish) of Wojtyła's poetry and *Brother of Our God* are included in *Collected Poetry and Drama.*

CHAPTER 12

182–188: Most of the material on Primate Wyszyński and the Polish Church's problems comes from Micewski's biography, the author's interviews with Micewski, Stanisław Stomma, an adviser to the primate, Turowicz, and from Jacek Żakowski's *Anatomia Smaku* account of *Tygodnik Powszechny*'s troubles in the 1950s (see bibliography).

188–192: The history of *Opus Dei* is largely based on *El Itinerario Jurídico del Opus Dei* by Fuenmayor et al., in Spanish (see bibliography), and on the author's interviews with the late Monsignor Escrivá in Spain in 1967, and the late Bishop del Portillo in Rome in 1993, and Father Flávio Capucci, the postulator general, also in 1993.

192–197: *Kalendarium,* Szczypka, author's interviews with Professor Jacek Hennel, Father Michal Heller, Professor Stefan Swieżawski, and Father Obtułowicz.

CHAPTER 13

198–211: *Kalendarium,* Szczypka; the material on Wyszyński comes from Micewski's biography; author's interviews with Father Feliks Bednarski in Rome, Professor Swieżawski in Warsaw, Professor Jerzy Kłoczowski in Lublin, Father Tadeusz Styczeń in Lublin, Father Maliński in Kraków; citations from Wojtyła's addresses to physicians are in *Kalendarium.*

CHAPTER 14

215–229: *Kalendarium,* Szcyzpka, *Spotkania.* Author's interviews with Father Andrzej Bardecki, Father Maliński, Father Kuczkowski, Father Obtułowicz in Kraków, and Father Michał Jagosz in Rome. Documents concerning Wojtyła and the communist authorities were made available to the author in Rome. Citations from his books and plays are from Polish texts in *Collected Poetry and Drama* and *Miłość i Odpowiedzialność, Aby Chrystus,* published by Znak and the Catholic University in Lublin (see bibliography).

CHAPTER 15

230–241: *Kalendarium,* Szcyzpka, *Spotkania.* Author's interviews with the late Cardinal Rubin in Rome in 1979,

Cardinal Deskur in Rome in 1993 and 1994, Father Bardecki in Kraków, Professor Swieżawski in Warsaw, Professor Williams in Cambridge, Massachusetts, Father Maliński in Kraków, and Cardinal König in Vienna. Wojtyła's poems appear in the *Collected Poetry and Drama*.

CHAPTER 16

242–256: *Kalendarium,* Szczyzpka, *Spotkania.* Author's interviews with Cardinal Deskur in Rome, Andrzej Micewski, Stanisław Stomma and Professor Swieżawski in Warsaw, Father Bardecki and Father Maliński in Kraków. The account of the Holy Land trip is in *Kalendarium.*

CHAPTER 17

257–260: *Kalendarium,* Szczyzpka.
260–264: Polish secret police (UB) documents on Wojtyła were made available to the author in Rome.

CHAPTER 18

269–278: *Kalendarium,* Szczyzpka, *Spotkania,* Peter Hebblethwaite, *Paul VI.* Author's interviews with Bishop Tadeusz Pieronek, Father Jagosz, Father Heller, Father Bardecki, Cardinal Deskur.
278–281: *Kalendarium,* Szczyzpka. Author's interview in Rome with Archbishop Wesoły on travel with Wojtyła.
285–286: *Kalendarium,* Szczyzpka. Author's interviews with Cardinal Deskur in Rome, Father Obtułowicz in Kraków.

CHAPTER 19

289–305: *Kalendarium,* Szczyzpka, *Spotkania,* for chronology of events before, during, and after the conclave.

Quotations from John Paul II upon and after the election are in OR and *Tygodnik Powszechny.* The reconstruction of events before and during the conclave is based on 1979 interviews with Cardinals Vicente Enrique y Tarancón in Madrid and Leo Jozef Suenens in Brussels; a 1993 interview with Cardinal Krol in Philadelphia; 1994 interviews with Cardinal König in Vienna and Cardinal Deskur in Rome. For the conclave description, the author's 1994 interview with Cesare Tassi at the Sistine Chapel. Also see Giancarlo Zizola's *Il Conclave: Storia i segretti, L'elezione papale da San Pietro a Giovanni Paolo II* (see bibliography).

CHAPTER 20

307–315: The Soviet and Warsaw regimes' reactions to John Paul II's election are based on the author's 1993 and 1994 interviews with General Jaruzelski and Mieczyslaw Rakowski in Warsaw. The Gierek quotes are from *Edward Gierek: Przerwana Dekada* by Janusz Rolicki (see bibliography). John Paul II's quotes are in OR.

317–319: *Notes Rzymski* by Adam Boniecki (see bibliography), author's interview with Marek Skwarnicki; *A Shepherd's Diary* by Archbishop Oscar Romero (see bibliography).

CHAPTER 21

320–335: The account of the negotiations and preparations for the papal visit to Poland is based on the author's interviews with Pieronek, Skwarnicki, Jaruzelski, and Rakowski. Micewski's biography of Wyszyński. All official texts are in OR and John Paul II, *Przemówienia, Homilie, Polska: 2 VI 1979–10 VI 1979* (see bibliography).

326–337: The account of the Soviet Communist Party Central Committee Secretariat's "Decisions" on

Wojtyła, etc. are based on documents obtained by the author in Rome in 1994. They have never before been published.

CHAPTER 22

340–344: The crisis in the Church is discussed in Riccardi's *Il Potere del Papa* and Peter Hebblethwaite, *Paul VI;* also in the author's 1993 interview with Dr. Harvey Cox at Harvard Divinity School. The conversation between Cardinal Villot and the pope is from an unpublished manuscript by a French journalist friend of the cardinal.

344: Statistics are from *Statistical Yearbook of the Church, 1991.*

345–346: Archbishop Marcinkus's remarks are from an interview with the author in Rome in 1979; Marcinkus, now retired in Arizona, refused to be interviewed in 1993 and 1994.

347–352: Archbishop Romero's *Diary;* author's interviews with Harvey Cox at Harvard and Cardinal Pironio in Rome in 1993.

352–355: Author's interviews with members of the Society of Jesus. Anonymity requested.

355–357: Discussion of dissent is based on the author's 1994 interviews with the Reverend Charles E. Curran and Harvey Cox. Also, Curran's *The Living Tradition of Catholic Moral Theology* (see bibliography).

357–359: Material on Opus Dei is from Fuenmayor et al., *El Itinerario,* and the author's interviews with Portillo and Capucci.

CHAPTER 23

365–380: The account of the rise of Solidarity is based on the author's interviews with Lech Wałęsa in Gdańsk in 1981 and with Monsignor Hilary Franco, Jaruzelski, Rakowski, Skwarnicki, and Micewski in 1993 and 1994; Micewski's biography of Wyszyński, *The Po-*

ish August by Neal Asherson, and *Tajne Dokumenty, PaństwoKościół,* Rolicki's book on Gierek, Wałęsa's *The Struggle and the Triumph,* and Zbigniew Brzeziński's *Power and Principle* (see bibliography for all the above).

380–381: Author's interview with Father Pittau, 1993.

CHAPTER 24

382–398: The accounts of the assassination attempt appear in Frossard's *"Be Not Afraid!"* (including the quotes from Monsignor Dziwisz) and in Boniecki's *Notes Rzymski;* medical information is contained in Frossard's *"Be Not Afraid!";* also in author's 1993 interview with Dr. Navarro-Valls. Background on Agca appears in Reuters News Agency 1981 dispatches, and in Claire Sterling's *The Time of the Assassins* (see bibliography). KGB cables to Moscow were reported by David Wise in the *New York Times Magazine* in 1994. The accounts of the CIA activities are based in part on the Senate Select Committee on Intelligence hearings, 1987 and 1991 (see bibliography), and in part on the author's own reporting (which also covers references to the NSA). The Warsaw regime's reactions appear in *Tajne Dokumenty* (see bibliography). Author's interview with Father Bardecki.

CHAPTER 25

399–414: *Tajne Dokumenty,* Boniecki's *Notes Rzymski,* author's interviews with Jaruzelski, Rakowski, Bogdan Lewandowski, Micewski, and General Walters. Author's Vatican conversations.

417–419: Author's interview with Jerzy Kuberski.

CHAPTER 26

420–431: The John Paul II–Jaruzelski–Gorbachev relationship is discussed in detail in a series of Jaruzelski's interviews with the author in 1993 and 1994; also author's interviews with Rakowski and Kuberski. Jaruzelski made available the texts of his letters to John Paul II. Also author's Vatican conversations. *Tajne Dokumenty.*

431–432: Author's conversations with Cardinal Lustiger.

433: Boniecki, *Notes Rzymski.*

CHAPTER 27

436–438: The survey of Polish religious attitudes is in *Tajne Dokumenty.*

438–444: Author's interviews with General Jaruzelski; author's Vatican conversations; author's interviews with Rakowski; *Tajne Dokumenty.*

444–451: The Vatican missions to Moscow and Gorbachev's visit to Rome are discussed in interviews with the author by Dr. Navarro-Valls and Bishop Duprey.

CHAPTER 28

456–457: Author's interview with Dr. Navarro-Valls; Boniecki, *Notes Rzymski.*

458–461: Author's reporting on travel with John Paul II; texts in OR.

461–477: All papal texts on Cairo conference, ordination of women, and Ratzinger documents appear in OR.

477–478: Reporting on the Bible translation controversy and the annual meeting of U.S. bishops appears in the November 1994 issues of *National Catholic Reporter, America,* and *Commonweal.*

479–481: Author's interview with Father Coyne. *John Paul II on Science and Religion* by George V. Coyne; *Galileo: per il Copernicanesimo e per la Chiesa* by Annibale Fantoli (see bibliography).

NOTES

CHAPTER 29

483–488: John Paul II's views on the post-communist world are best expressed in his *Centesimus Annus* encyclical (see bibliography), his speech at Riga University on September 9, 1993 (in OR), and in an interview in Jas Gawroński's *Il Mondo di Giovanni Paolo II* (see bibliography).

488–493: John Paul II's role in establishing Israel-Vatican relations is described in interviews with the author by Ambassador Avi Pazner in Rome in 1993.

493–495: John Paul II's explanation of Vatican diplomatic relations with Israel appears in his interview with the author in *Parade* magazine of April 3, 1994.

494–495: Author's notes from the concert he attended.

CHAPTER 30

503: Papal text in OR.

506: Interview with Hillary Rodham Clinton by Kenneth Woodward, *Newsweek,* October 31, 1994.

509: The number of Russian monasteries was reported at the October 1994 Bishops' Synod in Rome by Russian Orthodox Archimandrite Joseph Poustooutov (OR).

510–514: All figures are from the *Statistical Yearbook of the Church,* 1991. Author's interview with Archbishop Weakland. Evangelical sects are discussed in the author's interview with Dr. Harvey Cox, and the CEBs in an interview with Cardinal Pironio.

520: Mrs. Steinfels's article appears in the November 18, 1994, issue of *Commonweal.*

521: The Catholic commentator's views appear in *National Catholic Reporter.*

523: Author's conversation with Cardinal Etchegaray.

524–525: John Paul II's most up-to-date (end of 1994) travel statistics appear in the Vatican Radio's booklet on the September 1994 trip to Zagreb.

525–527: Canonization and beatification totals as of January 1995 were provided by the Congregation for the Causes of Saints. Kenneth Woodward's *Making Saints* is the best work on the subject (see bibliography).

NOTES

532: The pope's schedule is based on the author's Vatican conversations.

533: John Paul's quote on Paul VI appears in the compendium *Przemówienia i Wywiady w Radio Watykańskim* (see bibliography).

BIBLIOGRAPHY

The letter (P) denotes books available in Polish only; (I) denotes books available in Italian only; (S) denotes books available in Spanish only; (F) denotes books available in French only.

BOOKS

Accattoli, Luigi. *Io ho Avuto Paura a Ricevere Questa Nomina.* Societá Editrice Internazionale, Torino, 1993 (I).

Accattoli, Luigi, and Domenico Del Rio. *Wojtyla: Un Nuovo Mosé.* Arnoldo Mondadori Editore, Milano, 1988 (I).

Aristide, Jean-Bertrand. *Téologie et Politique.* Les Éditions du CIDIHCA, Montréal, Canada, 1992 (F).

Aristotle. *Ethics, Book I; Politics, Book I.* Henry Regnery, Chicago, 1970.

Armstrong, Karen. *A History of God.* Alfred A Knopf, New York, 1993.

Asherson, Neal. *The Polish August: The Self-Limiting Revolution.* Viking Press, New York, 1982.

St. Augustine. *The Confessions.* Collier Books, Macmillan, New York, 1961.

BIBLIOGRAPHY

Bardecki, Andrzej. *Kościół Epoki Dialogu.* Społeczny Instytut Wydawniczy Znak, Kraków, 1966 (P).

Berrigan, Philip. *Prison Journals of a Priest Revolutionary.* Holt, Rinehart and Winston, New York, 1967.

Berry, Jason. *Lead Us Not into Temptation: Catholic Priests and the Sexual Abuse of Children.* Doubleday, New York, 1992.

Betto, Frei. *Fidel y la Religión: Conversaciones con Frei Betto.* Oficina de Publicaciones del Consejo de Estado, La Habana, 1985 (S). English edition: *Fidel and Religion: Castro Talks on Revolution and Religion with Frei Betto.* Simon and Schuster, New York, 1987.

Bianchi, Eugene C., and Rosemary Radford Ruether (editors). *A Democratic Catholic Church: The Reconstruction of Roman Catholicism.* Crossroad, New York, 1992.

Boniecki, Adam, M.I.C. *Notes Rzymski.* Three volumes. Wydawnictwo Znak, Kraków, 1988 (P).

________.*Kalendarium Zycia Karola Wojtyły.* Wydawnictwo Znak, Kraków, 1983 (P).

Brumberg, Abraham (editor). *Poland: Genesis of a Revolution.* Random House, New York, 1983.

Brzeziński, Zbigniew. *Power and Principle.* Farrar, Straus and Giroux, New York, 1983.

Bujak, Adam. *Miejsce Piotrowe.* Wydawnictwo O. O. Bernardynów "Calvarianum," Kalwaria Zebrzydowska, Poland, 1987 (P).

Burns, Gene. *The Frontiers of Catholicism.* University of California Press, Berkeley, 1992.

Carrier, Hervé, S.J. *The Social Doctrine of the Church Revisited.* Vatican Polyglot Press, Vatican City, 1990.

Casaroli, Agostino. *Nella Chiesa per il Mondo: Omelie e Discorsi.* Rusconi Libri, Milano, 1987 (I).

Cateura, Linda Brandi. *Catholics USA: Makers of a Modern Church.* William Morrow, New York, 1989.

Chamberlayne, Elizabeth (editor). *The Life of Christ: As Portrayed by the Old Masters and the Words of the Holy Bible.* Bantam Books, New York, 1961.

Chamberlin, E. R. *The Bad Popes.* Dorset Press, New York, 1969.

Cooney, John. *The American Pope: The Life and Times of Francis Cardinal Spellman.* Times Books, New York, 1984.

Cornwell, John. *A Thief in the Night: The Mysterious Death of Pope John Paul I.* Simon and Schuster, New York, 1989.

Cox, Harvey. *The Secular City.* Collier Books, Macmillan, New York, 1990.

———. *The Silencing of Leonardo Boff.* Meyer-Stone Books, Oak Park, Illinois, 1988.

Coyne, George V. (editor). *John Paul II on Science and Religion.* University of Notre Dame Press, Notre Dame, Indiana, 1990.

Cragg, Gerald R. *The Church and the Age of Reason: 1648–1789.* Penguin Books, New York, 1990.

Crossan, John Dominic. *Jesus: A Revolutionary Biography.* HarperCollins, San Francisco, 1994.

Curran, Charles E. *The Living Tradition of Catholic Moral Theology.* University of Notre Dame Press, Notre Dame, Indiana, 1992.

Daim, Wilfried. *The Vatican and Eastern Europe.* Frederick Ungar, New York, 1970.

D'Antonio, William V., and Frederick B. Pike (editors). *Religion, Revolution and Reform: New Forces for Change in Latin America.* Frederick A. Praeger, New York, 1964.

Della Rocca, Fernando. *Papi di Questo Secolo.* Cedam, Padova, Italy, 1981 (I).

Del Rio, Domenico. *Wojtyla: Un Pontificato Itinerante.* Edizioni Dehoniane, Bologna, Italy, 1994 (I).

Dionne, Robert J. *The Papacy and the Church.* Philosophical Library, New York, 1987.

Dobrowolski, Tadeusz. *Polish Painting from the Enlightenment to Recent Times.* Ossolineum, Warsaw, 1981.

Dolan, Jay P. *The American Catholic Experience: A History from Colonial Times to the Present.* University of Notre Dame Press, Notre Dame, Indiana, 1992.

Dudden, F. Homes, B.D. *Gregory the Great: His Place in History and Thought.* Two volumes. Longmans, Green, London, 1905.

Dunn, Joseph. *No Lions in the Hierarchy.* Columba Press, Dublin, Ireland, 1994.

Dziewanowski, M. K. *Poland in the Twentieth Century.* Columbia University Press, New York, 1977.

Eliade, Mircea. *Essential Sacred Writings from Around the World.* HarperCollins, San Francisco, 1967.

Evangelisti, David. *Joannes Paulus II: Light in the Church.* Libreria Editrice Vaticana, Vatican City, 1980.

Fantoli, Annibale. *Galileo: per il Copernicanesimo e per la Chiesa.* Libreria Editrice Vaticana, Cittá del Vaticano, 1993 (I).

Fedorowicz, Tadeusz. *Drogi Opatrzczności.* Norbertinum, Lublin, Poland, 1991 (P).

Filibeck, Giorgio. *Les Droits de l'Homme dans l'Enseignement de l'Eglise: De Jean XXIII à Jean-Paul II.* Libreria Editrice Vaticana, Cittá del Vaticano, 1992 (F).

Finke, Roger, and Rodney Stark. *The Churching of America: 1776–1990.* Rutgers University Press, New Brunswick, New Jersey, 1992.

Fox, Matthew. *The Coming of the Cosmic Christ.* HarperCollins, San Francisco, 1988.

Fremantle, Anne (editor). *The Social Teachings of the Church.* New American Library, New York, 1963.

Frossard, André. *Portret Jana Pawła II.* Wydawnictwo Znak, Kraków, 1990 (P). Original edition: *Portrait de Jean-Paul II,* Éditions Robert Laffont, Paris, 1988 (F).

Frossard, André, and Pope John Paul II. *"Be Not Afraid!"* St. Martin's, New York, 1984.

de Fuenmayor, A., V. Gómez-Iglesias, and J. L. Illanes. *El Itinérario Jurídico del Opus Dei: Historia y Defensa de un Carisma.* Ediciones Universidad de Navarra, Pamplona, Spain, 1989 (S).

Gail, Marzieh. *The Three Popes.* Simon and Schuster, New York, 1969.

Gawroński, Jas. *Il Mondo di Giovanni Paolo II.* Arnoldo Mondadori Editore, Milano, 1994 (I).

Gorbachev, Mikhail. *Perestroika: New Thinking for Our Country and the World.* Harper and Row, New York, 1987.

Gorczyca, Roman. *Ojciec Święty Jan Pawe[msp II w Polsce: IV Pielgrzymka 1991.* Wydawnictwo Ycagra Ltd., Warszawa, 1991 (P).

Gray, Francine du Plessix. *Divine Disobedience: Profiles in Catholic Radicalism.* Alfred A. Knopf, New York, 1970.

Greeley, Andrew M. *A Catholic Myth: The Behavior and Beliefs of American Catholics.* Collier Books, Macmillan, New York, 1990.

Gremillion, Joseph. *The Other Dialogue: The Catholic Commitment in the Social Problems of the Contemporary World.* Doubleday, New York, 1965.

Gutiérrez, Gustavo, Francis McDonagh, Cândido Padin, O.S.B., and John Sobrino, S.J. *Santo Domingo and After: The Challenges for the Latin American Church.* Catholic Institute for International Relations, London, 1993.

Hageman, Alice L., and Philip E. Wheaton (editors). *Religion in Cuba Today: A New Church in a New Society.* Association Press, New York, 1971.

Halecki, Oscar. *Borderlands of Western Civilization: A History of East Central Europe.* Ronald Press, Company, New York, 1952.

Hanson, Eric O. *The Catholic Church in World Politics.* Princeton University Press, Princeton, New Jersey, 1987.

Hebblethwaite, Margaret. *Basic is Beautiful: Base Ecclesial Communities from Third World to First World.* HarperCollins, London, 1993.

Hebblethwaite, Peter. *Paul VI: The First Modern Pope.* Paulist Press, New York/Mahwah, New Jersey, 1993.

Higgins, George G., with William Bole. *Organized Labor and the Church.* Paulist Press, Mahwah, New Jersey, 1993.

Hochhuth, Rolf. *The Representative.* Methuen, London, 1963.

Hofman, Paul. *O Vatican!: A Slightly Wicked View of the Holy See.* Congdon and Weed, New York, 1984.

Hurley, Mark J. *The Unholy Ghost: Anti-Catholicism in the American Experience.* Our Sunday Visitor Publishing Division, Huntington, Indiana, 1992.

Jaruzelski, Wojciech. Stan Wojenny: Dlaczego . . . Polska Oficyna Wydawnicza "BGW," Warszawa, 1992 (P).

John Paul II. *Crossing the Threshold of Hope.* Alfred A. Knopf, New York, 1994.

________.*Tertio Millennio Adveniente: Apostolic Letter on Preparation for the Jubilee of the Year 2000, November 10, 1994.* Libreria Editrice Vaticana, Cittá del Vaticano, 1994.

________.*Truth's splendor: Tenth Encyclical Letter, August 6, 1993.* Office for Publishing and Promotion Services, United States Catholic Conference, Washington, D.C., 1993.

________.*Centisimus annus (Commemorating the centenary of Rerum novarum by Leo XIII): Ninth Encyclical Letter, May 1, 1991.* Office for Publishing and Promotion Services, United States Catholic Conference, Washington, D.C., 1991.

________.*On the permanent validity of the Church's missionary mandate: Eighth Encyclical Letter, January 22, 1991.* Office for Publishing and Promotion Services, United States Catholic Conference, Washington, D.C., 1991.

________.*Per la Pace nel Golfo.* Libreria Editrice Vaticana, Cittá del Vaticano, 1991 (I).

________.*W. Polsce: Przemówienia i Homilie 1979, 1983, 1987.* Instytut Wydawniczy Pax, Warszawa, 1991 (P).

________.*W Indiach: Homilie i Przemówienia: 31–11 II 1986.* Instytut Wydawniczy Pax, 1990 (P).

________.*W Wielkiej Brytanii 28 V 1982–2 VI 1982 i Argentynie 11 VI 1982–12 VI 1982: Homilie i Przemówienia.* Instytut Wydawniczy Pax, Warszawa, 1989(P).

________.*Na Dalekim Wschodzie: Homilie i Przemówienia: 2 V 1984–11 V 1984.* Instytut Wydawniczy Pax, Warszawa, 1988 (P).

________.*On the Dignity and Vocation of Women: Apostolic Letter, August 15, 1988.* Office for Publishing and Promotion Services, United States Catholic Conference, Washington, D.C., 1988.

———.*On social concerns: Seventh Encyclical Letter, December 30, 1987.* Office for Publishing and Promotion Services, United States Catholic Conference, Washington, D.C., 1987.

———.*On the role of Mary in the mystery of Christ: Sixth Encyclical Letter, March 25, 1987.* Office for Publishing and Promotion Services, United States Catholic Conference, Washington, D.C., 1987.

———.*Przemówienia, Homilie: 9 VI 1987–14 VI 1987.* Wydawnictwo Znak, Kraków, 1987 (P).

———.*On the Holy Spirit in the life of the Church and the world: Fifth Encyclical Letter, May 18, 1986.* Office for Publishing and Promotion Services, United States Catholic Conference, Washington, D.C., 1986.

———.*The Apostles of the Slavs (Commemorating Sts. Cyril and Methodius): Fourth Encyclical Letter, June 2, 1985.* Office for Publishing and Promotion Services, United States Catholic Conference, Washington, D.C., 1985.

———.*Przemówienia, Homilie: 16 VI 1983–22 VI 1983.* Wydawnictwo Znak, Kraków, 1984 (P).

———.*On human work: Third Encyclical Letter, September 14, 1981.* Office for Publishing and Promotion Services, United States Catholic Conference, Washington, D.C., 1981.

———.*On the mercy of God: Second Encyclical Letter, November 30, 1980.* Office for Publishing and Promotion Services, United States Catholic Conference, Washington, D.C., 1980.

———.*Przemówienia, Homilie: Polska: 2 VI 1979–10 VI 1979.* Wydawnictwo Znak, Kraków, 1979 (P).

———.*Redeemer of man: First Encyclical Letter, March 4, 1979.* Office for Publishing and Promotion Services, United States Catholic Conference, Washington, D.C., 1979.

John XXIII. *Peace on earth: Encyclical Letter, April 11, 1963.* Office for Publishing and Promotion Services, United States Catholic Conference, Washington, D.C., 1963.

Johnson, Paul. *A History of Christianity.* Atheneum, New York, 1976.

Kaiser, Philip M. *Journeying Far and Wide: A Political and Diplomatic Memoir.* Charles Scribner's Sons, New York, 1992.

Kant, Immanuel. *Groundwork of the Metaphysic of Morals.* Harper and Row, New York, 1964.

Karolak, Tadeusz. *John Paul II: The Pope from Poland.* Interpress Publishers, Warsaw, 1979.

Kelly, George A. *Keeping the Church Catholic with John Paul II.* Ignatius Press, San Francisco, 1993.

Korboński, Stefan. *W Imieniu Rzeczypospolitej . . .* Instytut Literacki, Paris, 1954 (P).

Kurón, Jacek. *Spoko! Czyli Kwadratura Koła.* Polska Oficyna Wydawnicza "BGW," Warszawa. 1992 (P).

Kydryński, Juliusz (editor). *Młodzieńcze Lata Karola Wojtyły: Wspomnienia.* Oficyna Cracovia, Kraków, 1990 (P).

Lader, Lawrence. *Politics, Power and the Church: The Catholic Crisis and Its Challenge to American Pluralism.* Macmillan, New York, 1987.

Łapinski, Zdzislaw. *Norwid.* Wydawnictwo Znak, Kraków, 1984 (P).

Leach, Catherine S. (editor). *Memoirs of the Polish Baroque.* University of California Press, Berkeley, 1976.

Lernoux, Penny. *People of God: The Struggle for World Catholicism.* Viking Press, New York, 1989.

Lustiger, Jean-Marie. *Wybór Boga.* Wydawnictwo Znak, Kraków, 1992 (P). Original edition: *Le Choix de Dieu.* Êditions de Fallois, Paris, 1988 (F).

Maffeo, Sabino, S.J. *In the Service of Nine Popes: 100 Years of the Vatican Observatory.* The Vatican Observatory and the Pontifical Academy of Sciences, Vatican City, 1991.

Magdziak-Miszewska, Agnieszka. *Kamień Węgielny.* Wydawnictwo Sw. Stanisława B.M. Archidiecezji Krakowskiej, Kraków, 1989 (P).

Maliński, Mieczysław. *Dlaczego Chrześcianie nie są Hydami.* TUM, Wroclaw, Poland, 1993 (P).

________*Pontyfikat Jana Pawła II: 1983–1988.* Księgarnia Sw. Wojciecha, Poznań, Poland, 1991 (P).

________*Wezwano Mnie z Dalekiego Kraju.* Pallottinum, Poznań, Poland, 1987 (P).

———. *Pope John Paul II: The Life of Karol Wojtyła.* Seabury Press, New York, 1979.

Martin, Malachi. *The Decline and Fall of the Roman Church.* G. P. Putnam's Sons, New York, 1981.

May, William W. (editor). *Vatican Authority and American Catholic Dissent.* Crossroad, New York, 1987.

McLaughlin, Loretta. *The Pill, John Rock, and the Church: The Biography of a Revolution.* Little, Brown, Boston, 1982.

Melady, Thomas Patrick. *The Ambassador's Story: The United States and the Vatican in World Affairs.* Our Sunday Visitor Publishing Division, Huntington, Indiana, 1994.

Messori, Vittorio. La Sfida della Fede. Edizioni San Paolo, Torino, 1993 (I).

Micewski, Andrzej. *Katolicy w Potrzasku.* Polska Oficyna Wydawnicza "BGW," Warszawa, 1993 (P).

———. *Cardinal Wyszyński: A Biography.* Harcourt Brace Jovanovich, Orlando, Florida, 1984.

Michałowska, Danuta. "*. . . Trzeba dać świadectwo:" 50-lecie Powstania Teatru Rapsodycznego w Krakowie.* ArsNova-Zjednoczenie Wydawcy, Kraków, 1991 (P).

Michnik, Adam. *The Church and the Left.* University of Chicago Press, Chicago, 1993.

———. *Letters from Prison and Other Essays.* University of California Press, Berkeley, 1985.

Mickiewicz, Adam. *OPan Tadeusz.* Książka i Wideza, Warszawa, 1950 (P).

———. *Dzieła Poetyckie.* Nakładem Komitetu Mickiewiczowskiego, Nowogródek, Poland, 1934 (P).

Morawski, Dominik. *Pomost na Wschód: Obserwacje i Refleksje Watykanisty.* Wydawnictwo "Polonia," Warszawa, 1992 (P).

Mumford, Stephen D. *The Pope and the New Apocalypse: The Holy War Against Family Planning.* Center for Research on Population and Security, Research Triangle Park, North Carolina, 1986.

Murphy, Francis X. *The Papacy Today.* Weidenfeld and Nicolson, London, 1981.

Mysłek, Wiesław. *Socjalizm i Katolicyzm: Polskie Spotkania w Dialogu.* Krajowa Agencja Wydawnicza, Warszawa, 1978 (P).

Nichols, Bruce J. *The Uneasy Alliance: Religion, Refugee Work, and U.S. Foreign Policy.* Oxford University Press, New York, 1988.

Nichols, Peter. *The Pope's Divisions: The Roman Catholic Church Today.* Faber and Faber, London, 1981.

Niewęgłowski, Wiesław (editor). *Moje Spotkania z Janem Pawłem II.* Wydawnictwo Rok, Warszawa, 1991 (P).

Nogar, Raymond J., O.P. *The Lord of the Absurd.* Herder and Herder, New York, 1966.

Nowak, Michael. *The Catholic Ethic and the Spirit of Capitalism.* The Free Press, New York, 1993.

O'Carroll, Michael, C.S.Sp. *Pius XII: Greatness Dishonoured.* Laetare Press, Dublin, Ireland, 1980.

Papafava, Francesco (editor). *The Sistine Chapel.* Musei Vaticani, Vatican City, 1992.

Paul VI. *On the regulation of birth: Encyclical Letter (Humanae vitae), July 25, 1968.* Office for Publishing and Promotion Services, United States Catholic Conference, Washington, D.C., 1968.

________. *On the development of peoples: Encyclical Letter, March 26, 1967.* Office for Publishing and Promotion Services, United States Catholic Conference, Washington, D.C., 1967.

Pelikan, Jaroslaw. *The Melody of Theology: A Philosophical Dictionary.* Harvard University Press, Cambridge, 1988.

Perea, Francisco J. *El Papa en México.* Editorial Diana, México, D.F., 1979 (S).

Piekarski, Adam. *The Church in Poland.* Interpress Publishaers, Warsaw, 1978.

Pieronek, Tadeusz, and Zawadzki, Roman M. (editors). *Karol Wojtyła Jako Biskup Krakowski.* Wydawnictwo Sw. Stanisław B.M. Archidiecezji Krakowskiej, Kraków, 1988 (P).

Rakowski, Mieczyslaw F. *Lata, Listy, Ludzie . . .* Polska Oficyna Wydawnicza "BGW," Warszawa, 1993 (P).

________. *Gorbaczow: Pierwszy i Ostatni.* Polska Oficyna Wydawnicza "BGW," Warszawa, 1992 (P).

———. *Czasy Nadziei i Rozczarowań*. Two volumes. Wydawnictwo Czytelnik, Warszawa, 1987 (P).

———. *Trzech na Jednego*. Czytelnik, Warszawa, 1986 (P).

———. *Od Sierpnia do Grudnia 1980*. Czytelnik, Warszawa, 1981 (P).

———. *Rzeczpospolita na Progu Lat Osiemdziesiątych*. Państwowy Instytut Wydawniczy, Warszawa, 1981 (P).

Ramet, Pedro (editor). *Catholicism and Politics in Communist Societies*. Duke University Press, Durham, North Carolina, 1990.

Ratzinger, Joseph Cardinal. *Turning Point for Europe?* Ignatius Press, San Francisco, 1994.

———. *The Meaning of Christian Brotherhood*. Ignatius Press, San Francisco, 1993.

———. *L'Angoscia di Un'Assenza*. Editrice Queriniana, Roma, 1971 (I).

Ratzinger, Joseph Cardinal, with Vittorio Messori. *The Ratzinger Report*. Ignatius Press, San Francisco, 1985.

Redmond, Jane. *Generous Lives: American Catholic Women Today*. Triumph Books, Liguori, Missouri, 1992.

Reese, Thomas J., S.J. *A Flock of Shepherds: The National Conference of Catholic Bishops*. Sheed and Ward, Kansas City, 1992.

———. *Archbishop: Inside the Power Structure of the American Catholic Church*. Harper and Row, New York, 1989.

Riccardi, Andrea E. *Il Potere del Papa: da Pio XII a Giovanni-Paolo II*. Editori Laterza, Roma, 1993 (I).

———. *Il Vaticano e Mosca: 1940–1990*. Editori Laterza, Roma, 1993 (I).

Richard, Lucien, O.M.I., Daniel Harrington, S.J., and John W. O'Malley, S.J. (editors). *Vatican II: The Unfinished Agenda: A Look to the Future*. Paulist Press, Mahwah, New Jersey, 1987.

Richardson, Cyril C. (editor). *Early Christian Fathers*. Collier Books, Macmillan, New York, 1970.

Rodríguez, Pedro Ocariz, and José Luís Illanes. *El Opus Dei en la Iglesia*. Ediciones Rialp, Madrid, 1993 (S).

Roeck, Jefd. *Juan Pablo II: El Hombre Que Vino de Polonia*. Verlag Altiora, Averbode, Belgium, 1978 (S).

Rolicki, Janusz. *Edward Gierek: Przerwana Dekada.* Wydawnictwo Fakt, Warszawa, 1990 (P).

Romero, Oscar Archbishop. *A Shepherd's Diary.* St. Anthony Messenger Press, Cincinnati, 1986.

Roncagliolo, Rafael, and Fernando Reyes Matta. *Iglesia, Prensa y Militares: El Caso Riobamba y los Obispos Latinoamericanos.* Instituto Latinoamericano de Estudios Transnacionales, México, D.F., 1978 (S).

Rowny, Edward L. *It Takes One to Tango.* Brassey's, McLean, Virginia, 1992.

Santini, Alceste. *Agostino Casaroli: Uomo del Dialogo.* Edizioni San Paolo, Torino, 1993 (I).

Sebes, Joseph, S.J. *The Jesuits and the Sino-Russian Treaty of Nerchinsk (1689): The Diary of Thomas Pereira, S.J.* Institutum Historicum S.I., Rome, 1961.

Sheed, F.J. *God and Politics.* Sheed and Ward, New York, 1960.

Sipe, A.W. Richard. *A Secret World: Sexuality and the Search for Celibacy.* Brunner-Mazel, New York, 1990.

Six, Jean-François. *Church and Human Rights.* Saint Paul Publications, Middlegreen, Slough, United Kingdom, 1992.

Skwarnicki, Marek. *Intensywna Terapia: Poezje.* Wydawnictwo Biblos, Tarnów, Poland, 1993 (P).

________.*Australijska Wiosna.* Społeczny; Instytut Wydawniczy Znak, Kraków, 1988 (P).

Spasowski, Romuald. *The Liberation of One.* Harcourt Brace Jovanovich, Orlando, Florida, 1986.

Spengler, Oswald. *The Decline of the West.* Two volumes. Alfred A. Knopf, New York, 1926.

Sterling, Claire. *The Time of the Assassins: Anatomy of an Investigation.* Holt, Rinehard and Winston, New York, 1983.

Stoll, David. *Is Latin America Turning Protestant?* University of California Press, Berkeley, 1990.

Studnicki, Gustaw. *Pierwsza Wsród Równych: Dzieje Gimnazjum i Liceum w Wadowiacach.* Towarzystwo Miłośników Ziemi Wadowickiej, Wadowice, Poland, 1991 (P).

Styceń, Tadeusz, S.D.S. *Solidarność Wyzwala.* Towarzystwo

Naukowe Katolickiego Uniwersytetu Lubelskiego, Lublin, Poland, 1993 (P).

———. *Urodziłeś się, by Kochać.* Towarzystwo Naukowe Katolickiego Uniwersytetu Lubelskiego, Lublin, Poland, 1993 (P).

Styczeń, Tadeusz, and Edward Balawajder. *Jedynie Prawda Wyzwala: Rozmowy o Janie Pawle II.* Polski Instytut Kultury Chrześcijanskiej, Rome, 1986 (P).

Suenenes, Léon Joseph Cardinal. *Ecumenism and Charismatic Renewal.* Darton, Longman and Todd, London, 1978.

Svidercoschi, Gian Franco. *Letter to a Jewish Friend.* Hodder and Stoughton, London, 1994.

Szajkowski, Bogdan. *Next to God . . . Poland: Politics and Religion in Contemporary Poland.* St. Martin's, New York, 1983.

Szczypka, Józef. *Jan Paweł II: Rodowód.* Instytut Wydawniczy Pax, Warszawa, 1991 (P).

Tazbir, Janusz. *Dzieje Polskiej Tolerancji.* Wydawnictwo Interpress, Warszawa, 1973 (P).

Teilhard de Chardin, Pierre. *The Heart of Matter.* Harcourt Brace Jovanovich, Orlando, Florida, 1978.

———. *L'Avenir de l'Homme.* Éditions du Seuil, Paris, 1959 (F).

———. *Le Milieu Divin.* Éditions du Seuil, Paris, 1957 (F).

Tuschner, Józef. *Myślenie Według Wartości.* Wydawnictwo Znak, Kraków, 1993 (P).

———. *Nieszczęsny Dar Wolności.* Wydawnictwo Znak, Kraków, 1993 (P).

Trasatti, Sergio, and Mari, Arturo. *Journey in Suffering.* Editrice Velar, Bergamo, Italy, 1981.

Turowicz, Jerzy. *Kosciół Nie Jest Łodzią Podwodną.* Społeczny Instytut Wydawniczy Znak, Kraków, 1990 (P).

Tymieniecka, Anna-Teresa. *Analecta Husserliana: The Yearbook of Phenomenological Research: Volume VI.* D. Reidel, Dordrecht, Netherlands/Boston, 1977.

Vircondelet, Alain. *Jean-Paul II: Biographie.* Édition Juilliard, Paris, 1994 (F).

Wahle, Hedwig. *Wspólne Dziedzictwo: Judaizm i Chrześcianstwo w Kontekscie Dziejów Zbawienia.* Biblos, Tarnów, Poland, 1993 (P). Original Edition: *Das Gemeinsame Erbe Judentum und Christentum in Heilsgeschichtlichem Zusammenhang.* Verlagsanstalt Tyrolia, Innsbruck, Austria, 1980 (German).

Wałęsa, Lech. *The Struggle and the Triumph: An Autobiography.* Arcade, New York, 1992.

———. *Un Chemin d'Espoir: Autobiographie.* Fayard, Paris, 1987 (F). English edition: *A Way of Hope: An Autobiography.* Henry Holt, New York, 1987.

Wieczorek, Adam. *Apostoł Pokoju.* Instytut Wydawniczy Pax, Warszawa, 1991 (P).

Wilkes, Paul. *The Education of an Archbishop: Travels with Rembert Weakland.* Orbis Books, Maryknoll, New York, 1992.

Willebrands, Johannes Cardinal. *The Church and Jewish People: New Considerations.* Paulist Press, Mahwah, New Jersey, 1992.

Willey, David. *God's Politician: Pope John Paul II, the Catholic Church, and the New World Order.* St. Martin's, New York, 1993.

Williams, George Huntston. *The Contours of Church and State in the Thought of John Paul II. Institute of Church-State Studies, Baylor University Press, Waco, Texas, 1983.*

———. *The Law of Nations and the Book of Nature.* St. John's University Press, Collegeville, Minnesota, 1984.

———. *The Mind of John Paul II: Origins of His Thought and Action.* Seabury Press, New York, 1981.

Wills, Garry. *Under God: Religion and American Politics.* Simon and Schuster, New York, 1990.

Winn, Wilton. *Keepers of the Keys: John XXIII, Paul VI, and John Paul II: Three Who Changed the Church.* Random House, New York, 1988.

Wojtyła, Karol. *Czlowiek Drogą Kościóła.* Fundacja Jana Pawła II—Ośrodek Dokumentacji Pontyfikatu, Rome, 1992 (P).

———. *Człowiek w Polu Odpowiedzialności.* Instytut Jana Pawła II, KUL, Rzym-Lublin, Poland, 1991 (P).

———. *Zagadnienie Wiary w Dziełach Sw. Jana od*

Krzyża. Wydawnictwo O. O. Karmelitów Bosych, Kraków, 1990 (P).

———.*Obecność: Karol Wojtyła w Katolickim Uniwersytecie Lubelskim. Redakcja Wydawnictw KUL, Lublin, Poland, 1989 (P).*

———.*Poezje i Dramaty*. Wydawnictwo Znak, Kraków, 1987 (P).

———.*Przemówienia i Wywiady w Radio Watykańskim*. Fundacja Jana Pawła II, Ośrodek Dokumentacji Pontyfikatu Jana Pawła II, Rome, 1987 (P).

———.*Wykłady Lubelskie: Człowiek i Moralność*. Wydawnictwo Towarzystwa Naukowego Katolickiego Uniwersytetu Lubelskiego, Lublin, Poland, 1986 (P).

———.*Miłość i Odpowiedzialnośc*. Wydawnictwo Towarzystwa Naukowego Katolickiego Uniwersytetu Lubelskiego, Lublin, Poland, 1985 (P). Italian edition: *Amore e Responsabilitá*. Marietti, Milano, 1978 (I).

———.*Brat Naszego Boga: Tekst i Reżyseria*. Prapremiera Światowa 13 grudnia 1980. Teatr Imienia J. Słowackiego w Krakowie, Kraków, 1980 (P).

———.*Sources of Renewal: The Implementation of the Second Vatican Council*. Harper and Row, New York, 1980.

———.*"Aby Chrystus się Nami Posługiwał."* Wydawnictwo Znak, Kraków, 1979 (P).

———.*The Acting Person*. D. Reidel, Dordrecht, Netherlands/Boston, 1979.

———.*La Bottega Dell'orefice*. Libreria Editrice Vaticana, Cittá del Vaticano, 1979 (I).

———.*Easter Vigil and Other Poems*. Translated by Jerzy Peterkiewicz. Random House, New York, 1979.

———.*La Fede della Chiesa*. Editzioni Ares, Milano, 1978 (I).

———.*Kazania: 1962-1978*. Wydawnictwo Znak, Kraków, 1979 (P).

———.*Sign of Contradiction*. Seabury Press, New York, 1979.

Wood, Jr., James E., and Davis, Derek (editors). *The Role of Religion in the Making of Public Policy*. Baylor University Press, Waco, Texas, 1991.

Woodward, Kenneth L. *Making Saints: How the Catholic*

Church Determines Who Becomes a Saint, Who Doesn't, and Why. Simon and Schuster, New York, 1990.

Żakowski Jacek. *Anatomia Smaku Czyli Rozmowy o Losach Zespołu Tygodnika Powszechnego w Latach 1953–1956.* Wydawnictwo Wolne Pismo Most, Warszawa, 1988 (P).

________. *Trzy Ćwiartki Wieku: Rozmowy z Jerzym Turowiczem.* Wydawnictwo Znak, Kraków, 1990 (P).

Zielinska, Barbara. *Kolumna Zygmunta III w Warszawie.* Wydawnictwo Sztuka, Warszawa, 1957 (P).

Zizola, Giancarlo. *Il Conclave: Storia i segreti, L'elezione papale da San Pietro a Giovanni Paolo II.* Newtown Compton Editori, Rome, 1993.

Życzynski, Józef (editor). *Sprawa Galileusza.* Wydawnictwo Znak, Kraków, 1991 (P).

CHURCH TEXTS AND RELIGIOUS DOCUMENTS

After 1991: Capitalism and Ethics. A Colloquium in the Vatican 1992. Pontifical Council for Justice and Peace, Vatican City, 1992.

Annuario Pontificio 1994. Libreria Editrice Vaticana, Cittá del Vaticano, 1994 (I).

The Cambridge Bible Commentary on the New English Bible: The Gospel According to Matthew. Cambridge University Press, New York, 1963.

Catechism of the Catholic Church. English translation. United States Catholic Conference, Libreria Editrice Vaticana, Paulist Press, Mahwah, New Jersey, 1994.

Catholic Almanac. Our Sunday Visitor Publishing Division, Huntington, Indiana, 1994.

Challenge or Crisis?: Texts by Pope John Paul II on Religious Life. Seamus O'Byrne (editor). Veritas Publications, Dublin, Ireland, 1987.

Constitution on the Church in the Modern World: Second Vatican Council. Office for Publishing and Promotion Services, United States Catholic Conference, Washington, D.C., 1965.

Constitution on the Church: Second Vatican Council. Office for Publishing and Promotion Services, United States Catholic Conference, Washington, D.C., 1964.

Conversations with Monsignor Escrivá de Balaguer. Scepter, Princeton, New Jersey, 1993.

Directory for the Application of Principles and Norms on Ecumenism. Pontifical Council for Christian Unity, Vatican City, 1993.

Dictionary of the Bible. John L. McKenzie, S.J. (editor). Collier Books, Macmillan, New York, 1965.

Documentos de la Conferencia del Episcopado Dominicano: 1955–1990. Colección Quinto Centenario, Santo Domingo, República Dominicana, 1990 (S).

Ethical and Pastoral Dimensions of Population Trends. Pontifical Council for the Family, Libreria Editrice Vaticana, Vatican City, 1994.

"Fasting and Solidarity": Pontifical Messages for Lent. Pontifical Council Cor Unum, Vatican City, 1991.

A Handbook of Theological Terms. Van A. Harvey (editor). Macmillan, New York, 1964.

The Holy See at the Service of Peace: Pope John Paul II's Addresses to the Diplomatic Corps (1978–1988). Pontifical Council for Justice and Peace, Vatican City, 1988.

Human Rights and the Church: Historical and Theological Reflections. Pontifical Council for Justice and Peace, Vatican City, 1990.

International Economics: Interdependence and Dialogue. Pontifical Commission for Justice and Peace, Vatican City, 1984.

Islam and Family Planning: Summary of the Proceedings of the International Islamic Conference, Rabat, Morocco, December 1971. International Planned Parenthood Federation, London, 1986.

John Paul II and the New Evangelization. Laurence J. McGinley Lecture by Avery Dulles, S.J., Fordham University, Bronx, New York, December 4, 1991.

John Paul II in the United States. The John Paul II Foundation, Rome/S.S. Cyril and Methodius Seminary, Orchard Lake, Michigan, 1988.

The Koran. Rodwell's translation. J.M. Dent & Sons, London, 1948.

Letter to the Bishops of the Catholic Church on the Pastoral

Care of Homosexual Persons. Congregation for the Doctrine of the Faith, Vatican City, 1986.

More Than Words: Materials for Christian Education. Seabury Press, Greenwich, Connecticut, 1960.

Path from Puebla: Significant Documents of the Latin American Bishops Since 1979. Secretariat of the Bishops' Committee for the Church in Latin America, National Conference of Catholic Bishops, Washington, D.C., 1989.

Pietnaście Lat Pontyfikatu Jana Pawła II: Wydarzenia, Dokumenty. Instytut Jana Pawła II, KUL, Lublin, Poland, 1993 (P).

Pope John Paul II on Jews and Judaism: 1979–1986. With Introduction and Commentary by Eugene J. Fisher and Leon Klenicki (editors). Office for Publishing and Promotion Services, United States Catholic Conference, Washington, D.C., 1987.

Portrety Jana Pawła II: Wystawa Fotografii Adama Bujaka. Wydawnictwo "Calvarianum," Kalwaria Zebrzydowska, Poland, 1987 (P).

Refugees: A Challenge to Solidarity. Pontifical Council for the Pastoral Care of Migrants and Itinerant People, Libreria Editrice Vaticana, Vatican City, 1992.

Rozmowy w Castel Gandolfo: Europa i co z tego wynika. Instytut Nauk o Człowieku, Vienna, Austria, 1987 (P).

Rozmowy w Castel Gandolfo: O Kryzysie. Instytut Nauk o Człowieku, Vienna, Austria, 1986 (P).

Santo Domingo Conclusions: New Evangelization, Human Development, Christian Culture. Fourth Conference of Latin American Bishops, October 12–28, 1992. Secretariat, Bishops' Committee for the Church in Latin America, National Conference of Catholic Bishops, Washington, D.C., 1993.

Statistical Yearbook of the Church. Secretaria Status, Rationarium Generale Ecclesiae, Vatican City, 1991.

Tajne Dokumenty, Państwo Kościół: 1980–1989. Aneks Publishers, London, 1993 (P).

Vatican Council II: The Conciliar and Post Conciliar Documents. Volumes 1 and 2. Costello, Northport, New York, 1992.

Ważniejsze Daty Pierwszego Pięciolecia Pontyfikatu Jana

Pawła II. L'Osservatore Romano, Wydanie Polskie, Rome, 1984 (P).

CONGRESSIONAL HEARINGS AND INTELLIGENCE MATERIALS

Hearings Before the Select Committee on Intelligence of the United States Senate on Nomination of Robert M. Gates, to Be Director of Central Intelligence: February 17 and February 18, 1987. U.S. Government Printing Office, Washington, D.C., 1987.

Hearings Before the Select Committee on Intelligence of the United States Senate on Nomination of Robert M. Gates, to Be Director of Central Intelligence: September 16, 17, 19, 20, 1991. U.S. Government Printing Office, Washington, D.C., 1991.

Hearings Before the Select Committee on Intelligence of the United States Senate on Nomination of Robert M. Gates, to Be Director of Central Intelligence: September 24, October 1, 2, 1991. U.S. Government Printing Office, Washington, D.C., 1991.

Hearings Before the Select Committee on Intelligence of the United States Senate on Nomination of Robert M. Gates, to Be Director of Central Intelligence: October 3, 4, 18, 1991. U.S. Government Printing Office, Washington, D.C., 1991.

Executive Report, 102nd Congress: Nomination of Robert M. Gates to Be Director of Central Intelligence. Report for the Select Committee on Intelligence. October 24, 1991. U.S. Government Printing Office, Washington, D.C., 1991.

The Holocaust Revisited: A Retrospective Analysis of the Auschwitz-Birkenau Extermination Complex. Central Intelligence Agency, Washington, D.C., 1979.

PAPAL BIBLIOGRAPHIES

Bielska, Krystyna. *Jan Paweł II w Utworach Muzycznych: Bibliografia.* Fundacja Jana Pawła II, Ośrodek Dokumnetacji Pontyfikatu, Rome, 1993 (P).

_______ *Jan Paweł II w Dokumentach Dzwiękowych: Bibliografia 1978–1988.* Fundacja Jana Pawła II, Ośrodek Dokumentacji Pontyfikatu, Rome, 1990 (P).

Chrostowski, Waldemar. *Papież Pielgrzym: Jan Paweł II na Znaczkach Pocztowych Świata, 1978–1990.* Oficyna Przegladu Powszechnego, Warszawa, 1991 (P).

Gramatowski, Wiktor, and Zofia Wilińska. *Karol Wojtyła w świetle publikacji: Bibliografia.* Libreria Editrice Vaticana, Cittá del Vaticano, 1980 (P).

_______ *Jan Paweł II: Bibliografia Polska 1978–1983.* Fundacja Jana Pawła II, Ośrodek Dokumentacji Pontyfikatu, Rome, 1987 (P).

Gramatowski, Wiktor, Zofia Wilińska, and Danuta Guźajewska. *Jan Paweł II: Bibliografia Polska 1984–1986.* Fundacja Jana Pawła II, Ośrodek Dokumentacji Pontyfikatu, Rome, 1991 (P).

Macinska, Krystyna. *La Papo Johano Paulo II en Esperantaj Publikajoj: Bibliografio 1978–1986.* Fundacja Jana Pawła II, Ośrodek Dokumentacji Pontyfikatu, Rome, 1989 (in Esperanto).

PERIODICALS AND NEWSPAPERS

"Alcune forme di fondamentalismo." *La Civilitá Cattolica,* Rome, April 1994 (I).

"Base Ecclesial Communities: A Meeting Point of Ecclesiologies." *Theological Studies,* Baltimore, December 1985.

"Czy Katolicyzm Będzie dla Polaków Religią XXI Wieku?" *Więz,* Warsaw, March 1993 (P).

"La Liberación Integral en América Latina." Monsignor Oscar A. Romero. *Opiniones Latinoamericanas,* Coral Gables, Florida, June 1979.

"Michelangelo's 'Last Judgment.' *National Geographic,* May 1994.

"Papal Foreign Policy." J. Bryan Hehir. *Foreign Policy, Spring 1990.*

"Polska jest Jedna." *Nowe Drogi,* Warsaw, May 1987 (P).

"The Sistine Restoration: A Renaissance for Michelangelo." *National Geographic,* December 1989.

"Socialism and Atheism." *Dialectics and Humanism, The Polish Philosophical Quarterly*, Warsaw, January 1987.

"Treasures of the Vatican." *National Geographic*, December 1985.

PRINCIPAL PUBLICATIONS CONSULTED FOR GENERAL INFORMATION

America
Commonweal
La Croix, Paris
The *National Catholic Reporter*, Kansas City
The *New York Times*
L'Osservatore Romano—daily Italian edition
L'Osservatore Romano—weekly English edition
L'Osservatore Romano—monthly Polish edition
The *Tablet*, London
Tygodnik Powszechny—Kraków
The *Washington Post*

GLOSSARY

Abbot: The male superior of a monastic community of men.

Absolution: The Act by which a priest grants forgiveness of sins.

Adoration: The most important act of religious worship; love and reverence to God in acknowledgment of his perfection and goodness.

Adventists: Members of several Christian sects whose doctrines are dominated by a belief in an imminent second coming of Christ.

Aggiornamento: An Italian word meaning bringing up to date, renewal, or revitalization, often used to describe the spiritual renewal and institutional reform in the Catholic Church fostered by the Second Vatican Council.

Anathema: A Greek word with the root meaning of cursed or separated, used in Catholic Church documents to refer to excommunication.

Angelus: A devotion that commemorates the Incarnation of Christ. The Angelus is recited in the morning, at noon, and in the evening.

Apostasy: The total repudiation of the Christian faith.

Apostolate: The ministry or work of an apostle. In Catholic usage, a term covering all kinds of work for the service of God and the Church.

GLOSSARY

Archdiocese: An ecclesiastical jurisdiction headed by an archbishop.

Atonement: The redemptive activity of Christ, who reconciled man with God through his life, especially his suffering and resurrection.

Base Ecclesial Communities: A conceptual and operational model of basic Christian communities that envisions relatively small communities of the faithful integrated for religious and secular life, with maximum potential for participation in worship, pastoral ministry, apostolic activity, and for personal and social development.

Beatification: A preliminary step toward canonization of a saint.

Beatitude: A literary form of both the Old and New Testaments of the Bible in which blessings are promised to persons for various reasons.

Biretta: A stiff, square hat worn by clerics.

Bull, Apostolic: The most solemn form of papal document, beginning with the name and title of the pope.

Canon: A Greek word meaning rule, norm, or standard.

Canonization: An infallible declaration by the pope that a person who died as a martyr and/or practiced Christian virtue to a heroic degree is now in heaven and worthy of honor and imitation by all the faithful—in other words, is now a saint.

Catechesis: Religious instruction.

Catechism: A summary of doctrine.

Cathedra: A Greek word for chair, designating the chair or seat of a bishop in the principal church of his diocese.

Catholic: A Greek word meaning universal.

Celibacy: The unmarried state of life, required in the Roman Catholic Church of candidates for holy orders and of men already ordained to holy orders.

Chamberlain: The cardinal who administers the property and revenue of the Holy See. On the death of the pope he becomes the head of the college of cardinals and summons and directs the conclave until a new pope is elected.

Charisms: Gifts or graces given by God to persons for the good of others and the Church.

GLOSSARY

Christ: The title of Jesus, derived from the Greek translation *Christos* of the Hebrew term *Messiah,* meaning the Anointed of God, the Savior of his people.

Christians: The name first applied about the year 43 to followers of Jesus at Antioch, the capital of Syria.

Clergy: Men ordained to holy orders, commissioned for sacred ministries, and assigned to pastoral and other duties for the service of the people and the Church.

Collegiality: A term in use especially since the Second Vatican Council to describe the authority exercised by the College of Bishops.

Concelebration: The liturgical act in which several priests, led by one member of the group, offer Mass together, all consecrating the bread and wine.

Concordat: A church-state treaty with the force of law concerning matters of mutual concern.

Consistory: An assembly of cardinals presided over by the pope.

Constitution: An apostolic or papal document in which a pope enacts law. Also, a formal and solemn document issued by an ecumenical council on a doctrinal or pastoral subject, with binding force in the whole Church.

Covenant: A bond of relationship between parties pledged to each other.

Curia: The Roman Curia is the personnel and offices through which the pope administers the affairs of the Church. Similarly, a bishop administers a diocese through a diocesan curia.

Declaration: An edict or ordinance issued by a pope and/or by an ecumenical council, with binding force in the whole Church.

Devotions: Pious practices of members of the Church, including not only participation in various acts of the liturgy but also in other acts of worship generally called popular or private devotions.

Diocese: An ecclesiastical jurisdiction under the pastoral direction of a bishop.

Discalced: A word of Latin derivation meaning without

shoes, applied to religious orders or congregations whose members go barefoot or wear sandals.

Dispensation: The relaxation of a law in a particular case.

Ecclesiology: Study of the nature, constitution, members, mission, functions, and other aspects of the Church.

Ecumenism: The movement of Christians and their churches of various denominations toward unity in one church.

Episcopate: The office bestowed upon a bishop at his ordination, or the body of bishops collectively.

Eschatology: Doctrine concerning the last things: death, judgment, heaven and hell, and the final state of humankind and the kingdom of God at the end of time.

Eucharistic congresses: Public demonstrations of faith in the Holy Eucharist, combining liturgical services and other public ceremonies.

Evangelization: Proclamation of the Gospel, the Good News of Salvation in and through Christ, among those who have not yet known or received it.

Excommunication: A penalty or censure by which a baptized Roman Catholic is excluded from the communion of faith, for committing and remaining obstinate in certain serious offenses specified in canon law.

Free will: The faculty or capability of making a reasonable choice among several alternatives. Freedom of will underlies moral responsibility.

Friar: Term applied to members of mendicant orders to distinguish them from members of monastic orders.

Genuflection: Bending of the knee, a sign of reverence.

Hagiography: Writings or documents about saints and other holy persons.

Hail Mary: A prayer addressed to the Virgin Mary.

Heresy: The obstinate denial or doubt by a Catholic of any truth that must be believed as a matter of Catholic faith.

Holy See: The diocese of the pope, or the pope himself and/or the various officials and bodies of the Church's central administration at Vatican City.

Holy Year: A year during which the pope grants the plenary Jubilee Indulgence to the faithful who fulfill certain conditions.

Incardination: The affiliation of a priest to his diocese. Every secular priest (that is, a priest who is not part of a religious community) must belong to a certain diocese.

Index of Prohibited Books: A list of books that Catholics formerly were forbidden to read, possess, or sell.

Inquisition: A tribunal for investigating and judging heretics, authorized by Gregory IX in 1231.

INRI: The first letters of the words in the Latin inscription on the top of the cross on which Jesus was crucified: Iesus Nazareanus, Rex Iudaeorum—Jesus of Nazareth, King of the Jews.

Interregnum: The period of time between the death of a pope and the election of his successor.

Laicization: The process by which a man ordained to holy orders is returned to the status of a layperson.

Liberation Theology: Deals with the relevance of Christian faith and the mission of the Church to advance efforts for the promotion of human rights, social justice, and human development.

Litany: A prayer in the form of responsive petition.

Magnificat: The canticle or hymn of the Virgin Mary.

Mendicants: A term derived from Latin, meaning beggars, applied to members of religious orders without property rights.

Millennium: A thousand-year reign of Christ and the just upon earth before the end of time.

Novice: A man or woman preparing, in a formal period of trial called a novitiate, for membership in a religious order.

Opus Dei: Organization founded in 1928 in Madrid by Monsignor Josemaría Escrivá de Balaguer y Albás (beatified in 1992) with the aim of spreading throughout society an awareness of the universal call to holiness and apostolate in the ordinary circumstances of life, especially through one's professional work.

Papal election: Election of the new pope by members of the College of Cardinals in a secret meeting normally convened in the Vatican Palace between fifteen and twenty days after the death of the standing pope.

Parish: A community of the faithful served by a pastor.

Peter's pence: A collection made each year among Catholics for the maintenance of the pope and his works of charity.

Prie-dieu: A French phrase (meaning pray God) for a kneeler or bench suitable for kneeling while at prayer.

Purgatory: The state in which those who have died in the state of grace, but with some attachment to sin, suffer for a time before they are admitted to heaven.

Ring: In the Catholic Church a ring is worn as part of the insignia of bishops, abbots, and others.

Rosary: A form of mental and vocal prayer centered on events in the lives of Jesus and Mary.

Saints, Cult of: The veneration, called *dulia*, of holy persons who have died and are in glory with God in heaven.

Scapular: A part of the habit of some religious orders; a nearly shoulder-wide strip of cloth worn over the tunic and reaching almost to the feet in front and behind.

Schism: Derived from a Greek word meaning separation, the term designates formal and obstinate refusal by a Catholic, called a schismatic, to be in communion with the pope and the Church.

Seminary: A house of study and formation for men, called seminarians, studying for the priesthood.

Stations of the Cross: A form of devotion commemorating the Passion and death of Jesus.

Stigmata: Marks of the wounds suffered by Jesus in his crucifixion, in the hands and feet by nails, and in the side by the piercing of a lance.

Synod, Diocesan: Meeting of representative persons of a diocese—priests, religious, laypersons—with the bishop, called by him for the purpose of considering and taking action on matters affecting the diocese.

Te Deum: The opening Latin words, "Thee, God," of a hymn of praise and thanksgiving.

Titular sees: Dioceses where the Church once flourished but which were later taken over by non-Christians and now exist only in name or title.

Viaticum: Holy Communion given to those in danger of death.

Vicar general: A priest or bishop appointed by the bishop of a diocese to serve as his deputy.

Vocation: A call to a way of life. Generally, the term applies to the call of all persons to holiness and salvation.

INDEX

The abbreviations JPII and KW denote Pope John Paul II and Karol Wojtyła.

INDEX

INDEX

INDEX

INDEX

INDEX

INDEX

INDEX